THE PUSHCART PRIZE IX

"What makes the Pushcart Prize editions so valuable is that they unearth otherwise neglected achievement. The editors have good, discerning ears, tuned in to what's important. Annually, the Pushcart collection reasserts the piercing potential of the muffled voice."

The New York Times
Book Review

THE
PUSHCART PRIZE, IX:
BEST OF THE
SMALL PRESSES
1984-85 Edition

THE PUSHCART PRIZE, IX:

BEST OF THE SMALL PRESSES

. . . WITH AN INDEX TO
THE FIRST NINE VOLUMES

EDITED BY BILL HENDERSON
with the Pushcart Prize editors

Introduction by JAYNE ANNE PHILLIPS

AVON
PUBLISHERS OF BARD, CAMELOT, DISCUS AND FLARE BOOKS

Note: nominations for this series are invited from any small, independent, literary book press or magazine in the world. Up to six nominations—tear sheets or copies selected from work published in that calendar year—are accepted by our October 15 deadline each year. Write to Pushcart Press, P.O. Box 380, Wainscott, New York 11975 if you need more information.

Pushcart Press sends special thanks to The Helen Foundation of Salt Lake City for its generous awards to the authors of our lead short story, poem, and essay.

Acknowledgments

The following works are reprinted by permission of the publisher and author.

"Hiding" © 1983 Grand Street Publications
"Self/Landscape/Grid" © 1983 *New England Review and Bread Loaf Quarterly*
"Ground Zero" © 1983 *Field*
"Consolation" © 1983 *Home Planet News*
"Duckwalking" © 1983 Sun & Moon Press, from *Contemporary American Fiction*.
"Over The Mountain" © 1983 *Antaeus*
"Winter Flight" © 1983 *New England Review and Bread Loaf Quarterly*
"Totems" © 1983 *Thunders Mouth Press*
"Caviar" © 1983 *Antaeus*
"The Power of Toads" © 1983 *The Iowa Review*
"Peacock Display" © 1983 *Prairie Schooner*
"Fish Fucking" © 1983 *Missouri Review*
"Recovering" © 1983 *Triquarterly*
"Making Poetry A Continuum: Selected Correspondence" © 1983 Georgia Review
"The Trickle Down Theory of Happiness" © 1983 *Poetry*
"The Unbroken Diamond: Nightletter to the Mujahadeen" © 1983 Telescope
"Crossing" © 1983 *Shenandoah*
"The Explosion" © 1983 *Ironwood*
"Oranges" © 1983 *Poetry*
"The Gift" © 1983 *American Poetry Review*
"The Soroca Girls" © 1983 Micah Publications, from the book *Kaputt*, originally published in 1946
"A Winter's Tale" © 1983 *Writers Forum*
"Careful" © 1983 *The Paris Review* © 1983 Alfred Knopf Inc.
"Poetry and Ambition" © 1983 *The Kenyon Review*
"Emotion Recollected In Tranquillity" © 1983 *Quarterly West*
"Lavonder" © 1983 *Northwest Review*
"A History of Speech" © 1983 *Poetry Northwest*
"L. A. Child" © 1983 *Story Quarterly*
"Cambodian Diary" © 1983 Antaeus, from the novel to be published by Simon & Schuster, *A Wilderness Called Peace*.
"Gise Pedersen Sets Me Straight on A Matter of Natural History" © 1983 *Cumberland Poetry Review*
"The Annunciation" © 1983 *Ironwood*
"Ukiyo-E" © 1983 Calliopea Press, from the book *Twelve Pages From The Floating Island*.
"Paul Goodman and The Grand Community" © 1983 *American Poetry Review*
"Copies" © 1983 *The Agni Review*
"Asilomarian Lecture (The Dirmal Life of the Inhabitats)" © 1983 *Chicago Review*
"Trying To Name What Doesn't Change" © 1983 *Domestic Crude*
"Coming of Age on the Harlem" © 1983 *Hudson Review*
"from *A Minor Apocalypse*" © 1983 Farrar, Straus and Giroux. Translated by Richard Lourie.
"As the President Spoke" © 1983 University of Nebraska Press.
"Tenebrae" © 1983 O. ARS. Translated by Cola Franzen.
"The Gala Cocktail Party" © 1983 Sun & Moon Press and North Point Press, from *Contemporary American Fiction*.
"Lot's Wife" © 1983 Alice James Books from the book *Bonfire*.
"The Form and Function of the Novel" © 1983 Ontario Review Press from the book *Original Light: New & Selected Poems 1973-1983*.
"High Adventures of Indeterminacy" © 1983 Poetry In Review Foundation.
"Tumor" © 1983 Dragon Gate Inc. from the book *Poems & Stories*.
"The Mystery of the Caves" © 1983 Michael Waters, reprinted from *Stories In The Light* (Thunder City Press).
"Physical Universe" © 1983 Ticknor & Fields and BOA Editions from *The Best Hour of the Night* and *People Live Here: Selected Poems 1949-1983*.
"The Cigarette Boat" © 1983 Word Beat Press from the book *A Small Cartoon*. Originally appeared in *The Paris Review*.
"Ground Zero" © 1983 *New England Review and Bread Loaf Quarterly*. Also appeared in *Dalmo'ma Anthology* (Empty Bowl).
"Claire's Lover's Church" © 1983 Grand Street Publications.
"Oh, Joseph, I'm So Tired" © 1983 Wampeter Press, from the anthology *Matters of Life and Death* edited by Tobias Wolff. Originally published in *Liars in Love* (Seymour Lawrence Inc.) Also appeared in *The Atlantic* and in *The O'Henry Awards*, 1977.
"John Cheever: The Novelist's Life As A Drama" by Malcolm Cowley appeared originally in *Sewanee Review* © 1983 by Malcolm Cowley, and will be included in the forthcoming work *The Flower and The Leaf* by Malcolm Cowley to be published by Viking Penguin Inc. Reprinted by permission of Viking Penguin Inc.
Note: the editor regrets a typographical error in Gilbert Sorrentino's "The Gala Cocktail Party" in the hardbound edition. The version in this edition is correct.

For
GENIE
and
LILY FRANCES

THE

PEOPLE WHO HELPED

FOUNDING EDITORS—*Anaïs Nin (1903-1977), Buckminster Fuller (1895-1983), Charles Newman, Daniel Halpern, Gordon Lish, Harry Smith, Hugh Fox, Ishmael Reed, Joyce Carol Oates, Len Fulton, Leonard Randolph, Leslie Fiedler, Nona Balakian, Paul Bowles, Paul Engle, Ralph Ellison, Reynolds Price, Rhoda Schwartz, Richard Morris, Ted Wilentz, Tom Montag, William Phillips. Poetry editor: H. L. Van Brunt.*

EDITORS—*Walter Abish, Ai, Elliott Anderson, John Ashbery, Robert Bly, Robert Boyers, Harold Brodkey, Joseph Brodsky, Wesley Brown, Hayden Carruth, Raymond Carver, Malcolm Cowley, Paula Deitz, Steve Dixon, M. D. Elevitch, Loris Essary, Ellen Ferber, Carolyn Forché, Stuart Friebert, Jon Galassi, Tess Gallagher, Louis Gallo, George Garrett, Jack Gilbert, Louise Glück, David Godine, Jorie Graham, Linda Gregg, Barbara Grossman, Michael Harper, DeWitt Henry, J. R. Humphreys, David Ignatow, John Irving, June Jordan, Karen Kennerly, Galway Kinnell, Carolyn Kizer, Jerzy Kosinski, Richard Kostelanetz, Seymour Krim, Maxine Kumin, Stanley Kunitz, James Laughlin, Seymour Lawrence, Naomi Lazard, Herb Leibowitz, Denise Levertov, Philip Levine, Stanley Lindberg, Thomas Lux, Mary MacArthur, Daniel Menaker, Frederick Morgan, Howard Moss, Cynthia Ozick, Jayne Anne Phillips, Robert Phillips, George Plimpton, Stanley Plumly, Eugene Redmond, Ed Sanders, Teo Savory, Grace Schulman, Harvey Shapiro, Leslie Silko, Charles Simic, Dave Smith, William Stafford, Gerald Stern, David St. John, Bill and Pat Strachan, Ron Sukenick, Barry Targan, Anne Tyler, John Updike, Samuel Vaughan, David Wagoner, Derek Walcott, Ellen Wilbur, David Wilk, Yvonne, Bill Zavatsky.*

CONTRIBUTING EDITORS FOR THIS EDITION—*Diane Ackerman, John Allman, John Balaban, Bo Ball, Jim Barnes, Charles Baxter, Philip Booth, Michael Dennis Browne, Michael Blumenthal, Richard Burgin, Kathy Callaway, Siv Cedering, Kelly Cherry, Amy Clampitt, Naomi*

Clark, Christopher Clausen, Andrei Codrescu, Henry Coulette, Philip Dacey, John Daniel, Jean Davidson, Susan Strayer Deal, Janet Desaulniers, William Dickey, Rita Dove, Patricia Dobler, Andre Dubus, Louise Erdrich, Raymond Federman, Jane Flanders, H.E. Francis, Ellen Gilchrist, Matthew Graham, Thom Gunn, James Baker Hall, Lyn Hejinian, Don Hendrie Jr., Elizabeth Inness-Brown, Josephine Jacobsen, Janet Kauffman, Jane Kenyon, Carolyn Kizer, Marilyn Krysl, Li-Young Lee, Gerry Locklin, David Madden, Oscar Mandel, Adrianne Marcus, Bobbie Ann Mason, Dan Masterson, Cleopatra Mathis, Robert McBrearty, Michael McFee, Thomas McGrath, Heather McHugh, Joe Anne McLaughlin, Sandra McPherson, Judy Moffett, Charles Molesworth, Hilda Morley, Jennifer Moyer, Naomi Shihab Nye, Sharon Olds, Raymond Oliver, Linda Pastan, Joyce Peseroff, Mary Peterson, Robert Phillips, Jarold Ramsey, William Pitt Root, Michael Ryan, Sherod Santos, Lynne Sharon Schwartz, Philip Schultz, Richard Smith, W. D. Snodgrass, Nat Sobel, Gary Soto, Marcia Southwick, Elizabeth Spires, Ann Stanford, Maura Stanton, Timothy Steele, Pamela Stewart, David Swickard, Ellen Bryant Voight, Elizabeth Tallent, Mary Tallmountain, Barry Targan, Julia Thacker, Barbara Thompson, Sara Vogan, Richard Wilbur, Anita Wilkins, C. K. Williams, Harold Witt, David Wojahn, Christine Zawadiwsky, Patricia Zelver, Paul Zimmer

DESIGN AND PRODUCTION—*Ray Freiman*

EUROPEAN EDITORS—*Andrew Motion, Kirby and Liz Williams*

MANAGING EDITOR—*Helen Handley*

ROVING EDITORS—*Gene Chipps, Lily Frances*

EDITOR AND PUBLISHER—*Bill Henderson*

PRESSES FEATURED IN THE PUSHCART PRIZE EDITIONS

Agni Review
Ahsahta Press
Ailanthus Press
Alcheringa/Ethnopoetics
Alice James Books
American Literature
American PEN
American Poetry Review
Amnesty International
Anaesthesia Review
Antaeus
Antioch Review
Apalachee Quarterly
Aphra
The Ark
Ascent
Aspen Leaves
Aspen Poetry Anthology
Assembling
Barlenmir House
Barnwood Press
The Bellingham Review
Beloit Poetry Journal
Bilingual Review
Black American Literature Forum
Black Rooster
Black Scholar
Black Sparrow

Black Warrior Review
Blackwells Press
Blue Cloud Quarterly
Blue Wind Press
BOA Editions
Bookslinger Editions
Boxspring
Burning Deck Press
Caliban
California Quarterly
Calliopea Press
Canto
Capra Press
Cedar Rock
Center
Chariton Review
Chelsea
Chicago Review
Chouteau Review
Chowder Review
Cimarron Review
Cincinnati Poetry Review
City Lights Books
Clown War
CoEvolution Quarterly
Cold Mountain Press
Columbia: A Magazine of Poetry and Prose
Confluence Press
Confrontation
Conjunctions
Copper Canyon Press
Cosmic Information Agency
Crawl Out Your Window
Crazy Horse
Cross Cultural Communications
Cross Currents
Cumberland Poetry Review
Curbstone Press
Cutbank
Dacotah Territory
Daedalus
Decatur House
December

Dragon Gate Inc.
Domestic Crude
Dreamworks
Dryad Press
Duck Down Press
Durak
East River Anthology
Empty Bowl
Fiction
Fiction Collective
Fiction International
Field
Firelands Art Review
Five Trees Press
Frontiers: A Journal of Women Studies
Gallimaufry
Genre
The Georgia Review
Ghost Dance
Goddard Journal
David Godine, Publisher
Graham House Press
Grand Street
Graywolf Press
Greenfield Review
Greensboro Review
Hard Pressed
Hills
Holmgangers Press
Holy Cow!
Home Planet News
Hudson Review
Icarus
Iguana Press
Indiana Writes
Intermedia
Intro
Invisible City
Inwood Press
Iowa Review
Ironwood
The Kanchenjunga Press
Kansas Quarterly

Kayak
Kenyon Review
Latitudes Press·
L'Epervier Press
Liberation
Linquis
The Little Magazine
Living Hand Press
Living Poets Press
Logbridge-Rhodes
Lowlands Review
Lucille
Lynx House Press
Manroot
Magic Circle Press
Malahat Review
Massachusetts Review
Michigan Quarterly
Milk Quarterly
Montana Gothic
Montana Review
Micah Publications
Mississippi Review
Missouri Review
Montemora
Mr. Cogito Press
MSS
Mulch Press
Nada Press
New America
New England Review and Bread Loaf Quarterly
New Letters
North American Review
North Atlantic Books
North Point Press
Northwest Review
O. ARS
Obsidian
Oconee Review
October
Ohio Review
Ontario Review
Open Places

Oyez Press
Painted Bride Quarterly
Paris Review
Parnassus: Poetry In Review
Partisan Review
Penca Books
Pentagram
Penumbra Press
Pequod
Persea: An International Review
Pipedream Press
Pitcairn Press
Ploughshares
Poet and Critic
Poetry
Poetry Northwest
Poetry Now
Prairie Schooner
Prescott Street Press
Promise of Learnings
Quarry West
Quarterly West
Rainbow Press
Raritan: A Quarterly Review
Red Cedar Review
Red Clay Books
Red Earth Press
Release Press
Revista Chicano-Riquena
River Styx
Rowan Tree Press
Russian *Samizdat*
Salmagundi
San Marcos Press
Seamark Press
Seattle Review
Second Coming Press
The Seventies Press
Shankpainter
Shantih
Shenandoah
A Shout In The Street
Sibyl-Child Press

Small Moon
The Smith
Some
The Sonora Review
Southern Poetry Review
Southern Review
Southwestern Review
Spectrum
The Spirit That Moves Us
St. Andrews Press
Story Quarterly
Sun & Moon Press
Sun Press
Sunstone
Tar River Poetry
Telephone Books
Telescope
Tendril
Texas Slough
13th Moon
THIS
Threepenny Review
Thorp Springs Press
Three Rivers Press
Thunder City Press
Thunder's Mouth Press
Toothpaste Press
Transatlantic Review
TriQuarterly
Truck Press
Tuumba Press
Undine
Unicorn Press
Unmuzzled Ox
Unspeakable Visions of the Individual
Vagabond
Virginia Quarterly
Wampeter Press
Washington Writers Workshop
Water Table
Western Humanities Review
Westigan Review
Wickwire Press

Willmore City
Word Beat Press
Word-Smith
Writers Forum
Xanadu
Yale Review
Yardbird Reader
Y'Bird

CONTENTS

EDITOR'S NOTE

Jayne Anne Phillips writes the Introduction to this *Pushcart Prize* edition. In 1977 a portion from her book *Sweethearts* (Truck Press) was reprinted in *Pushcart Prize II*. Since then we have been privileged to feature her stories "Home" (*Iowa Review*, IV), "Lechery" (*Persea*, IV) and "How Mickey Made It" (Bookslinger Editions, VII). She is the author of the fiction collection *Black Tickets* and the just-published novel *Machine Dreams*, both from Seymour Lawrence.

Pushcart Press is honored by her past and present contributions to this series.

BILL HENDERSON

INTRODUCTION
by JAYNE ANNE PHILLIPS

Pushcart Prize IX underscores, more than any other volume in the Pushcart series, the importance of small press publishing to American writers and American literature. It is a paradox that much of what is evolving in current American writing evolves in relative secrecy, unreflected in the more obvious media: television and film, and the handful of commercial magazines which continue to publish fiction and poetry and essays. Even in such magazines, space is limited, and what fills the space is often dictated by marketing considerations. The climate fostered by such conditions, especially for young writers, is daunting. What is its effect on the continuum of American letters, and on our culture as a whole? Few writers write because they expect to be heard, but contemporary writers have become more than usually isolated, unsure even of a potential of effect beyond what they have achieved in themselves. And the United States, like most highly industrialized countries, is more and more isolated from its artists—those aberrations whose one-of-a-kind products can be assigned only uncertain market value.

The breach continues to widen, and the small presses inhabit the breach itself like a varied and dedicated brigade of messengers. Since they have no "targeted" readerships and few advertisers, small presses often first publish work that is unconventional in subject matter or technique. They publish long works in their entirety, works that commercial magazines would not consider. And they publish unknown writers, with only the work as criteria. I owe a debt to small presses because my earlier work was published only in literary magazines—interesting magazines with names like *Io* and *Truck, Attaboy, Canto,* and magazines still well-known, like *Ploughshares, Iowa Review, North American Review.*

I never considered sending my stories to commercial magazines, and those same stories were first introduced to a wider audience through the prize anthologies, including *Pushcart Prize*, which has the special distinction of selecting work only from small press publications. Pushcart is an effective and highly successful marriage of the editorial freedom (freedom on a shoestring) inherent in the small press and the greater powers of production and distribution available through commercial presses. Such marriages should occur with more regularity. Ted Solataroff's *New American Review*, a magazine/paperback devoted only to literature, widely and inexpensively distributed, is still sorely missed. Writers and small presses have begun editing anthologies themselves (*Matters of Life and Death*, edited by Tobias Wolff, published by Wampeter Press, is a good example), partially to fill a need for current collected work in workshops they themselves teach. Many other writers are publishing first books and bodies of work—not only of poetry but of fiction—with small presses.

What are the advantages of such publication? My identity as a writer was already fixed in my mind (though certainly in no one else's) when Truck Press accepted the manuscript of my first short collection, a book of twenty-four one-page fictions. I was able to go to North Carolina where Truck Press was then located and contribute, along with David Wilk and David Southern, to a design for the book which followed naturally from the material. I was a teacher's aide in a rural school near my hometown then, completely out-of-touch with the "real" world, and I remember leaning against a pick-up in the parking lot of the school at noon hour, hurriedly reading the galleys for mistakes. I was trying to save money to buy a $1500 car that winter, so I could drive my typewriter and my dog and me to Iowa City. I didn't know how to drive yet but I had been cross-country to California three or four times; I figured the road was mostly super highway and I wouldn't have to worry much about steering. While at Iowa I became involved in a second small press project, a selection of short fictions published by Annabel Levitt's Vehicle Editions. I had known Annabel when we both lived out West, and she bound five hundred copies of the edition in the kitchen of her Mott St. walk-up in New York. Then and now, she owes the continued existence of her press mostly to rent control. She has always used original works by artists as covers for her books, but has now fashioned Vehicle Editions into a forum for artists as well as writers. This fall I will do another story publication with Vehicle, and the book will feature a series of drawings by artist Yvonne Jacquette.

Other small presses to whom I owe thanks are Bookslinger Editions and Palaemon Press, Limited. Both published my prose in small, fine editions during the long interim between full-length book publications, when I still wasn't sure if I could finish the book I'd promised myself I'd write. Seeing a small portion of that narrative in print between covers helped keep me going.

Nationally, poetry and fiction comprise a kind of associative history, a narrative on a much broader scope. We all have family stories and self-made traditions; we all live within a context larger than the length of our own lives—though anyone watching American prime-time (the most highly successful and highly exported television programming in the world) would assume we are living in the past ten minutes. It is heartening to see in *Pushcart IX* such a spectrum of pasts fully rendered, from Gail Godwin's resonant and unforgettable "Over The Mountain" to Richard Yates' classic "Oh Joseph, I'm So Tired" from the Wampeter Press anthology to Susan Minot's quietly lethal "Hiding." Positioned as it is directly before Terrence Des Pres' timely "Self/Landscape/Grid" ("we are resigned in our knowledge that things will start exactly forty miles away"), "Hiding" becomes a kind of familial metaphor for a national political stance: the mother and flock coping with a father, an overlord, whose distant presence becomes ever more threatening and disconnected. Des Pres' assertion that current American work is not reflecting these concerns is somewhat answered by writing collected here. Sharon Doubiago's long poem, "Ground Zero," moves across a spectrum of the personal, pulling everything it touches into an inclusive clarity—even confusion, dread, mourning, become active, honed forces.

The "hunted and haunted" of Doubiago's poem have always existed in American letters. In Hayden Carruth's "Paul Goodman and The Grand Community," we hear Goodman, "the perpetually fading echo that reverberates between the cliffs of consciousness," telling us our society "is in a chronic low-grade emergency," and that writers bring the "social conflicts in their souls to public expression." Malcolm Cowley's moving reminiscence, "John Cheever: The Novelist's Life As A Drama" seems an illustration of those words. There are many other poets in this volume, (and

27

Cheever was a poet, as are we all who attempt a psychic survival through reading and/or writing), poets like Williams, Eberhart and Stafford, speaking to and of each other; Merwin, Bly and Wright in McGrath's poem "Totems." This too is tradition and narrative—the work, the discussion, the thread of effort and story, the bearing on lives. Writers form a continuum. That continuum forms what is, to the country at large, almost an underground knowledge. The knowledge is needed now. It is that knowledge which informs Kooser's poem about the speaking President, that knowledge which sees the hideous vision of what is "spun out and away" from the finger in question. That knowledge, a sense larger than self evolving from what is most intimate, is present in Keeley's "Cambodian Diary," Konwicki's "From A Minor Apocalypse," Malaparte's "The Soroca Girls."

I believe there is a great deal of urgently applicable work being written—work that can inform and instruct and illuminate, if only it is read. How many of the pieces in *Pushcart IX* were you aware of? How many of the magazines from which this work was taken have you read? Writers have collectively edited this book. These are voices that are speaking now, and I am grateful to Pushcart Press for once again making them heard.

THE

PUSHCART PRIZE IX:

BEST OF THE

SMALL PRESSES

(1984-85 edition)

HIDING

fiction by SUSAN MINOT

from GRAND STREET

nominated by GRAND STREET, *Helen Handley, Daniel Menaker, and Seymour Lawrence*

OUR FATHER doesn't go to church with us but we're all down-stairs in the hall at the same time, bumbling, getting ready to go. Mum knuckles the buttons of Chicky's snowsuit till he's knot-tight, crouching, her heels lifted out of the backs of her shoes, her nylons creased at the ankles. She wears a black lace veil that stays on her hair like magic. Sherman ripples by, coat flapping, and Mum grabs him by the hood, reeling him in, and zips him up with a pinch at his chin. Gus stands there with his bottom lip out, waiting, looking like someone's smacked him except not that hard. Even though he's nine, he still wants Mum to do him up. Delilah comes half-hurrying down the stairs, late, looking like a ragamuffin with her skirt slid down to her hips and her hair all slept on wrong. Caitlin says, "It's about time." Delilah sweeps along the curve of the banister, looks at Caitlin who's all ready to go herself with her pea jacket on and her loafers and bare legs, and tells her, "You're going to freeze." Everyone's in a bad mood because we just woke up.

Dad's outside already on the other side of the French doors, waiting for us to go. You can tell it's cold out there by his white breath blowing by his cheek in spurts. He just stands on the porch, hands shoved in his black parka, feet pressed together, looking at the crusty snow on the lawn. He doesn't wear a hat but that's because he barely feels the cold. Mum's the one who's warm-blooded. At skiing, she'll take you in when your toes get numb. You sit there with hot chocolate and a carton of french fries and the other mothers and she rubs your foot to get the circulation back. Down on the driveway the car is warming up and the exhaust goes straight up, disappearing in thin white curls.

"Okay, Monkeys," says Mum, filing us out the door. Chicky starts down the steps one red boot at a time till Mum whisks him up under a wing. The driveway is wrinkled over with ice so we take little shuffle steps across it, blinking at how bright it is, still only half-awake. Only the station wagon can fit everybody. Gus and Sherman scamper in across the huge backseat. Caitlin's head is the only one that shows over the front. (Caitlin is the oldest and she's twelve. I'm next, then Delilah, then the boys.) Mum rubs her thumbs on the steering wheel so that her gloves are shiny and round at the knuckles. Dad is doing things like checking the gutters, waiting till we leave. When we finally barrel down the hill, he turns and goes back into the house which is big and empty now and quiet.

We keep our coats on in church. Except for the O'Shaunesseys, we have the most children in one pew. Dad only comes on Christmas and Easter, because he's not Catholic. A lot of times you only see the mothers there. When Dad stays at home, he does things like cuts prickles in the woods or tears up thorns, or rakes leaves for burning, or just stands around on the other side of the house by the lilacs, surveying his garden, wondering what to do next. We usually sit up near the front and there's a lot of kneeling near the end. One time Gus got his finger stuck in the diamond-shaped holes of the heating vent and Mum had to yank it out. When the man comes around for the collection, we each put in a nickel or a dime and the handle goes by like a rake. If Mum drops in a five-dollar bill, she'll pluck out a couple of bills for her change.

The church is huge. Out loud in the dead quiet, a baby blares out *DAH-DEE*. We giggle and Mum goes *Ssshhh* but smiles too. A baby always yells at the quietest part. Only the girls are old enough to go to Communion; you're not allowed to chew it. The priest's neck is peeling and I try not to look. "He leaves me cold," Mum says when we leave, touching her forehead with a fingertip after dipping it into the holy water.

On the way home, we pick up the paper at Cage's and a bag of eight lollipops—one for each of us, plus Mum and Dad, even though Dad never eats his. I choose root beer. Sherman crinkles his wrapper, flicking his eyes around to see if anyone's looking. Gus says, "Sherman, you have to wait till after breakfast." Sherman gives a fierce look and shoves it in his mouth. Up in front, Mum, flicking on the blinker, says, "Take that out," with eyes in the back of her head.

Depending on what time of year it is, we do different things on the weekends. In the fall we might go to Castle Hill and stop by the orchard in Ipswich for cider and apples and red licorice. Castle Hill is closed after the summer so there's nobody else there and it's all covered with leaves. Mum goes up to the windows on the terrace and tries to peer in, cupping her hands around her eyes and seeing curtains. We do things like roll down the hills, making our arms stiff like mummies, or climb around on the marble statues which are really cold, or balance along the edge of the fountains without falling. Mum says *Be careful* even though there's no water in them, just red leaves plastered against the sides. When Dad notices us he yells *Get down*.

One garden has a ghost, according to Mum. A lady used to sneak out and meet her lover in the garden behind the grape trellis. Or she'd hide in the garden somewhere and he'd look for her and find her. But one night she crept out and he didn't come and didn't come and finally when she couldn't stand it any longer, she went crazy and ran off the cliff and killed herself and now her ghost comes back and keeps waiting. We creep into the boxed-in place smelling the yellow berries and the wet bark and Delilah jumps— "What was that?"—trying to scare us. Dad shakes the wood to see if it's rotten. We run ahead and hide in a pile of leaves. Little twigs get in your mouth and your nostrils; we hold still underneath listening to the brittle ticking leaves. When we hear Mum and Dad get close, we burst up to surprise them, all the leaves fluttering down, sputtering from the dust and tiny grits that get all over your face like grey ash, like Ash Wednesday. Mum and Dad just keep walking. She brushes a pine needle from his collar and he jerks his head, thinking of something else, probably that it's a fly. We follow them back to the car in a line all scruffy with leaf scraps.

After church, we have breakfast because you're not allowed to eat before. Dad comes in for the paper or a sliver of bacon. One thing about Dad, he has the weirdest taste. Spam is his favorite thing or this cheese that no one can stand the smell of. He barely sits down at all, glancing at the paper with his feet flat down on either side of him, ready to get up any minute to go back outside and sprinkle white fertilizer on the lawn. After, it looks like frost.

This Sunday we get to go skating at Ice House Pond. Dad drives. "Pipe down," he says into the back seat. Mum faces him with white fur around her hood. She calls him Uncs, short for Uncle, a kind of joke, I guess, calling him Uncs while he calls her Mum, same as we do. We are making a racket.

"Will you quit it?" Caitlin elbows Gus.

"What? I'm not doing anything."

"Just taking up all the room."

Sherman's in the way back. "How come Chicky always gets the front?"

"Cause he's the baby." Delilah is always explaining everything.

"I en not a baby," says Chicky without turning around.

Caitlin frowns at me. "Who said you could wear my scarf?"

I ask into the front seat, "Can we go to the Fairy Garden?" even though I know we won't.

"Why couldn't Rummy come?"

Delilah says, "Because Dad didn't want him to."

Sherman wants to know how old Dad was when he learned how to skate.

Dad says, "About your age." He has a deep voice.

"Really?" I think about that for a minute, about Dad being Sherman's age.

"What about Mum?" says Caitlin.

This isn't his department so he just keeps driving. Mum shifts her shoulders more toward us but still looks at Dad.

"When I was a little girl on the Boston Common." Her teeth are white and she wears fuchsia lipstick. "We used to have skating parties."

Caitlin leans close to Mum's fur hood, crossing her arms into a pillow. "What? With dates?"

Mum bats her eyelashes. "Oh sure. Lots of beaux." She smiles, acting like a flirt. I look at Dad but he's concentrating on the road.

We saw one at a football game once. He had a huge mustard overcoat and bow tie and a pink face like a ham. He bent down to shake our tiny hands, half-looking at Mum the whole time. Dad was someplace else getting the tickets. His name was Hank. After he went, Mum put her sunglasses on her head and told us she used to watch him play football at BC. Dad never wears a tie except to work. One time Gus got lost. We waited until the last people had trickled out and the stadium was practically empty. It had started

34

to get dark and the headlights were crisscrossing out of the parking field. Finally Dad came back carrying him, walking fast, Gus's head bobbing around and his face all blotchy. Dad rolled his eyes and made a kidding groan to Mum and we laughed because Gus was always getting lost. When Mum took him, he rammed his head onto her shoulder and hid his face while we walked back to the car, and under Mum's hand you could see his back twitching, trying to hide his crying.

We have Ice House Pond all to ourselves. In certain places the ice is bumpy and if you glide on it going *Aauuuuhhhh* in a low tone, your voice wobbles and vibrates. Every once in a while, a crack shoots across the pond, echoing just beneath the surface, and you feel something drop in the hollow of your back. It sounds like someone's jumped off a steel wire and left it twanging in the air.

I try to teach Delilah how to skate backwards but she's flopping all over the ice, making me laugh, with her hat lopsided and her mittens dangling out of her sleeves. When Gus falls, he just stays there, polishing the ice with his mitten. Dad sees him and says, "I don't care if my son is a violin player," kidding.

Dad played hockey in college and was so good his name is on a plaque that's right as you walk into the Harvard rink. He can go really fast. He takes off—*whooosh*—whizzing, circling at the edge of the pond, taking long strides, then gliding, chopping his skates, crossing over in little jumps. He goes zipping by and we watch him: his hands behind him in a tight clasp, his face as calm as if he were just walking along, only slightly forward. When he sweeps a corner, he tips in, then rolls into a hunch, and starts the long side-pushing again. After he stops, his face is red and the tears leak from the sides of his eyes and there's a white smudge around his mouth like frostbite. Sherman, copying, goes chopping forward on collapsed ankles and it sounds like someone sharpening knives.

Mum practices her 3s from when she used to figure skate. She pushes forward on one skate, turning in the middle like a petal flipped suddenly in the wind. We always make her do a spin. First she does backwards crossovers, holding her wrists like a tulip in her fluorescent pink parka, then stops straight up on her toes, sucking in her breath and dips, twisted, following her own tight circle, faster and faster, drawing her feet together. Whirring around, she lowers into a crouch, ventures out one balanced leg, a twirling whirlpool, hot pink, rises again, spinning, into a blurred pillar or a tornado, her arms going above her head and her hands like the eye of a needle. Then suddenly: stop. Hiss of ice shavings, stopped. We clap our mittens. Her hood has slipped off and her hair is spread across her shoulders like when she's reading in bed, and she takes white breaths with her teeth showing and her pink mouth smiling. She squints over our heads. Dad is way off at the car, unlacing his skates on the tailgate but he doesn't turn. Mum's face means that it's time to go.

Chicky stands in the front seat leaning against Dad. Our parkas crinkle in the cold car. Sherman has been chewing on his thumb and it's a pointed black witch's hat. A rumble goes through the car like a monster growl and before we back up Dad lifts Chicky and sets him leaning against Mum instead.

The speed bumps are marked with yellow stripes and it's like sea serpents have crawled under the tar. When we bounce, Mum says, "Thank-you-Ma'am" with a lilt in her voice. If it was only Mum, the radio would be on and she'd turn it up on the good ones. Dad snaps it off because there's enough racket already. He used to listen to opera when he got home from work but not anymore. Now we give him hard hugs and he changes upstairs then goes into the TV room to the same place on the couch, propping his book on his crossed knees and reaching for his drink without looking up. At supper, he comes in for a handful of onion-flavored bacon crisps or a dish of miniature corn-on-the-cobs pickled. Mum keeps us in the kitchen longer so he can have a little peace and quiet. Ask him what he wants for Christmas and he'll say *No more arguing*. When Mum clears our plates, she takes a bite of someone's hot dog or a quick spoonful of peas before dumping the rest down the pig.

In the car, we ask Dad if we can stop at Shucker's for candy. When he doesn't answer, it means *No*. Mum's eyes mean *Not today*. She says, "It's treat night anyway." Treats are ginger ale and vanilla ice cream.

On Sunday nights we have treats and BLTs and get to watch Ted Mack and Ed Sullivan. There are circus people on almost every time, doing cartwheels or flips or balancing. We stand up in our socks and try some of it. Delilah does an imitation of Elvis by making jump rope handles into a microphone. Girls come on with silver shoes and their stomachs showing and do clappity tap dances. "That's a cinch," says Mum behind us.

"Let's see you then," we say and she goes over to the brick in

36

front of the fireplace to show us. She bangs the floor with her sneakers, pumping and kicking, thudding her heels in smacks, not like clicking at all, swinging her arms out in front of her like she's wading through the jungle. She speeds up, staring straight at Dad who's reading his book, making us laugh even harder. He's always like that. Sometimes for no reason, he'll snap out of it going, "What? What? What's all this? What's going on?" as if he's emerged from a dark tunnel, looking like he does when we wake him up and he hasn't put on his glasses yet, sort of angry. He sits there before dinner, popping black olives into his mouth one at a time, eyes never leaving his book. His huge glass mug is from college and in the lamplight you can see the liquid separate. One layer is beer, the rest is gin. Even smelling it makes you gag.

Dad would never take us to Shucker's for candy. With him, we do things outside. If there's a storm we go down to the rocks to see the waves—you have to yell—and get sopped. Or if Mum needs a nap, we go to the beach. In the spring it's wild and windy as anything, which I love. The wind presses against you and you kind of choke but in a good way. Sherman and I run, run, run! Couples at the end are so far away you can hardly tell they're moving. Rummy races around with other dogs, flipping his rear like a goldfish, snapping at the air, or careening in big looping circles across the beach. Caitlin jabs a stick into the wet part and draws flowers. Chicky smells the seaweed by smushing it all over his face. Delilah's dark bangs jitter across her forehead like magnets and she yells back to Gus lagging behind. Dad looks at things far away. He points out birds—a great blue heron near the breakers as thin as a safety pin or an osprey in the sky, tilting like a paper cutout. We collect little things. Delilah holds out a razor shell on one sandy palm for Dad to take and he says *Uh-huh* and calls Rummy. When Sherman, grinning, carries a dead seagull to him, Dad says, "Cut that out." Once in Maine, I found a triangle of blue and white china and showed it to Dad. "Ah, yes, a bit of crockery," he said.

"Do you think it's from the Indians?" I whispered. They had made the arrowheads we found on the beach.

"I think it's probably debris," he said and handed it back to me. According to Mum, debris is the same thing as litter, as in Don't Be a Litter Bug.

When we get home from skating, it's already started to get dark.

Sherman runs up first and beats us to the door but can't open it himself. We are all used to how warm it was in the car so everybody's going *Brrrr*, or *Hurry up*, banging our feet on the porch so it thunders. The sky is dark blue glass and the railing seems whiter and the fur on Mum's hood glows. From the driveway Dad yells, "I'm going downtown. Be right back," slamming the door and starting the car again.

Delilah yells, "Can I come?" and Gus goes, "Me too!" as we watch the car back up.

"Right back," says his deep voice through the crack in the window and he rounds the side of the house.

"How come he didn't stop on the way home?" asks Caitlin, sticking out her chin.

"Yah," says Delilah. "How come?" We look at Mum.

She kicks the door with her boot. "In we go, Totsies," she says instead of answering and drops someone's skate on the porch because she's carrying so much stuff.

Gus gets in a bad mood, standing by the door with his coat on, not moving a muscle. His hat has flaps over the ears. Delilah flops onto the hall sofa, her neck bent, ramming her chin into her chest. "Why don't you take off your coat and stay awhile?" she says, drumming her fingers as slow as a spider on her stomach.

"I don't have to."

"Yah," Sherman butts in. "Who says you're the boss?" He's lying on the marble tile with Rummy, scissor-kicking his legs like windshield wipers.

"No one," says Delilah, her fingers rippling along.

On the piano bench, Caitlin is picking at her split ends. We can hear Mum in the kitchen putting the dishes away.

Banging on the piano fast because she knows it by heart, Caitlin plays "Walking in a Winter Wonderland." Delilah sits up and imitates her behind her back, shifting her hips from side to side, making us all laugh. Caitlin whips around, "What?"

"Nothing." But we can't help laughing.

"Nothing what?" says Mum coming around the corner, picking up mittens and socks from the floor, snapping on the lights.

Delilah stiffens her legs. "We weren't doing anything," she says.

We make room for Mum on the couch and huddle. Gus perches at the edge, sideways.

"When's Dad coming back?" he says.

"You know your father," says Mum vaguely, smoothing Delilah's hair on her lap, daydreaming at the floor but thinking about something. When Dad goes to the store, he only gets one thing, like a can of black bean soup or watermelon rind.

"What shall we play?" says Sherman, strangling Rummy in a hug.

"Yah. Yah. Let's do something," we say and turn to Mum.

She narrows her eyes into spying slits. "All rightee. I might have a little idea."

"What?" we all shout, excited. "What?" Mum hardly ever plays with us because she has to do everything else.

She rises, slowly, lifting her eyebrows, hinting. "You'll see."

"What?" says Gus and his bottom lip loosens nervously.

Delilah's dark eyes flash like jumping beans. "Yah, Mum. What?"

"Just come with me," says Mum in a singsong and we scamper after her. At the bottom of the stairs, she crouches in the middle of us. Upstairs behind her, it's dark.

"Where are we going?" asks Caitlin and everybody watches Mum's face, thinking of the darkness up there.

"Hee hee hee," she says in her witch voice. "We're going to surprise your father, play a little trick."

"What?" asks Caitlin again, getting ready to worry but Mum's already creeping up the stairs so we follow, going one mile per hour like her, not making a peep even though there's no one in the house to hear us.

Suddenly she wheels around. "We're going to hide," she cackles.

"Where?" we all want to know, sneaking along like burglars.

Her voice is hushed. "Just come with me."

At the top of the stairs it is dark and we whisper.

"How about your room?" says Delilah. "Maybe under the bed."

"No," says Sherman breathlessly. "In the fireplace." We all laugh because we could never fit in there.

Standing in the hall, Mum opens the door to the linen closet and pulls the light string. "How about right here?" The light falls across our faces. On the shelves are stacks of bed covers and rolled puffs, red and white striped sheets and pink towels, everything clean and folded and smelling of soap.

All of a sudden Caitlin gasps, "Wait—I hear the car!"

Quickly we all jumble and scramble around, bumbling and

knocking and trying to cram ourselves inside. Sherman makes whimpering noises like an excited dog. *Sshhhh*, we say or *Hurry Hurry*, or *Wait*. I knee up to a top shelf and Sherman gets a boost after me and then Delilah comes grunting up. We play in here sometimes. Gus and Chicky crawl into the shelf underneath, wedging themselves in sideways. Caitlin half-sits on molding with her legs dangling and one hand braced against the door frame. When the rushing settles, Mum pulls out the light and hikes herself up on the other ledge. Everyone is off the ground then, and quiet.

Delilah giggles. Caitlin says *Ssshhhh* and I say *Come on* in a whisper. Only when Mum says *Hush* do we all stop and listen. Everyone is breathing; a shelf creaks. Chicky knocks a towel off and it hits the ground like a pillow. Gus says, "I don't hear anything." *Sshhh*, we say. Mum touches the door and light widens and we listen. Nothing.

"False alarm," says Sherman.

Our eyes start to get used to the dark. Next to me Delilah gurgles her spit.

"What do you think he'll do?" whispers Caitlin. We all smile, curled up in the darkness with Mum thinking how fooled he'll be, coming back and not a soul anywhere, standing in the hall with all the lights glaring not hearing a sound.

"Where will he think we've gone?" We picture him looking around for a long time, till finally we all pour out of the closet.

"He'll find out," Mum whispers. Someone laughs at the back of his throat, like a cricket quietly ticking.

Delilah hisses, "Wait—"

"Forget it," says Caitlin who knows it's a false alarm.

"What will he do?" we ask Mum.

She's in the darkest part of the closet, on the other side of the light slant. We hear her voice. "We'll see."

"My foot's completely fallen asleep," says Caitlin.

"Kick it," says Mum's voice.

"Ssshhh," lisps Chicky and we laugh at him copying everybody.

Gus's muffled voice comes from under the shelf. "My head's getting squished."

"Move it," says Delilah.

"Quiet!"

And then we really do hear the car.

"Silence, Monkeys," says Mum and we all hush, holding our breaths. The car hums up the hill.

The motor dies and the car shuts off. We hear the door crack, then clip shut. Footsteps bang up the echoing porch, loud, toe-hard and scuffing. The glass panes rattle when the door opens, resounding in the empty hall, and then the door slams in the dead quiet, reverberating through the whole side of the house. Some-one in the closet squeaks like a hamster. Downstairs there isn't a sound.

"Anybody home?" he bellows, and we try not to giggle.

Now what will he do? He strides across the deep hall, going by the foot of the stairs, obviously wondering where everybody's gone, stopping at the hooks to hang up his parka.

"What's he doing?" whispers Caitlin to herself.

"He's by the mitten basket," says Sherman. We all have smiles, our teeth like watermelon wedges, grinning in the dark.

He yells toward the kitchen, "Hello?" and we hunch our shoul-ders to keep from laughing, holding onto something tight like our toes or the shelf, or biting the side of our mouths.

He starts back into the hall.

"He's getting warmer," whispers Mum's voice, far away. We all wait for his footsteps on the stairs.

But he stops by the TV room doorway. We hear him rustling something, a paper bag, taking out what he's bought, the bag crinkling, setting something down on the hall table, then crum-pling up the bag and pitching it in the wastebasket. Gus says, "Why doesn't he—?" *Ssshhh*, says Mum like spitting and we all freeze. He moves again—his footsteps turn and bang on the hollow threshold into the TV room where the rug pads the sound.

Next we hear the TV click on, the sound swelling and the dial switching *tick-ah tikka tikka tick* till it lands on a crowd roar, a football game. We can hear the announcer's voice and the hiss-breath behind it of cheering.

Then it's the only sound in the house.

"What do we do now?" says Delilah only half-whispering. Mum slips down from her shelf and her legs appear in the light, touching down.

Still hushed, Sherman goes, "Let's keep hiding."

The loud thud is from Caitlin jumping down. She uses her regular voice. "Forget it. I'm sick of this anyway." Everyone starts

41

to rustle. Chicky panics, "I can't get down" as if we're about to desert him.

"Stop being such a baby," says Delilah, disgusted.

Mum doesn't say anything, just opens the door all the way. Past the banister in the hall it is yellow and bright. We climb out of the closet, feet-feeling our way down backwards, bumping out one at a time, knocking down blankets and washcloths by mistake. Mum guides our backs and checks our landings. We don't leave the narrow hallway. The light from downstairs shines up through the railing and casts shadows on the wall—bars of light and dark like a fence. Standing in it we have stripes all over us. *Hey look,* we say whispering, with the football drone in the background, even though this isn't anything new—we always see this, holding out your arms and seeing the stripes. Lingering near the linen closet we wait. Mum picks up the tumbled things, restacking the stuff we knocked down, folding things, clinching a towel with her chin, smoothing it over her stomach and then matching the corners left and right, like crossing herself, patting everything into neat piles. The light gets like this every night after we've gone to bed and we creep into the hall to listen to Mum and Dad downstairs. The bands of shadows go across our nightgowns and pajamas and we press our foreheads against the railing trying to hear the mumbling of what Mum and Dad are saying down there. Then we hear the deep boom of Dad clearing his throat and look up at Mum. Though she is turned away, we can still see the wince on her face like when you are waiting to be hit or right after you have been. So we keep standing there, our hearts pounding, waving our hands through the flickered stripes, suddenly interested the way you get when it's time to take a bath and you are mesmerized by something. We're stalling, waiting for Mum to finish folding, waiting to see what she's going to do next because we don't want to go downstairs yet, where Dad is, without her.

🔥 🔥 🔥

SELF/LANDSCAPE/GRID

by TERRENCE DES PRES

from NEW ENGLAND REVIEW AND BREAD LOAF QUARTERLY

nominated by NEW ENGLAND REVIEW AND BREAD LOAF QUARTERLY and
Joyce Carol Oates

> *Miller owns this field, Locke that, and Manning the woodland
> beyond. But none of them owns the landscape. There is a
> property in the horizon which no man has but he whose eye
> can integrate all the parts, that is, the poet.*
>
> —Emerson
>
> *Every appearance in nature corresponds to some state of
> mind. . . .*
>
> —Emerson

I LIVE IN UPSTATE NEW YORK, rural countryside and lovely hills,
a place my neighbors like to call "the village." It's small, quiet,
great for raising kids. Forty miles to the north, however, lies
Griffiss Airforce Base, known locally as Rome, because Rome is the
town the base uses. Out of there fly the B-52's that control our part
of the sky. There too the Pentagon keeps its brood of cruise
missiles. So nobody doubts, in this part of the country, that Rome
(when it happens) will be the spot where the warheads hit. At one
time we thought that the Russians had size but no technical
finesse. That gave us a stupid sort of hope. An overshot might land
on our heads, but if incoming missiles fell short, they would come
down way north, maybe on Edmund Wilson's old stone house in
Talcottville, and we, at least, would be well out of range. Now we
are told that the Soviets have refined their delivery. Their guid-
ance systems are on target, not least because the Russians have
used American technology, computers, micro-chips, ball-bearings,
made and sold by American firms. That, no matter how we look at

43

it, is ugly news. And with Rome at the nub of a nuclear arc, we are resigned in our knowledge that things will start exactly forty miles away. How far the firestorm will reach is what we mainly wonder. We don't know, but we are counting on these upstate hills to block the worst of the blast. If the horizon works in our favor, we shall then have time to consider the wind. In the meantime, B-52's cross and recross above us. They gleam with their nuclear payload. Two or three are up there always, and once I counted thirteen. The air is creased with vapor trails, and in the afternoons, when the sun starts down, the sky looks welted with scars.

That, anyway, is the prospect I share with my neighbors, our part of the nuclear grid. Not a landscape of the mind, no inner weather sort of scene, it's just life's natural place for those who live here. Even so, the bombers overhead keep me reminded that this landscape possesses, or is possessed by, some other will, some demonic grand design or purpose not at all my own. Nor would that kind of death be mine. An all-at-once affair for almost everyone is how that death would come, impersonal but still no accident. That way of dying would be the ultimate instance of political intrusion, for that is what has brought us to this pass, politics, and by political intrusion I mean the increasing unsettlement and rending of our private lives by public force. We do what we can as citizens, but when it comes to nuclear war we can't do much. The hazard is before us and won't budge. How to live with it is our problem, and some of us, at least, resort to magic. We turn to words which give the spirit breathing space and strength to endure. As in any time of ultimate concern, we call on poetry.

I can read *Ecclesiastes* or *King Lear* for a language equal to extremity, but such language isn't of my time, not of my landscape perhaps I should say. I find a little of what I need in poets like Akhmatova or Mandelstam or Milosz, but American poetry? and among poets of the present generation? Not much, in fact hardly anything. I'm writing in early February (1983) and I've just gone through the recent issue of *American Poetry Review*, which offers forty-eight poems by twenty-one poets. Some few good poems, but only two touch upon our nuclear fate, which leaves forty-six in worlds elsewhere. In "Against Stuff" Marvin Bell follows the possibility—this is a night-thoughts poem—that all our forms and habits, including those of poetry itself, may have been wrong, wrong enough to bring us to "the coming instantaneous flaming" of all creatures and things "which could not suffer/that much light at one time." The poem spreads disquiet and resists reply, and in the following lines the pun on "not right" keeps the poet honestly uncertain:

> and, if we are shortly to find ourselves
> without beast, field or flower,
> is it not right that we now prepare
> by removing them from our poetry?

Under nuclear pressure, should poetry contract its domain? The other poem in *APR*, Maxine Kumin's "You Are In Bear Country," moves with wit and nice inevitability to the imagined moment when the grizzly attacks—and then jumps to this question in italics:

> *Is death*
> *by bear to be preferred*
> *to death by bomb?*

The question seems to intrude out of nowhere, and the poet closes by answering yes. The point, I presume, is that any thought of death, even one so unlikely, recalls the nuclear alternative. And grotesque though it would be, death "by bear" does seem preferable, one's own at least, and natural, part of the order of things and an order, too, as timeless as the wilderness. Bizarre consolations, but once the nuclear element intrudes, these are the sorts of ludicrous lengths to which we feel pushed. And the either/or is not even a choice, but only a preference. The absence of *a* and *the* before *bear* and *bomb* suggests two categories of death, only one of which is humanly acceptable.

After *APR* I went on to *Poetry*, where there was nothing relevant, and after that I rummaged randomly through the library's stock of recent journals and magazines, all I could manage in two afternoons. I am sure I read more than two hundred poems, most of them quite short, some very good, but none informed by nuclear awareness. I realize, of course, that any successful poem must authorize itself, must utter its world with self-certainty, but even so, reading so many poems one after the other left me rather shocked by the completeness, the sealed-up way these poems deny the knowledge or nearness of nuclear threat. The other striking thing about most of these poems was their sameness, and especially the meagerness. These observations are not original, of course. Lots of poetry gets written and published in America just now, and if one reads even a small but steady portion of it, one starts to see that the current talk about a "crisis" in our poetry is not unfounded. The trivialization, the huddled stance, the seemingly deliberate littleness of so much poetry in the last few years— how shall we account for it?

Perhaps the rise of the "work-shop" poem has had something to do with it. Maybe also the new careerism among younger poets bent on bureaucratic power in the universities; those who, as Marx would say, have gone over to the management. And surely the kind of literary criticism now in vogue, hostile to the integrity of language, doesn't help. But these are as much symptoms as causes, and the larger situation comes down to this: In a time of nuclear threat, with absolutely everything at stake, our poetry grows increasingly claustrophilic and small-themed, it contracts its domain, it retires still further into the narrow chamber of the self; and we see in this not only the exhaustion of a mode and a tradition, but also the spectacle of spirit cowed and retreating.

The retreat has been swift because American practice invites it. Founded on Emersonian principles, our poetry has drawn much of its strength from an almost exclusive attention to self and nature. Typically we have conceived of the self *as* a world rather than of the self *in* the world. Things beyond the self either yield to imagination or else they don't matter, and the world becomes a store of metaphor to be raided as one can. The "strong" poet turns any landscape to private use, and solipsism wins praise as the sign of success. Emerson didn't invent these attitudes, but he was good at summing them up. "Every natural fact is a symbol of some spiritual fact," he wrote, and "the Universe is the externization [sic] of the soul." Thus the road was open for Whitman and poets to come, and thus Emerson delivered his mandate: "Know then that the world exists for you," and "Build therefore your own world." Partly, this is the mythology of our national experience, with its determination to deny social-political limits and focus instead on individual destiny. Partly, too, this is the American brand of Romanticism, part of a larger movement that on the continent peaked in its influential French example. Baudelaire called the world a "forest of symbols," and Mallarmé thought that everything external, *la cité, ses gouvernements, le code*, could be dismissed as *le mirage brutal*.

Stated thus, the whole business seems outlandish—but not really. The Emersonian mandate supports maximum belief in the poet's potency, not in itself a bad thing. Then, too, poets in our century have held some very odd convictions, Yeats for example, or for that matter, Merrill. But in one respect there is no doubting: American poetry has rejected history and politics on principle. Despite Lowell's example and more recent exceptions like Rich and Forché, our poets in the main have been satisfied to stick with Emerson, and few would find anything to take exception with in the following lines from Emerson's *Ode:*

> I cannot leave
> My honeyed thought
> For the priest's cant,
> Or statesman's rant.
>
> If I refuse
> My study for their politique,
> Which at the best is trick,
> The angry Muse
> Puts confusion in my brain.

American contempt for politicians runs deep. As a sort of common-sense cynicism it allows us to go untroubled by crime in high places and, more to the point, it bolsters our belief that personal life exists apart from, and is superior to, political force and its agencies. But also, as Gunnar Myrdal demonstrated in *An American Dilemma*, our sort of political cynicism goes hand in hand with a remarkably durable idealism. We take for granted that governments are corrupt, then feel that some other power, providential and beyond the meddling of men, governs our destiny finally. Where there's a will there's a way, and everything comes right in the end. But does it? Even without the Bomb to put such faith into question, Emerson's example—Poland, for God's sake!—invites scepticism:

> The Cossack eats Poland,
> Like stolen fruit;

47

Her last noble is ruined,
Her last poet mute:
Straight, into double band
The victors divide;
Half for freedom strike and stand:—
The astonished Muse finds thousands at her side.

The Muse might well be befuddled, given the logic of Emerson's syntax. But of course, Emerson's faith in the future—disaster compensated by renewal—can't mean much to us. With the advent of the nuclear age there is no assurance that anything will remain for the phoenix to rise from.

We have fallen from the Garden, and the Garden itself—nature conceived as an inviolate wilderness—is pocked with nuclear waste and toxic dumps, at the mercy of industry, all of it open to nuclear defilement. Generations come and go, but that *the earth abideth forever* is something we need to feel, one of the foundations of poetry and humanness, and now we are not sure. That is the problem with nuclear threat, simply as threat; it undermines all certainty, and things once absolute are now contingent. To feel that one's private life was in the hands of God, or Fate, or even History, allowed the self a margin of transcendence; the dignity of personal life was part of a great if mysterious Order. But now our lives are in the hands of a few men in the Pentagon and the Kremlin, men who, having affirmed that they would destroy us to save us, have certified their madness—and yet their will determines our lives and our deaths. We are, then, quite literally enslaved, and assuming that this bothers poets no less than the rest of us, why do they so seldom speak of it? It is not too much to say that most poetry in America is written against experience, against first feelings and needs. Whether the Emersonian tradition is a trap or a last-ditch defense is perhaps a moot point. But the poetry of self still predominates, with nature as its cornerstone, despite Los Alamos, a lovely spot in the mountains.

Nuclear wipe-out is possible, perhaps probable, and every day I talk with people who are convinced it will happen. No soul is free of that terror, nor of that knowledge; and simply as a state of mind or way of knowing, it drastically alters how we receive and value our experience. Birth, for example, or one's own death; surely having children troubles us in ways not known before, and we need to feel that each of us shall have a death of his or her own, simply in order to feel fully possessed of our lives. These are common feelings, and it's clearer than it used to be that no man (no, nor woman neither) is an island. Our surface lives are individual and unique, but human existence itself—the being that all of us share and feel threatened—gives us our most important sense of ourselves and, I should also think, gives poetry its most significant themes. Can it be, then, that the shallowness of recent poetry reveals a desperate clinging to the surface?

I do *not* ask for poems directly about the Bomb or the end of the world, although with the Bell poem in *APR* as evidence, a theme of this kind can be as legitimate as any other. I don't expect poems of protest or outrage or horror either, although again, I can't see that they would hurt. I do, however, try to keep in mind that some subjects are more human, and more humanly exigent than others—Forché on Salvador compared to Leithauser on dandelions—and also that poets are often scared off by subjects which, precisely because of the fear, signal a challenge worth the risk. But what I'd mainly hope to see, in this case, is poetry that probes the impact of nuclear threat, poetry informed by nuclear knowing, poems that issue from the vantage of a self that accepts its larger landscape, a poetic diction testing itself against the magnitude of our present plight, or finally just poems which survive their own awareness of the ways nuclear holocaust threatens not only humankind but the life of poetry itself.

Nature, for example, remains the mainstay of our poetry. Natural imagery makes us trust the poem, suggests a permanence at the root of things, and every poem about nature bears somewhere within it the myth of renewal and rebirth. But from the nuclear perspective, these ministrations falter. Permanence? Rebirth? Emerson's response to nature was genuinely poetic, and the measure of our present loss may be judged by the degree of nostalgia rather than assent we feel when he says: "In the woods, we return to reason and faith. There I feel that nothing can befall me in life,—no disgrace, no calamity (leaving me my eyes), which nature cannot repair." Well, his notion of calamity isn't ours. And nature, for all its proven renovative power, could never repair the worst that might befall us. Nature suffers the same division we observe in ourselves and in the landscape generally. We are what we are, yet some deep part of selfhood has been invaded by forces wholly alien to personal being, political forces of which the worst is nuclear threat. In the same way, the landscape belongs to us and yet it does not. This concrete place we share is also a site on the nuclear grid. And when, therefore, Emerson tells us that "Every appearance in nature corresponds to some state of mind," we must inquire not only What state of mind? but also Whose mind?

No doubt the crews in the bombers are bored. And no doubt bureaucratic haggling keeps the commander of the base in Rome bogged down in mindless detail. The chiefs in the Pentagon, on the other hand, definitely share a state of mind which must, now and then, get rather dizzy with the glamour of their global strategy. What the Russians have in mind we don't know. But for all of them, we and the landscape are expendable; to think that way, after all, is their job. We cannot say, then, that the landscape corresponds to their minds and to ours in the same way. Rather, what expresses their state of mind, provokes and negates our own. In a traditional landscape, points of correspondence for us would be, among other things, the sky's infinity and the sense of permanence arising from the land itself. But exactly this kind of metaphor-making has been undermined by the transformation of the landscape into a sector on the grid. Or we might look at it this way: the military state of mind becomes an alien element *in* the landscape as we behold it, the B-52's, the proximity of the missile site, the grid and its planners. These forces have broken into our world, they have defiled its integrity, and the new points of correspondence between ourselves and the landscape are the condition of vulnerability and the threat of terminal defacement. Self and world, nature and landscape, everything exists in itself *and* as acceptable loss on the nuclear grid.

I've gone on at length about the landscape in my part of the country to suggest what Emerson's poetic principle—"Every appearance in nature corresponds to some state of mind"—might mean in the nuclear age. Every person has his or her own place, of course, and in a country as vast as ours the variety of landscape must be nearly infinite. The kinds of personal vision to which a landscape corresponds must also, then, be fairly limitless. But all vision converges in the fact that every landscape is part of the nuclear grid. I have the air base in Rome to remind me of this, whereas people living in, say, New York City are reminded by the city itself—its status as a prime target; the difficulty of maintaining life-support systems, water, energy, even in normal times; traffic's five o'clock entrapment every afternoon, not to mention the way the city is mocked by officials in Washington who suggest that in the event of an alert, nine million people will please evacuate the area. Then too, there are the nuclear power plants nearby; these are also targets, and when hit will spout radiation like the fourth of July. The citizenry can always avail itself of shovels, as another Washington wit has proposed, but no, there's no real hope. So that landscape too has its message.

Meanwhile, poets write about "marshes, lakes and woods, Sweet Emma of Preservation Hall, a Greek lover, an alchemist, actresses, fairy tales, canning peaches in North Carolina," stuff like that, to quote from the ad for a recent anthology. The apology for poems of this kind (triviality aside) is that by celebrating modest moments of the human spectacle—little snaps of wonder, bliss or pain—poetry implicitly takes its stand against the nuclear negation. To say Yes to life, this argument goes, automatically says No to the Bomb. And yes, a grain of truth sprouts here. I expect many among us read poetry that way in any case. The upshot, however, is that poets can go on producing their vignettes of self, pleased to be fighting the good fight without undue costs—except *the* cost, which is the enforced superficiality, the required avoidance of our deeper dismay.

Nuclear threat engenders cynicism, despair, allegiance to a mystique of physical force, and to say No to such destructive powers requires an enormously vehement Yes to life and human value. What's called for, in fact, is the kind of poetry we once named "great," and my suspicion is that today the will to greatness is absent. Great poems, Wordsworth's or Whitman's for example, confront their times; they face and contain their own negation. The human spirit draws its strength from adversity, and so do poems. Examples like *The Prelude* and *Song of Myself* incorporate and thereby transcend that which, if they ignored it, would surely cancel their capacity for final affirmation. And having mentioned poems of this calibre, I might also add that the "American sublime," as critics call it, has been missing in our poetry at least since late Stevens. The sublime, as observers like Burke and Kant and Schopenhauer insist, arises from terror, terror beheld and resisted, the terror of revolution for Wordsworth, of the abyss for Whitman, of nuclear annihilation for any poet today who would make a language to match our extremity.

I can see, though, why we try to avoid what we know. Terror will flare up suddenly, a burst of flame in the chest, and then there is simply no strength. Other times the mind goes blank in disbelief. The temptation to retreat is always with us, but where can we go, where finally? Sometimes I let it all recede, let silence be enough, and go for a walk through the fields and apple hedge above my house. The horizon then is remarkably clear, the sky is still its oldest blue. Overhead, the planes are half a hemisphere ahead of their thunder. It's hard not to think of them as beautiful, some-times; humankind took so long to get up there. I wind my way through milkweed in the meadow and remember how Emerson, crossing an empty field, felt glad to the brink of fear. We know what he means, the elation that sweeps through us at such moments. And then I think of Osip Mandelstam and an old Russian proverb; life, he wrote, is not a walk across a field. We know what he means too, the inhuman hardship of centuries, the modern horror of being stalked to death. But it's all of this, isn't it? the grimness and the glory. Why should we think to keep them apart? We fear, maybe, that dread will undermine our joy, and often it does. To keep them wed is poetry's job. And now that the big salvations have failed us, the one clear thing is that we live by words.

GROUND ZERO

by WILLIAM STAFFORD

from FIELD

nominated by Siv Cedering, John Daniel and Joyce Carol Oates

While we slept—
   rain found us last night, easing in
from The Coast, a few leaves at first,
then ponds. The quietest person in the state
heard the mild invasion. Before it was over
every field knew that benediction.

At breakfast—
   while we talked some birds passed, then slanted
north, wings emphasizing earth's weight
but overcoming it. "There's no hope,"
you said. Our table had some flowers
cascading color from their vase. Newspapers
muttered repression and shouted revolution.
A breeze lifted curtains, they waved
easily. "Why can't someone do something!"
My hand began its roving, like those curtains,
and the flowers bending, and the far-off bird wings.

GROUND ZERO

by SHARON DOUBIAGO

from NEW ENGLAND REVIEW AND BREAD LOAF QUARTERLY
and EMPTY BOWL

nominated by Carolyn Forché, Howard Moss and William Pitt Root

1.

We met on an evening in July
in one of the old taverns of this town,
two poets, unable to write, newly arrived,
hunted and haunted. For me,
the escape. For you,
the return.

You said you would show me
the Olympic Peninsula.

The road was overgrown.
In the headlights of your car I cleared the trees.
The cabin was vandalized, gutted,
the twenty-six oddshaped windows
opening onto the Straits, Canada and all the northern sky
shot out. The sink, the pump, the stoves,
even the doors, stolen.
You wandered around, then out to the deck,
seeming to forget me in the debris.

Victoria, the only human light,
shimmered on the foreign shore.
I heard the groan of a fishing boat below the bluff,
a strange cry from the woods, like a woman,
your ex-wife, the children.

We lay on a narrow mattress in the loft,
amidst bullet shells, beer cans, mold and glass,
the cold, hard bed of delinquent teenagers.

The moon was a broken boat through the bullet shattered
   skylight.
We told each other.
First words. I said
one night stand. You said ground zero.
I said I lost my children, my lover.
You said submarine, fucking vandals.
I said kids with no place to go, kids forbidden
to love. You said holocaust. Apocalypse.
I pulled you over on me. The volcano erupted.
The world turned to ash. I screamed
love cannot be gutted.
The moon, the stars, the giant trees watched
through a bullet hole.

2.

You moved in, installed sink, stoves, water pump.
Sixty oddshaped windows. You sat here
pissed as the eagle that stared from the bluff,
the greasepen numbers on the glass around your brooding head
like cabala, some secret military code.
When I visited, I felt a vandal.
When I left you cried deserted.
Betrayed.

In November I moved in.
Sheetrock. Yellow paint named Sunlight.
My white dog, Moonlight.
I said I'd stay until the place
became a landscape in my dreams.
By moon's light through the bullet hole
I began to write.
Your words: The Duckabush, The Dosiewallips, The Hamma
   Hamma.

It snowed in December.
You followed Coyote's tracks to the log where he slept.
A trapper came on the deep path.
He had Coyote. He gave you his card.
He boasted he'd get the rest.
He hinted that for money he could get them for you.

You were not easy to love.
You couldn't speak. Your tongue was cut out.
I left, screaming down the interstate,
avoiding the road over the mountains
to my old, equally beautiful, home.
You wrote me. One Trident submarine equals
two thousand and forty Hiroshimas.

In the cities I was weighted with cedar, an inland sea,
like provisions carried on my back.
Friends I'd always respected said
they couldn't live without culture
I was weighted with the culture of eagle, coyote, people
like weather, like stars, functions of nature, not
human will, money, concrete.

3.

I came back to study the language of gulls,
the stories they scream to each other
as they fly off their sanctuary,
Protection Island.

You pulled me up the stairs.
Beyond your head I watched the moon through the bullet hole.
You said six layers of mountains
from the road, you said rivers
without end. You quoted Rilke's
Neptune of the blood and his terrible trident.
You said Trident
submarine. You said
zero.

I came back to stare back at Eagle,
to cut, carry, and chop our firewood,
to piss in the tall fern, to shit
in *the first little house you ever built*.
I came back and broke my habit at last
of the electric typewriter.
I came back to our cruel and grinding poverty,
never enough kerosene, gasoline, postage, paper or pens.
We turned off the propane. It is so cold in our house
the little food on our shelves is naturally iced.

I came back to listen to the woods,
gulls squawk and moandance of cedar, fir and alder,
the high scream of wind through the mouth of Haro,
Rosario, Deception Pass
where the ships disappear on the inward passage.
I came back to listen to your breath
as you sleep beside me. Poet. Your words.
Puma. Ish. Milosz. The children
who once lived here.

4.

You weighted me with your poems,
like provisions. I left, drove home.
My children were grown, gone.
Your words pulled me back.

We climb the stairs together.
The roof leaks, the cabin is for sale.
I say it is ours for now. Our one night stand,
our two hundred nights.

You tell me of this thing that is coming,
the deadliest weapon ever made.
Two football fields, four stories high.
Two thousand and forty Hiroshimas.

It can be anywhere in the world, undetected,
and hit its target within half a foot.

It can be anywhere in the world and no one,
not the President, not the Computer
will be able to find it.

One day soon it will enter the Straits of Juan de Fuca.
The most evil thing ever created
will float beneath our cabin, then down
the Hood Canal.

You say four hundred and eight cities
from a single submarine. You say
First Strike Weapon. You say
shoot out their silos. You say
U.S.S. Ohio.

5.

I came upon an old man
teaching his granddaughter and grandson
how to shoot.

I sat here alone.
The door banged open and four kids
burst in. Perfume, six packs, party clothes.
I think I frightened them
as much as they frightened me.

On clear days the islands rise up.
San Juan. Lopez. Orcas, white skyscrapers
on Vancouver. How many ships, my love,
have come and gone since we came? How many whales,
eagles, coyotes and gulls?
I finished my epic poem here.
You finished *The Straits*.

Every night the human city
shimmers and beckons on the Canadian shore.
Every night of one whole week
the sky wove and unwove
the rainbow flags of all the north

delicately over us. The Aurora
Borealis.

Two seasons of snow, now the season of light again.
My one night stand, our four hundred
nights.

I saw car lights descend Protection Island
to the water.
The leaks in the roof washed away
my nightwritten words.
We saw six killer whales
rise and fall through the water.
You said my rejected poems. I said
your smallminded editors. I said
I can almost understand now
what the gulls are saying.

6.

My dreams take place on an inland sea,
a land soaked in silver shadows and blue.
We are traveling to the heart of the continent.
We are looking for a room to rent. We are having a baby.
We are building a house.
You say unrecognized. Unpublished. I say just
wait. You say holocaust. You say apocalypse. I say
love.

Once you went with me.
Once you came for me.

We climb the loft together. This, you say
is your home now. This northwest corner. This last place
we can run.

This bed of outlaws, circle of mountains, finger
of glacier water, dark sun of winter behind
Mt. Olympus.

7.

Light shoots through the skylights.
Twenty full moons awake us.
Moonlight sleeps below by the fire, cries from nightmare.
The Manx, the Siamese watch us through the bullet hole.
We lie in terror,
watch the giant trees arch and blow over us,
rain and wind so fierce
we wait without words to be crushed.
Finally I say maybe we should leave. You say
where would we go?
You say death like a storm that might/might not
blow over. You say Puma.
I say Tatoosh means Thunderbird.
Like Phoenix, like rebirth.
You say the last crisis is not death,
but how to be beautiful.
How to die
beautifully.

8.

Say the word Hiroshima.
Reflect on its meaning for one second.
Say and understand Hiroshima again.
Say and understand Hiroshima two thousand and forty times.

Assuming you are able to understand Hiroshima in
one second, you will be able to understand Trident
in thirty four minutes. That's one Trident submarine.
To understand the destructive power of the whole
Trident fleet, it will take you seventeen hours
devoting one second to each Hiroshima.*

9.

The real estate agents are lost on Old Dump Road.
Coyote yelps. The last hunter shoots.

---

*from Jim Douglass' Lightning East and West.

The kids break through the woods
still looking for the party.
I throw open the window. "Here's your bed!
Come join us! We've kept it warm for you!"
You always pull me back to weep in your arms, where

are my teenagers?

10.

The volcano erupted. The world turned to ash.
Now the planets line up: *six hundred days and nights*.
The sun comes north
falls into the mouth of the Straits.
Rhododendron. Honeysuckle. Calypso. Trillium.
The stunted shrub blazes up
like a flaming heart.

And snow circle of mountains! Ring of fire!
Rainier, Mt. Baker, Glacier Peak, St. Helens!
Olympic Home of the Gods: *Sappho, Makah, Joyce, Quinault.*
Shi Shi, La Push, Ozette, Kalaloch.
How many nights, my love, how many poems, my great poet
we have awakened
to the low moan of a fishing boat,
someone's voice, almost,
heard in the trees

> *It has already left. It is on its way.*
> *It is coming around from the other side of the continent.*
> *the date is a secret.*
>
> *It will enter the mouth of the Straits,*
> *then slip down the Hood Canal..*
> *It will move beneath your cabin.*
> *It will come through your windows.*
>
> *You will be anywhere in the world*
> *and it will find you.*

for Michael Daley
March 25, 1982

AS THE PRESIDENT SPOKE

by TED KOOSER

from PRAIRIE SCHOONER

nominated by PRAIRIE SCHOONER *and Sara Vogan*

As the President spoke, he raised a finger
to emphasize something he said. I've forgotten
just what he was saying, but as he spoke
he glanced at that finger as if it were
somebody else's, and his face went slack and gray,
and he folded his finger back into its hand
and put it down under the podium
along with whatever it meant, with whatever he'd seen
as it spun out and away from that bony axis.

𝆶 𝆶 𝆶

LOT'S WIFE

by CELIA GILBERT

from ALICE JAMES BOOKS

nominated by ALICE JAMES BOOKS *and DeWitt Henry*

> *Then the Lord rained upon Sodom and Gomorrah brimstone and fire from the Lord out of heaven;*
> *And he overthrew those cities, and all the plain, and the inhabitants of the cities, and that which grew upon the ground.*
> *But his wife looked back from behind him, and she became a pillar of salt.*

Genesis: 24–26

> hibakusha: (hi bak' sha),
> explosion-afflicted person. The term
> coined by the Japanese to signify those who
> were exposed to the radiation of atomic bombs
> in Hiroshima and Nagasaki.

The moment I saw the strangers at the door,
men, without women, I was afraid.
I begged Lot not to take them in.
Muffled in dusty cloaks
they accepted hospitality
as if they were superior beings.
They were too beautiful—
faces hard and polished—
the light couldn't enter them,
it fell away, baffled.
But Lot was impressed by their authority,
he loved authority, loved
to use it. The men, we
thought they were men then,
they didn't care for us.
You could see they had a job to do

and that was all. They were looking
at us but thinking about the job.

> "Sweeney was like most bomber pilots who have formed a
> defensive armor about their particular role in war. Their
> function is to drop bombs on targets not on people. Were
> they to think otherwise, to be ordered to drop a bomb on
> say, 2,567 men, women, and children, they would probably
> go mad. A target was a different matter . . ."

Lot and the strangers talked about good and evil
while our daughters and I served them
at table. And Lot bowed low when they said
that he was a God-fearing man who would never
do anything wicked like his neighbors.

I knew my neighbors,
women like myself, going to the well,
weaving and spinning,
raising the family.
The little boys were noisy,
dirty, and quick,
the little girls, shy, quieter,
but sturdy.

> ". . . girls, very young girls, not only with their clothes torn
> off but with their skin peeled off as well. I thought should
> there be a hell this was it—the Buddhist hell where we were
> taught people who could not attain salvation always went."

I saw the strangers look at our daughters
not as men look at women
but as we might look at dumb brutes—
no, not even that—for often we recognize
ourselves in their uncomprehending
helplessness. They simply looked
but did not see.

> "The most impressive thing was the expression in people's
> eyes . . . their eyes looking for someone to come and help

them. The eyes—the emptiness—the helpless expression
were something I will never forget . . . they looked at me
with very great expectation staring right through me."

While we feasted the strangers,
the city hummed outside our doors,
the buzzing of the hive, moving,
agitating. Most people were like us
busy with small schemes. Lot called
our city wicked because he abhorred
the men in it who loved men and the women
who loved women, practices of love
he held unclean, claiming
Jews were different from other people.
But our city was like any other city.
And there were violent gangs of men
who raped men, and that seemed to many
especially horrible. When women were raped
that was wrong, they said,
but there was no special horror to it.

Then came the screams of drunks,
the obscene cries, the beating
at our doors.
    And they called unto Lot,
and said unto him, Where are
the men which came in to thee
this night? bring them out
unto us, that we may know
them.
    And Lot went out at the
door unto them, and shut the
door after him,
    And said, I pray you,
brethren, do not so wickedly.
    Behold now, I have two
daughters which have not known
man; let me, I pray you, bring
them out unto you, and do ye to

them as is good in your eyes:
only unto these men do nothing;
for therefore came they under
the shadow of my roof.

Dishonor and shame await those who
behave dishonorably.
We owed the guests at our table protection,
that was the custom,
but how could Lot offer
our virgin daughters to the mob?
He took the side of the angels—
for so they later revealed themselves—
or did he take the side of the men out there?

> "Sweeney's regular plane, *The Great Artiste,* named by the
> crew in honor the bombardier's technique with a bombsight
> and the opposite sex, had already been outfitted with special
> instruments."

"Take my daughters, but not
the strangers within my gates—,"
words spoken with high seriousness.
The house of Lot was only Lot,
we were chattels and goods.
We women were his animals to breed.
Why didn't he offer himself to the men?
The strangers smiled.
They had their orders, and their secret
knowledge: God was created in the image of man,
him only.
The rape of women and children
is sanctioned.
Our lives were spared,
because of Lot's godliness.

> ". . . all had skin blackened by burns . . . no hair . . . at a
> glance you couldn't tell whether you were looking at them
> from in front or in back. They had their arms bent . . . and
> their skin—not only on their hands but on their faces and

bodies, too—hung down . . . like walking ghosts they didn't look like people of this world."

We covered our heads,
my weeping daughters and I, and ran
with Lot and the strangers through the blinding
light that tore
and shattered and broke in a rain of fire and ash.

"I climbed Hijiyama Mountain and looked down. I saw that Hiroshima had disappeared . . . Hiroshima had become an empty field."

My neighbor was gone. I remembered her,
worn with children, disagreeable,
her harassed look, bent back,
how she came one day when my daughter
was sick, with a special broth.
"Take it, it might help."

With every step my blood
congealed with unshed tears;
my body thickened.
For what were we saved?
To turn our backs on slaughter
and forget? To worship
the power that spared our lives?

Those who died are my children now,
my other children, destroyed in the fire,
neighbors, women and their young,
the animals, the green of our simple
gardens.
How can I spit out
the bitter root I gnaw, foraged from the rubble,
more sour than the apple, the knowledge
of what power rules our lives,
the evil that knows but does not care,
that values men at nothing, and women less,

behemoth in love with death
and willing, to that end, to extinguish
even itself to celebrate its own spending?

The stench of flesh my skin breathes in
cannot be washed away.
What life could I have surviving
the second's flash that revealed
the sight of the world as it is?
Seared and defiled, scorched
and silenced, I turn back,
refusing to live God's lies,
and will my body, transfixed by grief,
to rise in vigil
over the ashen cities.

CONSOLATION

by DANIEL BERRIGAN

from HOME PLANET NEWS

nominated by Home Planet News

Listen
if now and then
you hear the dead
muttering like ashes
creaking like empty
rockers on porches

filling you in   filling you in

like winds in empty
branches   like stars
in wintry trees—
so far
so good

you've mastered finally
one foreign tongue

𝄞 𝄞 𝄞

DUCKWALKING

fiction by JOE ASHBY PORTER

from SUN & MOON PRESS

nominated by SUN & MOON PRESS *and DeWitt Henry*

I WAS DOWN IN THE MOUTH, Martha was upstairs with the kids, in his first tube series Rick Montalban was playing a DA—a welcome switch from the detective cycle according to Hearst Motion Picture Editor Dorothy Manners (HMPEDM). I'd had flak that day from the boss about some quantification, it was quite a flap and I was feeling like chucking it. Being a 'puter programmer (PP) I knew I wouldn't lack for work. I'd popped a Quaalude and Rick was wrapping up a smack baron when down the stairs comes Martha doing it. I said, "Oh really?" She gave me a Bronx cheer through the bannister rails.

We'd talked about it but I hadn't expected her to start just like that. I think she'd been practicing in secret cause she got down the stairs okay. She kicked off her mukluks and came over and stood with her elbow on the coffee table. A laxative ad, a melmac ad, some gag-rule claptrap on the news before she looks away from the screen. "Doc Purdy says forget bursitis."

"Purdy's no doc, he's. . . ."

Martha interrupted, "I've made up my mind, Bill, and I'm not backing out. Noon news showed Jackie doing it at a function. If you want to look like a cracker that's your problem." They were showing Iraqi quake damage footage before back to Rick, who was in hot water. Catherine Spaak, a skyjacker, had winged him. Martha said, "It's easier than I thought though."

"You fracture me. Five'll getcha ten you don't make it through the weekend." That was a Friday.

That weekend we backpacked with Arch and Tiffany Drake. Arch was a PP too, freelancing at the time. We'd talked about leaving kids home but decided not to. Bill Jr. was fifteen and

Martha Jr.'d've been eleven, with Arch and Tiff's in the same bracket. Ours had tried it now and again around the house, and Martha Jr. could already roller skate doing it. Saturday morning when we took stuff out to the car they and their mother were all doing it. They all stayed down most of that weekend and from then on, except that for half a year Martha Jr. might pop up for a laugh.

Arch and Tiff tooted and waved (T&W): "Let's book." I backed out and followed them to the wilderness area parking lot. The kids didn't stop yakking. They were playing tic tac toe in the back and when one won he or she would give the other a good thwack. I was too sicky-poo about employment snafus to mind. Arch parked his Wankel Mach II smack-dab at the end of the lot and when he and Tiff stepped down out I saw that they were doing it. Their kids were too.

The Joy of Cacking, the conglom that owned the one I'd been PPing for for a couple of years, had a knack for diversification. They'd just bought into Cunard, and office platitude had it the next step was to work some Peking action as a decoy to wangle tax shrinkage. That would draw ack-ack, but J of C had a gaggle of tricks up its sleeve and its future looked anything but lackadaisical. It was playing glitz ball, so what was racking my brains that Saturday was all I stood to lose or gain moving to a new conglom or freelancing like Arch. Arch and I'd been chums years and so had Tiff and Martha. Arch and Tiff are Quakers but you wouldn't want to meet a wackier couple, so I aimed to bend Arch's ear about my job sometime during the weekend.

All the rucksacks but mine dragged, and seeing how slow the going up the trail was didn't make me eager to get down. On the other hand they all chatted like mad and I kept having to bend over to follow. We hit the site about two and pitched camp. After a macaroon snack the kids waddled off to gather kindling, the girls were chewing the cud about a boutique and Arch and I broke out a six-pack and axes and split a few logs. Handling the axe down there was easier for him than I'd expected. Then we sat on the woodpile and rapped.

"What's eating you, Bill? You look like you want to duke it out with somebody." I got worked up letting off steam about the job but Arch didn't crack a smile. He said, "Listen, Mac, that's hooey. I'd hang tight in your place. This rickrack with the boss'll blow over. You and Martha should invite him and Khakeline bowling."

He said J of C's quark angle looked good and in fact he himself planned to hook up on a permanent basis since freelancing was getting too flaky too quick. The kids were moving back into the clearing over by the douches. Martha Jr. missed a softball from Arch Jr. that would've beaned me if I hadn't bobbed my head down in time. Arch grinned, "Dangerous up there, Bill," as he scooted off his log and started toward the fire. I rose to follow and old Arch looked up and said, "Why not give it a try?"

It was dusk, and I remember the crackling of the campfire as I thought, "Why not?" And I remember how the trees wagged as I squatted. Arch and I ambled over to the fire where the wives were cooking a lip-smacking wokload of sprouts. "I knew you were up to it," Martha cooed, and she planted a peck on my kisser. I stayed down the rest of that weekend, kayaking through quagmires and brackish shallows, nearly losing tackle to a bull mackerel I finally landed, relaxing at Tiff's after-lunch songfest cacophony, I stayed down. It sure was good to take a gander right or left and ogle smirks instead of empty air.

That was, oh, seven or eight years ago, when to lots like me duckwalking (DW) looked weak on staying power and thin on consequence. Little did we know. To backtrack, I had first heard of it a year or so before on a wrap-up of what older young adults had been into. One segment dealt with a Texas airforce base brouhaha where a Big Mac maitre d' who'd channelled incoming customers flat south of a DWing waitress got hooted by a WAC claque. I remember I said, "Those squirts." Martha said yes, but she'd scanned a Sunday supplement piece a while back about it that made it sound fun. Later you heard about it more frequently and then somebody said he'd seen a gentleman doing it here in town, over on 33rd near the shellac factory. The exact reason why it eventuated is still in question, but discos were one of the places it seemed to catch on first. The Cow-cow Mooie, the Wigwag and the Macaque were only three of the steps it hatched. *TV Guide* ran a New Year's spread about it with a snap of that month's Neilsen pinup doing it with the Whackers' quarterback at New York's Bimbo's overlooking Central Park. Videoland in fact was a pacesetter. A daytime game show anchorlady sometimes came on doing it, and then on a novelty series about a paramedic and his favorite Tommy gun the whole cast did it. Flicks caught on and novelizations followed fast on their heels.

In the sports world the change raised a few hackles. Most squawks centered on the gridiron cause it slowed the game so much. But that was true of all the running sports, and rule changes must've had umps cracking books even when they went potty. Fans groused but there was no denying that tactics, especially blocking and tackling, were easier to qualitate. Backboards got lowered for hoopsters, batters' and pitchers' styles underwent more far-reaching changes than catchers'. With these like other team sports the field of play naturally shrank so playtime could approximate foregoing commitments to duration length. Ditto for track, double-dog ditto for broad and high jump. The underhand disappeared from tennis, but in swimming the breast- and back-stroke needed only slight kick modifications. Billiards survived intact on a lowered table, and jockeys required minimal stirrup strap hitches.

The Presidential lackey squad gave out he personally affirmed DW's gassiness for some months until after one State of the Union Gossipcast (SUG) he slid off the official banquette and didn't stand but instead did it off the stage. Some hacks penned quasi clucks, others marked it up to sprightly daffiness. The short podium at his next confab told us we were eyeballing the beginning of an era. Armed forces were quick to follow suit. I recall some bivouacked Cossacks surviving a surprise attack with no more than dented helmets.

Of course it infused new fuel into the economy. Take slacks: looser knees cried out for alterations in factory process-components that themselves had to be designed and produced in other factories. Ripples big as tidal waves raced every which way.

My own life has taken several new tacks. For a month after that memorable weekend I sometimes thought of standing back up, but I stayed down and my relations with Martha and the kids waxed smoother pronto. One evening as we gathered on our tatamis around the dindin table Bill Jr. turned to me and cackled, "Pap, hunkering here with you and the big M and Sisface makes me sure I'm the luckiest little pecker alive." My ticker got gooey.

As far as old Martha and me are concerned, that weekend beside the picnic table we started to re-relate (RR) and as the new stance grew on us we found ourselves chitchatting more. The mechanics of sex haven't had to change too much of course, and the actual act gets done at least as often as before duckwalking (BD). At the drop of a hat she'll say, "Drag those knackers over here, Bill"—she's still in bed, it's Sunday, I've showered and before I even dry my back we're banging. We sleep streetcar. Sometimes in the beginning I'd stretch the gams in bed but now the fronts of my knees nuzzle the backs of hers. She's still stacked. The other day we were readying to step next door for drinkypoos and an Also Sprach tape. Old Martha had on a black Shantung poly mini and platform flippers. The placket wobbled like a raccoon tail and I went gaga all over again when she sidled over for a buss.

Like everybody we enjoyed a spate of redecorating in the beginning. We were in a semidetached bungalow in hock up to our necks so we made do with ladders and step-ups, our old gimcrack furniture, lowered macrame and spice racks and shorter wastebaskets. Now we're in the condo with all new chopped Louis XIV and a recessed waterbed. Marth's acquired some slick bricabrac at the Knickknack Shack down the block. A set of Now Faces in Composition Matter Plaques (NFCMP) tops the period baseboard.

Bosso got kicked upstairs soon after my little contretemps and with the new helmsman things have been cricket. Work's the same, but better. Puters' capacities explode monthly simultaneous to monthly hardware shrinkages, and programming's several magnitude notches above prior, but office routine's distinctly similar. So wall urinals have become straddle troughs, so what: everybody still wears baseball caps, gagsters stock whoopee cushions and the muzak's never run dry.

As to social life. The fam and I get off on floor tubefests with the neighbors now and again, as I've hopefully specified. Roller rink Saturday matinees are a hoot, especially when we tap a keg. Golf is always golf even with lateral swings, and the Cheer Club plays nine when it's not hawking loquat pie and sausage for the subteen skateoramas. Bill Jr. and Martha Jr. have Transams with glass packs. He plays wahwah in the marching band and shortstop in the summer. She majorettes—her squad's the Whirlybirds. They both have part-time jobs and heartthrobs.

J of C's had more than its share of the DW prosperity. Somebody must've had an inside line cause just at the start, when most congloms had kissed off construction for a cash flow bottleneck cork, and starts were scarcer than hen's teeth, J of C shifted its diversification exactly that way. As DW became a fait accompli, other gloms moved in for some pie too. Horizontal bisection of existing units was the rule, though some spaces accommodated tri- and hypertrisection, and none of the new plexes and rises has ceilings above four feet. Housing's had megabucks for a demidecade now and J of C's led the pack so I have plenty to crow about. True, some Jack or other over cocktails occasionally still gets nostalgic about the upright posture we abandoned. But I say, after all, was it really ever more than a posture?

THE MYSTERY OF THE CAVES

by MICHAEL WATERS

from THUNDER CITY PRESS

nominated by Stanley Lindberg and Elizabeth Spires

I don't remember the name of the story,
but the hero, a boy, was lost,
wandering a labyrinth of caverns
filling stratum by stratum with water.

I was wondering what might happen:
would he float upward toward light?
Or would he somersault forever
in an underground black river?

I couldn't stop reading the book
because I had to know the answer,
because my mother was leaving again—
the lid of the trunk thrown open,

blouses torn from their hangers,
the crazy shouting among rooms.
The boy found it impossible to see
which passage led to safety.

One yellow finger of flame
wavered on his last match.
There was a blur of perfume—
mother breaking miniature bottles,

then my father gripping her,
but too tightly, by both arms.
The boy wasn't able to breathe.
I think he wanted me to help,

but I was small, and it was late.
And my mother was sobbing now,
no longer cursing her life,
repeating my father's name

among bright islands of skirts
circling the rim of the bed.
I can't recall the whole story,
what happened at the end . . .

Sometimes I worry that the boy
is still searching below the earth
for a thin pencil of light,
that I can almost hear him

through great volumes of water,
through centuries of stone,
crying my name among blind fish,
wanting so much to come home.

WINTER FLIGHT

by JOHN ENGELS

from NEW ENGLAND REVIEW AND BREAD LOAF QUARTERLY

nominated by Donald Hendrie Jr., Philip Levine, Cleopatra Mathis, Sherod Santos and Paul Zimmer.

Just now, here on the runway at Milwaukee,
already three hours late into Ontario,
by way of Denver, which is filled
beyond all possibility with snow,

my invalid father, who has always feared
to fly, comes back just long enough
to ask me who is shepherding him west
are we airborne? an hour yet from taking off,

and he, the whole time here beside me
so far as I can tell, half-dead,
mouth agape, a dark stain down
one trousers-leg, eyes rolled into his head,

asking so as to display some shape
of interest, staring out the window
into the garish nightmare of blue runway lights,
each in its pool of blue snow, that snow-

flood in a cold place neither of us
is likely to see again nor cares to see;
then, sagging back into his seat on the dead
leg, dead arm, sour smell of the old meat

giving way, asks again *how high are we?*
goes still, tries himself once hard to shove
himself upright, and fails. And I cannot help or speak
for being one who, wishing to move, moves.

2

In the thrust and vigorous angle
of the aircraft when at last
it rises and we enter the black sky
of winter that arcs from here and west

and east of here to as far as we might
in order of safety wish to go—when
at last it rises, piercing the night clouds,
entering the watery currents of the high wind,

it is as he has been promised he should fear:
earth-pull as he could never have
imagined it, stony masses of the continent,
power of water calling after him *come back!*

flesh of belly, breast and balls
hauled at, even the smallest
of small bloods hauled at,
and in tumult to the east and west

the great seas he has never seen
about to spill out over the cold land,
below him the angry shallows of the lakes,
below him the forests of Wisconsin

lashing away, and ahead the mountains
sharply in wait, rising and hardening, ahead
and beneath him nothing with much
in the way of promise to it. Half-dead,

he is for the first time flying,
and the last, over the calm flowering
of the moonlit clouds, torn loose
from the entire beloved matter of things,

moving himself to move, fearing it is
in any but the most formal of descents
nothing but annihilation, flesh strewn
about the icy fields of the blue-lit planet,

which, as it turns out, falls away,
thrusts up, billows with snow or salt, surges
together, calls after him, calls after him,
boils up at its ravenous verges.

TOTEMS

by THOMAS MCGRATH

from THUNDERS MOUTH PRESS

nominated by THUNDERS MOUTH PRESS

(I)

In the fall
Feathers appear in the tassels
On Robert Bly's serape.

Without his knowledge or consent
His feet start a heavy dance
Like the dance of a prairie chicken.
All at once he is spinning
Like the reel of an old fanning mill,
Glowing in many colors as his phases change.

Lifting light as a top
He lofts up onto a fence post
The soles of his shoes smoking
In a smell of burning cedar.

Slowly geese appear in the sky.
He leaps up to join them,
Laughing and honking south.

(II)

A slow and heavy work horse—
A Clydesdale or Percheron—
Like a fenced-in cloud
Moves in the little pasture
Aimlessly. It is Jim Wright.

He moves delicately, avoiding
The round puffs of the clover
With his huge hooves. His fetlocks
Are hairy and melancholy.

Toward evening he goes
To the old watering trough.
He stands looking at the mossy stones on the bottom.
After a while he remembers
To lower his head and drink.

(III)

If you follow his tracks in the deep snow you can't believe it—
Sometimes a two-legged, sometimes a four-legged, sometimes a
   winged,

                              sometimes
A boat—or a barn door—it's certainly Merwin!
After a while you notice the tracks going off in several directions
                              at once.
Then a hand flies past, calling out in many tongues!
It is the left hand—the other has gone ahead
Looking for wood and water . . .

When the parts of the body have all disappeared,
We hear the voice speaking from the edge of darkness . . .
The voice speaking out of the ground
Out of the air
Speaking inside our heads . . .

🔥 🔥 🔥

From
A MINOR
APOCALYPSE

fiction by TADEUSZ KONWICKI

from TRIQUARTERLY

nominated by TRIQUARTERLY

Hᴇʀᴇ ᴄᴏᴍᴇs ᴛʜᴇ ᴇɴᴅ ᴏғ ᴛʜᴇ ᴡᴏʀʟᴅ. It's coming, it's drawing closer, or rather, it is the end of my own world which has come creeping up on me. The end of my personal world. But before my universe collapses into rubble, disintegrates into atoms, explodes into the void, one last kilometer of my Golgotha awaits me, one last lap in this marathon, the last few rungs up or down a ladder without meaning.

I woke at the gloomy hour at which autumn's hopeless days begin. I lay in bed looking at a window full of rain clouds but it was really filled with one cloud, like a carpet darkened with age. It was the hour for doing life's books, the hour of the daily accounting. Once people did their accounts at midnight before a good night's sleep, now they beat their breasts in the morning, woken by the thuds of their dying hearts.

There was blank paper close at hand, in the bureau. The nitroglycerin of the contemporary writer, the narcotic of the wounded individual. You can immerse yourself in the flat white abyss of the page, hide from yourself and your private universe, which will soon explode and vanish. You can soil that defenseless whiteness with bad blood, furious venom, stinking phlegm, but no one is going to like that, not even the author himself. You can pour the sweetness of artificial harmony, the ambrosia of false courage,

the cloying syrup of flattery onto that vacant whiteness and everyone will like it, even the author himself . . .

The first sounds of life could be heard in the building. This
building, this great engine, moved slowly into daily life. And so I
reached for my first cigarette. The cigarette before breakfast tastes
the best. It shortens your life. For many years now I have been
laboring at shortening my life. Everybody shortens their existence
on the sly. There must be something to all that. Some higher
command or perhaps a law of nature in this overpopulated world.

I like the misty dizziness in my head after a deep drag of bitter
smoke. I would like to say some suitable farewell to the world. For
ever since I was a child I have been departing from this life but I
can't finish the job. I loiter at railway crossings, I walk by houses
where roof tiles fall, I drink until I drop, I antagonize hooligans.
And so I am approaching the finish line. I am in the final turn. I
would like to say farewell to you somehow or another. I long to
howl in an inhuman voice so that I am heard in the most distant
corner of the planet and perhaps even in neighboring constellations or perhaps even in the residence of the Lord God. Is that
vanity? Or a duty? Or an instinct which commands us castaways, us
cosmic castaways, to shout through the ages into starry space?

We've become intimate with the universe. Every money-hun-
gry poet, foolish humorist, and treacherous journalist wipes his
mouth on the cosmos and so why can't I too hold my head up high
to where rusted Sputniks and astronaut excrement, frozen bone-
hard, go gliding past.

And so I would like to say farewell somehow. I dreamed of teeth
all night. I dreamed I was holding a pile of teeth like kernels of
corn in my hand. There was even a filling in one, a cheap Warsaw
filling from the dental cooperative. To say something complete
about myself. Not as a warning, not as knowledge, not even for
amusement. Simply to say something which no one else could
reveal. Because before falling asleep or perhaps in the first passing
cloud of sleep, I begin to understand the meaning of existence,
time, and the life beyond this one. I understand that mystery for a
fraction of a second, through an instant of distant memories, a brief
moment of consolation or fearful foreboding and then plunge
immediately into the depths of my bad dreams. In one way or
another everyone strains his blood-nourished brain to the breaking

point trying to understand. But I'm getting close. I mean, at times I get close. And I would give everything I possess, down to the last scrap but, after all, I don't own anything and so I would be giving a lot of nothing, to see that mystery in all its simplicity, to see it once and then to forget it forever.

I am a biped born not far from the Vistula River of old stock and that means I inherited all its bipedal experience in my genes. I have seen war, that terrible frenzy of mammals murdering each other until they drop in exhaustion. I have observed the birth of life and its end in that act we call death. I have known all the brutality of my species and all its extraordinary angelicalness. I have traveled the thorny path of individual evolution known as fate. I am one of you. I am a perfect, anonymous *homo sapiens*. So why couldn't a caprice of chance have entrusted me with the secret if it is, in any case, destined to be revealed?

These words have a sort of day-off quality, the luxury of an idler, the twists of a pervert. But after all, all of you who from time to time put the convolutions of your own lazy brains into gear are subject to these same desires and ambitions. The same fears and self-destructive reflexes. The same rebellion and resignation.

Two drunken deliverywomen have knocked over a tall column of crates containing milk bottles. Now, standing stock-still, they are observing the results of the cataclysm, experiencing the complicated and yet at the same time simple process which transforms a mess into some light-minded fun. The transparent rain has caught its wing on our building, which is rotting with age. A Warsaw building built late in the epoch of Stalinism, when Stalinism was decadent and had become Polonized and raggedy.

I have to get up. I have to rise from my bed and perform fifteen acts whose meaning is not to be pondered. An accretion of automatic habits. The blessed cancer of tradition's meaningless routine. But the last war not only took the lives of scores of millions of people. Without intending to, accidentally, the last war shattered the great palace of culture of European morality, aesthetics, and custom. And humankind drove back to the gloomy caverns and the icy caves in their Rolls-Royces, Mercedes, and Moskviches.

Outside, my city, beneath a cloud the color of an old, blackened carpet. A city to which I was driven by fate from my native city, which I no longer remember and dream of less all the time. Fate

85

only drove me a few hundred kilometers but it separated me from my old unfulfilled life by an entire eternity of reincarnation. This city is the capital of a people who are evaporating into nothingness. Something needs to be said about that too. But to whom? To those who are no longer with us, who are sailing off into oblivion? Or perhaps to those who devour individuals and whole nations?

The city was beginning to hum like a drive belt. It was stirring from the lethargy of sleep. Moving towards its fate, which I know and which I wish to avoid . . .

I am free. I am one of the few free people in this country of patent slavery. A slavery covered by a sloppy coat of contemporary varnish. I have fought a long and bloodless battle for this pitiable personal freedom. I fought for my freedom against the temptations, ambitions, and appetites which drive everyone blindly on to the slaughterhouse. To the so-called modern slaughterhouse for human dignity, honor, and of something else, too, which we forgot about a long time ago.

I am free and alone. Being alone is a small enough price to pay for this none-too-great luxury of mine. I freed myself on the last lap when the finish line could already be seen by the naked eye. I am a free, anonymous man. My flights and falls occurred while I was wearing a magical cap of invisibility, my successes and sins sailed on in invisible corvettes, and my films and books flew off into the abyss in invisible strongboxes. I am free, anonymous.

And so I'll light up another cigarette. On an empty stomach. Here comes the end of my world. That I know for certain. The untimely end of my world. What will be its harbingers? A sudden, piercing pain in the chest beneath the sternum? The squeal of tires as a car slams on its brakes? An enemy, or perhaps a friend?

Outside, those women were still discussing the catastrophe with the milk. They sat down on the old, dark gray, plastic cases, lit up cigarettes and were watching the watery milk trickle down the catch basin, which was belching steam because, no doubt, hot water from the heat and power plant had again gotten into the water main by mistake. And then I suddenly became aware that no one had delivered milk for years, that I had forgotten the sight of those women workers of indeterminate age pushing carts of milk bottles long ago and in my mind that image was associated with those distant green years when I was young and the world was too.

They're probably making a period film, I told myself, and pressed my forehead against the damp windowpane. But all I saw was an everyday normal street. Small crowds of people hurrying by the buildings on the way to work. As usual when the temperature rises in the morning, a crumbling block of stone facing tore loose from the Palace of Culture and flew crashing down into the jagged gulley of buildings. It was only then that I noticed the eagle on the wall of that great edifice, an eagle on a field of black—that is, on a field of red blackened by rain. Our white eagle is not doing too badly because it is supported from below by a huge globe of the world, which is tightly entwined by a hammer and sickle. The gutter spoke with the bass of an ocarina. Then the wind, perhaps still the summer wind or maybe now a winter wind, came tearing from the Parade Field and turned the poplars' silver sides to the sun, which was confined in wet clouds.

I was out of cigarettes. And when you run out of cigarettes you are suddenly seized by a desire to smoke. And so I opened the next drawer of my treasure chest where I keep outrageous letters and old accounts, broken lighters and tax receipts, photographs from my youth and sleeping powders. And there, among tufts of cotton batting and rolls of bandages from the good old days when it was still worth my while to submit to operations, in those age-encrusted recesses I found a yellowed page from many years ago, a page like a cartouche on a monument or a gravestone, a page where I once began a piece of prose I have not finished yet. I began this work in that wonderful time around New Year's, right after New Year's Eve, with a nice hangover still throbbing healthy in my head. I began on New Year's Day because I had indulged in superstition and wanted to celebrate the new biological and astronomical cycle with some work. Later I realized that my own New Year's begins at the end of summer or the beginning of fall and so that is why I stopped writing and have not written a word since.

And so there was that page, once white, now yellow, for long months, seasons, years, never finished, never completed, with its faded motto which was to bless the wistful scenes, the exalted thoughts, the lovely descriptions of nature. I blew the dust from Warsaw's factories off that waxen corpse of my imagination and read the words, which were the credo of an old Polish magnate in the nineteenth century: "If Russia's interests permit, I would gladly turn my feelings to my original fatherland." What was it I had in mind then? Did I want to read that avowal every morning to my children before breakfast? Or did I intend to copy it out at Christmas to be sent to the magnates of science, literature, and film, my contemporaries? Or was I trying to win the favor of the censor for a piece that had come stillborn from an anemic inspiration?

The windows rattled painfully. Hysterical police sirens leapt from some side street. I glanced at the watch my friend Stanislaw D. had once brought me back from a trip to the Soviet Union. It was going on eight. I knew what that meant. Each day at that hour, an armored refrigerator truck carrying food supplies for the ministers and the Party Secretaries raced through the city escorted by police vans. The cavalcade of vehicles flashed past my buildings splashing the puddles of milk on the street. The archaic milk deliverers, let out of some old-age home for the day, ground out their butts on the muddy sidewalk, exchanging furtive goodbyes.

Suddenly the gong by my door rang. I froze by the window, not believing my ears, certain that device had not been working for years. But the elegant, xylophone-like sound was repeated, and more insistently this time. Pulling on an old robe, a present from my brother-in-law, Jan L., I moved guardedly toward the door. I opened the door. Hubert and Rysio, both wearing their Sunday best, suits which reminded me of the carefree middle seventies, were standing at the top of the stairs.

Hubert was holding a cane in his right hand and in his left a sinister-looking black briefcase. My heart began beating rapidly, and not without cause, for they came to see me only about twice a year and each of their visits marked a radical change in my life.

"May we come in? It isn't too early?" asked Hubert jovially.

I was well acquainted with those artificial smiles of theirs which concealed attacks on my comfort.

Now smiling freely myself, I opened the door hospitably and, as they entered with much ceremony on their part, I instantly divined the purpose of this visit. Thanks to them, I had signed dozens of petitions, memorials, and protests sent over the years to our always taciturn regime. A few times it cost me some work, and many times I was secretly dispossessed of my civil rights; practically every day I was subjected to some petty, invisible harrassments which are even shameful to recall but which, adding up over the years, helped estrange me greatly from life. So, we exchanged cordial hugs, smiling all the time like old cronies, but I was already quite tense and my throat had gone dry.

Finally we found ourselves in my living room and we sat down in the wooden armchairs, all in a row as if we were on an airplane flying off to some mysterious and exciting adventure.

"You look good," said Hubert, setting the sinister-looking briefcase down beside him.

"You seem to be holding up too," I said in a friendly tone.

For a moment we looked at each other in embarrassment. Hubert was resting his sinewy hand on his cane. His one blind eye was motionless, the other kept blinking and regarding me with something between affection and irony. Once long ago he had been tortured, perhaps by the anti-Communist underground or perhaps by investigating offices of the Security police and, because of that incident, now long forgotten by everyone, he walked with a cane and was in poor health. Rysio, whom I remembered as a blond angel, was now balding and had put on weight, the high priest of the plotless allegorical novel without punctuation or dialogue.

We looked good, for old fogeys, that was true. But then the moment of silence lengthened out a bit and something had to be said.

"Would you like a drink?"

"A drink couldn't hurt," said Hubert. "What do you have?"

"Pure vodka. Made from potatoes. Imported potatoes."

"All the more reason not to refuse." Hubert's voice was thunderous, as if he were in some space larger than my cluttered room.

While I was getting the bottle and the glasses from the cupboard, they were both looking discreetly about the room. The liquid made from imported potatoes began to gurgle as I cowered at the edge of my chair. A cigarette on an empty stomach is bad for you but a hundred grams of potato vodka is death itself. Or maybe it's better. I raised my glass.

"Good luck."

"Your health." Rysio finally said something, and quickly tossed off the contents of his glass.

Outside, the wind had died down for the moment and the poplars had turned their solid green toward us. My building was, as bad luck would have it, exceptionally quiet and our silence was becoming increasingly louder. But I made a firm decision not to speak and to force them to show their cards.

Hubert set his glass aside with a certain deliberation.

"You're not going out much," he said.

"That's right. Autumn puts me out of sorts."

"A little depression?"

"Something like that."

"Are you writing?"

"I had just started."

He seemed to be looking at me in disbelief. Rysio poured himself another glass.

"What's it going to be?"

"No revelations. I just felt like writing a little nonsense about myself."

"You always wrote about yourself."

"You could be right. But I wanted to write about other people."

"It's high time you did."

"To drown myself out."

The whole thing looked like an examination. And I felt like a high school senior taking his finals. But, after all, I had felt that way my whole life, a student at best.

"Well, Rysio," said Hubert all of a sudden. "Time to get down to business."

Rysio nodded.

"Something to sign?" I hazarded a guess, squinting accomodatingly over at the black briefcase.

"No, this time it's something else. Perhaps you might begin, Rysio."

"Go on, go on, since you started," said Rysio eagerly.

A sort of goofy warmth was rising in me. I reached for the bottle automatically, wanting to pour Hubert a glass while I was at it.

"Thanks, that's enough." He stopped me with a somewhat official tone. I took that as a bad sign.

Really I was indifferent. I am a free person who has been suspended high above this city and who from a distance and with serene amazement observes the strange humans and their strange doings. Without thinking, I turned on the television on the table. I heard the sound of wind howling, the flutter of cloth, but after a moment, the image of a festively decorated airport emerged out of the silvery dots. An honor guard was frozen across the screen, some civilians were shielding themselves against the wind with their overcoats while, above the honor guard and the civilians, red,

90

sail-like flags swelled in the wind, and shyly interspersed among them were red and white Polish flags.

"Well now," said Hubert, deciding to break the silence. "We haven't spoken with you for some time now."

I took a deep breath, which made me feel ashamed, and I sank deeper into my chair.

"Yes, we lost contact with each other," I said in a worldly tone. "We're a vanishing breed."

"Everyone's out for himself," added Rysio.

"But I've been observing your activities."

"What activities," said Hubert with a dismissive wave of one hand. "We're keepers of a dying flame."

"That's a fact. I have the impression that this country is really dying," I said, without knowing what they were driving at.

"So many years of struggle. We've grown old, we've gone to pot putting out those semilegal bulletins, periodicals, appeals which are read by next to no one. Of course the young people read them. But young people get married, have babies, buy little Fiats, give up on action and start growing tomatoes. We've been overrun by the bourgeoisie, a Soviet bourgeoisie."

"It's the end, the grave," added Rysio, pouring himself another glass.

Water was dripping onto the floor through the leaky balcony door. I should have looked for a washcloth to prevent any damage but I didn't much feel like it and I would have been a little embarrassed to do it in front of my colleagues. Our conversation was not going well. It was hard to chat about the things we thought about all day long and which we even dreamed about in our lousy sleep. Things had looked better at one time. We were children of the nineteenth century. Our fathers had been members of Pilsudski's Legions or his secret army, and during World War II we had been in the Home Army or the Union of Fighting Youth. That means, how to say it now, that means, how to explain it after all those years, that means, the hell with it, that doesn't mean anything, now, at the end of our splendid twentieth century, a century of tyranny and unbridled democracy, foolish holiness and brilliant villainy, art without punch and graphomania run rampant.

I saw Hubert's good eye fixed on me.

"Are you listening?" he asked.

"Yes, of course."

"We have a proposition for you. On behalf of our colleagues."

My spine went cold and very slowly I put my unfinished glass aside.

"What is it you wish to propose?"

"That today at eight p.m. you light yourself on fire in front of Central Party Headquarters."

Nothing had changed on the screen—wind, the violent flapping of the flags, the waiting. Only then could the reverent, solemn music broadcast from the studio be heard.

My throat gulped saliva mixed with vodka.

"Are you joking, Hubert?"

"No, I'm not joking." He wiped some invisible sweat from his brow.

"But why me? Why are you coming to me with this?"

"Who else? Somebody has to do it."

"I understand, I understand everything, I just don't understand why me."

Hubert glanced over at Rysio. "I told you this would happen."

Rysio looked down at the floor.

"Listen," he finally said in some anguish, "we've been discussing this for a long time. We've analyzed all the possible candidates. And it came out you."

My tree of happiness stood by on the windowsill. Only then did I notice how much it had shot up lately and grown thick with young, strong leaves. It was sickly for many years and now, suddenly, without any external cause, it had surged upward, sending out a large number of powerful, knotty branches.

"You see," said Hubert softly, "an act like this can only make sense if it shakes people here in Poland and everywhere abroad. You are known to the Polish readers and you have a bit of a name over there in the West too. Your life story, your personality, are perfect for this situation. Obviously, we can't talk you into it and we won't even try—it's up to you and your conscience. I only wish to pass on an opinion which is not only mine or Rysio's, but that of the entire community which is attempting to put up some resistance. You'll pardon me for my lack of eloquence."

"I doubt whether my death would play the part you expect. I know people whose sacrifice would become a symbol the world over."

They looked at me with curiosity. Hubert rubbed his fingers, which were turning insistently bluish.

"No doubt you're thinking of Jan?" he asked.

"Naturally. The whole world knows his films and his books are read in many countries in courses on world literature. Every year we're on tenterhooks waiting to see if he'll win an Oscar or the Nobel."

A barely perceptible smile appeared on Hubert's face.

"That'd be too high a price to pay. Too high a price for the country and our community. You've answered your own question."

"All right. But what about our filmmakers, our composers? I can give you a few names better than mine right off."

"You're the one, old man," said Rysio and reached for the bottle. He clearly felt I was weakening, which gave him heart.

"Life and blood have to be disposed of intelligently," said Hubert wearily. "Those others have a different role to play. Every nugget of genius possesses the highest value in this massacred nation. Their deaths would not enrich us very much and would impoverish us terribly."

"But why not you, or Rysio?"

They glanced at each other with distaste. My blubbering embarrassed them.

"Then why would we have come to you?" asked Hubert. "Let's be frank. Your death will be spectacular, another order up. Don't you see that?"

"You're the one, old man," added Rysio, who was softhearted and was now suffering along with me.

"Listen to me, Hubert. I never interfered in the functioning of our artistic life. I never butted into your affairs, the affairs of a careworn opposition in a country no one cares about. But now I must tell you what I think. You have bred blind, deaf demiurges, who in their marvelous artistic passions create beautiful, universal art but do not notice us crawling in the mud or the daily agonies of our society. They worked hard at guarding the flame of genius that burned in them and gladly exploited the claque of the regime's mass propaganda which boasted of them every day and fed its own complexes with their world renown. You, the emaciated opposition, did not spare them the claques either, anointing them with the charisma of moral approval. They grew fat on our exile, our humiliations, our anonymity. They hopped freely from one sacred grove of national art to another, for we had been driven out of them or had left of our own free will. When you went around pleading with them to sign even the most modest of humanitarian appeals

93

which would displease our team of wanton rulers, they arrogantly sent you packing empty-handed, winking at their coteries to say that you were provocateurs, secret police agents. Their greatness came from our being voluntarily dwarfed. Their genius sprang from our graves as artists. Why shouldn't one of them pay for their decades of solemn, superhuman greatness with a cruel, physical death?"

I turned off the television, where the civilians and soldiers were impatiently waiting for someone. A sudden downpour flew past the balcony, knocking a condom withering on the iron balustrade off into the abyss. Those condoms—bouquets of lilies of the valley, presents to me from my neighbors on the upper floors from their days off.

"We're all racked by envy to one degree or another," said Hubert, somewhat taken aback. He was pale and strenuously rubbing his fingers, which were turning blue. "But let's not talk about that today. Maybe some other time."

"But when are we going to talk if I carry out your command?"

"But, old man, you know," said Rysio, setting his glass aside, "these arguments are indecent."

"I never said anything even though my guts were turning. Hubert, do I need to tell you the names of the people who spent their whole lives walking hand in hand with the government while pretending to go their own way? And their works, which the more clever ones clothed in the garb of universal fashion, world frustration, western melancholy and what is a sort of the neuralgia of the left. And when we became Sovietized to such a degree that a cult of the illicit erupted here, an ambiguous desire for a lick of the forbidden, a pitiful delight in political pornography dressed in the lingerie of allusion, when there arose in Poland that aberration, that scheming contest of self-justification for all the sins of collaboration, they were the first, greedy for applause, anxious for success, they fastened onto the new state of affairs and littered art with the phony gestures of cunning Rejtans, they muddied our poor art, they stomped out the last of their own conscience in it. Why do you fall down before them when they climb on your crosses looking for the golden apples which feed their pride? Why do you pour admiration on them when their fate is opposed to yours?"

"You chose your own fate. This is not the time for that sort of discussion. Rysio, isn't it time for us to be going?" Hubert bent

94

forward heavily and drew the black briefcase out from under the table, the briefcase which could contain an appeal for the abolition of the death penalty, a volume of uncensored poetry, or an ordinary homemade bomb.

"Wait a minute, Hubert." I stopped his hand. "Tell me here, in private, man to man, why have you designated me?"

He tore his hand from mine.

"I don't designate. I have the same rights as you do. And the same duties."

"But there must be something about me that makes me suitable and others less so."

The rain had hazed the windows over. Nearby a child was playing a melody with one finger, a melody which I remembered from years back, many years back.

"After all, you've always been obsessed with death," whispered Hubert hoarsely. "I never treated your complex as a literary mannerism. You are the most intimate with death, you shouldn't be afraid of it. You have prepared yourself and us for your death most carefully. What were you thinking about before we arrived?"

"Death."

"You see. It's at your side. All you have to do is reach out."

"Just reach out."

"Yes, that's all."

"Today?"

"Today at eight o'clock in the evening when the party congress is over and the delegates from the entire country are leaving the building."

"What about the others?"

"Who?"

"The people necessary to the nation."

"In sin and holiness, in conformism and rebellion, in betrayal and redemption, they will bear the soul of the nation into enternity."

"You're lying. You're choking on that garbage, your eyes are popping out of their sockets."

Rysio leapt from his chair, knocking over his glass.

"Leave him alone!" he shouted and began rummaging in Hubert's shirt. Hubert had gone stiff and extended his legs as if he wanted to look at his muddy boots. Rysio began pushing pea-like pills through his lips, which had turned blue. He forced a few drops of water between his clenched teeth. Hubert moved his jaw, closed his eyes then bit one pill in half and tried to swallow it.

Someone rang the bell. I opened the latch with trembling hands. A man, a bit on the drunk side, stood in the doorway, holding onto the doorframe.

"You should run yourself some water because we're going to turn it off," he said, belching a cloud of undigested alcohol.

"I don't need any water."

"I suggest you run your tub and your other faucets. We'll be cutting it off for the whole day."

"Thank you. So did a main burst then?"

"Everything burst. May I sit down here for a minute? I'm dead on my feet."

"I'm sorry but my friend isn't feeling well. I have to go fetch an ambulance."

"No one's feeling good these days. I won't bother you then. Stay well."

"The same to you."

He went off to knock on my neighbors' doors. I returned at a run down the hall. Now Hubert was sitting up straight in his chair. He smiled painfully to hide his sudden panic.

"Should I call a doctor?"

"No need to. I'm all right now. Where were we?"

A swath of sunlight moved across the rooftops of the city like a great kite. My friend the sparrow hopped onto one bar of the balustrade and was surprised that I did not greet him.

"Hubert, is there any sense to all this? Do you really believe there is?"

"Now you're asking?"

"Why have you been so unrelenting all your life? In all ways. Is it hormones or some higher force commanding you?"

"Leave him alone, he has to go home." Rysio pushed me away.

"Isn't it a short way to the party building?"

"Not all deaths are the same, you see," said Hubert in a muffled voice. "We all need the elevated, the majestic, the holy. That is what you can offer us."

"For your sins, old man," added Rysio and attempted a smile. "You have plenty of yours, and ours, on your conscience."

"But they have just as many," I said in despair, affected by the hysteria of that foul autumn day.

"They're not here. You're all alone with God or, if you prefer, with your conscience."

"And where are they?"

"Far away on a small, unhappy planet."

"Hubert, what a stupid joke. Someone put you up to it."

"No, it's not a joke. You know that perfectly well yourself. You've been waiting for us for years. Be honest for once and admit you were waiting."

He looked at me for a long moment with his one good eye and then began searching for his briefcase, which he had kicked under the table during his attack.

"Hubert, answer me—do you believe this is necessary?"

He walked heavily over to me, put his arms around me, and kissed both my cheeks with his cold lips.

"Be at number sixty-three Vistula Street at eleven. Halina and Nadezhda will be waiting for you there. They're in engineering."

"The engineering of self-immolation?"

"Don't make things more difficult, old man," interjected Rysio.

A sudden fury seized me. "And what are you supposed to be, just one of the guys? You better start using commas and periods, goddammit."

At a loss, Rysio began retreating toward the door.

"The lack of periods bothers you?" he said uncertainly.

"If you used punctuation, then maybe we wouldn't need to show deaths in this country."

A lazy peal of thunder rolled from one end of the city to the other. The wind drove the balcony doors groaning open. I would have closed them but the handle had come off.

"Lend us five thousand for a taxi. It's too much for him to walk home in this weather." Rysio took Hubert's enchanted briefcase from him and then glanced out into the dark corridor.

I dug a five-thousand-zloty note out of my pocket. They took it without thanking me and started for the front hall. And then we were greeted by a sort of a droning, the high-pitched sound of telephone wires presaging bad weather. They had been making that glassy moan for years now, since the days when the world had still been a calm and normal place.

Hubert stopped before a heap of old slippers which had some-how or other accumulated over the course of a lifetime.

"When did you stop writing? I can't remember anymore," he

said, looking askance and unseeing at the junk strewn about the floor.

"But I'm still writing."

"You've started writing again now. You're writing your testament. But I was asking about your fiction."

"I don't recall. Maybe five, maybe seven years ago. That's when I rid myself of two censors in one fell swoop, my own and the state's. I wrote a story for some little underground journal and that was my last piece. After that I was free and impotent."

"You were born to be a slave. Slavery emancipated you, it lent you wings, it made you a provincial classic. And then to punish you, it took everything away like some evil witch."

"Slavery has always perished at the hands of slaves," said Rysio. "You see what I mean, old man?" . . .

For some reason they loitered when leaving. Hubert began reading my neighbor's calling card tacked beside his bell. They were always a bit curious about my life though good form required contempt for my existence. So he read that card, the shop sign of a Secretary on the Central Committee, without knowing that behind that door an old pensioner had been dying for ten years, had been trying to die day after day but with no success. From above, drops of dirty water dripped from the steps and the edges of the stairs. Our janitor, or as he is to be called these days, the building superintendent, an incorrigible lunatic, was washing the landing. He had already been on television and been written up in the papers and still on he went washing our stairs, the only building superintendent in the country still doing it.

"Don't punk out, old man," said Rysio.

"I have to think it over."

"They're expecting you at eleven, Halina and Nadezhda," added Hubert.

"And if I don't do it?"

"Then you'll go on living the way you've lived till now."

They began down the stairs, supporting each other like two saints, like Cyril and Methodius. And naturally I remembered Rysio from those years long ago when we both were young. I remember one mad drunken night on some farm near Warsaw, the two of us sleeping side by side on a bed of straw. At that time Rysio was something between a critic and a filmologist. There was a drunken girl lying between us, a girl I never saw again. We were both lying semiconscious on my green poncho which I had obligingly spread out for us. The girl was moaning in her deep, drunken sleep. Rysio was fooling around with her, panting hoarsely with sudden desire and so she turned her back to him. Then she was facing me and I could feel her damp, sleepy breath on my cheek. Rysio did not give up; unconscious but hard at work, he was fumbling at her, tearing at her clothes, slipping under her inert body, breathing wildly. And then, when I was already falling into a delirious fever, Rysio clearly achieved his end, for he suddenly began moaning and pulling himself free on the frantic hay. Unaware of his ecstasies, she breathed her light, calm breath on me. It was only in the morning when, hungover, we were all collecting ourselves on that rustic bed, that I struggled into my raincoat and automatically put my hand in the pocket and to my horror discovered that in the darkness of the night, my pocket had been the victim of Rysio's passion, that he had made love to my pocket with a fierce and youthful love, perhaps even the first of his life.

Now Rysio wrote unpunctuated amorphous prose, played adjutant to Hubert, and was a venerable figure in the literary world. I returned to my room to watch them through the window. Just then, by some miracle, an empty taxi happened by, but they missed it and walked off with dignity toward Nowy Swiat. I was curious if they were being followed. But no car pulled away from the curb and no one came running out from the half shadows of any neighboring building.

At one point Hubert had hanged himself in his wardrobe; he had been mercilessly baited during one campaign, for at that time, toward the end of the sixties, the regime still had strength enough for cruel spectacles and sinister campaigns. So, Hubert hanged himself, but of course it was the first time he had ever done it and he didn't have the knack yet. The rod broke, the wardrobe turned over, and Hubert survived. Yes, he survived so that years later he could bring me my death sentence.

There was another peal of thunder in the low, cramped sky. I went to the bathroom to wash up. The pipes began gurgling something awful, they hiccupped, but what was left of the water came out. I washed mechanically, wondering if it were right to wash and dress, considering what was in store for me. But, after all, one should take death like communion, neatly dressed and

99

with reverence. But did I have to die? Was someone going to force me off a bridge or douse me with gasoline? The decision was mine, wasn't it? I could die with honor or go on living dishonorably.

The gong resounded again. I thought that Rysio and Hubert had forgotten something or were returning to call off the sentence. Dripping with the little water there was, I ran to the door. An old man with a large, leather bag was sitting on the steps.

"Are you here to see me?" I asked.

"Yes, I am. I've been instructed to turn off the gas."

"But you've already turned it off three times this year."

"What do I know, first they tell me turn it off, then they tell me turn it on. They don't know what they're doing. Every day a house blows up, so to make it look like something's being done about it, they tell me to turn off the gas. It's a lucky thing your apartment's still here because I've got the numbers here of places which are gone." He showed me a dirty slip of paper.

"Well, then why don't you turn off the electricity while you're at it? It doesn't matter to me."

"It doesn't matter to you," said the old man with a sly smirk, and he sprang nimbly into the bathroom. "But it matters to me. I've only got authority for the gas."

And indeed, in a fraction of a second, he had turned the valve, had taken apart the grate on the heater and was already sitting on the edge of the bathtub, lighting up a cigarette that was coming unglued.

"It's nice to take a warm bath, if only to wash your butt, you'll pardon the expression," discoursed the old man, glancing about the bathroom. "But what can you do, orders are orders. Maybe you should have a little talk with the manager, you know what I mean. Speak to his hand."

"I don't feel like talking with the manager. I'm going to die today."

The old plumber began chuckling merrily.

"Why'd you think that one up for today, isn't there enough going on? That Russian Secretary's coming today. They've got the whole town decked out. There's been bands playing everywhere since this morning. They say there's a sort of festival going on, some big holiday of theirs, maybe it's one of ours too. They've filled up the stands with goods, everywhere, by the Palace of Culture, down by the Vistula, people have been standing in line since early this morning and you're getting set to die."

"I'll be dying to spite them."

The gray-haired tradesman wiped away tears of joy.

"You're a funny man. If we started dying to spite them, there'd be no Poles left. You know what, I'll connect up your gas, but I'll seal up the valve handles. I'll leave it open wide enough so you can use the gas, just you be careful."

"I don't have need for gas. Why don't you take the little heater as a souvenir?"

"You're pretty touchy. If you don't want to, you don't have to. Sign here please."

I accompanied him back to the hall. He took the opportunity to feel my coat, which was hanging by the door.

"Nice wool. Foreign."

"Take it. Wear it in good health."

"What are you talking about? I can pay you. I'll give you fifty thousand."

"I'll give it to you for nothing. The only thing is, when you put it on, give a sigh for my soul, would you?"

"You must be an artist, right? You like a good laugh, right?"

But he rolled the coat up skillfully, packed it in his bag and then was already at my neighbor's door, pressing the doorbell, a severe look on his face.

translated by Richard Lourie

CAVIAR

fiction by T. CORAGHESSAN BOYLE

from ANTAEUS

nominated by David St. John

I OUGHT TO TELL YOU right off I didn't go to college. I was on the wrong rung of the socioeconomic ladder, if you know what I mean. My father was a commercial fisherman on the Hudson till the PCBs got to him, my mother did typing and filing down at the lumberyard, and my grandmother crocheted doilies and comforters for sale to rich people. Me, I took over my father's trade. I inherited the shack at the end of the pier, the leaky 14-foot runabout with the 35-horse Evinrude motor and the seine that's been in the family for three generations. Also I got to move into the old man's house when he passed on, and he left me his stamp collection and the keys to his '62 Rambler, rusted through till it looked like a gill net hung out to dry.

Anyway, it's a living. Almost. And if I didn't go to college I do read a lot, magazines mostly, but books on ecology and science too. Maybe it was the science part that did me in. You see, I'm the first one around here—I mean, me and Marie are the first ones—to have a baby this new way, where you can't have it on your own. Dr. Ziss said not to worry about it, a little experiment, think of it as a gift from heaven.

Some gift.

But don't get me wrong. I'm not complaining. What happens happens, and I'm as guilty as anybody, I admit it. It's just that when the guys at the Flounder Inn are sniggering in their beer and Marie starts looking at me like I'm a toad or something, you've got to put things in perspective, you've got to realize that it was her all along, she's the one that started it.

"I want a baby," was how she put it.

It was April, raw and wet. Crocuses and dead man's fingers were poking through the dirt along the walk, and the stripers were running. I'd just stepped in the door, beat, chilled to the teeth, when she made her announcement. I went straight for the coffee pot. "Can't afford it," I said.

She didn't plead or try to reason with me. All she did was repeat herself in a matter-of-fact tone, as if she were telling me about some new drapes or a yard sale, and then she marched through the kitchen and out the back door. I sipped at my coffee and watched her through the window. She had a shovel. She was burying something. Deep. When she came back in, her nose was running a bit and her eyes were crosshatched with tiny red lines.

"What were you doing out there?" I asked.

Her chin was crumpled, her hair was wild. "Burying something."

I waited while she fussed with the teapot, my eyebrows arched like question marks. Ten seconds ticked by. "Well, what?"

"My diaphragm."

I've known Marie since high school. We were engaged for five years while she worked for *Reader's Digest*, and we'd been married for three and a half when she decided she wanted some offspring. At first I wasn't too keen on the idea, but then I had to admit she was right: the time had come. Our lovemaking had always been lusty and joyful, but after she buried the diaphragm it became tender, intense, purposeful. We tried. For months we tried. I'd come in off the river, reeking of the creamy milt and silver roe that floated two inches deep in the bottom of the boat while fifty- and sixty-pound stripers gasped their last, come in like a wild bull or something, and Marie would be waiting for me upstairs in her nightie and we'd do it before dinner, and then again after. Nothing happened.

Somewhere around July or August, the sweet blueclaw crabs crawling up the riverbed like an army on maneuvers and the humid heat lying over the valley like a cupped hand, Marie went to Sister Eleazar of the Coptic Brotherhood of Ethiop. Sister Eleazar was a black woman, six feet tall at least, in a professor's gown and a fez with a red tassel. Leroy Lent's wife swore by her. Six years Leroy and his wife had been going at it, and then they went to Sister Eleazar and had a pair of twins. Marie thought it was worth a try, so I drove her down there.

The Coptic Brotherhood of Ethiop occupied a lime-green building the size of a two-car garage with a steeple and cross pinned to the roof. Sister Eleazar answered our knock with a scowl and a little crescent of egg yolk on her chin. "What you want?" she said.

Standing there in the street, a runny-eyed chihuahua sniffing at my heels, I listened to Marie explain our problem and watched the crescent of egg on Sister Eleazar's face fracture with her smile. "Ohhh," she said, "well why didn't you say so? Come own in, come own in."

There was one big room inside, poorly lit. Old bottom-burnished pews stretched along three of the four walls and there was a big shiny green table in the center of the floor. The table was heaped with religious paraphernalia—silver salvers and chalices and tinted miniatures of a black man with a crown dwarfing his head. A cot and an icebox huddled against the back wall, which was decorated with magazine clippings of Africa. "Right here, sugar," Sister Eleazar said, leading Marie up to the table. "Now you take off your coat and your dress, and less ex-amine them wombs."

Marie handed me her coat, and then her tight blue dress with the little white clocks on it, while Sister Eleazar cleared the chalices and whatnot off the table. The chihuahua had followed us in, and now it sprang up onto the cot with a sigh and buried its nose in its paws. The room stank of dog.

"All right," Sister Eleazar said, turning back to Marie, "you climb up own the table now and stretch yourself out so Sister 'Leazar can listen to your insides and say a prayer over them barren wombs." Marie complied with a nervous smile, and the black woman leaned forward to press an ear to her abdomen. I watched the tassel of Sister Eleazar's fez splay out over Marie's rib cage and I began to get excited, the place dark and exotic, Marie in brassiere and panties, laid out on the table like a sacrificial virgin. Then the Sister was mumbling something—a prayer, I guess—in a language I'd never heard before. Marie looked embarrassed. "Don't you worry about nothin'," Sister Eleazar said, looking up at me and winking, "I got just the thing."

She fumbled around underneath the cot for a minute, then came back to the table with a piece of blue chalk—the same as they use in geography class to draw rivers and lakes on the blackboard—and a big yellow can of Colman's dry mustard. She bent over Marie like a heart surgeon, and then, after a few seconds of deliberation, made a blue X on Marie's lower abdomen and said, "Okay, honey, you can get up now."

I watched Marie shrug into her dress, thinking the whole thing was just a lot of superstitious mumbo jumbo and pissantry, when I felt Sister Eleazar's fingers on my arm; she dipped her head and led me out the front door. The sky was overcast. I could smell rain in the air. "Listen," the black woman whispered, handing me the can of mustard, "the problem ain't with her, it's with you. Must be you ain't penetratin' deep enough." I looked into her eyes, trying to keep my face expressionless. Her voice dropped. "What you do is this: make a plaster of this here mustard and rub it on your parts before you go into her, and it'll force out that 'jaculation like a torpedo coming out a submarine—know what I mean?" Then she winked. Marie was at the door. A man with a hoe was digging at his garden in the next yard over. "Oh yeah," the sister said, holding out her hand, "you want to make a donation to the Brotherhood, that'll be eleven dollars and fifty cent."

I never told Marie about the mustard—it was too crazy. All I said was that the Sister had told me to give her a mustard plaster on the stomach an hour after we had intercourse—to help the seeds take. It didn't work, of course. Nothing worked. But the years at *Reader's Digest* had made Marie a superstitious woman, and I was willing to go along with just about anything so long as it made her feel better. One night I came to bed and she was perched naked on the edge of the footstool, wound around three times with a string of garlic. "I thought that was for vampires?" I said. She just parted her lips and held out her arms.

In the next few weeks she must have tried every quack remedy in the book. She kept a toad in a clay pot under the bed, ate soup composed of fish eyes and roe, drank goat's milk and cod liver oil and filled the medicine chest with elixirs made from thimbleweed and rhinoceros horn. Once I caught her down in the basement dancing in the nude around a live rooster. I was eating three meals a day to keep my strength up. Then one night I came across an article about test-tube babies in *Science Digest*. I studied the pictures for a long while, especially the one at the end of the article that showed this English couple, him with a bald dome and her fat as a sow, with their little test-tube son. Then I called Marie.

Dr. Ziss took us right away. He sympathized with our plight, he said, and would do all he could to help us. First he would have to run some tests to see just what the problem was and whether it could be corrected surgically. He led us into the examining room and looked into our eyes and ears, tapped our knees, measured our blood pressure. He drew blood, squinted at my sperm under a microscope, took X-rays, did a complete pelvic exam on Marie. His nurse was Irene Goddard, lived up the street from us. She was a sour, square-headed woman in her fifties with little vertical lines etched around her lips. She prodded and poked and pricked us and then had us fill out twenty or thirty pages of forms that asked about everything from bowel movements to whether my grandmother had any facial hair. Two weeks later I got a phone call. The doctor wanted to see us.

We'd hardly got our jackets off when Mrs. Goddard, with a look on her face like she was about to pull the switch at Sing Sing, showed us into the doctor's office. I should tell you that Dr. Ziss is a young man, about my age I guess, with narrow shoulders, a little clipped mustache and a woman's head of hair that he keeps brushing back with his hand. Anyway, he was sitting behind his desk sifting through a pile of charts and lab reports when we walked in. "Sit down," he said, "I'm afraid I have some bad news for you." Marie went pale, like she did the time the state troopers called about her mother's accident; her ankles swayed over her high heels and she fell back into the chair as if she'd been shoved. I thought she was going to cry, but the doctor forestalled her. He smiled, showing off all those flossed and fluoridated teeth: "I've got some good news too."

The bad news was that Marie's ovaries were shot. She was suffering from the Stein-Leventhal syndrome, he said, and was unable to produce viable ova. He put it to us straight: "She's infertile, and there's nothing we can do about it. Even if we had the facilities and the know-how, test-tube reproduction would be out of the question."

Marie was stunned. I stared down at the linoleum for a second and listened to her sniffling, then I took her hand.

Dr Ziss leaned across the desk and pushed back a stray lock of hair. "But there is an alternative."

We both looked at him.

"Have you considered a surrogate mother? A young woman

106

who'd be willing to impregnate herself artificially with the husband's semen—for a fee, of course—and then deliver the baby to the wife at the end of term." He was smoothing his mustache. "It's being done all over the country. And if Mrs. Trimpie pads herself during her 'pregnancy' and 'delivers' in the city, none of your neighbors need ever know that the child isn't wholly and naturally yours."

My mind was racing. I was bombarded with selfish and acquisitive thoughts, seething with scorn for Marie—*she* was the one, *she* was defective, not me—bursting to exercise my God-given right to a child and heir. It's true, it really is—you never want something so much as when somebody tells you you can't have it. I found myself thinking aloud: "So it would really be half ours, and, half—"

"That's right, Mr. Trimpie. And I have already contacted a young woman on your behalf, should you be interested."

I looked at Marie. Her eyes were watering. She gave me a weak smile and pressed my hand.

"She's Caucasian, of course, attractive, fit, very bright: a first-year medical student in need of funds to continue her education."

"Um, uh," I fumbled for the words, "how much, I mean if we decide to go along with it, how much would it cost?"

The doctor was ready for this one. "Ten thousand dollars," he said without hesitation, "plus hospital costs."

Two days later there was a knock at the door. A girl in pea coat and blue jeans stood there, flanked by a pair of scuffed aquamarine suitcases held shut with masking tape. She looked to be about sixteen, stunted and bony and pale, cheap mother-of-pearl stars for earrings, her red hair short and spiky as if she were letting a crewcut grow out. I couldn't help thinking of those World War II movies where they shave the actresses' heads for consorting with the Germans, I couldn't help thinking of waifs and wanderers and runaway teen-agers. Dr. Ziss's gunmetal Mercedes sat at the curb, clouds of exhaust tugging at the tailpipe in the chill morning air; he waved, and then ground away with a crunch of gravel. "Hi," the girl said, extending her hand, "I'm Wendy."

It had all been arranged. Dr. Ziss thought it would be a good idea if the mother-to-be came to stay with us two weeks or so before the "procedure," to give us a chance to get to know each other, and then maybe stay on with us through the first couple of months so we could experience the pregnancy firsthand—when she began to show, she'd move into an apartment on the other side of town, so as not to arouse any suspicion among the neighbors. He was delicate about the question of money, figuring a commercial fisherman and a part-time secretary, with no college and driving a beat-up Rambler, might not exactly be rolling in surplus capital. But the money wasn't a problem really. There was the insurance payoff from Marie's mother—she'd been blindsided by a semi coming off the ramp on the Thruway—and the $3,500 I'd got for delivering spawning stripers to Con Ed so they could hatch fish to replace the ones sucked into the screens at the nuclear plant. It was sitting in the County Trust, collecting five and a quarter percent, against the day some emergency came up. Well, this was it. I closed out the account.

The doctor took his fee and explained that the girl would get $5,000 on confirmation of pregnancy, and the balance when she delivered. Hospital costs would run about $1,500, barring complications. We shook hands on it, and Marie and I signed a form. I figured I could work nights at the bottling plant if I was strapped.

Now, the girl standing there before me, I couldn't help feeling a stab of disappointment—she was pretty enough, I guess, but I'd expected something a little more, well, substantial. And red hair. It was a letdown. Deep down I'd been hoping for a blonde, one of those Scandinavian types you see in the cigarette ads. Anyway, I told her I was glad to meet her, and then showed her up to the spare room, which I'd cleaned up and outfitted with a chest of drawers, a bed and a Salvation Army desk, and some cheery knickknacks. I asked her if I could get her a bite to eat, Marie being at work and me waiting around for the tide to go out. She was sitting on the bed, looking tired; she hadn't even bothered to glance out the window at the view of Croton Bay. "Oh yeah," she said after a minute, as if she'd been asleep or daydreaming, "yeah, that would be nice." Her eyes were gray, the color of drift ice on the river. She called me Nathaniel, soft and formal, like a breathless young schoolteacher taking attendance. Marie never called me anything but Nat, and the guys at the marina settled for Ace. "Have you got a sandwich, maybe? And a cup of hot Nestlés? I'd really like that, Nathaniel."

I went down and fixed her a BLT, her soft syllables tingling in my ears like a kiss. Dr. Ziss had called her an "ah pear" girl which I guess referred to her shape. When she'd slipped out of her coat, I saw that there was more to her than I'd thought—not much across the top, maybe, but sturdy in the hips and thighs. I couldn't help thinking it was a good sign, but then I had to check myself: I was looking at her like a horse breeder or something.

She was asleep when I stepped in with the sandwich and hot chocolate. I shook her gently and she started up with a gasp, her eyes darting around the room as if she'd forgotten where she was. "Oh yes, yes, thanks," she said, in that maddening, out-of-breath, little girl's voice. I sat on the edge of the desk and watched her eat, gratified to see that her teeth were strong and even, and her nose just about right. "So you're a medical student, Dr. Ziss tells me."

"Hm-hmm," she murmured, chewing. "First year. I'm going to take the spring semester off, I mean, for the baby and all—"

This was the first mention of our contract, and it fell over the conversation like a lead balloon. She hesitated, and I turned red. Here I was, alone in the house with a stranger, a pretty girl, and she was going to have my baby.

She went on, skirting the embarrassment, trying to brighten her voice: "—I mean, I love it and all—med school—but it's a grind already and I really don't see how I can afford the tuition without, without—" She looked up at me. "Without your help."

I didn't know what to say. I stared into her eyes for a minute and felt strangely excited, powerful, like a pasha interviewing a new candidate for the harem. Then I picked up the china sturgeon on the desk and turned it over in my hands. "I didn't go to college," I said. And then, as if I were apologizing, "I'm a fisherman."

A cold rain was falling the day the three of us drove down to Dr. Ziss's for the "procedure." The maples were turning, the streets splashed with red and gold, slick, glistening, the whole world a cathedral. I felt humbled somehow, respectful in the face of life and the progress of the generations of man: *My seed is going to take hold,* I kept thinking, *in half an hour I'll be a father.* Marie and Wendy, on the other hand, seemed oblivious to the whole thing, chattering away like a sewing circle, talking about shoes and needlepoint and some actor's divorce. They'd hit it off pretty well, the two of them, sitting in the kitchen over coffee at night, going to movies and thrift shops together, trading gossip, looking up at me and giggling when I stepped into the room. Though Wendy didn't do much around the house—didn't do much more than lie in bed and stare at textbooks—I don't think Marie really minded. She was glad for the company, and there was something more too, of course: Wendy was making a big sacrifice for us. Both of us were deeply grateful.

Dr. Ziss was all smiles that afternoon, pumping my hand, kissing the girls, ushering us into his office like an impresario on opening night. Mrs. Goddard was more restrained. She shot me an icy look, as if I were conspiring to overthrow the Pope or corrupt girl scouts or something. Meanwhile, the doctor leaned toward Marie and Wendy and said something I didn't quite catch, and suddenly they were all three of them laughing like Canada geese. Were they laughing at me, I wondered, all at once feeling self-conscious and vulnerable, the odd man out. Dr. Ziss, I noticed, had his arm around Wendy's waist.

If I felt left out, I didn't have time to brood over it. Because Mrs. Goddard had me by the elbow and was marching me down the hallway to the men's room, where she handed me a condom sealed in tinfoil and a couple of tattered girlie magazines. I didn't need the magazines. Just the thought of what was going to happen in the next room—Marie had asked the doctor if she could do the insemination herself—gave me an erection like a tire iron. I pictured Wendy leaning back on the examining table in a little white smock, nothing underneath, and Marie, my big loving wife, with this syringelike thing . . . that's all it took. I was out of the bathroom in sixty seconds, the wet condom tucked safely away in a sterilized jar.

Afterward, we shared a bottle of pink champagne and a lasagna dinner at Mama's Pasta House. My treat.

One morning about a month later I was lying in bed next to Marie and I heard Wendy pad down the hallway to the bathroom. The house was still, and a soft gray light clung to the windowsill like a blanket. I was thinking of nothing, or maybe I was thinking of striped bass, sleek and silver, how they ride up out of the deep like pieces of a dream. Next thing I heard was the sound of gagging. Morning sickness, I thought, picking up on a phrase from one of the countless baby books scattered around the house, and suddenly, inexplicably, I was doubled over myself. "Aaaaargh," Wendy gasped, the sound echoing through the house, "aaaargh," and it felt like somebody was pulling my stomach inside out.

110

At breakfast she was pale and haggard, her hair greasy and her eyes puffed out. She tried to eat a piece of dry toast but wound up spitting it into her hand. I couldn't eat either. Same thing the next day, and the next: she was sick, I was sick. I'd pull the cord on the outboard and the first whiff of exhaust would turn my stomach and I'd have to lean over and puke in the river. Or I'd haul the gill nets up off the bottom and the exertion would nearly kill me. I called the doctor.

"Sympathetic pregnancy," he said, his voice cracking at the far end of a bad connection. "Perfectly normal. The husband identifies with the wife's symptoms."

"But I'm not her husband."

"Husband, father: what difference does it make. You're it."

I thought about that. Thought about it when Wendy and I began to eat like the New York Jets at the training table, thought about it nights at the bottling plant, thought about it when Wendy came into the living room in her underwear one evening and showed us the hard white bulge that was already beginning to open her navel up like a flower. Marie was watching some soppy hospital show on TV; I was reading about the dead water between Manhattan and Staten Island, nothing living there, not even eels. "Look," Wendy said, an angels-in-heaven smile on her face, "it's starting to show." Marie got up and embraced her. I grinned like an idiot, thrilled at the way the panties grabbed her thighs—white nylon with dancing pink flowers—and how her little pointed breasts were beginning to strain at the brassiere. I wanted to put my tongue in her navel.

Next day, while Marie was at work, I tapped on Wendy's door. "Come on in," she said. She was wearing a housecoat, Japanesey, with dragons and pagodas on it, propped up against the pillows reading an anatomy text. I told her I didn't feel like going down to the river and wondered if she wanted anything. She put the book down and looked at me like a pat of butter sinking into a halibut steak. "Yes," she said, stretching it to two syllables, "as a matter of fact I do." Then she unbuttoned the robe. Later she smiled at me and said: "So what did we need the doctor for anyway?"

If Marie suspected anything, she didn't show it. I think she was too caught up in the whole thing to have an evil thought about either one of us. I mean, she doted on Wendy, hung on her every word, came home from work each night and shut herself up in Wendy's room for an hour or more. I could hear them giggling.

111

When I asked her what the deal was, Marie just shrugged. "You know," she said, "the usual . . . girls' talk and such." The shared experience had made them close, closer than sisters, and sometimes I would think of us as one big happy family. But I stopped short of telling Marie what was going on when she was out of the house. Once, years ago, I'd had a fling with a girl we'd known in high school—an arrow-faced little fox with starched hair and raccoon eyes. It had been brief and strictly biological, and then the girl had moved to Ohio. Marie never forgot it. Just the mention of Ohio—even so small a thing as the TV weatherman describing a storm over the Midwest—would set her off.

I'd like to say I was torn, but I wasn't. I didn't want to hurt Marie—she was my wife, my best friend, I loved and respected her—and yet there was Wendy, with her breathy voice and gray eyes, bearing my child. The thought of it, of my son floating around in his own little sea just behind the sweet bulge of her belly . . . well, it inflamed me, got me mad with lust and passion and spiritual love too. Wasn't Wendy as much my wife as Marie? Wasn't marriage, at bottom, simply a tool for procreating the species? Hadn't Sarah told Abraham to go in unto Hagar? Looking back on it, I guess Wendy let me make love to her because maybe she was bored and a little horny, lying around in a negligee day and night studying all that anatomy. She sure didn't feel the way I did—if I know anything, I know that now. But at the time I didn't think of it that way, I didn't think at all. Surrogate mother, surrogate wife. I couldn't get enough of her.

Everything changed when Marie taped a feather bolster around her waist and our "boarder" had to move over to Depew Street. ("Don't know what happened," I told the guys down at the Flounder, "she just up and moved out. Low on bucks, I guess." Nobody so much as looked up from their beer until one of the guys mentioned the Knicks' game and Alex DeFazio turned to me and said, "So you got a bun in the oven, is what I hear.") I was at a loss. What with Marie working full time now, I found myself stuck in the house, alone, with nothing much to do except wear a path in the carpet and eat my heart out. I could walk down to the river, but it was February and nothing was happening, so I'd wind up at the Flounder Inn with my elbows on the bar, watching the mollies and swordtails bump into the sides of the aquarium, hoping somebody would give me a lift across town. Of course, Marie and I would drive over to Wendy's after dinner every couple of days or so, and I could talk to her on the telephone till my throat went dry—but it wasn't the same. Even the few times I did get over there in the day, I could feel it. We'd make love, but she seemed shy and reluctant, as if she were performing a duty or somthing. "What's wrong?" I asked her. "Nothing," she said. It was as if someone had cut a neat little hole in the center of my life.

One time, a stiff windy day in early March, I couldn't stand the sight of four walls any more and I walked the six miles across town and all the way out Depew Street. It was an ugly day. Clouds like steel wool, a dirty crust of ice underfoot, dog turds preserved like icons in the receding snowbanks. The whole way over there I kept thinking up various scenarios: Wendy and I would take the bus for California, then write Marie to come join us; we'd fly to the Virgin Islands and raise the kid on the beach; Marie would have an accident. When I got there, Dr. Ziss's Mercedes was parked out front. I thought that was pretty funny, him being there in the middle of the day, but then I told myself he was her doctor after all. I turned around and walked home.

Nathaniel Jr. was born in New York City at the end of June, 9 pounds, 1 ounce, with a fluff of orange hair and milky gray eyes. Wendy never looked so beautiful. The hospital bed was cranked up, her hair, grown out now, was fresh-washed and brushed, she was wearing the turquoise earrings I'd given her. Marie, mean-while, was experiencing the raptures of the saints. She gave me a look of pride and fulfillment, rocking the baby in her arms, cooing and beaming. I stole a glance at Wendy. There were two wet circles where her nipples touched the front of her gown. When she put Nathaniel to her breast I thought I was going to faint from the beauty of it, and from something else too: jealousy. I wanted her, then and there.

Dr. Ziss was on the scene, of course, all smiles, as if he'd been responsible for the whole thing. He pecked Marie's cheek, patted the baby's head, shook my hand, and bent low to kiss Wendy on the lips. I handed him a cigar. Three days later Wendy had her $5,000, the doctor and the hospital had been paid off, and Marie and I were back in Westchester with our son. Wendy had been dressed in a loose summer gown and sandals when I gave her the check. I remember she was sitting there on a lacquered bench, cradling the baby, the hospital corridor lit up like a clerestory with sunbeams. There were tears—mainly Marie's—and promises to keep in touch. Wendy handed over Nathaniel as if he were a piece of meat or sack of potatoes, no regrets. She and Marie embraced, she rubbed her cheek against mine and made a perfunctory little kissing noise, and then she was gone.

I held out for a week. Changing diapers, heating formula, snuggling up with Marie and little Nathaniel, trying to feel whole again. But I couldn't. Every time I looked at my son I saw Wendy, the curl of the lips, the hair, the eyes, the pout—in my distraction, I even thought I heard something of her voice in his gasping howls. Marie was asleep, the baby in her arms. I backed the car out and headed for Depew Street.

The first thing I saw when I rounded the corner onto Depew was the doctor's Mercedes, unmistakable, gunmetal gray, gleaming at the curb like a slap in the face. I was so startled to see it there I almost ran into it. What was this, some kind of postpartum emergency or something? It was 10:00 a.m. Wendy's curtains were drawn. As I stamped across the lawn, my fingers began to tremble like they do when I'm tugging at the net and I can feel something tugging back.

The door was open. Ziss was sitting there in T-shirt and jeans, watching cartoons on TV and sipping at a glass of milk. He pushed the hair back from his brow and gave me a sheepish grin. "David?" Wendy called from the back room, "David? Are you going out?" I must have looked like the big loser on a quiz show or something, because Ziss, for once, didn't have anything to say. He just shrugged his shoulders. Wendy's voice, breathy as a flute, came at us again: "Because if you are, get me some sweetcakes and yogurt, and maybe a couple of corn muffins, okay? I'm hungry as a bear."

Ziss got up and walked to the bedroom door, mumbled something I couldn't hear, then strode past me without a glance and went on out the back door. I watched him bend for a basketball, dribble around in the dirt, and then cock his arm for a shot at an imaginary basket. On the TV, Sylvester the cat reached into a trashcan and pulled out a fish stripped to the bones. Wendy was standing in the doorway. She had nothing to say.

"Look, Wendy," I began. I felt betrayed, cheated, felt as if I were the brunt of a joke between this girl in the housecoat and the curly-headed hotshot fooling around on the lawn. What was his

114

angle, I wondered, heart pounding at my chest, what was hers? "I suppose you two had a good laugh over me, huh?"

She was pouting, the spoiled child. "I fulfilled my part of the bargain."

She had. I got what I'd paid for. But all that had changed, couldn't she see that? I didn't want a son, I didn't want Marie: I wanted her. I told her so. She said nothing. "You've got something going with Ziss, right?" I said, my voice rising. "All along, right?"

She looked tired, looked as if she'd been up for a hundred nights running. I watched her shuffle across the room into the kitchnette, glance into the refrigerator and come up with a jar of jam. She made herself a sandwich, licking the goo from her fingers, and then she told me I stank of fish. She said she couldn't have a lasting relationship with me because of Marie.

"That's a lot of crap, and you know it." I was shouting. Ziss, fifty feet away, turned to look through the open door.

"All right. It's because we're—" She put the sandwich down, wiped a smear of jelly from her lip. "Because we move in different circles."

"You mean because I'm not some fancy-ass doctor, because I didn't go to college."

She nodded. Slow and deliberate, no room for argument, she held my eyes and nodded.

I couldn't help it. Something just came loose in my head, and the next second I was out the door, knocking Ziss into the dirt. He kicked and scratched, tried to bite me on the wrist, but I just took hold of his hair and laid into his face while Wendy ran around in her Japanese housecoat, screeching like a cat in heat. By the time the police got there I'd pretty well closed up both his eyes and rearranged his dental work. Wendy was bending over him with a bottle of rubbing alcohol when they put the cuffs on me.

Next morning there was a story in the paper. Marie sent Alex DeFazio down with the bail money, and then she wouldn't let me in the house. I banged on the door halfheartedly, then tried one of the windows, only to find she'd nailed it shut. When I saw that, I was just about ready to explode, but then I figured what the hell and fired up the Rambler in a cloud of blue smoke. Cops, dogs, kids and pedestrians be damned, I ran it like a stock car eight blocks down to the dock and left it steaming in the parking lot.

Five minutes later I was planing across the river, a wide brown furrow fanning out behind me.

This was my element, sun, wind, water, life pared down to the basics. Gulls hung in the air like puppets on a wire, spray flew up in my face, the shore sank back into my wake until docks and pleasure boats and clapboard houses were swallowed up and I was alone on the broad gray back of the river. After a while I eased up on the throttle and began scanning the surface for the buoys that marked my gill nets, working by rote, the tight-wound spool in my chest finally beginning to pay out. Then I spotted them, white and red, jogged by the waves. I cut the engine, coasted in and caught hold of the nearest float.

Wendy, I thought as I hauled at the ropes, ten years, twenty-five, a lifetime: every time I look at my son I'll see your face. Hand over hand, Wendy, Wendy, Wendy, the net heaving up out of the swirling brown depths with its pounds of flesh. But then I wasn't thinking about Wendy anymore, or Marie or Nathaniel, Jr.—I was thinking about the bottom of the river, I was thinking about fins and scales and cold lidless eyes. The instant I touched the lead rope I knew I was on to something. This time of year it would be sturgeon, big as logs, long-nosed and barbeled, coasting up the riverbed out of some dim watery past, anadromous, prepro-grammed, homing in on their spawning grounds like guided missiles. Just then I felt a pulsing in the soles of my sneakers and turned to glance up at the Day Liner, steaming by on its way to Bear Mountain, hundreds of people with picnic baskets and cool-ers, waving. I jerked at the net like a penitent.

There was a single sturgeon in the net, tangled up like a ball of string. It was dead. I strained to haul the thing aboard, six feet long, two hundred ten pounds. Cold from the depths, still supple, it hadn't been dead more than an hour—while I'd been banging at my own front door, locked out, it had been thrashing in the dark, locked in. The gulls swooped low, mocking me. I had to cut it out of the net.

Back at the dock I got one of the beer drinkers to give me a hand and we dragged the fish over to the skinning pole. With sturgeon, we hang them by the gills from the top of a ten-foot pole and then we peel back the scutes like you'd peel a banana. Four or five guys stood there watching me, nobody saying anything. I cut all the way around the skin just below the big stiff gill plates and then made

116

five vertical slits the length of the fish. Flies settled on the blade of the knife. The sun beat at the back of my head. I remember there was a guy standing there, somebody I'd never seen before, a guy in a white shirt with a kid about eight or so. The kid was holding a fishing pole. They stepped back, both of them, when I tore the first strip of skin from the fish.

Sturgeon peels back with a raspy, nails-on-the-blackboard sort of sound, reminds me of tearing up sheets or ripping bark from a tree. I tossed the curling strips of leather in a pile, flies sawing away at the air, the big glistening pink carcass hanging there like a skinned deer, blood and flesh. Somebody handed me a beer: it stuck to my hand and I drained it in a gulp. Then I turned to gut the fish, me a doctor, the knife a scalpel, and suddenly I was digging into the vent like Jack the Ripper, slitting it all the way up to the gills in a single violent motion.

"How do you like that?" the man in the white shirt said. "She's got eggs in her."

I glanced down. There they were, wet, beaded and gray, millions of them, the big clusters tearing free and dropping to the ground like ripe fruit. I cupped my hands and held the trembling mass of it there against the gashed belly, fifty or sixty pounds of the stuff, slippery roe running through my fingers like the silver coins from a slot machine, like a jackpot.

THE POWER OF TOADS

by PATTIANN ROGERS

from THE IOWA REVIEW

nominated by THE IOWA REVIEW, *John Allman and David Wojahn*

The oak toad and the red-spotted toad love their love
In a spring rain, calling and calling, breeding
Through a stormy evening clasped atop their mates.
Who wouldn't sing—anticipating the belly pressed hard
Against a female's spine in the steady rain
Below writhing skies, the safe moist jelly effluence
Of a final exaltation?

There might be some toads who actually believe
That the loin-shaking thunder of the banks, the evening
Filled with damp, the warm softening mud and rising
Riverlets are the facts of their own persistent
Performance. Maybe they think that when they sing
They sing more than songs, creating rain and mist
By their voices, initiating the union of water and dusk,
Females materializing on the banks shaped perfectly
By their calls.

And some toads may be convinced they have forced
The heavens to twist and moan by the continual expansion
Of their lung-sacs pushing against the dusk.
And some might believe the splitting light,
The soaring grey they see above them are nothing
But a vision of the longing in their groins,
A fertile spring heaven caught in its entirety
At the pit of the gut.

And they might be right.
Who knows whether these broken heavens
Could exist tonight separate from trills and toad ringings?
Maybe the particles of this rain descending on the pond
Are nothing but the visual manifestation of whistles
And cascading love clicks in the shore grasses.
Raindrops-finding-earth and coitus could very well
Be known here as one.

We could investigate the causal relationship
Between rainstorm and love-by-pondside if we wished.
We could lie down in the grasses by the water's edge
And watch to see exactly how the heavens were moved,
Thinking hard of thunder, imagining all the courses
That slow, clean waters might take across our bodies,
Believing completely in the rolling and pressing power
Of heavens and thighs. And in the end we might be glad,
Even if all we discovered for certain was the slick, sweet
Promise of good love beneath dark skies inside warm rains.

PEACOCK DISPLAY

by DAVID WAGONER

from PRAIRIE SCHOONER

nominated by Louis Gallo and Joyce Carol Oates

He approaches her, trailing his whole fortune,
Perfectly cocksure, and suddenly spreads
The huge fan of his tail for her amazement.

Each turquoise and purple, black-horned, walleyed quill
Comes quivering forward, an amphitheatric shell
For his most fortunate audience: her alone.

He plumes himself. He shakes his brassily gold
Wings and rump in a dance, lifting his claws
Stiff-legged under the great bulge of his breast.

And she strolls calmly away, pecking and pausing,
Not watching him, astonished to discover
All these seeds spread just for her in the dirt.

FISH FUCKING

by MICHAEL BLUMENTHAL

from MISSOURI REVIEW

nominated by MISSOURI REVIEW

This is not a poem about sex, or even
  about fish or the genitals of fish.
    So if you are a fisherman or someone interested
    primarily in sex, this would be as good a time
As any to put another worm on your hook
  or find a poem that is really about fucking.

This, rather is a poem about language,
  and about the connections between mind and ear
And the strange way a day makes its tenuous
  progress from almost anywhere.

Which is why I've decided to begin with the idea
  of fish fucking (not literally, mind you,
But the *idea* of fish fucking), because the other
  day, and a beautiful day it was, in Virginia
The woman I was with, commenting on the time
  between the stocking of a pond and the

First day of fishing season, asked me if this
  was perhaps because of the frequency with which
Fish fuck, and—though I myself know nothing at all
  about the fucking of fish—indeed, I believe

From the little biology I know that fish do not
  fuck at all as we know, but rather the male
Deposits his sperm on the larvae, which the female,
  in turn, has deposited—yet the question

Somehow suggested itself to my mind as the starting
   point of the day, and from the idea of fish

Fucking came thoughts of the time that passes
   between things and our experience of them,
Not only between the stocking of the pond and our
   being permitted to fish in it, but the time,

For example, that passes between the bouncing
   of light on the pond and our perception of the
Pond, or between the time I say the word *jujungawop*
   and the moment that word bounces against your
Eardrum and the moment a bit further on when the
   nerves that run from the eardrum to the brain

Inform you that you do not, in fact, know
   the meaning of the word *jujungawop*, but this,
Perhaps, is moving a bit too far from the idea of
   fish fucking and how beautifully blue the pond was

That morning and how, lying among the reeds atop
   the dam and listening to the water run under it,
The thought occurred to me how the germ of an idea
   has little to do with the idea itself, and how
It is rather a small leap from fish fucking to the .
   anthropomorphic forms in a Miro painting,

Or the way certain women, when they make love,
   pucker their lips and gurgle like fish, and how
This all points out how dangerous it is for a
   man or a woman who wants a poet's attention

To bring up an idea, even so ludicrous and
   biologically ungrounded a one as fish fucking,
Because the next thing she knows the mind is taking
   off over the dam from her beautiful face, off
Over the hills of Virginia, perhaps as far as Guatemala
   and the black bass that live in Lake Atitlan who

Feast on the flightless grebe, which is not merely
   a sexual thought or a fishy one, but a thought
About the cruelty that underlies even great beauty,
   the cruelty of nature and love and our lives which

We cannot do without and without which even the idea
   of fish fucking would be ordinary and no larger than
Itself, but to return now to that particular day, and to
   the idea of love, which inevitably arises from the
Thought that even so seemingly unintelligent a creature
   as a fish could hold his loved one, naked in the water,

And say to her, softly, *Liebes, mein Liebes;* it was
   indeed a beautiful day, the kind filled with anticipation
And longing for the small perfections usually found only
   in poems; the breeze was slight enough just to brush

A few of her hairs gently over one eye, the air was
   the scent of bayberry and pine as if the gods were
Burning incense in some heavenly living room, and
   as we lay among the reeds, our faces skyward,
The sun folding our cheeks, it was as if each
   time we looked away from the world it took

On again a precise yet general luminescence when we
   returned to it, a clarity equally convincing as pain
But more pleasing to the senses, and though it was not
   such a moment of perfection as Keats or Hamsun

Speak of and for the sake of which we can go on for
   years almost blissful in our joylessness, it was
A day when at least the possibility of such a thing
   seemed possible: the deer tracks suggesting that
Deer do, indeed, come to the edge of the woods to feed
   at dusk, and the idea of fish fucking suggesting

A world so beautiful, so divine in its generosity
   that even the fish make love, even the fish live
Happily ever after, chasing each other, lustful
   as stars through the constantly breaking water.

𝅘𝅥 𝅘𝅥 𝅘𝅥

RECOVERING

by WILLIAM GOYEN

from TRIQUARTERLY

nominated by TRIQUARTERLY, *Louis Gallo and Robert Phillips*

THE STORY—AND TRAVAIL—of two brothers has been on my mind: Jacob and Esau, twins. Esau was born first, "coming forth red and all his body hairy, like a mantle," and Jacob followed, clutching onto his brother's heel. As though he wanted to hold back Esau, pull him back and go on ahead of him, "supplant" him. For this Jacob was called "The Supplanter." I suppose we've all felt the grabbing hand, the clutch on the heel as we were making our own natural headway, at some time or another; something—not good—pulling us back, stumbling us, even: a grasper, a potential supplanter. This is what Esau felt.

These brothers were, then, struggling brothers from the start, contending, even, for their birthright and blessing, as you may remember. Esau was a hunter and a man of the field, Jacob a quiet, indoors man. At a time in their youth their brotherhood became murderous out of jealousy and disharmony—as though they had been cursed; and Rebekah, Jacob's mother, heard of Esau's vow to kill his brother and advised Jacob to leave home. Once, Esau, the red and hairy, had been so hungry when he came in from the fields that he offered his birthright to his quieter, domestic brother for some soup he was making. The brother, Jacob the Supplanter, accepted the bargain and so took his brother's birthright. And another time—this time by deceit—the wild, red brother of nature lost his father's blessing to his softer, more cunning brother. When the brothers' father Isaac was an old, failing blind man (he'd been sixty when his twin sons were born), he craved some good venison

This lecture was delivered at the Writer at Work Series, Gallatin Division, New York University, on April 13, 1983.. William Goyen died on August 29, 1983, in Los Angeles.

soup once more before he died and begged Esau, his favorite, to provide it. Esau's mother, Rebekah, whose favorite was Jacob, overheard the request and made the soup herself. Take the soup to your father, she urged, and thereby gain his blessing. A blessing was a powerful gift and coming from venerable beings or from certain people of unusual power was carried by the blessed person for a lifetime like an anointing, a protective benediction, a redemption, sacred. So Rebekah, Jacob's mother, hoping for the blessing of Isaac upon her favorite son, made this suggestion to Jacob. "But he'll feel my hands and see that they are smooth where my brother's are hairy," said Jacob, "and know that I am not his beloved Esau; and then he'll curse me instead of bless me." "We'll dress you in Esau's clothes and cover your hands and neck with the bristling skin of an animal," the mother said. When Jacob brought the soup to his father, his father said, "The voice is Jacob's voice but the hands are the hands of Esau." So Jacob ate the venison and gave his impersonating son the vaunted blessing: it said that nations might serve him and people bow before him, receiving obeisance from his mother's sons. Jacob, again the supplanter, had stolen his brother's blessing.

But soon came Esau with *his* dish of venison. "Bless me, father," asked Esau. "Who are you?" cried his father. "Who was it who has already brought me venison? I've eaten my fill and given *that* one my blessing, and on him the blessing will come. Thy brother, coming in disguise, has snatched thy blessing from thee." "He's rightly named the Supplanter!" cried Esau. "First he took away my birthright and now he has stolen my blessing. Father," he implored, "have you no blessing left for me?" "No," answered Isaac, "I have designated your brother your master, I have condemned all his brothers to do him service; I have assured him of corn and wine; what claim have I left myself to make for you, my son?" "But," Esau pled, "have you only one blessing to give, father?" Esau wept. Then Isaac was moved and said, "All thy blessings shall come from earth's fruitfulness, and from the dew of heaven. Thy sword shall be the breath of life to thee, but thou shall be subject to thy brother until the day comes when thou wilt rebel and wilt shake off his yoke from thy neck." Esau begrudged this blessing and made a plan to kill his brother as soon as his father died. When Jacob's mother heard of this threat, she sent her son Jacob away from home. Thus the hostile separation of the two brothers began, fed by deceit and jealousy and contention. But Jacob, the heelclutcher, had got ahead of his brother.

Years passed and Jacob had seen the fruits of his blind father's misplaced blessing: he was very rich with cattle and sheep, wives and servants and eleven children. He had not seen his estranged brother Esau for a long time, but now a meeting was at hand. It was time to go home again, to reenter the promised land of home and to meet his brother, to make amends. Jacob was returning as a prosperous and successful man and sent ahead to Esau gifts of abundance, cattle and sheep and camels and corn and oil. This returning home again is hard when there has been no increase, no fulfillment, no "success"; it is often bitter; as such a returnee I remember well some empty-handed homecomings; but Jacob came back covered in glory. But his fear was great. He had wronged his brother and was afraid of him and had amends to make. His brother had vowed to kill him. He hoped to disarm his anger with gifts sent ahead, but he was going to have to face his brother whom he had cheated, deceived, swindled, impersonated, "supplanted."

The story, in the book of Genesis (32: 22-32), of Jacob's return home to meet his brother, encloses the ancient and beautiful incident of an angelic encounter by a river. It is concerned with the themes of loss and recovering of self, of wounding and healing, of discovery of true self through spiritual struggle. It is about an all-night, mysterious wrestling between two silent men, opponents; or one silent man, *himself* his own contestant: which is it? The silent wrestling is broken only by the approaching dawn, when each asks the other's name and by one wounding, crippling— "halting"—the other in order to subdue him, and by the subduer asking the subdued to bless him! The passage reads: "The same night Jacob arose and took his two wives, his two maids, and his eleven children, and crossed the ford of the Jabbok river. He took them and sent them across the stream, and likewise everything that he had. And Jacob was left alone; and a man wrestled with him until the breaking of the day. When the man saw that he did not prevail against Jacob, he touched the hollow of Jacob's thigh; and Jacob's thigh was put out of joint as he wrestled with him. Then the man said, 'Let me go, for the day is breaking.' But Jacob said, 'I will not let you go, unless you bless me.' And the man said to him, 'What is your name?' And he said, 'Jacob.' Then the man said,

'Your name shall no more be called Jacob, but Israel; that is, He who strives with God and prevails. For if you have held your own with God, how much will you prevail over men?' Then Jacob asked him, 'Tell me, I pray, your name.' But he said, 'Why is it that you ask my name?' And there he blessed him. So Jacob called the name of the place Phenuel (that is, the face of God), saying, 'For I have seen God face to face, and yet my life is preserved.' The sun rose upon him as he passed Phenuel, limping because of his thigh."

Jacob's recovering his name and spirit, his redemption by the night river, is one of the most mysterious and enigmatic scenes of literature and has meant a great deal to me in the experience of recovering. Relating to my work it is direct metaphor. I've limped out of every piece of work I've done. It's given me a good sock in the hipbone in the wrestling. My eyes often open when I see a limping person going down the street. That person's wrestled with God, I think. I don't know when I ever rose from that contest as hale and whole as when I began. For me every accomplishment of work has been a wounding that brought new strength, new vision. I've always felt new, changed when the work was done. And in a new—or different—relation with life. Work, for me—writing, that is—has been that renewal through wrestling, that naming, that going home, that reconciliation with old disharmony, grief, grudge. For me that was recovery. Now I am not here—thank God—to define functions and meanings of literature, of the art of writing for anybody but myself—and that only by way of sharing my experience in living the life of an artist, in creating fiction (which is and has long been a way of life for me). I am sharing my own very personal experience in writing life, in recovering life. I am speaking of recovery of spirit where it had been lost, of finding again, as though it were new, fresh, what had been thought to have gone; of renewed vitality where there was debilitation; of replenishment where there had been emptiness. That kind of wrestling. "Recovery" involves a transformation. It is not simply a dead replacement, a lifeless exchange of one thing for another. And the transformation I speak of is spiritual—of the spirit. Art recovers life through spirit—that is, not through physical action. Nostalgia, the use of flat memory, in recalling the thing itself, calling back what once was, and in self-pity, is not what I'm talking about when I speak of recovery, of recovering life as art. In nostalgia, the element of lifeless longing is present, and so it is sentimental in that it wishes, yearns for things to be once again the way they used to be, exactly—a dead transference from then to now, stamped down. The Now, the present moment, the livingness of life, the world of "lived, ordinary lives," are dammed back, buried over by grieving over what was. I speak entirely from my own feelings and my own experience, from my own personal adventures. Everything is autobiography for me. Long ago I knew that another could not give me my life, only help to find it. I could only know life through myself, or recover it myself. I continue to be astonished by my own history. My own experience keeps justifying living. Others' experience in history has supported and inspirited me; but finally my *own* has got me through. The most I have been able to offer others and can now is this self-consciousness, ferocious protection of *personal feeling*. I am astonished by what has happened to me. More than anyone else, I am most curious about myself, my own hidden behavior, the secret services of my mind. Of all people, I am the person closest to my own feelings. It is, above all, *my* journey, that long and close association with myself that has been the signal value of my existence. The journey with myself is more remarkable than any other journey I have ever taken. Therefore, writing life for me is (and has been) a spiritual endeavor, and is transforming and redemptive. Wrestling and getting named and demanding "blessing," I limp.

In speaking of the writer recovering, one can ask, why recover? Why not just give back what was, as it was, what is as it is? Why recover? Why not just let everything alone? Why wrestle, why not surrender; why not die? The unhealed must think this. In the fifties there was a vogue of the unhealed and unhealable. The poet was mad and lost. Some feared that "getting well" might mean the loss of poetry. If addictions were removed, by the grace of God, would art be removed along with them? Did a poet's songs live in speed and gin? These poets were exalted as lost and damned. Could writing heal them? Were poems cures? The recovering poet was the creating poet, the fertile, producing poet. I've sat in university halls and listened to visiting unrecovering poets who could not be understood behind drunkenness and dope. Could new poems heal them? If they could again in clear head write their poems, would they get well? Could the will, the willingness to make new poems, heal them? *Ex opera operandis*. In the power of the work itself, the power of the person.

The unhealed. I have not only known the unhealed but have been among them and one of them. The unhealed will not let go of the sickness, that is, come awake. The unhealed choose the hypnotism of illness and will not only not wrestle with it but certainly not ask a blessing of it. But pain and affliction do carry a blessing in them, I believe. Illness is a spiritual condition. It brings us to see something we had not seen before—seeing the meaning of our suffering. Thus, being healed—recovering—in this manner can cause great joy and even gratitude over having been sick. "Ordinarily, people feel sorry for themselves for having suffered," writes Dr. Thomas Hora in *Dialogues in Metapsychiatry*; "but in cases where real healing takes place, there is a sense of gratitude for the experience because it has brought about a realization which is of great value to the individual. Once we understand the true nature of healing, there is a valuable lesson in it for us all. If we have a problem, we do not have to seek fast relief, or even a quick healing to get rid of the problem as soon as possible. We may embrace the problem and say the same thing that Jacob said: 'I will not let thee go, except thou bless me.' If we quickly get rid of a problem and find relief, we are missing an opportunity to learn something vitally important. The mode of being-in-the-world changes and our character undergoes a transformation. That's the greatest healing." I will not let thee go, except thou bless me. Dr. Hora and others have shown me that in my stricken life and in my recovering life there has been a deep change within me; I am no longer the same person; I am somewhere made new. And I make new things out of this vision and out of this reality. In no longer holding onto my sickness in isolation and self-nursing, I have let go and have found new prowess, a new relationship to life and to others.

Which brings to mind, again, my friend the Greek archer: Philoctetes, about whom I have spoken before. Philoctetes was, you'll remember, given a bow of great power—a blessing in terms of what we have been saying. On a wild island where he and his fellow warriors had stopped to pray to a local god, Philoctetes was bitten by a snake. A person with a magical gift had been wounded, lamed, "halted." The wound was incurable, and what's more, gave off an unbearable odor, which drove the gifted youth's friends from him. More than that, seizures periodically rendered Philoctetes frightening—he looked and acted crazy. He was abandoned on the forlorn island. He hid himself further away from the world in a cave by the ocean. He limped.

Philoctetes was so concerned with his wound that he forgot his bow. He knew utter loneliness. But he had his wound, morbid companion. Years passed. Suddenly he was urgently needed by others: a crucial war could be won if he would come again among his family and his fellows, return to his homeland with bow. But, the young man reasoned with himself, there is this wound. Philoctetes refused to return; he was of no use. A famous doctor was offered. He would heal the wound. He asked to be left alone; he rejected the healing physician. Philoctetes was now in a position of power. A person with a handicapping wound and a priceless gift in demand by his society! He could sleep on, in self-pity and sickness, or accept healing and come back to the use of his gift, doubly empowered by his long suffering, by the long contest with himself, by his wrestling. You know the rest of the story, or can find it. It is the situation of the unhealed that serves us here.

For as I see it, the singer is the song; the poetry is the poet; the archer is the bow. In the power of the work itself, the power of the person. The two conditions are inseparable. I do not mean that a person must be wounded in order to use his gift. Isolate either the bow or the archer and you have no whole, a fatal division, a fragment. A person who sees life and others exclusively in terms of his own affliction is out of literature we all know, and a seductive literature at that: we can name poets and novelists who have lured us into the darkness, given us opiate visions that have seemed to be life itself. Exclusive self-nursing, tending the "curse," the "difference" that separates, produces darkness, a sunless, festering creation. Exclusive magic produces sentimentality, heartlessness, silvery confection, a doll. At any rate, there is a conversation I must have with Philoctetes, my brother. For it is clear that he and I have met with the same choice, suffered together that crucial struggle, lain day after day, night after night, in the same haunted cave, "unhealable," dozing undelivered in the uterine glow, held by sucking death from pushing out into the explosion of life, heel in the grasp of a seductive supplanter. The deadly wound was all. The life-robber, the death sore, had taken over life. The radiant, the life-thrusting—the bow—lay untouched in the darkness. But brother Philoctetes, your healer arrived, the wound was closed, the bow won the battle; and O brother of the cave and the pain, I too have once again shaken free, flipped like a fish from the hand that stretches toward me; I kick towards light, but the fingertouch is on my heel. Lend me your bow! Come before me!

From what I have said, it is clear that writing—recovering life—for me is a spiritual task. No matter what the craft of it, writing for me is the work of the spirit. Style for me is the spiritual experience of the material of my work.

Art and Spirit endure together. Art heals, puts the precious bow in our hands again; binds up and reconciles; recovers the dignity and the beauty in us that keep getting wounded by the wrestling with the angel in us, with the God in us, or—in the absence of angels or God—with the mystery in each of us, waiting in the night by the river that we shall surely come to, on our way home to meet our brother.

🔥 🔥 🔥

OH, JOSEPH,
I'M SO TIRED

fiction by RICHARD YATES

from WAMPETER PRESS

nominated by WAMPETER PRESS

W HEN FRANKLIN D. ROOSEVELT was President-elect there
must have been sculptors all over America who wanted a chance to
model his head from life, but my mother had connections. One of
her closest friends and neighbors, in the Greenwich Village courtyard where we lived, was an amiable man named Howard Whitman who had recently lost his job as a reporter on the *New York
Post*. And one of Howard's former colleagues from the *Post* was
now employed in the press office of Roosevelt's New York headquarters. That would make it easy for her to get in—or, as she said,
to get an entrée—and she was confident she could take it from
there. She was confident about everything she did in those days,
but it never quite disguised a terrible need for support and
approval on every side.

   She wasn't a very good sculptor. She had been working at it for
only three years, since breaking up her marriage to my father, and
there was still something stiff and amateurish about her pieces.
Before the Roosevelt project her specialty had been "garden
figures"—a life-size little boy whose legs turned into the legs of a
goat at the knees and another who knelt among ferns to play the
pipes of Pan; little girls who trailed chains of daisies from their
upraised arms or walked beside a spread-winged goose. These
fanciful children, in plaster painted green to simulate weathered
bronze, were arranged on homemade wooden pedestals to loom
around her studio and to leave a cleared space in the middle for the
modeling stand that held whatever she was working on in clay.

Her idea was that any number of rich people, all of them gracious and aristocratic, would soon discover her: they would want her sculpture to decorate their landscaped gardens, and they would want to make her their friend for life. In the meantime, a little nationwide publicity as the first woman sculptor to "do" the President-elect certainly wouldn't hurt her career.

And, if nothing else, she had a good studio. It was, in fact, the best of all the studios she would have in the rest of her life. There were six or eight old houses facing our side of the courtyard, with their backs to Bedford Street, and ours was probably the show-place of the row because the front room on its ground floor was two stories high. You went down a broad set of brick steps to the tall front windows and the front door; then you were in the high, wide, light-flooded studio. It was big enough to serve as a living room too, and so along with the green garden children it contained all the living-room furniture from the house we'd lived in with my father in the suburban town of Hastings-on-Hudson, where I was born. A second-floor balcony ran along the far end of the studio, with two small bedrooms and a tiny bathroom tucked away up-stairs; beneath that, where the ground floor continued through to the Bedford Street side, lay the only part of the apartment that might let you know we didn't have much money. The ceiling was very low and it was always dark in there; the small windows looked out underneath an iron sidewalk grating, and the bottom of that street cavity was thick with strewn garbage. Our roach-infested kitchen was barely big enough for a stove and sink that were never clean, and for a brown wooden icebox with its dark, ever-melting block of ice; the rest of that area was our dining room, and not even the amplitude of the old Hastings dining-room table could brighten it. But our Majestic radio was in there too, and that made it a cozy place for my sister Edith and me: we liked the children's programs that came on in the late afternoons.

We had just turned off the radio one day when we went out into the studio and found our mother discussing the Roosevelt project with Howard Whitman. It was the first we'd heard of it, and we must have interrupted her with too many questions because she said "Edith? Billy? That's enough, now. I'll tell you all about this later. Run out in the garden and play."

She always called the courtyard "the garden," though nothing grew there except a few stunted city trees and a patch of grass that

133

never had a chance to spread. Mostly it was bald earth, interrupted here and there by brick paving, lightly powdered with soot and scattered with the droppings of dogs and cats. It may have been six or eight houses long, but it was only two houses wide, which gave it a hemmed-in, cheerless look; its only point of interest was a dilapidated marble fountain, not much bigger than a birdbath, which stood near our house. The original idea of the fountain was that water would drip evenly from around the rim of its upper tier and tinkle into its lower basin, but age had unsettled it; the water spilled in a single ropy stream from the only inch of the upper tier's rim that stayed clean. The lower basin was deep enough to soak your feet in on a hot day, but there wasn't much pleasure in that because the underwater part of the marble was coated with brown scum.

My sister and I found things to do in the courtyard every day, for all of the two years we lived there, but that was only because Edith was an imaginative child. She was eleven at the time of the Roosevelt project, and I was seven.

"Daddy?" she asked in our father's office uptown one afternoon. "Have you heard Mommy's doing a head of President Roosevelt?"

"Oh?" He was rummaging in his desk, looking for something he'd said we might like.

"She's going to take his measurements and stuff here in New York," Edith said, "and then after the Inauguration, when the sculpture's done, she's going to take it to Washington and present it to him in the White House." Edith often told one of our parents about the other's more virtuous activities; it was part of her long, hopeless effort to bring them back together. Many years later she told me she thought she had never recovered, and never would, from the shock of their breakup: she said Hastings-on-Hudson remained the happiest time of her life, and that made me envious because I could scarcely remember it at all.

"Well," my father said. "That's really something, isn't it." Then he found what he'd been looking for in the desk and said, "Here we go; what do you think of these?" They were two fragile perforated sheets of what looked like postage stamps, each stamp bearing the insignia of an electric light bulb in vivid white against a yellow background, and the words "More light."

My father's office was one of many small cubicles on the twenty-third floor of the General Electric building. He was an assistant regional sales manager in what was then called the Mazda Lamp Division—a modest job, but good enough to have allowed him to rent into a town like Hastings-on-Hudson in better times—and these "More light" stamps were souvenirs of a recent sales convention. We told him the stamps were neat—and they were—but expressed some doubt as to what we might do with them.

"Oh, they're just for decoration," he said. "I thought you could paste them into your schoolbooks, or—you know—whatever you want. Ready to go?" And he carefully folded the sheets of stamps and put them in his inside pocket for safekeeping on the way home.

Between the subway exit and the courtyard, somewhere in the West Village, we always walked past a vacant lot where men stood huddled around weak fires built of broken fruit crates and trash, some of them warming tin cans of food held by coat-hanger wire over the flames. "Don't stare," my father had said the first time. "All those men are out of work, and they're hungry."

"Daddy?" Edith inquired. "Do you think Roosevelt's good?"

"Sure I do."

"Do you think all the Democrats are good?"

"Well, most of 'em, sure."

Much later I would learn that my father had participated in local Democratic Party politics for years. He had served some of his political friends—men my mother described as dreadful little Irish people from Tammany Hall—by helping them to establish Mazda Lamp distributorships in various parts of the city. And he loved their social gatherings, at which he was always asked to sing.

"Well, of course, you're too young to remember Daddy's singing," Edith said to me once after his death in 1942.

"No, I'm not; I remember."

"But I mean really remember," she said. "He had the most beautiful tenor voice I've ever heard. Remember 'Danny Boy'?"

"Sure."

"Ah, God, that was something," she said, closing her eyes. "That was really—that was really something."

When we got back to the courtyard that afternoon, and back into the studio, Edith and I watched our parents say hello to each other. We always watched that closely, hoping they might drift into conversation and sit down together and find things to laugh about, but they never did. And it was even less likely than usual that day because my mother had a guest—a woman named Sloane Cabot who was her best friend in the courtyard, and who greeted my father with a little rush of false, flirtatious enthusiasm.

"How've you been, Sloane?" he said. Then he turned back to his former wife and said "Helen? I hear you're planning to make a bust of Roosevelt."

"Well, not a bust," she said. "A head. I think it'll be more effective if I cut it off at the neck."

"Well, good. That's fine. Good luck with it. Okay, then." He gave his whole attention to Edith and me. "Okay. See you soon. How about a hug?"

And those hugs of his, the climax of his visitation rights, were unforgettable. One at a time we would be swept up and pressed hard into the smells of linen and whiskey and tobacco; the warm rasp of his jaw would graze one cheek and there would be a quick moist kiss near the ear; then he'd let us go.

He was almost all the way out of the courtyard, almost out in the street, when Edith and I went racing after him.

"Daddy! Daddy! You forgot the stamps!"

He stopped and turned around, and that was when we saw he was crying. He tried to hide it—he put his face nearly into his armpit as if that might help him search his inside pocket—but there is no way to disguise the awful bloat and pucker of a face in tears.

"Here," he said. "Here you go." And he gave us the least convincing smile I had ever seen. It would be good to report that we stayed and talked to him—that we hugged him again—but we were too embarrassed for that. We took the stamps and ran home without looking back.

"Oh, aren't you excited, Helen?" Sloane Cabot was saying. "To be meeting him, and talking to him and everything, in front of all those reporters?"

"Well, of course," my mother said, "but the important thing is to get the measurements right. I hope there won't be a lot of photographers and silly interruptions."

Sloane Cabot was some years younger than my mother, and strikingly pretty in a style often portrayed in what I think are called Art Deco illustrations of that period: straight dark bangs, big eyes, and a big mouth. She too was a divorced mother, though her former husband had vanished long ago and was referred to only as "that bastard" or "that cowardly son of a bitch." Her only child was a boy of Edith's age named John, whom Edith and I liked enormously.

The two women had met within days of our moving into the courtyard, and their friendship was sealed when my mother solved the problem of John's schooling. She knew a Hastings-on-Hudson family who would appreciate the money earned from taking in a boarder, so John went up there to live and go to school, and came home only on weekends. The arrangement cost more than Sloane could comfortably afford, but she managed to make ends meet and was forever grateful.

Sloane worked in the Wall Street district as a private secretary. She talked a lot about how she hated her job and her boss, but the good part was that her boss was often out of town for extended periods: that gave her time to use the office typewriter in pursuit of her life's ambition, which was to write scripts for the radio.

She once confided to my mother that she'd made up both of her names: "Sloane" because it sounded masculine, the kind of name a woman alone might need for making her way in the world, and "Cabot" because—well, because it had a touch of class. Was there anything wrong with that?

"Oh, Helen," she said. "This is going to be wonderful for you. If you get the publicity—if the papers pick it up, and the newsreels—you'll be one of the most interesting personalities in America."

Five or six people were gathered in the studio on the day my mother came home from her first visit with the President-elect.

"Will somebody get me a drink?" she asked, looking around in mock helplessness. "Then I'll tell you all about it."

And with the drink in her hand, with her eyes as wide as a child's, she told us how a door had opened and two big men had brought him in.

"Big men," she insisted. "Young, strong men, holding him up under the arms, and you could see how they were straining. Then you saw this *foot* come out, with these awful metal braces on the shoe, and then the *other* foot. And he was sweating, and he was panting for breath, and his face was—I don't know—all bright and tense and horrible." She shuddered.

"Well," Howard Whitman said, looking uneasy, "he can't help being crippled, Helen."

"Howard," she said impatiently, "I'm only trying to tell you how

137

ugly it was." And that seemed to carry a certain weight. If she was an authority on beauty—on how a little boy might kneel among ferns to play the pipes of Pan, for example—then surely she had earned her credentials as an authority on ugliness.

"*Any*way," she went on, "they got him into a chair, and he wiped most of the sweat off his face with a handkerchief—he was still out of breath—and after a while he started talking to some of the other men there; I couldn't follow that part of it. Then finally he turned to me with this smile of his. Honestly, I don't know if I can describe that smile. It isn't something you can see in the newsreels; you have to be there. His eyes don't change at all, but the corners of his mouth go up as if they're being pulled by puppet strings. It's a frightening smile. It makes you think: This could be a dangerous man. This could be an evil man. Well anyway, we started talking, and I spoke right up to him. I said 'I didn't vote for you, Mr. President.' I said 'I'm a good Republican and I voted for President Hoover.' He said 'Why are you here, then?' or something like that, and I said 'Because you have a very interesting head.' So he gave me the smile again and he said 'What's interesting about it?' And I said 'I like the bumps on it.' "

By then she must have assumed that every reporter in the room was writing in his notebook, while the photographers got their flashbulbs ready; tomorrow's papers might easily read:

GAL SCULPTOR TWITS FDR
ABOUT "BUMPS" ON HEAD

At the end of her preliminary chat with him she got down to business, which was to measure different parts of his head with her calipers. I knew how that felt: the cold, trembling points of those clay-encrusted calipers had tickled and poked me all over during the times I'd served as model for her fey little woodland boys.

But not a single flashbulb went off while she took and recorded the measurements, and nobody asked her any questions; after a few nervous words of thanks and good-bye she was out in the corridor again among all the hopeless, craning people who couldn't get in. It must have been a bad disappointment, and I imagine she tried to make up for it by planning the triumphant way she'd tell us about it when she got home.

"Helen?" Howard Whitman inquired, after most of the other visitors had gone. "Why'd you tell him you didn't vote for him?"

"Well, because it's true. I *am* a good Republican; you know that."

She was a storekeeper's daughter from a small town in Ohio; she had probably grown up hearing the phrase "good Republican" as an index of respectability and clean clothes. And maybe she had come to relax her standards of respectability, maybe she didn't even care much about clean clothes anymore, but "good Republican" was worth clinging to. It would be helpful when she met the customers for her garden figures, the people whose low, courteous voices would welcome her into their lives and who would almost certainly turn out to be Republicans too.

"I believe in the aristocracy!" she often cried, trying to make herself heard above the rumble of voices when her guests were discussing communism, and they seldom paid her any attention. They liked her well enough: she gave parties with plenty of liquor, and she was an agreeable hostess if only because of her touching eagerness to please; but in any talk of politics she was like a shrill, exasperating child. She believed in the aristocracy.

She believed in God, too, or at least in the ceremony of St Luke's Episcopal Church, which she attended once or twice a year. And she believed in Eric Nicholson, the handsome middle-aged Englishman who was her lover. He had something to do with the American end of a British chain of foundries: his company cast ornamental objects into bronze and lead. The cupolas of college and high-school buildings all over the East, the lead-casement windows for Tudor-style homes in places like Scarsdale and Bronxville—these were some of the things Eric Nicholson's firm had accomplished. He was always self-deprecating about his business, but ruddy and glowing with its success.

My mother had met him the year before, when she'd sought help in having one of her garden figures cast into bronze, to be "placed on consignment" with some garden-sculpture gallery from which it would never be sold. Eric Nicholson had persuaded her that lead would be almost as nice as bronze and much cheaper; then he'd asked her out to dinner, and that evening changed our lives.

Mr. Nicholson rarely spoke to my sister or me, and I think we were both frightened of him, but he overwhelmed us with gifts. At first they were mostly books—a volume of cartoons from *Punch*, a partial set of Dickens, a book called *England in Tudor Times* containing tissue-covered color plates that Edith liked. But in the summer of 1933, when our father arranged for us to spend two weeks with our mother at a small lake in New Jersey, Mr. Nicholson's gifts became a cornucopia of sporting goods. He gave Edith a steel fishing rod with a reel so intricate that none of us could have figured it out even if we'd known how to fish, a wicker creel for carrying the fish she would never catch, and a sheathed hunting knife to be worn at her waist. He gave me a short axe whose head was encased in a leather holster and strapped to my belt—I guess this was for cutting firewood to cook the fish—and a cumbersome net with a handle that hung from an elastic shoulder strap, in case I should be called upon to wade in and help Edith land a tricky one. There was nothing to do in that New Jersey village except take walks, or what my mother called good hikes; and every day, as we plodded out through the insect-humming weeds in the sun, we wore our full regalia of useless equipment.

That same summer Mr. Nicholson gave me a three-year subscription to *Field and Stream*, and I think that impenetrable magazine was the least appropriate of all his gifts because it kept coming in the mail for such a long, long time after everything else had changed for us: after we'd moved out of New York to Scarsdale, where Mr. Nicholson had found a house with a low rent, and after he had abandoned my mother in that house—with no warning—to return to England and to the wife from whom he'd never really been divorced.

But all that came later; I want to go back to the time between Franklin D. Roosevelt's election and his Inauguration, when his head was slowly taking shape on my mother's modeling stand.

Her original plan had been to make it life-size, or larger than life-size, but Mr. Nicholson urged her to scale it down for economy in the casting, and so she made it only six or seven inches high. He persuaded her too, for the second time since he'd known her, that lead would be almost as nice as bronze.

She had always said she didn't mind at all if Edith and I watched her work, but we had never much wanted to; now it was a little more interesting because we could watch her sift through many photographs of Roosevelt cut from newspapers until she found one that would help her execute a subtle plane of cheek or brow.

But most of our day was taken up with school. John Cabot might go to school in Hastings-on-Hudson, for which Edith would always yearn, but we had what even Edith admitted was the next best thing: we went to school in our bedroom.

During the previous year my mother had enrolled us in the public school down the street, but she'd begun to regret it when we came home with lice in our hair. Then one day Edith came home accused of having stolen a boy's coat, and that was too much. She withdrew us both, in defiance of the city truant officer, and pleaded with my father to help her meet the cost of a private school. He refused. The rent she paid and the bills she ran up were already taxing him far beyond the terms of the divorce agreement; he was in debt; surely she must realize he was lucky even to have a job. Would she ever learn to be reasonable?

It was Howard Whitman who broke the deadlock. He knew of an inexpensive, fully accredited mail-order service called The Calvert School, intended mainly for the homes of children who were invalids. The Calvert School furnished weekly supplies of books and materials and study plans; all she would need was someone in the house to administer the program and to serve as a tutor. And someone like Bart Kampen would be ideal for the job.

"The skinny fellow?" she asked. "The Jewish boy from Holland or wherever it is?"

"He's very well educated, Helen," Howard told her. "And he speaks fluent English, and he'd be very conscientious. And he could certainly use the money."

We were delighted to learn that Bart Kampen would be our tutor. With the exception of Howard himself, Bart was probably our favorite among the adults around the courtyard. He was twenty-eight or so, young enough so that his ears could still turn red when he was teased by children; we had found that out in teasing him once or twice about such matters as that his socks didn't match. He was tall and very thin and seemed always to look startled except when he was comforted enough to smile. He was a violinist, a Dutch Jew who had emigrated the year before in the hope of joining a symphony orchestra, and eventually of launching a concert career. But the symphonies weren't hiring then, nor were lesser orchestras, so Bart had gone without work for a long time. He lived alone in a room on Seventh Avenue, not far from the courtyard, and people who liked him used to worry that he might not have enough to eat. He owned two suits, both cut in a way that must have been stylish in the Netherlands at the time: stiff, heavily padded shoulders and a nipped-in waist; they would probably have looked better on someone with a little more meat on his bones. In shirtsleeves, with the cuffs rolled back, his hairy wrists and forearms looked even more fragile than you might have expected, but his long hands were shapely and strong enough to suggest authority on the violin.

"I'll leave it entirely up to you, Bart," my mother said when he asked if she had any instructions for our tutoring. "I know you'll do wonders with them."

A small table was moved into our bedroom, under the window, and three chairs placed around it. Bart sat in the middle so that he could divide his time equally between Edith and me. Big, clean, heavy brown envelopes arrived in the mail from The Calvert School once a week, and when Bart slid their fascinating contents onto the table it was like settling down to begin a game.

Edith was in the fifth grade that year—her part of the table was given over to incomprehensible talk about English and History and Social Studies—and I was in the first. I spent my mornings asking Bart to help me puzzle out the very opening moves of an education.

"Take your time, Billy," he would say. "Don't get impatient with this. Once you have it you'll see how easy it is, and then you'll be ready for the next thing."

At eleven each morning we would take a break. We'd go downstairs and out to the part of the courtyard that had a little grass. Bart would carefully lay his folded coat on the sidelines, turn back his shirt cuffs, and present himself as ready to give what he called airplane rides. Taking us one at a time, he would grasp one wrist and one ankle; then he'd whirl us off our feet and around and around, with himself as the pivot, until the courtyard and the buildings and the city and the world were lost in the dizzying blur of our flight.

After the airplane rides we would hurry down the steps into the studio, where we'd usually find that my mother had set out a tray bearing three tall glasses of cold Ovaltine, sometimes with cookies on the side and sometimes not. I once overheard her telling Sloane Cabot she thought the Ovaltine must be Bart's first nourishment of the day—and I think she was probably right, if only because of the way his hand would tremble in reaching for his glass. Sometimes she'd forget to prepare the tray and we'd crowd into the kitchen and fix it ourselves; I can never see a jar of Ovaltine on a grocery shelf without remembering those times. Then it was back upstairs to school again. And during that year, by coaxing and prodding and telling me not to get impatient, Bart Kampen taught me to read.

It was an excellent opportunity for showing off. I would pull books down from my mother's shelves—mostly books that were the gifts of Mr. Nicholson—and try to impress her by reading mangled sentences aloud.

"That's wonderful, dear," she would say. "You've really learned to read, haven't you."

Soon a white and yellow "More light" stamp was affixed to every page of my Calvert First Grade Reader, proving I had mastered it, and others were accumulating at a slower rate in my arithmetic workbook. Still other stamps were fastened to the wall beside my place at the school table, arranged in a proud little white and yellow thumb-smudged column that rose as high as I could reach.

"You shouldn't have put your stamps on the wall," Edith said.

"Why?"

"Well, because they'll be hard to take off."

"Who's going to take them off?"

That small room of ours, with its double function of sleep and learning, stands more clearly in my memory than any other part of our home. Someone should probably have told my mother that a girl and boy of our ages ought to have separate rooms, but that never occurred to me until much later. Our cots were set foot-to-foot against the wall, leaving just enough space to pass along-side them to the school table, and we had some good conversations as we lay waiting for sleep at night. The one I remember best was the time Edith told me about the sound of the city.

"I don't mean just the loud noises," she said, "like the siren going by just now, or those car doors slamming, or all the laughing and shouting down the street; that's just close-up stuff. I'm talking about something else. Because you see there are millions and millions of people in New York—more people than you can possibly imagine, ever—and most of them are doing something that makes a sound. Maybe talking, or playing the radio, maybe closing doors, maybe putting their forks down on their plates if they're having dinner, or dropping their shoes if they're going to bed—and because there are so many of them, all those little sounds add up and come together in a kind of hum. But it's so faint—so very, very faint—that you can't hear it unless you listen very carefully for a long time."

"Can you hear it?" I asked her.

"Sometimes. I listen every night, but I can only hear it sometimes. Other times I fall asleep. Let's be quiet now, and just listen. See if you can hear it, Billy."

And I tried hard, closing my eyes as if that would help, opening my mouth to minimize the sound of my breathing, but in the end I had to tell her I'd failed. "How about you?" I asked.

"Oh, I heard it," she said. "Just for a few seconds, but I heard it. You'll hear it too, if you keep trying. And it's worth waiting for. When you hear it, you're hearing the whole city of New York."

The high point of our week was Friday afternoon, when John Cabot came home from Hastings. He exuded health and normality; he brought fresh suburban air into our bohemian lives. He even transformed his mother's small apartment, while he was there, into an enviable place of rest between vigorous encounters with the world. He subscribed to both *Boy's Life* and *Open Road for Boys*, and these seemed to me to be wonderful things to have in your house, if only for the illustrations. John dressed in the same heroic way as the boys shown in those magazines, corduroy knickers with ribbed stockings pulled taut over his muscular calves. He talked a lot about the Hastings high-school football team, for which he planned to try out as soon as he was old enough, and about Hastings friends whose names and personalities grew almost as familiar to us as if they were friends of our own. He taught us invigorating new ways to speak, like saying "What's the diff?" instead of "What's the difference?" And he was better even than Edith at finding new things to do in the courtyard.

You could buy goldfish for ten or fifteen cents apiece in Woolworth's then, and one day we brought home three of them to keep in the fountain. We sprinkled the water with more Woolworth's granulated fish food than they could possibly need, and we named them after ourselves: "John," "Edith," and "Billy."

For a week or two Edith and I would run to the fountain every morning, before Bart came for school, to make sure they were still alive and to see if they had enough food, and to watch them.

"Have you noticed how much bigger Billy's getting?" Edith asked me. "He's huge. He's almost as big as John and Edith now. He'll probably be bigger than both of them."

Then one weekend when John was home he called our attention to how quickly the fish could turn and move. "They have better reflexes than humans," he explained. "When they see a shadow in the water, or anything that looks like danger, they get away faster than you can blink. Watch." And he sank one hand into the water to make a grab for the fish named Edith, but she evaded him and fled. "See that?" he asked. "How's that for speed. Know something? I bet you could shoot an arrow in there, and they'd get away in time. Wait." To prove his point he ran to his mother's apartment and came back with the handsome bow and arrow he had made at summer camp (going to camp every summer was another admirable thing about John); then he knelt at the rim of the fountain like the picture of an archer, his bow steady in one strong hand and the feathered end of the arrow tight against the bowstring in the other. He was taking aim at the fish named Billy. "Now, the velocity of this arrow," he said in a voice weakened by his effort, "is probably more than a car going eighty miles an hour. It's probably more like an airplane, or maybe even more than that. Okay; watch."

The fish named Billy was suddenly floating dead on the surface, on his side, impaled a quarter of the way up the arrow with parts of his pink guts dribbled along the shaft.

I was too old to cry, but something had to be done about the shock and rage and grief that filled me as I ran from the fountain, heading blindly for home, and half-way there I came upon my mother. She stood looking very clean, wearing a new coat and dress I'd never seen before and fastened to the arm of Mr. Nicholson. They were either just going out or just coming in—I didn't care which—and Mr. Nicholson frowned at me (he had told me more than once that boys of my age went to boarding school in England), but I didn't care about that either. I bent my head into her waist and didn't stop crying until long after I'd felt her hands stroking my back, until after she had assured me that goldfish didn't cost much and I'd have another one soon, and that John was sorry for the thoughtless thing he'd done. I had discovered, or rediscovered, that crying is a pleasure—that it can be a pleasure beyond all reckoning if your head is pressed in your mother's waist and her hands are on your back, and if she happens to be wearing clean clothes.

There were other pleasures. We had a good Christmas Eve in our house that year, or at least it was good at first. My father was there, which obliged Mr. Nicholson to stay away, and it was nice to see how relaxed he was among my mother's friends. He was shy, but they seemed to like him. He got along especially well with Bart Kampen.

Howard Whitman's daughter Molly, a sweet-natured girl of about my age, had come in from Tarrytown to spend the holidays with him, and there were several other children whom we knew but rarely saw. John looked very mature that night in a dark coat and tie, plainly aware of his special responsiblities as the oldest boy.

After a while, with no plan, the party drifted back into the dining-room area and staged an impromptu vaudeville. Howard started it: he brought the tall stool from my mother's modeling stand and sat his daughter on it, facing the audience. He folded back the opening of a brown paper bag two or three times and fitted it onto her head; then he took off his suit coat and draped it around her backwards, up to the chin; he went behind her, crouched out of sight, and worked his hands through the coat-sleeves so that when they emerged they appeared to be hers. And the sight of a smiling little girl in a paper-bag hat, waving and gesturing with huge, expressive hands, was enough to make everyone laugh. The big hands wiped her eyes and stroked her chin and pushed her hair behind her ears; then they elaborately thumbed her nose at us.

Next came Sloane Cabot. She sat very straight on the stool with her heels hooked over the rungs in such a way as to show her good legs to their best advantage, but her first act didn't go over.

"Well," she began, "I was at work today—you know my office is on the fortieth floor—when I happened to glance up from my typewriter and saw this big old man sort of crouched on the ledge outside the window, with a white beard and a funny red suit. So I ran to the window and opened it and said 'Are you all right?' Well, it was Santa Claus, and he said 'Of course I'm all right; I'm used to high places. But listen, miss: can you direct me to number seventy-five Bedford Street?"

There was more, but our embarrassed looks must have told her we knew we were being condescended to; as soon as she'd found a way to finish it she did so quickly. Then, after a thoughtful pause, she tried something else that turned out to be much better.

"Have you children ever heard the story of the first Christmas?" she asked. "When Jesus was born?" And she began to tell it in the kind of hushed, dramatic voice she must have hoped might be used by the narrators of her more serious radio plays.

". . . And there were still many miles to go before they reached Bethlehem," she said, "and it was a cold night. Now, Mary knew she would very soon have a baby. She even knew, because an angel had told her, that her baby might one day be the saviour of all mankind. But she was only a young girl"—here Sloane's eyes glistened, as if they might be filling with tears—"and the traveling had exhausted her. She was bruised by the jolting gait of the donkey and she ached all over, and she thought they'd never, ever get there, and all she could say was 'Oh, Joseph, I'm so tired.' "

The story went on through the rejection at the inn, and the birth in the stable, and the manger, and the animals, and the arrival of the three kings; when it was over we clapped a long time because Sloane had told it so well.

"Daddy?" Edith asked. "Will you sing for us?"

"Oh, well, thanks, honey," he said, "but no; I really need a piano for that. Thanks anyway."

The final performer of the evening was Bart Kampen, persuaded by popular demand to go home and get his violin. There was no surprise in discovering that he played like a professional, like something you might easily hear on the radio; the enjoyment came from watching how his thin face frowned over the chin rest, empty of all emotion except concern that the sound be right. We were proud of him.

Some time after my father left a good many other adults began to arrive, most of them strangers to me, looking as though they'd already been to several other parties that night. It was very late, or rather very early Christmas morning, when I looked into the kitchen and saw Sloane standing close to a bald man I didn't know. He held a trembling drink in one hand and slowly massaged her shoulder with the other; she seemed to be shrinking back against the old wooden icebox. Sloane had a way of smiling that allowed little wisps of cigarette smoke to escape from between her almost-closed lips while she looked you up and down, and she was doing that. Then the man put his drink on top of the icebox and took her in his arms, and I couldn't see her face anymore.

Another man, in a rumpled brown suit, lay unconscious on the dining-room floor. I walked around him and went into the studio, where a good-looking young woman stood weeping wretchedly and three men kept getting in each other's way as they tried to comfort her. Then I saw that one of the men was Bart, and I watched while he outlasted the other two and turned the girl away toward the door. He put his arm around her and she nestled her head in his shoulder; that was how they left the house.

Edith looked jaded in her wrinkled party dress. She was reclining in our old Hastings-on-Hudson easy chair with her head tipped back and her legs flung out over both the chair's arms, and John sat cross-legged on the floor near one of her dangling feet. They seemed to have been talking about something that didn't interest either of them much, and the talk petered out altogether when I sat on the floor to join them.

"Billy," she said, "do you realize what time it is?"

"What's the diff?" I said.

"You should've been in bed hours ago. Come on. Let's go up."

"I don't feel like it."

"Well," she said, "I'm going up, anyway," and she got laboriously out of the chair and walked away into the crowd.

John turned to me and narrowed his eyes unpleasantly. "Know something?" he said. "When she was in the chair that way I could see everything."

"Huh?"

"I could see everything. I could see the crack, and the hair. She's beginning to get hair."

I had observed these features of my sister many times—in the bathtub, or when she was changing her clothes—and hadn't found them especially remarkable; even so, I understood at once how remarkable they must have been for him. If only he had smiled in a bashful way we might have laughed together like a couple of regular fellows out of *Open Road for Boys*, but his face was still set in that disdainful look.

"I kept looking and looking," he said, "and I had to keep her talking so she wouldn't catch on, but I was doing fine until you had to come over and ruin it."

Was I supposed to apologize? That didn't seem right, but nothing else seemed right either. All I did was look at the floor.

When I finally got to bed there was scarcely time for trying to hear the elusive sound of the city—I had found that a good way to keep from thinking of anything else—when my mother came blundering in. She'd had too much to drink and wanted to lie down, but instead of going to her own room she got into bed with me. "Oh," she said. "Oh, my boy. Oh, my boy." It was a narrow cot and there was no way to make room for her; then suddenly she retched, bolted to her feet, and ran for the bathroom, where I heard her vomiting. And when I moved over into the part of the bed she had occupied my face recoiled quickly, but not quite in time, from the slick mouthful of puke she had left on her side of the pillow.

For a month or so that winter we didn't see much of Sloane because she said she was "working on something big. Something really big." When it was finished she brought it to the studio, looking tired but prettier than ever, and shyly asked if she could read it aloud.

"Wonderful," my mother said. "What's it about?"

"That's the best part. It's about us. All of us. Listen."

Bart had gone for the day and Edith was out in the courtyard by herself—she often played by herself—so there was nobody for an audience but my mother and me. We sat on the sofa and Sloane arranged herself on the tall stool, just as she'd done for telling the Bethlehem story.

"There is an enchanted courtyard in Greenwich Village," she read. "It's only a narrow patch of brick and green among the irregular shapes of very old houses, but what makes it enchanted is that the people who live in it, or near it, have come to form an enchanted circle of friends.

"None of them have enough money and some are quite poor, but they believe in the future; they believe in each other, and in themselves.

"There is Howard, once a top reporter on a metropolitan daily newspaper. Everyone knows Howard will soon scale the journalistic heights again, and in the meantime he serves as the wise and humorous sage of the courtyard.

"There is Bart, a young violinist clearly destined for virtuosity on the concert stage, who just for the present must graciously accept all lunch and dinner invitations in order to survive.

"And there is Helen, a sculptor whose charming work will someday grace the finest gardens in America, and whose studio is the favorite gathering place for members of the circle."

There was more like that, introducing other characters, and toward the end she got around to the children. She described my sister as "a lanky, dreamy tomboy," which was odd—I had never thought of Edith that way—and she called me "a sad-eyed, seven-year-old philosopher," which was wholly baffling. When the introduction was over she paused a few seconds for dramatic effect and then went into the opening episode of the series, or what I suppose would be called the "pilot."

I couldn't follow the story very well—it seemed to be mostly an excuse for bringing each character up to the microphone for a few lines apiece—and before long I was listening only to see if there would be any lines for the character based on me. And there were, in a way. She announced my name—"Billy"—but then instead of speaking she put her mouth through a terrible series of contortions, accompanied by funny little bursts of sound, and by the time the words came out I didn't care what they were. It was true that I stuttered badly—I wouldn't get over it for five or six more years—but I hadn't expected anyone to put it on the radio.

"Oh, Sloane, that's marvelous," my mother said when the reading was over. "That's really exciting."

And Sloane was carefully stacking her typed pages in the way she'd probably been taught to do in secretarial school, blushing and smiling with pride. "Well," she said, "it probably needs work, but I do think it's got a lot of potential."

"It's perfect," my mother said. "Just the way it is."

Sloane mailed the script to a radio producer and he mailed it back with a letter typed by some radio secretary, explaining that her material had too limited an appeal to be commercial. The radio public was not yet ready, he said, for a story of Greenwich Village life.

Then it was March. The new President promised that the only thing we had to fear was fear itself, and soon after that his head came packed in wood and excelsior from Mr. Nicholson's foundry.

It was a fairly good likeness. She had caught the famous lift of the chin—it might not have looked like him at all if she hadn't—and everyone told her it was fine. What nobody said was that her original plan had been right, and Mr. Nicholson shouldn't have interfered: it was too small. It didn't look heroic. If you could have hollowed it out and put a slot in the top, it might have made a serviceable bank for loose change.

. The foundry had burnished the lead until it shone almost silver in the highlights, and they'd mounted it on a sturdy little base of heavy black plastic. They had sent back three copies: one for the White House presentation, one to keep for exhibition purposes, and an extra one. But the extra one soon toppled to the floor and was badly damaged—the nose mashed almost into the chin—and my mother might have burst into tears if Howard Whitman hadn't made everyone laugh by saying it was now a good portrait of Vice President Garner.

Charlie Hines, Howard's old friend from the *Post* who was now a minor member of the White House staff, made an appointment for my mother with the President late on a weekday morning. She arranged for Sloane to spend the night with Edith and me; then she took an evening train down to Washington, carrying the sculpture in a cardboard box, and stayed at one of the less expensive Washington hotels. In the morning she met Charlie Hines in some crowded White House anteroom, where I guess they disposed of the cardboard box, and he took her to the waiting room outside the Oval Office. He sat with her as she held the naked head in her lap, and when their turn came he escorted her in to the President's desk for the presentation. It didn't take long. There were no reporters and no photographers.

Afterwards Charlie Hines took her out to lunch, probably because he'd promised Howard Whitman to do so. I imagine it wasn't a first-class restaurant, more likely some bustling, no-nonsense place favored by the working press, and I imagine they had trouble making conversation until they settled on Howard, and on what a shame it was that he was still out of work.

"No, but do you know Howard's friend Bart Kampen?" Charlie asked. "The young Dutchman? The violinist?"

"Yes, certainly," she said. "I know Bart."

"Well, Jesus, there's *one* story with a happy ending, right? Have you heard about that? Last time I saw Bart he said 'Charlie, the Depression's over for me,' and he told me he'd found some rich, dumb, crazy woman who's paying him to tutor her kids."

I can picture how she looked riding the long, slow train back to New York that afternoon. She must have sat staring straight ahead or out the dirty window, seeing nothing, her eyes round and her face held in a soft shape of hurt. Her adventure with Franklin D. Roosevelt had come to nothing. There would be no photographs or interviews or feature articles, no thrilling moments of newsreel coverage; strangers would never know of how she'd come from a small Ohio town, or of how she'd nurtured her talent through the brave, difficult, one-woman journey that had brought her to the attention of the world. It wasn't fair.

All she had to look forward to now was her romance with Eric Nicholson, and I think she may have known even then that it was faltering—his final desertion came the next fall.

She was forty-one, an age when even romantics must admit that youth is gone, and she had nothing to show for the years but a studio crowded with green plaster statues that nobody would buy. She believed in the aristocracy, but there was no reason to suppose the aristocracy would ever believe in her.

And every time she thought of what Charlie Hines had said about Bart Kampen—oh, how hateful; oh, how hateful—the humiliation came back in wave on wave, in merciless rhythm to the clatter of the train.

She made a brave show of her homecoming, though nobody was there to greet her but Sloane and Edith and me. Sloane had fed us, and she said "There's a plate for you in the oven, Helen," but my mother said she'd rather just have a drink instead. She was then at the onset of a long battle with alcohol that she would ultimately lose; it might have seemed bracing that night to decide on a drink instead of dinner. Then she told us "all about" her trip to Washington, managing to make it sound like a success. She talked of how thrilling it was to be actually inside the White House; she repeated whatever small, courteous thing it was that President Roosevelt had said to her on receiving the head. And she had brought back souvenirs: a handful of note-size White House stationery for Edith, and a well-used briar pipe for me. She explained that she'd seen a very distinguished-looking man smoking the pipe in the waiting room outside the Oval Office; when his name was called he had knocked it out quickly into an ashtray and left it there as he hurried inside. She had waited until she was sure no one was looking; then she'd taken the pipe from the ashtray and put it in her purse. "Because I knew he must have been somebody important," she said. "He could easily have been a member of the Cabinet, or something like that. Anyway, I thought you'd have a lot of fun with it." But I didn't. It was too heavy to hold in my teeth and it tasted terrible when I sucked on it; besides, I kept wondering what the man must have thought when he came out of the President's office and found it gone.

Sloane went home after a while, and my mother sat drinking alone at the dining-room table. I think she hoped Howard Whitman or some of her other friends might drop in, but nobody did. It was almost our bedtime when she looked up and said "Edith? Run out in the garden and see if you can find Bart."

He had recently bought a pair of bright tan shoes with crepe soles. I saw those shoes trip rapidly down the dark brick steps beyond the windows—he seemed scarcely to touch each step in his buoyancy—and then I saw him come smiling into the studio, with Edith closing the door behind him. "Helen!" he said. "You're back!"

She acknowledged that she was back. Then she got up from the table and slowly advanced on him, and Edith and I began to realize we were in for something bad.

"Bart," she said, "I had lunch with Charlie Hines in Washington today."

"Oh?"

"And we had a very interesting talk. He seems to know you very well.

"Oh, not really; we've met a few times at Howard's, but we're not really—"

"And he said you'd told him the Depression was over for you because you'd found some rich, dumb, crazy woman who was paying you to tutor her kids. Don't interrupt me."

But Bart clearly had no intention of interrupting her. He was backing away from her in his soundless shoes, retreating past one stiff green garden child after another. His face looked startled and pink.

"I'm not a rich woman, Bart," she said, bearing down on him. "And I'm not dumb. And I'm not crazy. And I can recognize

153

ingratitude and disloyalty and sheer, rotten viciousness and *lies* when they're thrown in my face."

My sister and I were halfway up the stairs jostling each other in our need to hide before the worst part came. The worst part of these things always came at the end, after she'd lost all control and gone on shouting anyway.

"I want you to get out of my house, Bart," she said. "And I don't ever want to see you again. And I want to tell you something. All my life I've hated people who say 'Some of my best friends are Jews.' Because *none* of my friends are Jews, or ever will be. Do you understand me? *None* of my friends are Jews, or ever will be."

The studio was quiet after that. Without speaking, avoiding each other's eyes, Edith and I got into our pajamas and into bed. But it wasn't more than a few minutes before the house began to ring with our mother's raging voice all over again, as if Bart had somehow been brought back and made to take his punishment twice.

" . . . And I said '*None* of my friends are Jews, or ever will be . . . ' "

She was on the telephone, giving Sloane Cabot the highlights of the scene, and it was clear that Sloane would take her side and comfort her. Sloane might know how the Virgin Mary felt on the way to Bethlehem, but she also knew how to play my stutter for laughs. In a case like this she would quickly see where her allegiance lay, and it wouldn't cost her much to drop Bart Kampen from her enchanted circle.

When the telephone call came to an end at last there was silence downstairs until we heard her working with the ice pick in the icebox: she was making herself another drink.

There would be no more school in our room. We would probably never see Bart again—or if we ever did, he would probably not want to see us. But our mother was ours; we were hers; and we lived with that knowledge as we lay listening for the faint, faint sound of millions.

THE CIGARETTE BOAT

fiction by BARBARA MILTON

from WORD BEAT PRESS and THE PARIS REVIEW

nominated by WORD BEAT PRESS, *J. R. Humphreys and Barbara Thompson*

IT WAS ST. PATRICK'S DAY IN MIAMI. Bryn Corley was looking in the mirror, deciding whether or not to curl her hair. When she curled it, it came out tight and blonde and emphatic like Jean Harlow's; when she sleeked it off her face the Grace Kelly came forward.

How she looked tonight was very important. She and Frank Kiernan had been invited to dine at the home of Maggie Bickle, a rich and very well-connected old woman. It was not inconceivable that Robert Mitchum would be there. Bryn thought she would curl her hair.

This could be her big break. She had an idea that if she walked into an office—any office, even in Hollywood—with a good tan they would offer her a job. And she very much wanted to be offered a job. For three years she had been out of the market and out of the country. But even in Europe the women she knew had interesting jobs and were making good salaries.

"I wonder if it's too late to get in as a starlet?" she asked herself. "I may be thirty-one but I've never been prettier. I'm thin and I'm tan and I speak French fluently."

She knocked over a warm bottle of Sasson Hair Oil and turned quickly to see if Frank had stirred. He was napping after a day of department stores. He was sixty-five years old and liked to buy her things.

Out of the room she tiptoed with her tape recorder and quietly shut the door to the bedroom. Slipping across the living room and into the kitchen she picked up a bottle of vitamin B-15. Bryn had been told it would keep you young forever but only if you pop

155

about eight at a time. She tossed twelve into her mouth and washed them down with six M&M's. Then she opened the refrigerator for a swig of Lite beer.

Beside the beer, in an almost empty refrigerator, stood a bottle of tonic water and an ancient alarm clock. Frank had six new-fangled clocks around the apartment but this was the only one that kept perfect time. Frank liked it because he knew how to set it. You turned the big knob in back and big hands moved; you turned the little knob and the little hand moved. Frank was obsessed with time but Bryn couldn't stand the ticking. It was her idea to keep the clock in the refrigerator.

"Really," she thought. "I have no concept of time at all." When her brother came down she asked him what month it was. "Oh, come on," he said condescendingly.

"It's St. Patrick's Day." She snapped her fingers. "I wish I had something green to wear."

Her fingers tapped the buttons on the recorder. One pushed the play button, another rolled back the volume. Wherever she went (except out to dinner) the tape recorder was with her. Her fingers governed it like an accountant's, a calculator.

Uh Uh Uh Uh Staying Alive

Bryn played disco music when she was free to dance and country and western when stillness was called for. But now the disco and vitamins filled her with boogie. Her teeth pressed in over her lower lip and her chin and shoulders harmonized in a series of small jerks. She had seen the movie *Saturday Night Fever* three times and John Travolta was her latest unrequited ethnic love.

Out on the terrace she leaned over the railing, smiling at the sun and her own good fortune. Seven stories below million dollar yachts sat motionless while cigarette boats rolled with the motion of the water.

"I want to be a star!" thought Bryn with the enthusiasm of a first thought. She had already told Frank that she wanted a career and preferably one that took place in L.A. He said he would ask Maggie Bickle. Maggie knew everyone, especially in Hollywood.

"Is she really very rich?" Bryn asked when Frank woke up.

"Yes, she's very rich."

Bryn decided on the Grace Kelly look and brushed and brushed and brushed back her hair.

Out into the pink and gray twilight that hung heavily over the concrete strips of Miami, Bryn drove Frank's Cadillac. Frank was sitting on her right in his blue and white seersucker, pressing an invisible brake with his loafer.

"Right here. Slow down to 50. Better get into the outer lane. Take this exit."

Though Bryn hated taking directions, she needed him tonight and would humour him with obedience. She glanced at herself in the rearview mirror just as the car passed under a street lamp. It was horrible what fluorescent lighting could do. You were driving along feeling your Grace Kelly bone structure and you checked into the mirror to be sure it was true but what the mirror gave back to you was the yellowing criss-cross of age by your eyes. Bryn looked at Frank. Except for his eyes, he was in pretty good shape.

A tall, thin, angular man, Frank was caught in the vortex between elegant and grotesque. The way that he dressed—the jacket, the polo shirt, the gray straight-legged trousers—was elegant. How he signalled waiters, turned his ear only when spoken to, said nothing when he had nothing to say—all this was elegant. But his disease: they called it moon-eyes in horses. Moon-eyes meant horses would eventually go blind. Frank had a year and half of sight to go. After that, the white half-moons that were invading his irises would rise up completely and block out the light. Even now Frank couldn't see at night. There was something terrifying in his look. Bryn had seen children refuse to approach him, but Frank was no martyr; he stayed away from children. He kept company instead with horses and women and preferred horses because they didn't pity him. That's why he liked Bryn because she didn't either. He often told her that she reminded him of his favorite mare who happened to be barren yet full of herself. He said she was feisty and quirky and lusty. No good for breeding but excellent for display.

Bryn parked the Cadillac at the dead end of one of the more delapidated streets, across from a high stucco wall covered with kudzu and broken glass. As she and Frank approached the gate, three fierce white dogs hurled themselves against the bars. The dry black skin around their teeth wrinkled up into the shiny wetness of their pink and freckled gums.

"Hoopla!" shouted a man who was standing in the doorway. One of the dogs bounded up to him and a uniformed houseboy rushed from the Spanish mansion to restrain the other two.

"Don't worry," said the Colonel. "They only bite delivery boys."

Colonel Bickle, known as Bic, looked like a Kentucky Colonel. His hair was white-yellow, his large face was bright red, his nose looked swollen and he had no beard.

"Shake the hand of the owner of the winner of today's race." He was friendly and gracious and held a large trophy.

"Who won it?" asked Frank.

"Big Duke."

Bryn shook his hand and entered the high, beamed living room. From the mantel up, the room looked like a church. Below, it was more like a storeroom for different periods of antique junk. In the Victorian cluster, plopped against the gold velvet of a Queen Anne's chair, sat Maggie Bickle. She didn't notice Bryn at first. She seemed far away, in her own meditation. Her face was still handsome; her profile was noble; one gray strand fell loose from her rider's knot. Bound up inside the sheen of a green and purple pantsuit, her large body was rigid. She could barely move her neck. At the nape of her neck the zipper was half-open. And she seemed angry. Glancing back at Bic who was getting credit for her race horse, she raised her eyes to Bryn.

"Who are you?"

"Oh, I'm Bryn Corley. What a marvelous room this is. I've heard so much about you."

Maggie didn't answer. Frank hurried toward her and stooped to embrace her while Bryn made herself comfortable and spread her skirt on the settee.

On the coffee table stood an unopened box of corn chips.

"May I have one?" Bryn asked.

"Help yourself," said Maggie dryly.

Dinner was to be served aboard a mahogany yacht. Mr. Mitchum would not be there. Bic led the way across the back lawn through the azaleas and the gardenias and the aloe plants, past the grand old cedars dripping globs of Spanish moss, along the cockled sea wall to the mahogany yacht. It gleamed like Bryn's mother's dining room table.

Frank stayed behind with Maggie. Both of them were horse-breeders. They had begun discussing an epidemic of gonorrhea among the horses in Maryland where both maintained their large farms.

Bryn crossed the gangplank ahead of Bic. She was startled at the expanse and dryness of the deck. She always assumed that in spite of massive exteriors, yachts were just boats, damp and claustrophobic inside.

Bic told her that this yacht was a Trumpie. The Trumpie was the Rolls Royce of yachts. This was no fragile floating thing subject to the wind or the current in the water. This yacht was a vault with its own handsome young Captain and a young Irish cook who had been educated by the best chefs in France. The cook did everything: cook, serve and keep the boat clean.

The yacht was immaculate. Every room was carpeted and curtained. The furniture was ample; the living room was wide. There was an organ, a television, a desk and an easy chair. Over the dining room table was a crystal chandelier.

And built into the wall along the staircase leading down to the sleeping quarters below were bookshelves filled with first-editions and leather bound books. In the master bedroom a color T.V. set sat on a shelf over the foot of the double bed. Smaller T.V. sets were placed between twin beds in two of the three other guest rooms. Even the bathroom was a normal-sized bathroom, but with luxurious trimmings. When Bryn sat down on the mahogany toilet seat she pulled out and read twelve astrological messages written on consecutive squares of the toilet paper. She reached for a handle that was not there and then noticed a brass pedal on the floor at her feet. A gentle swish of fragrant blue water circled and cleaned and refilled the bowl.

"The best thing about it," said Bic who had been waiting for Bryn by the staircase, "is that if you don't like your neighbors you can pick up and leave."

"It's better than fences!" joked Bryn. She liked her line and would store it for her memoirs. "To pick up and leave can be better than fences."

While they waited on the deck for their more businesslike partners, Allan, the cook, came to take orders for drinks. After he left there was a moment of silence while Bic looked out over the water. "It was the most terrible thing I ever saw," he said, "and it happened right out there in the harbor." His voice trembled, like a child telling a ghost story. "Out of the clear blue came this sharp, skinny speedboat—they're called cigarettes. This one buzzed right in front of us. It splashed us on purpose right up on the deck here then turned and headed straight for a small yellow yacht. A big, gray-haired woman was sitting on the deck fishing and —we couldn't believe it—the cigarette jumped over her and landed on the other side. It might have hit a wave or something but it looked so deliberate.

"We sped over to check on the woman thinking she must have been terrified—well, it was much worse than that. Her legs had been cut off just above the knees. We gave her our blankets. And all the ice we had with us. We phoned for the Coast Guard. What else could we do?"

"How old was she?" Bryn asked.

"Around sixty-five."

"Did she go into shock?"

"Of course she went into shock!"

"Is she alive?"

"Last I heard."

"I can't imagine a person of that age surviving a thing like that," said Bryn looking down at her own knees. She would rather lose one of her lungs than have either of her legs harmed. She had always admired her beautiful legs.

Bryn turned from the sea back to the gangplank where Maggie was crossing with the support of Frank's arm. As the two of them descended into the yacht, Bryn stood up to join them but Frank signalled her down.

"Dinner is ready," announced Allan politely.

"Get in here," yelled Maggie from below. "We want to eat."

Maggie was plunked sourly at the head of the table on a red leather bench that was built in the wall.

The first course was pompano. Bryn was very fond of pompano and her appetite was not curbed by Maggie's talk of gonorrhea.

"It all happened in the Queen's stables."

"Did the Queen know?"

"No, but her manager did."

"Why didn't he tell her?"

"He was too polite," said Frank.

"How did it get to America?"

"A French stallion brought it."

"Those French stallions!" said Bryn who had spent two years in Paris.

After the pompano Allan brought out the artichokes: four whole artichokes and two different sauces.

"I can't eat all that!" snapped Maggie.

Allan removed the plate and brought it back with half an artichoke. He then refilled the wine glasses and returned to the kitchen.

"Wonderful little fellow," said Bic. "We could never replace him."

"Remember Sonny?" asked Maggie. "That little pony we found in our front yard?"

"Sonny?" asked Bic.

"We found this pony in our front yard and nobody ever claimed him. We kept him around—he made a great little teaser."

"What's a teaser?" asked Bryn.

"A teaser," said Frank putting his elbows on the table. He coughed and cleared his throat and wiped his mouth with a napkin. His cloudy blue eyes, which were generally half-closed, were wide open. "It's like this. You don't want to get your stallion's balls kicked off by some bitch mare who's not in heat. So you get another, smaller horse—or maybe a pony—to tease her. You tie her down by all but one leg then you mount the tease on her. If she's in heat, she'll take him. Just as he's about to come you have a couple of men ready to yank his penis out and twist it to the side."

"The poor teaser!" said Bryn.

"Oh well. We give them a whore a couple times a year."

"The best teaser I ever saw had a crooked penis," said Maggie.

"What's a whore ?"

"A whore is a mare who is always in heat but never gets pregnant."

"Why call her a whore?"

"Because she loves it, that's why."

"Why not call her a teaser too?"

"No, the mares are called testers. When a stallion has just come down from the racetracks, he's either a virgin or hasn't screwed in six months. His first load of sperm is going to be stale. You don't want to put it into a good mare, so you bring the test mare in and the stallion unloads into her. Otherwise, it's just a waste." He turned his palms up, then returned them to his lap where he picked up his napkin and wiped off his hands.

The roast beef with mushroom sauce arrived in very thin slices on individual plates. A wedge of tomato sat like a rose to the side.

"Iggy?" called Maggie to an ugly yellow dog who was asleep on a chair in the corner. "Come over here, Iggy."

The dog jumped to the floor and crawled under the table where Maggie delivered several slices of beef.

"You should have seen him in the hospital," said Maggie.

"They smuggled him in in a blanket. I thought I was going to die and I wanted to say goodbye to him. I was kissing him one last time when Duke Wayne called. I was crying so hard I couldn't talk to him. He said, 'That's okay, Maggie. I understand. I'll call you tomorrow.' I love that man. He's got cancer. I think maybe I'll call him later tonight."

"Shall I bring you the phone?" asked Bryn enthusiastically.

"After dinner," said Maggie, looking a little taken back.

As Allan came out with a fresh bottle of wine, Bryn asked Maggie if she was going to eat her mushrooms.

"No," said Maggie. "I don't like mushrooms."

"Do you think I could have them? Unless, of course, Iggy wants them. Perhaps I could share them with Iggy."

"Iggy doesn't like mushrooms either," said Maggie coldly.

After Bryn had finished Maggie's mushrooms and the roast beef left on Frank's plate, she glanced at the beef still lying on Bic's, but Allan removed it before she could ask.

"Do you have coffee?" said Frank.

"Yes, sir. There's a fruit salad for dessert."

Maggie pointed to a large basket of fancy fruit. "Robert Mitchum sent us that. He was here last night."

"He was?" moaned Bryn, aching with disappointment. She asked Allan, "Do you have any ice cream?"

"I have chocolate ice cream."

"Ummmmm, my favorite."

"You *do* like to eat," observed Maggie. "How do you stay so slim?"

"I play a lot of tennis," said Bryn quickly. "I'm getting pretty good at it, wouldn't you say, Frank?"

Frank held his hand out and tipped it back and forth.

When Allan came back with dessert, Frank cleared his throat again. He was a three-pack-a-day man and had to do this often. His head gave an involuntary shake and he leaned back in his seat. "I want to ask you something," he announced to no one in particular.

"What is it, sweetheart?" said Maggie.

"Bryn wants to go to Hollywood. She wants to get a job there."

"What kind of job?"

"Something to do with the movies."

"You want to be an *actress?*" asked Maggie.

"No, no, I don't want to be an actress. I want to work in the production end of things. Maybe with an agent or something."

"An agent! What do you want to work with an agent for?"

"I know it's the armpit of the industry," Bryn said. "But you've got to start somewhere."

Maggie turned to Frank.

"She knows what I think of the idea," said Frank. "She knows that I think that it's futile and foolish. But she wants to go anyway. Is there anything you can do for her?"

"You want my advice, honey?" Maggie said to Bryn. "Stay away from it. There is no worse place in the world than Hollywood and I've known some lousy places. Look at the horse business! But let me tell you, the horse business is nothing compared to Hollywood. I ought to know. I was up for Scarlett."

"You were up for Scarlett!" Bryn's eyes opened wide and she lost her sophistication.

"And they damn near took me, too. But they put me on this train with David Selznick and he tried to get me to do something all the way from New York to Los Angeles. Can you imagine that? Listen, honey, you know what you have to do in order to make it in Hollywood? You have to sleep with Jews. You wouldn't want to do that."

"I'd like to enjoy my own mistakes."

Maggie shook her head. "Where's Liza?" she asked Bic. "Liza would take her around."

Bryn lifted the bowl and scooped out the last spoonful of ice cream, all the while keeping her eyes on Maggie. Then she put the bowl down, wiped off her chin, and became serious. Her voice lost its girlish impressionability.

"Look. I love the movies. It's been the one thing I've been

interested in all my life. When I lived in New York, I saw ten, sometimes twenty movies a week. A couple double features in an afternoon were nothing to me. I stood in line for two hours in the pouring rain to see the seven A.M. showing of *The Godfather* and I had already seen it the night before.

"And I've been in several movies. One in Switzerland with Al Pacino and a couple of others. And I write too. I've been writing my memoirs every day for a year. That's what I really want to be. I want to be a writer."

"Oh, pooh," said Frank. "She can't write."

Bryn put her chin in one hand and without looking at Frank flicked her lighter at his unlit cigarette. He took her hand and brought the flame forward.

"Well," said Maggie appraising Bryn like a race horse. "It shouldn't be too hard to find a job for a girl as smart and attractive as you are. Bic, let's call Sam Spiegel. He can get her a job. Maybe a small one at first."

"Oh, I don't mind," said Bryn, full of hope.

"When are you ready to start?"

"Well, I have to go to Paris. And, ummm, sublet my apartment. And I sort of thought I might go to Greece. God," she mused out loud, "I hate to work in the summer. Maybe at the end of August? Or the beginning of September?"

"Forget it, baby," said Maggie.

Bryn lowered her eyes and Frank leaned back in his chair.

"We'll see what we can do for you," the Colonel said sweetly.

Maggie turned all her attention to Frank and asked about an old girlfriend of his and how she was doing in the business he helped start. Frank said she was doing very well and had already paid back his initial investment. Bryn all of a sudden felt overwhelmingly tired and restless and bored and she wanted to go home.

"Maybe we ought to go," she said. "You've been ill. We shouldn't keep you awake."

"Oh, hell, I don't sleep anyway. I slept four hours after the operation and that was it. Haven't slept since," said Maggie.

"Take pills," said Bryn.

"Don't take pills," said Frank.

"I never take pills," said Maggie. "I'd rather not sleep than take pills."

"So would I," said Frank.

"At least I'm *doing* something. I know I'm alive."

Bryn took a cigarette from Frank's pack. He lit it for her as Maggie looked on disapprovingly. Maggie turned to Bic. "Let's call the Duke now."

"We could do that."

"Better yet, let's send him the trophy. We'll have it engraved: To the Duke from Big Duke. He'll love that. He's not going to last long. One lung and he's still smoking. Now it's his heart."

"How old is he?" asked Bryn inhaling.

"Seventy-one."

"How old are you?"

"Seventy-one." Maggie looked at Bryn and then turned to Frank. "He's got one of those breathers."

"He probably has pneumonia," said Bryn. "When you get old, pneumonia gets you."

Maggie winced and reached for Frank's hand. He looked at her with sad affection and nodded for Bryn to pass the cigarettes.

"They're all gone," Bryn said. "I guess we'll have to go."

"Don't go," said Maggie. "Just stop smoking cigarettes."

"It's just a habit."

"Get another habit. One that's good for you."

"But I like smoking. I just took it up."

From the galley they heard footsteps.

"Is that you, Captain?" she called out.

A young male voice said that it was. He came into the living room. The Captain was tall, blond and movie-star handsome.

"Oh," said Bryn brightening. "I bet you smoke Marlboros."

"He doesn't smoke," said Maggie coldly.

The Captain smiled. "Well, I just happen to have some cigarettes with me." He tossed a pack of Marlboros into Bryn's lap.

"Thanks," smiled Bryn.

Frank reached into her lap and took out the cigarettes, put two in his mouth, lit both, and gave one back to Bryn.

"We couldn't keep him if we didn't let him bring his beautiful playmates on board," said Maggie. "They stay a few days, then he starts flirting with the other girls. The first ones get mad and before you know it they're gone."

"Test mares," laughed Bryn flashing her blue eyes at the Captain.

"We'll need you to help Maggie back to the house," said Bic.

165

"Certainly," said the Captain who stood back with his arms folded.

Bryn went up to him and said, "Kiss me, I'm Irish."

He backed away and said, "Sorry, I'm not."

"May I have a light then?" she said holding a cigarette.

"Sure," he said lighting it and then, "keep the matches."

"You were talking to him for a half an hour!" said Frank as Bryn drove home.

"I was talking to him for *three* minutes," said Bryn.

"You have no sense of propriety."

"I'm not a piece of property."

"What are you then?"

Bryn turned to look at him. She looked at him until the car began to swerve off the road.

"I might have been something if you hadn't interfered."

"How did I interfere?"

"By telling Maggie you thought it was foolish for me to go to Hollywood. The whole point of tonight's dinner was to get me a job and I'm as unemployed now as I ever was. Frank, I think you could have tried harder."

Frank remained silent until they got back to his condominium. He sat down on the sofa and put his head in his hands. Bryn walked past him and into the kitchen. She stood at the counter clutching the alarm clock, waiting for him to go to bed so she could sleep on the couch. Finally, she got tired of waiting and went into the living room. He was sitting on the sofa in the same position she had left him. After a moment he looked up and narrowed his eyes as if he'd been thinking.

"You'll never find a job because you've never stayed with one thing long enough to pick up any skills. And if you think you'll find a husband, you can forget that too. You've no interest in house-keeping and you don't know how to cook. No man wants a wife who doesn't know how to cook. The only thing you're good at is being some man's mistress. And if you want my opinion you're not very good at that."

She threw the alarm clock at him. It ricocheted off his forehead into a picture of his favorite stallion. The glass cracked, the stand collapsed, and the picture slapped flat onto the surface of the table. There was a scratch above Frank's eye.

"I'm sorry!" Bryn cried, afraid he was going to hit her. "I'm really sorry, Frank. Let's not fight anymore."

"If only you'd touch me—show some sign of affection." It was hard for Frank to say this. The words got caught in his throat and he looked down at his hands. Bryn moved forward and set the picture straight up again and offered to have the glass replaced the next day.

That night, for the first time in their three months together, Bryn fell asleep in Frank's arms. He held her very gently and was careful not to apply the least bit of pressure. She felt so safe that when she fell asleep she dreamed that he was holding her. Then he nodded off and rolled over onto her shoulder. She woke from the pressure of the iron weight of his arm.

"Frank," she repeated in a low speaking voice until he turned over and away from her, leaving her once more alone. She couldn't sleep. She took a couple of sleeping pills out of the drawer and turned on the Merle Haggard tape just below Frank's hearing level. He began to snore. She took a pen light and shone it on the back of his neck. A thousand lines cracked the skin like a parched Mojave desert. The white hairs, sparse as cacti, stood up straight and short and stubbly. When she turned the light off, she could shut her eyes and see his neck.

Miami between four and five in the morning was jet grey. The pollution from the planes and the cars on the highway gelled with the light from the forthcoming dawn. Bryn drove Frank's Cadillac off an exit ramp toward the ocean.

The thick, black ocean rolled in like sleep. Bryn lay on her side, her head on her arm. "Think," she commanded, but thought didn't come easily. All she knew was that if she left Frank she would have to get a job.

She *should* have had a job by now. All of that travelling and all those celebrities. All of those people who were going to do something for her. She had been in *one movie:* one. Playing a girl with a broken arm. Every morning they spent forty-five minutes putting the cast on. Before lunch, they took it off; after lunch, they put it on again. Not once was it ever seen in the movie. All that was seen was the back of her head. She got the part by doing a tap-dance. Imagine that. Doing a tap-dance to play the part of a cripple.

Bryn fell asleep on the edge of the shoreline. When she woke up her knees were floating in water. The tide deposited a small shell beside her and quickly drew back leaving a long wrinkled wake in the soft wet sand.

Then something happened. Something Bryn had never seen before. There was a catch in the water, a hesitation. And then, in a moment, she saw a definite shift. The next wave didn't quite reach the foam left over from the last one and the one after that lapped to a lower mark still.

"I just saw the exact moment the tide changed! It must mean something," she sighed.

All around her the waves rushed up hopefully and even more quickly were sucked back to sea.

When Frank got up Bryn was sitting on the terrace drinking tea with three tablespoons of honey and reading the *National Enquirer*.

"Oh," she grabbed her stomach. "Jackie Wilson died. That really saddens me."

"Who's Jackie Wilson?" asked Frank.

"He sang 'Tears on My Pillow'."

Frank sat down and took her hand and looked at her tenderly. She could tell he was thinking of how she fell asleep in his arms.

"Do you remember?" he asked.

"Remember what?" She didn't want to hurt him but she couldn't stand it when he mooned this way. Besides, she had decided to be a stewardess and she had to get away.

"You know, Frank, I was thinking. I really have to earn some money."

"I'll give you money."

"No, I mean I have to earn my own."

"Well?"

"What do you think about my becoming a stewardess?"

"A stewardess! That's just a waitress in the sky. Why not be a pilot?"

"I hate responsibility."

"Well then travel around with me. I have to go to Europe at the end of May."

"Frank, really, I have to get out on my own. I have no identity here. I'm tired of being a 'Frank Kiernan' girl."

"You think you're going to find your identity serving coffee, tea and milk?"

"I love travelling and I love serving people. My very favorite job involved serving people."

"What was that?"

"I sold ice cream from a truck when I was sixteen."

"Look. I was thinking about going to Alaska."

"Alaska! I've always wanted to go to Alaska."

"I want to go this summer."

"But it's just March!" groaned Bryn.

"It's too damn cold to go up there in March."

"Alaska," Bryn sighed. It was becoming a mantra.

"Well, think about it and let me know what you're thinking."

Bryn thought about it all through her tennis lesson. After the lesson she stopped at the bar.

"Iced tea," she said to the bartender. "Have you ever been to Alaska?"

"No," he said serving up the iced tea.

Bryn took out her cigarettes and matches the Captain had given her. Inside of the matchbook which was white on the outside was a note that read "You can reach me at" and then gave the number.

"He likes me!" cried Bryn. "I knew that he liked me."

She slid off the barstool and crossed the dance floor, languidly placing one foot in front of the other. She pressed a white cube and a red one on the jukebox, thinking, "Maybe the Captain would like to go to Alaska." She had a burning desire to go to Alaska. "Or maybe I'll take a Greyhound and go all by myself."

🔥 🔥 🔥

MAKING POETRY
A CONTINUUM:
SELECTED
CORRESPONDENCE

letters by RICHARD EBERHART AND
WILLIAM CARLOS WILLIAMS

from THE GEORGIA REVIEW

nominated by THE GEORGIA REVIEW *and Maxine Kumin*

INTRODUCTION
by Stephen Corey

WHEN RICHARD EBERHART and William Carlos Williams met at
The Yaddo artists' colony in 1950, Eberhart was forty-six and
Williams was sixty-seven. Although they only saw one another
occasionally between that summer and Dr. Williams' death in
1963, they maintained a correspondence which indicates they had
been immediately and permanently drawn to one another. Emily
Dickinson and Walt Whitman could scarcely have made stranger
literary bedfellows: Eberhart, with his belief in the poet as an
exaltant, inspired seer in the Platonic tradition, one who cried, "If
only I could live at the pitch that is near madness"; Williams, with
his equally strong belief (most beautifully phrased in his *Autobiography*) that true poetry was to be found in the plain speech and
inarticulate hearts of the patients who passed every day through

his general practitioner's office in Rutherford, New Jersey. Yet, despite this and other differences in their theories and practices of writing, Eberhart and Williams developed a personal bond which allowed them to speak with unusual frankness about one another's work. And this meeting of friendly adversaries gave a latitude to their letters which resulted in lively, historically valuable discussions of American poetry and poetics.

At the time of their first meeting, both men were established as career poets with multiple book publications behind them, but for each the future held much greater recognition and acclaim. Williams had already been praised by a small following for his dogged attempts to create a distinctively "American idiom" in poetry: he had called repeatedly for subject matter, diction, and rhythms that would break what he saw as the stranglehold of the English poetic traditions. But not until the 1950's and 1960's did Williams achieve widely acknowledged status as one of the century's key figures. In the early 1950's the poets associated with Black Mountain College in North Carolina, especially Robert Creeley, took up Williams' call for a poetry whose language was superbly simple, and whose rhythms were—to many ears—indistinguishable from prose. A few years later, the young Allen Ginsberg traveled to Williams' home in Rutherford and literally sat at the feet of the man he considered to be a poetic master. Ginsberg, who later would move in directions that Williams would have had trouble approving, had been captivated by the older poet's efforts to extend (in a conversational tone) William Blake's cry that "every thing that lives is holy." Williams was awarded the Pulitzer Prize posthumously for his *Pictures from Brueghel,* and in the twenty years since his death he has been one of the most widely read, discussed, and written-about American poets. Much of Williams' more recent acclaim has gone to *Paterson,* the book-length poem he published piecemeal between 1946 and 1961. Encompassing Williams' personal mythos of America within the multiple aspects of the title word—Paterson the man, city, and demi-god—the poem is alluded to often in the letters here.

Richard Eberhart was no acolyte or quiet follower when he met Williams at Yaddo. Although he clearly felt affection and respect for the older poet's work, Eberhart was secure enough in his own middle career that he felt no inclination to cry quarter during any phase of their relationship. By the late 1940's, when the correspondence began, Eberhart's first book (*A Bravery of Earth,* 1930) was far behind him, and he had published several others at regular intervals. While he never carried the designation of "innovator," his lyrical and philosophical poems had already made him one of the best-known poets in America. During the 1950's he was offered teaching residencies at the University of Washington, the University of Connecticut, Wheaton College, and Princeton, and in 1956 took the permanent position he still holds at Dartmouth. Like Williams, Eberhart would discover that his reputation did not crest, but kept building: Oxford University Press and Chatto & Windus became his regular publishers, while additional work came out from New Directions, the University of Illinois Press, and a number of small presses. Among the honors he earned during the 1960's and 1970's were the Bollingen Prize (1962), the Pulitzer Prize (1966), the Fellowship of the American Academy of Poets (1969), and the National Book Award (1977). Most recently, in 1982, Eberhart was elected to the fifty-member American Academy of the National Institute of Arts and Letters.

The Dartmouth College Library, repository for nearly all of Eberhart's papers, has a file of Eberhart-Williams correspondence which includes forty-one pieces from Williams and twenty-one from Eberhart, and spans the years 1949–1960, from one year before their first meeting until three years before Williams' death. A number of the letters, especially in the earliest and latest years, are merely occasional: travel plans, family news, or a simple "how-have-you-been-doing-lately?" However, literary talk was always there waiting beneath the veneer of small talk, and neither poet (especially the opinionated, sometimes cantankerous Williams) could stay on the social surface for long. Williams sets the pendulum in motion during an early letter (27 April 1949): speaking of the ultimate isolation and mystery of the poetic process, he notes that nonetheless "one does lay his colors beside those of others as he goes along to the enhancement, often, of both."

The enhancement did not come easily or quietly for these two writers, and the best of their letters poured forth when they raised their voices almost to the pitch of anger and condemnation. On 19 August 1957, Williams wrote to Eberhart about the latter's new collection of poems, *Great Praises*: "The first half of the book typified by the superbly modulated sestina is the better, flashes of insight and gentle but penetrating wit and humor wake the eye here and there with a jolt. . . . But in the latter half you seem to have entirely run out of ideas. I don't call them poems at all." Three weeks later, stung but not convinced, Eberhart wrote that "criticism is essential, natural, partial, and dangerous. It is always faulty and human. Everyone has to hue to his line. It is good to have a definite line. By now you have precisely defined yourself, gaining in this direction in the last ten years and I take this to be a triumph. One can take it or leave it. What gives me the pip, however, is assumption of absolute authority. Your letter gives your absolute authority on my new book, but I must immediately take this as relative."

Williams' "precise self-definition" shows itself again and again in his letters to Eberhart, and it has the apparent effect of forcing Eberhart sometimes into a defensive position. Eberhart, interested in Williams' theories but unwilling to be cramped by them, comes across repeatedly as the voice of relativism and experimentation. Williams, so often hailed as a radical voice of American poetics, is ironically caught in the hardening of his own system. (In 1952 Williams had a serious stroke which caused him to write to Eberhart, "I am in a bad way and don't know what the outcome will be. . . . Private, I don't think I will recover." Fortunately, he made a strong—although never complete—recovery; but the physical difficulties he had to deal with over the last years of his life might certainly have contributed to the moodiness he exhibits in some of the late letters.)

Eberhart was particularly interested in coming to grips with Williams' theory of measure, asking Williams several times to provide a specifically illustrated explanation of his elusive use of this key term. Williams tried to oblige in a two-page letter on 23 May 1954 by setting forth a series of maxims, and then quoting as examples two short passages of his own composition. What Williams succeeds in showing us is that his *theory* of measure is enticing and apparently clear—but his practice, at least as evinced by the (presumably carefully chosen) lines he quotes, seems finally to be dependent upon Williams' own quirky ear. The beat (the measure) according to which we are supposed to hear the lines in question is at best dubious, and at worst bizarre. Williams would have done well to hold in mind his own words to Eberhart in a letter from the previous year, when he proposed that the poem and its processes are inexplicable: "It is something which is there and gone while you try to hold it."

The sampling of letters that follows is ballasted by the poets' discussion of literary subjects, but there were other things as well that held the two men close. In the Eberhart letter quoted earlier, where he admonishes Williams for claiming absolute authority as a critic, the younger writer goes on to say, "and as for truth, where the hell is it? You leave out everything true in re the Library of Congress about both me and you. Think that over for a while." In the early 1950's, Eberhart had been caught up by that small, odd thresher of American bureaucracy known as literary politics: he thought he had been affixed as the person to succeed Conrad Aiken as Poetry Consultant to the Library of Congress in late 1951, but then some personal (and evidently irrational) attacks by Aiken blocked Eberhart's appointment. Williams became trapped in the same swirl, but with an added twist: he was contacted about the possibility of taking the Consultant's chair, but then came under investigation by Senator Joseph McCarthy's infamous Committee on Un-American Activities. Williams was cleared of all charges, but not before the situation had caused him deep distress—a distress compounded by his having to deal with the after-effects of his stroke at the same time.

This crisis showed as well as anything the unusual closeness which had come to Eberhart and Williams. By 1952 they had exchanged only a few letters and spent a few days together; but when Williams suddenly had to back out of a teaching commitment because of his various problems, he thought first of writing to Eberhart for help. After the crisis passed, Williams wrote "no one shall know what it cost me to write those letters . . . to you or how grateful I am to you for handling the matter as you did. I was desperate for reasons which you will have to surmise. I mean that you shall have to believe me that I did not know where but to you to turn." Nothing inside or outside the letters of these two men fully explains their rapid and continuing intimacy. Some chemistry of spirits went to work, and kept on working. If it hadn't, the friendship would likely have been detonated by its own candor.

In 1959 Williams quickly obliged when Eberhart asked him to write dust-jacket copy for a volume of his collected poems set to be published the following year. In his remarks (sent attached to a letter on 10 October) Williams modulates, but does not abandon, his dual feeling about Eberhart's poetry. Just days later, Eberhart wrote back to thank Williams—not a simple thank-you letter, but one in which he explicates the explication, explores his own work in relation to Williams' most recent words about it. This particular exchange reads as if the poets somehow knew their correspondence was drawing toward a close, and as if therefore the controversies and discussions had to take on some warmer sheen of reconciliation. And indeed, although there were several notes back and forth over the next year, there was nothing with a substance approaching that of these two last letters reproduced here.

Several times Eberhart wrote to Williams about letter-writing itself, once noting (on 15 October 1956) that "I never write letters with an eye to one's public stance. That is a heavy burden, I am not for it." But all good letters, like all other good writings, have a way of multiplying and broadening their authors' intentions and meanings. Eberhart's final letter concludes by speaking of both Eberharts—Dick and Betty—and both Williamses—Bill and Flossie: "Our love to you both and many thanks, Bill, for your stirring words." The phrase "stirring words" is a *mot juste* that suddenly clarifies the real attraction for us in the correspondence of fine writers: we can think not only of the words in Williams' commentary on the collected poems of Eberhart, but of all the criticism these two men have exchanged—and of *all* their words back and forth through the mails—and even, I believe, of their published works and the works of all those other writers whom Eberhart and Williams discuss or mention. All good letters are metaphor.

Making Poetry a Continuum

Rutherford, N.J.
Feb. 9, 1953

Dear Dick:

What is it that makes a poem now-a-days? I suppose, as always, it's something of which the poet, whether it's Auden or Eliot or whoever it is, is entirely unconscious. So, finding it impossible to control it, Eliot, for one, has given up writing poems. But Auden, not knowing what else to do with all his dexterity, keeps on making his constructions. And who has the knowledge to say that they are

175

not poems? They certainly often look like poems but we are convinced that they are not poems. Invention is lacking.

Maybe it is simply that—try as one may the poem is not to be captured.

Clifford McKee has caught the authentic feel of a poem in what he writes. I don't think what he says is world shattering. It isn't. But it rings true and that for a young poet is everything.

It is something which is there and gone while you try to hold it.

Sincerely,
Bill

Rutherford, N.J.
5/14/53

Dear Dick:

I have before me your letter of last March enclosing two poems upon which you ask me to comment. But first I want to be sure that you know all that has happened to me in recent months. Oh, well, now that I come to tell it there seems not much to tell except that I was in a hospital which the less I speak of the more I am pleased. But I'm home again now and though I'm not yet cured I'm much better. When the old bean goes wrong it apparently takes time to put it to rights again. Meanwhile I've done quite a bit of writing, prose and verse, and for some [of] it I've even on occasion got a publisher. I am very limited as to what I can do but as long as I can do something I must be content.

As to the verses which you sent me my feelings are somewhat mixed. I like very much the poem "To Evan" which with its use of refrain is very moving. It has about it the sense of recurrence, as much as to say, this has happened before and it will happen again and such is the fate of man and how beautiful and inevitable and sad it is. This is in the spirit of the Greek epitaph, a spirit which is wholly resigned and so at peace. The beauty of the verse is its only excuse for being so that you make it as sensuously beautiful as you can make it. The catch in the voice should not be too apparent.

Of the other poem I am not so sure. I am as you know a stickler for the normal contour of phrase which is characteristic of the language as we speak it. It gives to a poem a distinction which it can get in no other way. For the most part you respect that rule but sometimes you appear to forget it and it is easy to forget it with results which are not good.

It is hard to say what makes a poem good but if it is not in the detail of its construction it is in nothing. If the detail of the construction is not to the smallest particular distinguished the whole poem might as well be thrown out. And when you invert a phrase even such an innocuous phrase as "great are" or "quietly I" or "violated is" etc. the effect is for me disastrous. The thought that you CAN do such a thing makes me look for it to occur in other places. The exercise which comes to you in fighting the phrase to make it obey your orders always pays off.

The second half of the long second poem is verbose in any case, there are few telling images in it anyway and the pace of it is not varied enough. You asked for it and I thought I might as well give it to you straight. But that doesn't mean a thing except that it is not one of your good poems.

Time flies! Best love to Betty and the kids. Take care of yourself.

Bill

Cape Rosier, Maine
August 27, 1953

Dear Bill:

We drove 6500 miles and landed safely in Maine. Now in a two day fog. I hope this finds you feeling OK.

I have been asked to select the poetry for #5 of *New World Writing* to come out early next year. Deadline November. Do you have a recent poem you would like to contribute to this? They pay .50 a line and as you probably know print 100,000 copies right off, 50,000 more shortly thereafter. It is a Mentor book. Maybe you saw my *The Visionary Farms* [a verse play] in #3. I would love to have a poem of yours in #5 if you have something you would like to print there.

We will be care of the English Department, The University of Connecticut, Storrs, Conn. after Sept. 8. Let me hear from you.

We all send our love and all the best,

yrs
Dick

Rutherford, N.J.
9/18/53

Dear Dick:

Yesterday was my 70th birthday and this morning I had a note from *The Yorker* saying that they had accepted my latest poem sent them two weeks ago. I don't know when they'll print it but I think it won't be long.

As I was thinking of sending the poem to you if they rejected it I shall now have to think again about you. But since I had already thought of that it remains only to tell you that in a few days you'll get the first part of a poem I've been working on for a long time. It is a continuation of the *Paterson* series, *Paterson V*, the first 4 or 5 pages under the usual title of such pieces, *Work in Progress*.

Is it too much to expect you to take as much as 5 pages of such a work? When I have heard again from you I'll begin making a final draught of it. What is the name of the publication where it will appear?

Sincerely yours
Bill

Rutherford, N.J.
10/20/53

Dear Dick:

Two sections of the so called *Paterson 5* will appear, not more than 2 pages of each, in publications during the coming months. They are not the parts that I have given you and which I have included in my forthcoming book. So you cannot claim priority of publication.

My book will come out in February so that, unless you can think of a real good solution, drop the *New World Literature [sic]* idea entirely because I do want the piece to appear in my book. It's up to you.

If, in spite of all you insist on including it (and I still hope you can find a way), please drop the idea of calling it by any name associated with its origin. The title should in that case be simply, *Work in Progress*. O.K.?

If not, I shall have to find you something else to publish though at present I have nothing to offer. Do what you can.

Going on to something more pleasant: when Floss began to read what you sent on of your own work I stopped her to say, that is the best Dick has ever written! I was thrilled. But somehow you seemed to lose the thread and when you began to speak of ideas without a visual image appearing, I lost interest. Compare the first part of the poem, which is brilliant, with the second part and you will see what I mean. And remember that Dante, Homer, Shakespeare and Milton also, if you want to include him, had an object intermediate to all they wrote about which forced them always to be objective and *never* to deal with ideas and feelings but only with their effects as shown upon [the] world about them. When you do that you write like an angel but failing to do that you are lost.

It shows first when you begin to invert the normal order of your phrases. It isn't flagrant but it has its effect. You have already taken your eye off the definite object and allowed your mind to wander. It is almost imperceptible but it gives you away.

The exact place it begins is the first sentence of the fifth quatrain, "Quietly I lie" and from then on it builds up. The construction of the sentences becomes forced, abnormal, not the language which we speak and should speak and use in our compositions if we are to remain effective. Obviously it should be, "I lie quietly" etc. "Safely time passes," "Softly I maintain," "Great are," "Violated is"—These are all indefensible in modern verse and in getting rid of them the mind is put on its mettle and will see more clearly what is lacking.

Mind you I am aware that you may not agree with me but I am convinced, by the excellent writing of your best work which I admire so much, that you yourself will agree with me when I call them to your attention. Old practices tend to dominate us all, it is ingrained in us to allow some ancient practice, some lilt of the phrase to carry us on when we know it but find ourselves unable to free ourselves from its influence.

Otherwise it is a good poem. Your work is growing better and better and I am getting to like it more and more. When you are good you are very moving to me, a true lyrical touch full of music.

Best luck.

Sincerely
Bill

Dear Bill:

Thanks for your good letter. I am sure we will use your poem in NWW5 if it can be done: your publishers want it in there too. I will be glad to call it *Work in Progress* (i.e., to stand as a poem—or thing-in-itself) but don't quite get the idea. If it is part of *Pat V* why not say so. Or say *Work in Progress*, with a line under "From Paterson V." Let me know definitely. Whatever you want is of course OK.

You are probably right about "Independence & Resolution." Magazine publication is a try-out. Apparently they have set up the whole thing in Paris and I won't see proof. I'll lynx-eye it. In my next book I will make a final determination, possibly truncate it. You are nothing if not keen in seizing on just the word where you feel the mind-body changes, tires, whatever. But no more of that now.

I suppose one could argue all day about inversion. I like to think of your principle toward absolute order, but it may be a simplification. It is right for you, but there is nothing absolute about language in the sense of the vast richness and possibility of English. Somebody in 2053 may use the instrument in ways you and I do not dream. For how could old Milton have dreamed of you, Bill?

Here is a class-room sort of argument. But you may not like Yeats or may not wish to take him as authoritative. He wrote (or published) "Sailing to Byzantium" in 1927. There is no inversion in it. It is the better of the two Byzantium poems. But "Byzantium" appeared in 1930, that is, later, and in this poem there are quite a few things you would not approve.

St. $_3$ Miracle, bird or golden handiwork,
     More miracle than bird or handiwork,
     Planted on the star-lit golden bough,
     Can like the cocks of Hades crow,

Now if he wrote "Can crow like the cocks of Hades," with what follows, is not a technical excellence lost? The line becomes prose, and too harsh.

Next st.   At midnight on the Emperor's pavement *flit*
     Flames that *no faggot feeds*, nor steel has lit,
     Nor storm disturbs, etc. . . .

The inversions cannot be extricated. Since you don't use rhyme you would probably throw out a justification on that account.

Last st.   Marbles of the dancing floor
                Break bitter furies of complexity,
                Those images that yet
                Fresh images beget,
                That dolphin-torn, that gong-tormented sea.

Again, if he said "Beget fresh images," in this case it would be possible, but where prose sense would be enhanced repetitions of sound running back through the other rhyme schemes of the poem would be lost, or altered for the worse.

I conclude at present that it can be done both (and many) ways—more than one way to skin a cat. I admire your definiteness, hope I will be as definite on some aesthetic theory sometime.

We love you both and send deepest affection.

                        Yrs,
                        Dick

P.S. Stevens had us over to The Canoe Club the other day. We drank martinis all afternoon.

                        Rutherford, N.J.
                        10/23/53

Dear Dick:

I remember when Ezra Pound first went to London and met Yeats. Yeats asked him what he, Ezra, thought of his, Yeats's, poems. Ezra was forced to say that he admired them greatly, as was the truth, but that they were marred by a deforming inversion of the phrase which was deplorable. Yeats at once set about correcting the defect and worked diligently at it for several years. The evidence of it appears in many of his finest pieces.

But the style of the older man had been set long and if, as you say, he reverted to the use of inversions, of an abnormal contour of the phrase in his last work (if it is true), you can put it down to a dominance of a measure to which he had become accustomed and which he did not find it easy to escape.

What Pound did not realize, nor Yeats either, is that a new order had dawned in the make-up of the poem. The measure, the actual measure, of the lines is no longer what Yeats was familiar with. Or Pound either except instinctively. Hopkins, in a constipated way with his "sprung" measures, half realized it but not freely enough. To escape the prosiness of the lines or the threat of prosiness in the line, the foot has to be expanded to make a freer handling of the measure possible. That's what Yeats was up against without realizing it. It had him restless under the restrictions of criticism. It makes you restless under the same restrictions. You, as Yeats was, are dominated by a concept of the line which comes from an old (pre-Whitman) prosody which stems from traditional english (and french, german, scandinavian, russian, chinese and perhaps greek) verse. Only in the present day are we beginning to realize how it restricts us. It restricts our lives as well to be measured after the standard and so, unless we become aware of it, our poems rather than freeing, as they should do, throw us back on old modes of behavior.

Whitman with his so called free verse was wrong: there can be no absolute freedom in verse. You must have a measure but a relatively expanded measure to exclude what has to be excluded and to include what has to be included. It is a technical point but a point of vast importance. The question of the inversion or refusal to invert our poetic phrases is locked up in that.

All right, call the poem in question:

Work in Progress

(Paterson 5)

With all the love in the world,

Bill

Rutherford, N.J.
11/17/53

Dear Dick:

Contract received, signed and returned herewith. It makes me very happy that it is you who has brought this about. There is only one thing about it that I do not particularly like, that is the use of "Paterson V" in the title. If you can persuade the editors to omit that I would be pleased but if they insist all I can do is to let it stand. I have decided not to use that title at all in the finished work. Instead the sub-title should be "(Of Asphodel)." It's up to you.

How is the work going, I mean your work as teacher? Was your work on the coast of much help? I'll bet it was. I'd be happy to sit in on one of your classes sometime to witness what a teacher of poetry nowadays puts over on his unsuspecting students. I probably have a lot to learn. Best of luck.

Sincerely
Bill

Storrs, Conn.
12/2/53

Dear Bill:

I think I owe you two letters. I hope you are both feeling fine. It is brisk, cold and windy here today.

Yours of 10/23 fascinated me and I will quote a pregnant part to warm up. "Only in the present day are we beginning to realize how it restricts us. It restricts our lives as well to be measured after the standard and so, unless we become aware of it, our poems rather than freeing, as they should do, throw us back on old modes of behavior." In the next paragraph, turning from the bonds of Yeats (before his final attempts) to Whitman, you go into the matter of inversion again. But to the above quote from your letter. This fascinates me. I would be the first to agree with you that old modes of behavior (verbal as well as societal) are hard to transcend. It is up to you now to put in print somewhere precisely what you mean as to your theory. Some would say that that is unnecessary: look at the poems, the theory is in the work. And you have spoken it on platforms and in various writings in recent years. Yet it still wants an absolute statement. I find paradox and conflict in it. For instance, you have lived in one house for forty years. You practiced medicine in a stable way for all that time. Everybody admires you for it. Is it not true then that there has been nothing new, radical, strange, or revolutionary in your mode of behavior? Yet you have invented a new way in poetry. This I take it has been accomplished in spite of living conditions and is a triumph over them as far as art goes. You seem to suggest that if you or I or any poet has "the new measure," throws off traditional diction, etc. he will be leading a new life and that that life will therefore be better. Does not your actual day-to-day life disprove this? Would you not have to posit

183

somebody like Rimbaud, only somebody like him? Yet in his case the wandering, the new life came after, not before (of course there was a lot of moving about when he was in his teens), the invention of his new system. And would it follow that if I, or anybody, lived in a new way (whatever that would be) that he or I would therefore necessarily write better poetry? I probably don't state this well. I have never been able to figure it out. Your "new measure" has been invented and perfected while doing the same thing over year to year in your practical medical life. Is there maybe not a psychological reason for this? It is not like the clamor of all artists to transcend their limitations? Have you not got the cart before the horse? Now there! That is an old-timer, one should use something about the jet before the fuselage. (Fuselage is probably out-moded!).

I think of poetry as a gift of the gods. One never knows when the fire will strike.

Is No. 5 to be the final part of *Pat*, or do you plan to continue it indefinitely?

Stevens told me somebody named Philbin or Philbrick was writing your life. I see in the *Times* 11/29 John C. Thirwall asks for letters. Is this the same man? I thought to send him some of our recent correspondence (only on literary matters, nothing really personal) but as I have never done this sort of thing I thought I would ask you if you think it pertinent?

Lots of love to you both. We can't yet realize we will not see Dylan again. The least I can do is to read next Sunday at Harvard for the passing of the hat.

Yrs
Dick

Rutherford, N.J.
12/4/53

Dear Dick:

Received your book a week ago and Flossie has read it aloud to me from beginning to end. This, as you may imagine was not done in one session. Depending on the mood we were in at the time the impression it made on us was now great pleasure and less. It is always so with me, sometimes all poetry bores me, even the sonnets of Shakespeare or my own writings. I have recently looked at much that I have perpetrated with anything but satisfaction. We can all take a leaf from T. S. Eliot's book, he wrote few poems in his life and, as far as he could be sure of himself, he has not repeated the things he has undertaken. All the rest of us on this score have much for which we must be forgiven.

You need room to make your effects, rhyme does not become you or at least your rhymed poems or lyrics do not come off well for me. They do not have Pound's delicate ear to support them. But when you come to something like "Fragment of New York, 1929" you cannot be surpassed. Really impressive work. I enjoyed Flossie's reading of it from beginning to end. There were several poems in that section of the book from which that authentic thrill or chill of exaltation reached me. All I could say was, That's swell! he really did it that time!

I won't say that I didn't thrill as well from an occasional briefer, tightly organized poem but often those seemed to go astray. Apparently when you get an intense and clear idea, at the start of a poem, something to carry the thought all the way through, you do well. But when you have to stop to think over an abstract idea your abstractions trip you and you forget that you are writing a poem, an objective work of art, and run off into something I don't like. It's just a lot of words. The ideas engendered by the thing and not the thing itself have you by the balls. You seem to want to *explain* something. Never explain a poem.

I wish I could remember all the poems I liked and catalogue them but you don't need that. They were quite a few, about a third of the book. Almost always the longer ones.

As far as what I understand by modern is concerned I'll have to refer you to my new book which is due to appear in March or April. It concerns almost entirely, measure. Inversions of the phrase or lack of inversions are purely incidental. It's very simple.

Never heard of Philbrick. *Thirlwall* is the guy I am working with. Please send him the letters you have, he's all right. Oh, I meant to ask you: Do you, when you write a poem, let the first draft of it stand or work over it? It looks as if the first draft is the final poem—as the first draft of a poem by Eliot must be anything but the final poem. With him the poem looks as if it had gone through all three of the cow's stomachs most of which are contained in her head rather than her belly but I cannot say that it might not be to our advantage to learn that a good digestion is a disadvantage.

Love and kisses
Bill

Storrs, Conn.
12/10/53

Dear Bill and Flossy:

Just a note to thank you for your wonderful and generous letter of the 4th.

I would like to make a cold-headed study of my poems in light of your question on revisions. In general I distrust revision, but then, it depends on what kind of a poem it is. They are written under all sorts of physical or psychological situations. You liked "Fragment of New York, 1929." That was written as prose about that time. It was turned into verse most laboriously, and with great love of every nuance of every syllable, and left for years. A couple of years ago I read it again and liked it. I revised again, taking off a whole passage at the end, and made it what it is. That poem has waited c. twenty years for print.

"An Herb Basket" was written off in a sort of trance, in complete control of one dominant slow quiet movement and rhythm, but then I must have made twenty or thirty changes with a cold mind.

Many of them come off almost clean, though "The Verbalist of Summer" I recall writing in a spate of itself.

Do you recall the war poem "The Fury of Aerial Bombardment"? The first three stanzas were written at one throw as a lyric. Later I appended the fourth "Of Van Wettering I speak, and Averill" which ended on the belt holding pawl. If this last stanza had not been put on as an afterthought the poem would probably never have been put into anthologies. What does one make of all this?

If I get time and the spirit maybe I'll go through some of my books and try to reconstruct just what the process in each poem was. I'll send you a copy—if I ever do it!

Sanders Theater was jam-packed (maybe a thousand) last Sunday night when we read to gain money for Dylan Thomas, i.e., for Caitlin and the kids. Jack Sweeney was in the chair, impeccable as always. John Brinnin led off, was amusing and drew applause, and gave the audience a sense of Dylan. All the while my heart was pounding in my chest as if I were a nervous schoolboy! Hell, I wait on 50. I came next and gave. Archie [Archibald MacLeish] followed, rather low in voice, very melodious. Then Dick Wilbur, who did fine as always. Then Ivor Richards took the podium. It is hard to realize that it was 26 years ago when I first loved that man way back in 27 at Cambridge. He has great nervous aliveness, did a sort of ballet dance when seen from the rear (also, I noted Dick W. taps with his long left foot when he reads—I tried to time the beats with the words, but couldn't see that it was regular—Richards read Dylan masterfully, some from *Milkwood*—and ended tremendously on "Do Not Go Gentle into That Good Night." Then Dennis Johnson made an appeal. I haven't yet heard how much they took in. Archie and Ada gave us a fine dinner beforehand in the new house they have bought around the corner from Longfellow's. Then some of the Poets' Theater people came back to Betty's mother's house for a drink.

What has been your opinion in recent years of Thomas?

I am going to Chicago after Xmas to read a paper at MLA on The Poets' Theater, and to read my poems that night at U Chi. This week-end I am going to Cambridge to hear the PT's production of two Yeats plays—*The Player Queen* and *Purgatory*. Wish you were both going too.

This is a brand new Royal portable but it makes as many misses as my old one—the machine age is always falling apart. Or am I?

Love and a happy Christmas,
Dick

Storrs, Conn.
5/22/54

Dear Bill and Floss:

I have been meaning to write you for weeks which is just to say that I think of you frequently whether I have communicated to you or not. Term ends. Betty has had virus pneumonia but is now recovered. The children thrive and grow, are constantly amazing and time-consuming—O the beautiful ways of childhood, so quickly grave and gay—a fight one minute and a kiss the next.

When you read "The Meaning of Indian Summer" in the Stevens # of the *Trinity Review,* read "The" for "That" in line 2 of the last stanza—otherwise it does not make sense. Morse sent no proof. I also wrote both poems for myself; they have nothing to do with Stevens. The fact that Morse put "For Wallace Stevens" would make some think, perhaps, that "Closing off the View" has to do with the psyche of Stevens. Actually, it has to do with mine. So there are all sorts of obscurities in every thing about poetry.

Your "Desert Music," though, tries to make things clear. It has a beautiful composition to the eye. Do we become what we are or are we what we become? This new-looking spaced verse is very you, and wonderfully pleasing.

I liked your piece in the Stevens number, yet it intrigues me to ask you for a plain statement of what you mean by measure. I don't think you have thoroughly stated this, although you have talked a lot about it and I recall hearing you talk about it when we met at Bard some years ago. Now you mention it again on Stevens, yet you do not specify. Would you please get out a poem of Stevens and give me your theory with your finger right on the lines of one stanza? I get maybe 90% of your meaning from the general tone of your remarks in the prose on Stevens; I would like to be satisfied to the 100th degree.

Next year we will be at Wheaton, near Providence. 500 girls. They elected me to a new chair there, a one year stand—or sit— with a skyey salary and a 3-bedroom house thrown in free. That will put us only an hour and a half away from Cambridge.

Utah for a while late June, then Yaddo (unless I give it up to go at once to Maine), then Maine and water.

Our love to you as always. Let me hear your news.

Dick

Rutherford, N.J.
May 23, 1954

Dear Dick:

Glad to hear from you. But sorry to hear about Betty's illness. The only thing I can add is that it is fortunate that the pneumonia occurred today and not when I was practicing. Today they have means of fighting it that we didn't possess. Glad she's well again.

I have never been one to write by rule, even by my own rules. Let's begin with the rule of counted syllables, in which all poems have been written hitherto. That has become tiresome to my ear.

Finally, the stated syllables, as in the best of present day free verse, have become entirely divorced from the beat, that is the measure. The musical pace proceeds without them.

Therefore the measure, that is to say, the count, having got rid of the words, which held it down, is returned to the *music*.

The words, having been freed, have been allowed to run all over the map, "free," as we have mistakenly thought. This has amounted to no more (in Whitman and others) than no discipline at all.

But if we keep in mind the *tune* which the lines (not necessarily the words) make in our ears, we are ready to proceed.

By measure I mean musical pace. Now, with music in our ears the words need only be taught to keep as distinguished an order, as chosen a character, as regular, according to the music, as in the best of prose.

By its *music* shall the best of modern verse be known and the *resources* of the music. The refinement of the poem, its subtlety, is not to be known by the elevation of the words but—the words don't so much matter—as by the resources of the *music*.

To give you an example from my own work—not that I know anything about what I have myself written:

(count):—not that I ever count when writing but, at best, the lines must be capable of being counted, that is to say, *measured*—(believe it or not)—At that I may, half consciously, even count the measure under my breath as I write—

(approximate example)

(1) The smell of the heat is boxwood
    (2) when rousing us
        (3) a movement of the air
(4) stirs our thoughts
    (5) that had no life in them
        (6) to a life, a life in which

or
　(1) Mother of God! Our Lady!
　　(2) the heart
　　　(3) is an unruly master:
　(4) Forgive us our sins
　　(5) as we
　　　(6) forgive
　(7) those who have sinned against

Count a single beat to each numeral. You may not agree with my ear but that is the way I count the line. Over the whole poem it gives a pattern to the meter that can be felt as a new measure. It gives resources to the ear which results in a language, which lends itself to a language which we hear spoken about us every day.

Hope I have been helpful and not confused the issues even more than they were formerly. Write again. Your plans for the next year can't be more encouraging.

By the way, may I have a transcript of this letter, as I do not make use of carbon paper.

Best
Bill

Rutherford, N.J.
Nov. 28, 1954

Dear Dick:

I want to tell you how much I enjoyed and appreciated your critical article, which I have just read, in the *Saturday Review of Literature,* of my book of essays. It is extremely well written as well as thoughtful and perspicacious. I had not noticed the subjects not touched on in the book, including the religious. It is a just comment and one I welcome, it is strange to me to notice how in a person as strongly inclined as I to think of the "other world" how disinclined I feel to talk of it—it is probably due to the damned rot spoken of it in the pulpit and among other devotional writers. Thank you for calling it, my reluctance to talk of it, to my attention.

Your eternal kindness and selflessness toward me and in all you write are very much appreciated. I have not been easy in my appreciation of your poems, I find them irregular in their worth and not to my mind sufficiently developed—but sometimes I am moved. That is a topic for friends to develop among themselves. Floss sends her love, she is one of your most passionate defenders. This last article has done more to convince me of your ability than anything of yours I have ever read.

Sincerely yours
Bill

Hanover, N.H.
Oct. 15, 1956

Dear Bill:

Thanks for your letter. I have been thinking of writing to you for some time. In any case, we think of you often, both of you, and knew that if you had wanted to or could you would have got in touch with us in Maine.

We have a very good house here and things are shaping up. It is a fine place, as you suggest, and a wonderful place to raise children. But more of all that some other time.

The fact is, Bill, I sent Mr. Thirlwall a few, I forget how many, letters from you and carbons of my replies two or three years ago. Please check with him and see what he has got. I will be quite mad at him if he has lost or misplaced them. I sent them along without having them photostated, I think on your suggestion that he should have them and would return them eventually. It was this packet that had some give and take between us on your notions of measure, all that. I have a few letters from you during the past year or so but these are not professional in the above sense—however I add that they are all loveable, all your and Flossy's words give us light and life. Are you collecting *all* your letters? If so I could send you these recent ones, but I don't suppose that is the point. Also, if he or you intend to publish my replies to yours I would like to see proof. I never write letters with an eye to one's public stance. That is a heavy burden, I am not one for it.

My book supposedly will be out in spring, but I keep on accreting poems so in a sense every book is out of date when it appears. In another sense they are supposed to last forever. I have written several I like quite recently. Another thing, I am often amazed to find poems (now that I have piles and piles of mss. around in trunks, boxes, files) written years ago which read well now. I sent one off the other day which is 25 years old but I'll bet it will be as hard and solid 25 years from now.

I enjoyed your introduction to Ginsberg but think you got the time or dates wrong in the beginning. By my count he is 29 now. Look at your text again and see if it adds up. But that is a minor point—you gave him a lively send-off. It is very hard for me to have absolute values about poetry. It is all relative, yet I recognize this attitude as an absolute itself, so where are we?

I wish you would come up here and read this year. I am not in charge of arrangements but if you think you could I wd. love to put in a plug for such an event. You were last here quite a while ago with a prose essay, were you not? I remember reading it with pleasure.

On my letters. For years I have kept carbons of almost all letters just as a practical matter; otherwise I could never remember what I said at a given time. So I have right here in my study 35 cases of letters going way back to the twenties—Good Lord what some scholar could find out about me if he had the colossal diligence! I would hate to think of wading through such a mass. I thought dimly long ago sometime I might be able to make a huge synthesis of my life, hence keeping all these letters, but the Comic spirit gives that a hee-haw.

So long for now, love to you from 4 of us
Dick

Rutherford, N.J.
Aug. 19, 1957

Dear Dick:

Thank you for your *Great Praises*. If I had to give out an award I'd probably give you the nod but not for reasons I would myself approve. The poems are too hopeless, too resigned in the face of an overwhelming fate without protest to give me much of a kick.

The first half of the book typified by the superbly modulated sestina is the better, flashes of insight and gentle but penetrating wit and humor wake the eye here and there with a jolt. Several of the lyrics are worthy of *Palgrave's Golden Treasury*. But in the latter half you seem to have entirely run out of ideas. I don't call them poems at all. The neat and appealing form is maintained in many cases but that is all, death time and again has possessed your imagination which is not worthy of you. I protest.

I have always objected to the use of the godhead as a figure in a poem. If the total appeal is not to that, or That as you may prefer, it is completely tautological and redundant. What are you writing poems for anyhow but to assert that in some form no matter how irreligious a man may think himself? But to cry out with an appeal to God is pure stupidity, it is no better than entirely to quit the job of an artist, to refuse to attempt to create and that is the effect on me. It is in the imagery of Mr. Eliot to give yourself to the Devil.

You're not that disgusted with life nor have been so thoroughly defeated. You ought to get hold of Allen Ginsberg's *Howl!* published by the City Lights Press of San Francisco and read it. It will do you good to find out how this Jew raises his voice.*

Well, Dick, you can see by this how I feel about this new book of poems of yours. I'm out of sympathy with it and we're too good friends not to have me speak outright about that. Wish we could visit you in Hanover to sit down to a knock down and drag out fight with you over the issues involved but you're too God damn far away and the time's too short for me to do anything about it. Love to Betty and the kids from both of us.

Bill

*Flossie tells me you reviewed the book!

Hanover, N.H.
Sept. 7, 1957

Dear Bill:

I appreciate your letter and am quite as realistic as you are about life and letters. If you had thoroughly approved of my work to date I should no doubt be happy, but there is a negative quality in such happiness. I am delighted that you thoroughly approve of Rexroth, my old friend, delighted that he is gaining cumulative dues. If you couldn't like my work at all I should be sad, but wouldn't be able to do anything about it. There are those who don't like yours. I alluded to them at Brandeis in my remarks at your left side saying hopefully that your British detractors would be won over yet.

Criticism is essential, natural, partial and dangerous. It is always faulty and human. Everyone has to hue to his line. It is good to have a definite line. By now you have precisely defined yourself, gaining in this direction in the last ten years and I take this to be a triumph. One can either take it or leave it. What gives me the pip, however, is assumption of absolute authority. Your letter gives your absolute authority on my new book, but I must immediately take this as relative. Others have quite other reactions. And no poet of any force wants to be the darling of his elders. One wants honesty and compassion; these you give me.

Curious about ambiguities: do you mean *Palgrave*-worthy poems as praise or insult? There is the hint in my consciousness that to be embalmed in a *Palgrave* would be a calamity. Or, if you meant praise, I assume your *Palgrave* would have to be one limited to your specifications. Is this right?

I don't think I have run out of ideas and I am not a defeatist. Quite the contrary. You say I talk too much about death. Perhaps I do. It is time for the life-poems as there have been too many death-poems, I agree. Your *Paterson* is a life-poem as are your later love poems. Yet I always thought you thin and limited, up to your last-decade work, which suggests also a lack of profundity, just because you had nothing to say about death, one of the three four or several great subjects. Love is another. "Life" is another (I put it in quotes) and your all-embracing stimulus. In reading your letters now, however, I find you have said quite a bit about death. You thrust it aside. I asked you in your house a year or so ago what you felt about it and you had no answer, or rather the universal answer that there is no answer.

To castigate me as negative for having brooded about death, or being defeatist as you say, is absurd. I could as well castigate you for claiming that there are no ideas but in things, a limited concept put out as if it were all-embracing or universal. There are many ways to catch the world's fish, all kinds of fish in the poetic seas.

Your truth is your truth, with a certin wide-applying relevance. It is something to say that truth is what is. It seems an easy belief, tainted with the obvious. You are not a Blake-type but critics (*The Times Lit Sup* last month, again) say I am. You hate mysticism because you are of a scientific, clear-headed, rationalistic bent or type. You can't help that. And if you don't like poems about God all you have to do is say so in so many words. But when you start

194

preaching that God is no subject for poetry and that I am either defeatist, Eliotic, or "unworthy" I have to laugh. Milton, Blake, Hopkins—and Dante whom you also shun—cannot be tossed out of poetic reality so easily. Nor can I. Take that straight as meant— without comparison, as attitude.

I think your letters should have the replies, but they are fascinating reading when dipped into. I wouldn't read them straight through.

And as for truth, where the hell is it? You leave out everything true in re the Library of Congress about both me and you. Think that over for a while.

I write as I please and when I can. I don't do it to order. I hope for a large synthesis as the years go by, [but] the problems deepen. You are a hard-hitter and have packed a lot of truth about Pound in the letters. I am glad that you have had the force to combat Eliot, but I take this as verbal game, intellectual wit, policy-making; you can't wipe him away. In many ways he is deeper and more profound than you. What I love in you is a sort of amazing one-to-one relationship with what I feel as American reality—the dynamics of the present, the feel of things. This is mighty good. The world of Stevens is grand, you love him in a certain way. So good we have all of you few of your generation, not one having the whole truth, each adding something to total poetic consciousness.

Later the 10th

There are a lot of other points to talk about, wish you were here and we could assail them. We wanted you to fly up to Maine but assumed you wouldn't but maybe next summer you will. Almost every time I went out in our 36-foot boat REVE I thought of your "Yachts," certainly a great poem and one of your best, a poem I have very deeply enjoyed many times. I learned to navigate through fog by dead reckoning and got into two storms which were quite enough—the waves were trying to defeat the hull but she withstood the enormous force that is always out to defeat man. I love the danger—but I wouldn't want to get fresh with the ocean. It is a battle of wit against Whatall.

On being called a genius. This does no good. A man has got to eat, hasn't he? I'd rather note the skip of my blond, six-year-old daughter. I recall AE's using that on me after my first book, 1930, in the last number of his *The Irish Statesman*. But you wouldn't have liked anything about AE I suspect. The next one was Ransom.

Well Bill this is just running on. I send you two all the love in the world, worlds of admiration and heady delight in your poetry. O yes on *Howl* I first lauded it in the *NY Times* summer of 56, Allen wrote me a 30 page letter on his principles, which Don Allen was to have printed the summary of in *Evergreen* this summer but I see he left it out. I like young Ginsberg a lot. I hadn't seen him for five plus years when I arrived in California. After a reading of mine at the Y, in a blurred room full of poets and smoke and fumes he came over, sat at my feet, then very young, with blazing black eyes, said he had encountered my poetry in an anthology when in a mental hospital, that "The Groundhog" gave him an extraordinary illumination that lasted for days, but concluded, "But then, Mr. Eberhart, your poem—or was it poems—made me feel worse and I had to go back to the psychiatric ward." Something like that, probably not accurate. Then I forgot all about him for years. What a pleasure to see this bright man again in California. You can't take too much credit, Bill, for only announcing your surprise that he finally wrote a poem.

I'm tossing in two enclosures, one some current answers about poetry & religion and a copy of *The Dartmouth* of last Jan. with some words I gave the boys at that time. Please have Flossy return these. I only send them as I have the happy picture of you with lots of time to do nothing but read and write.

Dikkon and Gretchen started to school yesterday. O the beautiful bright eternal vanishing world of childhood.

Love,
Dick

Rutherford, N.J.
Sept. 119 [sic], 1957

Dear Dick:

I'll return the enclosure as soon as I have a chance to look at it carefully. When I read your book I was disappointed at what I took to be your conservatism when I had always thought of you if not a radical at least more of a liberal in your style than apparently you are. You may be right in your attitude toward your art. No offense intended.

When I spoke of *Palgrave's Golden Treasury* I meant only to say that your style dated from some years back. Again, no offense I hope. And again you may be right. Who am I to say. If I said in the excitement of the moments anything that is offensive I offer you my sincere apologies.

The final quarter of the book was not up to the first part. Comparatively you seem to have run out of ideas, ideas at least that interest me. Since every important idea in our lives may be ascribed to God I do not in my poems want continually to ascribe them to the primal source. To do so is in my opinion tautological. Merely a preference on my part, of no basic significance. Sorry.

We think differently about our lives. Plenty of room in the world for both of us. Did you see the reception Frost got at Oxford and Cambridge, wonderful. I'm glad it wasn't me. I wouldn't know where to hide my face. Maybe he enjoyed it. God help him.

I didn't much appreciate being greeted at Brandeis as the Buffalo Bill of the American poets. Maybe that's what you think of me, and maybe that's what I am but there are many connotations to the epithet which should be explained before it is accepted. The old boy was hardly a writer. Nuts with that, I know, but I have been kicking around in the arts for a long time, too long to be classed as a cow-hand. Let's leave that to such a naive poet as Carl Sandburg, no offense to Carl, by the way.

Maybe that was what was rankling in my heart when I read your book! I just thought of it! What asses we all are about our own. See you sometime when we can have a drink together and forget the whole thing. I still love you—as does Floss also, you bastard.

Bill

Hanover, N.H.
Sept. 26, 1957

Dear Bill:

I hasten to clarify my usage of Buffalo Bill. There is always something to be said against any national figure but what made them national figures was the most important thing about them. I recall seeing Buffalo Bill when I was a small boy, in my home town, and then I forgot about it for about fifty years. But to me, as to many others, he was a dazzling man with a long, flowing beard who rode on a magnificent white horse and I can still see him today tossing up balls in the air and bursting every one with a loud-cracking six-shooter. He became a mythical figure to all America, although I read reviews of a book about him a year or two ago which depicted the sorry life he led, the glum reality of his all too human lot. I intended no reference whatever to a cow-hand in giving you what I thought a glowing, passionate tribute. I thought it would be evident that poetry is at the heart of life, is thus youthful, never-dying; that you as one of our best poets have wonderful youthfulness, vigor, life-likeness; and that to equate you with a symbol of greatness to the youth of America would be something that I could in fact do for no other of my elders. I meant it as an electrifying absolute—and not to be taken critically or made into something dubious in a literary way. So that's that! I'm sorry if it didn't come off for you. I vowed I would not mouth a lot of university platitudes in new-critical jargon. But to hell with it, as you so aptly say!

As a matter of fact, if you want to be really critical one could look with a jaundiced eye on any such convocations and have nothing to do with them. But that's not right, they are and this one was based on love, respect, devotion and I for one enjoyed the affair very much. The poem you read brought scowls from some ladies! I thought it direct and right and honest and clear.

On hearing of a colleague who went off the rails recently I felt a harsh brunt and wrote this:

> A fierce, enraged beast,
> Ready to kill, is man
> Rampant. Too bad!
>
> A deep disappointment
> Never to be unravelled.
> He destroys himself. Gone mad!
>
> Will mercy acquit him,
> Will love again fill him,
> Will it come right? I'd be glad.
>
> The fate of the mind
> When savage and destructive
> Banishes Sir Galahad.

Up with defenses
Against the totally enraged
And lock him in a quad, by God!

> Yours   as   it
> seems to me,
> *Dick*

Rutherford, N.J.
Oct. 5, 1959

Dear Dick:

Ever since your letter arrived this morning I have been working on a draft of something for your jacket, as soon as I have got it copied I'll forward it to you. I think it will do, hope you like it.

I wish I still had a head but I'm afraid that is too much to ask. I can write only out of the past. I do wish that I had a look at some of your later poems but when your new book arrives you'll no doubt take care of that.

I have to thank you Dick for not having completely forgotten me—a very easy thing to do under the circumstances. Isn't [it] a thrill to be having overflow audiences to hear your poetry read to them. Congratulations on your success. Best luck for the future. Love to Betty.

> Affectionately yours
> *Bill*

Rutherford, N.J.
Oct. 10, 1959

Dear Dick:

Here 'yare. I had my typist run it off for me so as not to lose my nerve about whether it should or should not be thrown out. I like it but that's no saying that you should or will. I had quite a tussle with myself to determine if it was precisely what I wanted to say in a short writing and there it is, I think it does us both justice, but is that enough? Chuck it back at me if you want to. In any case let me have a word from you how you feel about the piece.

You must be having fun with yourself and your students in the classes you are giving them. There must be many skeptics in such a gang which you have to consider and if you are not on your feet they will think you soft therefore I have to needle you whenever I get the chance—I'm not too confident of the modern radical movement the so called "Be Bop" originators for they do not originate anything. They're going back fast in my opinion.

Take care of yourself in the national capital and if you see any sign of life in literature there, drop me a word about it. It is that I am speaking about when I talk as I have done about your new poems, you have a marvelous opportunity to keep them alive.

Best
Bill

[Enclosure to letter of Oct. 10, 1959]

The Collected Poems of Richard Eberhart

A dichotomy possesses this man out of which emerges some unusual poems. I am not completely one with him on the character of his genius. He, being one of my closest friends, knows this best of all others. What poet is at peace within himself? None. Of Richard Eberhart this is true to an outstanding degree. On one side he would be happiest as a conventional poet, the man who could write such poem as "Villanelle," a poem as conventional, and as conventionally beautiful, as any modern poem I have ever seen. On the other hand this poet will be possessed by a madness as it were out of Goethe's *Walpurgis Nacht*.

Who is a man going to champion, the wild originator of a world opening his own astonished eyes, a world which he anticipates when he uses such a title as "If I could only live at the pitch that is near madness," a demonic mood of which, wrongly, he scarcely acknowledges himself to be possessed?

You have to make up your mind when submitting yourself to the reading of such a poet: the staid disciplines of the latter choice, which Eberhart for the most part elects to follow, or the other more Blakean mood of his rarer initiatives. There are two men involved who struggle for the supremacy. I prefer the wilder man, as I think to myself, the man addicted more to the future. The struggle going on within Richard Eberhart's consciousness will not be decided in a day. Lucky for him, the best of his poetry, the most far-seeing, is being written now in his middle years.

William Carlos Williams

Consultant in Poetry
The Library of Congress
Washington, D.C.
Oct. 15, 1959

Dear Bill:

I couldn't thank you more for your statements. As usual you hit the nail on the head, or this time the heads. I readily admit the dichotomy, cannot write at will, wait for a time when some crisis is resolved in the creative act, and learned a lot from you in making poetry a continuum, that is, an active, dynamic affair over every day and month and year, as one is able. The drives under open consciousness must have a lot to do with it. I find I am able to hold many assumptions together at one time; I like to dissolve apparent disparities. For instance, here are two dichotomous notions about poetry: It is thrown out of the being due to irrepressible high spirits and argues a fine state of health with superabundant energy. Oppositely, it is the expression of what a man knows he lacks, coming not perhaps from real illness (although this would be possible too) as from a gnawing sense of inadequacy, an effort to build back something that was either always missing or is felt to be lacking at the time. I associate this with the Baudelairean view of the poet not as passive filament but dark sufferer, a man with psychic wounds which never heal. These are two different ideas about what a poet is or from what he operates. I feel both within myself, but I do not feel anything unnatural in feeling this way. Of course, black and white is too obvious, there are all sorts of shadings in between. However, your picking out the opposites was good, astute, true. Night-day, life-death, hope-despair, good-evil have always been present to me as Devils and Angels of the world.

* * * * *

Did I tell you that a 3rd Secy from the Russian Embassy came in with a package. It was a present from Sholokhov of a boxed, 4-volume set of his *And Quiet Flows the Don*, signed, printed in English and published in Moscow. A friendly gesture after his one panel-meeting here before they all left for home. I had never read him before but note that we are of an age, but for a year or two. How ignorant one is! I lived over 50 years without ever hearing of Sholokhov. And wd. probably have to live as long again before I could send him in return a book of my poems printed in Russian and published in New York.

Our love to you both and many thanks, Bill, for your stirring words.

As ever,
Dick

THE TRICKLE-DOWN THEORY OF HAPPINESS

by PHILIP APPLEMAN

from POETRY

nominated by David Ignatow and Maura Stanton

It starts in the penthouses, drizzling
at first, then a pelting allegro
falling nowhere except the high places,
and Dick and Jane pull on bikinis
and go boogieing through the azaleas,
and Daddy, ecstatic, comes running
with pots and pans, glasses, and basins
and tries to keep all of it up there,
but no use, it's too much, it keeps coming,
and pours off the edges, down limestone
to the buckets and pails on the ground floor
where delirious citizens catch it,
and bucket brigades keep it moving
inside, until bathtubs are brimful,
but still it keeps coming, that shower
of silver in alleys and gutters,
all pouring downhill to the sleazy
red brick, and the barefoot people
who romp in it, squishing, but never
take thought for tomorrow, all spinning
in a pleasure they catch for a moment;
so when somebody turns off the spigot
and the sky goes as dry as a prairie,

then Daddy looks down from the penthouse,
down to the streets, to the gutters,
and his heart goes out to his neighbors,
to the little folk thirsty for laughter,
and he prays in his boundless compassion:
on behalf of the world and its people
he demands of the sky, give me more.

🔥 🔥 🔥

TENEBRAE

by SAUL YURKIEVICH

from O. ARS

nominated by O. ARS *and Loris Essary*

11th OF SEPTEMBER embrace of armored arm with swastikaed arm with braceleted arm THE PUBLIC FORCE an index finger with a dirty accusing nail fires at you FORMED CONSTITUTIONALLY Neruda: *dolls of death, charred/ by your hard and decorative ashes* BY THE FORCES OF LAND SEA AND AIR so that emboldened automatons assault you CONSTITUTES THE ORGANIZATION squad and squadron will gun you down the shadowy mathematics WHICH HAS BEEN SET UP BY THE STATE you will be tortured machinegunned by the patrol TO GUARANTEE ITS INTEGRITY tapping in time with the arrogant drumming PHYSICAL AND MORAL they will beat down your door and every word will be invalidated AND ITS HISTORICAL-CULTURAL IDENTITY *fauna of cold biters /of the city, terrible tigers, eaters of human flesh/ experts in the chase/ of the people sunk in darkness* ITS SUPREME MISSION because you are forever their danger IS TO MAINTAIN BEFORE ALL ELSE THE VALUES those who denounce you rejoicing join the army of shadows PERMANENT put on the boot of the exterminator OF THE CHILEAN NATION and execute you AGAINST INTRODUCTION OF A DOGMATIC IDEOLOGY (Hitler: "May God aid me in this fight . . . I would not have done away with Marxism if I hadn't been able to rely on force.") INSPIRED BY PRINCIPLES FROM ABROAD ("One must act radically . . . when you pull a tooth you have to do it with a single jerk . . . I didn't want the war nor the prison camps. Why did the Jews provoke this war?") THE SUPREME COMMAND TAKES OVER abolished every rule every letter twisted violated every measure IN ORDER TO RESTORE *establishing hostile margins/ zones of blind desolate shadow* THE CHILEAN VALUES ("And above all, no remorse!

205

We are not going to play at being good little boys . . . There is only one duty—Germanize this country") JUSTICE *bloody water, mud of salt marshes* ("I concede no importance to a legal end of the war in the East.") it is the moment of the predators they seek your entrails AND THE INSTITUTIONS praetorian peace pax *I am going to leave your number and your name/ nailed on the wall of dishonor* TO MAKE CHILE ADVANCE ("Hard men who act energetically, as I myself would . . . If the government is energetic, it will always be stronger than any revolutionary. Cruelty imposes respect.") ALONG THE PATH OF PROGRESS *The dust gathers/ rubber,/ mud, objects grow/ and walls rise up/ like an arbor of dark human skin* WILL GUARANTEE pieces of bodies ripped off as if by shark bites THE ATTRIBUTES *For him who gave the order of agony/ I demand punishment* OF THE JUDICIAL POWER blackout round-up cleaver REESTABLISHMENT OF ORDER undresses pulps swindles impedes hacks tortures shreds destroys ONLY OBJECT TO REESTABLISH ORDER put down with your leaden rage peoples silence waits works and stealthily TO SAVE THE COUNTRY *You will fight to erase the splotch/ of filth from the map, you will fight without a doubt* against the symmetrical mechanism of steel and silver whirlwind will come from gunpowder the explosion of the people

translated by Cola Franzen

THE UNBROKEN DIAMOND: NIGHTLETTER TO THE MUJAHADEEN

by WILLIAM PITT ROOT

from TELESCOPE and PIPEDREAM PRESS

nominated by Siv Cedering and Rita Dove

1.
Yes, your stories reach us

just as the grit once a summit in our country
reaches you, imperceptibly
dusting your upturned faces
                              calling on Allah,
scanning the indifferent blue skies
          armed with helicopters
—that iron nightmare politics has built
into your lives.

Our sunsets
intensified by that volcanic ash
remind us
of your tragedy, your sunsets
behind villages
                    in flames
from the bombings
where figures stumbling darkly up from rubble
search out
the others who do not rise.

Stories of
the unbroken diamond of your resistance.

2.
Here

those nine
spring days are called
The Children's Revolt—

as if
your children could be children, as if
the girl fifteen who tore her veil off

and handed it
to a soldier *Here, give me your rifle*
could any longer be a child

anywhere.

3.
                                        Or as if
at the head of the column of chanting students
Nahid Saed, first
                of seventy to die that day
—thirty
rounds pointblank in her body—, as if
that daughter
who became the daughter of your land
could turn
her ruined face
to answer a father again

4.
The stories reach us

—How you refuse
to attend an unveiling
turning away
from a new flag whose bright face is

the old lie of complicity,
and of how
troops fire into your faces,
Afghan troops
inexplicably your own.

Their faces freckle with your blood.

5.
                Yes, we do hear
how you stone the limousine
of the Soviet ambassador
until again
foreign guns in the hands of your countrymen
respond,
able to kill you,
                 unable
to stop your carrying of the dead and shattered
into a high school
where 5,000 students, male and female,
answer on the occupied streets of Kabul
crying,
       Death to Babrak Karmal
         Death to Bresnev
         Where is America
         Are we not human beings

6.
We hear the endless ten-minute slaughter
of students
by machine-gun fire, then hear
the charge of 2,000 horsemen
with swords drawn and cattle-prods high,
the ancient weapons and the new,
into the huddled dead and dying,
the screams of horses and your cries.
                   Finally
there is the low moaning,
arms lifting like fronds,
the thud of retreating hooves
muffled by earth trodden to red mud.

And we hear of your four more days of resistance.

7.
We hear
how when the armored unit
surrounding you
blazes, you answer
simply with your blood until 2,000 more
rise up,
grab one soldier,
stab out his eyes—
as if to kill him were too simple,
as if to blind him were to eradicate what he has seen.

8.
And we hear
of the puppet show that night
when televised officials
deny
those bodies
in whose wet flames of blood
your hands
burn and burn
until even the blinded soldier must see by their light.

9.
Yes, all these stories reach us
in blocks of black-and-white
we would hurl back

empowered by every mile and lie
between us
to scourge your nation clean.

If wishes were pumice.

If words were scouring stones.

10.
But all that reaches you
from us
is apolitical ash, proof
of an old magnificence
shocked to dust

—grit as hard
and fine
as the skin
of a pearl run across the tooth
of a mujahadeen skillfully determining
its true worth.
He spits
as he continues to watch
the hammered blue of the sky and chants
to himself
the ancient songs from a village turned
in 90 seconds
to light and the
smoldering limbs of family and friends,
the songs of shepherds
accustomed to solitude
now being used to keep armed men
aware of each other in the high passes.

11.
Those wornwood crooks
you manage your flocks with
cleverly tend
new herds now—
Soviet iron-tracks
your scouts lure
through ravines you seal with boulders
pried loose
by those staffs.

Trapped
and terrified
too late, they spatter

canon- and machine-gun fire
against the indestructible cliffs
where you are hidden, waiting
for the silence
you will break with dusty grins
and a calculated avalance of native stone.

12.
        Only once
have I stood on a summit
high as those passes
you guard like wives
—ten years ago,
while some of you were still children
playing among the billowing tents
at hoop-and-shadow games,
too shy
even to glance at those with whom
your children
have been born and raised.
                We'd driven east
through the thinning darkness,
those three friends and I, toward
dawn and the mountain
we climbed all morning long. Climbing
        we looked back
at a world all wilderness,
not unlike your own, and at the laketops,
each a remote
mirror to a bright fragment
of that vastness
no one sees all at once. Then
I began to comprehend
the Indian comparison of
climbing the mountain
to knowing God, ridge after ridge
beckoning, each
a false summit,
           until

only the euphoria
of feeling the mountain rise
to meet each step
kept us going—past excitement
and laughter, weariness
and silence,
past each new sense of limit
we imagined to be our last,
beyond pumice
                    to rockface,
into snow and ice
where the mountain disappeared
below us, leaving
us suspended
high on the rim of windfire and ice,
able to witness the world as a ring
to which our connection
has vanished.

13.
                    This is the mountain,
Fire Mountain,
whose summit circles the earth,
invisible to the eye where you are
except as a tint at sunset,
grit between your teeth
and the teeth of your wives and sons and daughters,
the teeth of your enemies—
this trace of Godhead inconspicuously everywhere.

14.
I am a man whose one power is telling.

I tell you this:
                    I would give you words
massive as boulders to roll against the tanks and iron-tracks,
delicate words to heal the roses
driven by dum-dum shells into your flesh,
words of silk and gut to restore each maimed limb
from the truckload

213

of arms and legs hacked off in a single village
and brought back
to be dumped in a square in Kabul,
words to re-root tongues
torn from the mouths
of those who warned you,
milk-words rich and white for the myriad infants
held to the shrunken breasts of mothers
                starving in Kohat and the dozens of camps
thousands flee to over Parachinar Pass
through the Speen Ghar Mountains.

15.
—I would give you
wind words to dispel the experimental gasses
                    of Soviet advisors,
to disperse the yellow rain and scatter
        mists of blue and green
dust,
each composed
to destroy in another way
the frail machinery of the human body,
hearts and minds betrayed by their own blood.

—I would give you
healing words to mend the lungs and shorted nerves
and bursting veins
of the hundreds, the thousands
of you who fall gasping
and hacking up sudden blood
with your nose-blood gagging you
and ear-blood hot along your necks,
anus-blood and manroot-blood scalding your legs
                to your boots and bare feet,
eye-blood blinding you as you look up
to take aim.

—I would give you
heatseeking words to bring down the observers taking
                notes in helicopters circling overhead

timing
on stop-watches
with cyrillic numerals
how long it takes before
you with your muzzle-loaders
and your women and children with slingshots and rocks
collapse, then
how much longer it takes you to stop writhing altogether
on sodden ground among the unscathed huts.

16.
Lastly
I would draw
          from Nahid Saed
the thirty traitorous pieces of lead
and give them to her
for charms. To the eyes
of your women
raped like the land, helplessly shamed
by the violence of men
whose shadows dark as vultures
seed the valleys with fire and char,
I would restore
the brilliance and tenderness
toward you,
toward themselves. Toward your children.

If words were scouring stones.

If wishes were pumice.

17.
With the stone of helplessness
huge under my tongue,
I tell you your story is heard.

Your story is being heard.

♨ ♨ ♨

CROSSING

fiction by BARBARA THOMPSON

from SHENANDOAH

nominated by SHENANDOAH

"Memsahib?" The tap at her door is light, tentative, like the scratch of a bird on a windowpane. Only bird cries and an occasional bicycle bell have interrupted the afternoon silence since an hour ago when the call to prayer rasped out from the loudspeaker at the neighboring mosque. It is an April Friday in the early Seventies in the old British part of Lahore. The willows that brush against the roshandon windows of Anne's dressing room were planted at the behest of some colonial official forty years ago. And the old habits too persist: in westernized households like this, only the menservants are at prayer in the mosque; the sahibs sleep in their beds after a heavy lunch.

Not Anne. She is American and even after twelve years she can rarely sleep in the daytime. For some minutes now she has been standing absently over an open suitcase, rummaging through a pile of woolens. Above her head the ceiling fan orbits slowly, making a sound like a drowsy insect.

"Memsahib?" Noiselessly the little maidservant pushes the door inward with the edge of a brass tray on which the telephone rests, its receiver beside it. "Trunk call from Karachi," she says softly. "From Libby Memsahib."

Anne takes the phone out into the passageway, away from the room in which her husband, Iqbal, is sleeping. Behind her the servant secures the connecting doors. She is young, hardly more than a child, but Anne is conscious how swift and purposeful she is, her bare feet gliding like silk over the parquet floor, the brass latches closing with one muted click. Anne feels again the hint of unacknowledged conspiracy between them, mistress and maidservant, against the hegemony of men. She has tacitly endorsed the girl's presumption by waiting these long moments before picking up the receiver.

"Libby?" Anne braces herself. Libby has a way of careening through other people's lives like a charge of static electricity, rendering everything momentarily more vivid but trailing a wake of confusion.

"There's been a balls up, Annie. Our Afghan visas aren't ready."

"But we're supposed to leave tomorrow morning!"

"That's all right, you have yours, and I've worked it so—"

"But there's no point in our going without Masood!"

"You *won't* go without Masood! Stop interrupting, Annie, I've fixed everything. I'll put Masood on the plane to Peshawar on Sunday morning just as we planned, only I won't be with him. You pick him up and drive to Kabul as scheduled and I'll collect both passports Monday morning and fly there straight. No one can stop *me*. It'll be fine. I made a hell of a row at the Afghan Consulate and they swore they'd give them Monday whether or not the authorization came from Kabul. OK?" Libby's voice is louder than necessary, higher pitched, and she is talking very fast. Anne is conscious she is meant to be overwhelmed.

"How can Masood cross the border without his passport?" she asks wearily.

"He'll have to use Sheriyar's. No one ever looks at kids."

"I'm *taking* Sheriyar, Libby. You know I'm taking both boys, that was the whole excuse for the trip. No one even knows about you and Masood."

"Stop fussing, Annie. Make something up. Tell Sher you'll bring him something wonderful from Kabul, a tribesman's banduq with an inlaid barrel, for Christ's sake. You'll think of something."

"I can't," she says sullenly.

"Annie, are you there? Damn it, this bloody telephone must be bugged. I can't hear a word you're saying."

"Then how do you know I'm saying anything?" Anne says. "Where are you, Libby? At your office?"

"I'm at a friend's flat. Listen, let's get this all straight before the line really dies. You collect Masood Sunday morning at the Peshawar airport and I'll catch up with you at the Kabul Hotel as soon as I can manage it, OK? Don't get fussed, Annie. Just make something up." There is a long pause in which Anne says nothing, and then Libby, her voice gentler, supplicating, adds, "you know how much it matters, Annie." And the phone goes dead. But not before Anne thinks she has heard another voice in the background, a man's deep laughter.

She goes back to her dressing room and takes up the packing, all her old hesitancies revived by Libby's call. It was a harebrained scheme from the beginning, based on lies and precisely synchronized movements, but Anne had been persuaded weeks ago that only with her help, and by these baroque means, could Libby get her twelve-year-old son away from his father. Koranic law gives Anwer custody and he is not one to negotiate against his own advantage.

There was too much risk in a direct escape by plane from the Karachi airport: the international departure lounge is full of people you meet at dinner, who know your private business and are given to meddling. If someone notified Anwer and he intercepted them, Libby would never have a second chance. And so they agreed that Libby would use the long Sunday she is permitted with Masood to fly with him to Peshawar where Anne would collect them for the drive across the border to Afghanistan—two ordinary American women on fourteen day tourist visas taking their children on a spring holiday.

But now Anne is supposed to do it alone, and she wants to balk. Libby is not that particular a friend. They have little in common beyond the bare fact that in the late Fifties each had married the Pakistani student she met at college and come here to raise children whose blood is mixed. The substance of their lives is very different, Anne's as tranquil and domestic as her mother's back in Indiana where Anne grew up. She does not think Pakistan has changed her very much except in superficial ways, matters of form—the routine of her day, the language she speaks to servants and shopkeepers, the clothes she wears. Even these changes came gradually. She gave up western dress only after her second son, Timmy, was born. It had become a bother, having her mother send things like shoes and pantyhose; and in the summer heat she felt buttoned up and clunky among the Pakistani women in their flowing silks and cottons.

Libby had come to Pakistan two years before her, embracing from the start every possible transformation of herself. She had met Anwer getting a graduate degree at Columbia in anthropology and she likes to say she is the only foreign wife she ever met who came here with both eyes open. She landed in Karachi knowing Urdu and a smattering of Gujerati and how to make a passable curry grinding her own spices. She wore local dress from the beginning, never bothering with the safety pin at the waist of her sari, as Anne still does. And when she left Anwer she had her right nostril pierced: a symbolically neutral way of wearing her engagement diamond, she said.

When Anne met her, Libby had just given birth to Masood, born as his father had been on a rope cot set in the middle of the women's courtyard to catch the sea breeze. A year later Anne went home in the early months of her own first confinement to be delivered of Sheriyar by the old doctor who had attended her own birth. Iqbal had understood without being told that at such a time she would want her own mother.

She had been surprised in those early years how well Iqbal understood her needs without any explanation. At first she tested him: does he mind her wearing sleeveless blouses in spite of the Koran? should she give in to his mother's insistence that she have a wet-nurse for the baby? does it embarrass him when she takes his hand, touches him, in the presence of others? But she soon saw that the questions made him uneasy, even when he answered, as he almost always did, the way she wanted him to. She was emphasizing differences between them that he did not wish to acknowledge. He often says that the lives of women are only superficially affected by culture—and then only to their detriment. A virtuous wife and mother is the same everywhere and forever.

How Anne wishes she could call Libby back. Why hadn't she insisted they postpone the trip to the following weekend? But how could she explain that to Iqbal, now that all the arrangements had been made, dinner parties declined on her behalf, Sher and Timmy given makeup assignments for this particular week of school. Anyhow there is no hope of reaching Libby today at any telephone number she knows.

Besides, through all her anxiety, Libby's last words throb like a pulse: Anne *does* know how much it matters that Masood should not be left where he is, at the mercy of his negligent father and the father's new young wife, running barefoot, eating with his hands, speaking pidgin English like a servant . . . And she goes on, mindlessly filling her case with a jumble of woolens and a few summer shifts leftover from visits to America. Libby has persuaded her they will be less conspicuous in their own old clothes than in the saris or shelwar kameezes that single them out as the wives or chattal of Pakistanis. She shakes out a yellow dress. Like everything else it smells of camphor and salty dust from years in tin trunks. She holds it up against herself and switches on the light over the long mirror.

She sees a tall thinnish woman, someone who would be called rangy if her movements were less instinctively cautious. The lemony yellow is too strong now for her pale skin and gray-smudged chestnut hair. It gives her the look of being unwell. In her youth she was on the verge of real beauty, and it is likely that in age she will regain it, with her fine bones and classical symmetries, but just now in her mid-thirties she has the diminished prettiness of a cut flower left too long in the sun.

Anne has never been particularly vigorous or energetic. She knows it is a wonder to Iqbal how capably she manages her household, controlling the often devious and contentious servants better than he dreamed a foreign woman could, better than his own mother does, though he would not admit it. And unlike his mother she never raises her voice.

Only once in their marriage has Anne come near setting herself against him, and that was—quite unexpectedly—in the matter of their children's religious upbringing. They had begun in full accord, Anne and Iqbal, the educated secularized offspring of devout parents. They chose to be married in the German Lutheran Church where Anne had been baptized and confirmed, because she had always imagined herself in the slipper-satin dress with the long train and her sorority sisters in attendance, but also because it reassured her parents, who were troubled that however decent and devoted he seemed, Iqbal came from a religion that allowed him four wives.

He was glad to pledge monogamy before their altar, in their words. And Anne, in the same concessionary spirit and with as little reflection, agreed that it would be best for their children to grow up like everybody else in Pakistan, which meant as Muslims. It would be sufficiently complicating to have a foreign mother.

But by the time her second son, Timur, was born, Anne had become uncomfortable with the laxness of Iqbal's observance. He is the Islamic equivalent of the Easter communicant, his sacramental impulses fully satisfied by abstention from pork and the formal prayers at the two major Eid celebrations. She saw Sher and Timmy growing up without any ordering beliefs, and with a decisiveness that surprised her she released herself from her promise. Every Sunday now she takes them to the watered-down Wesleyan service at the missionary college.

She steeled herself for a struggle, but Iqbal has never mentioned it or tried to deflect her. Perhaps he thinks she is acting out of devotional urgencies that she could not have anticipated, that it is something that happens to women when they have children. Perhaps he regrets not having followed his mother's admonition and insisted on her conversion. But it would have been out of character for him. He prized her foreignness.

Very little in their lives now proclaims her foreignness—certainly not the house in which they live. A single-story white bungalow from the heyday of the Raj, it was the choice Iqbal made when he returned to Lahore the month after their marriage, leaving Anne behind to spare her the first summer's heat. It is a house made for summer, a warren of high-ceilinged interconnecting rooms set along a stemlike corridor, each room with its cooling veranda. He furnished it with things from his mother's go-downs— carved walnut pieces which he had upholstered in rich dark colors, floorlamps that rise like giant silkcapped mushrooms fringed with iridescent beads. When Anne arrived in October she found the house gloomy and talked of lightening it with cane and wicker, fresher colors. But she had more pressing concerns—the language, Iqbal's mother, politics among the servants, her first pregnancy— and when she finally got around to it, the impulse had almost passed. She hung a few landscapes instead of the glum family portraits, taught the mali not to crush the flowers together in tight nosegays, and gave in to the dense Edwardian comfort.

There are guests tonight and Anne must consult with the cook. He has been in the family longer than she has and although he can concoct a baked Alaska that looks like a marble war memorial with meringue doves, she suspects that when she is not around he reverts to his old method of suspending the meat between his toes to pare away the fat and gristle. She makes a mild clatter as she goes down the corridor and when she pushes open the kitchen door, the old man is waiting for her in a clean apron, his hookah tucked away behind the charcoal brazier.

Mangoes are beginning to come into the bazaar, and Anne dictates a recipe for Mango Fool, translating it from an old issue of *Queen*. He takes it down laboriously in a mysterious shorthand. Watching his cramped fingers form the curly symbols that must mean 'castor sugar,' she feels suddenly dizzy, dislocated. It is more than the script, the Babel of Tongues. There are things she is trying not to think of now.

She wanders back through the hall into the drawing room, cool and dusky, its light an eerie blue from the navy linings of the bamboo shades that cover the tall windows. In the far corner a carved walnut game-table is set out with a half-finished jigsaw puzzle, Monet's water garden at Giverny. She lets herself down into the dimness, the intricate modulations of blue and green. Under her feet the Persian carpet is navy and dun, like an abstraction of mountain streams flowing past granite.

The afternoon falls away as other afternoons have since she discovered this way of summoning up and holding that inner stillness that other westerners have sought here in yoga and drugs. At the game table, over a jigsaw puzzle or one of her intricate varieties of solitaire, she can withdraw into a velvet darkness beyond thought. She is not aware that the grayish arch among the greens is a bridge, she is conscious only of matching shape and color. When Iqbal comes into the room an hour later she does not look up until his hands are on her shoulders. She sees from his slight smile that he finds her absorption charming: he has said with that same smile that if the house were burning Anne would finish her game of Patience.

She rings for tea and they sit together on the plum settee, talking of this and that—dinner parties, a holiday in August—the domestic conversation of the peacefully married who no longer need talk of intimate things, who have the perfect courtesy of strangers. But when the tea is poured she broaches the matter of Sheriyar's remaining behind. At first Iqbal hardly listens. He likes to say that the children are her department, though Anne wonders what that means when they both know that if he determines a vital interest is at stake he will prevail.

"I wonder if it isn't too close to his examination, Iqi," she says, tentatively. "I know this year isn't the decisive one, but—"

"What are you saying, Anne?" He is suddenly in full focus.

"Well, next year he'll be getting ready for Chief's College, and I thought . . . " Her voice trails off.

"I thought you cleared everything with the school," he says sharply.

"I did. I'm just having second thoughts."

"I wish you had come to me earlier," he says. "I would not have thought you would jeopardize his acceptance for a holiday."

"He's only eleven," she says.

"Exactly. He's almost a man."

They are interrupted by the tap of a walking stick against the door, Iqbal's old uncle—his father's only brother—who turns up periodically for a cup of tea to see how the foreign woman is rearing his nephew's sons. In spite of three marriages, he is childless; Sher and Timmy are all his family's future. Anne finds herself pulling the loose edge of her sari over her hair as she settles him into an armchair and rings for more tea. She knows he is embarrassed on Iqbal's behalf that she does not keep purdah like the women of his household. Once fresh tea and samosas are provided, she can leave the men to their own talk and find the ayah to tell her that only Timmy's things are to be packed for the next day's journey. Tonight when she tucks Sheriyar into bed she will find some way of explaining to him why he cannot go.

The moment comes: Anne is sitting on the edge of his bed on a scarlet silk quilt that Iqbal's mother had made for her when she came as a bride. The lights are out in the room and a single beam from the hallway throws her narrowed silhouette, twice longer than life, on the wall over Sheriyar's head. He himself is only a smudgy shadow with an aureole of unruly black hair against the white pillow.

She begins confidently—he has his examinations next month, someone should stay behind with Daddy. But when Sheriyar never questions, never dissents, she falters, spills out a rush of promises: gifts, a journey with her to Delhi or the Vale of Kashmir, the two of them alone. Her palms are damp, the shadow on the wall twists.

"Is there any other reason I can't go, Mummy?" he asks quietly, his voice so old in its tact and gentleness that for a minute she wonders if he knows something. But of course there is no way he could, and so she reassures him and kisses him, glad that in the darkness their eyes need not meet with anything like understanding.

The journey begins the next morning without any of the domestic ceremony that customarily attends a major departure. Even though it is Saturday, Iqbal has gone to his office and Sher is out on the polo grounds exercising his pony. Nor have the servants lined up for salaams as they do when she travels with Iqbal: is it their way of expressing disapproval that she is traveling unescorted? Only Fazal Dad, the driver, is here, sulkily polishing the already immaculate yellow Triumph, obviously hoping that at the last minute she will decide to take him along, at least as far as Peshawar, where his family is.

She honks the horn several times before Timmy scuffles out, the ayah trailing him with a wicker hamper of lunch, muttering ineffectually in Punjabi that his shirt tail is hanging out. He gets into the car without looking at Anne, but manages the obligatory "Good morning, Mummy" in a cross voice that she decides not to notice.

The sun is brilliant this morning, the first forewarning of the heat to come. Here on the plains spring is no more than ten April days, a temperate mirage of yellowy green and fragrant blossom before the blazing summer. Last night they had a wood fire in the grate, and now as Anne drives between the iron gateposts she sees in the rear-view mirror the servants assembling ladders to take the air conditioners down from their niches for spring cleaning.

Timmy hangs out of the car window, angling for a last look back.

"Well, we're off," she says with a heartiness that sounds false even to her.

"I don't see why Sher couldn't come."

"Daddy didn't want want him to miss school, Timmy."

"How come you just decided yesterday?" he says half under his breath, glaring out of the window as though he doesn't really expect an answer.

There is only one road up-country, one way to cross the Ravi River, and that is the Grand Trunk Road which the British built a century ago to connect the Bay of Bengal with the frontier of Afghanistan. As it cuts through Lahore it takes on many guises, mirroring the peculiarly disconnected districts of the city. Here where Anne joins it, it is the old Imperial Mall, lined by the walls and gardens of Government House, the colonial clubs and the botanical garden. The streets are clean and placid, empty except for a few cars and the odd cyclist in a crisp white servant's uniform. Here and there through ornate gates one catches sight of a mali brushing fallen leaves from a well-tended lawn with his broom of twigs.

But at the chawk, where a wedding-cake gazebo once housed a marble statue of Victoria, everything changes: the road becomes a trading street, the prosperous bazaar of the rich. Here pharmacies are air conditioned and the restaurants have deep awnings. Over the moon-door of the Cantonese restaurant a gilded dragon breathes scarlet flame. Beggars whine among the flower sellers and importune passers-by, but they do not follow or jostle them. Each seems to have his own agreed-upon station beside a doorway or parking place, and each his own unique affliction—the thin girl suckling the infant, the boy on the oversized skateboard whose legs stump at the knees, the humpback with the twisted face. . . .

In a few blocks the dragons and air conditioners are gone, the structures more tentative, exposed to the street, their paint peeling. Beggars wander randomly among the fruit and vegetable stalls, pushing spatulate fingers at the black-shrouded purdah women. The women shuffle along in pairs like nuns or are guided by a servant boy. Anne is alert to their movements; blinkered as they are, they sometimes panic and rush the traffic.

Nearer the University some younger women walk unveiled, with only muslim dopattas covering their head and breasts. Even they move as though conscious of peril, and none sit among the cigarette-smoking boys who lounge in the open-air tea stalls. One of these is built against the broken tomb of the little courtesan Anarkali whose Moghul lover had her immured alive for smiling at his eldest son.

The traffic is chaotic now, a flood of ill-assorted vehicles with no common rhythm. Anne's knuckles are white on the wheel. Suddenly, in front of the High Court, a wizened old man in a dhoti, crazed maybe, hurls himself in front of them—their fender strikes some part of his body with the dead sound of a palm on a metal drum—but he never slows down, only continues his frenzied weaving among the moving obstacles.

Anne brakes reflexively and kills the motor. The cars behind her set up a din of horns and curses, and at her left a villager perched atop a load of logs contemplates her with detached contempt. Timmy is ramrod stiff; she knows he is wishing he were somewhere else.

She manages to start the car without flooding it, and the shouts and hooting stop. They have come to the city wall now, its ancient mud-bricks festooned with bright silk beddings put out to air. The wall is breached in many places but it still defines the original city which has hardly changed in five centuries, still a maze of lanes that meander and cross and come to abrupt conclusions at open drains or the entrance to a courtyard of blue tile. Anne has never come there alone.

She rarely goes anywhere alone here. That is partly a matter of custom but also of populous households and elastic time: anyone who mentions a destination is likely to gain a companion. Anne prefers company. A foreign woman alone is always conspicious, however modest her demeanor, especially if she is still half-young. Timmy is a comfort to her, even his tentative masculinity is a shield, but when she planned this journey it was on Sheriyar's quiet strength that she had implicitly depended. He is the true native of this place, more Punjabi than his father, even—Iqbal willed some of that self away during his years abroad. Sher bears no sign at all of the foreign admixture, and Anne knows that she has come to invest him with a special authority, almost magical, that this society confers only upon its men. Timmy is frailer, still only a child, and he looks like her.

From these jumbled reflections a question arises: why was Iqbal so complacent about her setting out on this long journey with only the children? He would think it highly eccentric, unseemly even, for his sister to do such a thing. What does he think about Anne that makes it acceptable? Is it only her foreignness?

"Why do you think Daddy—" She stops. "That's Datta-Sahib's shrine over there," she says. "Daddy went there after your birth to offer prayers. There's a neem tree somewhere in the courtyard with a little packet of your baby hair." She thinks she is telling the truth. She remembers distinctly that Iqbal gave alms and made an offering of the shaved birth hair for Sheriyar, the firstborn.

Finally, beside the blood-colored minarets of Aurangzeb's great mosque, Anne catches sight of the bridge. They are underway. On the other side she will tell Timmy the first part, that tomorrow morning they will collect Masood Amin at the airport and take him with them to Kabul.

He studies her as she says it. "When did you decide that?"

"A while ago," she says.

"Yesterday?"

"No, weeks ago when Libby and Masood were in Lahore."

"Is his sister coming too?"

Anne has been trying not to think about Yasmin, the little daughter Libby is leaving behind. "Not now," she says. "It would be too hard." The logistics, she means; Libby said there was no way she could take them both at one time without arousing suspicion. Besides, she can come back for Yasmin, she said. The Koran gives mothers the custody of female children until they are twelve. Even if they are foreigners, infidels, kidnappers?

"What about his mother?"

"She'll meet us in Kabul Monday or Tuesday," Anne says. She doesn't want to go through the rigamarole about the visas.

"Why didn't you tell us before?"

He is still thinking of Sher. "I don't know," she says lamely. "Would it have mattered?"

She had told no one at all. This trip was presented as a fancy of hers, a celebration of spring, a tracing of history. The almond trees would be in bloom, pink against the immaculate snow of the Pamirs. She would show Sher and Timmy a different world—empty, with immeasurable sky. The harsh landscape tinted only in muted tones of dun and silver: infinite distance from the rich clutter of Lahore, where the hand of man is on everything.

Somewhere along the way they will cross the path of the Powindahs returning from winter on the plains of India. They have made this trek for a thousand years at least, cutting through passes of their own choosing, indifferent to roads and national boundaries. Their women are unveiled and powerful as men, striding along beside their camels burdened with grain, their flocks kept close by dogs as large and fierce as wolves . . . She would show them the high plateaus from which the Moghuls swept down upon the Indian subcontinent and changed its face. Iqbal's family has an Afghan thread, a grandmother on his father's side with slate-blue eyes, the story goes. Timmy's eyes, maybe. But she knew Iqbal

227

would never dream of coming with them. He prefers his holidays in the West or its counterfeit in Beirut. He has no hankering for his ancestral past, heroic and dismal.

They are in open country now, except for the small factories and one-room shops that line the road. There is little traffic, lorries mainly, but there are wandering goats to watch out for, and chickens, and an occasional darting child. In the empty spaces between settlements unglazed red pottery dries in the sun. Timmy has fallen asleep, his head taps loosely against the windowpane at each rut in the road.

She wonders why he is so cranky. He loves to be alone with her; she has always thought it is the second childs's deepest hunger to be singled out, to have his mother to himself. Of course there is Masood, but he didn't know that until an hour ago.

It has grown colder and Anne rolls up her window. But after a time she realizes that there is no single weather along this stretch of open road. It is as variable as her own spirits, changing as the angle of the road changes. From the Salt Range to the southwest comes a mild, spicy wind, bringing with it the first gritty heat from the wakening desert. And from the north and east the winds bring a dustless chill drawn from the melting snows of the Karakorams. Anne makes a game of it, opening and closing windows and sunroof, covering and uncovering Timmy with their cardigans. His nose is runny, he seems to have caught a cold. He snuffles in his sleep, and he sleeps or at least keeps his eyes closed until long after they have passed his favorite part of the journey, the gently rocking boat-bridge over the River Jhelum.

They are leaving the villages behind now, and the lonely spires of Anglican churches in the old cantonment towns. The road climbs through undulating fields, between softly rounded hills, as though this landscape was formed long ago by cyclonic winds or lashing waters. It is greener here, and in the distance Anne sees a grove of jacaranda trees in bloom, fountains of tumbling mauve. They are her favorite of all Indian trees, and they have the briefest flowering, as brief as spring itself. She half-consciously pushes away the sudden memory the jacarandas call up of the same mauve-colored wisteria vine that clings to the porch of the white wooden house where she grew up.

When Timmy wakes they stop for their picnic. He is better-tempered now, half-drugged from sleep in the enclosed car with the sun beating in. They speculate amiably about the pocked and gullied terrain. It looks like the ruin of a mud city, the rectilinear excavations of Harappa or Mohenjadaro. She is grateful to be back in her usual maternal role, teaching him about the things of the world. All morning in some indefinable way she has felt him to be the one in control.

At nightfall they check into Dean's Hotel in Peshawar. The old clerk remembers her from other visits and pretends to remember Timmy whom he has never seen. Timmy starts to correct him, but Anne cuts him off, and after a minute he understands that she is asking him not to embarrass the old man in his harmless flattery. Then, united by their consciousness of behaving decently, they go off to eat a good dinner of Peshawari rice and mutton, and sleep the heavy sleep of the reconciled in their white beds in the tall white hotel room.

When in the morning Anne comes out of the bathroom dressed in an eight-year-old summer shift, Timmy makes a face like a disapproving old Punjabi matriarch. "You're awfully white," he says, looking at her legs.

He means naked. "So are you," she snaps, sounding, she knows, like a taunted child. But he *is* very light-skinned. It has always been an ambiguous blessing here where fairness is the most prized attribute of a newborn baby or a potential spouse, but where too light a skin can alienate, raise questions about your belonging. Timmy still looks more like an American than like his brother's brother, even now that his hair has lost its first gold and turned a burnished brown. And he has those slate-colored eyes. Anne has come to feel their common fairness a form of vulnerability.

At the airport he won't get out of the car, though in Lahore he and Sher often straggle in hours late from school, having cozened Fazal Dad into driving home by way of the airfield so they can watch the planes take off and land. He loves especially the small ones, the Dakotas and Fokkers that PIA uses on these up-country runs. "I'd rather stay here," he says.

"Look, he's a nice boy, Tim. You'll like having him along." She can hear the plane circling overhead for a landing. "Remember? He has one blue eye and one brown one." She doesn't know why she said that, and she doesn't want to hear what Timmy will retort if he does, so she slams her door and hurries out to the landing strip. Whatever she meant to say, those mismatched eyes are Masood's most haunting feature—one a cold cyanic blue, the other the lambent brown of Moghul miniatures. At close range you can hardly look at anything else.

But now, watching him pick his way down the rickety metal steps, Anne thinks how beautiful he is, and at the same time how overburdened his thin twelve-year-old body seems by the large head of golden-brown curls. He reminds her of a statue of David she and Iqbal saw somewhere in Italy, spare and solemn, somehow androgynous. The boy's leaness is emphasized by the voluminous clothing he wears, a long tunic over baggy trousers; tissue-thin from washing on stones, and starched to the consistency of paper, they stand away from his body like a carapace. He wears dirty tennis shoes and no socks and he is empty-handed. Except for his coloring he could be the child of any one of Anne's servants, leaving for Urdu school with a dusty slate under his arm. This is what he has come to since Libby left his father's house.

"Here I am, Masood." Anne reaches out to touch his sleeve.

"Ussalam uleikum, Auntie." He bobs his head in an abbreviation of the formal greeting.

"Salaam uleikum, Masood," she says, hearing in her mind Sheriyar's patient voice correcting her: 'No, Mummy, you must say, 'valeikum ussalam' when it's a reply."

"Where is Sheriyar?"

"He couldn't come. You have to use his passport. Didn't your mother tell you?"

"No, Auntie, she didn't tell me anything. When she came to get me this morning she told Abu—she told my father—she would be taking me out to the beach hut at Hawk's Bay and would keep me very late. And then when we got into the taxi she told the driver to go to the airport, that I was going to my grandmother in America."

"It's all very complicated, Masood. I'm going to drive you as far as Kabul. Your mother was afraid—" Something in her resists saying Libby is afraid of anything. "She thought if she tried to take you straight from Karachi someone at the airport might see you and your father might stop her. So I said I'd drive you across to Kabul because no one bothers about people just going over for a holiday, especially women and children—"

"Is Ammi really coming, Auntie?"

"Of course she is. Your visas weren't ready, and she had to wait to pick them up tomorrow. She'll meet us in Kabul. But we had to travel on a Sunday when you could be away the whole day. We have to be out of Pakistan before the border closes at sundown."

"What will Abu do?"

"He'll be furious, I guess. But I don't think there's anything he can do once you're out of the country. Are you sorry, Masood? I thought you wanted to go."

"Oh sure," he says, and for the first time his voice is like her own children's voices: under the singsong Anglo-Indian rhythm, a strong American beat. "I hate it back there."

They are walking toward the old hangar that has been converted to a baggage shed. The early morning mist has burned off but the wind is still sharp. The feel of it against her arms and legs reminds her how bare she must seem to the people around her. Because this is Peshawar, not Lahore, the men do not smile hungrily as they stare at her; their eyes are as solemnly judgmental as the eyes of their womenfolk peering through the embroidered lattice-work of their white burqas. There are no other foreigners. Anne pulls the cardigan over her upper arms as the Koran demands.

"Do you remember America at all, Masood?"

"I remember the room I slept in had dark blue walls with white rabbits on them with very big teeth. I was afraid of them. But everything else was soft—my bed was soft and the seats in the drawing room. My grandmother's bathroom had mirrors all around and bottles that were cut like diamonds, and you could have anything you wanted to eat." He speaks as if by rote, as though he has repeated this litany to himself over and over again.

The coolies are dragging the baggage carts in now, a jumble of metal and cardboard suitcases, rolled-up beddings, and rush baskets of citrus fruit and early mangoes from outside Karachi. Anne looks to Masood to identify his things.

"I don't have any samaan, Auntie." He uses the Urdu word for luggage.

"But you have to have clothes to cross the border. Your mother said she'd have a bag packed for you. It's going to be freezing tomorrow in the Gorge and colder in Kabul—" And dressed this way he's conspicuous. For God's sake, Libby could at least have done that.

In the car Timmy is pretending to be asleep. Anne leans over to kiss him and his eyelids flutter. "Hi, darling," she says. "Masood's here."

231

He rouses himself with elaborate yawns. "Hi, Masood," he says coolly.

"Ussalam uleikum, Timur."

"Where's your mother?"

"In Karachi."

"When's she coming?"

"I don't know."

Because it is Sunday the shops are closed in the cantonment, but in the street of the cloth-sellers off the Qissakhani Anne finds a tailor who has some readymade clothes; she buys Masood a pair of khakis and a white shirt unsuitably appliqued with a blue duck but the only one that fits him, and a heavy olive-drab cardigan that looks to have been stolen from an army go-down. And, in case of trouble on the road, a red plaid blanket.

Before they leave the old city she buys apples and dried fruit and monkey nuts for the journey. At breakfast she had filled their thermos flasks with boiled water and milky tea. "We'll get kababs and nan at the border, but we have to get across as quickly as we can. I want to be in Jallalabad before dark."

They fill the gas tank and start out confidently on the last stretch of the Grand Trunk Road. But here, at the extent of the empire, the road suddenly branches out like the fingers of a hand. Choosing the logic of the central member leads Anne twice into the barren countryside—once to the new sugar mills, once to a Canadian dam project—before she gives up. With the sun making a longer shadow of the car she hurries back to the airport road to ask directions; even Timmy, whose Urdu and Punjabi are second-nature, can follow only the drift of the Pashtu: right, left, the number of miles, the names of the villages and check-points.

When they find it, the road to the Khyber Pass is unmarked, as though anyone who has any business there already knows where it is. Anne herself has been here before, but Fazal Dad was driving and Iqbal was in charge. Another time she came with a woman friend to Landhikotal, the smuggler's bazaar halfway along the road that the Government more or less officially tolerates as an informal subsidy to the Tribal Area. The Westinghouse refrigerator she bought that day turned up a month later in the middle of the night after a journey by camel and bullock cart and lorry. These passes have been the site of illegal and violent transit for a thousand years.

The Khyber Road does not cut through the actual Khyber Pass at all. The British, assessing its historical indefensibility, built their own border-crossing at another cut slightly to the east. For good measure they set out all along the subsidiary passes and dry gullies emplacements of dragon's teeth to hinder attempted invasion— from this high road they look like rows of lump sugar.

There is little traffic in either direction this Sunday. Once a brilliantly painted truck with Mianwalli license plates passes her on a downhill grade with a heavy load of pale pink rock salt. She catches up to it again when the grade reverses. The paint is fresh, its circus-poster images precise: the gold-maned Lion of Kashmir, scimitar in paw, lounges before the lotus-studded Dal Lake; hawks soar among cotton-candy clouds; and an old fashioned bridge arches over a river in which giant fishes leap. These are the icons of people who live in the plains: images of coolness, freedom and power.

The children are so quiet that she wonders if they are sick from the winding road, a pattern of hairpin turns. But as she is about to ask them if they need to stop, she sees around a broad curve the green-and-white flag of the border post, and then, clustered against the steep hillside, three or four freshly-whitewashed offices and sheds, their paths lined with blossoming spring bulbs. It's an Englishman's idea of a hostile border, she thinks. Not a soldier in sight except the one posted ceremonially at the flag. But behind them, all along the twisting road, she had been aware of stone lookouts, of deceptively empty-looking fortresses and parade grounds.

She parks at the side of the road and climbs the neat stone path to the bungalow marked Customs. She has never done this before: Iqbal has always been in charge of such things. She takes Timmy with her for moral support.

"Three passports here. Third passenger?" The official is polite but indifferent. American passports do not excite attention; Americans are tourists, not smugglers or fugitives.

"That's my other son. He's not feeling well, he's in the car."

"I will have to see the car." He is studying Anne's passport photograph. It is three years old and was flattering even then. "Chai pienge?" He motions to a coolie lounging by the door. "You will take a cup of tea?"

"No, thank you. We're rather in a hurry. I want to be in Jallalabad by dark."

He looks at her again. "You have a Muslim name, Memsahib."

"Yes, my husband is Pakistani."

"How does he permit you to travel unattended? Quite unsafe for ladies to travel unattended in the Tribal Area." He is annoyed. "You should have a servant."

"Oh, we'll be met at the border," she lies. "There was a . . . There was a death in the family."

His hauteur disappears. Death explains anything. "Your mummy or daddy?" he asks kindly, murmuring the prescribed blessing on the soul of the dead.

She is lost for a moment. "No, my husband's mummy," she says. Timmy's eyes are on her, watching the ease with which she lies.

"*He* is not coming?" The customs official is offended to the heart.

"Oh, he went ahead by plane." Yes, that is what he would do.

The customs man walks with her down the path to compare the description and identification numbers with those on the carnet. Following behind Timmy, he riffles the boy's light hair. "He is very fair. He looks like you, yes?"

Anne wonders how well he has taken in the image of Sheriyar on the third passport. Snapped on his tenth birthday, it shows him round-cheeked, laughing, his dark skin glowing—one of those plump, rosy children of Punjabi motion pictures, where the chief aesthetic is abundance and the sleek, round bodies that personify it. She has told Masood to keep his eyes closed and to stay under the blanket in the back seat, but the Triumph is too narrow for his long body and he is jackknifed like a grasshopper, his bright curls pressed against the sunny window.

"Sheriyar?" The customs man speaks gently, reaching through the front window to touch the boy's shoulder. "Sheriyar?" He makes music of the long vowels, pronouncing the name as Anne has never been able.

"Ji?" the boy responds, opening his wonderful eyes.

"Teek-tock?" asks the man. "Are you all right, baccha?"

"Teek-tock, officer-sahib," the boy affirms, and closes his eyes again.

"Thank you very much, Mukhtar-sahib," Anne says, remembering the name plate on his table. If he would only move away from the door so she could get in.

Mukhtar-sahib returns her documents. "You don't worry about him," he says, indicating with a motion of his head the boy in the back seat. "He'll be first-class when he sees his father." As she starts the motor he adds, "Very tall boy for ten years old, Ma'sh'Allah."

"My husband is very tall," Anne says, waving to him as she drives out of the manicured oasis into the barbed-wired-and rock-lined corridor of no-man's-land and the Kingdom of Afghanistan.

Here everything is different. She follows the sign marked Customs into a dingy shed full of people—mostly hippies of various nationalities—who are apparently being detained and have been allowed this place as a caravanserai or flophouse. Some few have chairs or benches, but the majority have made themselves as comfortable as they can on the cement floor, their goods about them. The air is heavy with tobacco, hashish, and cooking charcoal. Near the door a young blonde girl in a dirty sari is preparing a makeshift meal for herself and the dreamy-looking boy beside her. The room is peculiarly silent. Anne can't bring herself to ask for directions, but stumbles on to the next building, where a few dishevelled men in gray uniforms sit under bare light bulbs at tables strewn with teacups and official forms. Someone takes her passports and stamps them without even looking at her. It is clear that no one has the least interest in the identity of three American tourists who carry no threat of becoming a public charge.

The automobile is another matter. Anne waits for more than an hour while various officials debate among themselves the means of preventing her from taking the little yellow car into Kabul and selling it for an exhorbitant sum to a tribal malik without the government's receiving its proper tax. She cannot understand a word, but she knows that is what they are saying because every now and then one of them will snatch up the carnet and storm out to study the car again, as if its smooth yellow body contains the answer to their dilemma. She does not try to interfere, partly because she cannot imagine any way of being effective. So she sits quietly, grateful she has a chair when others, waiting as long, are still standing. The room smells of sour milk and dust. At length they give her several forms to sign—there is no English translation, she could be pledging anything—stamp her papers, and indicate that she is free to go, required to return within fourteen days to this same border crossing.

"Did they make trouble about me?" Masood asks when they are on their way again.

"Only about the car," she says. "It wouldn't matter except I didn't want to be on this road after dark."

"Why did we have to come?" Timmy's voice is so low she can't tell whether he is being sullen or is about to cry.

"Because Masood's mother wants him to go to America, where he can have a better life, and his father won't let him go." Neither of them says anything. "We're only driving him across the border, Timmy. His mother will get to Kabul tomorrow and you and I will have fun and see everything and buy presents for Daddy and Sher. Maybe we'll buy Sher a rifle. Would you like that?"

"Does Daddy know what we're doing?"

"Not yet. I didn't want him to have to lie or be embarrassed if Masood's father should get in touch with him or anything. But we'll tell him everything when we get home. He knows how unhappy Masood has been, Timmy." She is almost pleading.

Masood *has* been unhappy since the divorce. Or—Anne corrects herself—since Libby left her husband's house; it is not clear even now if Anwer ever divorced her. Though certainly he has taken a second wife, a girl of eighteen with a reputation as a folk singer, who came from a tribe of gypsies. He did so, Libby told Anne at the time, because the girl's father planned to marry her off to a rich old landowner who would lock her up and never let her sing again.

Libby said it as though she believed Anwer was just doing the girl a favor at the expense of no one. Libby, after all, would be the senior wife, dominant in her household: the mother of Anwer's son. Why should she mind fixing up a small room at the back of the house for another needy woman? Iqbal's comment was that Libby couldn't get malaria without claiming she'd done it on purpose for the sake of the hallucinations. He doesn't care for Libby: he says she is a stereotypical willful American woman who reflects badly on others, like Anne, who are so different.

Anne's feelings have always been mixed: she admires Libby's courage and zest, deplores her taste for dubious adventures, and sometimes, sheepishly and in private, pities her. Libby would not stand for pity, but it is pity nonetheless that brings Anne today to this desolate road: she cannot imagine a worse privation than the loss of a child.

Once Libby finally left Anwer she had no way of caring for a child. Apparently she never thought of going home then because the first year alone she went through half a dozen jobs ranging from handling up-country tours for a travel agency to acting as liaison for an Italian motion picture company. She left each of them in a mysterious flurry. Iqbal maintained it was always trouble with men, but Anne saw only how brave and uncomplaining she was, that when she could, she would swoop in on Sunday and carry Masood off to the beach, or to picnic where Metrovista was filming out near the blue ruins of Thatta.

How different this journey would be if Libby were here now. She would already have picked out a local guide from among the tribesmen they'd passed walking along the road, and by the time they reached Jallalabad tonight, they would have known all the lore of these barren passes through which Anne and the children are blindly driving—these undifferentiated peaks and strange wildflowers and seasonal rivers they will never have names for. The Afghan might have taken them to his village for a meal; he might have fallen in love with her—all the things Anne would never risk, she whose most passionate desire this deepening twilight is to reach Jallalabad in safety.

"Can you change a tire, Masood?"

"I don't know, Auntie. Abu doesn't keep a car."

"I know how," Timmy snaps. "I've helped Fazal Dad a million times."

"Don't be cross, Timmy. We won't get a flat. The road's fine. This is the one the Americans built. It goes all the way to Kabul. The Russians are building another one, from Kabul to the Russian border."

"Why would they want to?" Timmy says, peering out at the bleak dun-and-gray moonscape, the sheer black rocks.

"Is Ammi—is my mother—really coming for me?" Masood asks.

"Of course she is. Look at all the trouble she's gone to, just to get you here." All the trouble I've gone to, Anne thinks.

"What will happen to Yasmin?"

Yasmin. It is unfair that Anne should have to explain to him about Yasmin. There is something altogether wrong with Yasmin's being left behind, in spite of any explanation. "Your mother thought it would be impossible to take you both at one time, that your father would be suspicious if she tried."

Masood is silent.

"She can come back for Yasmin. She has the right to Yasmin until she's twelve, you know."

"Ji, Auntie," he says politely.

"Yasmin's so little, Masood. Your mother says Yasmin hardly even remembers her, that she's very fond of Bano and Bano is very kind to her. Isn't that so?" She stumbles over some of the words.

"Ji, Aunti," Masood says slowly. "Yasmin's very clever. When Bano comes in from the bazaar or the recording studio, Yasmin will be waiting for her, to press her feet. She knows Bano likes that."

Timmy sniffs loudly like an outraged old woman.

"Yasmin is very strong-headed for a little girl," he goes on. "After Ammi went away I would cry sometimes in the night, but Yasmin never cried even though she was only three. She would come to my room and press me until I fell asleep. I would pretend Ammi had come back, that the glass bangles were hers, not Yasmin's."

"Someday she'll come to America too," Anne says.

"No, she won't, Aunti. Ammi doesn't like her."

"I'm sure you're wrong, Masood. Mothers always love their children."

"She doesn't like Yasmin because she's dark. She says Yasmin can be Bano's child."

Anne has no answer to such enormity. She wonders if what he says is true. Perhaps Libby blames the child for Anwer's disaffection—she was carrying Yasmin when Anwer met Bano. Or has it to do with the Cleveland grandmother? Anne knows she deplored Anwer as much for his color as for his presumed calculations about Libby's eventual inheritance. After the marriage she had nothing to do with her daughter until Libby sent a photograph of Masood as a blonde curly-haired infant; her mother responded with tickets for a summer visit home. And after that there were regular gifts, carefully chosen not to constitute support or be convertible to cash. The Christmas Libby finally left Anwer, her mother had sent Masood—air mail from F.A.O. Schwarz—a full-sized bubble gum machine that would dispense its gumballs only after insertion of a U.S. penny. The customs duty equalled a week of Anwer's pay. There was no gift for Yasmin.

"Yasmin can't go because she's black," Masood says, his voice almost a whisper.

"So are you!" Timmy says.

"I am not!"

238

"Inside you are. Your father is!"

"So is yours!"

"I never said he wasn't!" Timmy is heaving, sobbing with rage.

"Stop it, both of you. I can't drive if you go on this way. Please, let's just get to Jallalabad, we'll have tikka kebabs and nice hot baths and everything will be all right. *Please.*"

They subside into angry silence, each withdrawing into a shadowed corner. And huddled apart that way they drive one last dark hour before Anne sees in the distance the smoky yellow light of Jallalabad.

"Now we could walk," she whispers to herself—hollow relief, for she has no idea how to find the hotel beyond its name and a vague location at the western edge of the city. But after the bleak and menacing passes even this strange city seems hospitable.

Her comfort is brief. Somewhere she has taken a false turn and the hard-surfaced road dwindles into a rutted city street with little shops pressing in at either side. Some are shuttered and dark, some lighted by a single dangling bulb or a sputtering acetylene lantern that throws grotesque dancing shadows over the car. There are no women anywhere.

Finally, they reach the intersection of a broad well-surfaced street. At one corner, like a warrant of welcome, is a large plateglass window crowded with giant scarlet geraniums, their heavy foliage pressed against the sweating glass like something tropical. It must be a restaurant, with great brass hamams of tea and boiling water. She yearns for the warmth and light.

The boys are awake now, silent and alert, searching with her for the column of street lights that will indicate a main thoroughfare. But when they find it, all the traffic is coming towards them. They can read nothing now, and there are no international symbols to reassure her that the road is two-way until, finally, far ahead, Timmy sees two donkey carts jogging along as they are, toward the north and west.

But it reminds her that all the great movements were in the opposite direction, since Babur made his first encampment here. Jallalabad has always been a staging platform, where tribes and armies paused to collect themselves for the assault on the subcontinent. Like tonight's traffic, they came from the north and west. Anne and the children are following the path of the defeated, of broken units withdrawing through the passes to their powdery steppes to renew themselves; north to the thinner air and sparse food, water so cold it hurts your teeth.

She feels soft and unequal to anything, even, now that they have finally found it, to going into this sprawling hotel to ask for rooms. In spite of a few scattered lights visible through the windows, it has the look of having been abandoned long ago. Since she came to Pakistan, Anne has never until last night gone into a hotel alone. She feels vulnerable, obliquely ashamed, as though she is doing something immoral.

The desk-clerk is slack and vague, with a stubble of beard and only rudimentary English, and the neon-lit lobby is dim with settled dust, but they have plenty of vacant rooms. She takes two, intending to put the boys together and have a room to herself for once. But Timmy, who is carrying her overnight case as well as his own green PIA flight bag, goes straight to the double room and defiantly drops them both on the huge hard bed. After a minute she hands Masood the two paper bags with the clothes he arrived in and the toilet articles she bought him in Peshawar, and lets him go to the small room across the hall. She doesn't feel up to a quarrel and she doesn't really want to be alone.

The water in the tap is tepid and brown and they dry their hands and faces on the edge of the bedsheet because there are no towels, but they are grateful to be here. It is with a certain weary peace that they go down to the dining room off the lobby.

They are alone in the domed cavernous room though there is evidence—a greasy teacup, a still-shiny turmeric stain on the cloth of the adjacent table—that someone was here earlier. Only a few tables are set up for dining, the rest are pushed against the walls with their chairs upended on them so that in the stark central light they cast shadows like giant spiders. Anne wonders what the season is in Jallalabad. It is hard to imagine that the bitter, dry winter would be pleasanter than this dusty spring, but she has the vague recollection that in some earlier time this was the winter capital of the Afghan royal house.

She orders the simplest of local food. The old waiter brings them grilled chunks of stringy mutton and flat rounds of bread. They split the bread and fill it with meat and onion and minted yogurt, and eat with their hands. The boys drink warm Coke and Anne tiny pots of pink Kashmiri tea from a mended porcelain cup. She tries to make conversation but her voice echoes mockingly in the domed room and the boys answer her in polite monosyllables.

Afterwards they are all too restless to go up to bed, so they retrieve their heavy sweaters and the plaid blanket from the car and set out to walk the cramps from their bodies in the garden they had seen through the dining room windows.

They reach it at the end of a winding cinder path, a stark geometrical park of dusty grass surrounded by brambly rose-trees just beginning to leaf out; in the darkness they look like the barbed-wire netting of no-man's-land. Beyond is a denser thicket of gray twisting branches that will in summer be a grape arbor. Timmy has seen something white in the distance—perhaps the reflection of the moon in an ornamental pool—and sets off with Masood in search of it. Their high-pitched voices are muffled and distorted in the vast emptiness. They seem to have patched up their quarrel in the subterranean way of children, without speaking of it again.

Anne doubles up the blanket and makes herself a seat at the center of the lawn, thinking this is where the sun-dial would be if the British had come this far. But of course they did, two or three times. She remembers an old etching of a lone man—Dr. Brydon it was—coming into Jallalabad slung over the back of his pony, the only survivor of his garrison. He had been ambushed again and again in the narrow passes, the river gorge between here and Kabul.

After a while she unfolds the blanket and lies back, gazing up at the immense indigo bowl of sky; the stars seem farther away than ever, though their pattern has never been so clear. The lemon-colored gibbous moon is halfway to the horizon, pierced by the bare branches of a cottonwood tree. The children's voices drift back intermittently like waves of ground fog. Anne occupies herself with the physical world as though it were a mantra: the black dome of sky, the circle of thorns around her resting place, the crisp, bittersweet odor of a nearby citrus grove in early blossom. But dark thoughts crowd back on her like bats that have lost their bearings and press in, brushing with agitated wings the very thing that is driving them away.

Far to the south Sheriyar is going to sleep. He has finished his schoolwork, and visited the stables to see his gray pony before

241

going to bed. His golden labrador sleeps next to him on the scarlet silk quilt, having outlasted the objections of the old ayah that the touch of dog is dirty and un-Islamic. The room is clear in every detail, down to the glass of water on the bedside table with its crocheted dust-cover weighted down by blue beads. But she cannot see Sher's face, only a dark shadow against the pillow, as it was the night she left him. She feels a terrible thrill of love for him, but it imposes itself like a portent, the love you feel for something you are losing.

"But I've lost nothing," her rational mind says. Anne says it aloud, for reassurance. Iqbal will be angry, she can admit that now. Not because he thinks Masood should have been left where he was, or that Libby could ever have obtained his custody by reason or recourse to law, but because it was Anne who lied and plotted, who exposed her husband as someone who is not in control of his wife. She has shown him that she is more than the mild, agreeable woman he trusts as simply as if she were a native woman. That she is capable of acting by stealth, reckoning for herself the hazards. It will be a long time before Iqbal sees her in the old way again.

But perhaps there will be no reckoning, no public acknowledgement of Anne's part in this. Libby is sure Anwer will do nothing, once the boy is irretrievably beyond his reach; anything else would be a public display of impotence. "Like announcing you've been cuckolded," Libby said. Anne will be able to explain everything to Iqbal first. It will be weeks before the whole story is known, if it ever is. Masood traveled from Karachi on a variant of his name, itself as common as sand; he never technically crossed the border at all—the passport Libby brings tomorrow will register neither exit or entry. And that kind border official, if he ever comes to recognize his error, will lie to save himself.

But it will not come to that. In this place events do not flow to such clearly defined conclusions. The habit of mind is not toward sharp discriminations or clear assessments of gain or loss, except where honor is at stake. There only the drift of things, a narrowing or broadening of possibility. As the country roads are at one place smooth and substantial, laid over a deep bed of crushed stone, but further on may dwindle to the width of a single vehicle or disappear altogether at the foothills or the edge of the desert, only to emerge a hundred miles beyond as mysteriously as a river gone underground. This is a country of few crossroads; nothing here happens once and for all time.

But as these thoughts pass through her mind, the threading of a maze to some eventual conclusion, the deeper part of Anne's consciousness holds a single, still image: the grave face of her elder son, his full lips and heavy-lidded eyes framed by the tall cerise-and-gold turban he wore at the great dinner to celebrate his circumcision. The image is like a miniature in an oval frame, confined and complete, never to be altered. Anne shivers, not entirely from the cold, and calls the children in to bed.

They are subdued when they return, and for the first time since Peshawar seem kindly disposed toward one another. At Masood's room she unlocks the door and goes in to check the blankets and the light by his bed. As she turns to go, she thinks how confused he must be as he goes to sleep tonight, and impulsively kisses him in promise of something she has not defined. Then Timmy, with a little low howl, hurls himself at Masood in a clumsy embrace, and bolts to the hall. Masood turns his back. Anne knows he is crying but she has no words to help him.

She makes Timmy brush his teeth and tucks him in pajamas and clean socks into his side of the broad bed. Then she takes the flask of Murree gin from her overnight bag and makes herself a weak gin-and-water. She switches out the light and puts on her flannel nightgown, drawing the plaid blanket around her like a cloak as she stands at the window with her drink, looking out at the pale lawn and the black sky with its bleak field of stars.

The wind is coming up. It tears at the shutters, shifting the loose panels. The dry wood rubbing together makes a sound like crying.

"She tried to get Sheriyar to do this," Timmy says. Anne looks back and sees that his eyes are wide open, he is staring up at the ceiling. She puts her drink on the sill and goes over to sit next to him. He doesn't make room for her.

"What do you mean, Timmy?"

"When they were in Lahore at Easter she tried to get Sheriyar to take Masood across the desert to India. She said Fazal Dad would do it if Sher gave the order. She said she'd give Sher her watch, the one with all the dials the pilot gave her."

"Why didn't you tell me?"

"We didn't think you'd be so dumb." He is crying now.

They didn't think she'd be so dumb. . . . So they had discussed it, Sher and Timmy, had speculated about this journey to Afghanistan, but had decided she couldn't be so dumb as not to know what sort of woman Libby is. That she can't be trusted, that she is capable of sending two little boys and a half-baked driver out into a desert full of border patrols, two irritable armies facing each other in terrain with no clear line of demarcation.

Even if they made it past the pickets, what reception would they have found in India? Libby might have arranged for Masood, but what about Sher and Fazal Dad, who would still have had the journey back? Every month there are reports of villagers who stray too near the border and are shot; the military says they are smuggling gold or grain.

"They could have been shot," she says.

"Yeah."

She tries to put her arms around him, but he has rolled himself into a ball, rigid and sealed against her. Now she understands what his tight little body has been showing her for two days, that he no longer trusts the perfect wisdom and benevolence of mothers.

Sher could be dead. Anne sees in her mind's eye the jeep bounding breakneck over the dunes. Fazal Dad keening tribal songs at the top of his lungs. She knows he takes bhang. He would have done whatever Sher asked. Twice last winter he took Sher deep into the Thar in search of antelope. He would make no distinctions. At least once, he had let Sher urge him within sight of Bikaner State. . . . Iqbal had threatened to sack him.

"But it didn't happen," she says, as much to herself as Timmy. "And tomorrow everything will be over. Libby will meet us in Kabul, and—"

"She won't come. Masood says she won't. She's got some man. She won't come, and we'll never be able to go back." He is sobbing hard, silently except for an occasional hiccough. "It's your fault, you took him. You took him instead of Sheriyar."

She lies on the bed holding the rigid little form, as though there were a windstorm or some other violence of nature against which she can shield him only with her body. She will not think of what he is saying now. Masood has to be wrong. Libby is wayward but she is not evil: she will turn up tomorrow, or the day after or the day after that, getting off the plane in her proprietary way with the pilot carrying her bag. The bag will be filled with clean, warm clothes for Masood and clever gifts for her family in America. . . .

But for Anne there is still the journey. Timmy is asleep now, and she disengages herself from him and goes back to her place at the window. The wind tonight is full of rain. The road through the Gorge tomorrow will be narrow and slippery, the sky only a thin, gray ribbon a thousand stony feet above them. She feels it now, the damp shale walls of the chasm pressing in on the small yellow car, the two sun-haired children, herself in her inappropriate summer dress.

She will go through the Gorge tomorrow because . . . because she gave her word, because they have come so far already and there is no easy way to turn back. Because in her heart she believes, she thinks she believes, that Libby will come.

Anne pours herself another gin and climbs into bed, under the thin coarse blanket that smells of dust and hashish. If Libby doesn't come, what will she do here in this alien place with someone else's child, with false papers, a handful of traveler's checks and one suitcase and no one to turn to?

With an angry husband too far away for explanations, a man whose pride has been humbled. What would Iqbal do if Anwer went to him, made it a point of honor between men? He has Sher, the eldest son, the one who looks like the portrait of his grandfather. Is he capable of abandoning her to the limbo she has made for herself, of leaving her to drift here until she finds her way back to her own people, the alien woman with her light-eyed son. Is that what Timmy thinks?

She lies in the dark listening to his deep breathing, interrupted now and then in sleep by a small reflexive sob. There is no hope or purpose in these speculations and she puts them away from her, and makes a conscious effort to empty her mind, to concentrate on natural things, the steady beat of her heart, the susurration of their two breaths.

After a time she is aware that her breathing has regulated itself to match his. She listens to the soft animal noises with which he lets himself drift into a deeper slumber where there are no sobs. She too is calmer but no nearer sleep. The deepest part of her is straining for an impossible certainty: that she will hear again those basal rhythms of the soft dark child she left behind.

♨ ♨ ♨

THE GALA
COCKTAIL PARTY

fiction by GILBERT SORRENTINO

from NORTH POINT PRESS and SUN & MOON PRESS

nominated by SUN & MOON PRESS *and David Wilk*

PAIN, THE SAGACIOUS DR. BONE WAS SAYING, flits through my sensibilities, accompanied by no small modicum of embarrassment, since it is my tortured yet stern duty to inform you, my dear Gavottes, that Dr. Poncho, embroiled as he needs must be in administrative tasks, will not be able to greet you tonight. He will, however, see you tomorrow, and lay, as the hep phrase runs, some heavy sounds on you. In the meantime, I have, with Dr. Poncho's blessing, arranged a small yet gay, if not gala, cocktail party for you, at which you may meet some of our most distinguished administrators and faculty. Shall we repair to the Dan'l Boone Room?

Thus saying, they . . . and so forth.

And there they were! What cascades of academic glitter! What a fine madness of the intelligentsia! What milling and wheedling! The wonderful persons circulated and chatted, drank and staggered, consumed "dip" (whatever that may be), and the like festive routine. Sing, Muse, of this catalogue of shits!

There came Brenda Fatigue, Regius Professor of Office Fashion; Ed Flue, Associate Professor of Logging; Burnside Marconi, Instructor in Televiewing; Syrup Concoct, Poet-in-Residence; Benjamin Manila, Chairman of the Stationery Department; G. Root Garbage, Counselor in Venereal Diseases; Jedediah Mange, Vice-President for Member Development; Winifred Zinnia, Corsetiere for Rector of the College; Socks O'Reilly, Chief of Tension Calisthenics; Marcus Podium, Ellsworth Harelip Professor of Speech and Drama; Heinz Pogrom, Horst Wessel Professor of German Philosophy; Gladys Bung, Dietary Tactician; Fifi Galleon, Instructor in French Jobs; Catherine Thigh, Director of Sexual Services; Nicholas Syph, Bureaucracy Professor Emeritus; Yvette Risque, Associate Professor of Auto-Erotism; Francis-Xavier Silhouette, S. J., Chaplain; Pedro Manteca, Professor of Fast Food Studies; Chastity Peep, Instructor in Vaginal History; Angelo Bordello, Disciplinary Dean of Women; Manatee Brouillard, Connecticut Professor of Fertilizer Studies; Idyott Dymwytte-Pyth, Instructor in Ur-Critique; Rastus X. Feets, Professor of Black English.

And circulating, smiling, chatting, laughing, the Gavottes moved as if . . . as if . . . in a dream!

"Alas! One acknowledges, sadly, sadly, that ladies' intimate garments are unattractive in direct proportion to their comfort."

"The sturdy old oak, falling heavily, crashed spang through the dorm windows, whereupon a cloud of flies rose up, buzzing in terror and chagrin."

"The first television 'sighting' took place in Dublin in 1904, when one Francis Aloysius McGlynn dropped his transistor radio and a little man, holding a bar of lemony soap, crawled painfully from the wreckage."

"Night is/and life is/what means/means be life."

"After being dated and stamped, then stamped and dated, the incoming mail is sent to the Dating-Stamping clerk."

"You've got your basic buboes, your running chancre, your clapperoo sacred and profane, your gleet malaise, your Spanish pox."

"Caught the lad in the act of self-gratification, so the benighted Scoutmaster stripped him of his Personal Health Merit Badge."

"I'm most proud, I think, of the fact that General Champagne, while dictating the peace terms, was marvelously trig in my featherweight foundation in ecru with black nylon-lace panels."

"The old Army dozen cures your basic born-again Christian in about three or four weeks."

"Duh perfeck eckshershize izh: 'Hash dow sheen budda bride lilygrow?' "

"Some uff mein goot Chewish frents from zuh fordies seem to haff . . .disappeared!"

"The fatback is then gently sauteed in two ounces of King Kong and a quarter-cup of oleo."

"It is permissible, even salutary, for the modern woman to fantasize a touch of sodomy with the office boy while in lawful embrace with her spouse."

"When the boys returned, simply *mad* for some clean, blond, smiling American poon, what was this once-great nation's inadequate response?"

"The truly efficient office should be able to complicate *everything* in just under six months, taking into account, of course, the zeal of the staff."

"With the skirt discreetly lifted to the upper portion of the lower limbs, and the underpants crisply rolled to that point at which said lower limbs are jointed, the clitoris may be surreptitiously massaged while dining, at the theater, or even in the office."

"I also serve who only blandly prate."

"We have almost achieved a breakthrough in the instant wiener."

"The vagina, long since accepted as reality in Mesopotamia, was first observed beyond that state's borders in the fourth millennium."

"I take absolutely no pleasure in chastising these remarkably lovely, luscious, desirable, nubile, and altogether terrific young women."

"We actually had to turn a thousand people away the evening Shecky Green gave a dramatic reading from *October Light*."

"The progression is crystal clear: Joyce, Beckett, Costain, Jong."

"When ah be's gwine, ah be's gwine to Jericho!"

". . . invented by a gay Presbyterian minister—pantyhose, I mean."

"No tenure *yet*, though I am known everywhere as Johnny Acorn!"

"I entered and saw Mrs. Marconi in the most *extraordinary* position."

"They/v himper."

"I don't exactly know what an 'envelope' *is*."

"The affected member is plunged into warm Pepsi."

"Putting it into a honeydew is also recommended."

"The new gym shorts offer just a wisp of gentle control."

"Leaping high into the air, you intertwine the index fingers."

"Yethhir! That'th mah baby!"

"So've burned der files."

"After four in the afternoon, the supple birch switch is best."

"Who dreamt that the dead salmon would grow into a lusty azalea?"

"The walking-stick is always a symbol for a specific Western angst."

"The baddest dude be's Gentian Washington."

". . . the *cruel* corset? Cruel? . . ."

". . . lifts his meaty hands to prey . . ."

". . . during the commercial break, large amphibians . . ."

". . . cer/tain/ly . . ."

". . . the tongue, now crisscrossed by small paper cuts . . ."

". . . the vast warehouse, filled with impounded toilet seats . . ."

". . . *bursting* through his BVD's, it . . ."

". . . her lacings, whipping through the air, caught the Monsignor . . ."

". . . now, the full bosom, during the eight-count pushup . . ."

". . . wit duh lipz inna shmirk . . ."

". . . undt vhen der rosy dawn lighted up Auschwitz . . ."

". . . the hamburger, partially rotted in the soil . . ."

". . . Havelock Ellis, delirious in the ladies' room . . ."

". . . even the most modest will lift her skirts if . . ."

". . . having typed it on green tissue instead of light blue . . ."

". . . the role of the pleated skirt in spontaneous orgasm implies . . ."

". . . in baseball cap and cassock, I often wander through . . ."

". . . the tuna is tossed with tiny marshmallows . . ."

". . . imagine Danae's surprise when all this gold . . ."

". . . while one young lady is spanked, another sometimes . . ."

". . . the piccadills and stoccadoes, well irrigated . . ."

"Yes, radishes! Skewered along with soybean balls and okra."

"The beautiful poems of Miss Flambeaux have saved many marriages."

"Yes, my famous 'Tuesdays' *are* booked months in advance."

"If it calls for eight copies, make twelve."

"The woman then places her ankles alongside her ears."

"In Indianapolis, God's hand is everywhere seen."

"What precisely is 'bread?' "

"Recent studies suggest that men who wear athletic supporters suffer from vagina envy."

". . . herring-motif in Malamud's juvenilia . . ."

". . . Dean Bordello an' me, man, we be's whoppin' an' whompin' on . . ."

". . . curious linguistic apparatus that often in disciplines that favor a particular array of the marvelous stretchiness of that postwar if you do understand a latex well can it be a swell campus support for what? is that the various social services or can it be a kind of utter lovely parameter when just a tiny bit of although they are a kind of 'fingers' if that's the specific kind of pastrami did you ever understand for instance what array of the most dedicated Doctorow? Gardner? Styron? often at mass it is in my mind that this campus this hallowed ground this garter belt flushed but it's most tough when in the very middle of the squash surprise a gentle zephyr at the egress of the people from Washington are there skirts just quietly lifting and the marvelous slice of Bermuda that decorates but also wraps the old ribbon in the same cellophane that the unfettered thigh decides to plant itself alongside the beloved peonies that have oft buried a mackerel like the Indians? sure enough into the gym fell a large bag in which the ivy mixed with an odd how shall I say 'novel' that makes one almost dense with flannel and yet not quite tweed although it is in a sense marinated in a cheaper wine your zinfandel your kosinski your screamingly boring onslaughts of what in Algiers? but of course not something for every day they dub it 'dub' is a bitch 'dub' it anyway the maniacal Jung deep in Mein Kampf and dosed up good with what? with what? oh dear sweet Jesus the tailored suit the bull clap because it can give you the tenure that you would suck spit for and knock a bull down on his knees if they have such articles of apparel unknown and not given the respect that ensues in Scranton that city of lost marines and the dry rot in the great nodding elms and if tenure is the guerdon of those who lift skirts and bull trousers and spaghetti soft and mushy the way it be's when they's be's got the lesson plan and the rosy reddened and tingling how shall I say in Tunis in the darkened office around five or so of a winter evening the sound of Marrakech and the soft sobbing as we watch the snap beans and the impeccable white of the knee hose and down there around the ankles is the mimeo machine andhg therzwx wehytu eogghji wh tuouh to thyrhtyyehyheuuhr jo joyk blamdurf oi gurdhujhut uh uh uhh uhhhh uh uh uh uh oooooooohhhh . . ."

Supper, with Dr. Bone, was, the doctor being the soul of genial warmth, a small yet festive occasion of genial warmth. They looked forward to the morrow with benign alacrity. Things were certainly looking "up."

Well, sweat-face, Blue said to Helene. Things are "looking" up! He seemed almost . . . happy!

OVER THE MOUNTAIN

fiction by GAIL GODWIN

from ANTAEUS

nominated by Marilyn Krysl and Richard Smith

If YOU HAVE GROWN TO LOVE YOUR LIFE, it seems ungrateful to belabor old injustices, especially those that happened in childhood, that place of sheltered perspectives where you were likely to wake up and go to bed without anyone ever disabusing you of your certainty that all days were planned around you. After all, isn't it possible that the very betrayal that flags your memory and constricts your heart led to a development in character that enabled you to forge your present life?

This is not a belaboring. I know by now that behind every story that begins "When I was a child" there exists another story in which adults are fighting for their lives. It is because I accept this that I am ready to go back and fill in some of the blank spaces in the world of a ten-year-old girl whose mother takes her on an overnight train journey. The train carries them out of their sheltered mountains to a town some thousand feet below. The mother and daughter walk around this town, whose main attraction is that the mother spent her happy girlhood years there. The mother and her little girl stay the night in a respectable boarding house. The next day, they get on the northbound version of yesterday's train and go back to the mountains.

Why do I remember nothing particular about that journey? I, with my usually prodigious memory for details? Except for a quality of light and atmosphere—the lowland town throbbed with a sociable, golden-yellow heat that made people seem closer, whereas our mountain town had a cool, separating blue air that magnified distances—I have no personal images of this important twenty-four hours. I say important because it was a landmark in my life: it was the first time I had gone away alone with my mother.

252

Despite the fact that I believe I now know why that excursion lies blank among my memory cells, there is something worth exploring here. The feeling attached to that event, even today, signals the kind of buried affect that shapes a life.

We were not, our little unit of three, your ordinary "nuclear" family, but, as I had known nothing else, we seemed normal enough to me. Our living arrangements were somewhat strange for a trio of females with high conceptions of their privileges in society, but, as my grandmother hastened to tell people, it was because of the war. And when the war ended, and all the military personnel who had preempted the desirable dwellings had departed from town, and we continued to stay where we were, I accepted my mother's and grandmother's continual reminders that "it was only a matter of time now until the right place could be found."

The three of us slept in one gigantic room, vast enough to swallow the two full-sized Persian carpets that had once covered my grandmother's former living room and dining room and still reproach us with its lonely space, even when we filled it with all the furniture from the two bedrooms of her previous home. The rest of her furniture crowded our tiny living room and dark, windowless kitchen and then spilled out into the shabby public entrance hall of our building, euphemistically called "the lobby" by our landlord and my grandmother. My grandmother spent a lot of time trying to pounce on a tenant in the act of sitting on "our" sofa in the lobby, or winding up "our" old Victrola. She would rush out of our apartment like a fury and explain haughtily that this furniture did not belong to the lobby, it was our furniture, only biding its time in this limbo until it could be resettled into the sort of room to which it was accustomed. She actually told one woman, whom she caught smoking while sitting on "our" sofa, to please "consider this furniture invisible in the future." The woman ground out her cigarette on the floor, told my grandmother she was crazy, and went upstairs.

Our building was still known in town by its old name: The Piping Hot. During the twenties, when Asheville overflowed with land-boom speculators and relatives visiting TB patients, this brown-shingled monstrosity had been thrown up on a lot much too small for it. It had come into existence as a commercial establishment whose purpose was to make money on not-too-elegant people willing to settle for a so-so room and a hot "home-cooked"meal. Therefore it had none of those quaint redeeming features of former private residences fallen on hard times. The reason our bedroom was so huge was simple: it had been the dining room.

It was a pure and simple eyesore, our building: coarse, square, and mud-colored, it hulked miserably on its half-acre with the truculent insecurity of a social interloper. It was a building you might feel sorry for if you were not so busy feeling sorrier for yourself for living in it. Probably the reason its construction had been tolerated at all on that leafy, genteel block was because its lot faced the unsightly physical plant of the proud and stately Manor Hotel which rambled atop its generous acreage on the hill across the street; moreover, the guests at the Manor were prevented by their elevation from seeing even the roof of the lowlier establishment. Our landlord had bought Piping Hot when it went out of business just before the war, chopped it up into as many "apartments" as he could get away with legally, and now collected the rents. Whenever he was forced to drop by, breathless and red-faced, a wet cigar clamped in one corner of his mouth, he would assure my grandmother he had every intention of sowing grass in the bare front yard, of having someone come and wash the filthy windows of the lobby, of cutting down the thorny bushes with their suspicious red berries that grew on either side of the squatty, brown-shingled "shelter" at the sidewalk's edge, where Negro maids often sat down to rest on their way to the bus stop from the big houses at the upper end of the street.

The most "respectable" tenants lived on the ground floor, which must have been some consolation to my grandmother. The Catholic widow, Mrs. Gannon, and her two marriageable daughters lived behind us in a rear apartment which had been made over from pantries and half of the old kitchen. (Our kitchen had been carved out of the other half.) When my grandmother or Mrs. Gannon felt like chatting, either had only to tap lightly on the painted-over window above her sink; they would gossip about the upstairs tenants while snapping beans or peeling potatoes at their facing sinks. The apartment across the lobby was inhabited by another widow, the cheerful Mrs. Rhinehart, who went limping off to work in a china shop every day; her numerous windowsills (her apartment was the Piping Hot's ex-sunporch) were crowded with delicate painted figurines. She suffered from a disease that made one leg twice the width of the other. Among the three widows existed a forbearing camaraderie. Mrs. Rhinehart did not like to gossip, but she always stopped and listened pleasantly if my grandmother waylaid her in the lobby; and, though both my grandmother and Mrs. Gannon thought Mrs. Rhinehart had too many little objects in her windows for good taste, they always amended that, at any rate, she was a brave lady for standing in a shop all day on that leg; and when sailors trekked regularly past our side windows on the way to call on the Gannon girls, my grandmother did not allow her imagination to run as wild as she would have if those same sailors had been on their way to one of the apartments upstairs.

Except for the policeman and his wife, whose stormy marital life thudded and crashed directly above our bedroom, the other upstairs apartments were filled with people my grandmother referred to simply as "the transients." They didn't stay long. You would have to be pretty desperate to stay long in those rear upstairs apartments, which were weird amalgams of former guestrooms, opening into hallways or one another in inconvenient, embarrassing ways, their afterthought bathrooms and kitchens rammed into ex-closets and storage rooms. We didn't even bother to learn their names, those constantly changing combinations of women, of women and children and the occasional rare man, who occupied those awkward upper quarters. They were identified merely by their affronts: the two working girls who clopped around most of the night in their high heels; the woman with the little boy who had written the dirty word in chalk on the sidewalk shelter; the woman who sat down on "our" sofa and stomped out her cigarette on the floor.

Those were the politics of our building. There were also, within our family unit, the politics of my mother's job, the politics of my school, and the subtler triangular dynamics that underpinned life in our apartment.

"Today has been too much for my nerves," my grandmother would say as we huddled over her supper at one end of our giant mahogany dining table which, even with its center leaf removed, took up most of the kitchen. "I was out in the lobby trying to wipe some of the layers of dust off those windows when I happened to look out and there was that little boy about to eat some of the

255

berries on those poison bushes. I rushed out to warn him, only to have his mother tell me she didn't want him frightened. Would she rather have him frightened or dead? Then, not five minutes later, the LaFarges' Negro maid came along and sat down in our shelter and I happened to see her hike her dress up and her stockings were crammed with eggs. I had to debate with myself whether I shouldn't let the LaFarges know. . . ."

"I hope you didn't," said my mother, rolling her eyes at me in that special way which my grandmother was not meant to see.

"No. You have to let them get away with murder if you're going to keep them. I remembered that. Do you remember Willy Mae, when we lived in Greenville?"

My mother laughed. Her voice was suddenly younger and she looked less tired. Greenville was the town on the other side of the mountain where, in a former incarnation, she had lived as a happy, protected young girl. But then a thought pinched her forehead, crimping the smoothness between her deep blue eyes. "I do wish that ass Dr. Busey could see through that snake Lu Ann Leach," she said.

"Kathleen. Lower your voice."

My mother gave an exasperated sigh and sent me a signal: We've got to get out of here. After supper we'll go to the drugstore.

"He hasn't said anything about her staying on at the college, has he?" asked my grandmother *sotto voce*, casting her eyes balefully towards the painted-over window above our sink behind which even a good friend like Mrs. Gannon might be straining to hear how other people's daughters were faring in this uncertain world without a man.

"No, but he hasn't said anything about her leaving, and now she's taken over the literary magazine. She was only supposed to fill in for Miss Pennell's operation and Miss Pennell has been back three weeks. The college can't afford to keep all three of us. There aren't that many students taking English. All the GI's want their math and science so they can go out and make *money*."

"Well, they have to keep you," declared my grandmother, drawing herself up regally.

"They don't have to do anything, Mother." My mother was losing her temper.

"What I mean is," murmured my grandmother in a conciliatory manner to ward off a "scene" which might be overheard, "they will naturally want to keep you, because you're the only one with your MA. I'm so thankful that Poppy lived long enough so we could see you through your good education."

"You should see the way she plays up to him," my mother went on, as if she hadn't heard. "She has that plummy, little-girl way of talking, and she asks his *advice* before she'll even go to the bathroom. If she weren't a Leach, people couldn't possibly take her seriously; she couldn't get a job in a kindergarten."

"If only Poppy had lived," moaned my grandmother, "you would never have had to work."

"My work is all I've *got*," blurted my mother passionately. "I mean, besides you two, of course."

"Of course," agreed my grandmother. "I only meant if he had lived. Then we could have had a nice house, and you could have worked if you wanted."

My mother's eyes got round, the way they did when someone had overlooked an important fact. She was on the verge of saying more, but then with an effort of her shoulders harnessed her outburst. She sat with her eyes still rounded, but cast down, breathing rapidly through her nostrils. I thought she looked lovely at such times.

"Can we walk to the drugstore and look at the magazines?" I asked.

"If you like," she said neutrally. But, as soon as my grandmother rose to clear the dishes, she sneaked me a smile.

"The thing is, no matter how much I wipe at those lobby windows from the inside," my grandmother said, as much to herself as to us, "they can never be clean. They need to be washed from the outside by a man. Until they are, we will be forced to look through dirt."

"It was on the tip of my tongue to say, 'If you stay *out* of the lobby you won't have to worry about the dirt,' " my mother told me as we walked to the drugstore a block away.

"That would have been perfect!" I cried, swinging her hand. "Oh, why *didn't* you?" I was a little overexcited, as I always was when the two of us finally made it off by ourselves. Here we were, escaped together at last, like two sisters from an overprotective mother. Yet even as the spring dusk purpled about our retreating figures, we both knew she was watching us from the window: she would be kneeling in the armchair, her left hand balancing her on the windowsill, her right hand discreetly parting the white curtains; she could watch us all the way to our destination. She had left the lights off in the apartment, to follow us better.

"It would have been cruel," my mother said. "That lobby is her outside world."

Though complaining about my grandmother often drew us closer, I could see my mother's point. It was not that we didn't love her; it was that the heaviness of her love confined us. She worried constantly that something would happen to us. She thought up things, described them aloud in detail, which sometimes ended up scaring us all. (The mother of the little boy about to eat the berry had been right.)

We had reached the corner of our block. As we waited for a turning car to go by, we looked up and saw the dining-room lights of the Manor Hotel twinkling at us. The handful of early spring guests would just be sitting down to eat.

I looked up at one of the timbered gables. "There's nobody in Naomi Benjamin's room yet," I said.

"The season will be starting soon. All the rooms will be filled. But never again will I ever write *anybody's* autobiography. Unless I write my own someday."

My mother and grandmother had been so excited last summer when Naomi Benjamin, an older woman from New York who had come to our mountains for her health, offered my mother $500 to "work with her on her autobiography." Someone at the Manor had told Naomi that my mother was a published writer, and she had come down from the hill to call on us at The Piping Hot and make her offer. We were impressed by her stylish clothes and her slow, gloomy way of expressing herself, as if the weight of the world lay behind her carefully chosen words. But, before the end of the summer, my mother was in a rage. Sometimes, after having "worked with" Naomi Benjamin all afternoon, and after typing up the results at night, my mother would lie back and rant while my grandmother applied a cold washcloth to her head and told her she was not too young to get a stroke. "A stroke would be something *happening*," snarled my mother, "whereas not a damn thing has happened to that woman; how dare she aspire to autobiography!" "Well, she is Jewish," reflected my grandmother. "They never have an easy time." "Ha!" spat my mother. "That's what I thought.

I thought I'd learn something interesting about other ways of suffering, but there's not even that. I'd like to tell her to take her five hundred dollars and buy herself some excitement. That's what she really needs." "Kathleen, tension can burst a blood vessel . . ." "I wish to God I could make it up," my mother ranted on, growing more excited, "at least I wouldn't be dying of boredom!" "I'm going to phone her right now," announced my grandmother, taking a new tack; "I'm going to tell her you're too sick to go on." "No, no, no!" My mother sprang up, waving the cold cloth aside. "It's all right. I'm almost finished. Just let me go walk up and down the street for a while and clear my head."

We had reached the drugstore in the middle of the next block, our oasis of freedom. We passed into its brightly lit interior, safe for a time behind brick walls that even my grandmother's ardent vision could not penetrate. Barbara, the pharmacist, was doing double duty behind the soda fountain, but when she looked up and saw it was us she went on wiping the counter; she knew that, despite her sign (THESE MAGAZINES ARE FOR *BUYING*, NOT FOR BROWSING), we would first go and look through the pulp magazines to see if there was any new story by Charlotte Ashe. But we always conducted our business as quickly and unobtrusively as possible, so as not to set a bad example for other customers; we knew it pained Barbara to see her merchandise sinking in value with each browser's fingerprints, even though she admired my mother and was in on the secret that Charlotte Ashe's name had been created from the name of this street and the first half of the name of our town.

There was no new story by Charlotte Ashe. It was quite possible all of them had appeared by now, but my mother did not want to spoil our game. It had been a while since Charlotte Ashe had mailed off a story. During the war, when my mother worked on the newspaper, it had been easier to slip a paragraph or two of fiction into the typewriter on a slow-breaking news day. But now the men had come home, to reclaim their jobs at the newspaper, and fill up the seats in the classroom where my mother taught; there was less time and opportunity to find an hour alone with a typewriter and let one's romantic imagination soar—within the bounds of propriety, of course.

We sat down at the counter. It would not do to make Barbara

wait on us in a booth. She was, for all her gruff tones, the way she pounced on children who tried to read the comic books, the pharmacist. As if to emphasize this to customers who might confuse her with a mere female employee, Barbara wore trousers and neckties and took deep, swinging strides around her store; she even wore men's shoes.

"Kathleen, what'll you have?"

"A Coke, please, Barbara, for each of us. Oh, and would you put a tiny squirt of ammonia in mine? I've got a headache coming on."

"How tiny?" Barbara's large hand with its close-clipped nails hovered over the counter pump that discharged ammonia.

"Well, not too tiny."

Both women laughed. Barbara made our Cokes, giving my mother an indulgent look as she squirted the pump twice over one of the paper cups. All the other customers got glasses if they drank their beverages in the store, but my grandmother had made us promise never to drink from a drugstore glass after she saw an ex-patient of the TB sanatorium drink from one. "Your cups, ladies," said Barbara ironically, setting them ceremoniously before us. She and my mother rolled their eyes at each other. Barbara knew all about the promise; my mother had been forced to tell her after Barbara had once demanded gruffly, "Why can't you all drink out of glasses like everybody else?" But Barbara did not charge us the extra penny for the cups.

We excused ourselves and took our Cokes and adjourned to a booth, where we could have privacy. As there were no other customers, Barbara loped happily back into her rear sanctum of bottles and pills.

At last I had my mother all to myself.

"How was school today?"

"We had field day practice," I said. "Mother Donovan was showing us how to run the three-legged race and she pulled up her habit and she has really nice legs."

"That doesn't surprise me, somehow. She must have had a real vocation, because she's certainly pretty enough to have gotten married. How are you and Lisa getting along?"

"We're friends, but I hate her. I hate her and she fascinates me at the same time. What has she *got* that makes everybody do what she wants?"

"I've told you what she's got, but you always forget."

"Tell me again. I won't forget."

My mother swung her smooth pageboy forward until it half-curtained her face. She peered into the syrupy depths of her spiked Coke and rattled its crushed ice, as if summoning the noisy fragments to speak the secret of Lisa Gudger's popularity. Then, slowly, she raised her face and her beautiful dark blue eyes met mine. I waited, transfixed by our powerful intimacy.

"You are smarter than Lisa Gudger," she began, saying her words slowly. "You have more imagination than Lisa Gudger. And, feature by feature, you are prettier than Lisa Gudger . . ."

I drank in this litany, which I did remember from before.

"But Lisa likes herself better than you like yourself. Whatever Lisa has, she thinks it's best. And this communicates itself to others, and they follow her."

This was the part I always forgot. I was forgetting it again already. I stared hard at my mother's face, I could see myself reflected in the small pupils, contracted from the bright drugstore lights; I watched the movement of her lips, the way one front tooth crossed slightly over the other. The syllables trying to contain the truth about a girl named Lisa Gudger broke into smaller and smaller particles and escaped into the air as I focused on my mother, trying to show her how well I was listening.

I partially covered up by asking, after it was over, "Do you hate Lu Ann Leach the way I hate Lisa?"

"Now that's an interesting question. Now, Lisa Gudger would not have had the imagination to ask that question. I do hate Lu Ann, because she's a real threat; she can steal my job. I hate her because she's safe and smug and has a rich father to take care of her if everything else falls through. But Lu Ann Leach does not fascinate me. If I could afford it, I would feel pity for her. See, I've figured her out. When you've figured someone out, they don't fascinate you anymore. Or at least they don't when you've figured out the kind of thing I figured out about her."

"Oh, what? What have you figured out?"

"Shh." My mother looked around towards Barbara's where-abouts. She leaned forward across our table. "Lu Ann hates men, but she knows how to use them. Her hatred gives her a power over them, because she just doesn't care. But I'd rather be myself,

261

without that power, if it means the only way I can have it is to become like Lu Ann Leach. She's thirty, for God's sake, and she still lives with her parents."

"But you live with your mother."

"That's different."

"How is it different?"

My mother got her evasive look. This dialogue had strayed into channels where she hadn't meant it to. "It's a matter of choice versus necessity," she said, going abstract on me.

"You don't hate men, then?" I could swear I'd heard her say she had: the day she got fired from the newspaper, for instance.

"Of course I don't. They're the other half of the world. *You* don't hate men, do you?" She gave me a concerned look.

I thought of Men. There was the priest at school, Father Lilley, whose black skirts whispered upon the gravel; there was Jovan, our black bus driver; there was Hal the handyman who lived in a basement apartment under the fifth-grade classroom with his old father, who drove the bus on Jovan's day off. There was Don Olson, the sailor I had selected as my favorite out of all those who passed our window on their way to see the Gannon girls; I would lie in wait for him at our middle-bedroom window, by the sewing machine, and he would look in and say, "Hi there, beautiful. I might as well just stop here." Which always made me laugh. One day my grandmother caught me in the act of giving him a long list of things I wanted him to buy me in town. "She's just playing, she doesn't mean it," she cried, rushing forward to the window. But he brought me back every item on the list. And there was my father, who had paid us one surprise visit from Florida. His body shook the floor as he strode through our bedroom to wash his hands in the bathroom. He closed the bathroom door behind him and locked it. My mother made me tell everybody he was my uncle, because she had already told people he had been killed in the war: a lie she justified because, long ago, he had stopped sending money, and because people would hire a war widow before they would a divorced woman. Still, I was rather sorry not to be able to claim him; with his good-looking face and sunburnt ankles (he wore no socks, even with his suit), he was much more glamorous than my friends' dull business fathers.

"Sure. I like men," I told my mother in the booth. I was thinking particularly of Don Olson. The Gannon girls were fools to let him get away.

"Well, good," said my mother wryly, shaking her ice in the paper cup. "I wouldn't want *that* on my conscience. That I'd brought you up to hate men."

As if we had conjured him up by our tolerant allowance of his species, a Man materialized in front of our booth.

"Well looky here what I found," he said, his dark brown eyes dancing familiarly at us.

My mother's face went through an interesting series of changes. "Why, what are *you* doing home?" she asked him.

It was Frank, one of her GI students from the year before, who was always coming by our apartment to get extra help on a term paper, or asking her to read a poem aloud so he could understand it better. Once last year, out of politeness, I had asked him to sign my autograph book; but whereas her other GIs had signed things like "Best of luck from your friend Charles," or "To a sweet girl," Frank had written in a feisty slant: "To the best daughter of my best teacher." His page troubled me, with its insinuating inclusion of himself between my mother and me; also, his handwriting made "daughter" look like "daughtlet." It was like glimpsing myself from a sudden unflattering angle: a "daughtlet." And what did he mean *best* daughter? I was my mother's only daughter. At the end of last spring, when I knew he would be transferring to Georgia Tech, I took a razor and carefully excised his page.

"I can't stay out of these mountains," said Frank, reaching for a chair from a nearby table and fitting it backwards between his legs. Barbara looked out from the window of her pharmacy, but when she saw who it was did not bother to come out.

"I should think it would be nice to get out of them for a change," said my mother.

"Well, what's stopping you?" asked Frank, teetering forward dangerously on two legs of his chair. He rested his chin on the dainty wrought-iron back of the chair and assessed us, like a playful animal looking over a fence.

My mother rolled her eyes, gave her crushed ice a fierce shake, and emptied the last shards into her mouth. They talked on for a few more minutes, my mother asking him neutral questions about his engineering courses, and then she stood up. "We've got to be getting back or Mother will start worrying that we've been kidnapped."

He stood up, too, and walked us to the door with his hands in his pockets. "Want a ride?"

"One block? Don't be silly," said my mother.

He got into a little gray coupe and raced the motor unnecessarily, I thought, and then spoiled half of our walk home by driving slowly along beside us with his lights on.

"I wish we could go off sometime, just by ourselves," I said in the few remaining steps of cool darkness. My grandmother had pulled down the shades and turned on the lamp, and we could see the shadow of the top of her head as she sat listening to the radio in her wing chair.

"Well, maybe we can," said my mother. "Let me think about it some."

We went inside and the three of us scrubbed for bed and the women creamed their faces. I got in bed with my mother, and, across the room, my grandmother put on her chin strap and got into her bed. We heard the policeman coming home; his heavy shoes shook the whole house as he took the stairs two at a time. "He has no consideration," came my grandmother's reproachful voice from the dark. There soon followed their colorful exchange of abuses, the wife's shrieks and the policeman's blows. "It's going too far this time," said my grandmother, "he's going to kill her, I'm going to call the police." "You can't call the police on the police, Mother. Just wait, it'll soon be over." And my mother was right: about this time the sound effects subsided into the steady, accelerated knocking against our ceiling which would soon lead to silence. "If Poppy had lived, we would not be subjected to this," moaned my grandmother. "Even he couldn't keep life out," sighed my mother, and turned her back to me for sleep.

Our trip alone together came to pass. I don't know how my mother talked my grandmother out of going with us. She was a respectful daughter, if often impatient, and would not have hurt my grandmother's feelings for the world. And it would have been so natural for my grandmother to come: she was the only one of us who could ride free. The widow of a railroad man, she could go anywhere she wanted on Southern Railways until the end of her life.

264

But, at any rate, after what I am sure were exhaustive preparations sprinkled with my grandmother's imaginative warnings of all the mishaps that might befall us, we embarked—my mother and I—from Biltmore Train Station south of Asheville. My grandmother surely drove us there in our ten-year-old Oldsmobile, our last relic of prosperity from the days when Poppy lived. I am sure we arrived at the station much too early, and that my grandmother probably cried. Poppy had been working at Biltmore Station when my grandmother met him. His promotions had taken them out of her girlhood mountains to a series of dusty piedmont towns which she had never liked; and now here she was back in the home mountains, in the altitude she loved—but old and without him. My mother and I were going to the first of the towns to which he had been transferred when my mother had been about the age I was now.

I do not remember our leaving from Biltmore Station or our returning to it the next afternoon. That is the strange thing about those twenty-four hours. I have no mental pictures that I can truly claim I inhabited during that timespan. Except for that palpable recollection of the golden heat which I have already described, there are no details. No vivid scenes. No dialogues. I know we stayed in a boarding house, which my grandmother, I am sure, checked out in advance. It is possible that the owner might have been an old acquaintance, some lady fallen on harder times, like ourselves. Was this boarding house in the same neighborhood as the house where my mother had lived? I'm sure we must have walked by that house. After all, wasn't the purpose of our trip— other than going somewhere by ourselves—to pay a pilgrimage to the scene of my mother's happy youth? Did we, then, also walk past her school? It seems likely, but I don't remember. I do have a vague remembrance of "downtown," where, I am sure, we must have walked up and down streets, in and out of stores, perhaps buying something, some small thing that I wanted; I am sure we must have stopped in some drugstore and bought two Cokes in paper cups.

Did the town still have streetcars running on tracks, jangling their bells; or was it that my mother described them so well, the streetcars that she used to ride when she lived there as a girl?

I do not know.

We must have eaten at least three meals, perhaps four, but I don't remember eating them.

We must have slept in the same bed. Even if there had been two beds in the room, I would, sooner or later, have crawled in with my mother. I always slept with her.

My amnesia comes to a stunning halt the moment the trip is over. My grandmother has picked us up from Biltmore Station and there I am, on Charlotte Street again, in the bedroom *née* dining room of the old Piping Hot.

It is late afternoon. The sun is still shining, but the blue atmosphere of our mountains has begun to gather. The predominant color of this memory is blue. I am alone in the bedroom, lying catty-cornered across the bed with my head at the foot; I am looking out the window next to the one where I always used to lie in wait for the sailor, Don Olson, on his way to call on the Gannon girls. The bedspread on which I am lying is blue, a light blue, with a raised circular pattern in white; it smells clean. Everything in this room, in this apartment, smells clean and womanly. There is the smell of linen which has lain in lavender-scented drawers; the smell of my mother's "Tweed" perfume, which she dabs on lightly before going to teach at the college; the acerbic, medicinal smell of my grandmother's spirits of ammonia, which she keeps in a small green cut-glass bottle and sniffs whenever she feels faint; the smell of a furniture polish, oil-based, which my grandmother rubs, twice a week, into our numerous pieces of furniture.

Where are they? Perhaps my grandmother is already in the kitchen, starting our early supper, hardly able to contain her relief that our trip without her is over. Perhaps my mother is out by herself in the late sunshine, taking one of her walks to clear her head; or maybe she is only in the next room, reading the Sunday paper, grading student themes for the following day, or simply gazing out at the same view I was gazing at, thinking her own thoughts.

I looked out at the end of that afternoon. The cars were turning from Charlotte Street into Kimberly, making a whishing sound. I could see the corner wall of the drugstore. But there was no chance of going there after supper, because we had already been away for more time than ever before.

An irremediable sadness gathered about me. *This time yester-*

day, we were there, I thought; *and now we are here and it's all over.* How could that be? For the first time, I hovered, outside my own body, in that ghostly synapse between the anticipated event and its aftermath. I knew what all adults know: that "this time yesterday" and "this time tomorrow" are often more real than the protracted now.

It's over, I thought; and perhaps, at that blue hour, I abandoned childhood for the vaguely perceived kingdom of my future. But the knot in my chest that I felt then—its exact location and shape—I feel now, whenever I dredge up that memory.

A lot of things were over, a lot of things did come to an end that spring. My mother announced that she would not be going back to teach at the college. (Lu Ann Leach took her place, staying on into old age—until the college was incorporated into the state university.) And then, on an evening in which my grandmother rivaled the policeman's wife in her abandoned cries of protest, my mother went out for a walk and reappeared with Frank, and they announced to us that they were married. The three of us left that night, but now we are talking about a different three; my mother, Frank, and me. All that summer we lived high on a mountain—a mountain that, ironically, overlooked the red-tiled roofs of the Manor Hotel. Our mountain was called Beaucatcher, and our address was the most romantic I've ever had: One Thousand Sunset Drive. Again we were in a house with others, but these others were a far cry from the panicked widows and lonely mothers of Charlotte Street. Downstairs lived a nightclub owner and his wife and her son (my age) from an earlier marriage; upstairs lived a gregarious woman of questionable virtue. One night, a man on the way upstairs blundered by accident into my room—I now had a room, almost as large as the one we three had shared in the life below—and Frank was so incensed that he rigged up a complicated buzzer system: if my door opened during the night, the buzzer-alarm would go off, even if it was I who opened it. That summer I made friends with the nightclub owner's stepson, learned to shoot out street lights with my own homemade slingshot, and, after seeing a stray dog dripping blood, was told about the realities of sex. First by the boy, the stepson, in his own words; then, in a cleaned-up version, by my mother. I invited Lisa Gudger up to play with me; we got into Frank's bottle of Kentucky Tavern and became roaring drunk; and I beat her up. My mother called Mrs. Gudger to come and get Lisa, and then hurriedly sewed onto Lisa's ripped blouse all the buttons I had torn off.

My grandmother, who had screamed she would die if we left her, lived on through the long summer. And through another summer, during which we were reconciled. Frank had quit Georgia Tech to marry my mother, and worked as a trainee in Kress's. Within a year, my mother and Frank had moved back to the old Piping Hot. They now had the former apartment of the policeman and his wife. My grandmother slept on in her bed downstairs, and I divided my time between them.

A few years later, we left my grandmother again. Frank was being transferred to a town on the other side of the mountain. One of those hot little towns a thousand feet below. After we had been away for some months, my grandmother shocked us all by getting her first job at the age most people were thinking about retiring. At the time most people were coming home from work, my grandmother pinned on her hat and put on her gloves and hid all of Poppy's gold pieces and his ring and his watch in a secret fold of her purse, and took the empty bus downtown to her job. She worked as night housemother at the YWCA residence for working girls. It was a job made in heaven for her: she sat up waiting for the girls. If they came in after midnight, they had to ring and she let them in with an admonition. After three admonitions she reported them to the directress, a woman she despised. We heard all about the posturings and deceptions of this directress, a Mrs. Malt, whenever we visited. My grandmother's politics had gone beyond the lobby into the working world; she was able to draw Social Security because of it.

When our brand new "nuclear family" arrived in the little lowland town where Frank was to be the assistant manager of Kress's, we moved into a housing development. Our yard had no grass, only an ugly red clay slope that bled into the walkway every time it rained. "I guess I'll never know what it's like to have grass in the front yard," I said, in the sorrowful, affronted, doom-laden voice of my grandmother. "Hell, honey," replied Frank with his mountain twang, "if you want grass in this world, you've got to plant it." I forgive him for his treachery now, as I recall the thrill of those first tiny green spikes, poking up out of that raw, red soil.

Years and years passed. I was home on a visit to my mother and Frank and their little daughter and their two baby sons. "You know, it's awful," I told Mother, "but I can't remember a single thing about that trip you and I took that time on the train. You know, to Greenville. Do you remember it?"

"Of course I do," she said, her eyes going that distant blue. "Mother took us to the station and we had a lovely lunch in the dining car, and then we went to all my old haunts, and we stayed the night at Mrs.————';s, and then we got back on the train and came home. It was a lovely time."

"Well, I wish I could remember more about it."

"What else would you like to know?" asked Frank, who had been listening, his eyes as warm and eager to communicate as my mother's were cool and elegiac.

But she suddenly got an odd look on her face. "Frank," she said warningly.

"Well hell, Kathleen." He hunched his shoulders like a rebuked child.

"Frank, please," my mother said.

"Well, I was there, too," he flared up.

"You were not! That was another time we met in Greenville." But her eyes were sending desperate signals and her mouth had twisted into a guilty smirk.

"The hell it was. The second time we went, it was to get married."

Then he looked at me, those brown eyes swimming with their eager truths. She had turned away, and I didn't want to hear. Fat chance. "I drove down," he said. "I followed your train. You were sick on the train and you had to have a nap when you got there. I waited till your mother met me on the corner after you fell asleep. And then after you fell asleep that night. Well, dammit, Kathleen," he said to the cool profile turned away from him, "it's the truth. Did the truth ever hurt anybody?"

He went on to me, almost pleading for me to see his side. "I don't know what we would have done without you," he said. "You were our little chaperon, in a way. Don't you *know* how impossible it was, in those days, ever to get her alone?"

THE EXPLOSION

by SUSAN MITCHELL

from IRONWOOD

nominated by Carolyn Forché, Stanley Kunitz and David Wojahn

No one is crying.
In fact, there isn't a sound, as if on this street
it has been snowing for years, muffling
the noises of three men and one woman
staring out of the factory window.
That is why it is so hard to find the children.
With so much silence, how could you hear
a child exploding?
The fathers, though, are easy enough to locate.
Theirs are the arms reaching in
from another world.
The children, when they find them, are absolutely white.
In another world they might be made of snow.
You think if a father brushed away the ashes
from his child's face,
he would remember.
The father knows better.
He knows if you saw his child in a dream
you would run away.
The miracle is its almost human form,
the arms spread wide like a snow angel's,
the pencil-thin legs sharpened to points so fine
you cannot see what they are writing on the pavement.
The miracle is the child hasn't blown away yet.
The child does this for the father.
It wants him to find it.

That is why the father is fighting the other men
to get at it. He points to the single shoe as proof.
The others know he is lying.
They know his child has vanished into the pavement.
His child is only that outline drawn hastily
with white chalk.

TUMOR

by RICHARD BLESSING

from DRAGON GATE INC.

nominated by DRAGON GATE INC.

for Lisa Arrivey

Like proud grandparents cornering a reluctant stranger,
they show me the pictures, pin them up, backlighting.
Left lobe and right, major and minor hemispheres,
they are walnuts, just as the textbooks say.
Let no poet improve on *that*.

                 And the left lobe,
my right hand, my noble and ignoble speech, sweet reason,
is whiter than the snow that surprised us last night
and which hangs still on the roofs of the modest houses
across the street.

            Ah, but the right! Blacker
than a coal miner's lung or a house new to mourning!
Is this what comes of them, my evil fantasies,
the sexual one guarded years like a microdot, my greed,
my pettiness, my unambiguous pleasure in a colleague's
bad reviews? Or is it only that, after all,
it has to be *someone,* has always been someone,
no trick to it really, no cause nor effect,
but always someone else. Today I am someone.

Take courage from this: it is not so bad as you think
it would be when you imagine it. I wouldn't lie to you.

It is only the minor hemisphere. All the things
I was never good for: singing and music, spatial relations,
the left-hand lay-in, the occult crafts and arts.
Always my tin ear, the one for listening when a bush
bursts suddenly into flame or when a whirlwind
has something it wants to say.

                    It is only
the minor hemisphere; that, and the fear on the faces
of friends, remembering I was young and more handsome
than any Phoenician, killing themselves being kind.

I set this down like a farmer planting at the bitterest end
of winter, perhaps before. I watch the sky. One way
    or another, I will outlive this all.

THE GIFT

by LI-YOUNG LEE

from AMERICAN POETRY REVIEW

nominated by Louise Erdrich and Linda Pastan

To pull the metal splinter from my palm
my father recited a story in a low voice.
I watched his lovely face and not the blade.
Before the story ended he'd removed
the iron sliver I thought I'd die from.

I can't remember the tale,
but hear his voice still,
a well of dark water, a prayer.
And I recall his hands,
two measures of tenderness
he laid against my face,
the flames of discipline
he raised above my head.

Had you entered that afternoon
you would have thought you saw a man
planting something in a boy's palm,
a silver tear, a tiny flame.
Had you followed that boy
you would have arrived here,
where I bend over my wife's right hand.

Look how I shave her thumbnail down
so carefully she feels no pain.
Watch as I lift the splinter out.
I was seven when my father
took my hand like this,

and I did not hold that shard
between my fingers and think,
Metal that will bury me,
christen it
Little Assassin,
Ore Going Deep for My Heart,
and I did not lift up my wound and cry,
Death visited here!
I did what a child does
when he's given something to keep.
I kissed my father.

THE SOROCA GIRLS

fiction by CURZIO MALAPARTE

from MICAH PUBLICATIONS

nominated by MICAH PUBLICATIONS

"Oh, how difficult it is to be a woman!" said Louise.

"Minister Baron Braun von Stum," said Ilse, "when he learned that his wife had committed suicide—"

"Did not bat an eye. He blushed a little. He said 'Heil Hitler!' That very morning he presided as usual at the daily conference of the foreign press at the Ministry of Foreign Affairs. He looked perfectly calm. No German women went to the funeral of Giuseppina, not even the wives of the colleagues of the Minister Baron von Stum. Following the hearse were only a few Italian women living in Berlin, a group of Italian workmen of the *Todt* organization and a few officials of the Italian Embassy. Giuseppina was not worthy of the sympathy of the German women. The wives of German diplomats take pride in the suffering, the want and the hardships of the German people. The German wives of German diplomats do not jump out of windows, they do not kill themselves. *Heil* Hitler! Minister Baron von Stum followed the bier in the uniform worn by Hitler's diplomats; now and then he looked around suspiciously; from time to time he blushed. He felt ashamed that his wife—*Ach!* he had married an Italian woman—had not had the strength to withstand the suffering of the German people."

"Sometimes I am ashamed of being a woman," said Louise softly.

"Why, Louise? Let me tell you the story of the girls of Soroca," I said, "of Soroca in Bessarabia, on the Dneister . . ."

They were poor Jewish girls who had fled into the fields and the woods to escape the hands of the Germans. The grain fields and the woods of Bessarabia, between Baltsiu and Soroca, were full of

276

Jewish girls hiding in fear of the Germans, in fear of the hands of the Germans.

They were not afraid of their faces, their terrible raucous voices, their blue eyes, their broad and heavy feet, but they were afraid of their hands. They were not afraid of their fair hair or their tommy guns, but they were afraid of their hands. When a column of German soldiers appeared at the end of the road, the Jewish girls hiding in the wheat and among the trunks of acacias and birches shook with fear; if one of them began crying and screaming, her companions jammed their hands over her mouth, or filled her mouth with straw; but the girl would struggle and howl—she was afraid of the German hands; she already felt those hard smooth German hands under her dress. She already felt those iron fingers penetrating her secret flesh. They lived for days hidden in the fields amid the wheat, stretched out between the furrows among the tall golden ears as in a warm forest of golden trees; they moved very slowly lest the golden ears should sway. Whenever the Germans saw the ears swaying in the windless air, they called "*Achtung!* Partisans!" and fired volleys with their tommy guns into the forest of golden wheat.

They were Jewish girls, about eighteen to twenty years old; they were the youngest and best looking. The others, the ugly and crippled girls of Bessarabian ghettos, remained shut up in their houses, and peered from behind the curtains to watch the Germans go by and shook with fear. Maybe it was not only fear, maybe it was something else that made all these unfortunate women tremble: the hunch-backed, the lame, the halt, the scurvy-scarred, the pock-marked or those with their hair devoured by eczema. They shook with fear as they lifted the curtains to watch the German soldiers go by, and they drew back frightened by the casual glance, the involuntary gesture or the voice of some soldier; but they laughed, red in the face and sweating, within those darkened rooms, and they ran limping and bumping against each other to the window of the next room to watch the German soldiers rounding the bend in the road.

The girls hidden in the fields and in the woods grew pale when they heard the rumble of motors, the clatter of horses, the creaking of wheels on the roads leading to Baltsiu in Bessarabia, to Soroca on the Dniester, and to the Ukraine. They lived like wild beasts, feeding on what little they could beg from the peasants, a few slices of *mamaliga* bread, some scraps of salted *brenza*. There were days when at sunset the German soldiers went out to hunt for Jewish girls in the wheat. They spread out like the fingers of a huge hand, raking the wheatfields, and they hailed one another, "Kurt! Fritz! Karl!" They had youthful slightly hoarse voices. They looked like sportsmen beating a moor to raise the partridges, quails and pheasants.

The larks, surprised and frightened, fluttered in the dusty sunset air. The soldiers raised their faces following them with their eyes, and the hidden girls held their breath, watching the hands of the German soldiers clutching their tommy guns and appearing and disappearing amid the grain—those German hands covered with light glistening down, those hard, smooth German hands. By now the hunters were close, they stooped a little as they advanced. They could be heard breathing noisily with a slightly hoarse hiss. At last one of the girls let out a shriek, then another, and still another.

One day the Department of Sanitation of the Eleventh German Army decided to open a military brothel in Soroca. But there were only old and ugly women in Soroca. Most of the town had been wrecked by mines and by German and Russian shells. Almost the entire population had fled and the young men had followed the Soviet Army toward the Dnieper. Only the part around the public gardens remained standing and the old castle which was built by the Genoese on the western bank of the Dniester in the midst of a maze of squat hovels made of mud and wood where wretched crowds of Tartars, Romanians, Bulgarians and Turks lived. From the top of the cliff overhanging the river, the town can be seen hemmed in between the river and the steep wooded bank. In those days the houses looked crumbling and gutted; a few beyond the public gardens were still smoldering. Such was Soroca on the Dniester when the military brothel was opened in a house close to the wall of the Genoese castle—a city in ruins, its streets cluttered with columns of soldiers, with horses and cars.

The Department of Sanitation detailed special patrols to hunt for the Jewish girls hiding in the grain and in the woods around the town. And so, when the brothel was officially opened with an inspection, very military in style, by the commander of the Eleventh Army, some ten pale trembling girls, their eyes scorched with weeping, received General von Schobert and his suite. All were very young, a few were still children. They did not wear those long silken loose gowns, red, yellow and green, with wide sleeves that are the traditional uniform of eastern brothels. They just wore their best dresses, the simple and honest clothes of middle-class girls in the provinces, so that they looked like students—some of them were students—who had gathered in the house of a friend to prepare for an examination. Their appearance was humble, shy and frightened. I had seen them go by in the street a few days before the opening of the brothel, about ten of them. They walked in the middle of the street with bundles under their arms or else carrying a leather suitcase or a parcel tied with string. Two SS men armed with tommy guns followed them. Their hair was gray with dust, wheat ears clung to their skirts, their stockings were torn; one of them limped with one bare foot, carrying a shoe in her hand.

A month later, when I was passing through Soroca, Sonderführer Schenck asked me one evening to go with him to see the Jewish girls in the military brothel. I refused and Schenck laughed, looking mockingly at me. "They are not prostitutes. They are girls who belong to good families," said Schenck.

I replied, "I know that they are decent girls."

"It isn't worth while feeling very sorry for them. They are Jewish girls."

I replied, "I know that they are Jewish girls."

"Well then," said Schenck, "perhaps you fear that they might feel hurt if we pay them a visit?"

I replied, "You cannot understand some things, Schenck."

"What is there to understand?" he asked.

I replied, "These unfortunate Soroca girls are not prostitutes. They are not selling themselves of their own free will. They are compelled to prostitute themselves. They are entitled to respect from everyone. They are war prisoners whom you exploit in an ignoble way. What percentage of the earnings of these unfortunate girls goes to the German Command?"

"The love of these girls costs nothing," said Schenck. "It is a free service."

"You mean compulsory work?"

"No, a free service," replied Schenck. "In any case, it's not worth while paying them."

"Not worth while paying them? Why?

The Sonderführer explained that when their turn was over, after a couple of weeks, they would be sent back to their homes and replaced by another team of girls.

"Home?" I asked. "Are you certain that they will be sent back to their homes?"

"Yes," replied Schenck with some embarrassment, blushing slightly, "home, maybe to a hospital; I don't know. Maybe to a concentration camp."

"Instead of those unfortunate Jewish girls, why don't you put Russian prisoners in that brothel?"

Schenck burst out laughing and kept laughing. He clapped me on the shoulder and laughed, "*Ach, so! Ach, so!*" But I was certain that he had not grasped what I had meant; he, no doubt, fancied that I had hinted at the story about a certain house in Baltsiu in which a *Leibesstandart* of SS men had a secret brothel for homosexuals. He had not fully grasped what I had meant, and he laughed open-mouthed, slapping me on the shoulder with his hand.

"If instead of those unfortunate Jewish girls," I said, "there were Russian soldiers, the fun would be greater, wouldn't it?"

At last Schenck thought he understood and began laughing louder. Then suddenly he asked in a serious tone, "Do you think that the Russians are homosexuals?"

"You'll find out at the end of the war," I replied.

"*Ja, ja, natürlich,* we'll find out at the end of the war!" said Schenck gurgling with laughter. . . .

One evening, very late, close to midnight, I set out for the Genoese castle. I went down to the river, turned into a lane of that miserable neighborhood, knocked at the door of that house and went in. In a large room lighted by an oil lamp hanging from the center of the ceiling, three girls were seated on the sofas placed along the walls. A wooden staircase led to the upper floor. From the rooms above came the squeakings of doors, light footsteps and a murmur of distant voices that seemed sunk in darkness.

The three girls raised their eyes and looked at me. They sat sedately on the low sofas covered with those ugly Romanian carpets of Cetacea Alba striped in yellow, red and green. One of them was reading a book that she put down on her knees to watch me as soon as I entered. It looked like a brothel interior painted by

Pascin. They watched me in silence; one of them smoothed with her fingers her black crinkly hair that had gathered on her forehead like a child's. In a corner of the room, on a table covered with a yellow shawl, stood several bottles of beer, of *zuica*, and a double row of glasses.

"*Gute Nacht*," said the girl after a while, as she smoothed her hair.

"*Buna seara*," I replied in Romanian.

"*Buna seara*," said the girl sadly attempting to smile.

At that moment I no longer remembered why I had gone to that house, although I was aware that without letting Schenck know, I had gone out of curiosity or from a vague feeling of pity, but for something that my conscience now refused to accept.

"It's very late," I said.

"We are closing soon," said the girl.

Meanwhile one of her companions had risen from the settee, and covertly glancing at me, lazily approached the gramophone standing on a little table in a corner; she turned the handle and placed the needle on the record. A woman's voice singing a tango rhythm came from the gramophone. I went over and lifted the needle from the record.

"Why?" asked the girl who with arms raised was getting ready to dance with me. Without waiting for a reply, she turned her back on me and went back to sit on the sofa. She was short and quite plump. Her feet were clad in light green cloth slippers. I joined her on the sofa and, staring intently at me, she tucked her skirt under her leg to make room for me. She was smiling, and I cannot tell why the smile irritated me. Just then a door opened at the top of the stairs and a woman's voice called, "Susannah!"

Down the stairs came a pale, thin girl holding a lighted candle shielded by a funnel of yellow paper. Her hair hung loosely over her shoulders. She wore slippers, a towel draped over her bent arm, her hand held up her dressing-gown—a sort of bath wrap tied around her waist with a cord—as if it were monk's cloak. She descended half way down the stairs, and looked me over attentively, frowning, as if my presence annoyed her, then she looked around with more suspicion than anger. She looked at the gramophone on which the record was still turning idly with a slight rustle. She looked at the untouched glasses, the orderly array of bottles and, opening her mouth in a wide yawn, she said in a slightly hoarse voice in which there was something harsh and rude, "Let's go to bed, Susannah. It's late."

The girl whom the newcomer had called Susannah laughed, looking at her companion mockingly, "Are you tired already, Lublia?" she asked. "What have you been doing to make you so tired?"

Lublia did not reply. She sat on the sofa opposite ours and with a yawn she carefully examined my uniform. Then she asked: "You are not German. What are you?"

"Italian."

"Italian?" The girls were now looking at me with curiosity. The one who was reading closed her book and looked at me in a tired, absent-minded way.

"Italy is beautiful," said Susannah.

"I would rather it were an ugly country," I said. "It's no use, just being beautiful."

"I would like to be on the way to Italy," said Susannah. "To Venice. I would like to live in Venice."

"In Venice?" asked Lublia, and began to laugh.

"Wouldn't you go to Venice with me?" said Susannah. "I've never seen a gondola."

"If I weren't in love I would start right now."

Her companions laughed and one of them said, "We are all in love."

The others began laughing again and casting strange glances in my direction.

"We have many lovers," said Susannah in French, with the soft accent of Romanian Jews.

"They would not let us leave for Italy," said Lublia lighting a cigarette. "They are so jealous!" I noticed that she had a long, narrow face and a small sad mouth with thin lips. It looked like the mouth of a child. But her nose was bony, the color of wax, with red nostrils. She smoked raising her eyes to the ceiling now and then, blowing the smoke into the air with a studied indifference. There was something resigned and at the same time despairing in her white glance.

The girl who had been sitting with the book in her lap rose and, clutching the book in her hands, said "*Nopte buna.*"

"*Nopte buna, Domnule Capitan,*" the girl said again bowing to me with a shy, clumsy grace. She turned and went up the stairs.

"Do you want the candle, Zoe?" asked Lublia following her with her eyes.

"Thanks, I am not afraid of the dark," replied Zoe without turning.

"Are you going to dream about me?" shouted Susannah after her.

"Certainly! I am going to sleep in Venice!" replied Zoe as she disappeared.

We were silent for a while. The distant roar of a truck broke gently against the windowpanes.

"Do you like the Germans?" Susannah suddenly asked me.

"Why shouldn't I?" I answered in a slightly suspicious tone that was not lost on the girl.

"They are very nice, aren't they?" she said.

"Some of them are very nice."

Susannah stared at me for a long time, then she said with inexpressible hatred. "They are very kind to women."

"Don't you believe her," said Lublia. "At heart she is very fond of them."

Susannah laughed and looked at me in a strange way. Something white and soft was lifting from the depths of her eyes; they seemed to be melting.

"Perhaps she has reasons to love them," I said.

"Certainly," said Susannah. "They are my last love."

I noticed that her eyes filled with tears, although she smiled. I gently stroked her hand and Susannah dropped her head on her chest, letting her silent tears stream down her face.

"What are you crying about?" said Lublia in a hoarse voice, as she threw away her cigarette. "We still have two more days of gay life. Do you want more? Haven't you had enough?" Then, raising her voice and her arms, shaking her hands above her head, as if she were calling for help, in a voice filled with hatred, revulsion and grief, she screamed, "Two days, two days more and then they will send us home! Only two days more and here you are crying! We'll be free, don't you understand? Free, free!" Dropping on the sofa, she buried her face in the cushions and began trembling, her teeth chattered violently and, now and again in that strange voice of fear, she repeated, "Two days, only two days!" One of her slippers dropped off her foot and hit the wooden floor; her bare foot as small as a child's was exposed reddish, wrinkled, seared by white scars. I thought that she must have walked miles and miles; who knows where she came from, who knows through how much space she had fled before she was caught and brought by force into that house.

Susannah was silent, her head lowered, her hand between my hands. She did not seem to breathe. Suddenly she asked softly, without looking at me, "Do you think they will send us home?"

"They cannot make you stay here all your life."

"Every twenty days they change the girls," said Susannah. "We have been here eighteen days already. Two days more and we shall be replaced. They have warned us already. But do you really think that they will let us go back to our homes?" I felt that she was afraid of something, but I could not understand of what. She told me that she had learned French in school in Kishinev, that her father was a Baltsiu merchant; that Lublia was a doctor's daughter; that three of her other companions were students, and she added that Lublia studied music, that she played the piano like an angel, and—she said—she would be a great musician.

"When she leaves this house," I said, "she will be able to resume her studies."

"Who knows? After all we went through! Besides, who knows where we shall end up?"

Meanwhile Lublia had raised herself on her elbows. Her face was tight as a closed fist; her eyes shone strangely in her waxen face. She shook as if she had a fever. "Yes, I shall certainly become a great musician," she said and began laughing as she searched through the pockets of her dressing-gown for a cigarette. She rose, went to the table, opened a bottle of beer, filled three glasses and offered them to us on a wooden tray. She moved lightly, without any noise.

"I'm thirsty," said Lublia drinking greedily with closed eyes.

The air was stiflingly hot; through the half-shut windows came the thick breath of the summer night. Lublia walked barefoot about the room, an empty glass in her hand, her eyes staring blindly. Her long, lean body swayed under the flabby bell of the loose red dressing-gown, her bare feet made a soft muffled noise on the wooden floor. The other girl, who all this time had not uttered a single word or given any sign of life—as if she had been gazing at us without seeing us—unaware of what was happening around her, had meanwhile fallen asleep; she lay on the sofa in her poor patched gown, one hand resting on her leg, the other clenched in a fist on her bosom. Now and then, from the public gardens, came the sharp crack of a rifle. From the opposite bank of the Dniester, down the river from Yambol, came a rumble of artillery that was stifled in the wooly folds of the sultry night. Lublia stood in front of her sleeping companion and gazed at her in silence. Then, turning to Susannah, she said, "We must put her to bed. She is tired."

"We have worked all day long," added Susannah, as if apologizing. "We are worn out. By day we have the soldiers; in the evenings from eight to eleven—the officers. We haven't a moment's rest." She talked in a detached way, as if she were discussing any ordinary sort of work. She did not even show any signs of disgust. While she spoke, she rose and helped Lublia to lift her friend who awoke as soon as her feet touched the floor; moaning, as if she were suffering from pain, she yielded and almost lay in the arms of her friends as they moved up the stairs, until her moans and the sound of their steps died away behind the closed door.

I was left alone. The oil lamp hanging from the ceiling was smoking. I rose to turn down the wick and the lamp continued to sway, rocking my shadow along the walls along with the shadows of the furniture, the bottles and other things. It would have been better if I had left at that moment. I was seated on the sofa looking at the door. I had a dim feeling that it was wrong for me to stay in that house. It would have been better if I had left before Lublia and Susannah came back.

"I was afraid we would not find you here," said Susannah's voice behind me. She had come noiselessly down the stairs; she moved slowly about the room as she arranged the bottles and glasses and then came over and sat next to me on the sofa. She had powdered her face and looked even paler than before. She asked me how long I would stay in Soroca.

"I don't know, not more than two or three days," I replied. "I have to leave for the Odessa front, but I shall be back soon."

"Do you think the Germans will take Odessa?"

"I care nothing about what the Germans do," I replied.

"I wish I could say the same," said Susannah.

"Oh, I am sorry, Susannah. I did not mean . . ." I said. After an uncomfortable pause, I added, "It does not matter what the Germans do. It takes more than that to win a war."

"Do you know who will win the war? Perhaps you imagine that the Germans or the British or the Russians will win the war? The war will be won by us, by Lublia, Zoe, Marica; by me and all those who are like us. It will be won by whores."

"Shut up," I said.

"It will be won by whores," repeated Susannah raising her voice. Then she broke into silent laughter and, finally, in a shaky voice, in the voice of a frightened child, asked, "Do you think that they will send us home?"

"Why shouldn't they send you home?" I replied. "Are you afraid that they will send you to another house like this?"

"Oh, no! After twenty days of this work we are not fit for anything. I saw them—I saw the other ones." She broke off and I noticed that her lips were trembling. That day she had had to submit to forty-three soldiers and six officers. She laughed. She could no longer bear life. The physical exhaustion was worse than the disgust. "Worse than the disgust," she repeated smiling. That smile hurt me; it seemed as if she meant to apologize, or maybe that there was something else in that ambiguous smile, something obscure. She added that the other ones, those who had been there before her, before Lublia, Zoe and Marica, when they had left that house had been reduced to a pitiful condition. They no longer appeared to be women. They were rags. She had seen them going out with their suitcases and with their bundles of rags under their arms. Two SS men armed with tommy guns had shoved them into a truck to take them no one knows where. "I would like to go back home," said Susannah. "I want to go back home."

The lamp was smoking again; a greasy smell of oil spread through the room. I gently held Susannah's hand between mine, and her hand trembled like a frightened bird. The night was breathing on the threshold like a sick beast; its warm breath penetrated the room together with the rustle of the leaves in the trees and the ripple of the river.

"I have seen them when they went out of here," said Susannah with a shudder. "They looked like ghosts."

We sat like that, in silence, in the twilight of the room, and I was filled with bitter sadness. I no longer trusted my own words. My words were false and evil. Our silence also seemed to me false and evil.

"See you soon, Susannah," I said softly.

"Don't you want to come upstairs?" she asked.

"It is late," I replied making for the door. "See you soon, Susannah."

"*Au revoir*," said Susannah smiling.

Her poor smile was shining on the threshold, and the sky was full of stars.

"Did you ever hear anything more about those poor girls?" asked Louise after a long silence.

"I learned that two days later they were taken away. Every twenty days the Germans provided a change of girls. Those who left the brothel were shoved into a truck and taken down to the river. Later Schenck told me that it was not worthwhile to feel so sorry for them. They were not fit for anything any more. They were reduced to rags, and besides, they were Jewish."

"Did they know that they would be shot?" asked Ilse.

"They knew it. They trembled with fear. Oh, they knew it! Everybody knew it in Soroca."

When we came out into the open, the sky was full of stars. They shone, cold and dead, like glass eyes. The raucous whistle of the train was heard from the station. A pale spring moon rose in the clear sky, the trees and the houses appeared to be made of a slimy, soft material. Over by the river a bird was singing. We walked along a deserted road to the bank and sat on the dam.

In the darkness, the river rustled like bare feet on grass. Then, in the branches of a tree that was already lighted by the pale flame of the moon, another began singing and others far and near replied. A large bird flew with silent wings through the trees, swooped down almost skimming the water and crossed the river in a slow and uncertain flight. There came back to my mind the summer night in the Roman prison, *Regina Coeli*, when a flight of birds settled on the roof of the prison and began singing. They certainly had come from the trees on the Gianicolo. They had nests in Tasso's oak, I thought. I thought that they had their nests in Tasso's oak and I began weeping. I felt ashamed of weeping, but

287

after such a long imprisonment, a bird's song is stronger that a man's pride. "Oh, Louise," I said and without meaning to, I took her hand and held it gently in mine.

Just as gently, Louise withdrew her hand and gazed at me with wonder rather than reproach. She was surprised by my unexpected gesture. Perhaps she regretted that she had evaded my sorrowful caress and the things I wanted to tell her. There rose in my mind Susannah's hand resting between mine—the small, sweating hand of Susannah—down there in the Soroca brothel; there rose in my mind the hand of the Russian working woman that I had covertly pressed one evening in a coach of the Berlin U-Bahn—that broad, lined hand, cracked by acids. It seemed to me that I was sitting with Susannah, the unfortunate Jewish girl, on the sofa in the Soroca brothel. A deep feeling of pity swept over me for Louise, Louise von Preusse, for the Imperial Princess, Louise von Hohenzollern. The birds were singing around us in the dark light of the moon. The two girls were silent as they gazed at the dull glint of the river flowing past the bank in the darkness.

"*J'ai pitié d'être femme,*" said Louise softly in that Potsdam French of hers. "I'm sorry I am a woman."

🔥 🔥 🔥

A WINTER'S TALE

fiction by CLARK BROWN

from WRITERS FORUM

nominated by WRITERS FORUM

By 1876 ENTHUSIASM HAD BEGUN TO WANE, yet the whole improbable business, even the sectioned heads (reproduced today on comic T-shirts), retained a respectful hearing on into the twentieth century, and as late as 1911 books appeared such as *Character Building and Reading,* a cheerful popularized treatise complete wth jargon and charts.

The foundations of the science were these: since the exercise of any corporeal organ increases in its size (Cuvier), and since certain portions of the brain control certain bodily responses and activities, it seemed reasonable to assume that strenuous exercise of, say, the intellectual faculties would increase the frontal lobes. And therefore, since brain size determined skull size, you could conclude merely from looking at a picture of Socrates (for example) that he was a man of profound thought. From such analogies there developed an elaborate system, quaint and ridiculous in our eyes (though no more so, some claim, than psychoanalysis), including the familiar diagrams of a hairless human head mapped and numbered like demarcated illustrations of cuts of beef. Wonderful qualities or "sentiments" were postulated, such as "bibacity"—"the love of liquids and the fondness for bathing, boating, swimming and marine life." Bibacity was thought to reside near the temple, half way between the eye and ear. Its "perversion" was drunkeness and excessive thirst.

One among many of the practitioners of this fanciful discipline (endorsed by Emerson, George Eliot, Herbert Spencer and Gladstone among others, and dignified with a chair at the University of Edinburgh) was Daniel Joseph Palmer, born in 1848 in Brookline, Massachusetts to Ephraim Leonidas Palmer, a manufacturer of stationers' supplies, and to Dorothy Wilcox Palmer, both robust Congregationalists who would convert to Christian Science soon after the publication in 1875 of *Science and Health*.

Matriculating at Harvard, Palmer graduated in 1869, having studied not medicine but theology and being attracted to the Unitarian faith which, now severed from the religion of his parents, would require him as minister to profess no particular doctrine or creed. He did not, however, enter the ministry but undertook a profitable career in his father's business, to which he brought an evangelical zeal.

It seems characteristic of Palmer to combine mercantile and religious fervor. He shied from a career as clergyman, fearing it would remove him from "the world of men," yet that very world—the world, in his case, of inventories, freight rates, price structures and sales volumes—demanded in his eyes some spiritual commitment, something to uplift and redeem what might otherwise remain a sordid grasping and scheming. He wished his life to be pure and worthy, yet he wished it to be active, virile and of this earth. A faith whose adherents dwelt apart held no charm for him. He wished not to renounce the world but to transfigure it.

In college he had read the works of Francis Gall (1758–1828) and John Caspar Spurzheim (1776–1832). He was familiar with the lectures of the Fowlers (Orson and Lorenzo), and he knew that Ferrier and others were even then applying a weak galvanic current to certain exposed portions of living animal brains and noting the muscular reactions. Like other physiognomists Palmer realized that these newly discovered motor centers corresponded to the psychic brain centers located much earlier by Dr. Gall, centers which positively expressed the feeling or emotion naturally arising from the activities of the faculties *in* sections of the brain. Whether this perception decided him or not is unclear, but at some point after graduation—and we do not know precisely when—Palmer journeyed to England where he studied with Dr. Henry Maudsley, F.R.C.P., Professor of Medical Jurisprudence, University College, London.

He—Palmer—was a short, stocky man with curly brown hair, a long square jaw and large, prominent dark eyes which in the few photographs that survive appear unusually lustrous and troubled. The lips are thick, almost pouting, and the face, which Palmer himself analysed or "read" numerous times (consulting, of course, a mirror), combines a suggestion of obscure and solemn sadness with a hint of boyish wonder. His vision was weak, and he usually wore a pince nez, but none shows in the pictures. This absence may explain the naked, surprised expression, the sense of a creature trapped.

From his journals and meditations—highly self-critical and analytical yet lighted by a stubborn optimism—we gather that he represented an unhappy combination of tenacity and shyness. Short but lacking the little man's compensating swagger, he was determined on self-improvement, and by a sheer assertion of will frequently compelled himself to do exactly what his nature most wished him to avoid. Any qualm or reservation which might, under Palmer's stern eye, be taken for cowardice or funk he resolved to extirpate. Thus he entered politics to the extent of campaigning for Rutherford B. Hayes, partly because he approved of the candidate's teetotaling convictions, but mainly as an opportunity to rid himself of a lifelong fear of public speaking. In the same way—or so we may speculate—he journeyed west in the late fall of 1875, intending to make scientific examination of what he persistently called the "savage temperament."

At that time white man and Indian enjoyed a theoretical peace. True, the Civil War had provided opportunities for sporadic rebellion, and there were still in several western territories small bands—mainly young braves—known as "hot-heads." In general, though, most Plains Indians had resigned themselves to treaties purporting to guarantee their territorial rights. Not all Indians understood such agreements, and the tribes' very democracy provided friction. A chief might sign and sincerely promise peace but compelling obedience was not always within his power. To be "chief" was to assume less authority than the white man often realized. Nevertheless, a truce of sorts prevailed. Then in 1873 the discovery of gold on the Yellowstone River altered these precarious arrangements.

That authorities could have stopped the influx of fortune seekers seems doubtful; that they were not interested in trying is certain. Tension rose. As the year in which Daniel Palmer journeyed west came to a close, people on the frontier wondered what the spring would hold. In winter, game and forage being scarce, Indians necessarily split into small scattered groups, but once the snows vanished, the grass got high and the ponies grew strong again, there might be war, and in the light of this dismal possibility a column of cavalry and mounted infantry left Fort Fetterman in the Wyoming Territory in late January ostensibly on reconnaissance. Daniel Palmer, making his own reconnaissance, traveled with it.

As a rule, Indian fighting was a more casual affair than history and cinema have portrayed. The pensions and commendations of "real" war did not apply, pitched battles were rare and since the army was shrinking and promotions were few, an ambitious officer had little chance to make a reputation against the "hostiles." One exception was Major Robert "Fighting Bob" Shannon, who at thirty-six had established himself, first during the Civil War, then in the brilliant if ambiguous confrontation at Deer Creek (near Cheyenne) in 1868. Presently, Major Shannon was north with a contingent of Crow scouts. He would join the column at a place known as Hanging Man's Fork, south of Sulphur Flats.

The soldiers themselves were not crack troops. Life on the frontier posts was dreary and unattractive, and many of those who signed on for the winter were simply "snowbirds," desperate for food and warm clothing and certain to desert in the spring. These and others were often debtors or worse who had fled the East. The army did not inquire scrupulously into anyone's past or worry overmuch about muster roll authenticity. The same tolerance extended to uniforms. Eccentricities of dress and weaponry were ignored, and some men fought in buckskin or outlandish costumes. Officers, too, could be whimsical. Captain Gideon J. Prowt (1821–1892) rode a mule, tied up his beard with bright ribbons and carried a shotgun.

There was, then, a Dickensian bustle and glamor to the whole business, a local "color" which journalists exploited. Then as now relationships between officers and the press were complicated. Rising stars such as George A. Custer (rumored to have Presidential ambitions) and Major Shannon, aware that Indian fighting was good "copy," encouraged publicity. Robert Shannon himself may well have written many of the dispatches printed under various reporters' names.

Certainly material existed for anyone with an eye to the picturesque. Wandering about the fort, you would see the officers in blues and shiny boots, the men in blues and dark forage caps, the muleskinner bearded and greasy in elkskin or buckskin, hung with revolvers and ammunition, butcher knives stuffed in their belts. Then there were scouts and friendly Indians, longhaired and brown, dressed in a motley of buckskin, blankets and cast-off uniforms. And always there was the noise: wagons clattering, bullwhips cracking, animals snorting, whackers swearing, officers snapping orders, boots thumping, rifles and carbines executing the manual with a slap and bang of stocks and barrels and the jingle of sling-belts.

Palmer, alive to this excitement, had arranged to travel as "scientific observer," eating at headquarters mess. His earnestness and his mysterious knowledge both amused and intrigued the officers, some of whom patronized him but made sure he was properly outfitted. His notebooks record the astonishing amount of gear: bedding, canvas, comforter, buffalo robes, beaver robe, mattress (to be rolled and tied to his horse), rubber poncho, a stock saddle instead of the pancake McClellans with their slots and pads and skirts, messkit (should he have to prepare his own rations), cup, canteen, extra clothes, boots, buffalo coat, muskrat cap with earflaps, fifteen pounds of grain (to be packed on the mules), extra horseshoes, wool face mask, fur gloves, mittens, buffalo overshoes and special issue gear for wrists and knees. For his protection he was equipped with a Springfield carbine rather than the infantry-man's "Long Tom" (unmanageable on horseback) and a Colt pistol. (Lithographs and films to the contrary, neither Palmer nor anyone else carried bayonets or sabers.)

On January 31st the column rode out—five troops of cavalry, the pack train and the infantry rear guard mounted on mules—moving north through the creek bottoms where the ground was flat, the riding easy, and thick woods kept off the wind. The first day's march was not arduous, but Palmer's journal notes displeasure— mainly, it appears, at himself.

At the fort he had "examined" various Indians, taking measure-ments and working his observations into a brief, tentative essay. The black eye, he observed, naturally indicated passion, intensity and impulse, but shape was equally significant. A narrow eye could mean secrecy and suspiciousness. The noses were usually aggres-sive and the straight thicklipped jaws pointed toward firmness and sensuality. The foreheads, he claimed, generally revealed a defi-ciency in the moral and intellectual sentiments, and the high prominent crowns (recalling Philip the Second of Spain) showed a desire to tyrannize. Then there was the hair. As a rule, Palmer wrote, the darkhaired races possessed more intensity but not necessarily more physical strength.

But all this was dissatisfying. These savages remained disappointingly unsavage. He felt cheated and balked yet relieved—and despised his relief. What exactly he hoped to find through such study is difficult to say, but it is clear in retrospect that he wished in some way to still within himself a kind of silent terror.

For Palmer was afraid—fearfully afraid—and he believed (or so we gather) that only by forcing himself to look unblinkingly upon the face of human darkness and depravity could he conquer his poisonous shame. But the Crow scouts and the copperskinned loafers at the post, though intriguing at first, failed to frighten him. He felt cravenly let off, deprived of his chance for self-mastery.

Whether at heart he *was* more or less a coward than most men is not the point. He *felt* himself a coward. He had sought a test and was privately grateful that none had arrived, and this gratitude, this obscene unconquerable joy at being spared, moved him to paroxysms of self-disgust. *Truly*, he wrote, *when I consider how my heart palpitates at the mere idea of danger, and when I look about me and remark how calmly other men accept the nearness of combat and the fact of their own mortality, I am filled with icy despair. Are they bluffers? Do they all wear masks? Even fat Captain Fenton—so clearly the lymphatic type with the characteristically active secreting glands, the languid pulse and the retarded vital functions—even he, I say, the least martial of men, seems undismayed by the frightening possibilities. There is nothing for it. I can only conclude that I am a wretch. . . .*

Then, on the third night, after the column had reached Hanging Man's Fork and pitched camp, Major Shannon and his scouts appeared from the north. With them they brought, as though for display, a captured Sioux brave.

Eight years older than Palmer, Robert Andrew Shannon looks, in photographs, several years younger. Though there is something youthful, even childlike in Palmer's glum dubious stare, there are in the pictures of Robert Shannon a blandness, a simplicity and even a lack of expression that suggest youth. The face is square, Irish and pale, with thin lips and the long, thin, not particularly prominent nose. In Palmer's jargon he represented the "motive temperament," characterized by "a tall, angular form, long, large bones, prominent joints, strong muscles and ligaments, large, strong, well defined features, and square or oblong face, hair and skin usually coarse, the movements and gestures abrupt and striking." The "mental attributes" of this species are, according to Palmer, "constructiveness, firmness, energy, executive power, stability, constancy and practical insight." *Such types make good builders*, Palmer wrote, *also construction engineers, surveyors, farmers, stock raisers and navigators*.

Certainly Shannon was tall, bony, rectilinear and dry. Certainly too he was laconic and arrogant, and in Palmer's presence affected a bored, half-lidded stare of contempt. He seems to have despised Palmer from the start, and Palmer quailed before his lofty gaze.

It appears not to have occurred to Palmer that much about Shannon might be pose. Such posturing Palmer never understood. He knew of course of Shannon's military record. West Point '61, Shannon had fought at the first battle of Bull Run and in McClellan's unsuccessful Peninsular Campaign. He had led the bloody but indecisive assault on Lee's left at Antietam, and with Sedgwick had driven Jubal Early from Mayre's Heights at Chancellorsville— before Early and Lee repulsed Sedgwick and Hooker. At Gettysburg he had helped turn back Longstreet. Finally, there was, as always, his stunning victory over the massed Sioux, Arapaho and Cheyenne at the battle (some said massacre) of Deer Creek. Thus when Shannon seated himself on a campstool and quietly, matter-of-factly (so softly officers strained to hear) made his recommendations, Palmer was stricken.

What would they do? someone asked. What would they *do?* said Shannon, lifting an eyebrow (his inflection could make you blush at your own words). Why, he said, they would rest that day, cut all the grass they could find for the animals and collect all the water they could carry. Then they would strike out across Sulphur Flats. Probably they would spend one night if they pushed themselves, two if they did not. But, someone objected, could it be done? Could it be *done?* Shannon asked with a laugh. Hadn't Hardass George Custer marched without water from the Republican River to the Platte—in a single day?

Technically, Shannon was not the commander. The commander was Colonel Hiram Bartholomew Chilldress, diminutive, silverhaired and vague, but no one doubted that the Major had assumed control and direction of the whole enterprise. He might defer—barely—to Chilldress, but there seemed to be in Shannon's bearing and speech and above all in his poised silences an expression of will that no one would oppose.

Palmer was shocked and fascinated. In Shannon he saw what he believed he wished to be, and yet there was something blind and stupid and hostile about the Major. He had made himself a force, yes, but a mindless force. Was he any better, Palmer wondered, than the savages themselves? Well, yes, certainly, but still. . . . Then Palmer no doubt stopped worrying about that. Other challenges confronted him.

Why and how Shannon captured the Sioux remain unclear even today. There was talk of the Crow scouts surprising the brave, who may have been sneaking upon them at night. Details are lacking. He was young—possibly seventeen or eighteen—skinny, proud, fierce and bitter, wrapped in a tattered blanket, his hands lashed behind him, a noose about his neck. He had been transported by horseback, but now he was seated among boulders, wrists and ankles bound, the blanket slipping off one bare shoulder while two carbine-bearing troopers stood guard. Palmer requested and was granted permission to make his "examination." How deeply he wished to do anything of the kind we may imagine.

Secretly, he was appalled. His whole being shrank from the task, from the very sight and smell—the mingled odors of dried sweat, damp wool and filthy buckskin. The lank dark hair, the glazed black eyes, the sharp facial bones, the snarling mouth, the blade of a nose—this was what Palmer had traveled two thousand miles to meet, and his spirit seemed to shriek and urge him to bolt. He realized that he was in no danger, that this miserable starving half wild creature—not much more than a boy—so securely bound and watched, could do nothing to him. All the same, Palmer trembled. Swallowing, he approached the man—*as though I were compelled to examine a leopard,* he wrote. *I could not help it. My very nerves seemed to clatter. I was consumed with fear!*

Yet he made his examination, even explaining briefly to those interested how cranial configurations might be mathematically classified (measuring the forehead slope against a perpendicular through the skull) and yielding such categories and "types" as—in ascending order—the Australian Bushman, the Uncultivated, the Improved, the Civilized, the Enlightened, and, at the apex, the Caucasian. Sometimes, he pointed out, with the Caucasian Type, foreheads actually exceeded ninety degrees. It was at this moment, one likes to think, that the captive broke into that unearthly wail which shook Palmer "to the very marrow of my bones."

. . . I inquired the reason for this eerie keening, and was informed that the subject was singing his death song. "He thinks you're going to torture him," someone volunteered, *"and he's telling you he don't think much of your medicine."*

At any rate, Palmer concluded his business, noticing that the Indian, seemingly bent on his own destruction, had refused all food—to the consternation of no one. *I pointed out that the subject would surely starve,* Palmer wrote, *to which I received the gratifying information that that was frequently the result of neglecting to take nourishment. I was not consoled.*

There was in fact a strong capacity for indignation within Palmer, an ability to resent, heatedly, injustice and cruelty. Whether his outrage at this callousness was in some way fanned by secret fear we cannot say. Possibly in protesting against the prisoner's treatment, Palmer was privately objecting to his own qualms. The truth is, he hated the man (hardly a man at that), hated him because the brave terrified and shamed him, and, as though to compensate or render some balance, Palmer felt compelled to speak out. He received little satisfaction. It was explained, reasonably enough, that the prisoner's hands *had* been untied and a tin dish of hardtack fried in pork grease (the usual staple of enlisted men) had been set before him, along with a cup of water. The "buck" had growled and overturned both offerings. Evidently, Captain Prowt suggested, the man lacked appetite.

"But surely," Palmer protested, "he must be dehydrated?"

It was conceded that such was very likely.

Palmer was distressed. *I do not understand,* he confided to his journal, *this indifference to the death of another human creature, even one so benighted as a savage sunk in barbarism. This heartless unconcern, I say, fills me with black misery.* Such were his sentiments that evening. Soon enough his misery would grow.

The wind shifted in the night. Rushing from the north now, it whistled through the pines. Dawn blew in grey and fiercely cold, the clouds dull pearl and scaly. The men turned out in the clumsy buffalo coats and the muskrat caps, and those with beards and moustaches seemed to bristle from head to foot.

After breakfast the column moved, the prisoner placed somewhere in the middle, bound in his blanket and set upon a mule, a rope around his neck held by the trooper behind.

"Does he have to have *that?*" Palmer objected.

"I'm afraid he does, Dan," Captain Fenton replied.

At the nooning Palmer went back with a tin dish of biscuit and beef. The Sioux sat the mule as though asleep. When Palmer showed the food, he averted his head.

That evening Palmer tried again.

"Eat!" I cried. "Eat! Eat! Eat!" And, rather comically, I think, I took a bite myself to show the way. "Meat!" I said.

Suddenly, to my astonishment, the subject snatched a morsel with his bound hands and popped it into his mouth.

"Mitt!"—he seemed to bark—or something like that.

"Meat!" I said.

"Mittuh!"

Palmer was trembling with excitement and confusion. *He has an ability with language, I think,* the physiognomist wrote. *The faculty, to be sure, is located in the inferior frontal convolution in the lower surface of the anterior lobe. Pressing upon the supraorbital plate, it throws the eye downwards and outwards. A clear enough sign all right, but somehow I missed it!*

But in the morning the brave was gone.

At first this disappearance seemed incredible, this vanishing like breath off a mirror. Then it was discoverd that several Crow scouts had also deserted. Apparently they had spirited away the prisoner, a Sioux and hence their hereditary enemy. Palmer flew upon Captain Fenton, who avoided his gaze.

There was much to admire about the Crows, Captain Fenton explained: tall, handsome, clean people, lighter than most savages and superb horse thieves. Some, however, were less than exquisite. These loafed about the forts with their squaws and papooses and dogs. When the urge seized them they could be magnificent scouts. Also, the pay attracted them, but they grew restive under discipline. Many were halfbreeds and squaw men. Some were thieves and bounty jumpers, the dregs of the agencies. Half the time they misdirected you or alerted the hostiles . . .

Yes, Palmer broke in, all that was fine, but what was the point? What were they going to *do* with the prisoner? Captain Fenton looked away again. About that, he said softly, he couldn't say.

Palmer understood—and was horrified. He sought out Shannon,

who, as it happened, was walking the picket line with an aide, the two men swollen-looking in the heavy buffalo coats. Shannon kept swinging his gloved fists together, making little pops.

". . . at Chattanooga," *he was saying when I arrived,* "the horses tried to eat bark, parts of wagons, tried to eat each other's manes and tails." *Ignoring me, he paused, knocked his fists together.* "Then," *he said,* "the men ate them."

"Major!" *I broke in.* "About the prisoner—how did the Crows get him?"

"No idea," *I was told.*

I persisted. Wasn't the brave someone's responsibility? I asked. Yes, Shannon agreed, and that someone had been fooled. Well then, I inquired, couldn't someone track the party? Couldn't some attempt be made? I pointed out that it still might not be too late.

The Major stopped and considered a horse. (All the mounts were covered with blankets and gunnysacks. They stood stamping and shivering and fluttering their nostrils, and their breath puffed out in little clouds.)

"Here's what I mean," *he said. Then he bent and lifted a hoof.* "No way to shoe a horse. Let a horse run barefoot, see how he wants to walk. Oh, it looks bully to shoe 'em so all four feet set the same, I know, but it's a bad idea." *Then Shannon straightened up.*

"Major!" *I cried—or rather barked, an intemperate burst.*

"Solferino!" *Shannon said, bewildering me.* "Before Solferino the French lost ten thousand horses. Think about it!"

Soon it began to snow. *The sky turned brown,* Palmer wrote, *the wind dropped. The first flakes fell, swirling down like tiny scraps of paper, powdering caps and shoulders, catching in beards and the horses' manes. A profound stillness reigns. I feel a throbbing between my eyes. My skull itself seems to ache, and the frozen air burns my lungs. . . .*

That evening, around the campfire at headquarters mess, he made some sort of official protest. What exactly he said or threatened we do not know, but that he intended to inform various authorities and newspapers seems certain, for a letter directed to the Commissioner of Indian Affairs still exists. Unfinished and unsent, drafted in pencil (his ink had frozen and burst the bottle), it begins: *On January 31st of this year, a column of United States cavalry and mounted infantry operating in response to rumors of hostile Indian movement was joined near Sulphur Flats in the*

Montana Territory by Major Robert Shannon and a party of Crow scouts. With him Major Shannon brought . . . Tersely the document continues, giving details, then asserts: *It is not these matters, distasteful as they are to anyone in whom the faculties of kindness, conscience and friendship are even moderately developed, which move me to write. Rather it is the negligence if not outright collusion.* . . .

Here the letter breaks off, and soon afterwards the story with it, for suddenly Palmer's journal, so voluble and indiscreet, the tight spidery prose (the ink portion a faded rust color today on·the brittle paper, the pencil almost indecipherable) becomes withdrawn, matter of fact, tightlipped. That inspired, sometimes tedious examination of conscience protracted over two thousand miles, three months and ten ragged notebooks (see the William T. Riggert Rare Book Collection, University of Montana, Missoula) stops abruptly. We are forced to speculate.

From Palmer's meager details, and from other firsthand accounts, it is possible to make some sort of reconstruction. There was a debate that night, possibly a "scene," the participants shaggy in their coats and caps like so many argumentative bears, their angry faces polished by firelight. We may imagine that Major Shannon sat his campstool and never raised his voice. We may assume that fat, good-natured Captain Fenton tried to make peace, that old goatbearded Captain Prowt was sarcastic and that Colonel Chilldress looked pained. What was said we do not know. Whether Palmer actually mentioned the letter he had begun and his intentions is questionable (though at some point Captain Fenton at least learned of such). What *is* certain is that Palmer, gripped with despair and misery, wandered off, wishing for solitude.

And how much of his suffering, one wonders, was due to some secret relief (which he hated)? Wasn't he glad, after all, the brave was gone? And was it once again himself he wished to assail and punish in his cries for justice?

And, too, one asks, was Major Shannon's hostility, his calculated contempt and pointed rudeness, were *they* in turn provoked by some fear and self-loathing? Did he despise Palmer—his very earnestness and ignorance, his childish persistance—because Palmer represented everything in himself which *Shannon* wished to destroy, every quality that seemed to the Major unmanly and base? Was Palmer the quintessential civilian in Shannon's eyes—a creature unworthy to bear arms? Further too, one asks, was the prisoner's very disappearance *arranged* by Shannon for precisely this result? And did Palmer suspect as much? Did this suspicion inflame him even further and fill him with anguish when he considered that he, in a sense, collaborated with the Major—that is, he wished, secretly, for just that outcome he felt compelled to deplore? Or did he? Did the image and sound of the brave inexplicably struggling to pronounce the white man's language return to haunt him?

Alone among the darkness and trees Palmer knew he must soon return to make a fire. A pale gibbous moon shone, yet it seemed that a few flakes dropped still. The wind had fallen. Palmer found that he was immensely tired. He sat upon a fallen tree, and dampness and cold seeped into him. He wondered if he could find his way back and recalled that he could, if necessary, fire a shot.

Fumbling out his knife, he dug at a dead tree, scaling bark and pricking out dry slivers. Then he rooted in the snow for seasoned twigs, threw down wet branches for a base and built a little cone of shavings. The feeling was already leaving his feet. His nose and cheekbones ached, "as though I had been beaten about the face."

. . . *The wood began to smoke,* Palmer wrote, in the last entry of any length, the last passionate moment. *I blew and a tiny leaf of flame fluttered up. I placed more twigs, pressing in, as though to embrace the heat, huddling in the pool of light. Outside, the trees rose in columns.*

I began to doze. Shadows flitted across the firelit trees and over the snow. Then I stiffened. Something seemed to move. I peered through the smoke and the wavering light. A twig snapped in the fire. Branches swayed and brushed together. I heard a plop—snow from a limb. Then my blood froze. Someone was standing among the trees.

He glided across the snow, the tracks stringing out behind. Limping, he approached and squatted. I saw the hawknose, the cheekbones like gleaming knuckles, the dark eyes burning with fever and hunger, the lips drawn tight. He stretched out his hands, flexing the long cold fingers. I stared at the buckskin leggings, the dirty bandage, the torn moccasins beaded with quillwork, the heavy blanket smelling of wet wool. He had followed the column. Somehow he had broken free and followed, sneaking in to steal the blanket and scraps of food. He had clung to us!

"Get warm!" I said. "You must get warm!" I whispered as though someone might overhear. I smiled. "Mittuh?" I said, though I had no meat. He gave no sign. Then, choosing a twig, he snapped and placed it on the fire, the long dark hands swift and agile now, like the hands of the blind. Quickly he began sorting my twigs, cracking them, setting them in place. The fire swept up.

"Mittuh?" I said.

He went on with his work. I too seized a twig and broke it. Then he let his hands hang, staring at the flames. The he looked at me.

He had drawn the blanket about him. Suddenly, I wondered what else he might have stolen. I saw the need to make him understand.

"If you are armed," I said, "so am I." I mimed pulling a trigger. It did no good. I drew off the mitten, undid the heavy coat and popped the holster flap. I drew the pistol slowly, hefting it, as though to guess the weight. I meant nothing more, only a show. At once he rose, shrinking back, his eyes never leaving me, dark and glittering in the firelight. Then he turned and began to run, the blanket flapping like coattails.

"Wait!" I cried. "Wait. You can stay. You must stay!"

I hurried after him, trees, rocks and shadows flashing by. I sucked the raw air.

He disappeared—then out from the trees, up a bank, down a gully and up again. Then I lost him, among a pile of snow-covered boulders. I wondered: was he waiting for me?

My chest was heaving, my heart slamming. I scooped snow and patted my feverish face. I could hear breathing—my own! The feeling was leaving my legs.

I feared moving, yielding my back, and yet . . . A shadow! I screamed. He darted away, but the scream was still in my ears and that burning rush of fear in my bowels.

"You!" I cried. "You!" And I saw him. The roar! The flash! "You!" I shouted. I fired again.

Emptying the gun it was as though I had burst from some great sea depth. My lungs filled with air. I could breathe. Only . . . the groaning, the noise, the smear of light . . . the shadow crumpling . . . and the joy, the joy, the joy! For a single instant scalding him as my scream scalded me . . .

A moment of reflection follows.

Here it must end. It is the knowledge of that obscene joy I cannot

302

bear. I seem to see the coppery bark of the pines and the bristling needles sprinkled with flakes and the dark half-buried rocks. Near the creek I can see the dingy frozen willows and the softly gleaming ice. Did they hear? I wondered. Would they come, dragging me back to their firelight and noise? I thought of Job: ". . . now shall I sleep in the dust; thou shalt seek me in the morning, but I shall not be."

But he was! The gunshot alerted the bivouac. Men did seek Palmer out, carried him back, slapping his shoulders and congratulating him, bringing him whiskey and coffee and blankets, rubbing his hands and feet with gunnysacks and ice and painting his extremities—and his nose—with iodine against frostbite. Huddled about the fire in the blankets, his face vivid with color, Palmer struggled feebly to explain, but, pressed for details, proved unhelpful. Did he look at Major Shannon? Did their eyes meet? Did some understanding flow? Did Shannon smile in faint bitter triumph? We do not know.

The column pushed on. By now, however, it had occurred to several officers that the mission itself was foolhardy and unnecessary. Captain Fenton in particular seems to have realized that the Indians were "up" to nothing—and couldn't be if they had tried—and though the Captain could not possibly have foreseen the course of history—the massacre at the Little Big Horn during the nation's centennial celebration, the outrage and resulting suppression of the Indians (ending in the bitter defeat at Wounded Knee), he saw clearly that war was *not* inevitable, that an assault upon some insignificant village could only be the spark to set the plains afire come spring. He—and others—privately consulted with Palmer, who at some point earlier *must* have threatened protest, not only via *The New York Herald* and *The Chicago Times* but also to General Terry in St. Paul, to General Crook in Omaha and to General Sheridan in Chicago. If there were some sort of objection, the officers insisted, some demand for an accounting—but a demand that for obvious reasons could not come from within the army itself—why if there could be an investigation of the battle of Deer Creek itself—much might be accomplished. Much too might be saved.

We lack Palmer's answer—or rather we find it in the empty pages, the brief notations. He simply records the pleas. If they stirred anything within him he does not mention it. When scouts returned with news of a village, a colloquy followed, more debate, and in the end Shannon prevailed, since no one except Palmer himself possessed a will sufficient to oppose his.

Thirty-five lodges, maybe a hundred fighting braves, Sioux and some Cheyenne camped across a lake in the mouth of a ravine.

"We don't need to do it!" Captain Fenton protested.

"We are at war," Shannon said smoothly, emphasizing each word.

"We're not at war!" Fenton objected.

Shannon made no reply (or so Palmer tells us).

The column left at night. No moon. A stiff wind flung snow in their faces and Shannon pushed everyone hard. They traveled light— a day's rations and ammunition. By midnight they reached the "sentinels"—three big peaks about the same distance apart. The column shoved through a pass and into a valley, rested and drove on, over bluffs and down slopes and into canyons, until the horses were panting and their flanks were streaming and flecked with curls of sweat. Then the troopers dismounted, scooped snow and rubbed their mounts.

Shannon forbade fires, and if a trooper sank into the slush and begged for rest, the officers would haul him up, cursing. Then they were all mounted and riding on, over flat ground until a ridge rose before them, as though from the sea.

Shannon sent a troop east, across the river, to lie in wait for the Indian ponies. Two more slipped around the west ridge, and the last two snuck north, to the ravine. Chilldress, Fenton and Palmer left their horses and climbed the ridge, looking into a wall of darkness, their breath clouding before them. The wind seemed to smother them. It was as though from the lake great wings beat forth waves of icy air, Palmer wrote, one of the few poetic touches he now allowed himself. Sometimes the tinkle of pony bells carried on the wind.

Slowly a pale white light began to flood the valley and the mist drifted into tatters, and they could hear the bells and see the river gleaming and the frozen lake covered with snow and all around, thick white mounds, and near the shore the ragged willows and cottonwoods casting grey shadows. Then, across the river, they saw the mules and ponies—small dark shapes, heads down, rumps to the wind. Then too, looking south, beneath the smoke and haze they saw the lodges scattered in the nooks of the old river bed.

Soon afterward the troopers formed in a company front, moved out, spreading across the valley—a long string of mouse-colored horses and blue-clothed men, coats gone, pistols cocked.

. . . *I could see,* Palmer wrote, *the tails switching and the heads lifted, ears back. I could see the glint of metal, the puff of breath— tiny sparkling clouds—and hear the jingle of bits and the squeak of leather. The troopers crossed the lake and mounted the shore, and behind them the prints and crushed snow rolled out. Then in the village someone hooted like a bird, a soldier whooped, the trumpet snarled, the men yelled and spurred, the horses squatted and sprang forward, tails flicking, snow kicking up behind. . . .*

At first it was only a trot, the men shouting and firing—spits of flame and the crackle and the smoke rising and drifting into a blue cloud. The Indians came swarming out, spinning and falling as they were hit, flinging up their arms or stumbling and dropping. Some escaped, most did not. The troopers tore down the lodges and piled them with dry cottonwood and fired everything— blankets and robes and buffalo meat and saddles and halters and powder. The fires smoldered; then the powder went up in great foamy sheets, and the long fir lodgepoles flung into the sky and down again. The snow began to melt; a dark cloud swept across the valley, and on the ridge you could smell the greasy stink of canvas and buffalo and elk hide burning.

They wouldn't leave the ponies and they couldn't handle them. The fires and the smell of white men spooked them, so to save ammunition the troopers bashed their skulls with axes or ripped their throats with knives, and the shrill trumpeting reached the ridge—the breath rushing from the slashed windpipes. Then came the *thoomp* of Captain Prowt's shotgun.

All this Palmer watched and noted, and if at some point his eyes met Major Shannon's we shall never know. In detail but without comment he leaves us his account.

"None of our men was killed," he concludes. "The wounded we dragged on travois."

🔥 🔥 🔥

CAREFUL

fiction by RAYMOND CARVER

from THE PARIS REVIEW

nominated by Jean Davidson, Elizabeth Inness-Brown, Robert Phillips, Sara Vogan and Patricia Zelver

AFTER A LOT OF TALKING—what his wife, Inez, called *assessment*—Lloyd moved out of the house and into his own place. He had two rooms and a bath on the top floor of a three-story house. Inside the rooms, the roof slanted down sharply. If he walked around, he had to duck his head. He had to stoop to look from his windows and be careful getting in and out of bed. There were two keys. One key let him into the house itself. Then he climbed some stairs that passed through the house to a landing. He went up another flight of stairs to the door of his room and used the other key on that lock.

Once, when he was coming back to his place in the afternoon, carrying a sack with three bottles of André champagne and some lunch meat, he stopped on the landing and looked into his landlady's living room. He saw the old woman lying on her back on the carpet. She seemed to be asleep. Then it occurred to him she might be dead. But the TV was going, so he chose to think she was asleep. He didn't know what to make of it. He moved the sack from one arm to the other. It was then that the woman gave a little cough, brought her hand to her side, and went back to being quiet and still again. Lloyd continued on up the stairs and unlocked his door. Later that day, toward evening, as he looked from his kitchen window, he saw the old woman down in the yard, wearing a straw hat and holding her hand against her side. She was using a little watering can on some pansies.

In his kitchen, he had a combination refrigerator and stove. The refrigerator and stove was a tiny affair wedged into a space between the sink and the wall. He had to bend over, almost get down on his knees, to get anything out of the refrigerator. But it was all right because he didn't keep much in there, anyway—except fruit juice, lunch meat, and champagne. The stove had two burners. Now and then he heated water in a saucepan and made instant coffee. But some days he didn't drink any coffee. He forgot, or else he just didn't feel like coffee. One morning he woke up and promptly fell to eating crumb doughnuts and drinking champagne. There'd been a time, some years back, when he would have laughed at having a breakfast like this. Now, there didn't seem to be anything very unusual about it. In fact, he hadn't thought anything about it until he was in bed and trying to recall the things he'd done that day, starting with when he'd gotten up that morning. At first he couldn't remember anything noteworthy. Then he remembered eating those doughnuts and drinking champagne. There was a time when he would have considered this a mildly crazy thing to do, something to tell friends about. Then, the more he thought about it, the more he could see it didn't matter much one way or the other. He'd had doughnuts and champagne for breakfast. So what?

In his furnished rooms, he also had a dinette set, a little sofa, an old easy chair, and a TV set that stood on a coffee table. He wasn't paying the electricity here, it wasn't even his TV, so sometimes he left the set on all day and all night. But he kept the volume down unless he saw there was something he wanted to watch. He did not have a telephone, which was fine with him. He didn't want a telephone. There was a bedroom with a double bed, a nightstand, and a chest of drawers. A bathroom gave off from the bedroom.

The one time Inez came to visit, it was eleven o'clock in the morning. He'd been in his new place for two weeks, and he'd been wondering if she were going to drop by. But he was trying to do something about his drinking, too, so he was glad to be alone. He'd made that much clear—being alone was the thing he needed most. The day she came, he was on the sofa, in his pajamas, hitting his fist against the right side of his head. Just before he could hit himself again, he heard voices downstairs on the landing. He could make out his wife's voice. The sound was like the murmur of voices from a faraway crowd, but he knew it was Inez and somehow knew the visit was an important one. He gave his head another jolt with his fist, then got to his feet.

He'd awakened that morning and found that his ear had stopped up with wax. He couldn't hear anything clearly, and he seemed to have lost his sense of balance, his equilibrium, in the process. For the last hour he'd been on the sofa, working frustratedly on his ear, now and again slamming his head with his fist. Once in a while he'd massage the grisly underpart of his ear, or else tug at his lobe. Then he'd dig furiously in his ear with his little finger and open his mouth, simulating yawns. But he'd tried everything he could think of, and he was nearing the end of his rope. He could hear the voices below break off their murmuring. He pounded his head a good one and finished the glass of champagne. He turned off the TV and carried the glass to the sink. He picked up the open bottle of champagne from the drainboard and took it into the bathroom where he put it behind the stool. Then he went to answer the door.

"Hi, Lloyd," Inez said. She didn't smile. She stood in the doorway in a bright spring outfit. He hadn't seen these clothes before. She was holding a canvas handbag that had sunflowers stitched onto its sides. He hadn't seen the handbag before, either.

"I didn't think you heard me," she said. "I thought you might be gone or something. But the woman downstairs—what's her name? Mrs. Matthews—she thought you were up here."

"I heard you," Lloyd said. "But just barely." He hitched his pajamas and ran a hand through his hair. "Actually, I'm in one hell of a shape. Come on in."

"It's eleven o'clock," she said. She came inside and shut the door behind her. She acted as if she hadn't heard him. Maybe she hadn't.

"I know what time it is," he said. "I've been up for a long time. I've been up since eight. I watched part of the *Today* show. But just now I'm about to go crazy with something. My ear's plugged up. You remember that other time it happened? We were living in that place near the Chinese takeout joint. Where the kids found that bulldog dragging its chain? I had to go to the doctor then and have my ears flushed out. I know you remember. You drove me and we had to wait a long time. Well, it's like that now. I mean it's that bad. Only I can't go to a doctor this morning. I don't have a doctor, for one thing. I'm about to go nuts, Inez. I feel like I want to cut off my head or something."

He sat down at one end of the sofa, and she sat down at the other end. But it was a small sofa, and they were still sitting close to each other. They were so close he could have put out his hand and touched her knee. But he didn't. She glanced around the room and then fixed her eyes on him again. He knew he hadn't shaved and that his hair stood up. But she was his wife, and she knew everything there was to know about him.

"What have you tried?" she said. She looked in her purse and brought up a cigarette. "I mean, what have you done for it so far?"

"What'd you say?" He turned the left side of his head to her. "Inez, I swear, I'm not exaggerating. This thing is driving me crazy. When I talk, I feel like I'm talking inside a barrel. My head rumbles. And I can't hear good, either. When *you* talk, it sounds like you're talking through a lead pipe."

"Do you have any Q-tips, or else Wesson oil?" Inez said.

"Honey, this is serious," he said. "I don't have any Q-tips or Wesson oil. Are you kidding?"

"If we had some Wesson oil, I could heat it and put some of that in your ear. My mother used to do that," she said. "It might soften things up in there."

He shook his head. His head felt full and like it was awash with fluid. It felt like it had when he used to swim near the bottom of the municipal pool and come up with his ears filled with water. But back then it'd been easy to clear the water out. All he had to do was fill his lungs with air, close his mouth and clamp down on his nose. Then he'd blow out his cheeks and force air into his head. His ears would pop, and for a few seconds he'd have the pleasant sensation of water running out of his head and dripping onto his shoulders. Then he'd heave himself out of the pool.

Inez finished her cigarette and put it out. "Lloyd, we have things to talk about. But I guess we'll have to take things one at a time. Go sit in the chair. Not *that* chair, the chair in the kitchen! So we can have some light on the situation."

He whacked his head once more. Then he went over to sit on a dinette chair. She moved over and stood behind him. She touched his hair with her fingers. Then she moved the hair away from his ears. He reached for her hand, but she drew it away.

"Which ear did you say it was?" she said.

"The right ear," he said. "The right one."

"First," she said, "you have to sit here and not move. I'll find a hairpin and some tissue paper. I'll try to get in there with that. Maybe it'll do the trick."

He was alarmed at the prospect of her putting a hairpin inside his ear. He said something to that effect.

"What?" she said. "Christ, I can't hear you, either. Maybe this is catching."

"When I was a kid, in school," Lloyd said, "we had this health teacher. She was like a nurse, too. She said we should never put anything smaller than an elbow into our ear." He vaguely remembered a wall chart showing a massive diagram of the ear, along with an intricate system of canals, passageways, and walls.

"Well, your nurse was never faced with this exact problem," Inez said. "Anyway, we need to try *something*. We'll try this first. If it doesn't work, we'll try something else. That's life, isn't it?"

"Does that have a hidden meaning or something?" Lloyd said.

"It means just what I said. But you're free to think as you please. I mean, it's a free country," she said. "Now, let me get fixed up with what I need. You just sit there."

She went through her purse, but she didn't find what she was looking for. Finally, she emptied the purse out onto the sofa. "No hairpins," she said. "Damn." But it was as if she were saying the words from another room. In a way, it was almost as if he'd imagined her saying them. There'd been a time, long ago, when they used to feel they had ESP when it came to what the other one was thinking. They could finish sentences that the other had started.

She picked up some nail clippers, worked for a minute, and then he saw the device separate in her fingers and part of it swing from the other part. A nail file protruded from the clippers. It looked to him as if she were holding a small dagger.

"You're going to put that in my ear?" he said.

"Maybe you have a better idea," she said. "It's this, or else I don't know what. Maybe you have a pencil? You want me to use that? Or maybe you have a screwdriver around," she said and laughed. "Don't worry. Listen, Lloyd, I won't hurt you. I said I'd be careful. I'll wrap some tissue around the end of this. It'll be all right. I'll be careful, like I said. You just stay where you are, and I'll get some tissues for this. I'll make a swab."

She went into the bathroom. She was gone for a time. He stayed where he was on the dinette chair. He began thinking of things he ought to say to her. He wanted to tell her he was limiting himself to champagne and champagne only. He wanted to tell her he was tapering off the champagne, too. It was only a matter of time now.

But when she came back into the room, he couldn't say anything. He didn't know where to start. But she didn't look at him, anyway. She fished a cigarette from the heap of things she'd emptied onto the sofa cushion. She lit the cigarette with her lighter and went to stand by the window that faced onto the street. She said something, but he couldn't make out the words. When she stopped talking, he didn't ask her what it was she'd said. Whatever it was, he knew he didn't want her to say it again. She put out the cigarette. But she went on standing at the window, leaning forward, the slope of the roof just inches from her head.

"Inez," he said.

She turned and came over to him. He could see tissue on the point of the nail file.

"Turn your head to the side and keep it that way," she said. "That's right. Sit still now and don't move. Don't move," she said again.

"Be careful," he said. "For Christ's sake."

She didn't answer him.

"Please, please," he said. Then he didn't say any more. He was afraid. He closed his eyes and held his breath as he felt the nail file turn past the inner part of his ear and begin its probe. He was sure his heart would stop beating. Then she went a little farther and began turning the blade back and forth, working at whatever it was in there. Inside his ear, he heard a squeaking sound.

"Ouch!" he said.

"Did I hurt you?" She took the nail file out of his ear and moved back a step. "Does anything feel different, Lloyd?"

He brought his hands up to his ears and lowered his head.

"It's just the same," he said.

She looked at him and bit her lips.

"Let me go to the bathroom," he said. "Before we go any farther, I have to go to the bathroom."

"Go ahead," Inez said. "I think I'll go downstairs and see if your landlady has any Wesson oil, or anything like that. She might even have some Q-tips. I don't know why I didn't think of that before. Of asking her."

"That's a good idea," he said. "I'll go to the bathroom."

She stopped at the door and looked at him, and then she opened the door and went out. He crossed the living room, went into his bedroom, and opened the bathroom door. He reached down behind the stool and brought up the bottle of champagne. He took a long drink. It was warm, but it went right down. He took some more. In the beginning, he'd really thought he could continue drinking if he limited himself to champagne. But in no time he found he was drinking three or four bottles a day. He knew he'd have to deal with this pretty soon. But first, he'd have to get his hearing back. One thing at a time, just like she'd said. He finished off the rest of the champagne and put the empty bottle in its place behind the stool. Then he ran water and brushed his teeth. After he'd used the towel, he went back into the other room.

Inez had returned and was at the stove heating something in a little pan. She glanced in his direction, but didn't say anything at first. He looked past her shoulder and out the window. A bird flew from the branch of one tree to another and preened its feathers. But if it made any kind of bird noise, he didn't hear it.

She said something that he didn't catch.

"Say again," he said.

She shook her head and turned back to the stove. But then she turned again and said, loud enough and slow enough so he could hear it: "I found your stash in the bathroom."

"I'm trying to cut back," he said.

She said something else. "What?" he said. "What'd you say?" He really hadn't heard her.

"We'll talk later," she said. "We have things to discuss, Lloyd. Money is one thing. But there are other things, too. First we have to see about this ear." She put her finger into the pan and then took the pan off the stove. "I'll let it cool for a minute," she said. "It's too hot right now. Sit down. Put this towel around your shoulders."

He did as he was told. He sat on the chair and put the towel around his neck and shoulders. Then he hit the side of his head with his fist.

"Goddamn it," he said.

She didn't look up. She put her finger into the pan once more, testing. Then she poured the liquid from the pan into his plastic glass. She picked up the glass and came over to him.

"Don't be scared," she said. "It's just some of your landlady's baby oil, that's all it is. I told her what was wrong, and she thought this might help. No guarantees," Inez said. "But maybe this'll loosen things up in there. She said it used to happen to her husband. She said this one time she saw a piece of wax fall out of his ear, and it was like a big plug of something. It was ear wax was what it was. She said try this. And she didn't have any Q-tips. I can't understand that, her not having any Q-tips. That part really surprises me."

"Okay," he said. "All right. I'm willing to try anything. Inez, if I had to go on like this, I think I'd rather be dead. You know? I mean it, Inez."

"Tilt your head all the way to the side now," she said. "Don't move. I'll pour this in until your ear fills up, then I'll stopper it with this dishrag. And you just sit there for ten minutes, say. Then we'll see. If this doesn't do it, well, I don't have any suggestions. I just don't know what to do then."

"This'll work," he said. "If this doesn't do it, I'll find a gun and shoot myself. I'm serious. That's what I feel like doing, anyway."

He turned his head to the side and let it hang down. He looked at the things in the room from this new perspective. But it wasn't any different from the old way of looking, except that everything was on its side.

"Farther," she said. He held onto the chair for balance and lowered his head even more. All of the objects in his vision, all of the objects in his life, it seemed, were at the far end of this room. He could feel the warm liquid pour into his ear. Then she brought the dishrag up and held it there. In a little while, she began to massage the area around his ear. She pressed into the soft part of the flesh between his jaw and skull. She moved her fingers to the area over his ear and began to work the tips of her fingers back and forth. After a while, he didn't know how long he'd been sitting there. It could have been ten minutes. It could have been longer. He was still holding onto the chair. Now and then, as her fingers pressed the side of his head, he could feel the warm oil she'd poured in there wash back and forth in the canals inside his ear. When she pressed a certain way, he imagined he could hear, inside his head, a soft, swishing sound.

"Sit up straight," Inez said. He sat up and pressed the heel of his hand against his head while the liquid poured out of his ear. She caught it in the towel. Then she wiped the outside of his ear.

Inez was breathing through her nose. Lloyd heard the sound her breath made as it came and went. He heard a car pass on the street outside the house and, at the back of the house, down below his kitchen window, the clear *snick-snick* of pruning shears.

"Well?" Inez said. She waited with her hands on her hips, frowning.

"I can hear you," he said. "I'm all right! I mean I can *hear*. It doesn't sound like you're talking underwater anymore. It's fine now. It's okay. God, I thought for a while I was going to go crazy. But I feel fine now. I can hear everything. Listen, honey, I'll make coffee. There's some juice, too."

"I have to go," she said. "I'm late for something. But I'll come back. We'll go out for lunch sometime. We need to talk."

"I just can't sleep on this side of my head, is all," he went on. He followed her into the living room. She lit a cigarette. "That's what happened. I slept all night on this side of my head, and my ear plugged up. I think I'll be all right as long as I don't forget and sleep on this side of my head. If I'm careful. You know what I'm saying? If I can just sleep on my back, or else on my left side."

She didn't look at him.

"Not forever, of course not, I know that. I couldn't do that. I couldn't do it the rest of my life. But for a while, anyway. Just my left side, or else flat on my back."

But even as he said this he began to feel afraid of the night that was coming. He began to fear the moment he would begin to make his preparations for bed and what might happen afterwards. That time was hours away, but already he was afraid. What if, in the middle of the night, he accidentally turned onto his right side, and the weight of his head pressing into the pillow were to seal the wax again into the dark canals of his ear? What if he woke up then, unable to hear, the ceiling inches from his head?

"Good God," he said. "Jesus, this is awful. Inez, I just had something like a terrible nightmare. Inez, where do you have to go?"

"I told you," she said, as she put everything back into her purse and made ready to leave. She looked at her watch. "I'm late for something." She went to the door. But at the door she turned and said something else to him. He didn't listen. He didn't want to. He watched her lips move until she said what she had to say. When she'd finished, she said, "Goodbye." Then she opened the door and closed it behind her.

He went into the bedroom to dress. But in a minute he hurried out, wearing only his trousers, and went to the door. He opened it and stood there, listening. On the landing below, he heard Inez thank Mrs. Matthews for the oil. He heard the old woman say, "You're welcome." And then he heard her draw a connection between her late husband and himself. He heard her say, "Leave me your number. I'll call if something happens. You never know."

"I hope you don't have to," Inez said. "But I'll give it to you, anyway. Do you have something to write it down with?"

Lloyd heard Mrs. Matthews open a drawer and rummage through it. Then her old woman's voice said, "Okay."

Inez gave her their telephone number at home. "Thanks," she said.

"It was nice meeting you," Mrs. Matthews said.

He listened as Inez went on down the stairs and opened the front door. Then he heard it close. He waited until he heard her start their car and drive away. Then he shut the door and went back into the bedroom to finish dressing.

After he'd put on his shoes and tied the laces, he lay down on the bed and pulled the covers up to his chin. He let his arms rest under the covers at his side. He closed his eyes and pretended it was night and pretended he was going to fall asleep. Then he brought his arms up and crossed them over his chest to see how this position would suit him. He kept his eyes closed, trying it out. All right, he thought. Okay. If he didn't want that ear to plug up again, he'd have to sleep on his back, that was all. He knew he could do it. He just couldn't forget, even in his sleep, and turn onto the wrong side. Four or five hours sleep a night was all he needed anyway. He'd manage. Worse things could happen to a man. In a way, it was a challenge. But he was up to it. He knew he was. In a minute, he threw back the covers and got up.

He still had the better part of the day ahead of him. He went into the kitchen, bent down in front of the little refrigerator, and took out a fresh bottle of champagne. He worked the plastic cork out of the bottle as carefully as he could, but there was still the festive *pop* of champagne being opened. He rinsed the baby oil out of his glass, then poured it full of champagne. He took the glass over to the sofa and sat down. He put the glass on the coffee table. Up went his feet onto the coffee table, next to the champagne. He leaned back. But after a time, he began to worry some more about the night that was coming on. What if, despite all his efforts, the wax decided to plug his other ear? He closed his eyes and shook his head. Pretty soon, he got up and went into the bedroom. He undressed and put his pajamas back on. Then he moved back into the living room. He sat down on the sofa once more, and once more put his feet up. He reached over and turned the TV on. He adjusted the volume. He knew he couldn't keep from worrying about what might happen when he went to bed. It was just something he'd have to learn to live with. In a way, this whole business reminded him of the thing with the doughnuts and champagne. It was not that remarkable at all, if you thought about it. He took some champagne. But it didn't taste right. He ran his tongue over his lips, then wiped his mouth on his sleeve. He looked and saw a film of oil on the champagne.

He got up and carried the glass to the sink where he poured it into the drain. He took the bottle of champagne into the living room and made himself comfortable on the sofa. He held the bottle by its neck as he drank. He'd never before drunk straight from the bottle, but it didn't seem that much out of the ordinary. He decided that even if he were to fall asleep sitting up on the sofa in the middle of the afternoon, it wouldn't be any more strange than somebody having to lie on his back for hours at a time. He lowered his head to peer out the window. Judging from the angle of the sunlight, and the shadows that had entered the room, he guessed it was about three o'clock.

POETRY AND AMBITION

by DONALD HALL

from THE KENYON REVIEW

nominated by THE KENYON REVIEW *and Robert Phillips*

1. I SEE NO REASON to spend your life writing poems unless your goal is to write great poems.

An ambitious project—but sensible, I think. And it seems to me that contemporary American poetry is afflicted by modesty of ambition—a modesty, alas, genuine . . . if sometimes accompanied by vast pretense. Of course the great majority of contemporary poems, in any era, will always be bad or mediocre. (Our time may well be characterized by more mediocrity and less badness.) But if failure is constant the types of failure vary, and the qualities and habits of our society specify the manners and the methods of our failure. I think that we fail in part because we lack serious ambition.

2. If I recommend ambition, I do not mean to suggest that it is easy or pleasurable. "I would sooner fail," said Keats at twenty-two, "than not be among the greatest." When he died three years later he believed in his despair that he had done nothing, the poet of "Ode to a Nightingale" convinced that his name was "writ in water." But he was mistaken, he was mistaken. . . . If I praise the ambition that drove Keats, I do not mean to suggest that it will ever be rewarded. We never know the value of our own work, and everything reasonable leads us to doubt it: for we can be certain that few contemporaries will be read in a hundred years. To desire to write poems that endure—we undertake such a goal certain of two things: that in all likelihood we will fail, and that if we succeed we will never know it.

Every now and then I meet someone certain of personal greatness. I want to pat this person on the shoulder and mutter comforting words: "Things will get better! You won't always feel so depressed! Cheer up!"

But I just called high ambition sensible. If our goal in life is to remain content, *no* ambition is sensible. . . . If our goal is to write poetry, the only way we are likely to be *any* good is to try to be as great as the best.

3. But for some people it seems ambitious merely to set up as a poet, merely to write and to publish. Publication stands in for achievement—as everyone knows, universities and grant-givers take publication as achievement—but to accept such a substitution is modest indeed, for publication is cheap and easy. In this country we publish more poems (in books and magazines) and more poets read more poems aloud at more poetry readings than ever before; the increase in thirty years has been tenfold.

So what? Many of these poems are often *readable*, charming, funny, touching, sometimes even intelligent. But they are usually brief, they resemble each other, they are anecdotal, they do not extend themselves, they make no great claims, they connect small things to other small things. Ambitious poems usually require a certain length for magnitude; one need not mention monuments like *The Canterbury Tales*, *The Faerie Queene*, *Paradise Lost*, or *The Prelude*. "Epithalamion," "Lycidas," and "Ode: Intimations of Immortality" are sufficiently extended, not to mention "The Garden" or "Out of the Cradle. . . ." Not to mention the poet like Yeats whose briefer works make great connections.

I do not complain that we find ourselves incapable of such achievement; I complain that we seem not even to entertain the desire.

4. Where Shakespeare used "ambitious" of Macbeth we would say "over-ambitious"; Milton used "ambition" for the unscrupulous overreaching of Satan; the word describes a deadly sin like "pride." Now when I call Milton "ambitious" I use the modern word, mellowed and washed of its darkness. This amelioration reflects capitalism's investment in social mobility. In more hierarchal times pursuit of honor might require revolutionary social change, or

318

murder; but Protestantism and capitalism celebrate the desire to rise.

Milton and Shakespeare, like Homer, acknowledge the desire to make words that live forever: ambitious enough, and fit to the O.E.D.'s first definition of "ambition" as "eager desire of honor"—which will do for poets and warriors, courtiers and architects, diplomats, Members of Parliament, and Kings. Desire need not imply drudgery. Hard work enters the definition at least with Milton, who is ready "To scorn delights, and live laborious days," to discover fame, "the spur, that last infirmity of noble minds." We note the infirmity who note that fame results only from laborious days' attendance upon a task of some magnitude: when Milton invoked the Heavenly Muse's "aid to my adventurous song," he wanted merely to "justify the ways of God to men."

If the word "ambitious" has mellowed, "fame" has deteriorated enough to require a moment's thought. For us, fame tends to mean Johnny Carson and *People* magazine. For Keats as for Milton, for Hector as for Gilgamesh, it meant something like universal and enduring love for the deed done or the song sung. The idea is more classic than Christian, and the poet not only seeks it but confers it. Who knows Achilles' valor but for Homer's tongue? But in the 1980s—after centuries of cheap printing, after the spread of mere literacy and the decline of qualified literacy, after the loss of history and the historical sense, after television has become mother of us all—we have seen the decline of fame until we use it now as Andy Warhol uses it, as the mere quantitative distribution of images. . . . We have a culture crowded with people who are famous for being famous.

5. True ambition in a poet seeks fame in the old sense, to make words that live forever. If even to entertain such ambition reveals monstrous egotism, let me argue that the common alternative is petty egotism that spends itself in small competitiveness, that measures its success by quantity of publication, by blurbs on jackets, by small achievement: to be the best poet in the workshop, to be published by Atheneum, to win the Pulitzer or the Nobel. . . . The grander goal is to be as good as Dante.

Let me hypothesize the developmental stages of the poet.
At twelve, the American poet-to-be is afflicted with generalized

ambition. (Robert Frost wanted to be a baseball pitcher and a United States senator: Oliver Wendell Holmes said that *nothing* was so commonplace as the desire to appear remarkable; the desire may be common but it is at least essential.) At sixteen the poet reads Whitman and Homer and wants to be immortal. Alas, at twenty-four the same poet wants to be in the *New Yorker*.

There is an early stage when the poem becomes more important than the poet; one can see it as a transition from the lesser egotism to the greater. At the stage of lesser egotism, the poet keeps a bad line or an inferior word or image because *that's the way it was: that's what really happened*. At this stage the frail ego of the author takes precedence over art. The poet must develop, past this silliness, to the stage where the poem is altered for its own sake, to make it better art, not for the sake of its maker's feelings but because decent art is the goal. Then the poem lives at some distance from its creator's little daily emotions; it can take on its own character in the mysterious place of satisfying shapes and shapely utterance. The poem freed from its precarious utility as ego's appendage may possibly fly into the sky and become a star permanent in the night air.

Yet, alas, when the poet tastes a little fame, a little praise. . . . Sometimes the poet who has passed this developmental stage will forget duty to the art of poetry and again serve the petty egotism of the self. . . .

Nothing is learned once that does not need learning again. The poet whose ambition is unlimited at sixteen and petty at twenty-four may turn unlimited at thirty-five and regress at fifty. But if everyone suffers from interest, everyone may pursue disinterest.

Then there is a possible further stage: when the poet becomes an instrument or agency of art, the poem freed from the poet's ego may entertain the possibility of grandeur. And this grandeur, by a familiar paradox, may turn itself an apparent 180 degrees to tell the truth. Only when the poem turns wholly away from the petty ego, only when its internal structure fully serves art's delicious purposes, may it serve to reveal and envision. "Man can *embody* truth"—said Yeats; I add the italic—"he cannot *know* it." Embodiment is art and artfulness.

When Yeats was just south of fifty he wrote that he "sought an image not a book." Many aging poets leave the book behind to search for the diagram, and write no more poetry than Michael Robartes who drew geometrical shapes in the sand. The turn toward wisdom—toward gathering the whole world into a book—often leaves poetry behind as a frivolity. And though these prophets may delight in abstract revelation, we cannot follow them into knowing, who followed their earlier embodiments. . . . Yeats' soul knew an appetite for invisibility—the temptation of many—but the man remained composite, and although he sought and found a vision he continued to write a book.

6. We find our models of ambition mostly from reading.

We develop the notion of art from our reading. When we call the poem more important than ourselves, it is not that we have confidence in *our* ability to write it; we believe in *poetry*. We look daily at the great monuments of old accomplishment and we desire to add to their number, to make poems in homage to poems. Old poems that we continue to read and love become the standard we try to live up to. These poems, internalized, criticize our own work. These old poems become our Muse, our encouragement to song and our discouragement of comparison.

Therefore it is essential for all poets, all the time, to read and reread the great ones. Some lucky poets make their living by publicly reacquainting themselves in the classroom with the great poems of the language. Alas, many poets now teach nothing but creative writing, read nothing but the words of children . . . (I will return to this subject).

It is also true that many would-be poets lack respect for learning. How strange that the old ones read books. . . . Keats stopped school when he has fifteen or so; but he translated the *Aeneid* in order to study it and worked over Dante in Italian and daily sat at the feet of Spenser, Shakespeare, and Milton. ("Keats studied the old poets every day / Instead of picking up his M.F.A.") Ben Jonson was learned and in his cups looked down at Shakespeare's relative ignorance of ancient languages—but Shakespeare learned more language and literature at his Stratford grammar school than we acquire in twenty years of schooling. Whitman read and educated himself with vigor; Eliot and Pound continued their studies after stints of graduate school.

On the other hand, we play records all night and write unambitious poems. Even talented young poets—saturated in S'ung, suffused in Sufi—know nothing of Bishop King's "Exequy." The syntax and sounds of one's own tongue, and that tongue's four-hundred-year-old ancestors, give us more than all the classics of all the world in translation.

But to struggle to read the great poems of another language—*in* the language—that is another thing. We are the first generation of poets not to study Latin; not to read Dante in Italian. Thus the puniness of our unambitious syntax and limited vocabulary.

When we have read the great poems we can study as well the lives of the poets. It is useful, in the pursuit of models, to read the lives and letters of the poets whose work we love. Keats's letters, heaven knows.

7. In all societies there is a template to which its institutions conform, whether or not the institutions instigate products or activities that suit such a pattern. In the Middle Ages the Church provided the model, and Guilds and secret societies erected their colleges of cardinals. Today the American industrial corporation provides the template, and the university models itself on General Motors. Corporations exist to create or discover consumers' desires and fulfill them with something that satisfies briefly and needs frequent repetition. CBS provides television as Gillette supplies disposable razors—and, alas, the universities turn out degree-holders equally disposable; and the major publishers of New York City (most of them less profitable annexes of conglomerates peddling soap, beer, and paper towels) provide disposable master-pieces.

The United States invented mass quick-consumption and we are very good at it. We are not famous for making Ferraris and Roll Royces; we are famous for the people's car, the Model T, the Model A—"transportation," as we call it: the particular abstracted into the utilitarian generality—and two in every garage. Quality is all very well but it is *not* democratic; if we insist on hand-building Rolls Royces most of us will walk to work. Democracy demands the interchangeable part and the worker on the production line; Thomas Jefferson may have had other notions but de Tocqueville was our prophet. Or take American cuisine: it has never added a sauce to the world's palate, but our fast-food industry overruns the planet.

Thus: our poems, in their charming and interchangeable quantity, do not presume to the status of "Lycidas"—for that would be elitist and un-American. We write and publish the McPoem—*ten billion served*—which becomes our contribution to the history of literature as the Model T is our contribution to a history which runs from bare feet past elephant and rickshaw to the vehicles of space. Pull in any time day or night, park by the busload, and the McPoem waits on the steam shelf for us, wrapped and protected, indistinguishable, undistinguished, and reliable—the good old McPoem identical from coast to coast and in all the little towns between, subject to the quality control of the least common denominator.

And every year, Ronald McDonald takes the Pulitzer.

To produce the McPoem, institutions must enforce patterns, institutions within institutions, all subject to the same glorious dominance of unconscious economic determinism, template and formula of consumerism.

The McPoem is the product of the workshops of Hamburger University.

8. But before we look into the workshop, with its training program for junior poets, let us take a look at models provided by poetic heroes of the American present. The university does not invent the stereotypes; it provides technology for mass reproduction of a model created elsewhere.

Question: If you manufacture Pac-Man, or a car called Mustang, and everyone suddenly wants to buy what you make, how do you respond? Answer: You add shifts, pay overtime, and expand the plant in order to saturate the market with your product. . . . You make your product as quickly as you can manufacture it; notions of quality control do not disturb your dreams.

When Robert Lowell was young he wrote slowly and painfully and very well. On his wonderful Library of Congress LP, before he recites his early poem about "Falling Asleep over the Aeneid," he tells how the poem began when he tried translating Virgil but produced only eighty lines in six months, which he found disheartening. Five years elapsed between his Pulitzer book *Lord Weary's*

Castle, which was the announcement of his genius, and its under-rated successor *The Mills of the Kavanaghs.* Then there were eight more years before the abrupt innovation of *Life Studies. For the Union Dead* was spotty, *Near the Ocean* spottier, and then the rot set in.

Now, no man should be hanged for losing his gift, most especially a man who suffered as Lowell did. But one can, I think, feel annoyed when quality plunges as quantity multiplies: Lowell published six bad books of poems in those disastrous last eight years of his life.

(I say "bad books" and would go to the stake over the judgment, but let me hasten to acknowledge that each of these dreadful collections—dead metaphor, flat rhythm, narcissistic self-exploitation—was celebrated by leading critics on the front page of the *New York Times Book Review* and the *New York Review of Books* as the greatest yet of uniformly great emanations of great poetical greatness, greatly achieved. . . . But one wastes one's time in indignation. Taste is always a fool.)

John Berryman wrote with difficult concentration his difficult, concentrated *Mistress Bradstreet;* then he eked out *77 Dream Songs.* Alas, after the success of this product he mass-produced *His Toy His Dream His Rest,* 308 further dream songs—quick improvisations of self-imitation, which is the true identity of the famous "voice" accorded late Berryman-Lowell. Now Robert Penn Warren, our current grand old man, accumulates another long book of poems every year or so, repeating himself instead of rewriting the same poem until it is right—hurry, hurry, hurry—and the publishing tribe celebrates these sentimental, crude, trite products of our industrial culture.

Not all poets overproduce in a response to eminence: Elizabeth Bishop never went on overtime; T. S. Eliot wrote bad plays at the end of his life, but never watered the soup of his poems; nor did Williams nor Stevens nor Pound. Of course everyone writes some inferior work—but these poets did not gush out bad poems late in their lives when they were famous and the market required more products for selling.

Mind you, the workshops of Hamburger University turned out cheap, ersatz Bishop, Eliot, Williams, Stevens, and Pound. All you want. . . .

9. Horace, when he wrote the *Ars Poetica,* recommended that poets keep their poems home for ten years; don't let them go, don't publish them until you have kept them around for ten years: by that time, they ought to stop moving on you; by that time, you ought to have them right. Sensible advice, I think—but difficult to follow. When Pope wrote "An Essay on Criticism" seventeen hundred years after Horace, he cut the waiting time in half, suggesting that poets keep their poems for five years before publication. Henry Adams said something about acceleration, mounting his complaint in 1912; some would say that acceleration has accelerated in the seventy years since. By this time, I would be grateful—and published poetry would be better—if people kept their poems home for eighteen months.

Poems have become as instant as coffee or onion soup mix. One of our eminent critics compared Lowell's last book to the work of Horace, although some of its poems were dated the year of publication. Anyone editing a magazine receives poems dated the day of the postmark. When a poet types and submits a poem just composed (or even shows it to spouse or friend) the poet cuts off from the poem the possibility of growth and change; I suspect that the poet *wishes* to forestall the possibilities of growth and change, though of course without acknowledging the wish.

If Robert Lowell, John Berryman and Robert Penn Warren publish without allowing for revision or self-criticism, how can we expect a twenty-four-year-old in Manhattan to wait five years—or eighteen months? With these famous men as models, how should we blame the young poet who boasts in a brochure of over four hundred poems published in the last five years? Or the publisher, advertising a book, who brags that his poet has published twelve books in ten years? Or the workshop teacher who meets a colleague on a crosswalk and buffs the backs of his fingernails against his tweed as he proclaims that, over the last two years, he has averaged "placing" two poems a week?

10. Abolish the M.F.A.! What a ringing slogan for a new Cato: *Iowa delenda est!*

The workshop schools us to produce the McPoem, which is "a mold in plaster, / Made with no loss of time," with no waste of effort, with no strenuous questioning as to merit. If we attend a workshop we must bring something to class or we do not contribute. What kind of workshop could Horace have contributed to, if he kept his poems to himself for ten years? No, we will not admit Horace and Pope to our workshops, for they will just sit there, holding back their own work, claiming it is not ready, acting superior, a bunch of *elitists*. . . .

When we use a metaphor, it is useful to make inquiries of it. I have already compared the workshop to a fast food franchise, to a Ford assembly line. . . . Or should we compare Creative Writing 401 to a sweatshop where women sew shirts at an illegally low wage? Probably the metaphor refers to none of the above, because the workshop is rarely a place for starting and finishing poems; it is a place for repairing them. The poetry workshop resembles a garage to which we bring incomplete or malfunctioning homemade machines for diagnosis and repair. Here is the homemade airplane for which the crazed inventor forgot to provide wings; here is the internal combustion engine all finished except that it lacks a carburetor; here is the rowboat without oarlocks, the ladder without rungs, the motorcycle without wheels. We advance our non-functional machine into a circle of other apprentice inventors and one or two senior Edisons. "Very good," they say; "it *almost* flies. . . . How about, uh . . . how about *wings*?" Or, "Let me just show you how to build a carburetor. . . ."

Whatever we bring to this place, we bring it soo soon. The weekly meetings of the workshop serve the haste of our culture. When we bring a new poem to the workshop, anxious for praise, others' voices enter the poem's metabolism before it is mature, distorting its possible growth and change. "It's only when you get far enough away from your work to begin to be critical of it yourself"—Robert Frost said—"that anyone else's criticism can be tolerable. . . ." Bring to class only, he said, "old and cold things. . . ." Nothing is old and cold until it has gone through months of drafts. Therefore workshopping is intrinsically impossible.

It is from workshops that American poets learn to enjoy the embarrassment of publication—too soon, too soon—because *making public* is a condition of workshopping. This publication exposes oneself to one's fellow-poets only—a condition of which poets are perpetually accused and frequently guilty. We learn to write poems that will please not the Muse but our contemporaries, thus poems that resemble our contemporaries' poems—thus the recipe for the McPoem. . . . If we learn one thing else, we learn to publish promiscuously; these premature ejaculations count on number and frequency to counterbalance ineptitude.

Poets who stay outside the circle of peers—like Whitman, who did not go to Harvard; like Dickinson for whom there was no tradition; like Robert Frost, who dropped out of two colleges to make his own way—these poets take Homer for their peer. To quote Frost again: "The thing is to write better and better poems. Setting our heart when we're too young on getting our poems appreciated lands us in the politics of poetry which is death." Agreeing with these words from Frost's dour middle-age, we need to add: and "setting our heart" when we are old "on getting our poems appreciated" lands us in the same place.

11. At the same time, it's a big country. . . .

Most poets need the conversation of other poets. They do not need mentors; they need friends, critics, people to argue with. It is no accident that Wordsworth, Coleridge, and Southey were friends when they were young; if Pound, H.D., and William Carlos Williams had not known each other when young, would they have become William Carlos Williams, H.D., and Pound? There have been some lone wolves but not many. The history of poetry is a history of friendships and rivalries, not only with the dead great ones but with the living young. My four years at college overlapped with the undergraduates Frank O'Hara, Adrienne Rich, John Ashbery, Robert Bly, Peter Davison, L. E. Sissman, and Kenneth Koch. (At the same time Galway Kinnell and W. S. Merwin attended Princeton.) I do not assert that we resembled a sewing circle, that we often helped each other overtly, or even that we *liked* each other. I do assert that we were lucky to have each other around for purposes of conversation.

We were not in workshops; we were merely attending college. Where else in this country would we have met each other? In France there is an answer to this question and it is Paris. Europe goes in for capital cities. Although England is less centralized than France or Romania, London is more capital than New York, San

Francisco, or Washington. While the French poet can discover the intellectual life of his times at a café, the American requires a degree program. The workshop is the institutionalized café.

The American problem of geographical isolation is real. Any remote place may be the site of poetry—imagined, remembered, or lived in—but for almost every poet it is necessary to live in exile before returning home—an exile rich in conflict and confirmation. Central New Hampshire or the Olympic Peninsula or Cincinnati or the soybean plains of western Minnesota or the lower East Side may shine at the center of our work and our lives; but if we never leave these places we are not likely to grow up enough to do the work. There is a terrible poignancy in the talented artist who fears to leave home—defined as a place *first* to leave and *then* to return to.

So the workshop answers the need for a café. But I called it the *institutionalized* café, and it differs from the Parisian version by instituting requirements and by hiring and paying mentors. Workshop mentors even make assignments: "Write a persona poem in the voice of a dead ancestor." "Make a poem containing these ten words in this order with as many other words as you wish." "Write a poem without adjectives, or without prepositions, or without content. . . ." These formulas, everyone says, are a whole lot of fun. . . . They also reduce poetry to a parlor game; they trivialize and make safe-seeming the real terrors of real art. This reduction-by-formula is not accidental. We play these games *in order* to reduce poetry to a parlor game. Games serve to democratize, to soften, and to standardize; they are repellent. Although in theory workshops serve a useful purpose in gathering young artists together, workshop practices enforce the McPoem.

This is your contrary assignment: be as good a poet as George Herbert. Take as long as you wish.

12. I mentioned earlier the disastrous separation, in many universities, of creative writing and literature. There are people writing poetry—teaching poetry, studying poetry—who find reading *academic*. Such a sentence sounds like a satiric invention; alas, it is objective reporting.

Our culture rewards specialization. It is absurd that we erect a barrier between one who reads and one who writes, but it is an absurdity with a history. It is absurd because in our writing our

328

standards derive from what we have read, and its history reaches back to the ancient war between the poets and the philosophers, exemplified in Plato's "Ion" as the philosopher condescends to the rhapsode. In the thirties poets like Ransom, Tate, and Winters entered the academy under sufferance, condescended to. Tate and Winters especially made themselves academically rigorous. They secured the beachheads; the army of their grandchildren occupies the country: often grandsons and daughters who write books but do not read them.

The separation of the literature department from the writing department is a disaster; for poet, for scholar, and for student. The poet may prolong adolescence into retirement by dealing only with the products of infant brains. (If the poet, as in some schools, teaches literature, but only to writing students, the effect is better but not much better. The temptation exists then to teach literature as craft or trade; Americans don't need anyone teaching them trade.) The scholars of the department, institutionally separated from the contemporary, are encouraged to ignore it. In the ideal relationship, writers play gadfly to scholars, and and scholars help writers connect to the body of past literature. Students lose the writer's special contribution to the study of literature. Everybody loses.

13. It is commonplace that, in the English and American tradition, critic and poet are the same person—from Campion to Pound, from Sidney to Eliot. This tradition started with controversies between poets over the propriety of rhyme and English meter, and with poets' defense of poetry against Puritan attack. It flourished, serving many purposes, through Dryden, Johnson, Coleridge, Wordsworth, Keats in his letters, Shelley, Arnold. . . . Although certain poets have left no criticism, there are *no* first-rate critics in the English tradition who are not also poets—except for Hazlitt. The poet and the critic have been almost continuous, as if writing poetry and thinking about it were not discrete activities.

When Roman Jakobson—great linguist, Harvard professor—was approached some years ago with the suggestion that Vladimir Nabokov might be appointed professor of Slavic, Jakobson was skeptical; he had nothing against elephants, he said, but he would not appoint one professor of zoology.

Oh, dear.

The analogy compares the elegant and stylish Nabokov—novelist in various languages, lepidopterist, lecturer, and critic—to the great, gray, hulking pachyderm, intellectually noted *only* for memory. . . . By jokes and analogies we reveal ourselves. Jakobson condescends to Nabokov—just as Plato patted little Ion on his head, just as Sartre makes charitable exception for poets in *What is Literature?*, just as men have traditionally condescended to women and imperialists to natives. The points are clear: 1) "Artists are closer to nature than thinkers; they are more instinctive, more emotional; they are childlike." 2) "Artists like bright colors; artists have a natural sense of rhythm; artists screw all the time." 3) "Don't misunderstand. We *like* artists . . . in their place, which is in the zoo, or at any rate outside the Republic, or at any rate outside tenured ranks."

(One must admit, I suppose, that poets often find themselves in tenured ranks these days. But increasingly they enter by the zoo entrance, which in our universities is the department of creative writing.)

Formalism, with its dream of finite measurement, is a beautiful arrogance, a fantasy of materialism. When we find what's to measure and measure it, we should understand style-as-fingerprint, quantifying characteristic phonemic sequence . . . or whatever. But it seems likely that we will continue to intuit qualities, like degrees of intensity, for which objective measure is impossible. Then hard-noses will claim that only the measurable exists—which is why hard-nose usually means soft-head.

Once I audited a course of Jakobson's, for which I am grateful; the old formalist discoursed on comparative prosody, witty and energetic and learned, giving verbatim examples from Urdu and fifty other languages, exemplifying the multiplicity of countable noise. The journey was marvelous, the marvel diminished only a little by its terminus. The last lecture, pointed to for some weeks, turned out to be a demonstration, from an objective and untraditional approach, of how to scan (and the scansion was fine, and it was the way one scanned the poem when one was sixteen) of Edgar Poe's "The Raven."

14. A product of the creative writing industry is the writerly newsletter which concerns itself with publications, grants, and

jobs—and with nothing serious. If poets meeting each other in 1941 discussed how much they were paid a line, now they trade information about grants; left wing and right united; to be Establishment is to have received an N.E.A. grant; to be anti-Establishment is to denounce the N.E.A. as a conspiracy. . . . Like Republicans and Democrats, all belong to the same capitalist party.

Poets and Writers publishes *Coda*, with chatty articles about self-publication, with lists of contests and awards. It resembles not so much a trade journal as a hobbyist's bulletin, unrelievedly cheerful, relentlessly trivial. The same organization issues the telephone-book, *A Directory of American Poets*, "Names and addresses of 1,500 poets. . . ." The same organization offers T-shirts and bookbags labeled "Poets and Writers."

Associated Writing Programs publishes *A.W.P. Newsletter*, which includes one article each issue—often a talk addressed to an A.W.P. meeting—and adds helpful business aids: The December 1982 issue includes advice on "The 'Well Written' Letter of Application," lists of magazines requesting material ("The editors state they are looking for 'straightforward but not inartistic work' "), lists of grants and awards ("The annual HARRY SMITH BOOK AWARD is given by COSMEP to . . ."), and notices of A.W.P. competitions and conventions. . . .

Really, these newsletters provide illusion; for jobs and grants go to the eminent people. As we all know, eminence is arithmetical: it derives from the number of units published times the prestige of the places of publication. People hiring or granting do not judge quality—it's so subjective!—but anyone can multiply units by the prestige index and come off with the *product*. Eminence also brings readings. Can we go uncorrupted by such knowledge? I am asked to introduce a young poet's volume; the publisher will pay the going rate; but I did not know that there was a going rate. . . . Even blurbs on jackets are commodities. They are exchanged for pamphlets, for readings; reciprocal blurbs are only the most obvious exchanges. . . .

15. Sigh.

If it seems hopeless, one has only to look up in perfect silence at the stars . . . and it *does* help to remember that poems are the stars, not poets. Of most help is to remember that it is possible for people to take hold of themselves and become better by thinking. It is also necessary, alas, to *continue* to take hold of ourselves—if we are to pursue the true ambition of poetry. Our disinterest must discover that last week's nobility was really covert rottenness, etcetera. One is never free and clear; one must work continually to sustain, to recover. . . .

When Keats in his letters praised disinterestedness—his favorite moral idea, destroyed when it is misused as a synonym for lethargy (on the same day I found it misused in the *New York Times*, *Inside Sports,* and the *American Poetry Review*), he lectured himself because he feared that he would lose it. (Lectures loud with moral advice are always self-addressed.) No one is guiltless of temptation, but it is possible to resist temptation. When Keats worried over his reputation, over insults from Haydon or *The Quarterly,* over Shelley's condescension or Wordsworth's neglect, he reminded himself to cultivate disinterest; to avoid distraction and to keep his eye on the true goal, which was to become one of the English Poets.

Yeats is responsible for a number of the stars in the sky, and when we read his letters we find that the young man was an extraordinary trimmer—soliciting reviews from Oscar Wilde and flattering Katherine Tynan, older and more established on the Celtic turf. One of the O.E.D.'s definitions of ambition, after "eager desire of honor," is "personal solicitation of honor." When he wrote, "I seek an image not a book," he acknowledged that as a young man he had sought a book indeed. None of us, beseeching Doubleday or Pittsburgh, has ever sought with greater fervor.

And Whitman reviewed himself, and Roethke campaigned for praise like a legislator at the state fair, and Frost buttered Untermeyer on both sides. . . . (Therefore let us abjure the old saw that self-promotion and empire-building mean bad poetry. Most entrepreneurs are bad poets—but then, so are most poets.) Self-promotion remains a side-issue of poetry and ambition. It *can* reflect a greed or covetousness which displaces the grand ambition—the kind of covetousness which looks on the life lived only as a source of poems; "I got a poem out of it." Or it can show only the trivial side of someone who, on other occasions, makes great art. At any rate, we should spend our time worrying not about other people's bad characters, but our own.

Finally, of course, I speak of nothing except the modest topic: how shall we lead our lives? I think of a man I admire as much as anyone, the English sculptor Henry Moore, eighty-four as I write these notes, eighty when I spoke with him last. "Now that you are eighty," I asked him, "would you tell me the secret of life?" Being a confident and eloquent Yorkshireman, Moore would not deny my request. He told me:

"The greatest good luck in life, for *anybody,* is to have something that means *everything* to you . . . to do what you want to do, and to find that people will pay you for doing it . . . *if* it's unattainable. It's no good having an objective that's attainable! That's the big thing: you have an ideal, an objective, and that objective is unreachable. . . ."

16. There is no audit we can perform on ourselves, to assure that we work with proper ambition. Obviously it helps to be careful; to revise, to take time, to put the poem away; to pursue distance in the hope of objective measure. We know that the poem, to satisfy ambition's goals, must not express mere personal feeling or opinion—as the moment's McPoem does. It must by its language make art's new object. We must try to hold ourselves to the mark; we must not write to publish or to prevail. Repeated scrutiny is the only method general enough for recommending. . . .

And of course repeated scrutiny is not foolproof; and we will fool ourselves. Nor can the hours we work provide an index of ambition or seriousness. Although Henry Moore laughs at artists who work only an hour or two a day, he acknowledges that sculptors can carve sixteen hours at a stretch for years on end—tap-tap-tap on stone—and remain lazy. We can revise our poems five hundred times; we can lock poems in their rooms for ten years—and remain modest in our endeavor. On the other hand, anyone casting a glance over biography or literary history must acknowledge: some great poems have come without noticeable labor.

But as I speak I confuse realms. Ambition is not a quality of the poem but of the poet. Failure and achievement belong to the poet, and if our goal remains unattainable, then failure must be standard. To pursue the unattainable for eighty-five years, like Henry Moore, may imply a certain temperament. . . . If there is no method of work that we can rely on, maybe at least we can encourage in ourselves a temperament that is not easily satisfied.

Sometime when we are discouraged with our own work, we may notice that even the great poems, the sources and the standards, seem inadequate: "Ode to a Nightingale" feels too limited in scope, "Out of the Cradle" too sloppy, "To His Coy Mistress" too neat, and "Among Schoolchildren" padded. . . .

Maybe ambition is appropriately unattainable when we acknowledge: *No poem is so great as we demand that poetry be.*

EMOTION RECOLLECTED IN TRANQUILLITY

fiction by JONATHAN PENNER

from QUARTERLY WEST

nominated by QUARTERLY WEST, *DeWitt Henry and Maura Stanton*

AFTER I GOT OUT OF THE SERVICE, I moved back in with my mother. Our temple was teaching contract bridge, and my mother drafted me as her partner, at least one generation younger than anybody else in the room. No matter which of us was declarer, my mother played the hand (her card sense was amazing, I give her that) while I sat behind the dummy.

Mrs. Leonard was another regular, a huge woman who always toadied up to my mother. I was the reason why. "Tell Philly," she'd beg my mother, as though we had food and she were starving, "to give Diane a little phone call." Then she'd squeeze my arm or sometimes, under the bridge table, always frightening me, my thigh. She was terrified her daughter would marry Richard Dean, a Gentile whose pharmacist uncle had been heard to pass anti-Semitic remarks.

"In addition to which," she would tell me sadly, taking me aside afterward during coffee and cake, "the boy is AC-DC."

Though this was close enough to the truth, I was silent out of loyalty. Mrs. Leonard thought I hadn't understood. She narrowed her eyes. "Do I need to spell it out?" She puffed at her cigarette in the way she used to signal sophistication. "A switch-hitter."

What Mrs. Leonard didn't know was that Diane had been on my mind as far back as my memory went. I had felt for her, starting in kindergarten, an unforgettable hatred. Even then she was considered pretty, which I especially hated, because it drew attention to her, therefore to me. Back then, and through the first six grades, she and I were the only Jews in our class.

Diane was incredibly stupid, incredibly something—nobody minding the store, was how my mother put it. In class, teachers had to yell at her to pay attention. It was always the same. Her vagueness, her dreamy sweetness, made me want to hit her, but I was afraid to. And year after year, fat Mrs. Leonard, whenever we met, would reach out a hand to stroke my head, which I didn't dare lean away more than slightly. The smell of her sweat and perfume intoxicated me, and I watched in fascination as the flesh hanging from her upper arm swung like a water-filled balloon.

"Philly, let me take you home," she'd say. "You'll write a little poem for me." Her voice was so melodious, humorous, and inviting that I would nervously feel myself falling under her spell.

"You and Diane are some pair. A little bride and groom."

The idea of my marrying anyone was humiliating. When her mother maneuvered us face to face at temple "events," I stared at Diane expressionlessly, while she wore a simple-minded smile and tried to back away. At last she would escape to the temple's front steps and sit reading a book, whose title she would hide when she saw me looking at it, and I would join my friends in back of the building, humming rocks at the garbage cans with as vicious a sidearm whip as possible.

In high school, to her mother's despair, she hung around with a brotherhood of tough guys we all called—I never knew why—the Baldies. Their leader, Rodney Cooper, would take her to movies, and then, late at night, to a deserted golf course. Big Ones, he always called her, Big Ones, and she'd only smile. Her mother was right to worry. Loathsome as Rodney was, he made himself the love of her life. Maybe it was just his being the first: Diane was soft, and would have retained anyone's impress.

"Sucks and fucks," he claimed, standing with his friends on the baseball field, all of them smoking and strewing the ground with butts. "Shakespeare!" Seeing me on the fringe of the group, he drew me apart and put his arm over my shoulder. "Jew girls are the best," he told me, as a compliment. "Right, Shakespeare?" I imagined myself dividing his grinning face into diamonds by pushing it through the chain-link backstop, but in a fight he would have destroyed me.

Oh, she loved him. He didn't go to college, so she didn't—she

336

enrolled in Hammersmith Secretarial School, whose billboard showed a giant hammer striking a door marked GOOD JOB, HI PAY. When Mrs. Leonard saw me at temple, escorting my mother to a bar mitzvah, she stared reproachfully. At the reception afterward she cornered us, holding out a paper napkin laden with pieces of rugaluch. "And you, Philly," she said bitterly. "What are your plans? Yale? Harvard? Brandeis?"

"I may go into the Army," I said.

She looked at my mother, who flushed but shrugged. Mrs. Leonard brightened. "A young man has time," she said, folding her napkin around the rugaluch and stuffing it into her pocketbook. "Are you still writing your lovely poems?"

"It's harder now."

"Explain to Mrs. Leonard about the Army," said my mother cruelly.

So I must have been able to explain my reasoning, then—I had to repeatedly, until the very day I left. But now don't ask me. It turned out I never wrote a poem about the Army. You see novels about the Army, but did you ever see a poem? They sent me to Germany—no poems about that, either. But once while I was there I got drunk and helped overturn some parked cars. And in jail I did write a poem, not about jail, but about Diane's face, which I remembered as too big, a pale floating target.

When I returned home she was working in a department store, going to the local college part-time. I enrolled there too. Rodney had gone to Texas to seek his fortune. Diane missed him badly, but was falling in love with someone new, the one her mother, squinting through cigarette smoke, called the switch-hitter, AC-DC.

This was unfair, but it was true that Richard Dean was (and God knows how Mrs. Leonard found out) a transvestite. Once a week or so he liked to go into the city dressed as a woman. Diane, who had taken to confiding in me (her oldest friend, she remarked sentimentally) about her love life, said that it was the deception he liked. That and the whiff of danger.

"He knows he isn't a homo," she explained. Saying the word made her squirm. "He just likes to see if he can pass. Can you understand that a little?"

"Sure," I said, and I thought I could. "When I was small I liked to go around the house in my mother's heels."

Our temple had started a theater group, and my mother was

there night after night for rehearsals. I usually stayed home alone. Though I met girls at college, they weren't right—that was all I would say whenever my mother raised the subject. To my surprise I'd turned out to be a serious, no, a gloomy person, and could hardly stand frivolity or even cheerfulness. Since getting out of the Army I'd had acceptances from a few literary magazines, and was starting to think about a book of poems. If I could accumulate forty I liked, I'd try for the Yale Younger Poets Award. That was enough to dream about.

But, as though I were forever back in jail in Germany, seeing her pale face float before me, I was upset to find myself—after all these years—contracting Diane like a kind of disease. I might have become infected in childhood. Like leprosy, its stain could have taken decades to surface. In any case, the way Richard Dean would slide his hand around under her armpit—as though he were sticking it between two cushions—made me furious.

It was Diane's cow-like submissiveness to him that bothered me most. She was pitifully afraid of his leaving her, already afraid—something I could hardly believe, in such a luscious girl—of being single all her life, and alone in her old age. "If I looked younger," she said (she wasn't yet twenty-five), craning to peer in my car's rear-view mirror, stretching her face with her fingertips to make it smooth. Her sweater rode up, exposing an inch of white back.

Richard, finally jealous, told her she shouldn't talk to me so much. That amazed Diane.

"It's natural," I told her.

"No. You don't understand," she said.

I thought I did. Sometimes now, after rehearsals, my mother was spending the night with her theater group's director, a retired actor. It wasn't the same, but upsetting enough in its way. "I'd be jealous too," I said, "in Richard's position."

"You wouldn't if I were your girl," said Diane—protesting her loyalty to him, and not hinting at anything at all.

Her mindless subservience made me angry enough to think she was right, he was certain to leave her—who could be happy with her for long? But at night, waiting to fall aleep, I had visions of Richard Dean dying in a car accident—sometimes my mother was in the car too—visions so clear that I frightened myself, and beamed into my pillow the thought that I didn't mean it.

At other times I imagined myself catching him in a homosexual act, and beating him up in spite of his being dressed as a woman, and telling him never to see Diane again. But I knew I would never lift a finger to him. He said he was a karate expert, and once, in a sudden rage, had half-squatted into combat position, hands stiffened like hatchets. "I can break twelve of your bones in two seconds," he told me softly. I laughed and backed away. Though the Army had tried teaching me a little of that, I had failed to learn it. In a fight he would demolish me.

Ghazir—he was a Christian Lebanese, raised in France, but an Arab was all Mrs. Leonard ever saw—was twenty years older than we were, with enormous shoulders and a walrus mustache. Divorced, he lived in a cottage he had built out in the country. Less than a month after she met him, Diane was living with him.

What, she asked me with a hopeless little smile, could she tell her mother? I didn't know. When Mrs. Leonard saw me in the supermarket, she rose from the freezer bin, a quart of ice cream in each hand. "Philly," she said distractedly, pointing at me with one of the quarts, the pendulous flesh of her arm swaying, the look on her face telling the world—while I pretended not to see, hurrying to the checkout—that I, my stubbornness, disloyalty, unmanliness, was the cause of it all.

I guess there are periods in everyone's life, like childhood, that seem to last forever, but when you look back at them later they're collapsed as flat as packing cartons, and everything's squashed together. That's what it started to be like for me now. Diane lived with Ghazir and finally married him. I got a job distributing newspapers, and didn't win the Yale Younger Poets Award. I began to send my book of poems to little presses named after things like planets and trees. Diane and Ghazir fought, were divorced, but continued to live together—their trouble was her fault, she was too demanding, she told me. Mrs. Leonard died. I wept at her funeral, but when I saw Richard Dean there, crying too, a guy who knew she'd hated him, I dried right up. My mother, svelte leading lady, was there with her boyfriend, the director of the Temple B'Nai Israel Players. "The weight this woman carried," said my mother, "she's got no kick coming."

Ghazir began to beat Diane. When I, drunk, tried to return the favor, he hugged me until one of my ribs cracked. I paid to have my book of poems published, and stacked the boxed copies in my bedroom. Ghazir was seeing other women, blaming Diane, who agreed that she was driving him crazy, she wanted so much to remarry him. My mother married her director, they bought a condo in Miami, and she gave me a hug and sold the house out from under me. "This is my chance for happiness," she explained. "Not so many years are left. What about you?" She made claws in the air. "When are you going to grab hold?"

I moved, then, to a furnished room near the university. My landlord was an old man who swept his sidewalk with painful care early each morning. He was completely deaf. I communicated with him in writing, but seldom, because my childish script irritated him. On a ledge in the dim downstairs hall, beside the disconnected telephone, lay a tract titled "What to Do in Time of Sorrow." It lay there, slowly growing a skin of dust, the three years I lived in that house.

Ghazir had been having an affair with a French girl who lived with a wealthy family as baby-sitter. She met him at his cottage, often bringing the children, when Diane was at work. Diane knew about it. Ghazir vehemently denied that anything sexual was going on. But when the girl returned to France he was broken-hearted, and wept with his face pressed into Diane's lap, she told me. Then he said he was going to Europe.

His picture postcards arrived with decreasing frequency, with no return address and no mention of his coming back. Diane still lived at the cottage, where, every time I visited her, she would talk to me for hours about nothing but Ghazir. The surrounding vegetation grew wild. I attacked it with a sickle. Winter came, and Ghazir wrote that he was working in a bicycle shop, thinking of getting married. He had asked his cousin to look into selling the cottage.

And a sign, FOR SALE, did appear, hammered through the snow into the frozen ground. No buyers came, Ghazir stopped writing. The cold wind oozed in; each time I visited I tacked up more cardboard. I left my deaf old man and slept in Diane's front room. Evenings, we made a fire and talked about our childhood, which she, to my amazement, remembered as perfect. Spring came early. I pounded open the windows, bruising the heel of my palm, and patched the torn screens. On a night with a full moon and a scented breeze, Diane and I became lovers. As we lay together in the valley of Ghazir's mattress, as she slept in my arms,

I beamed a promise into her damp forehead: to compensate her for every insult and betrayal.

We moved back to town, which had grown disturbingly since we were children, and rented a garden apartment in what I had remembered as empty marshland. I got a job at an aerospace plant—it had to do with missile nosecones, they said, but I never learned how. I emptied boxes of head-sized plastic hunks into a hopper atop a machine. They came out at the bottom fist-sized, warmed and smelling like model airplane glue. Diane, who was working as a secretary at the telephone company, joined their Executive-in-Training Program. We bought chairs and a sofa, rough-hewn wood slung with leather, the style that year. New sets of everything that came in sets—linens, pots and pans, china, glasses, silverware. It was the nicest place I ever lived in.

Except when we were at our jobs, we were together, even if I was just taking a ten-minute trip to the drug store. "You don't think I'm too clingy?" she asked.

"I love it," I told her. "Don't use that word."

Diane knew from the start how badly I was going to fail her, and her difficult job was to teach me that. She started practically at once asking whether she disappointed me, whether I was upset with her, as though I were a doctor withholding news of fatal illness.

"You look nervous," she'd say, or "You look unhappy," when I wasn't aware of feeling those things. If I did tell her something was bothering me, a backache, or something from work, she was more upset than I was, as though the trouble were her fault. She saw things in my expression that I never meant to be there. She heard them in my voice. She heard them in my silence.

And at last it became maddening, when I had been thinking about something, to look up and see her little smile of guilty fear. "I wasn't being cold," I'd shout, before she had a chance to say it.

But now I began to criticize everything about her. I said she spent too much on clothes—her dresses filled her closet and half of mine, many more than my mother had owned.

"That's because she threw them out whenever the style changed," said Diane. And it was true, I had been unfair, most of Diane's clothes were old, I thought I could remember some from the days of Richard Dean—old and unflattering, tight around the stomach and rear. And how strangely somber. When I saw them by the dozen, packed together on hangers, I realized that she never wore anything vivid.

"You should try bright colors," I told her.

But she only looked worried and asked me, smiling a little, her voice as hopeless as though I'd suggested she leap the moon, "Do you think I should?"

Diane. I saw now that I was stuck with her, she with me, forever. We weren't unhappy. I shouted, but not often; she rarely cried. We bought a second car, used. She dyed her hair to conceal the white. I had an extra drink each evening. We bought a little outboard cruiser and moored it in the river. I hardly remembered, would barely have wanted, any other life.

And then one night—out for supper at Howard Johnson's—we saw someone who looked familiar. "It couldn't be," said Diane.

I doubted it too. But Rodney Cooper recognized us at once, grinned, waved, and came to join us in our booth. "Shakespeare," he laughed, squeezing my hand. His face was deeply tanned, his hair silver, his wrinkles full of sly good humor. He was just back for a visit, he said—he came every year to see his family. He'd done, oh, pretty well in Texas, had his own business, now. Contractor, laying pipe, starting to bid on some pretty big jobs. His lawyers and his accountant were both Jews, he told us, then grinned, showing us that he admired the sharpness and shadiness of our race. Diane, with an unconscious half-smile, was staring at him—trying to read his face, I knew, wondering what he was thinking of her. It was exactly the same as always. "Big Ones," said Rodney, as he reached for our checks, "I gotta ask. You two married, or what?" Diane and I shook our heads slowly, as though in time to the same music.

They live in Houston, now—I know from the postmark on their Christmas card. It's the same card every year, the one his secretary must mail to his customers and suppliers. The signature, Rodney and Diane Cooper, is in red Old English type, within a wreath of green holly. I wonder how many others come to our town, whether he sends them to his grade school teachers in their retirement, or any of the old Baldies.

The missile nosecones business hasn't been good. But by the time the layoffs came, I had enough seniority to bump a younger man in what we call the Publications Division. Now I edit and mostly write *Inner Space*, a weekly that's distributed throughout the plant. News about the company, contracts we've been awarded, results from the bowling league, necrology—the Director of Publications lets me do whatever I want. Lately I've tried some light verse. I don't sign it, but the other publications people know who wrote it, and they say it's not bad. One of them is a woman, Lila. She hasn't been to where I live, but someday I'll open Diane's old closet and show her the boxes full of my book of poems.

Last week I saw Ghazir. He must be close to seventy, now. But he still has his swagger, and I stopped on the sidewalk to watch him. He emerged from a barbershop, thin hair and great mustache beautifully trimmed, and jaywalked across the street. I wanted to stop him there in the middle of traffic and ask when he'd gotten back from France. I'd have liked to know what he thought of his ex-wife's marriage, whether it would last or whether we'd see Diane back in town one of these years, alone in her old age as she'd always predicted. I wished we could go to a bar together, he and I, and have some drinks and talk about our lives. But Ghazir was across the street now. He hopped into an idling Thunderbird, where a young woman had just slid from the drivers' seat to make room for him, and drove away with his arm around her.

And when I saw that, I knew it was good I hadn't spoken to him. I might have told him that he'd never loved Diane, none of them had, that they'd ruined her. If we'd gone to that bar and had those drinks I'd probably have cried and said that I was the only one in the world who had tried to save her. If even a shadow of mockery crossed his face I might have grabbed his thick neck and squeezed. And it would have been the same as always—no matter how I fought, old as he was, he would have crucified me.

ORANGES

by GARY SOTO

from POETRY

nominated by Philip Levine

The first time I walked
With a girl, I was twelve,
Cold, and weighted down
With two oranges in my jacket.
December. Frost cracking
Beneath my steps, my breath
Before me, then gone,
As I walked toward
Her house, the one whose
Porchlight burned yellow
Night and day, in any weather.
A dog barked at me, until
She came out pulling
At her gloves, face bright
With rouge. I smiled,
Touched her shoulder, and led
Her down the street, across
A used car lot and a line
Of newly planted trees,
Until we were breathing
Before a drug store. We
Entered, the tiny bell
Bringing a saleslady
Down a narrow aisle of goods.
I turned to the candies
Tiered like bleachers,
And asked what she wanted—
Light in her eyes, a smile
Starting at the corners

344

Of her mouth. I fingered
A nickel in my pocket,
And when she lifted a chocolate
That cost a dime,
I didn't say anything.
I took the nickel from
My pocket, then an orange,
And set them quietly on
The counter. When I looked up,
The lady's eyes met mine,
And held them, knowing
Very well what it was all
About.

          Outside,
A few cars hissing past,
Fog hanging like old
Coats between the trees.
I took my girl's hand
In mine for two blocks,
Then released it to let
Her unwrap the chocolate.
I peeled my orange
That was so bright against
The gray of December
That, from some distance,
Someone might have thought
I was making a fire in my hands.

LAVONDER

by THOMAS RUSSELL

from NORTHWEST REVIEW

nominated by NORTHWEST REVIEW

Lavonder he played peacocks when he was three.
A white woman Miss Corley, owned a pair
in her farmyard up the road, and he toddle over
with one of us to see the racket. He played
dum deedee dum with both hands
till he got it right. Mother had patience.
Mother she was a quiet woman. She
never would speak down on nobody.
She just move straight along.
Ask in town if she was blind and they would say,
that little nigger woman with the peacock boy?
They didn't want to believe.

Lavonder he play all day rain on the roof
he play leaf in the wind he play
sunning up and sunning down
more peacock tunes than you ever want to hear
red peacocks blue peacocks. Mother
she know what she had
in that red dirt shanty house.
She had this well ear no one could take away
and she was dropping down Lavonder's soul
and hearing it fall.

A HISTORY OF SPEECH

by RODNEY JONES

from POETRY NORTHWEST

nominated by POETRY NORTHWEST

That night my sophomore date wanted kisses
I talked instead of the torn ligaments
in my ankle, crutches and Ace Bandages,
parading like any arthritic
the exotic paraphernalia of my suffering:
and, that failing, went farther, bobbing
in the thesaurus of pain: the iron lung,
the burn, torture with water and bamboo.
She twisted a frosted curl around one finger.
It was then she touched the skin along my neck.
It was then I noticed for the first time
    the strange wing beating in my mouth
    and kissed her in a kind of flight
that plummeted and clutched for branches.

Oh but Tahiti of a thousand Tahitis!
Among the suckling cars of the drive-in,
trays of pomegranates, lingerie of surf.
Days I hurled papers onto the porches of invalids.
June nights I only had to open my mouth,
out came a flock of multi-colored birds,
birds of all denominations and nationalities,
birds of nostalgia, the golden birds of Yeats,
birds trained in the reconnaissance of exclusive buttons.
Before I knew it, I was twenty-two.
I was whispering into the ear of Mary,

the mother of Jesus. I was dreaming
in two languages I did not understand.
I was sitting in the bar of the Cotton Lounge

railing against George Wallace when the fist
rang in my stomach, and I looked up
to a truckdriver shouting down at me
"Talk too much!" Talk too much into greasy
footprint, linoleum stinking of beer,
the thigh of that woman rising to leave.
Talk too much and understand I'm not to blame
for this insignificance, this inflation
in the currency of language. Listen:
Whenever I hurt, the words turned their heads.
Whenever I loved too much, they croaked and hopped away.
At my luckiest, I'm only saying the grace
the hungry endure because they're polite.
Learning speech, Demosthenes put pebbles in his mouth,
but my voice is haunted by softer things.

THE FORM AND FUNCTION OF THE NOVEL

by ALBERT GOLDBARTH

nominated by THE ONTARIO REVIEW, *Philip Booth and Joyce Carol Oates*

My parents have come to town for my wedding.
Because of some way a shadow falls, or a hand
in conversation cuts air as if laboring, my father
reminds me increasingly of a man in a small
Canadian village, who manufactures racks
for drying lace curtains, who catches shadow in
that same way, and who moves his hands as if against
a current, in a book

I've been reading but leave, to shop
for cheese, bouquets and the wedding trousseau.
While we pick over veils and daffodils, life
according to narrative forces set in motion
continues: the backlands
moon slips up like a washed dish, and a rig
clops heavily toward the main street's tethering-rail.
His son's come home, for that sturdy Canadian

349

spring with the flowers like nailheads everywhere,
home from study in Europe, his son the biologist
talking Darwin and opera these last two years
over cognac in snifters like goldfish bowls.
They argue. The father is oafish, gruff, a
squared-off man whose lips move reading.
The son knows quiche and genetics. He's
embarrassed. Their words are ugly weather. I

see, although the son ironically can't despite
his interests, how the distance between them is
nothing, you hear me?, nothing, compared to the first
irrepressible land plants over 400 million
years ago stretching familially to the flax
in the lace that's hung in the front display case
under the sign with the father's name but *and*
Son freshly painted out. I think he's special

in his plainness and hurt. In this chapter he's
alone. It's night, he paces in the store he loves, and
so the moon through the fine white nets of his trade
makes him a complicated figure at last,
doilied over by dark and silver, eloquent, pensive, oblique . . .
"Do you think she'll like this one?" I turn.
He's holding a lace dress up to the late deep light
and it's all I can do to stop crying.

L.A. CHILD

fiction by PAMELA BRANDT

from STORY QUARTERLY

nominated by STORY QUARTERLY

THEY SAY THAT L.A. has the filthiest air in the whole United States. Petulia and I tested this statement yesterday, outside her apartment next to the highway. We reached to the sky with our hands and waved them about for five minutes. Afterwards we checked for dirt and our hands looked clean. Our hands are always clean. Maybe they're referring to another sort of pollution. This guy I met at a party a few weeks ago, he told me that everyone goes to L.A. to die. What a downer he was and of course from New York. Buzz Martin he called himself even though Jack told me his name was Ricky Klein. I wish these N.Y. people stayed in the Big Apple and rot away by themselves. Petulia and I like L.A. This is where it is. Good bands, good clothes, lots of cruising and lots of guys. The people who aren't with us just aren't there.

I got fired yesterday for walking into the office with purple hair. Laney dyed it for me over at her Mom's beauty parlor and Christ how those blue-rinsed bags twitter. Not much different from their hair really. The head secretary, Miss Elliot, wasn't too happy. "Ginger" she says, "I took a lot because of your dear Mother but I can't and won't take this." I grounded my cigarette into the carpet and it left a dime-size hole. Fuck them. Jackson says I can get a job at his record store as soon as he's through with court. Who knows when that'll be and Jackson was goddamn stupid to be caught peddling ludes to eleven year olds. In the broad daylight. In the fuckin schoolyard, beneath the swings. What do you expect from a forty year old ex-yippie who refused to believe that Jim Morrison is dead?

Anyway, I'll get some job with or without Jackson. My Mom calls here at Petulia's and bugs me to go back to school but I won't

351

even answer her on that one. I stopped going to school after they threw Keith out for wearing the kilt to Geology. Plus the Mohawk didn't do him any favors either. What do you do my mother asks. I hang out by the hot dog palace, everyone who's here goes there. Morty, the owner and original founder, gets pissed off at times but he won't report us, no, it's great publicity; hey, he and his miserable hot dog palace were even written up in Penthouse. THE NEW PUNKS was the title. Crap stuff, all it talked about was the punks that died. How about us, the ones that live and are living, don't we count? No, they talked about Jasmine and Lars and Rex Jolt and made it seem like every L.A. kid eats speed for breakfast. Great photos too. Some asshole with a swastika on his shoulder and blood dripping from his chin. That's right, we're the new Gestapo and people actually walk to the other side of the street when they see us, clutching their pocketbooks and holding little Jimmy's hand a little tighter. Fuckin stupid it all is cause we're more scared of you. Scared you're going to brainwash us with soap operas and laundry commercials and twenty-four hour Wendy's and roller-skates with batteries, Christ, you even don't have to move. See this is the story. You call us punks cause we dress different and our hair is more colorful than a florist's and we see bands and buy records and none of us were cheerleaders or football players in high school. And sure, some of the guys get into headbanging, pogoing, knife fights, broken glass some nose bleeds but it's not Berlin, it's not Vietnam it's just messy fun. Get a job they always tell us. Christ, why would anyone want a job? I don't want a job, 9-5 burnout and you're hollowed eyed and you're dead. So I try to get in at the Roxy and go to the Chinese and listen to X and the Circle Jerks and that's life and that's breathing and if you get cut it's good to taste your own blood.

My boyfriend, Mike, is learning the guitar and he likes practising at 5 A.M. and some asshole always calls and Mike puts his amplifier right next to the receiver and cranks the volume all the way and does something nasty with the strings that can only cause permanent brain damage. And the bastard still calls for more. Mike is only sixteen but he's got this incredible goatee and wears lots of black eyeliner and people think he's thirty sometimes. Mike's story is everyone's story: parents split when he was nine, went to live with his father, the gas station attendant. Dad completely flipped when he realized that Junior didn't go in for sports.

But this is California, Pop screamed. Mike split and did a bit of hustling and did a bit of junk but after he woke up one night with a knife still stuck in his thigh he straightened out. My mom doesn't like him. She thinks he doesn't look real. California is not real and that is why none of us look real. The sun should not shine all the time. Suntans kill you, cancer creeping every minute. On Christmas there is fake snow, that's right, this crystal white stuff they sprinkle even on the highway and you always find some dead animal lying in it, freshly hit and it's red snow now. When I used to live at home I would look out the window and see all the lights in the buildings and the lights of the cars and the lights in the planes and I'd get sick all over myself and didn't give a shit that Carlotta, the maid, just vacuumed this morning.

After Belushi's death there were lots of weird stories. Okay, there was nasty stuff involved but this is L.A., not Scranton Ohio. Tom Snyder, that dick Donahue, they blab all about death in L.A. but they don't even know what death looks like. Death looks like Jilly after she made her first porn loophole standing at the sink washing the same dish over and over again. Death is Jason, Petulia's little brother whose face looks like sandpaper after all the trips he's taken. Shit, it makes me crazy watching the bright dots on television and they talking about L.A. and death. Mike tried to do himself in with a razor last year. This time it was downers and whiskey. A real Hendrix I told him. And you're not even black. He wears three earrings in one ear now. A cross, a ruby and a safety pin. More eyeshadow than me. When we make love one of us always falls asleep before it's finished. The shades are always down and I don't know if it's morning or night when I wake up.

Petulia. She slept with the biggies you name them: a couple of Stones (at the same time no less) a couple of movie stars a few game show hosts, and all they left were nasty infections. Never an orgasm either. How could I, she tells me, you're so totally into Them, you can't be bothered with yourself. She's so beautiful that if I still cried I would. Hair so golden like a fairy princess, spun gold and I look into her eyes and there are high towers and white horses in them with knights grieving beneath her window. She was born in the wrong century, Mike says. He's in love with her and I'm in love with her but Petulia, she's in love with no one. See, she's not really there. It happened at a pool party out by the Hills. Petulia fell in and was down under for ten minutes they said. Her heart was beating when they pulled her up but that's about it. I watched a cigarette burn between her fingers the other day and she didn't even flinch.

As soon as I get some money from dear Jackson who owes me more than a few favors I'm going to learn how to play guitar and stand on stage and look down, look down instead of being in the crowd and always looking up and your neck hurts and some goon is either getting sick on you or fuckin stomping your feet with Doc Martin boots. I'm going to play guitar and sing about Jasmine who was so dead when they found her that her skin just cracked when they touched it, that's right cracked like dried mud and fell into dusty pieces, sing about Mike, sing about Lacey found between her steering wheel in a Jack-In-The Box restaurant and it took them two hours before they found her hand and why it happens, sing about why, and Petulia and Gene her ex-boyfriend who blew his brains out in a movie theatre showing of course Rebel Without a Cause. My music will clear the air raise the fog raise the smog and no one will ever say that people go to L.A. to die.

🔥 🔥 🔥

CAMBODIAN DIARY

fiction by EDMUND KEELEY

from ANTAEUS

nominated by Paul Bowles, Harold Brodkey, Joyce Carol Oates and David Wojahn

APRIL 13. The city appears to be silent now. On the surface there has been no change, even though the Year of the Tiger has ended and we are beginning the Year of the Hare. Our government has declared a state of emergency and so there is to be no holiday, no celebration except in secret, business as usual. Most people have gone to work as on any other day, the healthy children play in the streets, the army fights on courageously according to our Prime Minister, the rocket fire from across the river is not much different from what it has been. But the city is waiting. One can tell from the way nobody talks in public about the Americans leaving, out of superstition, as though talk will influence what is going to happen to us and it is therefore better to remain silent and wait.

I'm not afraid to talk about the Americans leaving—why be superstitious when there isn't room for choice or argument?—but there's no one I care to trust now, even if talking might help one accept what seems both unacceptable and unalterable. At the same time, I feel an urge to record what is happening here, partly for your sake but mostly for my own. Maybe it will give me a certain liberation from the events themselves. Maybe it will serve in ways I don't yet fully understand to put some order into this absurd day-by-day chaos. Whether or not other eyes ever see this inelegant

Though the action and the characters in this excerpt from a novel are entirely fictional, I have drawn on the following sources in creating an image of actual events in Cambodia during April and May of 1975: conversations with Robert Keeley, Deputy Chief of Mission, Phnom Penh, 1974-75, a report by Sydney Schanberg for CBS News, William Shawcross's Sideshow *(Simon and Schuster, 1981), and, most of all, François Ponchaud's* Cambodia: Year Zero *(Holt, Rinehart and Winston, 1978).*

little notebook. I think it will most likely go with me into my next incarnation unread by you or anyone else, and since I'm sure that I will reappear among the lower orders of life—at best as a careless scavenger of a bird, at worst as a tick to suck your blood—even I will not be able to read it after the road ahead turns back on itself. And that too is a certain liberation.

You didn't know I had such Buddhist leanings, you don't take them seriously, not in a woman who could pretend for your pleasure to be so French in her thinking. Why should you understand very much about who I am after knowing me less than a year and knowing best what is now probably the least valuable part of me? My blood is of course very mixed and my loyalties confused— you were quick to recognize that—but what you came to know outside the language classes is mostly the imported part, from my father's side: those English and French and Chinese delicacies that you preferred for a while to your food at home. Yet the stronger, less reckless part that I will need to favor now comes from my mother's side, all Khmer. What can you really know about that, my American friend? And isn't it a shame you couldn't stay long enough to learn?

April 14. This city that I know so well has become suddenly unfamiliar. One grew so used to the shifting feel of danger, the constant movement of those who have nowhere to go, the changing smells of hunger and sickness, that this new activity hangs over us in our spring evening like an unwanted hot mist, bringing listlessness, apathy, disconnection. The rocket fire has increased, but mostly one no longer hears it. The streets seem almost empty, and not just because the government has declared a twenty-four-hour curfew in a futile attempt to keep the refugees and army deserters from crowding into the city and blocking all the roads (what cleared some roads this morning and stopped the few illegal festivities was the bombing of the army headquarters by a government plane, they say by mistake). It is as though this terrible waiting for the enemy, this anticipation, instead of heightening fear and vigilance, now lulls us into contemplation. It isn't just the curfew that keeps us inside. We turn more and more into ourselves. The waiting has become almost erotic in the way it induces self-absorption.

And it is supposed to be our New Year (I wonder, by the way, if your Embassy chose the date of its departure to conform with our

356

tradition of cleaning the house thoroughly of the dirt it has gathered before the old year goes out—forgive me if I'm being too unfair). I spent the day at home cleaning my apartment a bit late and with little enthusiasm, because there hardly seemed any point when I don't know how much longer I will be able to stay here. Maybe as a widow of the war I will have special dispensation. And with all this foreign blood in me, I may find some excuse that will counteract my having worked with the Americans in the small way I did (don't laugh; I speak strictly of the French lessons). The Chinese in me is not likely to help after the Khmer Rouge take over the city, because they are said to hate the Chinese merchants first among their local capitalist enemies despite the fact that it is China which has made their victory possible, as you yourself insisted. But maybe my English background through my grand-mother will somehow prove useful. Doesn't that carry as much weight as my Hong Kong grandfather? I suppose not, especially since my face and manners reveal too much of what my English nanny used to call "Oriental cunning" whenever she wanted to chastise me for behaving in a way that was less proper and British than she found acceptable. Or maybe the French in me—at least in my point of view. Aren't the French doing their subtle best these days to play the role of neutral? If it weren't for my face and the small remnant of Anglo-Saxon in my blood, I could pass for French, couldn't I? Not that either, I suppose.

Anyway, it wasn't my future as much as my past that kept me so self-absorbed this afternoon—not only our short past but years ago when the three-day New Year holiday often meant a trip to Kampot Province and the lower slopes of the Elephant Mountains by the Gulf of Thailand. My father had a Chinese friend who owned a pepper plantation there, one of those who remained in my father's debt for many years through loans. To go to that plantation was always exciting for me as a young girl, not only for the clear air of the mountains and the green forests, but finding the sea each time, so clean and unlimited, so different from our brown river—the endless free space it seemed to offer, as far as the low sun.

I think it was the discovery of that sea, always for the first time though often repeated, that made me less frightened of going away to France for my university studies when that became my father's plan. It seemed almost natural by then to follow the impulse it had slowly created—I was just eighteen but old for my age, at least by comparison to my schoolmates in the English-language school here—the impulse to fly clear of this country and to keep going on and on until one arrived at some new and unexplored space beyond the distance another's vision might reach. After I returned from France of course it wasn't the same sea any longer. I was too old and worldly-wise. I went to that region the last time with my husband for a week of vacation just before the army took him from me, a week mostly spent at the beach in Sihanoukville—there was a small but very good restaurant by the beach where you could get excellent oysters from Kep—and I would lie under our striped umbrella or under a palm tree in my very small bikini with the new concrete city at my back, lie there sipping Dubonnet and being very modern, very much loved, and sometimes look out at that sea with a feeling of hatred because I was beyond finding the challenge in it any longer.

It is now midnight. I did poke my head out in the early evening to see if anyone still cared that it's the New Year. Apparently the Khmer Rouge do, because the rocket fire has become the heaviest in weeks. But there was one final absurdity that made me rather cheerful. Against all the rockets some sweet fool sent up a fire-works display from somewhere near the Phnom, and for a few minutes the sky appeared ridiculously to belong to our city again.

April 16. The waiting, which had become as intolerably comfort-able as a disease that shows itself with less than the right pain day after day, now is over. We know the end is close, and this brings its own kind of excitement. There are reports that the Khmer Rouge have cut the road to the airport, that they have reached Kilometer 6 in the north and have crossed the Monivong Bridge in the south. We could see fires everywhere in the outskirts yesterday—factor-ies burning, munition depots exploding, who knows if anything is left. They say the last government tanks are retreating to surround the French Embassy.

Now that we are certain a change is at hand, some would say that this new knowledge is better than our continuing desperate lie: the government forces holding on valiantly, reinforcements coming in all the time from unnamed regions—after all, are there any regions left that haven't been "liberated"?—the city prepared for a long fight to the death, etc. Of course few people are fooled by these reports, and most of those who recognize that the government and the army are doomed have already begun to move beyond this certainty. Their direction is toward the uncertain future. And viewing the past we've had in recent months—recent years—some are apparently able to look that way with hope.

I can't, I must admit. Whatever change may come, I now realize that it surely means the end of life here as I have lived it for most of my thirty-six years. Not that what I've known here has been without its trials and complications, as you're well aware. And you're also well aware that I'm not afraid of new adventures. But it's clear that my situation is precarious now. I can't any longer count on my husband's connections—they will vanish with the government. And my connections to the royal family through my mother seem comically remote, as does the Prince himself. Now that the Americans have gone, it seems even my credentials in foreign languages are not likely to give me a means of support: refugees from the liberated zones report that the Khmer Rouge speak one language only when they speak at all. And other—what shall I call them?—assets and skills that an educated woman with a weakness for pleasure might be thought to have are even less likely to prove useful if this Communist regime turns out to be as ruthlessly puritan as the others in our part of the world. Can you in any case imagine me as the lady friend of some round little guerrilla officer from the northern provinces used to a pound of rice a day and dried fish and painfully boring sexual practices?

I suppose you can imagine it. I suppose from your point of view it is simply a matter of changing one's taste and standard of living and perhaps one's politics a bit in keeping with the reality of new conditions. I did it for you, I can do it again for the next regime. The charm of a civilized woman of the East is her flexibility, isn't that so? And need is ever the mother of invention, as I think your great Anglo-Saxon poet put it. Perhaps, we will see. But I spent yesterday rather depressed by it all—too much so to write about it. Not that I can really blame you for going away; you had no choice. And though you were good enough to offer to arrange my evacuation in one of your helicopters, I think you realized that I had no choice but to stay here, like so many others who worked for the Americans. How could I just abandon my sister and her children, all that's left of my family in this country? And where would I go in yours? You kept saying that we would work something out once we got there, but you never explained how I would support myself without finally becoming a burden to you—not to mention your wife. And I didn't want to embarrass you by raising such a direct and essential question.

I think we both understood the reality of our muddy circumstances here and in your country without having to spell it all out. But what has happened still isn't just, at least not for those of us here who took a road that we can't now reverse, whether by our will or someone else's. And the sudden discontinuity of the life you and I knew will make it difficult from now on for me to look back at our pleasure—yes, I think I can say our kind of love—with very much aftertaste of spice or longing.

I tried yesterday. Again I had the whole day to myself at home. And though it has been only five days since you left, I felt surges of desire that I finally had to release. But I could not do it under your image. Not because of any bitterness, just a sadness that came at the wrong moment and made it impossible. Maybe it was from the realization that you and I have nothing more that we can share now, no discovery, no useful remembrance, no irony even, only my one-sided language sent into the void. I suppose if I were a good Buddhist, this might be taken as another firm step toward liberation—not merely the necessary awareness that this is a life of suffering because of the unsatisfied cravings it brings with it but that the way to break the harsh cycle is by turning in on one's self to face the void without illusions. Oh, I wish it were that easy. The cravings, the cravings. They are still too holy for me. And the illusions also.

April 18. The Khmer Rouge began to enter the city yesterday morning, first from the south, they say, but very soon from every direction. I wasn't there to greet them personally. I thought that would be in bad taste. And I guess this bit of decorum is what makes it possible for me to write at all today from my refuge in the French Embassy. I did try to find out what was happening early yesterday morning by way of the radio, but of course the radio was dead, as it had been for hours. News came to me first from my landlady, who went down to Monivong Boulevard as soon as word reached us that the soldiers were arriving, only these soldiers turned out to be the wrong ones. She reported that there was much activity on the boulevard when she got there. The tanks near the French Embassy moved down to the Cathedral and pointed their guns toward the north. A group of long-haired young men dressed in black marched in that direction and were cheered on their way because the onlookers thought they were Khmer Rouge, especially when some of the tank crews climbed down to applaud and embrace them as liberating conquerors. But their flag had a cross on it, and the soldiers looked too fat to be revolutionaries. It turned out that these soldiers were mostly students who belonged to a new National Movement organized by the brother of your friend the former Prime Minister in a last-minute attempt to replace the current Prime Minister and so perhaps grasp victory from the Khmer Rouge by the power of political miracle, in keeping with our ancient tradition.

The true revolutionaries who came in soon afterwards to kill all this celebration were not so fat and much younger, children really, all in black except for a checkered scarf, with Chinese caps and sandals made out of old tires. And they carried large guns and grenades and strange new weapons in belts across their chests. My landlady reported that some of those watching thought these new soldiers looked confused, withdrawn, gaunt, ready to collapse, but she herself thought they just looked severe and determined, especially the girl soldiers—very unfeminine, she said. In any case, they were all silent, and the only time any of them smiled a little was when they found something interesting to steal from a shop that they could share with their comrades: a bottle of soda or a package of cigarettes or a handful of cheap wristwatches. They didn't have time for serious stealing. There was much business to be done. First they had to take over the city from one end to the other, small groups at every crossroad controlling the traffic, collecting all arms, emptying trucks and cars. Then, before the sun set, they had to empty the city itself. Completely.

They began with the hospitals, it seems. My landlady watched them clean out the Preah Ket Melea hospital, and then she decided she had better go home. The hospitals had become so filled with the heavy casualties in these last days since the Americans left that there had been little chance to remove the dead, and those watching the new soldiers at work assumed at first that they were making room for the seriously wounded by transferring those who could be made to walk and then by removing the dead bodies from the corridors. But the dead and the seriously wounded were all that was allowed to remain behind—no doctors, no nurses, no guards even. And those who could walk had to carry those who couldn't or push their beds down the street as though they were carts. It was a slow parade, she said, the crippled and wounded using each other for crutches. One woman had a child in each hand and a third in a blood-soaked sack tied around her neck. My landlady watched a man with no legs thump his way out of the hospital and up the street, picking his way as best he could through the crowd until his arms weakened.

That is when she decided to go home. And that is when she discovered that this bizarre exodus was just the beginning of the great evacuation that long before nightfall would clog every road leading out of the city, because the streets on her way back were already starting to fill with people leaving their homes under the direction of these young soldiers in black. Neighborhood after neighborhood was being liberated to the point of desolation, with only occasional shots fired for encouragement since the people were told that the Americans would soon begin to bomb the city and that everyone should leave quickly for the countryside, taking only what food they could carry under one arm. They were told to go as many kilometers as they could outside the city by the nearest road and not to bother locking up their houses, all would be protected for them until their return in a few days, after the city had been bombed and then cleaned up a bit. So it seems most people went without argument, tired of the rockets and mortars, happy that these young revolutionaries had taken over the city without much further bloodshed, ready for any sort of new beginning. Some of the more greedy apparently filled up their cars with belongings, but then they found that they weren't allowed to start their motors and had to push their cars through town until they were exhausted. And as more and more people moved into the streets, the journey out of the city became terribly slow, a few feet at a time, much stopping and starting again and always in a single direction after one got going, whatever direction some other member of one's family might have taken in the chaos of this mass departure.

It was my landlady who saved me to begin with. As you no doubt gathered, she always keeps very much to herself—a secretive woman, suspicious of almost everyone in the building, me in particular because of my "French" ways and my questionable foreign associations. So when she came back to my apartment so very agitated with her story about the hospital and her rumors about the streets beginning to fill with people ordered out of their homes by these armed children, I had to believe the fear in her voice. I packed a suitcase in less time than you are likely to believe—you who became so sullen over what you thought was my vanity when I made you wait half an hour or so while I packed my things for our helicopter trip to Siem Reap. I took with me only essentials (honestly, very little make-up) and what foreign currency I have collected, and I made my way quickly by the back streets to the French Embassy. I tried to convince my landlady to come with me, but she just stared at my feet and said: "What business could I have at that place?" So I gave her double what I owed her for rent in American money—the final absurdity—and left her there to gather up all the food I left behind.

The situation at the French Embassy was worse than I could have imagined. Of course it was the only place where Cambodians who had worked for the government or the Americans might hope to receive some kind of asylum, but I had not expected to find so many foreigners there as well, hundreds of them, diplomats, business men, correspondents, who knows what else, and of all nationalities, American included. It seems that the Khmer Rouge ordered the Hotel Phnom cleared out after they emptied the hospitals, and that eliminated the neutral zone for foreigners that was supposed to have been set up by the Red Cross. So the French Embassy became the only neutral zone, with the foreigners occupying two of the buildings and the Embassy staff the Consulate building. This rather complicated the situation for the Cambodians arriving there, even those like myself with a French—how shall I put it?—history. I don't mean only my intimate French friends and my years in Paris. I was counting on my father's past connections with the French community, not least the diplomatic community, which was often in his debt for matters of financial exchange and sometimes information, even in his last years, after he had more or less retired from business. But there was no chance of making a case of this kind at the Embassy yesterday afternoon with more than five hundred Cambodians and an even larger number of foreigners pushing into the Embassy grounds. The staff was simply overwhelmed by this swarming mass—no time for talk, it was all they could do to keep people from striking each other as they fought for space to squat, which is as much space as I found.

My only advantage under such conditions proved to be my face—that and a bit of luck. I happened to catch the eye of a clerk sitting behind a desk just inside the Consulate building. He was apparently assigned the duty of recording the names of Cambodian officials arriving on the scene, and the man recognized me. We met more than two years ago at a dinner party given by a friend of my father's shortly after my husband was reported missing. This clerk—a young Frenchman maybe thirty years old, a bit short for my taste—was at my table and at one point tried to flirt with me, saying in soft French that I struck him as a ray of Eastern moonlight, with the sort of complicated beauty that he would feel privileged to learn to decipher. But I wasn't in the mood for flattery that night and sweetly told him that though I appreciated his interest, my mind was still very much on my husband, recently reported missing in the war but not yet to be presumed dead. The poor man returned to his vichyssoise as though I had emptied the pepper shaker into his soup bowl.

I had not run into him since that evening as far as I can remember—of course my relations with the French generally diminished after my father's death and especially after you arrived in Phnom Penh. But yesterday he recognized me when I kept looking at him, and once we had exchanged smiles, he signalled me to make my way through the crowd and to put my suitcase among those beside his desk, as though I were the wife of some high official or foreign diplomat deserving such special treatment. I don't know what he wrote in his ledger—there was no chance even to exchange pleasantries—but with another gesture he motioned me to push beyond him into a small office that aready had three Cambodian women in it, all much older than me. And that is where I spent the night, mostly listening to one of them who somehow got separated from her husband weep inconsolably about her fate and the fate of her country.

She is right to weep. None of us can say this morning what is going to happen to us. I don't know how long I will be allowed to stay here or what this young clerk who was so kind to me yesterday will expect in return. The one thing we have been told is that our city is now dead.

April 19. One gets to see both the worst and the best of people under these conditions. We in our small office are lucky: we have been spared the fights and arguments that have begun in the crowded corridors outside our cell and apparently in the other buildings too. The problem is food, and it seems of special concern to the foreigners, though not all of them. Some—many of the French, for example—are not only eating well (they are the hosts, after all) but have enough left over for their pets. And the Russians, who arrived today, appear to have brought their own food and drink in large quantities but are unwilling to share what they have with anyone else. This means that the American correspondents and some of the other foreigners have to eat what the Cambodians eat, which is often of poorer quality than what the French pets get and much less in quantity than what the Russians are feeding themselves.

The food problem has created a series of international episodes, and things have been said that simply should not be said in a diplomatic environment. The tension seems to be especially high in the lines outside the toilets, which is where I gather most of the information I get. Those who complain to the French about their pets are called fascists, those who complain to the Russians about their self-sufficiency are called imperialists, those who complain to the Americans about their manners are called sons of bitches. The only true peace is in the toilet itself, where the language is entirely international.

I was visited yesterday afternoon by my clerk, who broke away from his duties long enough to bring me a bottle of French wine and some pastries to supplement my portion of rice. I tried to share these gifts with my Cambodian cellmates, but of course they wouldn't touch the wine and they were either too depressed or too insecure to try the other unexpected luxuries. The clerk was very sweet. He apologized for the spareness of our quarters—the four of us share an empty desk, a chair each, and enough floor space for two people to lie down—but he explained that our situation was better than most and in any case might improve as soon as the problem of asylum was negotiated with the Khmer Rouge. When I asked him what the problem was exactly, he answered that it was too early to define with precision but that I should not worry. The way he said it was hardly reassuring, and he must have seen my reaction, because he touched my hand gently for a second. I thanked him for his kindness to me and the others. Then he disappeared before I had a chance to ask him the twenty other questions that kept me and my companions awake through most of the night. Mine was spent in a chair, and I woke up from one period of dozing to find the old woman sitting next to me, mother of some minor government official, cradling me under her arm as though I were her daughter. At one point I even let her stroke my face, which she seemed to find fascinating.

Some of the questions we had were answered by talk in the toilet line this morning. A few of the foreign correspondents who did not seek asylum immediately were able to follow the exodus from the city at least long enough to learn from Khmer Rouge officials that the evacuation will be total and that it will probably include other cities as well. Cities have been declared evil, the refuge of capitalist exploiters and imperialist spies. There is a grand plan, it seems, to settle everyone in the countryside, those who have never worked with their hands along with those who have, and to convert all intellectuals, businessmen, technicians, civil servants, everyone with any education into peasant farmers. The "Supreme Organization," the "Angkar," is now in command of the new life we are meant to live. The past and its imported devils are to be wiped away completely, not only the most recent of these, French and American imperialism, but Buddhism too. Can you believe it? The correspondents were told that time in Cambodia begins now. The Khmer Rouge have been storing food on the highways, but there is clearly not enough for the more than two million people who are being forced to take this trip to the countryside. Those who do not have the strength to walk the whole way, wherever the end may be, will be left by the roadside. Those who protest will be executed on the spot. And those who get separated from their families must abandon hope of reunion because families no longer exist. All of Cambodia is now one family, with the Angkar as its sexless father.

What we have seen today leads us to believe that it will be a thoroughly ruthless father, as those of us who found no reason to disbelieve the many refugee stories of past weeks have suspected all along. This morning a delegation of three high-ranking Khmer Rouge arrived at the Embassy, supposedly to negotiate the question of asylum. There was no negotiation. They simply demanded the expulsion of all traitors, meaning anyone who had served the previous government. When the old vice-consul still in charge here objected that the people they had in mind had all asked for political asylum on what was after all diplomatic territory protected by international convention, the Khmer Rouge told him coldly that the land he was sitting on belonged to the Cambodian people, not France, and either the traitors were handed over to the people or the people's representatives would come in and take them without obligation to anyone in their way.

I wasn't there to witness the spectacle that followed, but I heard from other Cambodians who did that Prince Sirik Matak led the group of departing officials with great dignity—the president of the national assembly, the minister of health, Prince Sihanouk's Laotian wife—thanked France for its hospitality, shook hands with the vice-consul, and guided his companions into the jeep that was waiting to take them to their execution. The vice-consul stood there weeping, quietly telling his French colleagues over and over that he and they were no longer allowed to be men. Of course the vice-consul had no choice. Does any one of us now?

I imagine even you and your American friends with your bloodbath theory did not anticipate this kind of mass dispossession and the ideological viciousness that seems to go with it. I wonder what the Americans will think when they come to see what is happening. Will they look with new eyes on their secret violation of my country's attempt at neutrality before Prince Shihanouk was deposed? That early intervention surely helped to feed and strengthen this young monster called the Khmer Rouge which is growing fat on Chinese provisions and the blood of its own people. Of course nobody in a war can see clearly enough to do much about these kinds of evil until it is too late, but isn't there some final justice in acknowledging one's mistakes? I wish you were here to debate the issue with me in your rational, unemotional style. I find myself slipping into the sort of irrational passion that encourages hatred. At this moment I could do with a bit of your infuriating objectivity.

April 20. Early this morning two Khmer Rouge officials arrived at the Embassy to extend their greetings to all Cambodians, local Chinese, and resident Vietnamese in the Embassy grounds. One of the officials made a polite speech welcoming these groups in the name of the Revolution, accepting all Cambodians and resident aliens as brothers and sisters, and since we are all part of the same family now, requesting that we leave the Embassy grounds immediately and join the rest of the Cambodian people in rebuilding the country. There was of course immediate panic among those who heard this message. None of the Cambodians I have managed to talk to has any more illusions about what is going on out there. And some of our worst fears were confirmed by a French schoolteacher and his wife who were brought in last evening by truck from north of the city. They reported that the roads were still crowded with evacuees, as far as ten kilometers outside the city in that direction. Many of the sick and the wounded have died and are simply left unburied, creating a terrible stench in places, and many of the old people have had to be abandoned where they collapsed.

The Khmer Rouge are apparently selective in their outright killing: only those in uniform, or those with long hair, or those who complain. This teacher saw several corpses in uniform that had been run over on the highway again and again by trucks so that they were flattened out as though cardboard figures left there from a fallen advertisement. And they found a great shortage of food on the highways. When people ask the guards what they are to eat, they are told that the Angkar will feed them, and when they ask who the Angkar is exactly, the answer is "You. The people." One man, also a schoolteacher, tried to argue that this was absurd. The Khmer Rouge cut his throat right in front of his friends and left them his body to dispose of. So most people have to feed themselves by bartering what they have brought with them or gathering up what scraps they can find along the way. And if they are unlucky enough to stumble into a checkpoint, their jewelry and wristwatches are taken away for the Angkar. Then their money, because money doesn't exist any longer in Democratic Kampuchea, the Angkar has eliminated it. People who find a shelter of some kind to settle into for a while are perhaps in the greatest danger, because soon someone comes along to ask them to identify themselves and their profession, and if they admit to having been in the army or the city administration or if they show any connection to the old regime, they are separated out to be taken away nobody knows where. So most people continue to move as they can or find ways of hiding until the roads clear somewhat again.

After the Khmer Rouge welcome this morning, the vice-consul evidently tried to keep people calm by explaining that the Khmer Rouge had not yet actually entered the Embassy grounds on any occasion and would surely allow the Embassy staff to handle as best it could this new demand that all Cambodians leave the Embassy grounds. He won his point for the moment, and as it turned out he gained some valuable time by negotiating strenuously with the Khmer Rouge officials.

My clerk brought the news of the latest developments to our office cell. He explained that the Khmer Rouge had set down certain absolute terms: Cambodian men married to French women would have to leave, their wives joining them if they chose to. Cambodian women married to French men would be allowed to stay. That was that. Since no one of the four of us was married to a French man, we collected our things and filed out of our office to join the others outside the building who were preparing to leave, some seven to eight hundred people by that time. My clerk suddenly took my arm in the corridor and pulled me to one side. He told me that the vice-consul was going to save as many Cambodian women as he could in what time he had left by issuing marriage certificates and passports. He said the situation outside the Embassy was likely to be especially difficult for anybody with a commercial Chinese background, because the Khmer Rouge apparently considered the local Chinese merchants the worst of the capitalist exploiters and were systematically destroying their shops and businesses. The clerk was looking at me straight in the eyes, rather tenderly I thought, and despite the weakness from fear that I had begun to feel in my legs, I had a horrible impulse toward comedy. I almost told him: "Surely you cannot mean to propose marriage? I barely know you." He must have seen something in my face, because he said, still firmly holding my arm: "The marriages will of course be fictitious."

What could I say? I let him lead me into a room down the corridor where five or six Cambodian women were already in line, and within less than an hour each of us in there was married to a French name, in my case one Jacques Donnet, who may or may not be fictitious but is in any case not related to me nor to my clerk, M. Henri Baudrot. And for what it is worth, I now have a false French passport.

The marriage came just in time. By ten o'clock this morning the column of those leaving the Embassy grounds had begun to move through the gate. As a "French citizen" I was allowed to watch from a window of the Consulate building. I cannot remember an hour of more difficult emotion: the relief from fear, at least for the moment, the feeling of undeserved luck, and to match this, the

369

guilt of my staying behind as I watched my former cellmates go out through the gate, two of them leaning on each other as they wept freely, the third—the old woman who had played mother to me—trying to walk with her head high. And the courage of so many others that followed, for example the mountain troops of both men and women marching out smartly in formation as though invulnerable to history. And the few senior army officers left who must have realized fully that they were doomed but would not let it show, even joked among themselves. And some of the Cambodian men who decided at the last minute to leave their French wives behind to care for the children embracing too briefly, almost casually, as though trying to pretend they were just off for the weekend.

I don't know what to say about it now. Would you have gone out into that dead city if it were possible to avoid doing so? Was one supposed to survive where one could or join the long march into some unknown countryside and hope to survive that way? Whatever the right or wrong of it, my solution is temporary since I obviously can't stay in this Embassy forever, even with a fictitious husband.

I now have a proper bed, in a room on the second floor, Yes, it is M. Baudrot's room, but he insists that the bed is solely mine, he will make do elsewhere. I am both too tired and too grateful for much thought as to whether or not I should believe him.

April 22. It has been quiet here since my compatriots left. There are some six hundred foreigners still in the compound, but they are mostly in the two other buildings, and I now run across them only when I go outside for a walk in the grounds (no need to share communal toilet facilities any longer; my new bathroom is luxurious in contrast to the old, and it is open only to a few of the French staff). The city around us is also quiet, except for occasional rifle fire, I suppose from some place where a lone resister has been discovered in hiding or some army officer has finally given himself up for execution. There must be very few such individualists left, because we gather that the water and electricity are cut off in any neighborhood that still shows a sign of life. Yesterday we could sometimes see a cone of smoke rising over the city here and there, today not even that. And the stragglers we could occasionally make out leaving for the countryside beyond Tuol Kauk to the west are not there today. We have had no further contact with the Khmer Rouge except for those who bring us our ration of food—they say it is generous compared to their own—and a few young soldiers escorting some French people who joined the evacuation in the beginning but who have been brought back in trucks to share our asylum. It seems that we in the Embassy and the occupying forces "protecting" the city are now the only inhabitants of Phnom Penh, and as some have suggested, a few well-aimed rockets directed this way could complete the purification and dehumanization of this once beautifully corrupt heart of our princely republic.

I decided to put the insanity of politics behind me for a few hours yesterday and become domestic (I am after all a new, if somewhat soiled, bride). I began by cleaning up this room thoroughly, getting down on my knees and scrubbing the floor with a towel and bucket, dusting the easy chair and the desk—this too must be a converted office—shaking out the rug in the corridor. Then I took up the sheets, which smelled of overwork, and washed them in the bathroom, along with my dirty laundry and what little of M. Baudrot's I found in a bottom drawer of the desk. I spread the washed laundry all over the room, partly because I was too shy to go down and ask for a clothes line and partly to give the room some intimacy for a while. By the time I gathered up the laundry in the late afternoon, I had begun to feel more or less at home.

Of course one pressures oneself into these adjustments. The truth is that I'm still quite nervous about being here. Not that M. Baudrot has been anything but a model gentleman—rather irritatingly so. He came in yesterday evening to pick up a few things, very effusive in his thanks for my domestic labors, and he brought me a bottle of wine for my dinner but didn't stay long enough to share it. I had a number of questions to ask him. I think he didn't want me to get the slightest sense that he might try to take advantage of my new—how shall I put it?—circumstances. And I felt too awkward to tell him that there was certainly no need for him to run off so quickly, before I had a chance to find out what he now thinks is going to happen to all of us "foreigners" here, married and otherwise. I expect I'll have to be a bit bolder tonight.

I know what you will think: as I was with you. It's very different really. I'm not at all in love with M. Baudrot. In fact I'm not even attracted to him, except perhaps to that rather unexpected gentleness that comes into his face when the news he brings seems to be hopeless, a prelude to the very controlled pleasure he takes in offering a way around it. With you it was purely visceral. I had to break you down, crack through that surface of cold intelligence, that assured inaccessibility that you carried with you like a diplomatic privilege despite your very obvious attraction to me. In the beginning what I wanted most was to get through to your core, find out if I could bring you out of yourself so completely that you would end up crying like a child after you'd exhausted yourself making love to me. And I more less succeeded, didn't I? But what does that prove now?

April 23. I've been given a small radio. I accepted it because I thought it might be diverting,but so far all it has provided is military music and revolutionary songs on the hour, and a horrible long speech by Khieu Samphan, one of the great leaders now in charge of our lives. I'm sure you've heard of him. He is actually an old politician of the left who went underground, a former professor of political economy who once served in Prince Sihanouk's cabinet and who has always been a cold sexless fanatic. Especially after he was undressed in public many years ago by the royal police for having dared to offer his criticism of the Sihanouk regime before the People's Assembly, which was supposedly created for that purpose (can you imagine the humiliation and misanthropy that would bloom in a man as puritan as this standing in public with his bare bottom and his thing hanging there for everyone to see?). Now he speaks to us about the goal of his revolution in the same language that the guards outside our gate use, as though they have all been made to memorize a new catechism that will magically bring about happiness, equality, justice, and democracy in a country without rich or poor, without exploiters or exploited, where the young are the heroes and where the people enjoy independence, sovereignty, identity, integrity, neutrality, harmony, purity, I don't know what else, under a culture opposed to corruption, reaction, and oppression, especially by the colonialist and imperialist enemy which is still America and its fascist Lon Nol clique, whose culture gave us men wearing their hair to their shoulders like women and sometimes actually becoming women in the flesh. Whereas in Democratic Kampuchea there will be no gambling, prostitution, adultery, sexual intercourse outside of marriage, or other evil habits of any kind, in particular those stimulated by cities and their corrupt merchants, because those who will now reign like the princes of old will be the peasants and laborers living not in palaces or even houses but in undefined communities beside their ever multiplying rice fields and factories.

It seems that one way this new revolutionary program will be achieved is by a process of overnight selection that may soon leave only those without a name or a past still alive. This morning the Consulate admitted a return refugee from the caravan of local citizens who were liberated out of the Embassy and into the empty streets three days ago. This is a woman who was among the two or three foreign wives who decided rather heroically but also recklessly to go out into the unknown with their Cambodian husbands. One night of the new Democratic Kampuchea and both she and her husband reached the conclusion that she should make her way back here on her foreign passport and whatever cunning or bribery might be required to get her safely under French protection again.

From what the woman reported, those poor Cambodians forced out of the Embassy were herded into the Lambert Stadium just north of here and were immediately put through a simple, preliminary interrogation that consisted of identifying themselves and writing their names on one of three lists: military personnel, civil servants, people. This woman's husband was a minor civil servant, but he had the presence of mind to sign the list under people. Those on the first list, junior as well as senior officers, were taken away that night in trucks. The rest slept among the rats on the edges of the stadium, where the military had once set up huts for their families. The next day the Khmer Rouge arrived to read off the names from a new list they had prepared overnight, and those on this list—civil servants and who knows what other categories— were also driven off in trucks, one assumes never to be seen again. The remainder were told to go north on foot to join their compatriots in rebuilding the country. Anybody who asked "Where in the north?" was in danger of ending up on a truck going south. Occasionally one of the Khmer Rouge would actually smile and suggest that those on the "people" list head for their home village as quickly as they could, so long as they could get there without turning south through Phnom Penh, because Phnom Penh was no longer on the map of Democratic Kampuchea for people who belonged to the people. So the caravan, somewhat diminished and quite disorderly by now, moved north through the deserted countryside until it arrived at the rear of the earlier exodus from the city somewhere beyond the ten-kilometer mark, and that is where the woman and her husband separated with a pledge to find each other again across the border in Thailand. She may be lucky enough for that. It is hard now to believe that he will be too.

April 25. The calm that has come into my life since I moved into my new "quarters" has begun to prove more unnerving than the restlessness of my first days here when I was sharing the office downstairs with my properly hysterical compatriots. It is not just a matter of being alone day and night. I've known that often before, and with a special flavor of anxiety after my husband was reported missing. Here there is a dissociation that presses in from beyond one's private psyche. It's as though one has suddenly become a foreigner in one's home country, a visitor in the house where one grew up. Only that isn't exactly right, because the objects around me here do not rouse even a sensation of remembered familiarity, and the country outside has come to seem the foreign intrusion. Not that the Khmer Rouge have yet actually set foot inside the Embassy grounds. It's the idea of them, their inescapable presence beyond the walls. We are in a sanctuary that has taken on the aura of a prison surrounded by unseen guards, and the silence of these recent days, with only the occasional exchange of greeting in the corridors and little reliable news of the world outside, seems to have shaped us into a community of unconnected if crowded cells of which mine is the most isolated and solitary.

I suppose I may have these feelings more strongly than many of the others here because I am not waiting, however long and uncomfortably, to be repatriated to my homeland. My homeland is still out there where the Khmer Rouge are, whether I like it or not. Or else I have to carry it with me. I can't simply fly home in a helicopter. And what I can't carry with me under any circumstances worries me more and more: my sister and her family in Battambang and my cousins on my mother's side in the northern provinces. My sister is especially on my mind now. I don't want to believe the rumors about what is likely to happen in other cities, but the evacuation of Phnom Penh has been so cruel and thorough that one has to be prepared to believe anything.

Maybe it is our isolation here and my uncertainty about what lies in wait outside the Embassy compound that has worked to undermine my normal self-control—anyway, that has begun to make me vulnerable in unexpected ways. I mean specifically in my relationship with my—what shall I now call him?—my sweet benefactor. He came to me again yesterday, in the evening, bringing wine and French delicacies—pigeon terrine, goose-liver pâté, triple-crème goat cheese, where he got these only he knows—and this time he stayed. Through part of the night. I cannot tell you how marvelously delicious the meal was, beyond any reality. It has been barely three weeks since you and I last feasted ourselves in our usual uninhibited way, so I cannot say that the special delight of what he brought me last evening was the result of long abstinence. But it may have been partly the reverse of that: knowing that such luxury is doomed and that the great desert lies ahead. Every mouthful seemed to carry a titillation of finality. Of course such definition may be all afterthought. I can't really speak for anything but the intensity of what I felt at the moment, a pleasure that had to be savored in all its corners and no mind for hidden causes. And I know the effect was to put me off my guard, open me to possibilities that in the warm sadness afterwards also seemed to lie outside thought or defense.

Henri may have sensed my mood but he didn't take advantage of it until I gave clear signals. We talked for two, three hours over the Armagnac, talked about what was happening to my country—which he, incidentally, has come to love much as you have and which he knows better than you do—and we talked about France. Henri is convinced that the Khmer Rouge will allow all foreigners to leave the Embassy in due course, though he has no idea just when. He feels that this new regime, like all other new regimes, will want at least some degree of international legitimacy beyond recognition by the Chinese, and if it holds the refugees here as hostages or harms them in any way, it is not likely to get what it is looking for. The fact that the Khmer Rouge have not come into the Embassy grounds uninvited is a good indication, he thinks, though he has no illusions about the ruthlessness of these people. He actually went out into the empty city day before yesterday with an interpreter to help bring back a group of French people who had turned up some ten kilometers north of the city. He found the suburbs now completely deserted except for scavenging dogs and pigs and a few Khmer Rouge soldiers hunting down anyone still hiding among the litter that fills the side streets. His rescue truck came across a few stragglers evacuating their homes around Kilometer 9 and then suddenly a sea of people spread across the rice fields beyond, hundreds of thousands, the roads clogged except where army trucks forced a lane open, the war-ruined villages covered with people camping under any shelter they could find, the mass of them stretching as far as you could see, as though the whole city had come out at once to gather in the northern market place for a grim sale that offered no product but themselves. Henri said he could see terror in the eyes of some of those he thought he recognized but who could not respond to any gesture he made because of the guards accompanying him. But he saw no dead bodies. There was no room for bodies to lie on the ground in that section of the highway. The evidence for the killing of former officers and civil servants and teachers came from the French he rescued, each of whom had his own account of some murder seen or heard.

The brief trip outside the city had clearly shaken Henri. His description of what he'd seen was broken at times, and he couldn't bring himself to tell me the stories he'd heard from the French he'd brought back. I also found him too somber when we came to my personal situation, no sense of humor about it any longer, as though he now realized that the charade of my French citizenship had its special dangers if I were caught. At the same time he tried very hard to persuade me that I had no choice but to go out of the country on my new passport when he and the other foreigners were finally released. It was very touching. He insisted on sitting in a chair behind the desk with his cognac snifter square in front of him as though this post-dinner conversation were really an official consular exchange about my future, but his hand kept twisting the stem of the glass nervously, and for all his effort to seem impersonal and objective as he argued the case for my leaving with him, his gentle face kept giving him away.

I finally got up from the bed where I'd been curled around my Armagnac like an indifferent cat and came around the desk to kneel beside him. I told him that I simply couldn't go with him and the others. It was impossible for me to think of leaving my homeland and the few relatives I have left and wandering from one foreign country to another with a passport that didn't belong to me and no money, dependent on the generosity of strangers, however grateful I was to him personally for the kindness he'd shown and however much the prospect of staying behind frightened me. I was at least half smiling as I said all this, trying not to spoil the honest warmth I felt by the wrong kind of sentiment, the wrong language. But when I'd finished he looked down at me with such sadness that I couldn't resist touching his face. And when he took my hand to turn it so that my fingers crossed his lips, we both knew that one phase of our charade was over.

If I say that he was a quiet lover I hope you won't use that for getting even with me by indulging yourself in some private irony. He gave me what I needed at that moment, that's all I'm willing to say. And if I cried to myself after he was gone, it wasn't any reflection on him but on me for still wanting you, for still wanting the kind of life I'm going to lose, for not having had the courage to survive entirely on my own resources. I can't explain it. And I don't care if I can't. He held me for a while, flesh against flesh, our bodies alive, our breath hot. The rest doesn't matter.

April 26. Do you know that there were three days of festivities in Phnom Penh to honor the opening of the People's Representative Assembly and we in the Embassy here didn't even know about it? According to the radio the celebration began on April 21st and ended when the Assembly opened on the 24th. I suppose one reason we didn't know about it was the difficulty the new regime had in creating a festive atmosphere and the right kind of noise without any inhabitants to help them and with only hungry dogs and pigs to watch the parades. One of the French officials here did notice a streamer hailing the glorious victory of April 17th and the even more glorious revolution that followed, but one streamer drifting by does not make a holiday. And a few unelected guerrillas sitting in a room do not make a people's assembly. Though of course in time cavils such as these will belong to the forgotten history of reactionary revisionism.

At Henri's insistence I went downstairs this morning to speak to one of the French consular officials about my future. I knew that Henri's intention was to have the official persuade me to go out of the country with him and the others, and though I was quite prepared to resist such persuasion, I felt the least I owed my benefactor was the gesture of hearing whatever arguments he had arranged for me to hear.

It turned out that the official—a rotund, thickly spectacled, rather pompous little man—wasn't as ardent about my prospects officially as Henri had been informally. He said he assumed there would be no difficulty about my falling in with the foreigners when the expatriation was finally arranged since my "French" identity had already been established, and he also assumed that I would want to take advantage of this escape route that the vice-consul had been good enough to provide me since any other course was logically unacceptable, especially in view of my mixed background (by which he presumably meant my once wealthy Chinese father, apparently still to be counted among the most despised of Khmer Rouge enemies though dead these many months). At the same time, the official said, he could not offer me any assurance regarding what might happen once the evacuees from the Embassy arrived in Thailand or wherever their initial destination might be. In fact, he felt he had to make clear that the French government could take no further responsibility for my circumstances once I was out of Cambodia since I was not in reality a French national and would henceforth have to be regarded as a displaced person. Henri broke in at that point to suggest that the issue of nationality might be resolved by my asking for political asylum in France. The consular official turned to stare at him as though he had violated some kind of sacred trust by merely raising the question. "That is another matter entirely," the official said. "Quite beyond my personal competence or interest."

I decided to be equally cool in response. I thanked the gentleman and his French colleagues for the generosity they had shown me by taking me in and treating me so well despite my mixed background and my apparently dubious nationality, but I told him I felt I had to make two things clear, first, that I did not consider myself to be a displaced person but a free Cambodian citizen who had been robbed of her native country, and more immediately, of her native city, by a group of murderous fanatics under the influence of an alien ideology and supported by foreign arms, and second, though I was personally fond of France and indebted to her for much of my education, I did not have the remotest intention of settling there while I could still see any chance at all of helping to save my homeland from yet another period of domination by a foreign power after such a miserably long history of foreign domination, not least of all our recent hundred years under the so-called French protectorate. And with that I smiled sweetly, dipped my head humbly, and left the room.

Henri followed me upstairs full of embarrassment, apologies, hopelessness. I drew him inside my—his—room and calmed him with a wet kiss, then sent him back to his desk (he was on duty, so there was no time for further romance). I was strangely elated by what I'd done downstairs, as though some problem of conscience that had been burdening me was suddenly released. That feeling lasted for about an hour. I spent the remainder of the afternoon brooding over my encounter with the French official. I even began to wonder if that little puffed-up man didn't have a point. What was I if not a displaced person? I may have taken a certain naughty pleasure in becoming eloquent about my free Cambodian citizenship before a French audience, but it was another matter to examine the cold reality beyond that sort of rhetoric. Was there a country out there that I could still belong to? If there wasn't, didn't it become dangerously sentimental to think I should stay behind? On the other hand, how else could I find out what of mine was still there, my sister and her children most of all, and whether there was still some way to help them?

These thoughts were too private and unsettling for me to share with anyone (that is, anyone but you in this unanswerable form). I went to bed early, and though sleep didn't come for some hours, I pretended to be dead out when Henri finally knocked on the door.

April 27. There is a true holiday mood in the Embassy this evening, at least for all those who know exactly where their country is. A group of Khmer Rouge emissaries arrived this morning to settle the repatriation issue. All foreigners, some several thousand of them, are to be driven by truck to the Thai border via Battambang and Sisophon. The first convoy is scheduled to set out in three days. I gather from Henri that the negotiations were rather awkward at moments, especially when the vice-consul tried to insist that both the French nationals and the other aliens be transported by French planes. It seems this touched a sensitive spot in the Khmer Rouge official who is in charge of foreigners. "We have our own means of transportation," he said, his eyes slits. "We do not need your French planes. We do not need anything from anybody. All foreigners are in violation of the Angkar's proclamation of March last which ordered them to leave Cambodia or suffer the consequences. You are of course still free to suffer the consequences. If we now choose to let you go it is an act of perhaps stupid diplomacy on our part, and I warn you that you question it at your peril." The vice-consul accepted the offer of trucks.

Since this meeting was among the few contacts that French officials here have had with the Khmer Rouge authorities, much speculation resulted from the encounter. According to Henri, some of his colleagues thought that the idea of using French planes was so distasteful not because the planes were French but because they would give the departing foreigners a clear aerial view of what is happening in Democratic Kampuchea. Others suggested that this did not make sense because the view of Democratic Kampuchea from trucks across an expanse of over four hundred kilometers would be much more detailed and precise than any aerial view. Besides, everyone here assumes that the Americans are sending over their spy planes as usual to gather whatever information can be gathered from the sky. Henri thinks the arrangement is simply a matter of Khmer Rouge pride, further evidence of their fanaticism. They obviously do not care to hide anything because they fully believe in what they are doing, and it now seems they do not care what foreigners think or don't think or what they can or can't provide—with the exception, of course, of their Chinese patrons. All help that doesn't come directly from China is to be rejected, it appears, including a French plane full of medical supplies that is reported to be still on the runway in Bangkok after almost two weeks of waiting to be cleared for a landing here, this originally offered in exchange for French nationals housed in the Embassy. The French nationals will now be released as an act of Khmer Rouge generosity, and the medicine meant to serve the sick and dying of the old Cambodian protectorate will apparently go back home with the dispossessed protectors.

I have decided not to go with them. At least not across the border. It is obvious that staying behind in Phnom Penh would be some kind of suicide now that the city has been turned into a graveyard patrolled by vicious children. I don't have a definite plan yet, but my thought is to go with the convoy as far as Battambang and to search out my sister there. I'm sure that she can make room for me; she has a whole house. We haven't been as close in recent years as we once were, not since I went off to France to become the family bohemian and she moved north with her husband to take over the Battambang piece of my father's business and make up for the children I failed to provide (she has three). I don't know whether it was my self-consciousness about being educated and "different" or her bourgeois view of the world that made for the tension, but the few times all of us got together for a family reunion in Phnom Penh, I ended up feeling a failure for not settling down to breed children and promote the family business for its benefit as much as mine.

But much has happened since those days. My sister and I are both widows of the war now, the only family either of us has left in our generation, so we'll have to learn to get along again. And if they make us move out of Battambang, I suppose we can try to settle among other refugees in some new community of the anonymous that those of us in Cambodia who have lost a city and a past will have to create now. Even that isn't the last hope. Should it turn out that there is no such community or no chance of building one, I will simply have to take my sister and her children across the border into Thailand and wait there for a more favorable turn in our history. Given what we've known so far, such a turn is bound to come eventually, and at this point it is hard to conceive of it being for the worse. I don't imagine that it will be difficult to get from Battambang to the border west of the city, where there are mountain forests for cover. It is less than a hundred kilometers.

I'm not going to tell Henri about my decision. I don't feel that I know him well enough to trust him to accept what I have in mind, any more than he knows me well enough to understand my reasons for staying this side of the border, and I'm afraid he will find a way of trapping me in the convoy so that I can't get away when I have to. He knows even less about my Khmer side than you do. I haven't mentioned my family to him at all since that one remark about my missing husband that spoiled his vichyssoise two years ago, and I can hardly get him involved in the problem of my sister at this late date, especially after having allowed myself to be led in another direction.

Besides, she may be the most important reason but not the only one that is difficult to explain. I'm not sure how I can explain this other reason to you—or perhaps even to myself. It has something to do with being a witness. I can't imagine myself taking part in the new Cambodia beyond what is required for me and my sister to survive, but I may find that I can at least record what is going on in my own words, and I feel there could be value in this record, if only that which makes it possible for me to keep myself from becoming totally displaced. If this seems too self-conscious to you, I could say that there may be a certain fatalism in what I'm doing, a sense that I've been put where I am by events beyond my control and that I'm meant to confront this moment for purposes that may not be clear to me yet, as so many others who have been identified by their fate as threatened refugees in this cruel century—surely the cruellest of all for the evil man has done by killing or displacing his brothers in the name of some ideology. So let us say that like you, I find I simply have no choice but to do what I am doing.

April 29. Yesterday—the last of my days in the Embassy that I'll be able to record at leisure—was among the oddest of my long visit here. It started out feeling the freest of all, as might be expected when one has been released by a decision that seems both inevitable and right. My early morning euphoria was very evident to Henri, who responded to it by becoming more openly playful and flirtatious than I've seen him, and this despite a rather exhausting night together (before carrying up our breakfast he grasped the excuse of some quite innocent irony on my part to chase me around the room and then hold me prisoner on the bed, pinned there with surprising violence until I was willing to buy my freedom by suckling his nipples in turn), but of course he completely misread the causes of my mood. During breakfast he told me that he would make sure I went out with the first convoy, the one that is supposed to leave tomorrow, and though he wasn't certain when he and the other French officials might follow, I was simply to wait for him at the first camp set up to accommodate us on the other side of the border, and whenever he arrived he would take charge of me for the rest of the trip home.

The absolute confidence with which he pictured our reunion and what would follow assured me that he had no idea at all of what was really in my head. And for much of the rest of the morning he was irritatingly domestic, helping me gather up all my things for a final wash, hovering around the bathroom while I was in there working, then reorganizing our room so that I could hang things up out of the way at one end on the spread of clothesline he provided, all of which made me feel that he had actually begun to see our presumed reunion beyond the border as the first stage of a trial marriage. I finally told him that he was making me nervous hovering around like that and sent him downstairs. Then I began to feel guilty. He was probably just trying to be helpful, solicitous, and the domestic aversion he had generated in me was no doubt my own creation to compensate myself for secretly planning to betray him.

This thought killed my euphoria. And it led to an afternoon of self-absorbed reflection. I lay on my bed gazing at the laundry spread on three levels across the opposite end of the room, thinking not about where and when I might next have a chance to display my clean things like that but why my life seemed to depend so often on a delicate balance between loyalty and disloyalty, why my obsession with holding on to what I believed in was constantly threatened by a passion for adventure in unknown and sometimes dangerous places. You were such an adventure. And just when you had become among those things I believed in and needed to hold on to, another adventure came along to undermine my commitment to you and your American view of the world.

I never told you about that episode, of course—which was also disloyal of me. Anyway it was too brief to prove really dangerous. And I suppose there is nothing lost in telling you now since it was among my preoccupations yesterday afternoon and must therefore still gnaw at my conscience in some way. Do you remember the trip you took with your Ambassador to survey the Mekong north of here and the situation around Kompong Cham? I had a visitor during that time—a young soldier who belonged to a government battalion originally stationed in Siem Reap but deployed to this area when the Khmer Rouge began their January offensive. He had deserted when his unit was overrun south of here, and he drifted into the city with other army refugees looking for a place to scratch our survival until the war was over. He came to me after tracking down one of my husband's cousins who was a minor official in the city administration. The soldier said he had some documents to give this cousin, some letters and a picture that he'd been carrying around for months, ever since one of his former officers failed to return from a patrol up north and the foxholes they were in had to be abandoned. I think the soldier hoped to sell his documents to my husband's cousin, but when the cousin saw what they were, he simply sent the soldier to me.

He was a boy, really, no more than eighteen, absolutely filthy, very uncommunicative, what you would call spaced out by the war. He stood there in my apartment holding his envelope of trophies, unable to speak more than a few words. I think I frightened him out of any cunning he may have had left. Anyway, I had to go over and take the envelope out of his hand, and what I discovered in it were letters from me to my husband and a photograph I'd sent him from my bikini days. I tried to interrogate the boy about the circumstances of his finding the envelope and what it might tell me about my missing husband, but he wasn't any help: the officer had disappeared on patrol and the soldier had found the envelope among the things he'd left behind. My being the lady in the photograph clearly unnerved him, ruined the whole sale for him, destroyed all his expectations, especially when he saw how much it upset me to leaf through those letters. A rush of words finally came out of him. He begged me to keep the envelope, all he wanted was to deliver it to me safely, unless I might have a few cigarettes to give him for his fellow deserters from the battalion, and even that didn't matter since the missing officer was my husband. I finally ended up smiling at him through my tears because he looked so desperately pathetic. And so hungry. I told him that in a moment I'd be happy to get him something to eat, but before we got to that, I suggested he take a bath. The poor boy just stood there thoroughly miserable. So I finally went over and started undressing him, unbuttoning his torn shirt, trying to get him to help me. He wouldn't move. And I could feel him tremble every time my hands brushed against him. Who knows how long it had been since a woman touched him, even through his clothes. I had to undress him completely, then taken him by the hand into the bathroom and give him a bath.

He stayed with me the three days you were gone. I was both mother and lover to him, but more than this, I used his body to try and find my husband again. That was the way I betrayed you most. And when the vicarious pleasure failed to work any more and I finally sent him away with enough money to keep him going for a month or two, I was left with the same old quiet absence, only there was something new to go with it: I recognized that I could no

384

longer trust my feeling for you to take the place of what I'd lost. At least not in the long run. And as things have turned out, the gods were on my side in teaching me that.

I've put off my packing until now, really the last minute. Even without a firm sense of my purpose in keeping this diary, it seems to have become what I take up first, sometimes to the exclusion of all else. Don't let that go to your head. Though you are now my first audience, the living image I address my voice to, I now think that I would keep on writing even if that image were to vanish. I don't want it to, I'll give you that. But it will not be easy for me to write regularly from now on. I suppose I will find a way as long as it remains essential. And that is what it seems to have become, maybe the one presence in my life beyond any possibility of betrayal.

April 30. I'm in the prefecture at Kampong Chhnang. We had a good dinner of rice and fish about an hour ago, and since we're scheduled to leave at dawn, most people have already gone to sleep. I'm writing this under my pocket flashlight, so I can't be sure it will be entirely legible, but to worry about that seems rather precious in these circumstances.

This morning about twenty-five trucks arrived at the Embassy, some of them American GMCs captured from our army and the others Chinese Molotovas. Over five hundred of us crowded into the trucks. I can't say that it was even reasonably comfortable, but once we left the Embassy grounds, everything assumed a new relativity, so that in the end we had to see ourselves among the fortunate. We didn't head north as we expected to but west along Highway 4. We went through the empty suburbs, patches here and there wiped away by fire, and past the airport, where we could see the few planes left behind, skeletons burned clean. It was raining hard. At the edge of the city we came across a new cemetery, but only for cars, every kind of car you could think of, abandoned at all angles along the borders of the highway, some on their sides with bent doors open like broken wings, others over-turned with their wheels in the air, mostly stripped of their tires, I suppose to make Ho Chi Minh sandals for the army of liberation. Every large settlement we entered today had its cemetery of cars. It seems the rotting dead have now been gathered up from the roadsides along our route and disposed of elsewhere, but the cars are to stay indefinitely where they were abandoned, chaotic markers of the capitalist evil that has been expunged from the new Kampuchean paradise along with capitalists, intellectuals, and those classless peasants trapped on the wrong side of our capricious history.

We saw something of the new paradise after passing through Thnal Totung, where there was nothing left but a few ruined walls and cement staircases leading to the open sky, the sugar palms beheaded and stripped by our bombardments or burned to spikes by napalm, nothing alive to be seen, the landscape barren, all creatures now dead or gone off as they could elsewhere. We turned suddenly northward then, by design it seems, because they brought us through territory "liberated" by the Khmer Rouge several years ago, and there had been time for the villagers to learn to smile again. That was very refreshing. But the landscape they lived in was alien, the houses not on stilts as you would expect but built on the ground the way the Chinese and Vietnamese do, and the fields cultivated with yams, the Vietcong crop that grows fast and travels well: guerrilla food. At one point we saw an army of the young, hundreds and hundreds of them, working on dikes, and later some Buddhist monks rebuilding a bridge. Eventually we stopped for a meal beside a pagoda, and some villagers working nearby were allowed to come up and stare at us, we the curiosity now, especially awesome to them when they found out we had live Americans and Russians among us.

I had to act as interpreter for the group in my truck. Only a few of the villagers actually spoke, smiling men, those in charge it seemed. They talked easily about the war, the horror of the B-52 bombers and the government bombardments but especially the T-28s with their stubby wings, flying in just above ground so that they couldn't be seen. They said one could hear the B-52s coming over, so there was usually a chance to hide, and anyway the bombers spent much of their time bombing the forest aimlessly, and after a while one even got used to the bombardments, but the T-28s were too fast and unseen, anyone who heard them was already dead. They smiled at that. Now they were happy, they said. Now the war was over and they could live like normal people. And they said it in a way that made you actually want to believe them.

386

We drove north again in heavy rain, the heat steaming the water over the countryside, the sky black. They took us through Amleang, I imagine to show us that the Khmer Rouge command post which had been there for years still stood untouched for all the bomb craters scattered in the neighborhood, proof that their new gods had diverted the Americans from the most important target in the bombing. Beyond was forest land, kilometer after kilometer, the green of it heightened by the rain but finally oppressive in its abundance because it was so uninhabited, so silent, no sign of people or animals or even reptiles, as though it were too early in the Creation for living things. And then we suddenly found the living, thousands of them with their ox carts on the road ahead, moving slowly toward us, refugees from somewhere in the region going God knows where else, pans and bits of clothing and a few old people or children piled in cars like rubbish, skeletons really, the rest walking almost without visible motion, their faces—some of them—burned to dark leather by the sun, the eyes sometimes vacant or bewildered or openly terrified but never curious and most often afraid to look in our direction as we passed between them. That seemed to take hours. And all you heard in our truck were versions of "Mon Dieu" and "My God," no talk, nothing to mute the despair of it.

We didn't reach Kampong Chhnang until well after dark because there was a long stop at Romeas to visit—like tourists—the great cemetery of revolutionary soldiers buried there. It was impressive; those in charge of us made their point about how many had died fighting on the Khmer Rouge side for the liberation of the New Kampuchea. But it didn't work to quiet the image of those ox carts, any more than the special meal provided our convoy by the Angkar could fill the desolation of Kampong Chhnang when we finally settled here for the night. I remember this place as a small town on the river with a pottery works that I visited with my father the year before he sent me off to France. It became a city because of the refugees that swarmed in from the liberated zones late in the war. Now it's a desert as empty as Phnom Penh. Are there no cities left? Will those who lived in them have to keep crossing back and forth between one desert and another until there are no refugees either? I don't want to think any more about what I may find in Battambang tomorrow. I have to sleep.

May 1. I must have a secret source of luck, maybe those ancient Khmer spirits that have guaranteed long life to my mother's side of the family for generations (though they didn't quite manage to keep her from dying ahead of her time). We left Kampong Chhnang on schedule at dawn—a clearer day, actually bright at moments—and since the road took us through the same empty spaces between one deserted town and another, we traveled at a good speed. I began to worry about how soon we might reach the outskirts of Battambang. I still hadn't figured out how I was going to escape from my truck without getting myself shot, or at the least without having to leave my suitcase behind. It was tricky. One couldn't help but feel exposed in the truck, watched all the time by somebody, either those in charge of us or people one had never seen before who might prove to be enemies. So there seemed little chance of my finding someone I could take into my confidence if that became essential.

I tried to smile at the paradox of my situation: the sense of danger one is made to feel in attempting to escape from the best opportunity for survival. Yet I was sure the danger was real. To be caught leaving the convoy would bring my identity immediately into question. If I admitted who I really was, how could I explain my false passport and my days in the Embassy without becoming totally suspect? And if I succeeded in passing for a Frenchman's wife, what was I doing running away from the other foreigners and the road home? My best possible hope was to slip away unnoticed at some point after we entered the city and make my way to my sister's house like any other refugee from Phnom Penh. That wouldn't be too difficult once I was clear of the convoy; I knew the city fairly well having lived there with my sister for a month—a rather unhappy month—shortly after her husband was killed early in the war, so I was sure I could find her place again from any major intersection. But clearing the convoy with my suitcase seemed an almost impossible obstacle. At least my imagination didn't come up with a secure plan this morning, and I began to wish Henri would suddenly arrive on the scene with his gentle expression of hopelessness and the possible solution he would have hiding behind it.

I suppose if you are born lucky there is always an Henri. In any case, my solution arrived at noon when we reached Pursat and apparently entered a new military region. Without warning we were ordered by our young drivers to disembark from the American and Chinese trucks that had carried us for two days and to board a line of buses that would be driven by their replacements, soldiers who looked generally older and more relaxed and who were under the authority of the Battambang committee chairman. Our new leaders handed out food lavishly and told us before boarding that we could help ourselves to any fruit that appealed to us in the neighboring orchards because the trees were now the property of the people, which in the Battambang region appears to include even foreigners. The people who once owned the orchards were of course nowhere to be seen. House on house along the road stood empty, abandoned by those who had been ordered somewhere else to gather what fruit they could in the wilderness while they waited for the Angkar to bring forth the new Eden.

I was quick to see this change of the guard as an opportunity. I still had no specific plan, but it struck me as a chance to move closer to the rear of the convoy, where it might be easier for me to slip away. And it also struck me as a chance to find a seat beside somebody I felt I could trust. So I joined the others to pick some oranges from nearby trees, working my way down the road. Don't be unnecessarily flattered if I admit that I was looking for an American. My thinking was mostly objective: an American would be the least likely of my fellow aliens to create difficulties for me if I asked for help because he himself would feel among the more threatened. Also, given our particular nationalites, he might be among the more generous. In any case, what I ended up pursuing turned out to be a Canadian. Very blond, with a thick reddish moustache, big eyes, beautiful teeth. I spotted him under a mango tree as I was edging my way toward the last of the buses. I developed a sudden craving for mangoes. So I put my suitcase down by the side of the road, took out a new kerchief, went over to his tree to see if he might share some of the fruit he was picking.

We became friends quickly after settling in a seat near the back of the last bus—there was no time for normal reticence—and by the end of the afternoon, we were co-conspirators. He turned out to be a journalist-photographer representing several Canadian and one provincial British newspaper— I don't remember which—and I think what started out as his merely flirtatious interest in me, no doubt livened by my audaciousness, became more serious when I told him I was planning to leave the convoy as soon as I could work out a safe way of doing so. I had to make up a bit of biography to explain myself. I told him that besides being a Cambodian war widow who had worked for the Americans and who was now posing as a French housewife, I had some years ago been a stringer for several French newspapers and considered journalism my first profession, which was why I felt both a special opportunity and an obligation to record what was happening to my country as long as I was healthy enough to keep a record, and I planned to stay healthy first of all by tracking down my sister in Battambang and then, with her help, by making my way to a village near the border on the Battambang-Pailin road so that we could cross into Thailand quickly if that became a necessary route to survival.

I think Nicholas (that's what I'll call him: the closer I come to going out on my own, the less secure I feel about putting real names in this diary)—I think Nicholas actually played for a while with the idea of coming along with me, my white lie maybe stirring the jealous reporter in him whatever else I may have stirred. But the more we talked about the problems I might run into getting clear of the convoy and merging with what were after all my people speaking my language, the less sense that idea must have made to him. And of course I wouldn't have permitted it, blond beauty though he is—both for his sake and mine. Still, I found his boyish enthusiasm for my plan rather touching. And of course useful: he's now in charge of my suitcase.

The first scheme we worked out was to make ourselves a couple when we reached Battambang, where we assumed we would spend the night in some sort of official quarters. Then, at the right moment, maybe during the dawn washing, we would simply take a lover's stroll into the open air with the suitcase between us, and I would disappear down the first safe street we came to. It was a scheme that obviously appealed to Nicholas because it meant our spending the night together in some kind of intimacy, but the Khmer Rouge spoiled even that touch of romance. Our convoy stopped short of the city center, in the outskirts by Battambang's graveyard of cars, and our shelter for the night has become our bus. Nicholas is now sound asleep beside me. I haven't been able to sleep at all. We held hands like adolescents for hour on hour, until he finally dozed off and I eased myself free to write in my notebook, hoping that would tire me. Now I'll stay awake until dawn.

Our new scheme is to go our separate ways at the morning

washing—we'll surely be allowed one trip into the fields—and I will simply remain behind wherever they let the women go for their bit of privacy. Nicholas is to take care of my suitcase: he will leave it hidden behind one of the abandoned cars by the roadside where I can pick it up when the convoy has gone on its way. That seems to matter less to me now. I feel so near the edge of a beginning, the presence of some new confusion of good and evil, that it almost seems right for me to go into Battambang to find my sister and her unfamiliar children without any of my recent past to burden me.

May 7. It has taken nearly a week for me to come back to my notebook. I am in Treng on the Pailin road with my new family, waiting to be given a piece of forest land to clear and cultivate. There are thousands of us between here and Boeung Trasal waiting for the same thing, so I expect to have time on my hands for a few days. I spent yesterday resting from the trip here. Today I'm less exhausted but also less preoccupied, and images from Battambang and the long walk here crowd my mind uncomfortably. Battambang first of all. It was empty. More than Phnom Penh even, it seemed a ghost town, because I discovered only a few familiar landmarks to locate my memory of what had been. It had the feel of a great vacant set for an abandoned film, without actors, now partly dismantled, much of the expected landscape taken away. On the road going in I did come across some carts, the people with them death walkers mostly, too tired or terrified to do more than glance at me. So getting to my sister's place proved even simpler than I'd anticipated—too simple. There was no one at home. The house was open and all the furniture in place—the heavy, over-stuffed easy chairs and couch, the grand buffet and dining table, everything I used to detest because of its pretentious bourgeois provinciality, worse, its domestic complacency, which I had come to see during my irrational month there as a silent accusation. Now it seemed funereal, and it touched me at a level far deeper than that of taste or even of pride.

As I looked around the house it became clear that my sister and her children had left in a hurry and taken very little with them. The dishes hadn't been cleared from the table and the kitchen looked as though it had been burglarized. I went through every room in turn looking for I know not what, and then I sat down in the living room and gazed at that pathetic furniture I had hated so passionately until I felt myself beginning to cry. To put a stop to that I got up and cleared the dining room table, washed the dishes, went upstairs and made the beds. I couldn't stand having the place look as though life in it had been suddenly terminated in mid course by some quick and violent interruption.

The work calmed me. I decided I would simply have to determine what route they were most likely to have taken when the city was evacuated and try to catch up with them. That meant first of all getting rid of my suitcase. Nicholas, dear boy, had done his task brilliantly: he'd left the suitcase by the roadside in the open trunk of an abandoned car, a new one turned on its side, where it apparently seemed so at home that nobody took notice of it in the short time it was there. But it occurred to me that it might now become a dangerous liability: both too heavy to carry as far as I might have to go and too obviously out of place among those I would now join on the road. So I made another careful selection of my belongings—this time only what I considered truly essential— and transferred them to a rice sack that I found in the kitchen. I topped the sack off with the few tins of food my sister left behind and a box of British biscuits.

There was no one in the street outside or anywhere in the neighborhood to help me decide which way to head, but as I studied the situation it still seemed to me that the Battambang-Pailin road was my best route since, as far as I could tell at that moment, it would have given my sister her nearest escape exit from the city, and it was also the route that I thought led most directly to the Thai border. So I headed for the Pailin road, and I reached it without incident, my walking much aided—alas—by the lighter load I was carrying.

A few kilometers along that road I began to encounter remnants of the exodus that had apparently cleared the city overnight the previous week. The accounts were all the same. People had been told by loudspeakers in cruising military cars that they had three hours to make their way out of Battambang if they wanted to avoid being shot. Everything still alive in the city after the deadline would be killed where it was: citizens of all ages, dogs, other domestic animals. Nobody argued. People took what they could and fled for the outskirts, men and women, old and young jamming the roads in every direction, because this was only a few days after the reports had come in about the massacre of officers and noncommissioned officers belonging to the government army, and nobody had any illusions about who was now in charge and how they planned to maintain their authority.

The officers had been called in by radio the day the Khmer Rouge entered Battambang. The radio asked them to lay down their arms and assemble the following day in order to offer assistance to the new government in unspecified ways and to promote unity. So they gathered in front of the prefecture on the morning of the 18th and waited for further orders. When there were no further orders, they went home. They gathered again the next day and were marched first to the university and then to the Sar Hoeur primary school, where they stayed four days waiting for orders that never came. Then someone arrived to read all their names off a list that had been prepared for the occasion, as though they were to receive a special commendation for cooperating with the new government, and they were told to go home, put on their dress uniforms and all their decorations, say goodbye to their wives, and return to the prefecture to be transported to Phnom Penh to greet Prince Sihanouk on his arrival there from China. Of course there was no Sihanouk or even a ghost of Sihanouk. Six trucks loaded with officers in dress uniform moved slowly out of Battambang in single file, and that was the last anybody saw of them in that city or any other. Witnesses from the region of Phnom Thippadey reported that there is a mass graveyard of unburied officers in a field there, clearly marked by its stench. The noncommissioned officers were transported to Bat Kang, near Thmar Kaul, where they were lined up on the sides of Highway 5 with their hands tied behind their backs, shot one after the other, and left in piles along the highway for any traveler to see. The ordinary soldiers were sent elsewhere, some say to reeducation camps in the region of Phnom Sampeou, some say to the river.

Battambang is now the cleanest of the military districts. What war couldn't quite do in five years for all its dead, wounded, and still missing, peacetime completed in just over five days—at least in the case of those who chose the wrong army. Now the ordinary . citizens in the Battambang region find the question of choice much simpler: there is only one army left, and when that army gives you three hours to pack up and find a new life, you find a new life or none at all.

Mine began about thirty kilometers into the Pailin road, just beyond the Anglong crossing. I arrived there late in the third day, exhausted from two wet nights of little sleep spent on my rice sack by the side of the road under a yellow umbrella. I was lucky even so. Most of those camping on the roadsides had to take the rain as it came because they hadn't managed to get out of Battambang with anything as luxurious as an umbrella. During my first day on the road I inquired constantly about my sister and was greeted constantly by silence or suspicion. Nobody knew anything about anybody, and nobody wanted to talk except in general terms about what had happened. The mention of specific names, even specific streets, was somehow threatening. The talk—except for the storytellers—seemed to be confined within families. And I suppose there was something in my way of speaking Khmer that showed me to be an outsider.

All I learned that first day was that people had left the city from every direction in their hurry to get out, and some routes had proven more accessible than others at certain moments, depending on which of the main streets were the least crowded at a given time. Those I questioned turned out to come from various sections of the city, proving the point. So my sister could have taken any one of several routes. The farther I got that first day, the more hopeless I became about my prospects of finding her easily. And the more cautious I became about asking direct questions. The second day produced nothing new. I spoke less and concentrated on passing from one group to another in the hope of hearing anything that might give me a clue. I was worried that something I might say would reach the wrong person and cause trouble. By the third day I'd become as silent as the others. And almost as self-protective.

But of course when you're exhausted from walking and not sleeping you let your guard down. I did the third night, which I spent among refugees some of whom had been camping by the roadside for several days, waiting for a new rumor that might help them decide where to go next. They took me for a stranger to that region—I suppose not hard to do given how relatively fresh I must have looked to them—and the more courageous asked me if I had any news. I offered those nearest me some oranges from my convoy supply, but sharing news seemed more important for the moment than sharing food. So I told them what I could about Phnom Penh without revealing too much about myself, and I was repaid by an account in full detail of the Battambang massacres. The later it got, the more we crowded in together, gradually forming a tight circle against the dark and the dampness. It turned out that the people gathered there had come to the crossroads from three directions and most were as much strangers to each other as they were to me. Everybody new kept testing his neighbors with questions, small bits of personal history, never enough to prevent a retreat back into silence if it seemed one had suddenly become too exposed.

The talk opened out again when we began dividing up what each of us had to eat that wasn't likely to last. We picked over rumors and opinions from wherever they may have come, to see if there was any consistency in them that would help to tell the future. Those from the north, outside the towns, had heard that all population centers were being evacuated because the Khmer Rouge were afraid of spies left behind by the Americans, this after discovering secret radio transmitters in several cities. Others thought it was the Lon Nol government officials and certain conspiring military leaders they were afraid of, and that was why they had decided to kill everyone in uniform or government service either by murder or gradual starvation, and since they didn't have a new administrative service to replace the one they killed, the cities had to be abandoned. Some of those from Battambang said that it was the Khmer Rouge hatred for Chinese merchants and their capitalist exploitation that had caused them to close the cities and make everyone a farmer, as was proven by the way they had destroyed the market overnight by changing the cost of rice from 150 riels a kilo to 3 and pork from 300 riels to 12, thus clearing the market of food, emptying pockets of whatever money there was, and driving the Chinese merchants mad. But most from the city thought it was the problem of controlling so many people with so few soldiers, especially when it became apparent that there wasn't enough food for everybody. Some said they'd been told by the soldiers themselves that city people had to be sent into the country where the food was grown in order to prevent mass starvation. But those from villages didn't see how that explained why the Khmer Rouge were burning what they could of village houses and emptying the rest, even isolated farm houses, why almost everybody in the newly liberated areas was made to move elsewhere even if a farmer at work on his land, why the rice fields everywhere were deserted and so little cultivation was under way

395

when it should be nearing its end. The more we talked, the more it seemed the Khmer Rouge had in mind destroying absolutely everything that had been, so that they could start the country over again from the beginning. But what would the beginning be like? And what were we to do until we came to it?

These questions hung depressingly over our circle, and since there was no answer to them, we turned to things we knew, things actually seen or heard from witnesses who were beyond any need to lie. The stories built a horror too large to seem possible outside the world of myths, and places one had never heard of or seen only on the map became suddenly essential in the imagination's landscape, as though planted there by clever new fables meant to twist the mind. Mechbar, for example, an experimental farm in the north where a full company of soldiers were executed in front of their wives and children, then the wives were executed, and when the children began to cry they were told to stop crying over these enemies of their country or they too would be executed beside them. A man amongst us had traveled for a while with some people who had come down from the Mechbar farm. He said one of them talked without stopping, telling the story over and over again, but the others couldn't talk at all, as though their tongues had been cut out. And Pailin. Two trucks carrying government troops wearing the Black Cobra insignia crossed from Pailin into Thailand on April 17th but came back a few days later to surrender to the Khmer Rouge because the Thais wanted their weapons. They said they had told the Thais that their weapons were Khmer and would stay Khmer, and now they wanted to join the Khmer Rouge to fight the Thais. So the Khmer Rouge gathered up their weapons and then drove their noncommissioned officers out to Trapeang Ke near the first bridge on the Pailin-Battambang road and shot them all dead. The ordinary soldiers were sent out to found a War Prisoners' Village somewhere near Samlaut, as though they were permanent enemies of the new Cambodia they had hoped to defend. And it was at the Samlaut crossroads that a family from Pailin had to choose between going into the forest to face evil spirits or turning back to face the Prince of Death because they couldn't continue on the main road past the smell and disgrace of the slaughterhouse they found there in the shape of a mass open grave for officers and officials who once ran their city.

This is the family that has now become mine. The father is a mechanic who worked in a garage in Pailin, maybe forty years old (it is hard to tell because the cracked dark skin of his face seems much older than that, except around the eyes). His wife is a simple woman who looks both older than him and better fed, and she is evidently in constant terror of spirits. They have a daughter who is somewhere between a child and a woman, delicate, with the possibility of being beautiful—she could be fifteen or sixteen and simply undernourished. It was the daughter who brought me into the family. She was next to me on my left in our circle that third night on the road, and I could tell that she became increasingly upset by our talk because she ended up squatting there beside me with her head between her legs as though to hide from the sound of our voices. I could feel the whole of her body tremble at moments. Her mother, squatting on her far side, was apparently too frightened by different voices coming out of the darkness to pay attention to anything but her own silent dialogue with the invisible. I finally drew the young girl in close to me and put my arm around her. She wouldn't look at me, but at the same time she didn't resist, and she stayed that way through the night. After I fell asleep I would wake up every now and then and feel her cheek against my breast and her warm breathing, feel it with both more tenderness and more sensuality than I wanted to admit.

The next morning, as I was gathering my things to move on toward the Pailin hills, the father came over to me and shyly asked where I was planning to go. I told him I wasn't sure exactly: in the general direction of the border, where I hoped to find some place safe to settle while I tried to figure out if there was still any way I could trace my sister and her children. He squatted beside me and asked my permission to tell me something he preferred the others not to hear. Against my better instincts I gave him permission. He said softly that he was afraid his wife had gone mad. She hadn't been right since they'd come out of the forest beyond the Samlaut crossroads. Angry spirits had reached her during that passage through the forest, so near the unburied dead, and now he was afraid they would get his daughter as well. I told him the only spirits that I thought truly dangerous were those that living men carried in the dark half of their selves. He gazed at me without comprehension. He said that I had to help him with his daughter now that her mother was mad, I had to give her my protection as I had through the night. I kept shaking my head, but he went right on in his soft, desperately intense voice, breath close and vile. He had heard as they passed through Treng that the new government was going to distribute forest land to people for clearing and planting, as much as three hectares to a family depending on its size, and if I agreed to join his family to act as mother to his daughter and sister to him, he would be willing to turn around and head back for Treng, fearful though that was, and I could freely share in whatever lot came his way for as long as it served my needs.

Of course the idea was grotesque. But as he gazed at me with those unblinking eyes of his it suddenly occurred to me that, unlikely as it may have seemed in that wretched, desolate, absolutely godforsaken setting with that tattered, vile-smelling demon of a man squatting beside my rice bag, it was just possible that I had found myself a new Henri. And that is why I am now at Treng, still very tired, still waiting with my new family, still not sure whether it is angry or benevolent spirits that have guided me here, but quite certain now that I will have to be more lucky than I deserve to be if I'm ever going to find what is left of the real family I once had.

May 10. Today I have a new identity again. I am no longer Francine Donnet, wife of Jacques Donnet, as my French passport had it, but Phal Sameth, sister of Phal Saren, auto mechanic from Pailin, where I have lived with my brother and mentally sick sister-in-law to help care for their daughter since abandoning my profession of schoolteacher in Phnom Penh two years before Prince Sihanouk was overthrown. This is what I wrote in the autobiography that each of us in our ten-family group of "new people" was required to submit before we could qualify for our allocation of forest land in one of the settlements to be founded northwest of here.

The autobiography was to cover the last five years, since the Lon Nol coup deposed Sihanouk. I had not planned to mention anything about Phnom Penh, just pretend to have been a member of Phal Saren's family since leaving school, but my new brother convinced me that I had to create some excuse for my manners and my way of expressing myself if I wanted to avoid suspicion. And there has been much suspicion in the air since we reached Treng— though as far as we know it has not yet touched us personally. We

398

were told by those already camped here that spies have been planted everywhere and that we must be especially wary of children who are not attached to families—and even those who are. Now that the Angkar has disposed of the official enemy, they are apparently training the children to report on the hidden enemies among us, and every evening certain people have been summoned to meet with the Angkar Leu only to disappear into the night. There is still much weeding to be done, it seems, yet there is little time for official concern about what belongs in the new Eden and what doesn't. Word has spread among us that it is best to surround one's house with kapok trees and one's person with silence.

I began the process of insulation yesterday by disposing of everything alien in my rice sack, everything that might be regarded even remotely as capitalist or imperialist luxuries: the last of my makeup, two books, my one beautiful blouse—everything that once seemed essential. What I have left now fits into the bottom of my rice sack, which demonstrates how lavishly foreign and intellectual I've allowed myself to become these fifteen years under French and American influence.

I tried to be lighthearted about separating myself from this past, tried to cover my feelings with appropriate irony, but I wasn't very effective. What I found especially painful was ridding myself of my French passport, the most dangerous thing I was carrying—except, perhaps, for this notebook. The so-called luxuries I simply left in a gully by the side of the road, and I'm sure that bundle has been picked clean by now so that nothing I left in it can ever be traced back to me. But the passport and other papers that might have served for identification, both false and real, had to be taken care of more subtly, and that became complicated. My first plan was to rip everything into pieces and dispose of it in one of the toilets we've created here, the farthest I could get to. That worked for everything but the false passport. I simply couldn't bring myself to tear that up and watch it dissolve in filth. I didn't have time to understand whatever irrational hold it had on me, so I decided to exorcise the thing by making a small ritual out of giving it up. In the middle of the night I buried it under my head with a handful of my rice ration. We are camped under a stilted house, many of us packed in close, so it took me an eternity of careful scratching to clear the burial place, and when I was done I discovered that Phal Saren had been watching me with those unblinking eyes of his—for how long, I don't know. My scratching that way must have made him think I'd suddenly gone as mad as his poor wife.

But this morning he didn't say a word about it. Nor has he yet asked me about my scribbling in this notebook, which he and his daughter Thirith both pretend not to notice at all. I'm sure, though, that they realize it will do none of us any good if those in charge of us should find it among the few things we will be taking with us to our new home, and of course it would have been prudent of me to have buried it with the passport. I couldn't do that. This little notebook and the simple clothes I wear are all I have left outside myself from my other life, and this now seems to have become an essential part of me, like an implant. There is only one place to hide it that is safe, that I have to believe is safe: in my panties, flat against my belly. That is also where Phal Saren's wife keeps several rubies she must have rescued from Pailin, wrapped in a dirty handkerchief that she brings out and opens to explore whenever her mind's eye frees itself from whatever threatening presences inhabit her darkness.

Tomorrow we go northwest toward one of the mountain ranges that is supposed to stretch to the border. We have been told that each family in our group will be expected to clear a tract of land and build a bamboo house, then cultivate the land with cassava and yams. None of us in the group knows how to do that. And there are no animals to help. When someone asked our leader how we are to manage without the help of animals and tools, he smiled and showed his hands, the way a priest does.

May 26. Our village has no name, and it has no streets. It is a village only because we have decided to call it that as a defense against total anonymity. It consists of random huts that we have made with our own hands out of bamboo and branches in the area at the edge of the forest assigned by the Khmer Rouge to our group of families. The men go into the forest every day at six a.m. with hatchets to clear the land as they can. They return at dark. The women are planters in fields already cleared and in new land the men make and then plow in teams of eight because there are no oxen. The leader of the women in my group is a man, a Khmer Rouge veteran with one leg, who goes along ahead of us on his crutch and makes holes with a stake for us to drop our seeds in. We cover the holes by scraping earth over them with our feet. We have no tools. Our work also begins at six a.m., but we are given a recess between eleven and two so that we can return to the village to husk rice for our families. Sometimes, when we are not being watched too closely, we go into the forest to gather bamboo shoots, leaves, roots, anything edible we can find to supplement our daily ration of a half-tin of rice. Only the evenings are free for rest—most evenings, that is. Two so far have been given over to lectures by the village chairman, a stupid man, one of the few "old people" in the village, a reformed drinker and gambler who has been cured of his sins by our new religion. He has tried to teach us the catechism we are meant to know by heart, but his speech is not always clear, and it is hard to avoid laughing at him. Nobody does laugh. Laughter at a village meeting is taken to be a kind of complaint, and complaints will be allowed only at special meetings for self-examination which have been scheduled for some time in the future. To complain now is to take a trip at night to the rice fields far from here, where there is much need for fertilizer.

I got the catechism by heart in three languages today to keep my mind from fading out during the morning's planting. I give you my English version. The people are to become masters of earth and water, masters of rice fields, forests, and all plant life, masters of annual floods, masters of nature, masters of the future, masters of revolution, masters of factories, masters of both rainy and dry seasons. The four guiding principles for achieving the ideal society are independence-sovereignty, self-reliance, defense of the country, taking our destiny into our own hands. To arrive at the new society, justice must be simplified. For every crime, there will be one punishment: death. For those who do not want to be part of the new society, there will be one alternative: death. For those who protest the system of justice, there will be one satisfaction: death. We are told that the new code of justice has to be simple enough for a child to understand. And it is mostly children who are called on to administer it, young soldiers nicknamed A-ksae nylon and A-ksae teo because of the nylon rope or telephone wire they use to tie your hands before they break your neck with an axe handle to save ammunition.

Our life in the new village was almost good at first. After the long hours of waiting in Treng and the uncertain nights on the road, there was relief in arriving at a place that we could think of making into a kind of home, and even some pleasure in work that created a certain privacy and a shelter against the dampness. But the work in the forest and the fields has become cruelly exhausting for those of us not used to work of this kind. After the first days, Phal Saren would sometimes come home from the forest with his hands bleeding, but we had to keep that hidden so that he wouldn't be transferred to the plow, where they say the blood eventually comes into your throat. Fortunately I had some of your first-aid cream among the things I kept out of my suitcase—there is no medicine of any kind in the village and to ask for any special treatment is to raise suspicion or hostility. Our problem now is Phal Saren's wife, Hoon, who has a bad fever. No one wants to say that it is malaria, but our chief at work, who normally abides no suffering from us ("Think how we suffered during the war," he mumbles, baring his stump and pointing it at anyone who complains) is superstitious enough about malaria to raise no objection to Hoon's staying home from the fields. Since there is no quinine, we can do nothing for her but try to keep her warm when she shivers and cool when the fever begins to make her delirious. Thirith has been frightened deeper into silence by the noises her mother makes. She works beside me in the fields and husking rice and never says a word to me, but at night, after her father finally gives up attending to Hoon and falls asleep on the far side of the room (a manner of speaking, since there is only straw on the ground, as in a stable), she edges over next to me and I take her in my arms until she no longer hears her mother's hard breathing. I try to disengage myself after she has fallen asleep, but there are times when I can't, when I don't want to, and we stay that way until the light comes.

I spent the anniversary of your leaving on the road west of Treng. I was going to write something about it here when we camped for the night, but I found that I had a block. It seemed so remote, so sentimental to make something out of a past that has broken into too many fragments even in this short endless time. But I did think of you then, as I do now, and if it is without enough sentiment, that is no fault of yours. It is a measure of the road I've taken away from what I was, quite unwillingly.

May 28. Hoon died on Tuesday. It took less than a week for the malaria to kill her. Others in the village have died too, all quickly.

They are buried in the forest in the middle of the night—the village men help each other, our one voluntary communal project—so that a death doesn't become an excuse for the Khmer Rouge to move the survivors in the family out of their hut and away to some place unknown. We have heard that they transport people from one place to another on any pretense, supposedly to avoid epidemics but also to wear out the weakest, and the prospect of moving seems to have become more frightening to many than staying where one's fate is at least partly visible.

I don't know how Phal Saren feels about remaining here. He hasn't talked since Hoon died. When he comes back from the forest at the end of his day, he lies down on his side of the room and just stares up at the lattice of branches that we have made into a roof, his eyes rarely blinking, no response when Thirith or I speak to him. I think he has given up. It is as though he knows now that all of us in the village are going to die, it is just a matter of time. If it isn't the malaria, it will be starvation, because they are already cutting down our ration of rice, and there is little hope that we can last with this kind of exhausting work until we have the benefit of what we have planted—or whatever portion of it is meant to be shared by "new people." He must feel that if he talks, this is all he will be able to say to us, so he stares at the roof. And once in a while he glances at his daughter.

I have to tell him sometime soon that I've decided to leave. Maybe he already knows that too, which would explain why he never looks at me. Maybe he suspects that I want to take Thirith with me when I go. I wouldn't do so without his permission—at least I don't think I would. Of course he could come with us, but he probably can't bring himself to leave his wife, not so soon, and I can't wait. He must realize how dangerous it is not to go now, yet I'm certain the poor man won't move, just like most of the others. I don't know whether Thirith would be willing to leave him behind. And I'm not sure how best to persuade her.

June 1. A few lines before I put this away in its secret place and take up my rice sack again. Phal Saren has vanished. Deliberately. He finally spoke to me yesterday evening after he came in from the forest. I was asleep, trying to save my strength for today, and he must have noticed that my things were packed. He was bending over me as I woke up—cheeks hollow, eyes holes—and when he spoke he nearly scared me out of my skin. "You'll take her with you," he said. It was a statement, not a question. Thirith was watching us. She said "no." That is what she said to me when I told her I was planning to try to cross through the forests and mountains into Thailand and wanted her to come with me. She said "no" both times in a way that left no room for argument. I'm sure she realized that it was her only chance to survive, but nothing I could say budged her one bit, so I'd made up my mind to go without her, tonight, when the village would be asleep. And Phal Saren must have seen that she wouldn't move unless he went with us. Since he couldn't do that, he disappeared into the forest. When he didn't come back from work this evening, Thirith and I went out to see what had happened to him. Those who had been working with him said that he wandered off during the midday recess and simply didn't return. They thought he was gathering things to eat. Now Thirith says she has to go into the forest to look for him, and of course I will go with her. I think we both know that we're not going to find him, and she knows we won't come back, but in this way she can go with me without being disloyal. So we will leave with what we have left: this dying flashlight, my yellow notebook, the handkerchief with rubies that Thirith inherited from her mother, food for maybe a week, her youth, my luck. It isn't enough. But at least now neither of us has to worry any longer about questions of loyalty and choice.

GISE PEDERSEN SETS ME STRAIGHT ON A MATTER OF NATURAL HISTORY

by MICHAEL FINLEY

from CUMBERLAND POETRY REVIEW

nominated by CUMBERLAND POETRY REVIEW

'No, you've got this part all wrong,'
says Gise, swatting a poem about birds
with the back of one hand.

'You have whippoorwills sobbing in the limbs
of poplars, but whippoorwills don't perch
in poplars, whippoorwills don't perch anywhere,

because their legs are just tiny twigs,
they are gone into atrophy, no muscle left,
so all they can do is plop themselves

flat on the ground and make the best of it
there on their haunches. And furthermore,
what is this sobbing business? It's poetic

but hardly accurate. Their cry is more
like a cheer, it is a call my son Peter,
before he died, liked to imitate

on his walks home from school.
Many times, late summer nights in our cabin,
Hendrik and I would be feeling morose,

only to hear out there in the darkness
the cry of a creature pressed close
to the cold of this earth, shouting

to all who might hear him:
VIP-poor-VEE!'

THE ANNUNCIATION

by CHRISTOPHER JANE CORKERY

from IRONWOOD

nominated by Cleopatra Mathis

The angel of the Lord came unto me
carrying a dove with curious, blinking eyes.
The angel said to me in an accent I had heard
This is the spirit of the Word. And then
You are the one who shall bear it.
The words hung there, like inedible fruit,
while the angel stiffly cleared his throat.
Yet I rejoiced greatly, not knowing why,
but sensing that my pleasure,
once caught inside this room,
was suddenly boundless and that it let me see
beyond the dust in the fly-thick road
and the cankered chickens pecking at the door,
beyond my neighbor Isa whose sobs cut the air,
beyond the web of Father's swollen hands.
I am chosen? I asked again, as if I could be sure.
And the angel pointed. *See the dove? It stays.*
And indeed it had found a little perch
in the deepest slit of our one white wall.
You are blessed among women, a mellow tone now,
and all will rejoice when you bear your fruit.
The angel paused here and began to smile
and amazed, I understood, exactly, what was meant,
as if another voice were speaking inside me.
So I took the tally board that Father made for market
and the pot of nettle liquor, pulling out the cork.
Then I plucked and cleaned a quill from that quiet bird.
The angel seemed disturbed.
I began to write.

UKIYO-E

by SIV CEDERING

from CALLIOPEA PRESS

nominated by Michael Dennis Browne

What explanation is given for the phosphorus light
That you, as boy, went out to catch
When summer dusk turned to night.
You caught the fire-flies, put them in a jar,
Careful to let in the air,
Then you fed them dandelions, unsure
Of what such small and fleeting things
Need, and when
Their light grew dim, you
   Let them go.

There is no explanation for the fire
That burns in our bodies
Or the desire that grows, again and again,
So that we must move toward each other
In the dark.
We have no wings.
We are ordinary people, doing ordinary things.
The story can be told on rice paper.
There is a lantern, a mountain, whatever
   We can remember.

Hiroshige's landscape is so soft.
What child, woman, would not want to go out
Into that dark, and be caught,
And caught again, by you?
Let these pictures of the floating world go on
Forever, but when
This light must flicker out, catch me,
Give me whatever a child imagines
To keep me aglow, then
   Let me go.

PAUL GOODMAN AND THE GRAND COMMUNITY

by HAYDEN CARRUTH

from AMERICAN POETRY REVIEW

nominated by AMERICAN POETRY REVIEW, *Jack Gilbert, Carolyn Kizer, Li-Young Lee, and Joe Anne McLaughlin*

As an artistic personality Paul Goodman was so cohesive in his concerns and beliefs, so altogether yoked and bonded within himself, that one can make no analytical statement about him without falling immediately into paradox, by which I mean opposites held in tension, and this is one reason, probably, why his writing has so far been little tested by the critics. For my part, I have always preferred to call myself a reviewer, not a critic, because reviewing is what I have had to do most of my life; and the distinction is important to me, not only as a matter of exigency and degree, but more as a disclaimer, for myself, of any systematic view of literature, especially as derived from sociology, linguistics, esthetics, or any other standpoint outside literature as such. I do not mean to be falsely modest. It's no news that we live in a low and narrow literary age and that the lamentable consequences are evident everywhere. My kind of spadework is what we need now, I believe, both to sort out our jumbled tastes and to make possible a future criticism that will be in the fullest sense serious and responsive (as opposed to the Wimbletonian criticism we have now, the tennis match we can hear from somewhere on the other side of the hedge). More than eight years ago I began to attempt these sentences, and even now I do not know where they will lead.

Nevertheless there is point in my following my broadest impressions of Goodman's sensibility, since precisely these may lead me into the self-enclosure of his remarkable fluency, which was not a matter merely of words, but of thought, feeling, perception, cultural reference; in short, the pattern-making awareness of experience that he himself called "the continuum of the libido." It was in fact his natural facility of imagination, driven always by his pervasive, many-tempered lust, and it never deserted him.

The first thing to be said about Goodman, therefore, is that his integrated sensibility was in some manner achieved; not imposed, not revealed, not fortuitously agglomerated.

And I think the second thing—still staying within one's broadest impression—is that Goodman's integrated sensibility nevertheless had two foci. Culturally speaking, Goodman lived in two places at once. More than any other important American writer of the twentieth century, with the possible exception of Edmund Wilson, he was European. Hemingway, Faulkner and the others of the "southern renaissance," Williams, Stevens (in spite of his mannered elegance), even Eliot and Pound (in spite of their European allegiances), as well as such members of Goodman's own generation as Schwartz, Jarrell, Shapiro, Lowell, Bishop, etc.,—all were American, whether determinedly or unselfconsciously. It is not a question of style. (If it were, Stevens would be from Paris, circa 1880.) It is a question of vision, angle of approach, the way experience is seized and organized esthetically. Goodman was precisely *moderniste* in the European tradition, a companion of Kafka, Gide, Rilke, Brecht, Aragon, and Cocteau; especially Cocteau. He disdained the impersonal and conventional; he celebrated the personal and mythological. His procedure was that of dreaming awake, its wit as well as its profundity. He was absurd, practical, deeply moral, shocking, and polemical. He was a superb technician and had a philosopher's sensitivity to the humanity of language (somewhat akin to Heidegger, though I don't know if he had read him); at the same time he had little use for linguistics as such, for structuralism or concretism or any other conceptualist theory of art. He was devoted to *meaning*. In all these qualities he was a European man, and not simply European but Continental. He was a romanticist in the post-post-post-romanticism that this implies. I am reminded of the absolutely necessary apothegm written somewhere by Camus: "Classicism is nothing but romanticism with the excess removed."

Further, a point can be made I think about the deliberately "American" writers of the first half of the century, namely, that many of them, often including Williams (whose work I admire enormously), fell into a kind of rhetoric of America, exaggerated, in effect chauvinistic. The American Experience, etc. Goodman was far too sophisticated, too analytical, too well trained philosophically to fall into that. He knew how important the city of Paris was to the modernist movement. There really is a sense of place in the works of Cocteau, Gide, etc., to say nothing of Proust, whereas with American writers place tends to become exclusively subject, that is, to move from the background to the foreground. With Goodman, as with the Europeans, it is in both places. As for Whitman, I think at some deep level—below style, topic, and mode of thought—Goodman shared with him the bedrock humanism or artistic altruism, close to but never the same as messianism, that saved the older poet, if barely, from chauvinism. In some poems, though not many, I detect phrasings by Goodman that could have been taken word for word and rhythm for rhythm from Whitman.

Having said this about Goodman's Europeanism, however, I think at once of the ways in which he was so thoroughly American that my remarks seem absurd. No other American writer of his time dared to be patriotic in Goodman's fundamentalist sense. In the midst of his sophistication he was plain and straightforward, not to say homely; in the midst of castigating contemporary American civilization he would stop to proclaim, in tones of injury, his faith in the Jeffersonian archetype. It was almost a tic, but no less serious on that account. He truly believed that the Lockean presence in the American Constitution made it not only one of the world's most beautiful documents but still the best hope of mankind. He took off his hat when the flag went by. And his love of the American scene, urban or rural, was clear in everything he wrote. He called himself a "Jeffersonian anarchist." What's more, he made it stick, he turned the seeming contradiction into a unity. He was American even to the extent of accepting necessity in politics, moderating his revolutionary zeal and despair to a reformist optimism, at least from time to time—and what could be more American than that? Sometimes he seemed in danger of turning into an ordinary Anglo-American liberal, a fault his critics on the left were always glad to point out. At all events, he made us see that *radical* and *conservative,* if they remain useful terms at all, are only so in combination. We cannot say one without meaning the other. He was practical and a pragmatist, like all Americans; but always haunted, like all Americans, by the ideal.

But I see that already I must correct myself, the difficulty of dealing with so complex a personality. It was not so much that Goodman "moderated his revolutionary zeal"; he advocated short-range changes that in themselves were nothing basic but that he saw as necessary little elements of the social revolution (after Kropotkin) which, if it were accomplished, would make the later political revolution more secure. Something like that, at any rate. He felt, I believe, that it would be a mistake to leap over these little changes because they were not revolutionary in themselves. He also felt—and this may be the heart of the matter—that it was important to avoid despair, depression, etc., since political activity, especially revolutionary, requires energy and hope.

Yet how many times, again in paradox, he castigated Hope as the enemy of reasonable human endeavor!

Perhaps, refining the point further, it is possible to say that in effect Goodman believed in an underlying *nature,* in which human beings participate, though at the same time he recognized the danger of such a belief, its outworn transcendental simplicity. Cautiously but nevertheless clearly, he believed that at all moments of political or social vitality (in history) one will find glimpses of this underlying nature, and one will be able to say why the particular political form sustains it, frees it, nurtures it, etc. This thought, and his preference for simplicity, entered very actively into the aspects of his mind that can be called conservative. In an analogous recognition of its danger, he tempered his romanticism, his native libidinous exuberance, with a classical and historical mode of reasoning. And all this was deeply characteristic of western intellectual life during the years of Goodman's active maturity, 1940 to 1970, though it obviously appeared in many shapes and colors.

In the back of my copy of *The Empire City* I jotted some of the names that occurred to me in my rereading: Rabelais, Cocteau, Aristophanes, the Old Testament (but more *Genesis* than *Isaiah*), Swift and Hogarth, Proust, Joyce (but with a question mark),

Twain, Voltaire, Handel, Poulenc, Thurber, "even in parts Francis Ponge," "the orchestrations of *The Critique of Pure Reason*," and Buster Keaton. A random list; obviously many others were tributary to Goodman's confluence: Aristotle, Villon, Wordsworth, Freud, Louis Sullivan—the names keep surfacing—perhaps Kafka most of all. Two temperaments so unlike, Kafka and Goodman, their positions worlds apart, their concerns scarcely touching, yet clearly Goodman found in Kafka something necessary to himself. I think it was the figure of the alien first of all. If Kafka was an artist, too, so much the better. But the isolated man, the cut-off imagination, these were the paradigms Goodman needed for himself. If he loved America, he did not love Americans, any more than he loved Libyans, Finns, or Trobrianders. Before each act of thought he had to touch, as if it were his talisman, his own freedom in all its chordal changes—independence, solitude, alienation, horrible messianic loneliness. Otherwise he could not think deeply at all.

(And was he, parenthetically, touched by his own style of language and thought as it had surfaced occasionally in prior American civilization, in works by Thoreau, Alcott, the other tax-dodgers, or by Dickinson or Hawthorne? The styles were close to his in many ways, so similar that sometimes it seems like superimposition; yet the distances are also great. I feel that Goodman's cultural temperament made him think of his American forerunners as unwanted rivals, and of their Transcendentalism, especially in its withdrawal from social process, as too puny a human endeavor to warrant his attention. Yet Brook Farm was clearly important to him.)

Now in the course of a couple of pages, following my sentences where they go, I have been led already through a considerable number of opposing coordinates on the circle of Goodman. The European American, the socialized alien, the practical utopian, the radical conservative, the pragmatic idealist, the self-explaining mystery and self-disclosing secret; for like all writers, but more manifestly than most, he was an Indian giver. If he disclaimed, as he characteristically often did but sometimes did not, the conventional post-romantic role of prophet, *homme d'esprit*, and vatic spirit, nevertheless he promised what he could not deliver. This was not, as one might be tempted to say at first, the "unutterable" word; Goodman was too thoroughly Aristotelean and psychoanalytical in his bias to accept ultimately the idea of a secret, mystical, supraverbal *logos*. It was simpler than that. What he sought was the word, the combination of words, that could contain all his own contradictions. This was humanly impossible, itself a factor that would have to be incorporated in the "word," with emphasis on "humanly." So he wrote around it and around it, forty books on almost as many topics explaining himself again and again, laying everything bare except the one real object of his and our desire, that which has no name though a thousand synonyms. Goodman is the perpetually fading echo that reverberates between the cliffs of consciousness. Call them being and nothingness. That inexactitude will do as well as any other.

A system of opposites lined up like the intersectional points of radii along the circumference of a circle. As with all metaphor, this from geometry is wildly inaccurate in its application, yet it is useful, which is to say, functional. In its typicality it represents one observable and so to speak certifiable aspect of the continual negotiation between reality and human mental capacity; it is inevitable, it is there in our heads, beyond the control of "reason" or "will," and its success in any particular operation will be relative. This Kantian view (though Kantian only to the extent that much else proposed by Master Immanuel himself is disregarded) would have been agreeable to Goodman. He was an anarchist, meaning by definition a mind limited and undoctrinal; a pragmatist, a relativist, a humanist, a moralist, a personalist. I don't know if he read Nikolai Berdyaev, but he would have gone part way with that philosopher's peculiar Catholic anarchism, as he would have gone part way or further with Tolstoy and Buber and many other religious radicals; and the points of separation from them would have come over disagreement about terms—the definition of the social context—more than from conflict of ideas. Part way was Goodman's perennial journey.

So he chose more and more to live in the countryside of northern New England where some half-articulate philosopher might be milking cows on the next farm down the road. He was a city Jew drawn like a moth to the light of backwoods Yankee nonconformity. His place was as far from Cambridge as he could get without leaving New England, ideationally speaking. He shunned as well the objectivism of William Carlos Williams, Louis Zukofsky, and George Oppen, with their insistence on the purity and autonomy of the thing-in-itself. Yes, he might have said to them, metaphor has its dangers, including the risk of phenomenological distortion; but lo! (for he was our only modern writer who knew how to get away with the marvelous archaisms still resident in English) see that metaphor pure and shining in this poem by Wordsworth, and another! here in Villon. They work, they function, they are useful. How can one deny so natural an expedience of human invention? He demanded to be taken as a "practical" man, the esthetician of the possible. And in the same way that he shunned the objectivists, he shunned everyone else.

Goodman could make friends with no one who was not either a disciple or a dead man and the longer dead the better.

One cannot avoid the inference that Goodman's oppositionism was as much a matter of temperament as of principle. Yes, he complained of loneliness and he welcomed new friends eagerly; but he could stick with no group for long. He preached communalism, yet was the last man who could have accepted it. Notice how quickly, after he had attained success, and had won a following among the young advocates of counter-culture during the 1960s, he turned against them, or partly against them, and began writing books and essays to distinguish his positions from theirs. These distinctions were and are important, he was perfectly right to insist on them; but he could have written his books and essays as a leader, rather than as a critic. The chance of leadership was handed to him, the gift of history that most ambitious people pray for and that he himself had prayed for (e.g., in *Five Years*). But Goodman threw it away, abruptly, almost at times disdainfully. He knew what he was doing. Was he then unambitious? Not a bit of it; his need for recognition was enormous, a principal theme of his poems, a constant motive. But so was his need for independence. He was in conflict with himself—the point is worth repeating—and what is interesting, indeed crucial, is the way he kept his conflicts under control, brought them into the circle of tension that was his whole sensibility, and thus held himself and his work together.

But I have no wish to anticipate Goodman's biography. That job is being done—I am sure ably—by Taylor Stoehr, and we shall have the story in due course. (I knew Goodman only briefly in the time before his public success.) One point of biography is well known already, however, Goodman himself being always eager to publish it, and is important and worth emphasizing here. He belonged to the generation of New York intellectuals, mostly

Jewish, who dominated much of American political and literary thought in the late thirties, the forties, and into the fifties; such writers as Philip Rahv, Lionel Trilling, Hannah Arendt, Delmore Schwartz, and many others. A cardinal point with these brilliant men and women was precisely their alienation from the main currents of American life and thought; yet Goodman was alienated even among them.

It was an earlier instance of what happened in his relationship to the young people of the 1960s. But his estrangement from his own contemporaries was probably more fundamental, perhaps more painful, more damaging. He bitched about it endlessly. I think even he, however, knew how much he needed that damage, that extreme intellectual and even personal isolation. He continually took positions, consciously or unconsciously, that would reinforce it. No line could be laid down by the group, whether political, artistic, or philosophical, that Goodman would not bristlingly object to. He was an alien among aliens, ignored, scorned, refused access to the alien magazines and publishing houses. He complained about it, bitterly and with justice, yet it was his own doing as much as anyone else's, more than anyone else's, and his complaints were triumphs of exuberance.

Goodman was the self-justifying, self-congratulating pariah; not quite a martyr, he knew he was too intelligent to play that role convincingly; but he was wily enough to know, too, that he could be comfortably downtrodden and make a public virtue of his perpetual, autonomic dissidence. Not that the "virtue" was "public" at the time. The factions within intellectual life in New York during the late thirties, forties, and early fifties were many and minute; but they themselves produced hardly any public impact. How could the one who dissented from the dissidents expect recognition for it, all the more since the dissidents, when he attacked them, failed to counterattack? They simply ignored him. Yet I believe Goodman knew himself well enough to recognize that he could function best as philosopher and artist in an attitude of persistent opposition, and he hoped—he always hoped!—that ultimately this private necessity would become a public virtue. Indeed this is exactly what happened in the 1960s when all his works, earlier and later, came, however briefly, into public prominence.

Even anarchists, whose base in thought denies them the comfort of ideology, need something to rest on, i.e., that base itself, which thereby becomes a kind of ideal or absolute. It is, of course, the notion of freedom. Freedom complete and unconstrained by anything except considerations of "public safety." What ensues from this has been debated for a century and a half, with tactical and philosophical consequences to my mind both fascinating and illuminating; but I have no wish or need to try here even the sketchiest recapitulation. Goodman's use of the notion is my concern. His freedom was less that of the utopian theorists of Europe than of the nostalgic theorists of America. He called himself a "Jeffersonian anarchist." But the term did not satisfy him, and elsewhere he equated "anarchism" with "libertarianism" and "rebel humanism" in the attempt to pin down in a word his own undogmatic and ideologically unideological desire for freedom, practicality, and love. His view of the early history of the United States was sentimental, perhaps wrong; but it was crucial. "During the first thirty years of the Republic only 5 to 10 per cent were enfranchised and as few as 2 per cent bothered to vote. But the conclusion to be drawn from this is not necessarily that the society was undemocratic. On the contrary, apart from the big merchants, planters, clerics, and lawyers, people were likely quite content, freed from the British, to carry on their social affairs in a quasi-anarchy, with unofficial, decentralized, and improvised political forms. It was in this atmosphere that important elements of our American character were developed." And those elements were kept alive today, Goodman insisted, primarily in his own writing.

Yet he never forgot "our moronic system of morals and property," nor that this system emerged constitutionally from the political forms of the Republic, nor that the only recourse of honest men in America has almost always been political illegitimacy.

Goodman was a radical who dreamed backward more than forward, and whose view of the present was more often vague than precise, more often anxious than expedient, in spite of his commitment to "practicality." "Perhaps it is because I am so crazy with hope that I live in constant terror," he wrote. But also: "I fail to experience myself in groups that I cannot immediately try to alter by personal decision and effort." Again: "To dance into the present with the force of the endurance of the world." And elsewhere still: "With much of the business of our society, my intuition is to forget it." Finally: "On the advice of Longinus, I write . . . for Homer, for

Demosthenes, and other pleasant company who somehow are more alive to me than most of my contemporaries, though unfortunately not available for comment." But was that so unfortunate? If Homer had been alive in New York in 1940, I feel, Goodman would have dismissed his "comment" as inhuman and doctrinaire.

Goodman was not divided, he was torn. All his writing, seen from this standpoint, was an effort to patch himself together. It worked, and that is what is so remarkable.

The temptation at this point becomes obvious, namely, to reduce these various dualisms to the basic one that Goodman called his bisexuality. In one way or another sex is his tonic from first to last. Aside from the explicitly erotic poems and stories, sexual energy is present in all his writing; at least so I would argue. I don't know how to prove it. But when Goodman speaks of "the force of the endurance of the world," a statement that can be found in many different formulations throughout his works, I believe he is thinking of a nature that by no means excludes Newtonian, Darwinian, Freudian, Einsteinian, or any other modus of "objective contemplation," but that nevertheless is basically and simply generative—he is thinking, however metaphorically or unconsciously, of sex. His dualisms are sexually informed. His manner of argument the same. The sensuality of his style, by which I mean its "poetry" or "music," its syntactical sinuosity and almost tactility, is clear to me in even his most abstruse discussions. This uninhibited fluency, so remarkable in a writer given to making distinctions, is the one element that pervades all his writings: the fiction and poetry, of course, but also the declamations, the private jottings, the philosophical and critical exegeses—everything. And he kept this sexual energy flowing all his life, through to the final poems of sexual melancholy written when he sensed death not far away.

Yet I find none of these considerations convincing when it comes to assigning reasons for the dichotomies of intellect and feeling in Goodman's work. First, although he usually called himself bisexual, in at least one prominent passage of his writing he called himself homosexual. Secondly, one cannot avoid seeing that among his poems, the expressly erotic ones are to, for, or about men, while those addressed to his wife (and to his children as engenderings of his marriage) are distinctly different in tone; the latter being warmly and deeply affectionate, so that often they move the reader more genuinely than do the former poems of lust. And thirdly, I dislike and distrust any of these quasi-clinical, reductionist analyses in literature, and I would not resort to them even if I were competent to do so. For Goodman himself, psychoanalysis was without question the single self-enclosed structure of concepts that most clearly determined his view of reality, yet he was prudent, as he would say, in his application of Freudian theory, even in the derived Gestaltanalysis he favored, to artists or their works.

To my mind Goodman's propensity for dualistic modes of experience was forced on him, as on most of us, by his own temperament or by human temperament in general, and perhaps also by his early philosophical training, his graduate studies at the University of Chicago when Richard McKeon and Neo-Aristoteleanism were the vogue there. Aristotle's Pity and Woe, Pathos and Purgation, were important categories to the young intellectual of 1938 because, not only esthetically but socially and psychologically, they substantiated his instinctive awareness of art as a functioning thing, if not dialectical at least mediative. No doubt he found further support for his pragmatic view in the Kantian notion of a priori limits, popular with John Ransom and other New Critics. (Part of the avant-garde rejection of Hegel and Marx in general during the late thirties was expressed in a reversion to Kantian concepts, but bypassing the Romantic excess, along with new interest in such writers as Kierkegaard, Dostoyevsky, and Kafka.) But mainly Goodman had no interest in faddish philosophy. Conflict for him was a practical or procedural necessity, but he was always engaged in more or less holistic analysis, or at least the hope of it. He resorted, or was forced to resort, to dualistic modes in some books, e.g., *Compulsory Mis-Education* and *New Reformation*, but more often he regarded himself as a man in the main line of honest souls, from Aristotle, Longinus, Descartes, Spinoza (whom he reverenced), Kant, James, Nietzsche (though he discounted the superman as a form of neurotic yearning), Dewey, etc., down to his own knocked-together but generally unitary "system." He shows little liking for Cartesian or, in his own time, Sartrean examples. And if it is true that the more he insisted on the ideal oneness of society and the individual person, the more he found himself pushed toward equations, dichotomies, and oppositions, nevertheless he held the ideal—a functional unity—before him as the only reliable goal for anarchistic and loving ways of thought. If this meant, psychiatrically speaking, some scarcely appraisable but pervasive form of sexuality, so much the better.

Goodman's sexuality, however, does remain a question needing further explanation. He did not explain it himself, which is significant. He explained everything else about his poetry, repeatedly and lengthily, but he ignored this. He is rightly credited for his courage as a forerunner in the movement toward gay liberation; that is, for his open avowal of homosexuality in his poetry. But his silence elsewhere seems to indicate some deeper embarrassment. Goodman knew that his concept of love was unitary and that it was fundamental to his notion of the good community. Only love can hold people together (as Locke had said), and this love must be whole and wholly free. Yet community necessarily entails the ideas of fertility and generation, which were traditionally associated with the loving heterosexuality of the human animal. And Goodman himself was a traditionalist. He does not say, however, what his communalism means in this respect, beyond his insistence that love, like everything else, must be free.

It is as if the division of love into *eros* and *agape* dear to the Catholic theologians and invidious to at least some of the rest of us (so that we have denied it and said that the two are really one) does in fact exist in Goodman's life and work, and expresses itself in his attitudes toward his family on one hand and toward his sexual adventures with males on the other. Thus we come round to bisexualism again, but at a deeper level of meaning, and I think this is valid. Goodman tried to make a unity of *eros* and *agape*, and at times succeeded (or thought he did), but ultimately he really is stuck with some kind of separation. His inability to *rest* in any group and his obsessive need to keep talking, both of which he confessed readily, as well as his preference for being the critic in opposition, since he was always more adversary than advocate except in cases where he found himself in such primary opposition that he could "afford" to lean toward conciliation (e.g. his almost innate divergence from established religion and his final attempt to come to terms with it in *Little Prayers and Finite Experience*), all these elements of his own "nature" indicate to me a practical alienation from the social values of love. This would explain both his yearning for community and his inability to come to rest in a community. It was a deep duality, perhaps the deepest of all, far below his bisexuality. Nevertheless this is what I am talking about, this source, when I say that all his thought and writing are informed by his sexual energy.

Goodman was not famous, God knows, for laconism. By his own count he wrote "forty books," a nice round number such as authors are frequently heard to let fall. Yet in his case it seems that this may be an underestimation; his bibliography is huge, and since his death in 1972 newly uncovered works have continued to appear with regularity. He was a man of many words, for "to me it is panic to be speechless." At the same time he knew the values of brevity. (So complete was his proficiency that I find myself wanting to say, against reason, that he knew *all* the values of *all* literary strategies.) As he grew older and his imagination progressively consolidated and simplified his vision, he turned often to the Japanese hokku, for example, and wrote a few so poignantly right that they wring your heart.

> *If they were to say*
> *that this hokku was the last*
> *poem that he wrote*

Yes, he knew *all* the values: how the strict armature of traditional artifice glows and becomes alive in the broken language of unutterable, or nearly unutterable, feeling; the sentence left unfinished eternally. Yet he had a sharp wit.

> *I must be thirsty*
> *man, to make love to such a*
> *long drink of water.*

In the prose, too, which gives the impression of almost uncontrolled discursiveness, organization by caprice, one finds nevertheless embedded apothegms, these less the consequence of conscious effort perhaps than of the unmitigated force of invention. Imagine him at work. There he sits, hunched over the battered old typewriter, his pipe fuming and clenched between what remained of his teeth (for he was one of the world's great consumers of tobacco). The sentence, the *sentence* (look it up)—it was for him an act of imaginative compression, though he knew well how to hook them together and keep cadence rolling. Here are a few that have struck me particularly over the years of reading.

The giveness of Creation is surprise.

*

This world is purgatory. I have plenty of proof that I am not damned—I understand that it is heretical to say so—but I am being tried, I have no notion why. Maybe that's what I'm supposed to learn.

*

Yet men have a right to be crazy, stupid, or arrogant. It is our speciality. Our mistake is to arm anybody with collective power.

*

"Stand up for the stupid and crazy," Whitman said. Is there a connection? I can say only that either way I wouldn't be surprised.

*

When Isaac was saved on Mt. Moriah, Abraham must have gone into a towering anger. The Bible, written as God's history, tells us nothing about this. All that heartache for nothing.

*

There are too many missionaries among my friends.

*

Spite is the vitality of the powerless.

*

It is astounding how natural and few the fine arts are.

*

A style of speech is an hypothesis about how the world is.

*

Despite its bloodlessness, the tradition of literature is a grand community and, much as I envy the happy and the young, I doubt that they have as good a one.

*

The color of the Burning Bush is thought-passing-over-a-face color (but it must be a *thought*, not one of the vagaries of the likes of you).

*

Any workman putting away his tools is among the lovely dancers of this world.

*

For whatever is a human passion may be expressed in music, and whatever is music is in the human throat to imitate it.

*

. . . the bondage of peace. . . .

*

The thing is to have a National Liberation front that does not end up in a Nation State, but abolishes the boundaries.

*

Literature is not a "linear" unrolling of printed sentences and it is not a crude code; it is artful speech. And speech is not merely a means of communication and expression, as the anthropologists say, but is a chief action in our human way of being in the world.

*

The case is that our society is in a chronic low-grade emergency.

*

In the breakdown of repression, the artists do their part by first dreaming the forbidden thoughts, assuming the forbidden stances, and struggling to make sense. They cannot do otherwise, for they bring the social conflicts in their souls to public expression.

*

Certainly we are in a political crisis, for, though the forms of democracy are intact, the content is vanishing.

*

Yet it is a melancholy but common thing in the world (and makes for a melancholy world) that while the one fighter is for some reason single-mindedly bent on destroying a man, that man does not want this fight; he does not believe in it, he does not think that it is worth the hurt and damage involved. He has been forced into it, and it happens that he cannot quit the field.

*

Goodman could never quit the field. He would stalk off, muttering his disgust, but the next day—the same afternoon!—he would be back, his pipe fuming. Engaged willy-nilly against the enemy's "right to be crazy, stupid, or arrogant."

What made Goodman so blythe a philosopher was his understanding that philosophy is of the heart. He loved Kant almost because the Koenigsburgher was so often wrong; or rather, not wrong but incomplete—stopped by the limits of mentality. And this is the pathos that makes the Beautiful, surpassing every secondary esthetic principle of inclusiveness, dynamism, control, or whatever. *The Critique of Pure Reason*, read in this way, is western man's greatest oratorio of ideas, a triumph of art; so huge, so majestically orchestrated, touching so many of the unnotable, unsoundable limits.

In this Goodman was closer, on second thought, to his American forerunners than to his European. He was a little Emersonian, but of the jumbled Notebooks (though I don't know if he read them) more than of the finished Essays. An important distinction. In spite or because, whichever, of his haste and vitality, Goodman was always feeling his way, touching one after another of the objects, often books, presented to him by chaos, repulsing most, taking a few into himself. It was intuition at work, his rule of

425

thumb, which left him sometimes in contradictions he cared nothing about. But we, his readers, may care. Inconsistency is no hobgoblin, but it makes strangers where there should be friends.

". . . my trouble is that I have to be that kind of poet who is in the clear because he has done his public duty. All writers have hang-ups, and mine is To Have Done My Duty. It is an arduous taskmaster, but at least it saves me from the nonsense of Sartre's poet *engagé,* politically committed. How the devil could a poet, who does the best he can just to get it down as it is whispered to him, decide whether or not to be morally or politically responsible? What if the Muse won't, perverse that she is? What if the Truth won't, unknown that it is?"

"The ability of literature to combine memory and learning with present observation and spontaneous impulse remarkably serves the nature of man as the animal who makes himself . . ."

Strange. The terms are Sartre's yet the drift seems blindly anti-Sartrean. How is it that the "animal who makes himself" has a "nature"? Impossible, the Frenchman would say, unless mere self-consciousness is a "nature," which it is not. Can a person be both created and self-creating? Yes, Goodman would exclaim, why not! And then he would go on to say, perhaps, that the fact that a man "makes himself" does not contradict the idea of a prior givenness, or nature, but instead refers to the aspects of evolution that proceed from human culture. Science and technology, applied to agriculture, improve the diet, and after a few generations the average man is 5' 10", and has bad teeth instead of good ones. But obviously this takes more intellectual, more spiritual, forms as well.

Sometimes it seems as if Goodman ought to have found in Sartre, as he did in so many other European writers, a companion-at-arms. Very little necessary conflict existed between them. Sometimes Goodman's rejection of Sartre seems merely vanity, parochialism, defensiveness, the feelings that made him flare out at anyone who seemed, however distantly, to be treading on his own ground. But if there were no necessary differences between them, certainly there were practical differences, stylistic differences. Sartre was an ideologue, after all. In politics he supported the invasion of Hungary. To this Goodman could have uttered only a gigantic NO! Freedom and love come before ideas. And to Sartre's word-spinning, the house of cards built for Jean Genet, the strange tenuosity of "existential psychoanalysis," Goodman could have responded with only another negative.

For it is after all more than a question of vanity, parochialism, and defensiveness. And Goodman is closer to Emerson than to Sartre and the other European secular existentialists (though I wish he had written something about Camus). The poet "who does the best he can just to get it down as it is whispered to him," — what is he but the Kantian, the Emersonian, the Romantic?

I do not doubt for a moment Goodman's sincerity in avouching what was "whispered" to him. He is a poet of intuition. And yet, and yet—was he not as well a poet of "responsibility," of "authenticity"? Emerson had thought he was a Kantian, but was at best only loosely so. Goodman brought to American "romanticism" the inner moral voice, the imperative, of Kant, the poet's due to the Greater Spirit, his *intuition*. Goodman repaired the ruin of Transcendentalism with an esthetic accountability that could have come, but didn't, straight out of Sartre's theory of literature. For of course and without the slightest question, large parts of Goodman's poetry and fiction are political. He was being only petulant, denying the obvious, to say otherwise. The notion that somehow his polemical writing, his participation in rallies and demonstrations, left him free to be a "pure" poet was deeply at variance with many statements of his belief in the unit of literature and life and of his own sensibility. Even on the same page with that last quotation above he wrote: "The habits, genres, and tropes that have been developed in the long worldwide literary tradition constitute a method of coping with reality different from science, religion, political power, or common sense, but involved with them all. In my opinion, literature, although it is a method *sui generis*, is not a specialized department of learning but a good way of being in any department. It is a part of philosophy, which as a whole has no department."

Incidentally, watch out for Goodman when he says "in my opinion." It means a whopper—right or wrong—is on the way.

Yet, with nearly the whole span of twentieth-century American poetry before us—so many politically inspired poets who failed to transform their politics successfully into their poetry compared with the few who have—we can see how the trap that Goodman fell into was tempting enough; I myself have not avoided it. I used to think, indeed I said publicly, that Goodman's broadly political books which brought him to the attention of a wider audience than usually reads good poetry and fiction—I had in mind such books as *Growing Up Absurd, Compulsory Mis-Education,* and *People or Personnel*—were in some sense a misfortune, though no one could honestly say they should have been unwritten; a misfortune because they distracted attention from his "creative" writing; and I expressed the hope, I think even the belief, that in the long run these polemical works would be forgotten and his poems and fictions would remain alive in the American consciousness. I no longer make this distinction. His best poems and fictions *will* remain alive in the American consciousness (if the American consciousness survives in any functional degree of vitality, which it well may not), but so will many of his other books. They go together. Goodman's topics were many, but his theme was always himself; and he could no more refrain from inserting into his polemical works remarks about his own beliefs as an artist than he could refrain from breathing. He was an organic whole. No other writer in America of this century—not Pound, not Williams, not Olson, though these are more nearly identified with the concept— represents so well the organicity of sensibility implied in the title he gave himself, a Man of Letters.

Which is not to say that everyone must read every book in Goodman's "forty." Some are more important than others. For my part, I feel that the minimum for every reader's bookshelf is the following:

Art and Social Nature, The Copernican Revolution (edition of 1947), *Kafka's Prayer* (extremely important), *Communitas* (written with his brother Percival), *The Structure of Literature, The Empire City, Growing Up Absurd, the Lordly Hudson, Utopian Essays and Practical Proposals, Compulsory Mis-Education, Five Years, Hawkweed, Like a Conquered Province, Adam and His Works* (collected stories), *North Percy, Homespun of Oatmeal Gray, New Reformation, Speaking and Language, Little Prayers & Finite Experience.*

All these were published during Goodman's lifetime. Since his death more systematic collections of his short works (stories and essays) have been edited by Taylor Stoehr, including a few pieces not previously contained in books, and also one whole book found hidden away among other papers, the novel *Don Juan* written around 1940. Goodman always had a difficulty—a heartbreaking struggle; see his negative paean to despair and survival in *Five Years*—in seeking publishers for his work, and heaven knows (or maybe Mr. Stoehr) what further unknown works may still appear.

Finally, the *Collected Poems* of 1973. Goodman was working on this, assembling, cutting, revising, when he was struck down; the further work of completing the manuscript and seeing it through the press fell to Stoehr, who did his best to ascertain and follow Goodman's last wishes. He could do neither less nor more. But I have considerable doubt of the wisdom of Goodman's own revisions, as I shall explain hereafter. Probably the *Collected Poems* must be added to the list because it contains poems not included in any earlier books while some of the earlier books themselves are out of print and hard to find. But the original books of poems are to be preferred, at least for the present.

A month or six weeks ago I found myself needing a copy of *The Lordly Hudson,* published in 1962. Mine was in Vermont, but I was in Syracuse—Syracuse, New York, which is not exactly Alexandria but is still a big enough, rich enough American city, with some pretentions of civic intelligence. Well, the neglect of Goodman's work during much of his life and now still continuing has been a long, long source of pain to me, and of astonishment. I could not find the book in any library, public, academic, or private, in Syracuse, New York. And is it any different in Lexington, Kentucky; or Hot Springs, Arkansas; or Salmen, Oregon? (You other Americans, you pious four flushers and grandstanders, what the hell is one to say to you?)

I don't know how to account for the neglect of Goodman's work. Time after time I have met people who should be attracted by his poems and fictions, young and old, rich and poor, male and female. They have heard of him, they have read *Growing Up Absurd* or attended a symposium on alternative schools in which he took part, but beyond that he means no more than the statue of President Harrison in the park. They do not know, have not even heard of, his poems or *The Empire City*.

One explanation has occurred to me, wild as it seems, which is that Goodman's writing is too clear and that whatever explanations it needs have been given by Goodman himself. The critics have nothing to do, and of course readers will not bother with anything that hasn't been hashed over a dozen times in the fashionable maggot-scenes.

"As a man of letters, I am finally most like Coleridge," he wrote. Then in parentheses: "With a dash of Matthew Arnold when the vulgarity of liberalism gets me by the throat." It was true. There is, if I am not mistaken, a universal turning point between Enlightenment and Romanticism, in the histories of individual men and women as in the histories of civilizations. It is a dangerous point because, for the vulgar liberals, who are the vast majority of mankind, it devolves into sentimentalism. But for the few, including Coleridge when young, it is a point of extraordinary freedom, the well-trained mind releasing itself into spirit. That point was where Goodman lived.

"Poets contrive to make interjections an organic part of their language by inverting the word order, distorting the syntax, and adding rhythm and resonance. Ordinary folk in a passion give up on the language." To which one need add only Goodman's own innermost thought, that poets ultimately are ordinary folk, that poems ultimately also must give up, e.g. the hokku with no conclusion.

Kafka was Goodman's closest literary friend, the young Jew of Prague, the writer whose greatness was like a dreamt castle with its towers vanishing upward in the mist.

Why am I so polemical about recent language theory . . . ? Why don't I let those scholars do their thing, while I, as a man of letters, do mine? Frankly, I am made polemically uneasy by it, by the thrust of cultural anthropology, Basic languages, scientific linguistics, communications engineering, and the Theory of Communications. They usually treat human communication as far more mechanical than it is; they are technological in an antihumanistic sense. They suit State and corporate policy too well and have crashingly pre-empted too many research grants and university appointments. My own bias, to be equally frank, is to play up the animal, spontaneous, artistic, and populist forces in speech. These forces are both agitational and deeply conservative—as I think good politics is. And as a writer, I want to defend literature and poetry as the indispensable renovators of desiccated and corrupt language.

Agitational and deeply conservative: mind soaring into spirit. (Reason, order, objectivity submitting to love.)

A poem is one inseparable irregular conglomeration, chanted. The word order is likely to be twisted. The names are particularistic and anomalous. New metaphors are invented. There is use of echoic meaning and expressive natural signs. There is strong use of tone and rhythm, sometimes even meter. The syntax is manipulated more than is common, sometimes "incorrectly," to give it more meaning. The exposition of the sentence follows the speaker's exploration of the subject rather than a uniform rule. All of this is for the purpose of saying a feelingful concrete situation, rather than making discursive remarks about it.

*

A generalist is a man who knows something about many special sciences, in order to coordinate their conclusions in a system that has little relation to reality. A man of letters knows only a little about some major human concerns, but insists on relating what he does know to his concrete experience. So he explores reality. A generalist is inter-disciplinary. A man of letters finds that the nature of things is not easily divided into disciplines.

*

When I do what is called "thinking," muttering to myself, I never use words like God or Faith, and they are in no way premises for my behavior. When I talk to other people, I sometimes use them, but not authentically; I might use such language, as I have said, to facilitate earnest conversation with a believer, though I am not a believer; or I might use it to cut short a boring conversation with an unbeliever, when I am too tired to explain myself better. When I write, however, I readily use this vocabulary and apparently seriously. How is this?

*

In *Defense of Poetry*, I suggest a possible reason: "Maybe it is that when I think or talk to myself, I am embarrassed; but when I write, I am not embarrassed"—since writing is my free act. But there could be a simpler reason, more *prima facie*, more what it

431

feels like; I use this language because it is a poetic convention, a traditional jargon, like wearing old clothes because they are comfortable. It means what is the genius of the language of billions of human speakers—not my business. As a writer my business is only to be as clear as possible and say a work that has a beginning, middle, and end.

So we see Goodman clinging to his web of contrarieties.

Poetry is an empty act that is unfinishable but that has a beginning, middle, and end. But it is an *act*. Thinking is not an act. When the catcher signals to the pitcher, this is a thought; when the pitcher nods his head and goes into his windup, this is an act. Mind and imagination are connected, but the connection is tenuous, sometimes unlucky. The pitcher may shake off the sign, in which case the thought is useless. Or he may throw a bad pitch, in which case the act is a failure. But in all cases the pitcher's act is free, empty, isolated, internal, and its consequences, whatever they are, do not change it; no, not even if he beans the batter, who thereby suffers irreparable brain damage. Failure is failure, Goodman would say; it is a condition of human (self-conscious) existence, and so are punishment and misery and guilt. We can and must act with good faith and clarity, though these will never save us.

Thought is an argument with an imaginary companion. Making poetry is an act whose thought and content come from elsewhere, performed deliberately and in a conventional manner; its concreteness comes from its singularity—no act completely duplicates another, and a machine does not act but only moves in a meaningless transference of energy—and from the style imparted to it by the particular combination of attributes in the poet. (A machine is closer to thought than to a poem. A machine cannot have style.)

One may think at times that Goodman has painted himself into the same corner as the linguists and structuralists, as when he insists on the conventionality of language and artistic form. Yet the whole force of his argument, to say nothing of his poems, is to distinguish himself from those who would dismiss meaning from poetry. He too insists that the poem is "concrete," but he goes further. One must always remember that the poet does not believe in meaning as thought. Meaning is morality; morality is right feeling; and right feeling in concrete language is beauty. Sometimes I think Goodman yearned for "pure" poetry as much as Mallarmé before him. But I also think that such was not the case with poetry, no matter how he yearned. His poems are political. It is impossible to think of them as anything but political, moral, practical acts, "empty" and "free" only in their disconnection from objective determinants. Poetry is given. But so is life.

Another distinction, which Goodman did not make (as far as I recall) but which I want to make for him is this: on one hand, style with a small *s*, being the techniques of syntax, grammar, and prosody contained in the grand and good and almost immemorial poetic convention; on the other hand, Style with a capital *S*, being the self-consciously fabricated verbal idiosyncrasy of poetic caprice or, worse, poetic fraud. Goodman's style was the former, and in fact he does not think about style explicitly and rarely uses the word. Moreover, as he knew, as we all know, convention in Goodman's sense is not always reliable. John Berryman could compose his *Dream Songs* in a Style that gave them a consistent superficial tension and density, while Goodman's poems in a plain style are, as we say, more uneven. The fact that Berryman has been the darling of the critics while Goodman has been neglected demonstrates the insensitivity of critics, who are always suckers for artifice.

But if in his poems Goodman conventionally used the conventional signs of a conventional religious language, and if as an unbeliever he conventionally knew that they were conventionally worthless, this is by no means the whole story. He was a practical man, i.e. a poet, i.e. a man of faith. Often he adverts to the idea of the earth beneath him supporting his footsteps as he walks idly along, thinking of something else. *This* is his faith. He was able, I don't know how, to shrug off the truly immense apparatus of his learning, experience, and thought, and to put himself again into the attitude of a child; or, more rigorously, certain constellations of traits and actions in the mature man reveal a childlike quality, the panicky, needful child who is very much afraid, but at the same time reliant on an unselfconscious prudential wisdom and joy. A child does not touch a porcupine even though he has never seen one before. "Nothingness" is a useful concept, and it may well be, as many have said, that if one pursues it far enough it turns into the same thing as "somethingness." But Goodman was a practical man. He worked with his experience of "this only world," and for him

433

"somethingness" was truly somethingness: the given reality upon which we unselfconsciously, faithfully rely. He worked with his experience, which was this simple faith, through years and decades, writing poems in which the conventional signs took on more and more a personal, independent significance. Astonishing how simply and clearly he could say his complicated relationship to reality.

> O God, there must be some way
> that he and I (and many another)
> can be a little happier.
> Whisper it to me in my ear.

He was like a child. A wise, suffering, hopelessly hopeful child. Neither a literal nor a mystical way exists to define what the word "God" says in this quatrain. Yet I know what it says, and I am confident that my readers know what it says too. I don't have to try to explain it.

Goodman was *like* a child. But this is not to say that he was a child. On the contrary, it is to say he was in his yearning, which was how he was in the world. And the words of children were often—but others just as often—expressive of how he was. "Whisper it to me in my ear," he says.

And then many times this poignancy eluded him, and he spoke out like the tough existential man he was, the Jewish Yankee.

> For the beautiful arts
> are made of cheap stuff,
> of mud and speech
> and guts and gestures
>
> of animal gaits
> and humming and drumming
> daylight and rock
> available to anybody.

This also is saying how he was in the world. And the names in these eight lines are not as random as they may at first appear, but were chosen in long-accruing wisdom and placed with care. How else could he ever say how it *really* was for him in this world.

As for how it would be out of this world, Goodman did not write of death as much as one might have expected, knowing his metaphysical consternations. When he did write about it, he took it for what his experience—e.g. as a motorist (he loved the road)— told him it would be, and put it down on the paper more and more simply (though simplicity was one of his virtues from the beginning), and so in some sense dismissed it.

> *Chuangtze is dead as I shall die*
> *unnoticed by the wayside,*
> *his spirit does not haunt the world*
> *and his death-grip is relaxed.*

So. Finished and decomposing, no haunting spirit. Chuang-tzu, more than two thousand years ago, the great interpreter of Taoism to the world.

Returning again to the matter of style (with a small *s*), I wonder what poets were Goodman's models. He does not say much about this. Poets generally don't. Villon was obviously important to him, Wordsworth more than important—crucial. I know he read Milton's essays. I suspect he may have looked once at Donne's sermons and several times at Aubrey's *Brief Lives* and Pepys's *Diary*. And I am convinced myself, that he must have read Bradford's *History of the Plymouth Plantation*, that great, distressed American epic, though I have only intuition to support me. But one can multiply the inferred influences indefinitely: Anacreon, Swift, Woolman, Catullus, Burns, the Shepherd's Calendar, Baudelaire, and so on. Is there no contemporary instance? I can scarcely think of one (still adverting to style alone), though a wild guess might be that his deep interest in Kafka came through the translations of the Muirs, and that this might have led him to seek out Edwin Muir's own poems earlier than other Americans did; more than a trace of verbal similarity exists between the two. And then Robert Frost— what about him? In an astounding number of ways Frost and Goodman echo each other, in many more ways than the devotees of either poet are likely to accept. But see, for instance, Frost's

"The White-Tailed Hornet," especially its conclusion, which is Goodmanian in substance, tone, texture, and style.

But the point needing emphasis more than any other is that Goodman's instinct for the tradition took him not to individual models as much as in the direction of a persistent sub-part of the tradition, somewhat difficult to define but roughly identifiable in his own thought and feeling. It was the pathos and sweetness and power of plain song that held his loyalty. The mandarins, the official poets—no, from Virgil to Eliot, they were not for him, though he could pick out a genuine strain from any poetry wherever he found it. Thus his poem in praise of his brother Percival is in the "manner of Pindar"; and some of his poems in couplets have traces of Pope's last epistles and satires, though not of the earlier poems or of anything by Dryden but his songs. But not to individuals did he attach himself; rather it was to the company of poetic craftsmen who fashioned the long sigh of humanity; before them he knelt in genuine humility. In his polemical writing he could be as egomaniacal and offensive as anyone, and even worse in his private behavior if we are to believe those who knew and loved him best; but to the real achievements of human genius he paid nothing but respect. And shall we blame him if his respect was surer and more readily accorded the further back he looked? Time in its passage clears away our doubts, and Galileo seems a firmer friend than, for instance, Darwin (as Darwin in turn seems a firmer friend than the authors of *The Double Helix*).

Yet the paradox persists. Goodman's esteem for the tradition is a conspicuous part of his poetic attitude, both in explicit statements and in the intimations of his style; at the same time he was distinctly an experimental writer—perhaps more in his prose fiction than in his poetry—and probably the last of the important modernists in American literature of the present century. He stood at the end of the long tradition, but he cut out his immediate predecessors; he insisted on standing alone. The generation of Pound and Eliot did not much appeal to him, the generation of Auden and Spender even less. Whereas with all of his own prominent contemporaries—Jarrell, Schwartz, Shapiro, Lowell, Bishop, Rukeyser, Roethke, and so on—I can perceive immediate derivations from their forerunners, with Goodman I cannot. In a few other cases I see experiment and individuality—William Everson, James Laughlin, Kenneth Patchen, Charles Olson—but even with these I can trace immediate influences more easily than I can with Goodman, and besides they do not—for whatever reason, narrowness of view, smallness of output, confusion of cultural locus, quirkiness of temperament—stand in Goodman's rank.

Down, down, my dears, my students—I said it and I mean it. Paul Goodman was a better artist and arguer than Charles Olson, superior to him, and hence, if you but knew it, is more valuable to you in your present plight, you with your workshop verses! (Yet Olson at his best, in writing and I suspect in teaching, had the sweeter, more generous temper, and for this reason exerted the greater influence.)

The thing is that Goodman reached backward to go forward. He was a heretic, outcast in his era, like all his heroes of old. Better than anyone else he understood the poet's need to exist consciously in the continuum. Granted, Eliot and Pound in their own ways had said the same thing and to a certain extent had shared the same tastes; but their views of contemporary literary society were elitist and their politics disreputable. (Not that Goodman was free from elitism, the elitism of one, which he called—and so do I—independence.) Nor was Goodman a mannerist, not in the slightest degree, which is what one cannot say of any important poets in the earlier part of the century. His archaism of diction and syntax came naturally, came from the whole sound of the great writing of the whole past in every language and every region, from folk tales and legend, from hymns, from the private ceremonial utterances occasioned by love and death, from everywhere; and it was combined inextricably with the jargon and street talk of his own time. Goodman, in fact, levied upon every linguistic force at his command, shamelessly raiding both the elegances of gentility and the argot of hipsters. He made it all his own.

> *This lust that blooms like red the rose*
> *is none of mine but as a song*
> *is given to its author knows*
> *not the next verse yet sings along.*

No, this is genius, not typographical confusion. Stein, Proust, Joyce, and Faulkner made languages out of cultivated complexity, hard to unravel. Goodman is as clear as glass (or the peals of English bells, and indeed his songs remind me of the little changes rung by children there). But you will not find any grammarian after 1800—and before that who cared for grammar?—to parse Goodman's sentence logically. To my mind, to my ear—I having read this stanza many, many times—these four lines are magical, balancing backward and forward on the fulcrum of "author," that many-meaning, many-feeling word. (And only three polysyllables, in the whole quatrain.) This strange syntax is not, I insist, a mannerism. It is the spontaneous speech of a man as much immersed in *The Anatomy of Melancholy* as in *The Neurotic Personality of Our Time*, a man to whom Cardan, Emerson and Whitehead were all contemporaries.

How much would I have to quote to convince the reluctant reader that this is *typical*, that Goodman does it again and again (though naturally he became more skillful as he went on)? Too much. I refer the reluctant reader to the books. But still I will quote once more, this time an entire poem.

> *I lustily bestrode my love*
>   *until I saw the dark and poured my seed*
>   *and then I lay in sweetness like one dead*
> *whom angels sing around him and above.*
>
> *I lay with all my strength embraced*
>   *then swiftly to a quiet grave withdrew*
>   *like a grotto with the sea in view*
> *surging and pounding, till the spell was past.*
>
> *Since then, my hours are empty of*
>   *everything; beauty touches me*
>   *but is like pain to hear or see;*
> *absent among the tribes of men I move.*

I cannot imagine, after this, that I need say more about diction and syntax; the fourth line is to me a wonder, a plain magnificence. A few additional points may be helpful, however. First, I take this poem from the same place in the book where I found several other quotations used already, where the book fell open randomly on my table. Secondly, how rarely do poets have the courage to take up what seem utterly worn out metaphors—orgasm as death—and use them again and anew. Thirdly, the stanza suggests, but only suggests, the English lyric of the seventeenth century, a poem by Herrick perhaps (for Goodman too is a son of Ben, among other things); yet notice how the meter varies between tetrameter and pentameter and how the accents fall not quite in order. Many have tried it and some have succeeded—I think of Louise Bogan, Theodore Roethke, J. V. Cunningham, Stanley Kunitz, Richard Wilbur, and many others—but none quite as well as Goodman. He is, if only by a shade, the most himself within the tradition. Finally, notice the perfection of cohesiveness among the poetic elements, how archaism ("bestrode") and inversion ("swiftly to a quiet grave withdrew") and backward-harkening syntax ("whom angels sing around him and above") all combine without the least sense of rhetoric, overwriting, or strain. It is the most natural poem in the world. And I think the fundamental reason for this is precisely Goodman's humility, which so many doubt; his capacity to write simply with little words, yet always in deference—to time, to poets, to the poem, and to the reader—never in condescension.

It is a remarkable, an astonishing poem. It has no "right" to succeed. Bestrode, "my love," seed, angels, grotto, spell, beauty, tribes of men—no, this is a weird, romantic/biblical vocabulary, of attitudes as well as of words. The truly astonishing thing is that this vocabulary really is Goodman's, is not just literary. Yet one reads the poem, at first, with little tics of embarrassment along the way, embarrassment for the poet and his naive words; and then, such is the force of the poem that when one rereads it, as one inevitably does, the tics are gone. Something powerful is at work here, some strange alienation in the poem from the very beginning, deeply underlying the words, so that the sexuality of it disperses quickly and one is drawn down into the deeper matrix—of what, one hardly knows. The whole poem is about utter aloneness, but aloneness drained of its suffering. (Compare the *basic mood* with Frost's "Stopping by Woods.") Esthetically what happens in Goodman's poem is so complex that even in this apparently boundless essay I cannot try to analyze it. Why does the poem work? What is behind the poet's humility? Goodman not only respected experience, the what-happens of life, he was often enough overwhelmed by it, like a child exposed to too many things, too much to handle. He wanted to freeze it, hold it *out there*, control it; but he couldn't—he was too hungry for it. His earnest defenses continually broke down, and the world crashed through. Such pathos! On

439

the other hand Goodman would have defined an academic as one whose defenses are, alas, entirely successful. The question for him—and not only for him—was: how much experience can I stand?

But I pause, I haul myself down. As always when writing about poetry, I become diffident and I doubt myself. Do other people hear what I hear? And if not, how can I explain? The first line of the third stanza in the above poem, for instance: does Goodman get away with that contrived enjambment for the sake of the rhyme? Can one read it with any accent on "of" and still read in justified, justifiable English? I know I could never do it aloud; my voice will not hesitate on that syllable with the precisely needed degree of indeterminancy, though people tell me I am a good reader. In my head I can do it. But I am not willing for this reason to admit that the weak final accent is a flaw. No, it is, as I say, a contrivance, and not *all* contrivances are artificial. If Donne can get away with

> *Love's not so pure, and abstract, as they use*
> *To say, which have no mistress but their muse. . . .*

(and he does), then Goodman can bring off his irregular line as well. And if my ear is more attuned to convention, and my mind more ready to accept it, than is the case with many other readers nowadays, then I can only agree, though ruefully and wishing otherwise, that this is so. Contrivance works when it is conventional; and convention works when it is (1) not presently so widespread that it is meaningless, (2) not followed slavishly but with daring, and (3) not of the voice alone but of the mind and spirit. In short, the relationship between the artist and his convention must be inventive and must subsist in a nice proportion of humility and self-assurance. Contrary to popular belief, convention in itself is never alive nor dead, these being objective and verifiable conditions. It is an attitude, a feeling, almost a fantasy, and only its effects are demonstrable, never the thing itself.

Goodman had, like most full-time, long-time poets, many voices and many modes, and he was not shy in using them. I have already spoken of his hokku. Then there are his sonnets, the ballades and ballads, the blank verse, free-form poems, songs, and especially the quatrains composed of two loosely rhymed couplets with the second indented below the first, to which he turned more and more for his prayers and elegies as he grew older. The question is, what were his attitudes toward the different forms? Only the most meticulous, probably futile research could pin them down, and it is enough to say here that he did feel differently about them and turned now to one and now another, half instinctually, as his moods changed and different topics occupied his mind. And it is notable that in organizing his collected poems he lumped certain ones together by genre, the sonnets, the ballades, etc., showing that he had a purely literary feeling for them, even though the stronger linkages throughout the whole collection fall clearly within thematic, not generic, configurations. The further question is, did he have a single voice observable throughout? And the answer is yes, definitely, although again only the most painstaking statistical analysis could discover the particular verbal usages that embody it. They are there, I am certain of that. But beyond the few, which I think I recognize in my casual but intensive reading and which I therefore do not want to put on display, I can only point again to his remarkable control of syntax as the one talent that permitted him to move readily among and within the various forms; for all but a few of his poems were occasional and extemporaneous. (Which does *not* mean that he did not work hard or invest his poetry with the utmost seriousness.) Syntax, meaning the art of the putting together of sentences, as opposed to grammar, meaning the science of taking them apart: this is the quintessence. And perhaps his sonnets show it as well as anything.

For those who cannot perceive in the poems themselves Goodman's affection and respect for the sonnet as a special, long-standing convention that he could take to himself, among many other conventions, in his state of being as a poetic master—and I am not speaking invidiously, because I know many people today who through no fault of their own have tin ears when it comes to the great traditions—for such readers, I say, Goodman's analysis of Milton's sonnet on his blindness, done in the finest, most caring manner of *explication du texte* and contained in *The Structure of Literature*, will be helpful,as, for that matter, will all the rest of that book.

Goodman did not have a tin ear—anything but. Of the sixty sonnets included in the *Collected Poems*, only two or three seem to me unreadable. I have checked five as sufficiently superb to stand

441

in the first rank, meaning that for me they are alongside the sonnet by Milton and the one that begins "Let me not to the marriage of true minds" and the one made by Wordsworth when he was standing on the bridge in Westminster. Another way to say it: Goodman wrote the best American sonnets after Longfellow, although I like very well a few others by Lizette Woodworth Reese, E. E. Cummings, Edna Millay, Yvor Winters, and Allen Tate. This is astonishing, almost miraculous (maybe it was). Goodman wrote in a time when even the most determined traditionalists did not care much for fixed forms; the sonnet, in spite of its provenance at the very center of Renaissance poetry, was still thirty years ago too closely associated with Romanticism. Pound wrote many but published none. Even Yeats, who one might have thought would have taken to the sonnet eagerly, did not, but preferred instead the stanzaic forms of his own invention. And taking Goodman's poetic generation as a whole (1935-1970), its most popular model by far was precisely in the ambience of Yeats's later work. To all this Goodman paid no mind, going his own way in his "only world."

The first sonnet by Goodman that I read was "In Lydia," which I believe was submitted in a group of poems to *Poetry* when I was a member of the staff there, circa 1947-1950.

> *I am touring high on the Meander River*
> *the scenery ever varying. The land*
> *is Lydia, the wheat rich, the climate bland,*
> *and very sweet the modus of the zither.*
> *Our queen is Omphale, for never never*
> *cut was the curving cord in which we end*
> *—when shall we arrive? I round a bend,*
> *the view is changed, and forward is another.*
>
> *That's not a woman in the palace yard*
> *spinning! unwillingly—breathing hard—*
>
> *Hercules! here, for pity's sake*
> *the thread is long enough, it leaves the wheel*
> *and tangles, and the world is areel.*
> *My hands have hold upon it; shall I break?*

I don't know (oh, for the books, the books!) whether the wording here, taken from the *Collected P*, follows the original version (I suspect the thirteenth line may have once been stronger), but I do know definitely (because it struck me forcibly when I first read it and influenced the invention of a form I myself have often used, which I call the paragraph) that I have printed the poem in its original shape, i.e. with the couplet displaced from the end and set apart by space-breaks in the middle. For reasons I cannot fathom, Goodman chose to run the couplet into the last four lines when he revised his poems for the collected edition, thus deemphasizing his rearrangement of the usual form and giving the sonnet a more or less conventional sestet. It is a fine sonnet in any case, though I wish Goodman (in violation of his usual practice) had written "and the world's areel," thus making the thirteenth line a clear metrical equivalent to the short eleventh line, the whole final quatrain easier and stronger.

> God damn and blast and to a fist of dust
> reduce me the comtemptible I am
> if I again hinder for guilt or shame
> the blooming of my tenderness to lust
> like a red rose; I have my cock traduced
> to which I should be loyal. None to blame
> but me myself that I consort with them
> who dread to rouse me onward and distrust
> what has a future.
>   Let me bawl hot tears
> for thee my lonely and dishonored sex
> in this fool world where now for forty years
> thou beg'st and beg'st and again thou beg'st
> because this is the only world there is,
> my rose in rags among these human wrecks.

Is it half jocular? Of course, all poems about sex are; such is the human sensibility, primitive or refined. But notice the strong movement of the sentences through the octet, the power yet naturalness of the rhymes, and then in the sestet Goodman's giveaway, "the only world": whenever he says that, he is serious, let no one misunderstand him. This is a sonnet so packed with tonal, metrical, dictional, and thematic intricacies that I doubt a thorough *explication* could be made in less than many pages; I mean this—no exaggeration. Yet any reasonably experienced reader will be able to do it just in the reading. The poem is crystalline.

At the same time it is necessary to point out, not only in prudence but in the humility I more and more feel before my task, that Goodman's sonnets do not appeal to everyone, and that this sonnet in particular has been attacked by an extremely acute critic who is also one of Goodman's friendliest. The poem—I paraphrase him—is dishonest and spiritually ugly; only an intellectual, full of ideas as well as hurt and having a long history of attempts to heal the splits between mind and body, passion and thought, etc., could be so arrogantly *loyal* to his cock; "rouse me onward," ha!— Goodman was compulsive and fetishistic, self-aroused and continually so; how can diction, syntax, etc., be of any force when the poem itself (and the evidence is in the poem) displays such a disgusting mess of illness, attitudinizing, self-protective lying, etc. I can only answer that to my mind the literary quality of the poem does in fact overcome these ugly revelations. Goodman was a man of letters indeed. He revered prosody. The arrogance and dishonesty patent in the poem, especially in the octet, are retrieved for me by the prosodic power of the whole poem and by the authentic universalization of feeling in the sestet. A great many of us can "bawl hot tears" for our "lonely and dishonored sex." But see how crazy and silly the words sound when quoted outside the poem? They are. What can I say—except that for me they work in the poem? The whole verbal and structural and imagistic complex of the sonnet holds its substance together and elevates it to the plane upon which personal dishonesty and braggadocio become realized esthetic paradigms. It was a terribly risky sonnet to write. But I feel Goodman took the risks and surmounted them. This is, obviously, a subjective judgment. As for the sonnets in general, I have chosen to concentrate on them here, instead of taking poems more widely scattered in the collected edition, because they are short enough to quote, they are formally similar and comparable, and they contain some of Goodman's best writing. But by no means all. There are other poems that I myself prefer to any of the sonnets, which does not mean that I back away from the praise I lavished (the right word) on the sonnets earlier.

> Grief how into useless age away
> ebbed youth and I was unhappy all those years
> I also do not feel, for now new fears
> possess me and I steel myself today
> today's pain to endure, so I can die
> without a reckoning and weep no tears
> for promises deceived. Maybe my peers
> or my disciples will this tribute pay.
> Oh, when He bound my arms behind my back
> and threw me in the sea, I heard Him call
> "Swim! swim!" and so I have swum to this hour
> breathless in the cold water rough and black
> where many have already drowned and all
> shall *drown in the swells that sink and tower.*

Is it necessary to point out the poetic self-faith expressed in the metrical irregularity of the two opening lines? Yes, they are crabbed, incredibly so, arrogantly and intentionally so. (It would have been child's play to put those two lines in "right" order.) To me the force of feeling in them is the force that justifies and demands them, and they are beautifully expressive.

> One thing, thank God, I learned, the grisly face
> of Hope to abhor, her eyes bloodshot with dreams,
> her hair unkempt with fury. Lying streams
> out of her mouth and men drink it. Alas,
> if you look ever in a looking-glass
> and see an ugly Hope in hungry flames
> devouring you, so the unreal seems
> real and the impossible to come to pass
> possible, see, when you look again
> Disappointment! But this *face of pain*
> is mine, which I and all my family have,
> my mother wears it in her southern grave,
> my sister grown old woman has it, and
> my brother building buildings rich and grand.

The couplet at the end makes us think of the great tradition, and no one has better extended the sonnet's essentially Shakespearean movement, pushing the runovers and enjambments *just enough further*. Goodman's verbal instinct is here at its best. See "mother/ southern" in line twelve: did it fall accidentally that way? or did Goodman think it up? I know I feel the force of years of poetic thought behind it. Note also the movement of imagery in this fluent poem, from horror and Dantean grotesquerie to the more human "face of pain" and ending in the last line—the reference to his brother Percival, the architect, with whom he wrote *Communitas*, his most important early statement of social criticism and also, incidentally, a hopeful book—with "buildings rich and grand." Who could have expected such a swift, complex modulation of images and feelings?

Students have said to me that they dislike the inverted syntax and archaism because such writing seems to them awkward and forced. They wonder why Goodman let himself be pushed around by form. But there is no question of forcing. Goodman was a *writer*, a *versewriter*, among many other things, which entails a skill that young readers seem ill-equipped to recognize. Goodman wrote this way because he wanted to, because this was the effect consonant with his own temperament and feeling. He could just as easily have written:

> *Thank God I learned one thing, to abhor Hope's*
> *grisly face, her eyes bloodshot with dreams,*
> *her hair unkempt with fury. Lying streams*
> *from her mouth and men drink it. If you perhaps*
> *should look in a mirror and see Hope's hungry shapes*
> *of flame reaching to devour you, your own schemes*
> *raging there . . . , etc.*

This would have accorded well enough with his usual rhyming and metrical practice. Indeed something like this might have been a first draft of the poem. But Goodman *chose* the inversions, the archaic "Alas," the whole inner strategy, and his choice was intentional, if not at the moment of writing, then certainly in the long course of self-training that led up to it. In fact I am struck now by the possibility that some of Goodman's contemporaries may have had more influence on him than I suggested earlier; but a negative influence, not a positive one. Delmore Schwartz and John Berryman, for instance, were both writing sonnets at about the time Goodman was beginning his. He may have seen very early that he needed something different from their styles, plainer than Schwartz's Marlovian grandness, simpler and easier than Berryman's extreme contortedness. This would have been in keeping with Goodman's constant desire to be separate.

This sonnet is called "The Americans Resume Bomb-Testing, April 1962"

> *My countrymen have now become too base,*
> *I give them up. I cannot speak with men*
> *not my equals, I was an American.*
> *Where now to drag my days out and erase*
> *this awful memory of the United States?*
> *how can I work? I hired out my pen*
> *to make my country practical, but I can*
> *no longer serve these people, they are worthless.*
>
> *"Resign! resign!" the word rings in my soul*
> *—is it for me? or shall I make a sign*
> *and picket the White House blindly in the rain,*
> *or hold it up on Madison Avenue*
> *a silent vigil, or trudge to and fro*
> *gloomily in front of the public school?*

Clearly this is *in extempore*. Goodman's spontaneous anger is too great, forcing him into egomania and dishonesty, permitting him to make the easy identification of "my countrymen" with the State, which elsewhere he would never have done. The rhymes are too easy; only a trifle, but noticeable. And why when force, measure, and colloquial value demand it, did he not insert "out" after "gloomily" in the final line? Nevertheless I include it among my five because it shows so trenchantly how the surplusage, so to speak, of feeling can drive through the poetic form in Goodman's flexible syntax and carry all before it. This it does precisely *as* a sonnet: the movement from octet to sestet exactly what the original lyric impulse (back to Pier delle Vigne in the *trecento* as Arthur Symonds said) prescribes; *pre-scribes*, the word is worth considering.

Finally—

Foster excellence. If I do not
who will do it? The vulgarity
of this country makes my spirit faint, what we
have misdone to our history and what
to the landscape. The tasteless food we eat,
the music, how we waste day after day
child, woman, and man have stunned me to dismay
like an ox bludgeoned, swaying on his feet.

John, rescue me by becoming. I have well
deserved of the Republic, though it has
rewarded me with long oblivion.
Make you me proud and famous as the one
who thought that we could be what Florence was
when angry men made rough rocks beautiful.

Notice how Goodman has no metrical force-of-habit, but starts off this sonnet in a totally different, short and punchy syntax. Also how the hackneyed images follow one another in perfect originality because the language will not let them slump back on their cushions of hebetude. Lastly how Goodman, like the rest of us, was grandiose and greedy in his demands on his personal friend, in this case John. why should John do what the "Republic" will not? Because, goddamn it, *somebody* must! Who better than a lover to assuage the injury dealt by unjust Time and the State? Cattulus, Villon, Swift, Leadbelly, etc.

In part I chose to emphasize Goodman's use of the sonnet because it seems to fall more or less midway between his use of the larger fixed forms, especially the ballades, and his own invented forms, both the deliberate and the impromptu. But no consideration of his writing can be let go without at least a glance at the quatrains he came to appreciate more and more as the poetic shape most amenable to his verbal and emotional needs. Here is a bit of a poem, no more than a tag stuck on at the end of a sonnet about a glimpse of a handsome, inaccessible young man.

Some happy folk their faith
and some their calling doth
justify, but Lord,
I am justified

> *by the beauty of*
> *the world and my love*
> *of Your animals, though I*
> *may not be happy thereby.*

This is totally characteristic: the involved, pivoted sentence, the rhymes ranging from near to remote, the archaism both reinforced and contradicted by the irregularity of rhythm, and then the grand affirmation given and at once partly withdrawn. It occurs to me, too, that many, a great many, of Goodman's poems end in their beginnings, as here with the repetition of "happy." It is the lyric circle around whose perimeter the contraries align themselves.

I choose two more, untitled:

> *I ask the Lord, "Who are You?"*
> *though I know His name is "Spoken to."*
>   *Hoping but I am not sure*
>   *His name might be "I am who answer."*

> *With certain faith let me continue*
> *my dialogue with Spoken-To.*
>   *Hope has always been my curse,*
>   *it never yet came to pass.*

> *The crazy man that you meet*
> *talking to himself on the street*
>   *is I, please gently lead him home.*
>   *Creator Spirit come.*

Again a small poem, probably impromptu or near it. Technically it is very fine, revealing Goodman's faculty for reducing brilliance to what seems off-hand, so many fortuities that we know they cannot be fortuitous. I will point only to the second stanza, how there "certain" and "curse" are linked internally, as are "spoken" and "hope," "always" and "pass," so that the stanza is aurally compressed and unified, and then how the rhyme in the first couplet, "continue" with "Spoken-To," an unaccented sound rhymed with an accented one that nevertheless is a very small word, a preposition, how this assembles behind the meaning a huge power of prosodic reinforcement. But perhaps we have had enough discussion of technique. "Spoken-To" is a term used by some orthodox Jews as a euphemism for the divine name, which is taboo, and so Goodman's poem is immediately rooted not only in his own people's religion, a backward reach reinforced by further biblical-sounding language ("come to pass," "lead him home," etc.), but also in the structure of spiritual taboo in all human consciousness, as amplified sophisticatedly in our awareness of cultural anthropology and Jungian psychiatry. It is a poem about fear and craziness and unnamability, pathos, the gross matter of the human condition, profoundly Hebrew and also profoundly Greek; a poem which ends on our one solace as the poet utters his own euphemism, "Creator Spirit." This is no cheap-shot poetic aggrandizement; quote the contrary. The humility of utterance is plain, it is sincere. (Goodman did talk to himself on the street.) Yet the poem is far from any orthodoxy, and it does almost heretically link mankind's esthetic mentality with the sense of religion. It makes no claim for the poet as prophet, but every claim for poet inhabiting all human souls. It reaches back, far back, through the shadows of anonymity which time gathers around the early members of "the grand company," back to the earliest, the greatest Anonymity. I cannot help thinking of the painting that shows God touching Adam's finger. In this poem Adam (one of Goodman's favorite names) touches back. It is a poem as swift as lightning, a spark leaping across an infinite gap, and it is as succinct, lucid, and profound a statement of modern man's religious nature as Goodman or any other poet has written.

Now another in the same stanza, opening with the line that was the earlier poem's close, this one written a couple of months after the death of the poet's son Mathew.

> *Creator Spirit come*
> *by whom*
>   *I'll say what is real*
>   *and so away I'll steal*
>
> *When my only son*
> *fell down and died on Percy mountain*
>   *I began*
>   *to practice magic like a pagan.*

Around the open grave we ate
the blueberries that he brought
   from the cloud, and then we
   buried his bag with his body.

Upon the covered grave
I laid the hawkweed that I love
   which withered fast
   where the mowers passed.

I brought also a tiny yellow
flower whose name I do not know
   to share my ignorance
   with my son. (But since

then I find in the book
it is a kind of shamrock
   Oxalis corniculata,
   Matty, sorrel of the lady.)

Blue-eyed grass with its gold hexagon
   beautiful as the gold and blue
   double in Albireo
that we used to gaze on

   when Matty was alive
   I laid on Matty's grave
      where two robins were
      hopping here and there;

and gold and bluer than that blue
or the double in Albireo
   bittersweet nightshade
   the deadly alkaloid
      I brought for no other reason
      than because it was poison.

Mostly, though, I brought some weed
beautiful but disesteemed,
  plantain or milkweed,
  because we die by the wayside.

(And if spring comes again
I will bring a dandelion,
  because he was a common weed
  and also he was splendid.)

But when I laid my own forehead
on the withering sod
  to go the journey deep,
  I could not fall asleep.

I cannot dream, I cannot quit
the one scene in the twilight
  that is no longer new yet does
  not pass into what was.

Last night the Pastoral Symphony
of Handel in the key of C
  I played on our piano
  out of tune shrill and slow

because the shepherds were at night
in the field in the starlight
  when music loud and clear
  sang from nowhere.

Will magic and the weeks placate
the soul that in tumbling fright
  fled on August eighth?
  The first flock is flying south

and a black-eyed susan
is livid in the qutumn rain
  dripping without haste or strain
  on the oblong larger than a man.

> *Creator spirit come*
> *by whom*
> > *I say that which is real*
> > *and softly away I'steal.*

It was not so long after this that Goodman did steal away, joining Mathew, and he did it softly enough too, like the rest of us.

From this longer poem I have learned how not to care overmuch for the design I had chosen from artifice to suit my poem; the seventh stanza is shaped differently to accomodate the change of rhyming, yet the next-to-last stanza, which has the same rhyme in abba, is shaped like the rest. In the ninth stanza he thought of an extra couplet—before or afterward? I don't know. He could just as well have used the third couplet as the first of a new stanza. He didn't.

Another point. Goodman was his own closest reader. He remembered when he had found a scrap of language that suited him and compressed his meaning. He repeated it, using it as often as he liked, deepening its meaning in the variety of contents. In this poem "we die by the wayside," just as in the poem about Chuang-tzu.

And for a while I thought, foolishly, that I could leave this poem about the death of Mathew Goodman with no more than my few trifling technical observations. Perhaps I felt so fine a poem, so clearly embodying the elements of Goodman's practice I had already discussed, needed no further commentary. More likely, I think, I was attempting—but not consciously—to disguise or dispel my own and the reader's sense of self-revealment after reading this almost unbearably moving poem. Why are we overcome with shyness just as we find what we go to art to seek, this ultimate human actuality? I do not know, but I believe this phenomenon underlies the predicament of the arts in our civilization today, our willful concentration on mediocrity.

The poem is as fine an elegy as any I know. Do I mean it is as good as the dirge in *Cymbeline* that I have had tacked to my cowshed wall for twenty years? Yes. How do I know it is as good? Knowledge has nothing to do with it; both poems are pinchbeck to the *cognoscenti*. I feel the goodness, and I speak to those who feel it with me, or who may come to feel it. Shall I define the human heart in an essay?

At the beginning and again at the ending, the poem advocates magic, invokes our primal intellection. It is another reaching back; it is paleolithic. Indeed, the opening stanza and the closing one are the same, which gives the poem Goodman's characteristic circularity, but in this case gives it even more than that: the almost strict repetition is like the magician's clap at the beginning and end of his trick, for the poem occurs out of time, out of experience, as if in the science-fiction writer's favorite time warp. It is a true act of ecstacy (ex stasis). So simple the device, known well to children; so complex the psychic action. Then while we are "away," we live only ritualistically, the bringing of flowers again and again, their parts and properties named (with perfect correctness) in the magic of evoking the reality we can say but never understand, the music, the seasons. And the references all appear to us like waves from the same source, the mowers, the lady, the star, the poison, the music "from nowhere": all are the same, the waves falling on our shore of consciousness from "nowhere," from far out, from grief as the mythologos, the word that cannot be said. It is a poem of transcendent negation.

Milton praised Lycidas, Shelley Adonais, Goodman says of his "only son," Mathew, no more than that he was a "weed" and "splendid" and that he "fell down and died," having brought blueberries "from the cloud"; no more. Yet to my mind Goodman's elegiac intensity is greater, and on my ear his words fall, without loudness, without formal declamation, still with more resonance. I call it "transcendent negation" because I cannot define it except by saying what it is not, and even then only very imperfectly. An elegy without praise? It seems odd, yet now that I stop to think I see that this is the poem of our time, written again and again, by Ransom, Roethke, by many others, because our "hero" is always this young person who is "real." And "the oblong larger than a man" is real. But the reality is more than we can take, except in the time out of time, the poem, the myth. This movement, as of mercury in a balancing tube repelled by negative magnets at either end, myth and reality falling toward and away from each other, is the magic of minds reverting through mankind's ten thousand years or a man's ten thousand days of reason, to unending agony and fatigue again.

Goodman wrote:

> *I cannot dream, I cannot quit*
> *the one scene in the twilight*
> *that is no longer new yet does*
> *not pass into what was.*

I feel in this the ache of implacability as in few other pieces of literature. I know it is the simplicity of it, the negative refusal to say more, that makes it, technically, so effective; but I cannot hope to understand the means of it much further. So much does not pass into what was. Stonehenge. Ozymandias.

"The soul that in tumbling fright/fled on August eighth"—was it Matty's? Yes. Was it Paul's too? Yes. Was it the Creator Spirit, was it Death? Yes. Yes. Will it be placated? No. Do affirmation and negation mean the same thing? No. Yes.

Now approaching, if it hasn't long been passed, the permissible limit of an essay, still I have written almost nothing about Goodman's prose fiction. Obviously, anything near to an adequate discussion must wait for another occasion, and probably I won't do it, but will leave the job to others better fitted for it than I am. My own feeling—and I hope it does not come merely from my own greater interest in poetry—is that Goodman's mind and temperament were not quite as well suited to prose narrative as they were to poetry. Here I must make a clear distinction between Goodman's fictional prose and his philosophical, critical, and polemical prose. The latter is mostly superb. And the modes of poetry, though most people do not recognize this, are closer to argument than are the modes of prose narrative. To say it another way, his poems are more like his essays than either are like his novels and stories. This is hair-splitting, I admit. A dozen of his short stories are among the best by any American writer of this century. And his big novel, *The Empire City*, though it probably fails some of the ultimate tests, the standards of the creative writing workshop, is so spirited and intelligent that I would rather be amused and stimulated by it than sedated by any number of our pretentious current metafictions. Sometimes it is such joy to throw the "ultimate tests" out the window!

Goodman had great hopes once for *The Empire City*. The first section, entitled "The Grand Piano," enjoyed considerable success

when it was published separately in 1942. According to Taylor
Stoehr (see his introduction to *Don Juan*), one of Goodman's
friends wrote to him: "Paul, I congratulate you on your immortality." Statements like that were not made lightly in New York in
1942, when literature was still a serious and dangerous business,
not even among friends. But Goodman's reputation fell off sharply
after that. The second section, "State of Nature," was ignored.
When the third section of the novel was completed, Goodman
could find no publisher for it, though he tried and tried, as always,
even in his darkest despondency, indefatigable in promoting his
wares. At last he published "Dead of Spring" himself, and sold the
copies to friends through the mail, as I recall for $2 each; and
strange books they were, printed on stiff paper held in spiral metal
bindings, apparently produced in some job-shop that normally
specialized in calendars and appointment books. Now no doubt
they are collector's items; I wish I had mine, but it is gone, who
knows where? It seemed at the time a pitiable effort. How many
could he have sold? A couple of hundred if he was lucky. But now,
looking back, we see the courage of his persistence, a courage he
needed all his life, for although the novel was eventually published
in one volume—including the previously unpublished fourth section—by a commercial publisher and then later in a paperback
edition, and although I salute Bobbs-Merrill and Random House
for their editorial intelligence, *The Empire City* still did not
receive the attention it deserves from reviewers or readers, and
has not till this day.

Is it a novel? I don't know and I don't much care; call it whatever
you like, the internal monologue of the man in the moon. In
historical terms it can with perfect justice be denominated an
allegory, a picaresque tale, a philosophical novel, a comedy of
humor, a panoramic adventure, and possibly a tractatus. For
myself, though I am certain no one will ever define its essences in
a simple statement, I am content to say that *The Empire City* is a
phantasmagoria of ideas whose hero is Horatio Alger, whose
secondary personages are a very mixed group of imagined and real
people, whose structure is random, and whose purpose is to
investigate through episodes of comic pathos the *truth* of human
life at the middle of the twentieth century in the greatest city on
earth. Its antecedents are legion, but mostly from para-literature:
commedia dell'arte, Rabelais, *The Canterbury Tales*, Hogarth,

Artemus Ward and Mark Twain, Krazy Kat, Chaplin and Cocteau—the list could go on and on, and why do I call it "paraliterature?" That is an academic way of putting it. What I mean to say is that almost anything you can take from outside the "main current of literary evolution," anything from Petronius to Ring Lardner, will find its echo in *The Empire City*.

As for the short stories, they are various yet mostly also of adventuresome intents and methods. They are not well wrought in the Mansfieldean manner, nor in the Hemingwayan either, but effloresce from Goodman's exuberance with only his own cogent imagination to supply their limits. I cannot describe them, nor attempt to say in a paragraph how they were made. I think all of them are a delight to the mind, some a delight to the heart, and a few are, after the poems, extremely important. I do not think any reader can go into a bookstore and take up a copy of *Adam and His Works*, if he is lucky enough to find it, or one of the three new volumes of collected stories edited by Taylor Stoehr, if he is lucky enough to find that—I do not think he can pick it up and read one story, any story—say, "The Complaint of Richard Savage," but none will take more than a few minutes to read—and then walk out without buying the book. Like almost all true writing, the stories are immediately gratifying.

But Goodman was no perfectionist, never that. Rather he wrote at a dizzy pace, I think, his sentences of prose (more than his sentences of poetry) scarcely able to keep up with his flying thoughts, and he cared little about revision, so that sometimes he wrote stories which had no real purpose, no sufficient prior envisioning, such as the posthumously published novel *Don Juan*, which bears some connection to the early parts of *The Empire City* but becomes tedious after the first fifty or sixty pages because the theme is too tendentious for the narrative, being lyrical rather than active, to sustain.

Failure, especially youthful failure, is predicated if not by the limits of the human mind then by the nature of post-romantic ego and of post-impressionist language, both of them riddled with the sense of their own inadequacy. Yet the grand company continues in spite of all.

The hardest thing to say is what I have left till the end, which is not my custom. As a writer about writers, I have always preferred to extol where that was possible; and in extolling I have preferred to deal at the beginning with whatever reservations may have presented themselves to me, thus permitting the commentary to mount progressively toward affirmation at the end. In Goodman's case I have been unable to do this; I have kept putting off the difficult part. (It is, of course, the mess of the *Collected Poems*.) A number of reasons account for my hesitancy. First, I am a practical man in this only world, as Goodman would have said, and I know what publishers in current American "civilization" are likely to do and, worse, what they are likely *not* to do. Secondly, the topic of Goodman's achievement has been intimidating to me. (I wonder at those who can sit down at their tables and begin an essay on Sophocles or Dante.) Thirdly, I am hurt, deeply and indelibly, by this mischance, for I sense that it will not be corrected in my lifetime; hurt, that is, to such an extent that I cannot in my human experience find an analogue except an imagined one, namely, to come upon an edition of Shakespeare's Sonnets that had been set in type by a printer who thought he could improve the text by substituting words of his own for the author's.

It is a sorry business. I do not wish to exaggerate; readers may buy and use the *Collected Poems* safely, knowing they will get more than their money's worth. But they must bear in mind that some of the poems have been mistakenly revised and are not at their best. For me, anything less than the author's own best is useless. But readers—all of us—must also bear in mind that the mistaken revisions were made when Goodman was old and ill. Not old as longevity goes these days, he was only just past sixty, but old in the conditions of his own life, because those forty books plus all the teaching, lecturing, and political activity, all the anxieties and frustrations, had worn him out. Then there is another consideration, I believe. Goodman knew himself, his own methods, and that much of his poetry had been composed on the spot, extemporaneously; at the end he may humanly have regretted his haste and wished to make reparation to the Creator Spirit. If his revisions were no more than another hastiness, who will not smile in sorrow and compassion.

Here is the text of Goodman's best-known poem, "The Lordly Hudson," as it was printed in 1962.

> *"Driver, what stream is it?" I asked, well knowing*
> *it was our lordly Hudson hardly flowing,*

"It is our lordly Hudson hardly flowing,"
he said, "under the green-grown cliffs."

Be still, heart! no one needs your passionate
suffrage to select this glory,
this is the lordly Hudson hardly flowing
under the green-grown cliffs.

"Driver! has this a peer in Europe or the East?"
"No, no!" he said. Home! home!
be quiet, heart! this is our lordly Hudson
and has no peer in Europe or the East,

this is our lordly Hudson hardly flowing
under the green-grown cliffs
and has no peer in Europe or the East.
Be quiet, heart! home! home!

We all know many ardent wordings for a river, a mountain, a highway, a glen: our only world, the earth *in loco parentis.* After the wrack of sex, this is the singer's most passionate human news. But I know no other surpassing this in simple expressiveness. Such poems bear the authenticity of universal knowledge and feeling. They are beyond the bounds of judgment, beyond relativism, in the realm of objectivity, equivalence, and essential anonymity.

This is the text as from the *Collected Poems:*

"Driver, what stream is it?" I asked, well knowing
it was our lordly Hudson hardly flowing,
"It is our lordly Hudson hardly flowing,"
he said, "under the green-grown cliffs."

Be still, man! no one needs your passionate
suffrage to select this glory,
this is our lordly Hudson hardly flowing
under the green-grown cliffs.

"Driver! has this a peer in Europe or the East?"
"No no!" he said. Home! home!
be quiet, heart! this is our lordly Hudson
and has no peer in Europe or the East,

> *this is our lordly Hudson hardly flowing*
> *under the green-grown cliffs*
> *and has no peer in Europe or the East.*
> *Be patient, Paul! home! home!*

By such small stitches may passion be clothed in art, or left shivering and naked! Three alterations: the change from "heart" to "man" in the first line of the second stanza; the deletion of the comma between "no" and "no" in the second line of the third stanza; the substitution of "Be patient, Paul" for "Be quiet, heart" in the final line.

One can intuitively reconstruct Goodman's motives. "Heart" is a genteel and banal word; how much better to generalize and universalize by saying "man." Or maybe "man" was addressed to himself. But in his haste Goodman did not see that "man" points directly and reductively back to "Driver" in the stanza before, and is thus both a ruination of the poem's universality and a misplaced colloquialism. Moreover, the effect of the original poem was exactly *in* its repetitions: "heart, heart"; "lordly, lordly," etc.

The excision of the comma between the "no's" was in keeping with Goodman's later exterior style, and is not of much moment—I do not wish to be finicky. Yet I must add that for me the comma was part of the poem's celebratory, ode-like, formal (yet how individual) expressiveness, and I miss it.

The greatest damage is the final change. Yes, Paul wanted to get home; he was ill, he had been teaching (hard work!) in Hawaii. The exotic climate of the Islands suited him far less than the plain hayfields and hawkweed in New Hampshire. But "patient" is not the same as "quiet," again the telling repetition is lost, and "Paul" is a long, long way from "heart."

"The Lordly Hudson" is an early poem, probably from before 1940. I am told its occasion was Goodman's homecoming to New York after an unhappy stay in Chicago. He was strong, his poetic instinct was working beautifully, and he was in no haste. More than thirty years later when he revised the poem, he was coming home again, this time from Hawaii, where he had not much enjoyed himself either. He was in pain and knew that death was not far off. He made the three little changes, and a great poem was reduced to an ordinary one. It was a misfortune, yes, but not a disaster, for we have the great poem still. We must seek every means, as I am doing here, to get it back in print again.

I do not want to leave the *Collected Poems* without saying my admiration for the memoir by George Dennison that serves as the book's introduction. It is not the whole story, we shall have that only in the course of time; but for its good taste, acuity, and style I think it one of the finest works of its kind I have seen.

To the two sequences of poems he wrote for Mathew, Goodman gave the title "Sentences." Here is one of the poems.

> *"Great Tao is a ship adrift"—awakes*
> *at sunrise asking, where am I?*
> *and deviates forward slowly to nowhere.*
> *What does he know? to front afraid the gale*
> *and painfully climb the next oncoming wave.*
> *It is by an inevitable mistake*
> *that the ten thousand cheer and shake their flags*
> *lining the shore in the indifferent port.*

Nevertheless, and Goodman would have said so too, to be one of the ten thousand is something.

A sentence is an always potential construction of language. Goodman gave it his devotion for a lifetime. It is also "the opinion pronounced by a person on some particular question" (OED). Finally, it is what the judge says. Those who fail to recognize behind Goodman's Sentences the weight of all these meanings and the weight of some of his favorite word-works from the past, *The Testament* by Francois Villon or *The Trial* by Franz Kafka, will perhaps miss nothing essential. But those who do recognize these things will be enriched humanly by them, and will thereby become themselves in some part members of Paul Goodman's Grand Community. For the tradition is what we as mankind travel on, the Tao, wherever we are going.

ঌ ঌ ঌ

CLAIRE'S LOVER'S CHURCH

fiction by TERI RUCH

from GRAND STREET

nominated by Pat Strachan

THE CITY FATHERS did not like the church on the other side of the ditch by the welcome-to-our-city sign. They didn't like the dolls' heads with empty eye sockets in the churchyard dirt. They wondered about the midgets from out of town who appeared and disappeared at the rear of the church with stuffed duffel bags bouncing on their backs. They didn't appreciate the stained-glass windows showing naked women leaping around a handsome shepherd. And the glare of the church's gold front doors blinded people driving in and out of the city. The city fathers moved the welcome sign three feet to keep the church outside the city limits.

As a child Claire crawled down in the ditch, under the highway through the drainage pipe, and up the opposite bank. She pressed an ear to the glowing doors and listened to altos and sopranos hum the same three notes repeatedly. It reminded her of the chant she hummed herself to sleep with. The doors were always locked.

Rumor spread that a minister lived inside, that he kept many women with him. Claire started the rumor.

On Claire's twenty-first birthday, her mother gave her seven gilt-edged Bibles. "For your friends taking Philosophy of Religion 101 with you," she said. Her eyes were set so deep Claire wondered if she saw the edges of her sockets when she glanced left and right. Her straight thin lips reminded Claire of an equal sign.

By the gold doors of the humming church Claire dropped her seven Bibles. Twenty hands pulled her inside, ten naked women hugged her. "Remove your shoes," they said. "Shade your eyes.

Overwhelming is the brilliance of our lover, blinding is the radiance of the women he has taught. Close your mouth, ye who would enter, for your gasp echoes. Close your mouth, be silent, our lover may soon utter. Unerring is his wisdom, unending is his grace."

They guided Claire to the organ bench and pressed her shoulders until she lay on her back. They held her hands and feet. "Where is the minister?" Claire asked. They opened their mouths then closed them. No words, just three notes hummed in harmony. They unzipped Claire's skirt, removed her blouse, unbuckled her sandals. Was it unreasonable of her, Claire asked, to demand to see the minister? A woman held her hand on Claire's lips while another, with a sponge, dabbed frankincense on her. Two women touched her nipples, another leaned close to her lips. Three slid their hands along her neck, her arms, her waist. One held Claire's thighs. Then they dressed her in a surplice and said, "You are prepared to meet our lover."

In the east Cry Room, the women sat Claire on the floor. Before them, a gold-skinned man in a large paper bag ate biscuits. When he saw Claire he embraced her and offered her, with the others, biscuits and beer. Claire could not look at him directly, but held the sleeve of her surplice before her eyes. Not even the bag could hide this man's beauty. He addressed the women:

A woman gave birth to a handsome boy at the same moment another woman gave birth to a headless boy. The handsome and the headless boys became best friends. One day the handsome boy's father fell in love with the headless boy's mother and the headless boy's father fell in love with the handsome boy's mother. The parents swapped. Now the handsome and the headless boys had four parents. How happy and confused they were.

The handsome boy grew up bad. He robbed rich families of their grandparents. One day he borrowed a baby. This was too much. One of his fathers sought to whip him. "Where's your mother?" he asked the kid. "Which mother?" "My wife, your mother." "She's with my other mother and my other father," he said. "Where?" cried the father. "In bed," the bad kid said. The father ran off

with his whip and the handsome boy was never pun-
ished for his crimes.

But the headless boy was not intelligent enough to be
bad like his handsome brother. He had no head, poor
bastard. His life was sad and uneventful.

All afternoon the minister spoke in parables. At sunset a midget
opened a duffel bag for Claire. The minister held her hands. "We
enjoy our evenings here," he said. "You're always welcome back."
She thanked him. Unwillingly she took her surplice off, dressed
again in her clothes and climbed inside the bag.

Wild women fill Claire's lover's church, leaping pew to pew and
laughing. "All women will be bad," the lover says. They are.
Hymnals show teeth marks from gentle gnawing and indented
spines from being thrown against the pews, the altar, hip bones.
Singing Glorias, the naked women flip from altar to organ, from
organ to altar. They make love to each other, then dress in robes
made from the paraments pulled off the altar and the pulpit. They
practice scandals with bad boys bagged in from nearby cities. The
women grin. They are bad, bad, bad, and love it.
    None have seen the minister naked. He appears in the Cry
Room fully bagged for morning parables. Near noon he stands
behind the pulpit and guides the women in scandal practice. Late
afternoons he counsels them, on his knees. They kiss him and each
other.
    Claire is not satisfied. She wants to see the lover bagless. In the
men's room she lies on her back in a stall, peeking up as the
minister looks in the mirror. He pulls her up beside him and points
in the mirror. "Look how young you are," he says. He shows her
his hands, says, "Old," and hits them against the wall. Claire slaps
his golden ass and drags him to her mattress. She rips his paper off.
    The minister can't get Claire off his back. She clings to his neck
as he showers and shaves. While he bakes biscuits, she breathes in
his ear and presses her breasts against his shoulder blades. She
climbs off only so he can dress in his new paper bag and meet his
women for breakfast parables and popovers.
    He stares at Claire. He cannot concentrate on his parables. He
wants her on his back again.

The minister rearranges his schedule to spend more time with Claire than with the other women. "We can't let them know," he says. "It will disrupt my ministry."

"Why do you teach us bad?" Claire asks. "Bad will be with us always," he explains. "We must be thoughtful so our bad behavior hurts as few as possible. My women will be bad responsibly." Claire requests a sermon on the relationship of bad to sad.

Outside, spitters gather on the premises. It must be winter now, Claire thinks. Standing in their steamy breath, the spitters stare in the Cry Room windows. In packs they glare at their spit as it freezes on a stained-glass shepherd spitting golden biscuits on naked women. The spitters are jealous of the minister. So is Claire. According to the laws he created, Claire should love each woman and the minister equally. But she prefers the minister. She writes a parable:

> A man had eleven wives. One loved the man more than the others and the man loved her more than he loved the others. He threw a party and invited ten men, hoping they would take away ten of his wives. The ten men raped the wife he loved the most and left her behind ten casks of sour wine.

Claire throws the parable away. Outside, the spitters comb their hair. They practice jumping jacks.

On Sunday, the minister repeats a sermon he delivered two months earlier. His congregation regards the large log in his eye.

He writes a parable for Claire:

> A married man sowed pennies in a supermarket parking lot. Some rolled into a drain. Others fell before the front tires of a Mack truck. Wedged in the tire cracks, the pennies were slapped against cement repeatedly before they flew in weedy fields beside the freeways. Still others were swallowed by hungry babies. But one a young woman found and, considering it good luck, she slipped it into her bra. She fell in love with the married man. But the penny, which the frugal girl hid in her bedroom closet, grew into a young, well-speaking and warmhearted man who was not married. He and the

woman fell in love. The married man swore never again to sow his pennies in a supermarket parking lot.

The parable disturbs Claire and the minister. Claire tries to write one:

A young woman kept tickets to Iceland in her freezer. Each morning she defrosted them and read the itinerary. Each afternoon she replaced the tickets underneath the trays of ice. Her lover asked if he could go with her. She bought him tickets, but had to sell the last of her goat milk to do so. Grateful, the lover moved in with her. This made the young woman happier than she'd ever been.

The minister interrupts Claire. "This parable is horrible," he says. "It rambles. What's the point?"

"The point," says Claire, "is that the minister does not stay with his lover and he never goes to Iceland, so the young woman stays on ice forever, fucking young, blond men."

"I don't think the parable as you started it can hang together," he says. "And the relationship between the lovers isn't clear. What is it?"

"The man is interested in the woman's anxiety."

"Is that all? Does he love her?"

"It's not in the parable," says Claire. "That's all I know. It's not in the parable."

Claire writes another:

A greedy man took three fat women to bed. In the night, one stole his wallet. "Who's got it?" he asked at breakfast. None would confess. The women ate and ate— bacon, sausage, popovers—growing ever larger. The greedy man considered kicking them away, but he didn't want to sleep alone. He said, "She who confesses gets a foot-long ice cream sundae." The thief confessed and the greedy man gave her the sundae. She grew. Next morning the greedy man's gun was missing. Naked, he quaked. "Who's got it?" he cried. The women sat at the end of his bed gnawing on his feet. He offered them fried potatoes, shrimp and oysters. The villain pulled the greedy man's gun from behind her back. She ate, she grew.

All four hit the highways. This mobile mountain range struck terror in the hearts of hale pedestrians. The greedy man trembled.

Next morning he couldn't find his clothes. None of my ladies can fit into my clothes, he thought. He knew the evil in their hearts. "Ladies," he cried. "Why do you torture me?"

"What will you feed us?" they asked. He offered them fruit.

"No, no," they said.

"Celery, tomatoes."

"NO."

"Cheese cake?" The clothes fell on his face.

Now each woman measured fifteen feet by fifteen feet. The greedy man moved quickly, but not quick enough. Before the multitude of tow trucks came, the greedy women ate him.

In his room the minister tries to write his sermon on bad and sad. He's thinking of Claire. He wants to be with her, but the women would be upset. Why can't he please himself? Why does he have to be sad? Claire's parables disturb him. She says she has committed the worst bad yet, that she's in love with him. He tries to sleep.

Claire sits in the empty Cry Room. If the minister believes in bad, she thinks, why isn't he with her, now? He has responsibilities to his women. He promised he would train them in decent badness. Claire understands, but she does not feel loved. "Here is my body," she says. "Where is his?"

She looks outside at the spitters smearing each other's spit in their hair. Their primping disgusts her. Why is no handsome man among them, no man with heart and wisdom? Still, they are available. Claire undresses and steps outside. It's lovely weather here, she thinks. It's glorious to be in love, to fall in half-iced puddles, to grin in my sopping slip and bra, to freeze in my sopping slip and bra. I can even get a cold without worrying anyone. "Sick," Mom used to say. "Get ye the hell to bed then. Here's a box of tissues and a throw-up bucket. Best be well tomorrow. I'll have no messes in my house." And the teacher who wore elf-earrings isn't here to give me aspirin from the fat bottle she kept in her top desk drawer. Nor is my lover.

A horde of hungry spitters grabs Claire, wraps her in electrician's tape and rolls her behind a mound of dolls' heads. The spitters take turns raping her. At night they practice spitting by the fireside. Legs taped together, Claire tries to hop away. A spitter lassos her. "Where you going?" he asks. "Back to church," she says. "To praise your lord?" "To sing him hymns." "Sorry, sweetheart," he says. "Can't leave yet. Must pay for stepping out. I won't hurt you *too bad*. One bite here, a bit of blood, a bruise."

Three days Claire has been missing. The minister has not slept. He does not eat. At night he sees a body wrapped in silver, glowing in the light of the spitters' fire. He sends five bad boys out with duffel bags. The spitters toss the boys against the church walls. They run back to the minister. Dare the minister emerge in person? Will the spitters laugh to see he cares so much for Claire? Will they think he is too old? The minister paces the pew ways, looks outside, paces. He leaves the church. He lifts Claire in his arms. Silent, the spitters stare. None try to stop him. The gold man carries his silver lover back to the church. Realizing they cannot penetrate, the spitters slink away in single file.

The minister unwraps his lover and lies beside her on her mattress. He kisses her bruises and anoints her cuts. She wakes ungrateful, with one eye open. "You've been sleeping with your women," she says. "A different one each night."

"Ritual," he says.

"Crap," says Claire. "It ain't all pain, this late night partaking."

"You should leave," he says. "This isn't good for you. I can't give you what you want."

"Your women need you," she says.

He nods.

The minister is not well. He has begun to disappear while he is speaking. Several of the women question his existence. One claims she walked through him twice—once in the transept, once in the narthex. "He was the scent of caramel," she says. Another says he disappears when the choir sings high E. Only Claire can reach the note and she refuses to repeat it. "He belongs in this world he created," she says bitterly. "He is the minister."

The women are jealous of the minister's distraction. They have begun to misbehave their own way instead of following the minister's instructions. Some have bitten the bad boys. The boys will not come back. Some women have stuffed biscuits in the organ pipes. The organ will not play on key.

Claire is losing patience. Why hasn't the minister addressed his congregation on the relationship of bad to sad? Why does he say he wants to sleep with her forever, but sleep with her only once a month? Why does he say she makes him happy, then tell her he's unhappy?

Claire leaves notes in her lover's Bibles asking him to meet her. He doesn't. "The other women might . . . " "I know," says Claire. "They might get jealous." Claire has lost her patience.

Rumor spreads that those who enter a crack in the north wall of the men's room will be taken to a land where bad conscience does not accompany bad action, a land of no responsibilities. Claire started the rumor. One by one the women disappear.

The minister is depressed. He wants his women back. Claire hugs him. "Come to my mattress," she says. "You told me once you wanted to lie beside me forever, your left arm under my shoulder, your right arm around me."

The minister retreats behind his pulpit. "I am a minister," he says. "I need my women." He pauses. "And I need you."

"You're a bit too needy then," Claire says. "So am I." She packs her hymnal and her seven Bibles. She removes her surplice, dresses in the blouse and skirt she came in and steps outside in the dark. She hadn't realized it was night. In the church she lost her sense of endings and beginnings.

Beside the welcome-to-our-city sign, Claire watches the gold doors of her lover's church. She will give her lover three hours.

🔥 🔥 🔥

HIGH ADVENTURES OF INDETERMINACY

by JOAN RETALLACK

from PARNASSUS: POETRY IN REVIEW

nominated by PARNASSUS: POETRY IN REVIEW

WE'VE BEEN LOOKING for ways to get out of ruts for as long as we've been in them. About the third century B.C., when Epicurus had his prescient vision of a rush-hour stupor of atoms commuting through the void, bumper to bumper at uniform speed in parallel lanes spanning the cosmos, he surely cried out "there must be more to life than this!" We do know that he came up with the "swerve." For no reason at all, but often enough to account for variety and change in the universe, atoms just ran amok, swerving into adjoining traffic, creating in the mess of collision, new structures. Enter onto the scene of Western thought (albeit for a cameo appearance), indeterminacy and its refreshing artifacts, alleviating briefly the claustrophobia we've always been prone to in the confines of our small worlds. Is there nothing new under the sun?, we groan. Yes, more things than are dreamt of by Reason alone, says Epicurus, foreshadowing Shakespeare's reply to Ecclesiastes.

Despite Renaissance zest for play, the fragile spirit of indetermi-

Books considered in this essay—

Marjorie Perloff. *The Poetics of Indeterminacy: Rimbaud to Cage*. Princeton University Press 1981. 346 pp. $20.00.

Gertrude Stein. *The Yale Gertrude Stein*. Yale University Press 1980. 464 pp. $30.00. $6.95 (paper).

John Cage. *For the Birds*. Marion Boyars 1981. 239 pp. $20.00.

John Cage. *Themes & Variations*. Station Hill Press 1982. Unpaginated. $25.00. $9.95 (paper).

nacy seemed destined to be squeezed out between the Judeo-Christian God (who for some reason needed to know it all in advance) and the great weight of evidence brought to bear on everything during the Enlightenment and its aftermath. We've had problems ever since dealing with things like spontaneity, intuition, and, most of all, change. Does change really occur? How can it be possible? Is it really advisable? Determinism, Rationalism, Logical Positivism are such reassuringly traditional bedtime stories. All the well-wrought prose of history seems to be on their side.

We are obsessed with law—since Moses came down from the mountain with our first lawbooks; since Plato in his senescence wrote *The Laws,* his sequel to the *Republic,* to ensure that nothing would be left to the imagination. Somewhere along the way we invented laws of chance, confident there was nothing we couldn't tame. Einstein alarmed us with relativity but then reassured us: God doesn't play dice. Heisenberg's "uncertainty" principle, we are relieved to know, describes an uncertain observer, not uncertain events. Even sub-atomic behavior must be law-abiding and, hopefully, any day will enter the fold of the respectably predictable.

Predictable. But isn't that a synonym for dull? All this docility, this good citizenship, all this predictability should begin to make us a bit uneasy. Must we really resign ourselves to the same old patterns—birth, struggle, a few laughs, and old devil death, generation after generation, *ad nauseum*? Well, yes; but perhaps there could be a few more laughs, we say in all modesty. Or perhaps the struggle can take a new form, says the revolutionary. Suddenly there is hope—declarations of independence, manifestoes, constitutions, utopias filled with good will and free-play, not all practical, but envisioning something other than the structures we inhabit, the habits of our structures.

Buckminster Fuller has said that a structure is simply a division of an outside from an inside. If nothing else, we are curious about what lies outside. The more so since Whorf and others showed us the extent to which structures of language and culture engender and delimit our understanding of reality. Along with our tendencies toward biological conservatism, we harbor a genuine wish to enlarge the range of the possible. There will always be revolutionaries, anarchists, deconstructionists, experimentalists of one sort

471

or another. In short, an avant garde, defying the gravity of established order or just ignoring it, reinventing invention. There they are, folks, swerving into view, climbing up to the high wire—philosophical daredevils, *bêtes blanches, artistes noires*—a death defying act.

Meanwhile, down on the ground floor ("low culture" some call it) indeterminacy never did go out of style. Lots and dice and other forms of courting chance have been a firmly entrenched institution since ancient times. Never mind the rantings of preachers and teachers and police. We're no fools. We know you can't leave everything to logic. The willful indeterminist act in literature, however, of the sort we find in the work of Gertrude Stein or John Cage, appears to be a relatively recent development. Marjorie Perloff dates it from Rimbaud, though Hugh Kenner makes an intriguing case for an accidental indeterminacy that we've been negotiating as readers for as long as our pile of books has included works written in other cultures or other times.

First let me explain that much of what Perloff discusses under the rubric "indeterminacy" has to do with the effect of a text on the reader. This effect, which she sometimes calls "undecidability," is (in contrast to Heisenberg's particles) lodged in the nature of the event, the text, which because of random references or syntactical dislocations or illogical juxtapositions, resists the reader's attempts to pin down a coherent exegesis. (Text as irreducible enigma.) The reader may not even be able to perceive a correspondence of references to referents, signifiers to signifieds. All of this implies a theory of meaning in literature entirely different from the one we are accustomed to. Or does it?

In *The Pound Era,* Kenner claims there is a high degree of "undecidability" in any text removed from our experience, either through historical accident (the not so accidental passage of time transporting it beyond certainty) or cultural remove. It seems that we are in fact accustomed to reading with a surprisingly high tolerance for non-comprehension of one sort or another. We "intuitively grasp" while letting slip and slide the great deal that we don't understand; or radically misunderstand what we think is perfectly clear. But this doesn't inhibit our enjoyment in the least. It may even enhance it.

Take Shakespeare for instance. Kenner gives an example from *Cymbeline,* IV, ii, circa 1611:

Golden lads and girls all must
As chimney-sweepers, come to dust.

Social commentary foreshadowing Blake, yes/no? No. Kenner recounts this startling fact:

> . . . in the mid-20th century a visitor to Shakespeare's Warwickshire met a countryman blowing the grey head off a dandelion: "We call these golden boys chimney-sweepers when they go to seed."

And the point really isn't the same at all. The text has separated off from the referents we tend to think are necessary if it is to have meaning. It is only a chance encounter that restored the referent in this case. Before which we didn't miss a thing. We had been doing perfectly well without it. How can that be? Kenner again:

> Hanmer or Theobold, with Dr. Johnson, supposed that words denoted things. A language is simply an assortment of words, and a set of rules for combining them. Mallarmé and Valéry and Eliot felt words as part of that echoing intricacy, Language, which permeates our minds and obeys not the laws of *things* but its own laws, which has an organism's power to mutate and adapt and survive. . . . The things against which its words brush are virtually extraneous to its integrity. We may want to say that Shakespeare wrote about happenings in the world, the world that contains mortal men and sunlight and dandelions, and that a post-Symbolist reading converts his work into something that happens in the language, where "golden" will interact with "dust" . . . and "lads" and "girls" and "chimney-sweepers," and where "dust" rhymes with "must". . . . Thus the song seems to us especially fine when we can no longer say what the phrase "golden lads" was meant to name. (And "genuine poetry," wrote Eliot in 1929, "can communicate before it is understood.")

(*The Pound Era*, p. 123)

473

Ironically, though Kenner is describing a Symbolist aesthetic, we are on our way (not chronologically, but conceptually) to the view of language that makes Perloff's account of indeterminacy in non-Symbolist poetry possible. (Indicating, perhaps, that the division between the two is not so clear after all.) But we're not quite there. Kenner moves us further along. It seems that what we respond to is *"effect"* ("an effect being something hypnotic we cannot quite understand") produced by: the "extra-semantic affinities" of words, the "molecular bonds of half-understood words," the "structure of words, where the words exchange dynamisms in the ecology of language," the "chemistry of Language [which] supersedes meaning," the "characteristic force fields" of Language. Our view of language as reference pure and simple is assailed by new possibilities of linguistic impact, what with signifieds sliding out from under signifiers and meaning rudely detached from its transitional objects.

In Shakespeare it's not too disquieting. The rumor that he knew what he was talking about has survived four centuries intact. We relax on authority and experience words splendid in their burnished opacity. In our tardy arrival at *Cymbeline*, a certain loss of literal sense may well increase our susceptibility to images and raise our sense of what the old philosophers called "secondary qualities"—sound, rhythm, texture; and, for synesthesiacs, color and even taste. ("We do not discern nonsense," says Kenner.) These qualities are ingredients of the etymological elixir that suffuses the senses, awakening one as linguistic Lazarus to the play of language in the play. Those seventeenth-century Warwickshire locals shared with Shakespeare what Wittgenstein called a "form of life"—local culture, turns of phrase, familiar flora and fauna, habits of commerce, assumptions of value and rank. . . . We also share with Shakespeare a form of life, the English language. What he made of the English language has been part of our formation as linguistic creatures. His words replenish us with their dense textures. We do not require a vernacular translation.

As we approach the modern scene, indeterminacy as historical accident becomes indeterminacy as intentional effect—a structural principle of the Symbolists, according to Kenner:

> . . . we may say that Symbolism is . . . an effort to anticipate the work of time by aiming directly at the kind

474

of existence a poem may have when a thousand years
have deprived it of its dandelions and its mythologies, an
existence purely linguistic, determined by the molecular bonds of half-understood words. (130)

Eliot, Kenner says, "has withdrawn in favor of the language,"
calling the chapter in which he deals with this development
"Words Set Free." Set free as in: "the Symbolist willingness to lift
words out of 'usage,' free their affinities, permit them new combination." So the Symbolists, via the Romantics, did by choice what
Time did by default. But the point is that both processes enable us
to pay a new kind of attention to language; language is no longer
rendered invisible by dailiness or precise reference, because of
course when we "refer," we are attempting to point with language
at something beyond language. The point of reference is not
language, but its object.

In *The Poetics of Indeterminacy*, Marjorie Perloff locates the
first appearance of intentional indeterminist devices in the *Illuminations* which Rimbaud began in 1872. She offers us this quotation:

> . . . I flattered myself on inventing, some day, a poetic
> language accessible to all the senses. I withheld the
> translation.
>
> (Rimbaud, *Une Saison en enfer [Délires II]*)

The withholding of the translation, if we find Kenner's theory of
historical indeterminacy convincing, shouldn't seem so exotic. (We
are used to it, no?) But of course it does. It's one thing to come
upon incomprehensible passages in poetry from other eras; it's
quite another in poetry just off the press. Is the poet trying to put
one over on us, we ask irritably? It is thus the burden of a poetics of
indeterminacy to demonstrate that these intentional *de*constructions are indeed constructive; that the experience of indeterminacy in literature is not all frustration and disappointment; that it
can nourish us with a particular kind of linguistic feast, perhaps not
entirely dissimilar to the great wild game of free-playing signifiers
in portions of Shakespeare. Before such a demonstration can take
place, however, there is other work to do. Contexts must be
differentiated.

475

For Perloff this means primarily a distinction between the modes and intentions of Symbolism as against those of indeterminacy. Unlike Kenner who thinks *The Waste Land* (Symbolist exemplar) presents a code not intended to be broken, bearing no more than the "teasing implication of meaning" (characteristics she would find more appropriate to John Ashbery whom she locates in the anti-Symbolist tradition), Perloff firmly identifies Symbolism with reference. This position, though not implausible, tends to move the rationale for indeterminacy toward the negative ("non-Symbolist") camp, and to deprive it of the kind of historical depth one enjoys in *The Pound Era*. Though she agrees with Kenner's description of the effects of indeterminacy in literature, these effects appear in her account to have a sudden immaculate conception in Rimbaud ("There is no real precedent for the *anti-paysage* of the *Illuminations*.") in reaction to Baudelaire. The most fruitful (positive) explanation of the genesis of indeterminacy in literature probably lies in a selective synthesis of the views of Kenner and Perloff and even of Jacques Derrida who believes indeterminacy to be an inherent property of all texts. But Perloff is unequivocal on her point:

> For, unlike [Ashbery's] "These Lacustrine Cities," where tower, swan, and petal have no definable referents, *The Waste Land* has, despite its temporal and spacial dislocations and its collage form, a perfectly coherent symbolic structure. (13)

> However difficult it may be to decode this complex poem, the relationship of the word to its referents, of signifier to signified, remains essentially intact. (17)

And Perloff is a crack code-breaker. Like the New Critics' star pupil, she goes at passages from *The Waste Land* with gusto, efficiently unpacking symbols like bags at the start of a month's vacation, tucking everything into its proper spot; she refers to this exercise as a "Norton Anthology reading." Its purpose is to serve as a kind of negative model. This is what we should not attempt to do, cannot succeed in doing with indeterminist poetry.

What Perloff posits are two distinct literary traditions emerging out of the revolutionary milieu of the late nineteenth and early twentieth centuries (though the historical and social context is not discussed):

> . . . what we loosely call "Modernism" in Anglo-American poetry is really made up of two separate though often interwoven strands: the Symbolist mode that Lowell inherited from Eliot and Baudelaire and, beyond them, from the great Romantic poets, and the "anti-Symbolist" mode of indeterminacy or "undecidability," of literalness and free play, whose first real exemplar was the Rimbaud of the *Illuminations*. . . . we cannot really come to terms with the major poetic experiments occuring in our own time without some understanding of what we might call "the French connection"—the line that goes from Rimbaud to Stein, Pound, and Williams by way of Cubist, Dada, and early Surrealist art, a line that also includes the great French/English verbal compositions of Beckett. It is this "other tradition" (I take the phrase from the title of a poem by John Ashbery) in twentieth-century poetry that is the subject of my book. (vii)

> And although our own early Modernist poets generally resisted the indeterminacy model of the *Illuminations*, the notion of enigma, of the poem as language construction in which the free play of possible significations replaces iconic representation, began to gain adherence among avant garde writers. (66)

The "other tradition" as a label is not entirely first-class; shades of the "other network," the "other woman"—things we don't quite grant legitimacy—hover round. The "other tradition" has to my knowledge had only one fully positive, though not fully satisfactory, attribution, "language-centered poetry." ("Indeterminist," though still a negation, seems less pejorative since it is nonparasitic and non-hierarchical.) It is usual to oppose "traditional" poetry to something else, like "experimental" (read "arbitrary," "unstructured," "tentative") or even "non-traditional" as though this work had no tradition other than the reactive one of defying or denying what society has baptised "traditional." A currently fashionable opposition is "modern" vs. "post-modern" which Perloff's compelling argument implies is historically misleading. The two lines to which we apply these labels have in fact been flourishing alongside one another, despite partisans who periodically enjoy pronouncing the other side defunct.

The long habit of invidious comparison, the second class status of the "non," the "other," the "anti" is due to the virtual wholesale identification of the literary establishment with Symbolism, as though "Symbolism" were the generic term for poetry. Work coming out of the "other tradition" has been much abused because of this—interpreted within the Symbolist context as some sort of high Symbolism (e.g., mystical) or as failed Symbolism, or, because non-Symbolist, rejected out of hand as non-poetry. To read an Indeterminist work looking for qualities and effects of a Symbolist epiphany poem is an injustice, not to say a waste of time. Other critical methods are demanded.

Perloff identifies and explores a number of suggestive contexts, which together provide a framework for her illuminating discussions of Rimbaud, Stein, Pound, etc.: the concept of indeterminacy itself (more implicitly than explicitly); literary genealogy (Rimbaud . . . to David Antin); extra-literary influences (visual arts, cinema, ordinary speech . . .); the Indeterminist or "non-Symbolist" stance (intentions and effects). Some crucial issues related to this last context are raised in the first chapter of the book:

> Art becomes play, endlessly frustrating our longing for certainty. . . . poetic texts like "These Lacustrine Cities" . . . derive force from their refusal to "mean" in conventional ways . . . Contemporary poets have often commented on this situation, but no one has paid much attention, perhaps because readers seem bent on absorbing the unfamiliar into familiar patterns. From Charles Olson's "Projective Verse" (1950), with its call for "objectivism" . . . to John Cage's remark in *Silence* (1961) that "I'd never been interested in symbolism . . . I preferred just taking things in themselves, not as standing for other things"; to . . . David Antin's definition, in the mid-seventies, of poetry as "the language art," a form of discourse which, rather than "saying one thing

and meaning something else," returns to the literal but with the recognition that "phenomenological reality is itself 'discovered' and 'constructed' by poets," the question of how to create poetry in a post-Symbolist age has been a primary concern. (34–35)

To explore what I call "the mode of undecidability" in twentieth-century poetry is by no means to criticize the great Symbolist movement of our period. It is, rather, to suggest that much of the poetry now emerging has different origins and therefore makes rather different suppositions. It deserves to be read on its own terms. (44)

And this from the last chapter:

"Empty Words" is Cage's way of making us look at the world we actually inhabit, the sights and sounds we really see. So, from the opposite direction, Antin's talk poems force us to become aware of our natural discourse, to become sensitive to the way we actually talk and hence think. (338)

An interesting tacit assumption throughout much of Perloff's book is that the world we must construct or reconstruct in reading Symbolist poetry, the restoration of the lost half of the equation, symbol = thing, is a world less vital and less authentic, less "in process" than the immediate world of language which does not point beyond itself. This assumption is a complicated one and is intimately related to developments in philosophy of language in this century found in the work of, among others, Heidegger, Lacan, Derrida, Wittgenstein, and Dewey. It is also, not surprisingly, a controversial assumption which deserves, at least, another book. The inverse equation (thing = symbol) is equally offensive. Perloff quotes D. S. Carne-Ross on this point in her chapter on Pound:

Not merely does the thing, in Pound's best verse, not point beyond itself: *it doesn't point to us*. The green tip that pushes through the earth in spring does not stand

479

for or symbolize man's power of spiritual renewal. . . . .
The green thrust is itself the divine event. . . . Meant as
literally as Pound means it, this is very hard to take. Not
only does it offend against the ways we have been taught
to read literature, it is an offense against the great
principle of inwardness or internalization that has put us
at the center of things and laid waste to the visible
world. (198)

The Deconstructionists, following Lacan, would take this a step
further and say that the divine event is the word itself, which
creates its own peculiar tension-filled presence in the absence of
the thing.

But the critical question remains. If the poem primarily presents
us with a charged linguistic field, charged for instance by the
"tension between reference and compositional game, between a
pointing system and a self-ordering system," as Perloff describes
the dynamics in one of Gertrude Stein's poems, what is to be done
with it? What form can the act of criticism take? Clearly this is a
language game for which the Symbolist rules don't work. Here are
two samples of Perloff's approach to Pound:

> I would posit that Pound's basic strategy in the *Cantos* is
> to create a flat surface, as in a Cubist or early Dada
> collage, upon which verbal elements, fragmented im-
> ages, and truncated bits of narrative, drawn from the
> most disparate contexts, are brought into collision. Such
> "collage poetry," as David Antin points out, "no longer
> yield(s) an iconic representation, even of a fractured
> sort, though bristling with significations." It thus occu-
> pies a middle space between the mimetic on the one
> hand and the non-objective or "abstract" on the other;
> the referential process is not cut off but is subordinated
> to a concern for sequential or spatial arrangement. In-
> deed, in the case of the Malatesta Cantos, the text
> becomes a surface of linguistic distortions and contradic-
> tions that force the reader to participate in the poem's
> action. . . . Pound dislocates language so as to create new
> verbal landscapes. (181–82)

On Canto VIII:

> . . . the sonorous formality of the address is undercut by
> a series of incomplete words, meant to reproduce what is
> on the back of the envelope *("tergo")*. Here the reader
> has to fill in the first few letters of each word in order to
> make sense of the address. . . . The poet thus insists on
> our participation; it is up to us to fill in the blanks, to
> play the game. . . .
>
> The lines, in short, do not convey information; rather
> they take certain facts and present them from different
> linguistic perspectives (formal, florid Italian; broken
> Italian words; English translation) as if to undercut their
> historicity. . . . Such linguistic indeterminacy is one of
> the central devices of these Cantos. (183)

Much of the descriptive language in *The Poetics of Indeterminacy* reflects Perloff's considerable knowledge of the visual arts, an
excellent resource for getting at formal dynamisms in the partially
opaque linguistic surfaces that characterize much of the work she is
discussing. The book pushes continually toward a positive aesthetic, one divergent from but not necessarily in competition with
Symbolist poetics. The pervasive negatives—anti-Symbolist, absent whole, resistance to closure, decreation, decomposition, dis-
location, fragmentation, incompletion, deformation; reader described as frustrated or forced—are not an indication of
contrariness on Perloff's part. They rather reflect two things: the
extent to which the experimental swerve moves us out of the
reigning metaphysic; and the extent to which that metaphysic
governs our language—our concepts of form, structure, method,
the nature of the unit, etc. Though art is never primarily polemical, polemical terms seem always to dominate the early critical
evaluation of avant garde work. Rimbaud, Stein, Pound . . .
"early"? Yes, we are still having trouble assimilating the aftermath
of structural collisions that were the turn of the (nineteenth)
century origins of Modernism. "Early" can last a long time for the
avant garde.

Considering this persistent time lag, and the Princeton imprint,
Perloff's book is an almost pioneering contribution to the develop-

ment of critical approaches to Indeterminist poetry, heretofore confined to extremely small circulation journals. The strengths of the book far outweigh its infelicities, but some are annoying nonetheless—frequent (non-Steinian) repetitions; an utter misunderstanding of Wittgenstein's notion of silence; a surprising dismissal of Cage's chance operations as "not in themselves the mainspring of his poetic art." The treatment of Cage, in fact, has the feeling of a run-through, with no discussion of his musical sources. There are also a large number of descriptions of non or anti-Symbolist work as "dreamlike," a characterization which in our post-Freudian cultural age is almost a contradiction in terms. But the book is overridingly a valuable one, providing the best thing a critical work can—an informed and stimulating framework for further discussion.

The Yale Gertrude Stein happily makes accessible a large quantity of Stein's work selected from the eight-volume Yale collection of "The Unpublished Writings of Gertrude Stein," available otherwise only in expensive hardback editions. This selected edition is a long time in coming and yet has a look of haste about it. The work appears haphazardly arranged. The "Introduction" by Richard Kostelanetz, editor of the volume, is an article which first appeared in the Summer 1975 *Hollins Critic*. Though full of interesting comments on Stein's work, it is clearly appropriate to another occasion. Only two of the twenty-seven selections included in *The Yale Gertrude Stein* are (briefly) mentioned, while work that does not appear (mostly better known and less problematic) is copiously cited. Kostelanetz tells us in his Preface that he intentionally chose "more experimental works" for this selected edition—examples of "extended abstraction," "abstract prose," "minimal poetry," etc. This volume deserved its own introduction. The work would have been more profitably discussed than labeled.

The appearance of carelessness (on the part of Yale University Press as well) is compounded to insult when Kostelanetz ends his "Introduction" with the "curious fact that I will let others explain (of) the absence of visible [Steinian] influence upon subsequent women writers." Since we know that virtually all subsequent experimental writing in this country (probably in the English language) has been influenced one way or another by Stein, this is tantamount to saying there are no women experimental writers, or women writers who engage in some degree of experimentation. Let me name a few of the visibly influenced: Edith Sitwell, Barbara Guest, Anne Waldman, Rochelle Owens, Judith Johnson Sherwin, Laura Chester, Lyn Hejinian, Bernadette Mayer, Tina Darragh, Diane Ward, Carla Harryman, Rae Armantrout. . . . It is curious that Kostelanetz is unaware of these writers. They are all, except for Sitwell, contemporary Americans whose work appears widely in distinguished avant garde publications. Kostelanetz, as a leading advocate and impresario of experimental writing in this country, should find their work of interest.

"Fact is," Zeno of Elea (fifth century B.C.) might have said to Epicurus (in the history of ideas riposte can precede its object), "logic shows us that your so-called swerves are out. Too bad, old man. You see, before your capricious atom can go anywhere at all, it must first go half the distance. And before it can go half the distance, it must go half of that. And before it can go that half, it must again go half of that. And before . . . you get the drift . . . toward infinity and sweet stasis. 'Infinite regress,' some snide types call it. 'At my back I always hear Time's winged chariot not getting any nearer.' It's quite simply impossible to move through an infinite number of points in a finite amount of time. So much for your swashbuckling swerves! Motion of any kind is out of the question. ("If that piece of reasoning isn't a swerve, I don't know what is," mutters Epicurus into the future.) But don't worry, old man, in the twentieth century A.D. not getting anywhere will become fashionable. In athletic circles it will be called jogging or cycling 'in place.' In literature it will be given the lovely paradoxical name, 'continuous present.' "

By one Gertrude Stein. Or was it two? This large mythic corpus we call Gertrude Stein seems always to produce double images—female/male, playful/pretentious, fascinating/maddening, amusing/a bore. She has enlarged our range of possibilities in prose and poetry beyond comprehension, for which we are grateful/and annoyed. Her intentions, not to say her effects, are deeply disjunctive. There is for instance that complicated desire to say what she wants to say without actually saying it, to "mean names without naming them"; enough one would think to render a lesser being mute. But not Stein. She had what we like to call today chutzpah (supreme self-confidence, nerve, gall). And her spirit of adventure (or was it sometimes obsession?) never seemed to flag, though it has worn out many of the less hardy along the way.

Even her deathbed scene demonstrates the capacity for persistence—popping up for one more question—"What is the question?"—a last, finally economical repetition (of form and content) squeezed into the moment before Time's proto-period. But the last thing in any ultimate sense cannot be a question since a question implies yet another thing, an answer. Grammatically she was keeping the game open, stalling her myth at the pen-ultimate. *Mors Interrupta*, again and again and again would have been her scenario had she only been able to continue writing.

To continue writing is her indisputable objective, to "commence and re-commence," as she often said, like a perpetual procession into unending graduation exercises—steering clear of valedictory exhortations and other grand finales of "moral" or "message" or "aboutness." Stein isn't fond of endings, so they are, in her prose and poetry, like deaths, arbitrary conveniences to keep things from going on too interminably. There are none of those end points foreordained from the start—no climaxes, no epiphanies, no summings up or answers of any kind. The last sentence or line in a piece is formally indistinguishable from, and probably interchangeable with, any other except in its placement as the final item in a series of what are designed to be "continuous presents." The monumental end points, the crescendoes of implication which adorn the concluding lines or pages of Symbolist work, have been deflated to the status of a punctuation mark, generally a tidy but inconclusive period. Inconclusive, in part, because it is all-purpose, used even to punctuate questions. "What is the question," she would have put it on the page, thereby having yet another thing both ways. Part of her wasn't so open; part of her disliked the prying nature of the interrogative.

Which brings us back to that odd naming without naming business. If the implications of endings could be ignored, starting points, which for Stein were always tied up with reference, were not so easy to dismiss. She wanted, in fact, to do "portraits," to celebrate the datum, and therefore could never really entirely banish "aboutness," though she certainly did not want to engage in the (c)rude behaviour of pointing. Privacy must be protected. Her aim was to honor the referent without the intrusion of reference. Referents without reference became the poles of one of her working paradoxes, poles which appear, passionate and distinct, in these passages from the essay "Poetry and Grammar":

> (Homer, Chaucer, the Bible) . . . they were drunk with nouns, to name to know how to name earth sea and sky and all that was in them was enough to make them live and love in names, and that is what poetry is it is a state of knowing and feeling a name.

> As I say a noun is a name of a thing, and therefore slowly if you feel what is inside that thing you do not call it by the name by which it is known. Everybody knows that by the way they do when they are in love and a writer should always have that intensity of emotion about whatever is the object about which he writes. And therefore and I say it again more and more one does not use nouns.

> Was there not a way of naming things that would not invent names, but mean names without naming them.

> Of course you all do know that when I speak of naming anything, I include emotions as well as things.

As you can see, the rules of the game are challenging: the writer must have intensity of emotion about her objects without divulging either her objects or her emotions. To name without naming is a semantic paradox which, along with its logical class-mates, is susceptible to resolution through a rather peculiar means—language talking about language rather than about objects; language as analogue of, rather than reference to, object; words themselves playing the role of object, flashing secondary qualities without inhibition.

Consider these lines from "Yet Dish" in *The Yale Gertrude Stein:*

> A lea ender stow sole lightly.
> Not a bet beggar.
> Nearer a true set jump hum,
> A lamp lander so seen poor lip. (55)

Here Stein has vaulted over that high tension wire strung between the poles of the paradox, defying gravity and Zeno with the best of them. The swerve into indeterminacy has produced a surface which scintillates in an imbalance of mass to energy. The weight of denotation and connotation is lightened so we are free to return to language as primary process (prior to logical structuring), like young children or foreigners, aware of crisp textures (bet beggar), gentle phonemic transformations—"stow sole lightly," where the s and o move from "stow" to "sole," and the l from "sole" to "lightly" with a symmetrical balancing of s/s to l/l. There is pleasure in this elegantly textured, linguistic lunch. There is also the poignancy of language cut off from circumstance, juices still flowing: fleeting but vivid images, e.g., "lea ender stow" bringing with it a taste of things maritime; or "jump hum" evoking children's games; "beggar," "lamp," and "lip," good red-blooded nouns.

The effect is reminiscent of Middle English untranslated, full of glimpsed significations, but also studded with opacities confronting the reader primarily with tactile (phonemic or graphic) qualities. We are not in this experience of language undergoing abstraction *from;* we are being returned *to* words as objects in the process of becoming—a state of suspended arrival which engages our intellect and our senses and gives them permission to play, much as we play(ed) with language in nursery rhymes and word games. We needn't hunch over annotations to enjoy "Yet Dish" or the following Stein text:

> Age in beefsteaks age in pear shapes age in round and puzzle.
> Witness a pair of glasses. Extra win eager extra win eager.
> Piles piles of splinters piles piles of splinters.
> English or please english or please or please or please or please or please.

> ("Emp Lace")

One can easily imagine a group of children chanting this, perhaps even inventing a repertoire of movements to go with different parts, thoroughly caught up in the sheer vitality of language; not needing to worry about or defend its sense because they are so in touch with its sensations. They would be exercising themselves as linguistic creatures, just as they exercise themselves as bodily creatures when they play kickball. Adults continue to run and play tennis and other games (elevated to "sports") knowing they enhance health and prowess, and also are fun. But they (most of us) stop playing with language. What are the implications and consequences of this? Interesting question to play with. And here is another: Suppose we were to value some poets primarily for their symbolic structures and epiphanies and others for their invitations to play, to swerve, perchance even to collide—the latter lot (and many spanning both catagories) sought out for their ability to let us, with them, experience language, not as a reflection or description *of* reality, but as a reality itself in which we move, jump, hum?

This is not to suggest that Stein always proffers such irresistible invitations. In "A Birthday Book," a twenty-five-page poem included in the *Yale Gertrude Stein*, Zeno's laws against motion have overtaken her. This poem should be a quintessential intertwining of "continuous" and "present" since it is written in the form of a calendar diary. It begins,

> Who was born January first.
> Who was born in January first.
> Who was born and believe me who was born and believe me, who was born who was born and believe me.

> At that rate.
> Let us sell the bell.(73)

Not an entirely inauspicious beginning, especially had she taken her own good humourous advice in the last two lines. But she goes on, clanging a duller and duller bell throughout a full calendar year:

> January the twenty-fourth makes it as late, as late as that.
> January the twenty-fifth ordinarily.
> January the twenty-sixth as ordinarily.(75)

By this time, the third page of the poem, having rapidly flipped through the remainder to see if any relief is in sight, one realizes as Zeno's stunned runner must have, there is no way to go the distance; at least not as "reader," if that term presumes even a minimal engagement with the text. Stein herself is exercising in place. The mid-point (which we must first achieve in order to get to the end) finds her in this regressive state:

> June and so forth. June the twenty-fifth, June the
> twenty-fifth. June and so forth.
> June the twenty-sixth her name is June and very
> soon.(86)

To have gotten this far one must first have read half-way, and so on and so forth. The problem is as fundamental as Zeno's—how to get from one point to the next—because Stein too has presented us with a series of discrete units (lines), rather than a continuum. Without engines of plot or semantic development to push or pull us across the gaps, there must be a current of energy running throughout to draw us on and connect otherwise isolated parts. In the absence of this current we are psychologically, if not logically, stuck; unable even like poor quaking Kierkegaard to contemplate leaps of faith, since that strenuous athleticism is also dependent on an unusually high degree of energy—energy that a text like the Bible, not without its own share of repetition and illogic, seems somehow able to generate, unlike "A Birthday Book." This is not to imply a direct comparison between Stein and the Old Testament psalmist, though at least one respected critic has called her a mystic, but just to say that some texts are "charged," moving readers to take a great deal of active responsibility for missing links, and others are not. We must ask in the case of "A Birthday Book", why not?

Ironically, the stolidity of the poem is exacerbated by the superficial appearance of movement. After all, we are racing through the year, are we not? But the mechanics of this incessant series of dates, the pro forma pace of the familiar unto deadeningly habitual sequence, renders one as enervated as Beckett's "Unnamable"—"you must go on, I can't go on, I'll go on," knowing the next words will be "I can't go on," and so on and on to yet another infinity of fixation. But the major reason why there is no dynamic "continuous" in "A Birthday Book" is that, in contrast to "Yet Dish" and "Emp Lace," there are no lively "presents." The reader is starved rather than fueled. Rhymes, for instance, are of the order of clang associations—June/soon, door/more, stew/do: "May and might hold me tight, might and may night and day. . . ." This facile rattling on is childish, not child-like. Mother Goose would yawn. With virtually no surprising combinations, no interesting vocabulary to savor in its rigidly structured abstract language, the poem is like an obligatory form filled out with nonvital statistics.

Movement in Indeterminist poetry is generated to a large extent by the inherent interest of individual units (ripe in their presentness, as a Zen master would say), whether they be lines, sentences, phrases, or phonemes. These must whet the appetite for more. And they must spill over with excess energy—enough to create a lively magnetic field, a charged whole raised to a power significantly greater than the mere sum of parts. There is nothing to "find out at the end," no solution to the crime or the lovers' plight, no homily to live by, no punch line. There is the process of reader interacting with text, a process which must deliver an abundance unimaginable at the start. This, in contrast to logical conclusion ("December thirty-first. So much so."), which can never outgrow its premises.

In "A Birthday Book," the paradoxes which generated abundance and inventiveness in other work have resulted in absence and evasion. Perhaps this is the phenomenon of "protective" language about which William Gass has written. Love that wants to but dares not speak its name fosters an aversion to naming; caution about desire in language short-circuits linguistic intuitions. Or, perhaps some of Stein's strategies for naming without names are just too logically efficient. Paradox, though a creature of logic, won't tolerate an excess of it without losing its dynamic tension. Of course, these perhapses are not mutually exclusive.

The most logical of strategies is to excommunicate nouns altogether, along with their cheeky adjectives. The discreet pronoun can remain. But the really dependable parts of speech are active, non-referential elements—conjunctions, verbs, and prepositions. The poetry which logically follows resembles William James's image of language as a kind of algebra—anonymous variables exercising themselves with mathematical rigor, staying thin:

They must be always careful to just be with them
Or they will not only be but could be thought
To change which they will never know
Not only only all alike
But they will be careful . . .

("Stanzas in Meditation," Part II, Stanza X, 347)

The words in these five lines fade into invisibility even as we read them because they are almost pure syntax. Contrary to Stein's goal of "continuous present," the function of syntax is to move us right along. There is no syntactical present. This is why Stein in other work, along with contemporary writers attempting to achieve the effect of continuous present, has dislocated syntax or discarded it entirely. The abstract syntactical flight in "Stanzas in Meditation" not only avoids reference, it blocks resonance. Later in the poem Stein writes, "It is natural to think in numerals/If you do not mean to think."

One must question the judgment in devoting 148 pages (well over a quarter) of the Yale volume to this work. It is of interest to Stein scholars of course but should prove daunting and dull to the non-scholarly reader with a zest for language who, admirably, just wants to play.

In delightful contrast to "Stanzas in Meditation" there is "Dates," which presents words as things replete with pith, not variables, in a deliciously humorous compositional game that with its orderly but surprising permutations (mostly noun to noun) sustains a lively momentum:

II
Worry.
Wordly
Pies and Pies.
Piles.
Weapons.
Weapons and weapons.
World renown.
World renown world renown.

III

Nitches.
Nitches pencil.
Nitches pencil plate.
Nitches vulgar.
Nitches vulgar pencils.
Nitches plate.

V

Spaniard.
Soiled pin.
Soda soda.
Soda soda.

(197-98)

In section II, transformations from "worry" to "wordly" to "world"; and "pies" to "piles"; or "wordly . . . weapons" to "world renown" are pleasing in themselves, but they also give us enough semantic stimuli to conjure visions of an Achilles and the Tortoise armaments race ("worry" will never catch up with "world renown" anymore than Achilles can overtake the Tortoise in that other of Zeno's logical tales). This gives us both language as object *and* as analogue of object. In section III, crunchy nouns like "nitches" and "plate"—word salad garnished with "vulgar pencils," absurd and delightful as "soiled pin"—are of fully independent means. They do not require an "objective correlative" to support them. Nor does the phonemic unfolding of "Spaniard" into "soiled pin" and "soda"—a lighthearted, unpredictable assortment in the eclectic spirit of Dada. The words are free for the exhilaration.

The fifty-page poem, "Lifting Belly" which Kostelanetz calls a "lesbian classic," ranges high and low from the delightful to the tedious. First the former:

I have feathers.
Gentle fishes.
Do you think of apricots . . .

If this language is erotic, and I think it is, it is not because it refers to sexuality, but because it shares with sexuality a tense we might call "present sensual." The words don't direct us very far beyond themselves. They are largely ornamental. As with ornamental lacquered boxes, the aesthetic object is the outside; we forget to wonder what, if anything, is inside or behind or underneath:

> Say anything a mudding made of Ceasars.
> Lobster. Baby is so good to baby.
> I correct blushes. You mean wishes.
> I collect pearls. Yes and colors.
> All colors are gods. Oh yes Bedlington.
> Now I collect songs.
> Lifting belly is so nice.
> I wrote about it to him.
> I wrote about it to her. (24)

The contrast between the pleasantly flowing and the awkward or strained, between the lush and the restrained, creates an evocative tension. Though, as in the "feathers/fishes" lines, there is some transformational development of sounds, any budding lyricism is always interrupted ("Oh yes Bedlington"). Removed from "poetic" sentimentality, the poem does not attempt to whip the reader into unearned emotional peaks. Its engagement is in its sensuality of language and its fun.

When it is not fun, when it is tedious, it may be that it has fallen into a different sort of sentimentality, verging on private language—words like pet names, cherished and exclusive, self-contained units again with no overflow. Private language used in public arenas, like books or dinner parties, reveals conflict about sharing and condemns readers or companions to boredom. In Stein's case the language may have so crackled with private meaning that the drab surface went unremarked:

> Lifting belly is a third.
> Did you say third. No I said Avila
> I would not be surprised surprised if I added that yet.
> Lifting belly to me.
> I am fondest of all of lifting belly.
> Lifting belly careful don't say anything about lifting belly.

492

I did not change my mind.
Neither did you carefully.
Lifting belly and again lifting belly.
I have changed my mind about the country.
Lifting belly and action and voices and care to be taken.
Does it make any difference if you pay for the paper or not.

Here Stein is straddling, like a dilatory Hamlet, "to name or not
to name," "to open or close." The gaps have widened again,
yawning vacuums interspersing remote vacuities. Of the relatively
few nouns (other than "belly") most are abstract: "third," "mind,"
"action," "care," "difference." Tone and rhythm are unrelievedly
awkward and strained, though entirely devoid of active tension, as
straddling is bound to be. The minimal impact is that of a spat,
sotto voce and yet something we are not quite meant not to
overhear. We have the nagging impression that the matter at hand
could be of little interest to any but the interlocutors. In such
sections of the poem, language hasn't been given the substantive-
ness of object; neither is it transparent. We are, if not intentionally
excluded, subject to sensory deprivation. (Experiment: Lock subjects in bare rooms with abstract Stein texts. How soon will they
begin to hallucinate? Control group to be given portions of "Yet
Dish" or "Dates.")

The concluding lines of "Lifting Belly" are in the active, resonant voice of the poem. Curiously, they reveal virtually no "information" and yet are not "private language" in Wittgenstein's sense
of alienation from a shared context. They are pleasing to the
communal ear, tone deafness having undergone miraculous cure.
We share in the rhythmical grace of "Lifting belly enormously and
with song." We are pleased by the echo of "signs" in "Pauline," the
balance of "meantime listen" and "Miss Cheatham," by the open-
ness (even graphically), the spirit of affirmation and ebullience, the
amusing whimsy that brings together Miss Cheatham and Aunt
Pauline and a cow. The surface is so delightful that it totally
absorbs our attention:

> Lifting belly enormously and with song.
> Can you sing about a cow.
> Yes.
> And about signs.

Yes.
And also about Aunt Pauline.
Yes.
Can you sing at your work.
Yes.
In the meantime listen to Miss Cheatham.
In the midst of writing.
In the midst of writing there is merriment.

In the midst of Gertrude Stein's writing there is merriment or not, depending on the piece or the part. She is in that awkward but intriguing position of having proven both Epicurus and Zeno right. No mean feat. She can ride the currents of indeterminacy like a wonderful, mad balloonist, ornamenting an unsuspecting terminus, an otherwise ordinary field, with her colorful and regenerative improbability. She can also remain securely tethered, refusing to budge, grimly over-determined. Large enough to accommodate more opposition than most of us could bear, she is a formidable ancestor of much issue.

We are haunted by an odd bunch—Epicurus, the great paradoxical Buddha, even Pound—when we come upon John Cage's "nutshell" philosophy in *For the Birds:* "Get out of whatever cage you find yourself in." On the periphery lurk specters of prominent cage manufacturers—Western Rationalists and Academicians in whose shadow Epicurus would have entirely disappeared were it not for his reputation as a gourmet. It is the collision of currents East and West that makes Cage what he is, but though he became a student and practitioner of Eastern philosophy, he always remained with us, the quintessential American—pragmatist and experimentalist, not unlike one of his chief mentors, Buckminster Fuller. The following exchange between Daniel Charles (French philosopher and musician) and Cage in *For the Birds* tells a good deal of the story:

D.C.: What you just said about your last *Thunderclap* [composition by Cage] reminds me of McLuhan and his ideas on an electronic environment. But how has Fuller inspired you?

J.C.: But Fuller talks about that too. I remember the years 1949 and 1950 when I met him at Black Mountain. One day he told us that the wind around the earth always went from west to east. There were people who went with the wind, others against the wind. Those who went with the wind went to the East and developed the Eastern type of thought; those who went against the wind went to Europe and developed European philosophy. And he suggested that the two tendencies met in the United States, and that their meeting produced a movement upward, into the air.

D.C.: What is this movement into the air? Spiritual ascension?

J.C.: No, the invention of the airplane!

Cage, of course, has worked with another kind of aerodynamics—the movement of sound through the air to the ear. His methods for choosing (or not choosing) and launching these sounds have again combined East and West: East providing a philosophy of Indeterminacy as well as a *modus operandi*, the Chinese "Book of Changes," *I Ching*; West providing the active technological model. American experimental pragmatism (Cage's father was an inventor) and the sort of sunny disposition we identify with California have generated the humor to bring these qualities together in happy synergy. But the kind of optimism inherent in trusting to chance as one's primary guide in certain personal and most significant aesthetic matters could probably only have been nourished by Eastern philosophy. It involves a profound belief in the unity and value of all things, a kind of wholesomeness that ecologists exhort us to develop before it is too late. Though it largely characterized the world view of the early Greeks (who also began the process of breaking it down), it is no longer indigenous to the West.

What is indigenous is the logic of the laboratory: the idea of isolating the subject as a necessary purification in the search for truth, and belief in law. Jung, in his introduction to the Bollingen *I Ching*, comments on this:

> . . . we know now that what we term natural laws are merely statistical truths and thus must necessarily allow for exceptions. We have not sufficiently taken into account as yet that we need the laboratory with its incisive restrictions in order to demonstrate the invariable valid-

ity of natural law. If we leave things to nature, we see a very different picture: every process is partially or totally interfered with by chance, so much so that under normal circumstances a course of events absolutely conforming to specific laws is almost an exception.

Hence Cage, who wishes to imitate Nature not in her appearance, but in her manner of operation, employs the chance operations of the *I Ching* for the process of his art. Chance methods, he feels, enable us to explore the abundance outside our laboratories and logical structures (read "strictures"); to move our music, for example, beyond classical constraints inherent in harmonic arrangements of "pure" sound. They draw us out of intolerance and isolation, not into chaos, but into collaboration with Nature's processes. Cage's wish is to free our attention from habits of narrow focus, to turn it away from the static precedence of the art object toward the world with its inimitable, unimaginable, rich flux of sound, toward joyous appreciation of events around us. Cage, his own best exemplar, says he has never heard a sound he didn't like.

Daniel Charles, the persistent interviewer in *For the Birds,* worries that this attitude may be fostering yet another restrictive habit—that of adaptation:

D.C.: Then art as you define it is a discipline of adaptation to the real as it is. It doesn't propose to change the world, it accepts it as it presents itself. By dint of breaking our habits, it habituates us more effectively.

J.C.: I don't think so. There is one term of the problem which you are not taking into account: precisely, the world. The real. You say: the real, the world as it is. But it is not, it becomes! It moves, it changes! It doesn't wait for us to change. . . . It is more mobile than you can imagine. You are getting closer to this reality when you say as it "presents itself"; that means that it is not there, existing as an object. The world, the real is not an object. It is a process.

D.C.: There can be no custom or habit in a world in the process of becoming. . . . Is that your idea?

J.C.: Yes, it is an idea of changing, like all my music, which could be defined as a *Music of Changes*. And I found that title in the *Book of Changes*, the *I Ching*.

D.C.: I cannot help but believe that *logos*, logic, has only the slightest hold on this world as you define it.

J.C.: It's simply that I am not a philosopher . . . at least not a Greek one! Before, we wished for logical experiences; nothing was more important to us than stability. Today, we admit instability alongside stability. What we hope for is the experience of that which is. But 'what is' is not necessarily the stable, the immutable. We do know quite clearly, in any case, that it is we who bring logic into the picture. It is not laid out before us waiting for us to discover it. 'What is' does not depend on us, we depend on it. And we have to draw nearer to it. And unfortunately for logic, everything we understand under the rubric 'logic' represents such a simplification with regard to the event and what really happens, that we must learn to keep away from it. The function of art at the present time is to preserve us from all the logical minimizations that we are at each instant tempted to apply to the flux of events. To draw us nearer to the process which is the world we live in. (80-81)

Those familiar with Cage's distinctive voice will frequently miss it in *For the Birds*. The book is a reconstructed transcript (and a translation of a translation) from a series of interviews conducted by the knowledgeable and perceptive Daniel Charles in Paris in the late Sixties. Some of the original tapes were damaged or lost or accidentally erased; others were not entirely audible. The meticulous and repeated editing of the final manuscript (by both Charles and Cage) necessitated by these mishaps leaves us with an unprecedentedly logical unfolding of Cage's theoretical frame of reference, intricacies of technique, etc. Logic emerging out of accidental and contingent events did not offend Cage, who is, above all, not dogmatic. The result is an indispensable introduction and/or companion to the many books in which Cage demonstrates, but does not explicate, his Indeterminist approaches.

The work which appears in *Themes and Variations* came, according to Cage, "out of a need for poetry." This is bound to be an interesting need in one who says, "There is poetry as soon as we realize that we possess nothing" and "I hope to let words exist, as I have tried to let sounds exist." *(For the Birds)* As with most fundamentally simple things, the complications are enormous, because we must get around heaps of cultural paraphernalia. Marjorie Perloff says "what is really 'easy,' in the context of the present, is to write little epiphany poems in free verse, detailing a 'meaningful experience.' " This creates an artifact, poem as object, remnant of a process called "writing poetry." It is not, if it conforms to the criterion of easy access, in process itself. It is finished, fixed, mimetic, mirror image of things jelled in our habits of thought and perception. The reader is pampered, protected from uncertainties, unpredictabilities—the untidiness (the unHeidiness) and excitement of process. Like most of ordinary language, this poetry is designed to smooth out irregularities, to move us from one word to the next with a minimum of resistance.

We may thus be fooled into taking the continuity of syntax for ontological necessity. Cage warns us, "We forget that we must always return to zero in order to pass from one word to the next." There is no ontological glue between words. There is no ontological glue connecting certain words with certain ideas or feelings. Process is Indeterminacy is process:

> We would not have language if we were not in process. But I don't believe normal language can *provide* us with that process. That's why I insist on the necessity of not letting ourselves be dragged along by language. Words impose feelings on us if we consider them as objects, that is, if we don't let them, too, be what they are: process.

> *(For the Birds,* 151)

Themes & Variations combines "mesostics" (a variation of acrostics) with a traditional Japanese form called Renga. The mesostics are built around capitalized letters which run down the middle of the poems spelling fifteen names of men who have been influential in Cage's life and work. Words and phrases in the poems have been chosen by means of an intricate series of chance operation from a list of 110 ideas culled from five of Cage's previously published books. He developed the procedure "to find a way of writing which though coming from ideas is not about them; or is not about ideas but produces them." Here is a sample:

we coMe
to the sAnd

no Regrets

we Know
enTertainment
Or not
and Backwards
thE stones

ImpermanentlY

(42)

What Cage has to say about Japanese poetics in his Introduction is surprising. It turns out that haiku has a much greater element of indeterminacy built into it than we are led to believe from translations:

> A haiku in Japanese has no fixed meaning. Its words are not defined syntactically. Each is either noun, verb, adjective, or adverb. A group of Japanese of an evening can therefore entertain themselves by discovering new meanings for old haikus.

A literal translation of a Bashō haiku would go like this:

pine mushroom
ignorance   leaf of tree
adhesiveness

This group of words is left syntactically, and therefore semantically, free to stimulate a meditative or imaginative response in the reader as collaborator. Writing and reading, though two very different kinds of processes, become part of an active whole. The

499

free-floating condition of the words in the Bashō poem brings to mind a quotation, with a distinctly European point of view, that opens Roland Barthes' *The Poetics of Indeterminacy*:

> . . . modern poetry, that which stems not from Baudelaire but from Rimbaud. . . . destroyed relationships in language and reduced discourse to words as static things. . . . In it, Nature becomes a fragmented space, made of objects solitary and terrible, because the links between them are only potential. . . .

For the optimistic Oriental and for Cage, the response is not terror, but delight, and the words are dynamic in the potential of the negative space that surrounds them.

Cage goes on to explain Renga:

> Traditionally renga is written by a group of poets finding themselves of an evening together and having nothing better to do. Successive lines are written by different poets. Each poet tries to make his line as distant in possible meanings from the preceding line as he can take it. This is no doubt an attempt to open the minds of the poets and listeners or readers to other relationships than those ordinarily perceived. . . . Thus an intentionally irrational poem can be written with liberating effect. This is what is called purposeful purposelessness.

That old Buddhist swerve, and what Cage is referring to when he says, "Poetry is having nothing to say and saying it; we possess nothing."

Empty words. Empty words brimming with power to elicit active collaboration. That evocation from empty to full is desire in language, what we desire of language. Aristotle in one of many wise moments said happiness is activity of soul in accordance with its special capabilities. For "soul" we would today substitute "nature" as in human nature. If we take this to be a peculiar union of the sensual and intellectual, and language (that sensual/intellectual pièce de résistance) to be our special capability, then nothing should make us happier than the process of filling empty words with the process of filling empty words with the process . . . though not all empty words stimulate this process. The difference between those that do and those that don't is the great perennial question of poetics. But one thing is certain, immediately accessible "finished" texts which leave us in a state of unadulterated passivity won't do. Cage's poetic texts, "Empty Words" and "Mureau," are both in process, evocative of process. What about *Themes & Variations*?

nEed
betteR
to be wIthout

quicK
  Sound of children

A
waTer

superfIcial
aspEcts

fixEs itself

boRedom
or I
worK

Stones
And
unemploymenT

from heIght
rEgrets

What follows could be called "Notes from an Experimental Reader." They are based on a running record of my approaches to, and engagements with, the text of *Themes & Variations:*

(1) This is schematic, cool (Cage would say "empty") poetry that is formally engaging and open, so different from Stein's impacted abstractions which close the reader out. *Themes & Variations* is an

inviting book. It is "cool" in the sense Marshall McLuhan described in *Understanding Media*:

> . . . a cool medium [is] of low definition, because so little
> is given and so much has to be filled in. . . . On the other
> hand, hot media do not leave so much to be filled in or
> completed by the audience. Hot media are, therefore,
> low in particiation, and cool media are high in participation or completion by the audience.

> . . . the hot form excludes, and the cool one
> includes. . . .

> We . . . find the *avant garde* in the cool and the
> primitive, with its promise of depth involvement and
> integral expression.

(2) Looking at the graphic surface of the text, thinking of how to approach it, brings to mind Wittgenstein on "language games." *Themes & Variations* is clearly a text where familiar rules for reading won't work.

> Doesn't the analogy between language and games throw
> light here? We can easily imagine people amusing themselves in a field by playing with a ball so as to start
> various existing games, but playing many without finishing them and in between throwing the ball aimlessly into
> the air, chasing one another with the ball and bombarding one another for a joke and so on. And now someone
> says: The whole time they are playing a ball-game and
> following definite rules at every throw.
> And is there not also the case where we play and—
> make up the rules as we go along? And there is even one
> where we alter them—as we go along.

> *(Philosophical Investigations*, 83)

(3) The rules which generated the text of the mesostics did not dictate a finished game anymore than the rules of Renga do. In both cases, the writing procedure ensures an open field for the

reader who can in turn make up and alter her rules as she goes, all the while staying within the domain, the playing field, of the text.

(4) Turning the pages, I begin by looking for the names as in a "Find the ———" puzzle, as families and friends do at the Vietnam Name Memorial. Names *are* memorials—for the quick, the slow, and the dead.

(5) But these names on a vertical axis are somehow insubstantial. They are certainly not comfortably sedentary or complacent like the horizontally "Reclining Name." This is more like "Name Descending the Staircase" after MARCEL DUCHAMP (one of those honored in *Themes & Variations*). Or is it "Name Falling Down Stairs"? Or names suspended mid-Fall like Icarus in Breughel, like Icarus in Auden and Williams. Or perhaps these are linguistic atoms (letters) stuck in moments of collision.

(6) In Cage's poems these falling (but not fallen) names are just that—letters colliding with other letters, forming word structures along the way. There is both surprise and order.

(7) And humor and mnemonic resonance: names, flagrantly dangling their letters, bond with words in ragged columns that resemble the (flattened) helical structure of DNA. (In linguistics, they speak of "transformational strings.")

(8) Vertebral letters: stalk of central nervous system shoots off most regenerate of neural impulses, words. Trunk shoots off branches and twigs toward other electrobiological exchanges. Or, aerial view: narrow stream of names fed by tributary words.

(9) This could (maybe does) begin to look like *Snow White and Seven Types of Ambiguity*. Making connections is important. It's what the human brain is designed to do. But Fairy Tales and free associations take you where you've been before.

(10) Reading from left to right, there is no semantic tension between horizontal and vertical axes. Is there formal tension? Capitalized letters act as interference. Tendency is to stress them, silently or aloud. Feels/sounds like a stutter. Stutter, like foreign accent, heightens awareness of phonemic components of words.

(11) Becoming more accustomed to capitals. They are smoothing down, rounding off into pleasant lumps, like beads, something for fondling, relaxing one's attention. Is this the experience of the rosary (or sucking stones)—freeing the mind to operate on an intuitive plane?

12) But then, intermittently, the awkwardness returns—uppity,

upper case letters like grains of sand in oysters—formative irritations. Mellowing again, overhead view again, they become small ripples in flowing water—surface tension.

(13) I have discovered that I particularly like upper case Os and Zs: hOw, nOw, hOrn, wOrd, Organ, dOors. RevOlution and harmOny are one-word blue songs. Then there's bliZzard, wiZard, gaZing. . . . Os and Zs should probably always be in upper case. Also, there is the pleasant realization (sensual, not intellectual) of the role of the conciliatory H, how it softens the t in patH.

(14) False etymology game: taking parts of words beginning with capital letters as original concepts embedded in them—Egrets in rEgrets, Ravings in engRavings, Hots in sHots, Ape in tApe, Sic in muSic, Ion in salvatIon, Ted in unexpecTed . . . words in words—telescoping words.

(15) Before I read *Themes & Variations*, egrets were in regrets and ravings were in engravings. After I read *Themes & Variations* Egrets were in rEgrets and Ravings were in engRavings.

(16) Meanwhile, there is always the peripheral sense of names flowing by: "Sweet names run softly, till I end my song." No; one is not always conscious of their presence *as* names. They submerge and re-emerge quietly like dolphins, dolphins and river swimming together downstream, toward the sea. Not an end point; an opening out.

(17) Discovery that the last word in *Themes & Variations* is "river." I trust that this may have been coincidence—tribute (tributary) to a connectedness of things that needn't be forced, *bonne chance*.

(18) There are piquant juxtapositions, pleasantly recurrent words and phrases, but mostly the sense of gentle unfolding. The experience of reading Cage is similar to a summer's picnic by the edge of a stream: leaning back against a tree, letting the rhythms of events intermingle with one's own associative rhythms; every now and then being stirred into acute focus by a bird's song, a twig snapping, wind in the leaves, a fragment of a conversation taking place nearby. You go home rested and refreshed. What could it mean, to go home to Language rested and refreshed?

(19) Interesting question. Questions counter the centripetal force of association by moving you away from self, toward the appealingly gratuitous otherness of the unknown. Excitement of exploration. Not knowing what you will find. The experimental attitude: "That's it: research. I call that 'experimental' music: the kind where

you do research . . . but without knowing what the result will be," says Cage in *For the Birds*. ReSearch, QuestIon: Re Search Quest Ion. . . .

(20) Research question: where can language take us? If we know that we know only too little, and wish to explore, then we are onto indeterminate adventures: schemes and variations, swerves and collisions. . . .

🔥 🔥 🔥

COPIES

fiction by MARY MORRIS

from THE AGNI REVIEW

nominated by THE AGNI REVIEW, *Richard Burgin and Daniel Menaker*

Beverly stands at the model 2200, wondering why Doug hasn't looked at her all day. Doug, the man Beverly has been dating for the past six weeks, is busy at the color xerox. He is her third boyfriend this year. That is one less boyfriend than last year but it is still more than she wants.

Beverly always meets her boyfriends on the job. She met Andy, the one before Doug, at the Actor's Hotline where they sat side by side, answering the phone for other people who were getting jobs. One day Beverly answered a call and handed the phone to Andy. "It's for you," she said. It was a producer he'd met at a party a long time ago who had found just the right part for him and he moved to L.A. in a matter of days. A week after he moved he sent her a postcard of the hills of Hollywood, saying he knew she'd get there sometime.

Beverly met Doug after working at the copy center for a few hours. He is a tall, skinny Columbia dropout who is "trying to find himself" and who sits at the edge of her bed at night, playing the guitar while she sleeps. Beverly learned to sleep through anything when she was a little girl and lived with her parents in a little split-level just beyond the northeast approach runway at LaGuardia. Her father wasn't a pilot but a sales representative for a shoe company and she hardly ever saw him.

Beverly hates the 2200 because there is nothing to do but watch and make certain it doesn't break down. The 2200 can print a hundred pages a minute. When it breaks down, it is a disaster. The Ektaprint is much better than the 2200 but Doug always works on the Ektaprint. Her favorite machine is the binder. She likes the way the frayed edges of paper fall like confetti into the little pouch at the back of the machine. Beverly collects this confetti. She plans to give a party when she leaves the copy center and toss these bits of paper into the air.

It is a Monday morning and there is already a long line of customers with numbers in their hands, waving them at the people who work behind the pale oak counter that separates customer from employee. They wave their tickets as if they were seeing people off who are about to depart on a long cruise. The copy center is done in California-style oak paneling with neatly painted signs that read "Express Pick-Up" or "Take a Number, Please." When Beverly came to work here six months ago, she thought it must be a very orderly place but it isn't very orderly at all.

A nervous homosexual has already been in to complain about the quality of the copies on his last teleplay. Every Monday he comes in to have something copied. He always refuses to drop it off and sometimes he will wait an hour. Usually he wants thirty copies of everything, done by hand, collated, bound, with a two-tone cover. He is a tedious client and Doug does his jobs. But it is Robert, the store manager, who listens to the complaints.

Andrea, Beverly's friend and assistant manager of the store, is crazy about Robert but Beverly doesn't see why. Robert is a pale, skinny man with stringy brown hair and jagged buck teeth. He is one hundred percent Italian and Andrea, who studied Italian literature for a term at Pomona College, thinks he is passionate. But Beverly finds him dull and self-absorbed; she thinks the only time Robert ever seems to react to anything is when Mrs. Grimsely comes into the store.

Mrs. Grimsley is an old Irish lady who always thinks other people are butting in line in front of her. She thinks that somehow people can slip a number in between hers and the one they are currently attending to. Mrs. Grimsley writes novels. She once brought in a copy of a novel that survived Hurricane Agnes. The novel was water-stained, the ink was smeared. It was virtually illegible. She told Robert she wanted it copied so that it would become legible.

Robert always gets a headache when he sees Mrs. Grimsley because Mrs. Grimsley wants the impossible. She wants things made bigger so she can read them with her failing eyesight but Robert has explained to her many times that he can't make a page bigger. Mrs. Grimsley doesn't understand. She wants things darker than they are in reality. She wants fingerprint smudges, waterstains, ink blotches, removed from the page. She wants her copies to come out perfect.

Mrs. Grimsley had a son who looked just like Robert who was killed in one of the wars before Robert was born. Once she brought in a picture of her son and everyone agreed that Robert did look like him. Mrs. Grimsley thinks Robert is her son. She wants the impossible.

When Robert sees her come in, he shudders. He does not get along well with his own mother so the thought of having Mrs. Grimsley as his mother irks him more. He has tried to explain to Mrs. Grimsley that he is not her son but she won't take no for an answer. "Around the eyes," she says. "And the hair. Just like my Billy." Andrea tries to wait on Mrs. Grimsley this morning but she will hear nothing of it. "I want Billy," she shrieks. "I want my Billy."

This particular Monday has been terrible. The 2200 broke down twice and the repairman had to be called. It seems that every application to everything in the world is due by October 15 and everyone wants his or her copies made on 25% rag. Beverly can barely stand toward the end of the day and all she wants to do is to go to bed with Doug. But Doug tells her he is going down to the Village to jam with some friends. Beverly is disappointed but she doesn't say anything. "O.K., so maybe tomorrow." Doug smiles. "Maybe tomorrow." Beverly suspects Doug has another woman but she doesn't say anything.

Steven can't take his eyes off Beverly as she tries to yank paper out of the 2200. Unlike Doug, Steven will never lose interest in her. He doesn't know what Beverly sees in Doug, but he knows Doug has lost interest in her.

Steven thinks he is becoming sterile from the photocopying equipment. He is always careful not to get exposed to the light. Steven reads most of the information he copies and a few months ago he copied a report from the Journal of the AMA which suspects sterility from fluorescent lights. Once every few days Steven talks about going off to a sperm bank and putting some seeds on ice. "These machines are ruining us," Steven says in the middle of a busy Monday morning. "Aren't you people concerned?"

No one is terribly concerned. Steven wouldn't be so concerned either if he didn't want to have children with Beverly. He has been in love with her since she walked into the store. He is short and Jewish and he always falls for tall, blond women who are not going to be interested in him.

As they are leaving, Steven asks Beverly if she wants to get a bite at Bagel Nosh. It is just around the corner and Beverly has nothing better to do so she says, "Why not." She wanted to go home and take a shower. Instead she goes to Bagel Nosh. She hopes Steven will not talk about the sperm bank over dinner. She gets an onion bagel with chicken liver and he gets a sesame bagel with lox.

Steven feels he is duty bound to level with Beverly. "Well, you know, Doug likes women, I guess. Lots of women, I mean. I'm looking for something a little more secure." Beverly knows this. Steven is the kind of man who would be looking for something more secure. Things don't come to him easily and he isn't likely to get what he wants out of life.

As they are about to leave Bagel Nosh, Robert walks in with Andrea. They were doing the books and decided to get a bite. Andrea stares at Robert wide-eyed as if she were a fish he just caught on a line. Robert smiles brightly at Beverly and she can tell that Andrea is jealous. Andrea thinks Robert likes Beverly. It would make sense. Everyone else does, except Doug. Beverly looks at Andrea in the Bagel Nosh reflecting glass. She is a rather dumpy brunette with frizzy brown hair. Andrea is the kind of woman most men would like to marry; they just don't want to date her.

Robert and Andrea sit down and Steven is disappointed. He wanted to go to Beverly's and drink wine. He wanted to tell her about his deprived childhood in Buffalo. Steven thinks he is a marvelous storyteller and that he can charm her with his yarns. Then he wants to get her into bed. Once he is able to convince a woman to go to bed with him, she usually has no regrets. Robert and Andrea order bagels and coffee.

Robert says, "Boy, this is copy center night, huh. We just ran into Doug going uptown."

Beverly takes this in carefully as Andrea nudges Robert. "Uptown?"

Andrea says, "Oh, we didn't know which way he was going." Andrea, who helped Beverly get her the job, has watched Doug go through many women at the copy center. Every time a new woman comes in, Doug, who has wonderful grey-green eyes and thick black hair, gets interested. But then, after a month or so, he will lose interest and usually the girl will have a broken heart.

Andrea has thought about firing Doug several times, but he is the fastest copier she has ever seen. Doug can keep three machines going at the same time and be hand-feeding another machine as well. Because the copy center is the busiest one in the neighborhood, Andrea can't really afford to fire him. She has tried to hint to Beverly that Doug has lost interest in her. Andrea knows the signs because Doug lost interest in her once a few years ago.

Robert is somewhat oblivious. "No, he said he was meeting a friend at Empire Szechuan, don't you remember?"

Andrea doesn't know what else to say. "Yes, I remember."

Robert is the only one who doesn't know exactly what is going on in his store. He doesn't know, for example, that every chance she gets, Andrea tries to work beside him. He has no idea that the reason why Andrea, who once had ambitions of going to law school, has stayed at the copy center for the past three years, is because she is hoping someday Robert will pay attention to her.

After a few minutes, Beverly gets up. "I'm going home." Steven gets up to go with her but Beverly waves him down and away, as if she were the trainer of an animal act.

As Beverly climbs the stairs to her apartment, she hears the phone ringing. She counts almost fifteen rings but she is not in a hurry to get the call. If it is not her mother, it is Doug. If it is Doug, she is not sure she wants to talk to him. When Beverly gets inside, she is glad to be alone. She is especially glad because her apartment is so quiet and the copy center is so noisy.

Beverly calls her service and tries not to be upset when she learns no one has phoned her for auditions. Like everyone in the copy center, she wants to be doing something else. In high school she was named "Most Likely to Appear on Saturday Night Live." Once a month she has new pictures of herself made up with new resumes and she mails them to all the agents in New York. Andrea thinks there is no other actress in the city with that much determination. Because she is very beautiful, sometimes Beverly gets calls, but she never gets a part.

The phone rings again and Beverly answers on the fifth ring. Doug sounds anxious on the other end. "Where've you been? We

510

finished jamming a while ago. The tenor sax never showed. Can I come up?"

Beverly wants to say no, but she says all right. She wants to say no because the truth is that she want to be alone. She wants to read a book and wash her hair. She wants to watch *Family Feud* and call her mother. She wants to tell her mother she hasn't made it big yet and that she'd like to come home for Christmas but she can't afford it. Beverly's mother lives in a retirement village in Arizona; she always asks Beverly to visit but never sends her the money for a ticket.

There are a dozen things she wants to do but when Doug calls, she tells him to come on up. Beverly has always had a hard time saying no to men and she has spent too many nights with men she didn't want to be with. Doug arrives out of breath. He always runs up her steps, two steps at a time. She wonders why he does this since he is never all that happy to see her. Doug is seeing another woman as Beverly suspects. He was going to see her tonight but her husband called off his meeting so she had to be home.

Beverly kisses Doug perfunctorily on the cheek when he walks in. She wonders why she always falls for men who never pay much attention to her. Beverly's father died when she was fourteen and she's never felt so betrayed before or since. She knows Doug likes to be with more than one woman at a time. He has told her he has no desire to settle down. Doug's mother has been married three times and as far as Doug can tell, the new men were never improvements over the old ones.

After they make love, Beverly falls asleep and Doug strums his guitar. First he tunes it, then he plays "I Write the Songs That Make the Whole World Sing." In the middle of his tune, Beverly shoots out of bed. "Oh, my god," she cries.

Doug grabs her hand. "What was it?"

"Another DC 10." Since she was a little girl, growing up near LaGuardia, Beverly's dreams have been filled with airplanes crashing into her sheets. She can be in the middle of a dream about Yosemite, a place she visited with another boyfriend she met when she did mailings for the Sierra Club, and suddenly an airplane will crash into her sheets. Beverly always wakes up when there is a crash but otherwise she can sleep through anything.

He pulls the covers up over her chin. "You were just dreaming," he tells her. "Go back to sleep."

511

There are steady customers at the copy center and Beverly knows them all. She knows Mrs. Grimsley and she knows the homosexual playwright. She knows the Jehovah's witness, who sends prayers to his brother on Riker's Island, and the impatient woman who puts down her American Express gold card. She knows the music school teachers with dandruff on their collars, the desperate unemployed with their tattered resumes. And she knows a woman named Emily who has been coming to the copy center since she began working there.

Everyone who works at the copy center is jealous of at least one person who brings in work and stands at the other side of the oak counter. Robert is jealous of a graphic designer who does a lot of annual reports. Robert wants to have his own graphic design business some day. Doug is jealous of a musician who is always having his scores printed and bound for his publisher. Steven is jealous of a medical doctor and Andrea is jealous of a social worker. Beverly is jealous of Emily.

Emily comes in often. She has soft, doe-like eyes, and she cannot speak without smiling. She never comes up and says, "I'm 90. Why are you taking 91?" She always says, "Excuse me. Did you call 90?" Beverly knows Emily is happy and successful. Emily comes into the copy center calmly with the music for her newest concert to be run off. She has blurbs xeroxed in which Diana Ross says, "I'd be honored to sing any of Ms. Barkington's songs."

Beverly doesn't suspect that Emily curses the day she had her baby, that her work brings her no pleasure and she is married to a record producer for his money. She has no idea that Emily takes tranquilizers before going out and she has no idea that Emily is one of Doug's lovers. This isn't some strange coincidence. Emily and Doug worked together on a musical production in the Village two years ago and he's been her lover on and off ever since.

It is because of Emily that Beverly has decided to leave the copy center, give up her acting ambitions and go to school in public health. Beverly bought a copy of *Are You Really Creative?* and took the quiz in the book. Would you rather a) fix a clock, b) fly a plane, c) sit in a wild bird sanctuary? On New Year's Eve would you rather be a) the life of the party, b) the person who gives the party, c) the person who stays home from the party and reads a book?

Beverly has no idea how to answer these questions so she

answers at random. Then she adds up her score and learns that "You are too ambivalent about creativity but would work well with people. Why not try a helping profession?" Since she decided to go back to school in public health, her dreams of planes are increasing, only now she dreams of bombers, B-52s to be specific.

When Emily comes into the copy center in the afternoon, the mood is very tense. Mrs. Grimsley came in a little while ago. She wanted to make a hundred copies of a telegram from 1951 that read, "Dear Mr. and Mrs. Grimsley, We regret to inform you that your son, William, has been killed in action . . ." Mrs. Grimsley told Robert, whom she called Billy, that they were invitations to a party and she gave a copy to him. Even Robert who normally isn't shaken by anything was shaken by Mrs. Grimsley.

Beverly is a little upset when Emily walks in, and she calls out her number rather impatiently. "Forty-seven," Beverly snaps and Emily tells her she'd like to wait for Doug. Emily knows that Beverly and Doug are lovers, but Beverly has no suspicions at all. She does not even suspect when Emily hands Doug a note and Doug smiles. She thinks Doug is supposed to make a copy of the note.

That evening Doug tells Beverly he is going to jam downtown again and he'll be late so why don't they see one another the next night. She knows he is going to meet someone else, but she has no idea it is Emily. Doug and Emily could be drug dealers, they are so discrete. Beverly is disturbed but doesn't say a word. As she is leaving the store, Steven asks if she'd like to go to dinner with him uptown. Since she has no other plans, she agrees.

They go to a burger place near West 90th and Steven orders a bacon cheeseburger. Beverly orders the same thing because she can't make a decision. Even before their cokes arrive, Steven grabs Beverly's hand. "Listen," he says, "Doug Cransfield isn't worth this joint on your little finger." He extracts the joint from the mass of fingers he is holding. She pulls her hand away.

"It doesn't matter," she says. "I'm not looking for anything serious."

"Well, I am," Steven says boldly. "I'd like to see you more often."

"I already see you about eight hours a day." Beverly yawns and Steven frowns. "I just don't want to date much these days." She pats his hand gently. Steven and Beverly finish their burgers and walk downtown.

As they pass the 86th Street subway, they see Doug and Emily, coming out of the station. There is an odd moment of recognition as Beverly thinks to herself, "There's Doug with that woman." And Doug thinks he should do something but he doesn't know what. He smiles at Beverly and it is a strange mix of guilt and affection and confusion behind his smile. Beverly thinks he looks boyish, smiling at her, with Emily holding his arm.

Doug says, "Hello," and then Beverly says, "Hello." And not knowing what else to say, Doug says, "See you tomorrow."

Because she is somewhat disoriented, Beverly does something she would not ordinarily do. She asks Steven to come over. When they get to her apartment, a place Steven has wanted to get to for a long time, he praises her choice of furniture. He praises the posters that hang over her bed. He praises the cat, he praises a rather wilting lotus plant. Finally Beverly says, "Steven, let's face it. This place is a dump."

Beverly feeds the cat, named Walter, a can of Purina sardines, which he sniffs. Then he walks away. She dumps a glass of water on the plant. Then she puts on Keith Jarrett's Koln Concert and rolls a joint.

Steven is sure he will spend the night and he hardly knows what to do, he is so overjoyed. "I told you baby, that guy wasn't worth your tiny toenail."

Beverly doesn't want to think about Doug at all. She gets stoned and instead of thinking about Doug she thinks about her father. She thinks about how she used to be afraid of the airplanes that passed so closely over their house and so one day her father took her outside. He lay down in the grass and told her he was the runway and she should fly around the yard and come in for landings on his chest. So she spent the day running around their yard, making a buzzing noise, and then crashing into her father's rib cage.

Beverly is thinking about her father when Steven lunges across the candle between them and grabs her by the arm. He puts his thumb print into her muscle. Beverly pulls back, "I'm tired," she says. She gets up, goes into her bedroom, lies down and falls asleep.

Bewildered, Steven follows. He gets into bed with her and caresses her. Beverly wakes up screaming. "Oh, my god, two little private planes in mid-air." Then she looks at Steven, unsure of what he is doing there. "Please leave," she says, and Steven, because he has almost no will where she is concerned, gets up and leaves.

The next day when Beverly comes into work, Doug says "Hi" and Beverly says nothing. When Beverly is running off an actor's resume, Doug comes over. "How are you?" He waits but she doesn't reply. "Look, about last night . . ."

Beverly says, "There is nothing to say." And she says nothing.

She knows that Doug can stand anything but the silent treatment. His mother used to give him the silent treatment when he did anything she didn't like and it drove him crazy. Once his mother didn't talk to him for five days and they even ate their meals together. All afternoon Doug follows Beverly around, saying dumb things like, "You think they'd fix the fan in this place," that she won't respond to.

Beverly knows Robert and Andrea are watching her ignore Doug, but she doesn't care. She has decided to leave the copy center and go to school in public health. She can imagine herself working in a center for disease control. She knows Doug is exasperated. He stands next to her while she copies an entire book on how to grow a vegetable garden in a city apartment. "Don't be discouraged," one page reads. "You can grow fine tomato plants right in your window boxes."

Doug points to the line. "Isn't that stupid," he laughs. "You couldn't see out the window then."

Beverly doesn't say a word. Finally Doug says, "All right, so maybe I am a jerk but I'm trying to apologize."

She turns to him. "You are a jerk and I don't want your apology. I don't want to talk to you or see you. Just leave me alone."

When Doug walks away, Steven puts his machine on automatic. "Hey, Bev." He speaks loudly, hoping Doug will hear. "Can I see you tonight?"

She looks at Steven's small, frail body, his dark beard that hides his pock-marked face. He's not so terrible, she thinks, but she just can't stand him. "No," Beverly mumbles. "I've got plans."

515

Steven turns away in a huff and later when Beverly is leaving, he hands her an envelope. "Open this when you get home," he says to her. "It'll explain everything."

Beverly breathes a sigh of relief when she walks into her apartment. She puts a Weight Watchers veal with peppers TV dinner into the oven at 425 with the foil peeled back. She runs a bath. She calls her service and there are no messages. She gives herself a face sauna with honeysuckle herbs. She pours herself a glass of wine and gently eases her way into the bathtub.

Beverly often reads in the tub and so she dries her hands on a towel and opens the envelope Steven gave her as she left work. She opens it slowly, expecting to find a long letter, explaining why she should not care about Doug but about him. Instead what she finds is more to the point. What she finds is a color xerox of a portion of the male anatomy. At the bottom he has written, "You don't know what you're missing, baby."

The next morning Beverly walks into the copy center and screams at Steven. She holds up the color xerox so everyone in the store can see. "What is this? Is this your idea of a joke?"

Andrea is waiting on a customer and she turns around. Doug is making copies at two machines and he is stunned. Steven tries to grab the page out of her hand. "Of course it's a joke. What's your problem?"

Beverly pins the xerox to the bulletin board behind her. The place where she puts the pin makes all the men in the store wince. "This is no joke," Beverly shouts. "You're sick. I should call the police."

Doug smiles. He has never seen Beverly so passionate, so vital. Robert is not smiling. He rips the xerox off the board. "The customers are aware of what is going on," he says to them. "You're all fired if you don't get back to work."

"You should fire him," Beverly shouts. "He is sick."

Steven turns off his machine. "You can't even take a joke. I'll be back later." He slides out beneath the oak counter.

Just then Mrs. Grimsley comes in, checking numbers to make certain no one has butted in front of her. Everyone in the store is upset about Beverly's fight with Steven. Robert is especially upset because he is afraid he will lose business. When Mrs. Grimsley comes in, he decides to humor her. "How's my Billy today?" she says. She is an old woman with dark sunken eyes who probably hasn't long to live.

Robert reaches across the counter. "How'ya doing, Mom?" he pats her hand. "Boy've I missed you."

Mrs. Grimsley looks first stunned, then angry. She pulls her hand away. "Don't you call me that. You have no right. Only my son calls me Mom." And she walks out of the store, never to return.

Beverly also walks out of the store but she returns a few hours later. When she does, she finds a purple geranium, sitting on the 2200. She hopes it is from Doug, but she knows from the handwriting it is from Steven. She opens the card and reads, "Please accept this geranium for your apartment as an apology. I am sorry if I upset you." Beverly feels badly about having shouted at him. Sometimes she thinks, working here isn't so bad.

Because she took time off in the afternoon, Beverly agrees to stay late to finish up a doctoral dissertation. Doug decides to work late with her. It is dark out as they complete their jobs at different machines. They put on the radio and listen to a program of all Sinatra. Sinatra is singing "I Did It My Way."

They turn down the bright fluorescent lights which make them look pale green and now the lighting is amber. Doug works on a screenplay about corruption in the police department. He reads parts of it outloud to Beverly. They agree it sounds like all the police films they've ever seen.

Beverly is making seven copies of a dissertation on the abandonment/castration complex in men and women. As she is completing it, Doug comes up behind her. He puts his hands on her shoulders and kisses the back of her neck. He turns her to him. The green lights of the machines flash on and off. The amber lights are soothing. He takes her in his arms and pins her to the machine as he kisses her. She presses her body against Doug's and remembers what it was that made her like him in the first place. She feels the even, rhythmic pulsing of the 2200 against her spine. She prays it won't break down.

ASILOMARIAN LECTURE (THE DIRMAL LIFE OF THE INHABITATS)

fiction by BETH TASHERY SHANNON

from THE CHICAGO REVIEW

nominated by Gordon Lish

It is Maurine Biology. Upon my gret podium I stand to tell you. It is creats of the see. Voices from the deeep, whose language isnot our very owned, yet not without some lack of unfamiliality.

Squish squin, weave wim, creats of the see ar grack an slwee. The ar clawn an chuff, lorf an lee, the ar danky, dwark an brittetulous. Indee!

Som (as yo have herd) ar old. Som live in waives. Som liver seeweeds bulbous. Some even rockblack taverns far be neath. Hear comes a waive! Coms over, coms glisten. That is with see turkeys. With eyes bigger than their branes. The eat waives. If you ever wander where awaive goes, only see turkey knos. Still it is never far off inn the mind. how these creats of the sees clauster white on the swells. For see turnkeys cause the tides. Tiny, but when the mooon pauses over, the begin to goble. Goble an goble. Waives, floatbulbs, sharks, eveny ocean liners. (Littl do we reality underst and the benufayous snee turkey.) Whin the moonsets, the turkey spits it out.

Squish squim, leave lim, creats of the see ar dlooth within. An when thay wash up, you walk among the beech. Gret bones of strrom bleech by the cutfull face of rock. So tine lucine shellls. Bumbulous dritwood fromm a fishe's tree.

An shoes of the deeep. Upon my gret podium what viscious

518

creats the ar! With thir tongues al! awaggle backword thay go, thir switness among thee fluids! If the didnot look so much like feet shoes, woodnot be so dangeroo. The lie in wait in these unlikely places. Heaps off dritwood. Sandcrab holes. Only com fort is, when you sea shoe of the deeep, it has to be dead.

It is, Because creat shoes of the deeep neeed squids to eat, an drownd peops to breathe. With only air an sandy the ar harmless. We must be thankful.

Lick slosh, glin lost, creats the nights ghoststars tide poools.

Bouys too. Whin you se a bouy, you kno its stomack to catch fishes below. Bouys feeed by telepathy. On the line. Heave himm, whish whim, a bouy calls an yoo go inn! You can not help it. But you cannot help it. You get wet. Upon my gret podium, yooo mayget glinny scallles yoorslef   som daay

TRYING TO NAME WHAT DOESN'T CHANGE

by NAOMI SHIHAB NYE

from DOMESTIC CRUDE

nominated by Amy Clampitt and William Stafford

Roselva says the only thing that doesn't change is
train tracks. She's sure of it.
The train changes, or the weeds that grow up spidery
at the side, but not the track.
I've watched one for three years, she says,
and it doesn't curve, doesn't break, doesn't grow.

Peter isn't convinced.
He saw an abandoned track near Sabinas, Mexico,
and says a track without a train is a changed track.
The metal wasn't shiny anymore.
The wood was split, some of the ties were gone.

Next door butchers crack the necks of a hundred hens.
The widow in the tilted house spices her soup with cinnamon.
Ask her what doesn't change.

Stars explode.
The rose curls up as if there is fire in the petals.
The cat who knew me is buried under the bush.

The train whistle sounds like it used to sound,
only bigger. But when it goes away,
shrinking back from the walls of the brain,
it takes something different with it every time.

COMING OF AGE
ON THE HARLEM

by JOAN MURRAY

from THE HUDSON REVIEW

nominated by Joyce Carol Oates

for Kathy

I

My father would tie a life jacket
to a length of seaworn rope and dangle me
off the dock of The Harlem Boat Club float.
A strange baptism.
Down, down into the mad rushing river,
worm on a hook, a girl of six or seven,
I am let loose among water rats,
made sister to half-filled soda cans
floating vertically home from a picnic,
and to condoms that look like mama doll socks
in the unopened infant eye.
What man would toss his child to that swill?
He who can swim across the river,
whose arms churn a feud with the current.
He thinks he can hold me from any maelstrom.
Safe on the dock, I watch my father
float on his back from the Bronx
to Manhattan and back again.

II

Between the river edge and river park,
the New York Central tracks could fry a child.
How lucky to have this father with
long, strong arms to whisk me over
the wooden hooded, menacing third rail.
Can you remember when you reached your father's waist
and he told you of the serpent track where
only birds could land in safety?
But one day my father takes me home a different way:
up the wooden bridge above the tracks
where huge phallic shapes have been burned in black
along its walls. Don't look. Don't look.
That sight will fry you up like Semele.
Now my strong father, my never ruffled father
pulls me roughly over the wooden planks.
His dark face reddened tells of great,
unspoken danger. When we reach the street,
he makes me promise never to come this way again,
never to go to the river shore without him.
Over my shoulder I form an opposite determination.

III

The Harlem Boat Club is the man place.
My father slips down twice a week to shower,
on weekends plays a sweaty game
of four wall ball. Outside in the garden,
I wander six years old among lilies
of the valley, Queen Anne's lace,
the shoreline irises and great climbing rose
that began as someone's potted plant.
Elmer, the muscular black cat,
drags a water rat to the front door.
I follow inside to the boat room,
run my hand along the lean flanks
of polished rowing sculls,
then up the stairway, pause at the wooden roster,
the names with gold stars dead in some war.
Then the sweat smell of the lockers,

the place where they held a party
to welcome the Beatty brothers home from Korea.
Off to the side, three men stand
naked in the steamy, tiled shower.
Quiet, I sit down on a bench
beside a girl my own age, who has also come
to pretend she doesn't notice.

IV

Still my close, though distant, friend,
who sat with me in the men's locker room,
whose father had a strong right arm for handball,
whose mother and mine embarrassed
in their forties, had pregnancies,
who accompanied me through puberty
up and down the Harlem shore,
Kathy, in your Brahmin home in Brooklyn,
you say you want to rid your sleep
of those dirty years along the river.
But stop for a moment, stop trying
to make the river pass genteelly,
for there'll be no weaning from those waters.
Instead come back with me and watch
the sun glint off the rippling surface,
bearing the shore-hugging flow of turds and
condoms north to the Hudson.
You conjectured it all came from cabin cruisers
on some far-off glory ocean.
Kathy, would you have even looked
if you had known it came from humble tenements
on our Highbridge hill?
Could that one reflection
have darkened all your plans to sail?

V

"Mirror Mirror"
was the name you gave him,
a dexterous man with a pocket mirror
who could catch the Sunday morning sun

524

and flash it on our untouched child bodies.
A fairy tale gone haywire, Rapunzel in reverse:
"Mirror Mirror!"
we shouted from the bridge height,
and he below us in the river park
would hold his instrument to the sky like
a sextant and calculate his grotesque angles.
Then we'd race down the ramp
just beyond his unknown reach and dive
behind the safety of a tree.
Oh God! Oh God! the heavy breathing,
ours, his, the fear, the vague desire
that was always escaped in time to
run home at one for Sunday dinner and meet our
unsuspecting fathers coming home from mass.

VI

Just before ten, just before your father's curfew,
you can station yourself on the highway bridge,
where it joins the ramp from the river park,
to see the couples rise up on the evening tide:
the sooty venuses with dirty hand marks
on white and fondled blouses, and
their boyfriends swaggering in teenage jeans.
You laugh, and send your first awakening lust
to follow them back to the neighborhood
where someday all will notice that you've grown.
And small children will stand on bridges
to flank your path
as you make your debut entry
to the nightly river park cotillion, on the arm
of some lanky boy with a dangling black curl,
and the cleanest, oh the cleanest hands.

VII

It's the boys with sprouts of pubic hair
who have the manliness to strip and jump
while tourists on the Circle Line around
Manhattan watch with Brownie cameras.

Bright faced fathers and mothers, pointing out
the river life to their wondering children.
They look for street kids in straw hats,
the Tom Sawyers and Huck Finns of the Harlem
but only get an upraised finger.
Behind the nude boys who perch on river rocks
and invite the sun to their members,
a ring of girls, in tight black shorts and
pony tails, keep a coy but glancing distance.
And behind them all, a white-haired voyeur
drops his pants to masturbate.
The eyes of the Circle Line sail up river, still
hopeful that Becky Thatcher in eyelet bloomers
will wave a hanky from the shore.

VIII

In Undercliff Park, below Washington Bridge,
I play stretch and toe-knee-chest-nut with
my father's pocketed army knife.
A dangerous age. Threats are cutting through the air:
the flailing depantsings, the groping bra quests for
a wad of cotton or a nylon stocking.
A dangerous age, with the deadly fear
of being found a child.
To relieve it one day, we hang a tire in a tree and
swing in packs out over the cliff edge, until
the boy beside me loses grip and lies below,
as quiet as an infant in a lullabye.
Weeks later, we visit him at home, sign his casts
and giggle at his immature pajamas.
He lifts his mattress to show
an arsenal of thirty knives and ice picks,
and lets each girl pick a pocket lighter
shoplifted from Woolworth's.

IX

Hung by my hands above water,
I am dangled by boys from the ledge
of the Washington Bridge abutment.

Twelve years old, twelve feet from the surface,
I do not trust boys, but love their giddy danger
like a windflaw teasing with a sail.
And while we dangle, the boys hurl rocks
at the river, waiting for the splash that will leap
up to our blouses and clutch the outlines
of our forming breasts.
Soaked through, we climb the naked limbs
of a shore tree and sprawl in the afternoon sun.
Above a boy hovers in the branches,
reaches for my hand a moment and is gone,
leaving something growing in me
that holds me separate from my friends
as we walk together to our fathers' houses,
wearing our secret scent of the river.

X

My husband no more swims b.a.
I can no longer picture his shadow
rippling across the sidewalks to the Harlem.
A swaggering, older boy, once unattainable.
Now at night I cradle his black hair
to my breast and we share the river's secrets:
My splashing joyride pick-up
with three strange boys in a motor boat.
His first hesitating touch of Dodie, the hillbilly
girl on the fourteen steps below Macombs Dam Bridge.
The tales of all those years I was not permitted
at The Harlem, unless my father stood beside me,
gathering me into his safe garden.
All those years I learned the route to avoid his path.
Now I retrace it in the dark, step by step, till
again I watch The Harlem Boat Club burn,
and see the steps plucked from the river bridge
where no child can again take the path
that leads me nightly to this good bed.
Kathy, did we escape our fathers?
Or did they plan our turns and detours
just carefully enough to lead us here?

PHYSICAL UNIVERSE

by LOUIS SIMPSON

from THE HUDSON REVIEW and BOA EDITIONS

nominated by Jane Kenyon, Patricia Dobler and Philip Schultz

He woke at five and, unable
to go back to sleep,
went downstairs.

A book was lying on the table
where his son had done his homework.
He took it into the kitchen,
made coffee, poured himself a cup,
and settled down to read.

"There was a local eddy in the swirling gas
of the primordial galaxy,
and a cloud was formed, the protosun,
as wide as the present solar system.

This contracted. Some of the gas
formed a diffuse, spherical nebula,
a thin disk, that cooled and flattened.
Pulled one way by its own gravity,
the other way by the sun,
it broke, forming smaller clouds,
the protoplanets. Earth
was 2,000 times as wide as it is now."

The earth was without form, and void,
and darkness was upon the face of the deep.

*

"Then the sun began to shine,
dispelling the gases and vapors,
shrinking the planets, melting earth,
separating iron and silicate
to form the core and mantle.
Continents appeared . . ."
history, civilisation,
the discovery of America
and the settling of Green Harbor,
bringing us to Tuesday, the seventh of July.

Tuesday, the day they pick up the garbage!
He leaped into action,
took the garbage bag out of its container,
tied it with a twist of wire,
and carried it out to the toolshed,
taking care not to let the screendoor slam,
and put it in the large garbagecan
that was three-quarters full.
He kept it in the toolshed so the raccoons
couldn't get at it.

He carried the can out to the road,
then went back into the house
and walked around, picking up newspapers
and fliers for: "Thompson Seedless Grapes,
California's finest sweet eating";

"Scott Bathroom Tissue";

"Legislative report from Senator Ken LaValle."

He put all this paper in a box,
and emptied the waste baskets in the two
downstairs bathrooms,
and the basket in the study.

He carried the box out to the road,
taking care not to let the screen-door slam,
and placed the box next to the garbage.

Now let the garbage men come!

*

He went back upstairs.
Susan said, "Did you put out the garbage?"
But her eyes were closed.
She was sleeping, yet could speak in her sleep,
ask a question, even answer one.

"Yes," he said, and climbed into bed.
She turned around to face him,
with her eyes still closed.

He thought, perhaps she's an oracle,
speaking from the Collective Unconscious.
He said to her, "Do you agree with Darwin
that people and monkeys have a common ancestor?
Or should we stick to the Bible?"

She said, "Did you take out the garbage?"

"Yes," he said, for the second time.
Then thought about it. Her answer
had something in it of the sublime.
Like a *koan* . . . the kind of irrelevance
a Zen master says to the disciple
who is asking riddles of the universe.

He put his arm around her,
and she continued to breathe evenly
from the depths of sleep.

JOHN CHEEVER: THE NOVELIST'S LIFE AS A DRAMA

by MALCOLM COWLEY

from THE SEWANEE REVIEW

nominated by THE SEWANEE REVIEW *and Sherod Santos*

Late in the fall of 1930 John Cheever appeared in my office at the *New Republic*, where I was then a junior editor recently assigned to the book department. John was eighteen and looked younger.[1] He had a boyish smile, a low, Bay State voice, and a determined chin. We had just printed the first story he submitted to a magazine, a fictionized account of why and how he got himself expelled from Thayer Academy in South Braintree. Promptly John had come to New York to make his fortune as a writer.

The story—we called it "Expelled"—had come to us marked for my attention. I felt that I was hearing for the first time the voice of a new generation. There were some objections by the senior editors, who pointed out that we didn't often print fiction. "It's awfully long," Bruce Bliven said; he had the final voice on manuscripts. I undertook to cut it down to *New Republic* size, and it went to the printer. When John appeared we talked about the story. I didn't tell him that it had caused a mild dispute in the office. Instead I invited him to an afternoon party, the first that the Cowleys had dared to give in their bare apartment a few doors down the street.

---

1. John always said "seventeen" in telling the story; he was inexact about his age, since he was born May 27, 1912. He also said that his manuscript was addressed to me because he had been reading my first book of poems, *Blue Juniata*, and thought I might sympathize.

I had forgotten that party of Prohibition days, but John remembered it fifty years later when he went to Chicago and spoke at a dinner of the Newberry Library Associates. The library had acquired my papers and wanted to hold a celebration, with John as the principal speaker. "I was truly provincial," he said in evoking that long-ago afternoon. "Malcolm's first wife Peggy met me at the door and exclaimed, 'You must be John Cheever. Everyone else is here.' Things were never like this in Massachusetts. I was offered two kinds of drinks. One was greenish. The other was brown. They were both, I believe, made in a bathtub. I was told that one was a Manhattan and the other Pernod. My only intent was to appear terribly sophisticated and I ordered a Manhattan. Malcolm very kindly introduced me to his guests. I went on drinking Manhattans lest anyone think I came from a small town like Quincy, Massachusetts. Presently, after four or five Manhattans, I realized that I was going to vomit. I rushed to Mrs. Cowley, thanked her for the party, and reached the apartment-house hallway, where I vomited all over the wallpaper. Malcolm never mentioned the damages."

John must have walked or staggered back to what he called "the squalid slum room on Hudson Street" that he had rented for three dollars a week. At the time his only dependable income was a weekly allowance of ten dollars from his older brother Fred, who had kept his job during the Depression and who believed in John's talent. His only capital was a typewriter for which he couldn't often buy a new ribbon. That first winter in New York he had lived—so he reported—mostly on stale bread and buttermilk. As time went on he found little assignments that augmented his diet; one of them was summarizing the plots of new novels for MGM, which was looking for books that would make popular movies. John was paid five dollars for typing out his summary with I don't know how many carbons. The *New Republic* couldn't help him much except by giving him unreviewed books to sell; it was "a journal of opinion," mostly political, and John wasn't given to expressing opinions; by instinct he was a storyteller. He kept writing stories and they began to be printed, always in little magazines that didn't pay for contributions.

I told Elizabeth Ames about him. Elizabeth was the executive director and hostess of Yaddo, a working retreat for writers and artists in Saratoga Springs, and I had served on her admissions committee. She invited John for one summer, liked him immensely, and later renewed the invitation several times. John would never forget his indebtedness to Yaddo, which had fed and lodged him during some of his neediest periods.

In New York I sometimes gave him advice—not about his writing, which I had admired from the beginning, but about finding a market for it. Once I told him it was time for a novel that would speak for his new generation as Fitzgerald had spoken in *This Side of Paradise*. It turned out that John had already started a novel, and he showed me the first three or four chapters. They wouldn't do as the beginning of a book, I reported; each chapter was separate and came to a dead end. It might be that his present talent was for stories . . . Then why wouldn't editors buy the stories? he asked me on another occasion. By that time I had been divorced from Peggy and had remarried, this time for good. It was a Friday evening, and John had come for dinner in our new apartment. "Perhaps the stories have been too long," I said, "usually six or seven thousand words. Editors don't like to buy long stories from unknown writers." Then I had an inspiration. I suggested that he write four very short stories, each of not more than a thousand words, in the next four days. "Bring them to me at the office on Wednesday afternoon and," I said grandly, "we'll see whether I can't get you some money for them."

John carried out the assignment brilliantly. I doubt whether anyone else of his age—he was then twenty-two—could have invented four stories, each different from all the others, in only four days, but John already seemed to have an endless stock of characters and moods and situations. Although the *New Republic* seldom published fiction, one of the four could be passed off as a "color piece" about a burlesque theater. "Yes. Short and lively" was Bruce Bliven's comment when I showed it to him. The other three ministories, plainly fictions, I sent along to Katharine White, then fiction editor of the *New Yorker,* and she accepted two of them. That event, which I have told about elsewhere, was the beginning of John's career as a professional writer. The *New Yorker* was his principal market for more than thirty years and it would end by publishing 119 of his stories.

In the course of time John became impatient with the accurate reporting that was demanded of *New Yorker* writers, especially in the days when Harold Ross was editor. The magazine's editor set limitations on fiction, and John always wanted to go farther and deeper into life. "This table seems real," he later said in an interview; "the fruit basket belonged to my grandmother, but a madwoman could come in the door any moment." In the stories he wrote after World War II the madwoman appeared more often. Once she was a vampire; that was in "Torch Song." Once she assumed the shape of an enormous radio that picked up conversations from anywhere in a big apartment building. That story, his first with a touch of the impossible, was also his first to be widely anthologized.

Some future critic should trace John's development as a writer by reading his work from the beginning in its exact chronological order. The work changes from year to year and from story to story. "Fiction is experimentation," he was later to say; "when it ceases to be that it ceases to be fiction. One never puts down a sentence without the feeling that it has never been put down before in exactly the same way, and that perhaps the substance of the sentence has never been felt. Every sentence is an innovation." That is too seldom true of fiction, but it is true of John's best work, in which the sentences, apparently simple, are always alive and unexpected. Reading them makes me think of a boyhood experience, that of groping beneath roots at the edge of a stream and finding a trout in my fingers

There were times of crisis when his purposes changed rapidly. One of these must have been during his work on *The Wapshot Chronicle*, his first novel and still his most engaging book. Perhaps it isn't a novel so much as a series of episodes connected with the imaginary town of St. Botolphs, on the south or less fashionable shore of Massachusetts Bay, and with the fortunes of the Wapshot family; John was right to call it a chronicle. The characters are presented with a free-ranging candor that must have embarrassed the Cheevers, to whom the Wapshots bore a family resemblance, but also with an affection not often revealed in his New York or Westchester stories. John felt that he couldn't publish the book until after his mother died. It appeared in 1957 while the Cheevers were spending a year in Italy. John was happy about the *Chronicle*, and this without seeing the reviews, most of which were enthusiastic. Writing it seems to have given him a new sense of scope and freedom.

Nevertheless he was having trouble with his second novel, *The*

Wapshot Scandal, which was to be seven years in the writing. While work on it progressed slowly, or not at all, he published two more collections of stories (there would finally be six of these in all). One of the new collections bore a title that suggested another change in direction: *Some People, Places, & Things That Will Not Appear in My Next Novel.* In the title story he was performing what almost seems a rite of exorcism: he was presenting in brief, and then dismissing with contempt, a number of episodes that, in his former days, he might have developed at length. Not one of them, he now believed, would help him "to celebrate a world that lies spread out around us like a bewildering and stupendous dream."

He tried to present that dream in *The Wapshot Scandal,* but in writing the book he found little to celebrate. He had to record how the Wapshots, with their traditional standards, faced the new world of aimlessness, supermarkets, and nuclear bombs. They died or went to pieces—all of them except Coverly Wapshot, more solid and unattractive than the others, who found himself working in a secret missile base and lost his security clearance. The book is almost as episodic as the *Chronicle,* but with the episodes more tightly woven together. Each of them starts with a scene that is accurately observed—it might correspond to Cheever's real table and his grandmother's fruit basket—but then everything becomes grotesque, as if his madwoman had come in the door. On one occasion she is followed by a screaming crowd of madwomen in nightgowns with curlers in their hair. The book has an unflagging power of invention and was praised by critics when it finally appeared; it also had a fairly impressive sale. John himself "never much liked the book," as he was to say when he was interviewed much later for the *Paris Review.* "When it was done I was in a bad way. I'd wake up in the night and I would hear Hemingway's voice—I've never actually heard Hemingway's voice, but it was conspicuously his—saying, 'This is the small agony. The great agony comes later.'"

But first would come another agony that was not the greatest, but was not a small one either. After thirty years of intimate relations the *New Yorker* rejected one of his longer and more treasured stories, "The Jewels of the Cabots." John sold the story to *Playboy* for twice what the *New Yorker* would have paid, but still his pride had been hurt. There were other rejections, one or two of them inexcusable, and John stopped writing for the *New Yorker*. If one were plotting his life as a theater piece, one might say the curtain had fallen on a second act.

A few years later John published a third novel, *Bullet Park* (1969), that was more tightly plotted than the second. It pleased him more than the *Scandal*. "The manuscript was received enthusiastically everywhere," he reported, "but when Benjamin DeMott dumped on it in the *Times*, everybody picked up their marbles and went home. I ruined my left leg in a skiing accident and ended up so broke that I took out working papers for my youngest son." John was exaggerating, as he liked to do with gullible reporters. The son, then twelve years old, never thought about working papers; in due time he went off to Andover and Stanford. But John, horrified at going into debt, wasn't making progress with his writing, and he confessed to himself that he had become an alcoholic. He had a heart attack, nearly fatal, in 1972. Having recovered, he accepted teaching assignments, first at the Iowa School of Writing and then at Boston University, where, so he said, "I behaved badly."

For the black years that might be called a third act in his life, I'm not sure about the sequence of events, and I have to depend on his later accounts. I was seeing less of John. In 1967 our only son, Robert, had been married to John's daughter Susan in a high-church ceremony at St. Mark's in the Bouwerie. The elder Cowleys played no part in the preparations for an expensive wedding. At the reception, under an outsize tent in the churchyard, the Cheever connection drank their champagne on one side of the tent, while the smaller Cowley contingent sat grouped on the other. That marked a growing difference in styles of life between the two families. For ten years after *The Wapshot Chronicle* and before *Bullet Park* John had earned a substantial income: there were Hollywood contracts and what seemed to me huge advances from publishers. The Cheevers had bought and remodeled a big stone house in Westchester County, to the disapproval of some *New Yorker* editors, who felt that authors should defend their economic freedom by living on a modest scale. The Cowleys did live modestly, farther out in the country, and spent rather less than they took in. I came to suspect that the Cheevers, who traveled widely, always in first class, now regarded us as tourist-class country cousins. Then Rob and Susan were divorced, after eight years of marriage. It was an amicable divorce, with no children to argue about (only two golden retrievers) and with no hard feelings. Still it was the end of casual family visitings.

I was always overjoyed to see John, but was a little tongue-tied even when we met at Yaddo, where we were both on the board of directors, or at various committee meetings of the American Academy; there was never much time for confidences. Later John would tell the public about his misadventures. After Boston University he went home to the big stone house, where he fell into utter depression. He used to wash down several Valium tablets with a quart of whiskey. He was trying to abolish himself—but why? Clearly it was less a matter of his finances or his physical state than of his concern with the art of fiction; he felt that his life as a writer was at an end. He was also a sincerely religious man, though he wouldn't talk much about the subject, and he must have felt that he had fallen from grace forever. His family, deeply concerned, told him that alcohol would kill him, as it had already killed his loved and resented older brother. "So what?" he said, taking another drink. In 1975 he finally listened to the family and committed himself to Smithers, a rehabilitation center. He was to speak darkly, in later years, of going mad when deprived of liquor and of being wrapped in a straitjacket.[2] The treatment was prolonged, whatever it was, and it worked; after being released from Smithers John never again took a drink. He experienced a new sense of redemption, elation, and release from bondage. Almost immediately he set to work on a novel, which he finished in less than a year.

The novel, of course, was *Falconer,* published in 1977; John was to call it "a very dark book that displayed radiance." It was the story of Ezekiel Farragut, a moderately distinguished professor who becomes a drug addict, who kills his brother with a poker, and who is sentenced to ten years in Falconer Prison. There he is redeemed, partly through a homosexual love affair, and he loses his craving for Methadone. The book reads swiftly and displays John's gift for economical prose with not a misplaced word, besides his amazing talent for invention. Some of the episodes have a touch of the miraculous. A cardinal descends from the skies in a helicopter

---

2. The treatment of Smithers did not include a straitjacket, but John had been confined briefly in another institution.

and carries off Zeke's lover to freedom. A young priest appears in the cellblock and administers last rites to the hero. "Now who the hell was that?" Zeke shouts to the guard. "I didn't ask for a priest. He didn't do his thing for anybody else." Symbolically Zeke is about to die, be entombed, and rise again. In life his cellmate dies instead. Attendants come to put the corpse into a body bag. Farragut zips open the bag, removes the corpse, and takes its place; then he is carried out of the prison. Walking in the street a free man, his head high, his back straight, "Rejoice," he thinks, "rejoice."

Those are the last words of Cheever's longest continuous fiction. Judged purely as a novel, *Falconer* has obvious faults. There are loose strings never tied up and events left unexplained. The reader is forced to wonder how Zeke Farragut will survive in his new life, since he has no money and no identity, and is still dressed in his prison clothes. Then one reflects that the faults don't matter much; that *Falconer* is not a novel bent on achieving verisimilitude, but rather a moving parable with biblical overtones of sin and redemption; it is Magdalen redeemed by divine grace and Lazarus raised from the dead. That is how it must have been read by thousands, and the book had an astoundingly wide sale, enough to pay off its author's debts to publishers for the first time in years.

And the fourth act in the drama?

The success of *Falconer* led to another change in John's character, as well as in his public image. He had always managed to keep from being a celebrity. When he was twelve years old his parents had given him their permission to earn his future living as a writer—if he could earn it—but only after he promised them that he had no idea of becoming famous or wealthy. In later years he had kept that promise, though with some latitude in the matter of income, since he liked to support the family on a generous scale. He had refused several offers that promised to make him rich, though he had always been shrewd in a Yankee fashion (and his agent was known for striking hard bargains). In the matter of fame he had obdurately defended his privacy. Medals and honors he accepted when they came, if grudgingly, but he had done his best to avoid being interviewed—often by the simple device of getting drunk, or getting the interviewer drunk. But *Falconer* had made him a national figure as if by accident, and he found himself enjoying his new status.

For the first time in his life he gave interviews willingly—and brilliantly too, since he said without hesitation whatever was on his mind. Always the interviewers would mention his boyishness. I suppose the word was suggested by his lack of self-importance, his deprecatory smile, and his candor in speaking about intimate misadventures. In simple fact he was now an old man, wearied by the physical demands he had made on himself, so that he was older in body and spirit than his sixty-five years. He now had nothing to lose by telling the truth, so long as it made a good story. He was finding pleasure in addressing a new audience—as he explained more than once—but also he wanted to set things straight with himself and the world while there was still time.

His next book after *Falconer* would be a retrospective undertaking, *The Stories of John Cheever* (1978), collected at last in one big volume. He had chosen sixty-one stories for the book, after omitting all those printed before his army service in World War II (though some of that early work is worth preserving) as well as two or three stories written during his breakdown. Almost all the others he arranged in roughly chronological order. For the first time a wider public could note the changing spirit of his work over the years, not to mention its essential unity. John also had given the book a brief, illuminating preface that has been widely quoted. "These stories," he says at one point, "seem at times to be stories of a long-lost world when the city of New York was still filled with a river light, when you heard the Benny Goodman quartets from a radio in the corner stationery store, and when almost everybody wore a hat. . . . The constants that I looked for in this sometimes dated paraphernalia are a love of light and a determination to trace some moral chain of being. Calvin played no part in my religious education, but his presence seemed to abide in the barns of my childhood and to have left me with some undue bitterness."

That moral element is always present, if concealed, in a Cheever story. At first the bad people, whose commonest sin is heartlessness, seem hard to distinguish from the good people, but they end by indicting themselves; and Cheever was an inexorable judge (especially when faced by women bent on expressing themselves at everybody's cost). He was not a tender judge of his own work, and there are only two sentences of the preface that I think are in error as applied to himself. "The parturition of a writer, I think, unlike that of a painter, does not display any interesting alliances to his masters. In the growth of a writer one finds nothing like the early Jackson Pollock copies of the Sistine Chapel paintings with their interesting cross-references to Thomas Hart Benton." That seems to me far from the truth. Among the important writers of this later time Cheever reveals more alliances than others to three masters of the World War I generation.

Hemingway was his first master, as was evident in his early and now forgotten stories. These copied many features of Hemingway's style, notably the short sentences, the simple words, the paring away of adjectives, adverbs, conjunctions, and the effort to evoke feelings without directly expressing them, simply by presenting actions in sequence and objects seen accurately as if for the first time. I can testify that the novel John tried to write when he was twenty-one—and abandoned after three or four chapters—had as its obvious starting-point a story by Hemingway, "Cross-Country Snow." It would have been the equivalent, in his case, of Jackson Pollock's attempts to copy the Sistine Chapel. Very soon Cheever developed a style of his own that became more effective than Hemingway's later style; he never parodied himself. Still he retained what he had learned from that early master, including an enthusiasm for fishing and skiing. Hemingway as a father figure appeared in his dreams.

The resemblance to Fitzgerald was more often noted, especially during John's middle years. His characters, like Fitzgerald's, were mostly from the upper layers of American society (though Cheever didn't invest them with the glamor of great wealth). Like Fitzgerald he had the gift of double vision; he was both a partici-pant in the revels and, at the same moment, a fresh and honest-eyed observer from a different social world. Both men were at heart romantics, even if they had different dreams. Cheever's was not the dream of early love and financial success; he was more obsessed with the middle-aged nightmare of moral or financial collapse. Sometimes, however, he wrote sentences that might grace a Fitzgerald story—for example "The light was like a blow, and the air smelled as if many wonderful girls had just wandered across the lawn." Both men were time-conscious and tried to recapture the feeling, the smell, the essential truth of a moment in history. One can often guess the year when a Cheever story was written by internal evidence, without looking for the date of publication. It is the same with Fitzgerald, of whom Cheever was to say admiringly: "One always knows reading Fitzgerald what time it is, precisely where you are, the kind of country. No writer has ever been so true in placing the scene. I feel that this isn't pseudohistory, but the sense of being alive. All great men are scrupulously true to their times." It was one of the things that Cheever tried to be. His stories also imply moral constants that make them relatively timeless—but then Fitzgerald too was a moralist, "a spoiled priest."

And Faulkner? Here it is not at all a question of early influence or the relation between explorer and settler. I'm not sure that Cheever even read Faulkner during the 1930s, although he was an enormous reader. It is rather a question of natural resemblances in writing and in character as well. The two didn't look alike, but they were both short handsome men attractive to women and blessed from childhood with enormous confidence in their own genius. (The influence of mere stature on writers' careers is a subject that calls for more study. Often the Napoleons of literature—and the Balzacs—are short men determined not to be looked at from above.) Both Cheever and Faulkner were high-school dropouts and greedy readers. Like Faulkner from the beginning, Cheever was a storyteller by instinct: they both turned description into narration. (Note for examples the panoramic views of Bullet Park, at the beginning of the novel, and of St. Botolphs, in the first chapter of *The Wapshot Chronicle*. First we see the houses one by one, but each house recalls a family and each family suggests a story. That was how Faulkner proceeded too.)

Like Faulkner again, Cheever depended at every moment on the force and richness of his imagination. Faulkner was preeminent in that gift, but Cheever had more of it than other writers of his own time, and he too created his "little postage stamp of native soil": Westchester and St. Botolphs are in some respects his Yoknapatawpha. *Falconer*, the novel he liked best among his own works, was named for an imagined prison in Westchester County, but he usually pronounced the name in an English fashion: "Faulkner." Mightn't that be a form of tribute to the older novelist?

The two men had other points of resemblance, besides their common fondness for hard liquor. One trait of a different sort was their frequent use of symbols from the Bible, as if they were the last two Christians in a godless world. But I want to make the more general point about Cheever that he was carrying on a tradition. His generation or cohort has included many gifted novelists: Bellow, Welty, Updike, Malamud, to name only a few. I will never try to assign a rank to each of them like a schoolmaster noting down grades. Cheever may or may not be the best of them, but he is clearly the one who stands closest in spirit to the giants of the preceding era.

Most of the American authors admired in our time did their best work before they were forty-five. Many of them died before reaching that age. Most survived into their sixties, but their truly productive careers had been cut short by emotional exhaustion, by alcoholism, or by mere repetition and drudgery. Scott Fitzgerald said "There are no second acts in American lives." We produced no Thomas Hardys or Thomas Manns (an exception perhaps may be made for Robert Frost), and no one who made a brilliant rebeginning after a crisis in middle life. More recently there have been other exceptions and Cheever is one of them. His career in literature not merely started over but had a last act as brilliant in a different way as the acts that preceded it.

After he published *The Stories of John Cheever,* honors came pouring down on him like an autumn shower. Among them were a doctorate from Harvard (1978); a Pulitzer prize for the stories, which also received the award for fiction of the Book Critics' Circle, both in 1979; the Edward MacDowell Medal in that same year; and finally, in 1982, the National Medal for Literature. He accepted the honors gladly, not with the indifference he had displayed toward the few that had been granted him in earlier years. Once he had acted like Faulkner, as if on the assumption that readers didn't exist; now he was delighted by their response. He gave public readings of his stories, most often of two favorites, "The Swimmer" and "The Death of Justina." His face and his voice became admiredly familiar on television. He was photographed on horseback, like Faulkner in his last years. Meanwhile he had started a new novel for which he had signed, so we heard, a magnificent contract. To interviewers he said merely that it would be "another bulky book." There wasn't much time to work on it in the midst of distractions. After he had spent so many years in the shadows, even his New England conscience would have absolved him for basking a little in a transcontinental light.

Often there is an essential change in writers as they grow older, something beyond a mere ripening of earlier qualities. (I am thinking here mostly of men and not of women, who are likely to follow a different pattern.) The writer, if he has something of his own to say, begins under the sign of the mother, which is also the sign and banner of rebellion—against tradition, against the existing order, against authority as represented by the father. The change comes after a crisis in middle-age, or even before it in many cases. The writer becomes reconciled with his father, indeed with all the Fathers who suffer from having wayward sons. (Here again women are different: they are likely to sign a truce with their mothers.) Cheever said more than once that the Wapshot books were "a posthumous attempt to make peace with my father's ghosts."

Whether men or women, writers find themselves going back in spirit to the regions where they spent their childhoods. For more than forty years Cheever had been a Yorker, not a Yankee; he had been mistakenly called a typical writer for the *New Yorker*. Now he rebecame a New Englander. One can be more specific: he became a Bay Stater, a native son of the Massachusetts seaboard, which has a different voice and different traditions from those of the Connecticut Valley. If Bay Staters are of Puritan descent, they trace their ancestral histories back to the founder of the family. In John's case the founder was Ezekiel Cheever, a minister highly respected by Cotton Mather, who preached his funeral sermon. John quotes Mather as saying "The welfare of the Commonwealth was always upon the conscience of Ezekiel Cheever . . . and he abominated periwigs." The commonwealth of letters was always on John's conscience, and he abominated all sorts of pretension, almost as much as he abominated pollution and superhighways.

While writing *Falconer* he had still smoked furiously. "I need to have *some* vice," he explained. Now, after a struggle, he gave up smoking as well as drinking. In default of vices he practiced virtues, especially those native to the Bay State. That breed of Yankees are distinguished, and tormented as well, by having scruples; they keep asking themselves "Was that the right thing for me to do?" John must have asked that question often in his prayers.

Another Yankee precept is not to speak ill of people even when they are rivals. John, if he had grudges, now managed not to express them.

He had become conservative in the Bay State fashion—in manners though not always in politics, this last being a field that he continued to avoid. There was, however, another Yankee precept, Be reticent about yourself!, that he now flagrantly violated. I suspect this was because he had come to regard himself as a fictional person, the leading character of a novel that he was composing not in written words but in terms of remembered joys and tribulations.

The true Bay Stater discharges his obligations, and he sets high store by loyalty first to family, then to a few old friends and to chosen institutions. John became a devoted churchgoer, always attending early mass. He worked for the institutions that had befriended him, notably Yaddo and the American Academy, where he served for three years as chairman of the awards committee for literature. In that post he had to read some two hundred novels a year; it was another of his unrecompensed services to the commonwealth of letters. He paid off his moral debts to friends; one example was his making a trip to Chicago in order to speak at a dinner held in my honor. He was like a man who puts his affairs in order before setting out on a journey.

The journey started, as always, sooner than he had expected. In July 1981 John had an operation for the removal of a cancerous kidney. The operation appeared to be successful, but a few weeks later John was barely able to walk. The cancer had metastasized to the bones of his legs; then it appeared as a burning spot on his rib cage. There was no hope left except in chemotherapy and radiotherapy at Memorial Hospital. Once again John spoke of himself dispassionately, as if he were a character in fiction. He told an interviewer for the *Saturday Review*, "Suddenly to find yourself with thousands and thousands seeking some cure for this deadly thing is an extraordinary thing. It's not depressing, really, or exhilarating. It's quite plainly a critical part of living, or the aspiration to live."

Those were arduous months for John; I think one might call them heroic. Doggedly he prepared a manuscript for his publisher, though it was not the bulky novel he had planned. *Oh What a Paradise It Seems* was no more than a novella, but, like all the best of his work, it was accurate, beautifully written, and full of surprises. It appeared in the early spring of 1982. A few weeks later he wrote me: "I fully intend to recover both from the cancer, the treatment and the bills."

I last saw him in Carnegie Hall less than two months before his death. The occasion was the ceremony at which, among the recipients of lesser awards, he was presented with the National Medal for Literature. His face was gaunt after radiotherapy and almost all his hair had fallen out. I said that I admired him for having made the trip from Ossining and he answered: "When they give you fifteen thousand dollars you owe them an appearance." He hobbled out to the rostrum leaning on a cane—or was it two canes? From my folding chair in the wings I couldn't hear his little speech, but I heard the great rumble of applause; John had nothing but friends.

A few minutes later we met and embraced in an empty corridor; I remember feeling that the treatment at Memorial had altered his body. It was more than fifty years since John had first appeared in my office at the *New Republic*. We were two men who had grown old in the service of literature, but our roles had been transposed: John was now older than I and was leading the way.

♨ ♨ ♨

OUTSTANDING WRITERS

(The editors also wish to mention the following important works published by small presses last year. Listing is alphabetical by author's last name.)

FICTION

The Final Proof of Fate and Circumstance—Lee K. Abbott (Georgia Review)
The Place That Calls You Hence—Lee K. Abbott (Crazyhorse)
Alaska—Alice Adams (Shenandoah)
The Honeymoon—Dean Albarelli (Southern Review)
Shaking She Speaks This Time—Paula Gunn Allen (Spinsters Ink)
Finding The Women—Michael Alley (Missouri Review)
Kitty Partners—Max Apple (Antaeus)
Play, Bird Eyes—Madelyn Arnold (13th Moon)
Myrtie's Salvation—Bo Ball (South Carolina Review)
Trick Scenery—Frederick Barthelme (Chicago Review)
Legacies—Paulette Bates (Kansas Quarterly)
Weights—Charles Baxter (TriQuarterly)
Sheer Energy—Brian Bedard (Chariton Review)
Hadza—John Bennett (Crab Creek Review)
Grandma and the Eskimos—Richard Blessing (Dragon Gate Inc.)
Odori—Dielle Bowen (Mendocino Review)
The Barbecue—Mary Ward Brown (Threepenny Review)
The Settlement of Mars—Frederick Busch (TriQuarterly)
The Storytellers—Fred Chappell (TriQuarterly)
A Woman One Time—Fred Chappell (Crescent Review)
The Discipline—Austin Clarke (Confrontation)
Like One Redwood Tree To Another—Gina Covina (Barn Owl Books)

I Break Into Houses—E.J. Cullen (Apalachee Quarterly)
The Great Godalmighty Bird—Coleman Dowell (Conjunctions)
A Father's Story—Andre Dubus (Black Warrior Review)
Translations from the Mother Tongue—Lorraine Duggin (North American Review)
Father Abraham—William Faulkner (Red Ozier Press)
Naked To Naked Goes—Robert Flanagan (Ohio Review)
Passages from The Tunnel—William Gass (Conjunctions)
Suspicious Origin—Perry Glasser (New Rivers Press)
The Confessions of Friday—James B. Hall (New Directions)
Ride, Fly, Penetrate, Loiter—Barry Hannah (Georgia Review)
Children of the Valley—David Hellerstein (North American Review)
About Three Years Ago—John Helton Jr. (Missouri Review)
In The Cemetery Where Al Jolson Is Buried—Amy Hempel (TriQuarterly)
Inexorable Progress—Mary Hood (Georgia Review)
Baby You Belong To Me—Mary Howard (Ontario Review)
The Ruth Tractate—Fanny Howe (Fiction)
Johnny Rabbit's Dark Night of the Soul—T.R. Hummer (MSS)
El Condor—Harold Jaffe (Thunders Mouth Press)
Hook—David Jauss (Story Press)
Christine—Marie Luise Kaschnitz (Translation)
The Witch of Ballymadden—Herbert A. Kenny (Stories)
Women Friends—Sandra J. Kolankiewicz (Mississippi Review)
For Jerome—With Love and Kisses—Gordon Lish (Antioch Review)
Veterans—Evan K. Margetson (TriQuarterly)
Harvest—Bobbie Ann Mason (Bloodroot)
Daddy's Girl—Tia Maytag (Tendril)
The Birds and The Bees—Sue Miller (Ploughshares)
August Eschenburg—Steven Millhauser (Antaeus)
Rundle—Barbara Milton (Quarto)
The English Lesson—Stuart Mitchner (Raritan)
Sweet Cheat of Freedom—Ursule Molinaro (Top Stories)
The Men In Dark Suits—David Moser (Mississippi Review)
Mitrani—Barbara Mujica (Antietam Review)
The Year Between—Jay Neugeboren (Boston Review)
Unicycle—Howard Norman (Ploughshares)
The Love Child—Helen Norris (Sewanee Review)

Pablo Tamayo—Naomi Shihab Nye (Virginia Quarterly)

December—Joyce Carol Oates (Carolina Quarterly)

The Victim—Joyce Carol Oates (Iowa Review)

Kindred—T.R. Pearson (Virginia Quarterly)

Frankenstein Meets The Ant People—Jonathan Penner (Antaeus)

A Way of Life—Jonathan Penner (Story Quarterly)

The Fame of Price—Fred Pfeil (Sewanee Review)

The Pragmata of Baltasar Mung—Roberto Picciotto (Conjunctions)

Nam—C.E. Poverman (Canard Foundation)

The Rugged Rascal Ran. . .—Victor Power (The Long Story)

The Crescent—Peggy Rambach (Crazyhorse)

What The Meek Inherit At The End—Sallie F. Reynolds (Prairie
    Schooner)

Dogs—Kurt Rheinheimer (Michigan Quarterly Review)

Who's To Say This Isn't Love—William Pitt Root (TriQuarterly)

Sinners—Sarah Rossiter (North American Review)

An Incident At The Border—Larry Rudner (Croton Review)

A Man of Conviction—Ira Sadoff (Antioch Review)

Lost Sons—James Salter (Grand Street)

Virginia: or, A Single Girl—Susan Fromberg Schaeffer (Prairie
    Schooner)

Intelligent Life—S.M. Schwartz (Sequoia)

You Can't Get There From Here—Ludmila Shtern (Stories)

From The World About Us—Claude Simon (Ontario Review)

Crystal River—Charles Smith (Paris Review)

Hands—Gregory Blake Smith (Kenyon Review)

Kingdoms Are Clay—Madelon Sprengnether (New Rivers Press)

Ode To The Big School—Sharon S. Stark (New England Review/
    Bread Loaf Quarterly)

Pleasantly and Well Suited—Alma Stone (Shenandoah)

Caveat Emptor—Barry Targen (Missouri Review)

Silver Sugar From Bombay—Maria Thomas (North American
    Review)

Down From Coeur d'Alene—Dan Trapp (Missouri Review)

Gravedigger—Dan Trapp (Puerto del Sol)

The Girl Who Turned Into Cider—Luisa Valenzuela (Open Places)

Cyankali—Hart Wegner (MSS)

A Dwelling Place for Dragons—Gloria Whelan (Michigan Quar-
    terly)

White—Joy Williams (Antaeus)

Land Fishers—Robley Wilson Jr. (Antaeus)
The Barracks Thief—Tobias Wolff (Antaeus)
Fair—Tobias Wolff (Tendril)
Woe To Live On—Daniel Woodrell (Missouri Review)

NONFICTION

Universals of Performance; or, Amortizing Play—Herbert Blau
(Sub-stance)
On A Greek Holiday—Alice Bloom (Hudson Review)
He Beats His Women—Charles Bukowski (Second Coming Press)
Criticism and Invention—Michel Butor (Cream City Review)
How Dead Men Write to Each Other—Lori Chamberlain (O.ARS)
Stabs At Bewilderment—E.M. Cioran (Translation)
Tradition and The Adversarial Talent—Thomas DePietro (Poetry
East)
A Laurel For Richard Hugo—Andre Dubus (Black Warrior Re-
view)
Performance and Reality—Stanley Elkin (Grand Street)
Montale—Ross Feld (Parnassus)
Zelda: A Worksheet—Zelda Fitzgerald (Paris Review)
Who's Listening?—Reginald Gibbons (Missouri Review)
The Second Coming of Aphrodite—Sandra M. Gilbert (Kenyon
Review)
Business and Poetry—Dana Gioia (Hudson Review)
A Spectator Sport—Joan Givner (North American Review)
Nimsism and Kindred Delights—William Harmon (Parnassus)
Deep Song: Some Provocations—Michael Heller (Ironwood)
Originality—John Hollander (Raritan)
The Commerce of the Creative Spirit—Lewis Hyde (American
Poetry Review)
The Establishment of Science—Thomas H. Johnson (Georgia Re-
view)
Trial Balances—David Kalstone (Grand Street)
Some Ways Philosophy Has Helped Shape My Work—Jackson
Mac Low (Poetics Journal)
Reassembling the Dust: Notes on the Art of the Biographer—Paul
Mariani (New England Review/Bread Loaf Quarterly)

The Fascination of the Miniature—Steven Millhauser (Grand Street)

Two Women: Regina Nestle, 1910-1978, and Her Daughter, Joan—Joan Nestle/Regina Nestle (13th Moon)

Story—Jay Neugeboren (American Scholar)

The Orbiting Self—Walker Percy (Georgia Review)

Imagination on the Ropes—Sanford Pinsker (Georgia Review)

A Renaissance of Women Writers—Jed Rasula (Sulphur)

Attic Envy—Anna Rosen (A Jewish Journal At Yale)

At Play In The Paradise of Bombs—Scott R. Sanders (North American Review)

Aga Dawn—Bill Schermbrucker (Talonbooks)

The Neural Lyre—Frederick Turner and Ernst Pöppel (Poetry)

How to Die—Richard Watson (Georgia Review)

A Succession of Poets—Glenway Wescott (Partisan Review)

Song Without Words—Paul West (Parnassus: Poetry In Review)

Under The Bed—Jincy Willett (Massachusetts Review)

POETRY

Salmon—Roger Aplon (Dryad Press)

A Wave—John Ashbery (American Poetry Review)

When The Sun Went Down—John Ashbery (Conjunctions)

The Field—David Baker (New England Review/Bread Loaf Quarterly)

Mining The Second Baptist Church, 1936: My Father's Story—David Baker (Texas Review)

Night Blue Fishing on Block Island—Peter Balakian (New Directions)

The Summer of the Wild Artichokes—S. Ben-Tov (New England Review/Bread Loaf Quarterly)

Alakanuk—Mei-mei Berssenbrugge (Conjunctions)

Confessional—Frank Bidart (Paris Review)

The Fox—David Bottoms (Antioch Review)

Blackout, 1944—William Carpenter (American Poetry Review)

One Man's Family—Rosemary Catacalos (Pax)

Buffalo Evening—Robert Creeley (American Poetry Review)

In Texas We Get Persimmons—Judson Crews (Ahsahta Press)

☣ ☣ ☣

OUTSTANDING SMALL PRESSES

(These presses made or received nominations for this edition of *The Pushcart Prize*. See the *International Directory of Little Magazines and Small Presses,* Dustbooks, Box 1056, Paradise, CA 95969, for subscription rates, manuscript requirements and a complete international listing of small presses.)

Abraxas, 2518 Gregory St., Madison, WI 53711

Academic & Arts Press, P.O. Box 31, Helena, MT 59624

Acrobat Books, P.O. Box 480820, Los Angeles, CA 90048

Adastra Press, 101 Strong St., Easthampton, MA 01027

Adrift, 239 East 5th St., #4d, New York, NY 10003

Adz, 127 Charles St., Boston, MA 02114

The Agni Review, P.O. Box 229, Cambridge, MA 02138

Ahsahta Press, Dept. of Eng., Boise St. Univ., Boise, ID 83725

Akiba Press, Box 13086, Oakland, CA 94611

The Alchemist, P.O. Box 123, LaSalle, Quebec, Canada H8R 3T7

Alembic Press, 1424 Stanley Rd., Plainfield, IN 46168

Alice James Books, 138 Mt. Auburn St., Cambridge, MA 02138

Alta Napa Press, 1969 Mora Ave., Calistoga, CA 94515

The Altadena Review, P.O. Box 212, Altadena, CA 91001

American Poetry Review, 1616 Walnut St., Philadelphia, PA 19103

American Studies Press, Inc., 13511 Palmwood La.,
   Tampa, FL 33624

Anhinga Press, Dept. of Eng., Florida St. Univ., Tallahassee,
   FL 32306

Another Chicago Magazine, Box 11223, Chicago, IL 60611

Ansuda Publications, P.O. Box 158, Harris, IA 51345

Antietam Review, 33 W. Washington St., Hagerstown, MD 21740

The Antigonish Review, Antigonish, Nova Scotia, Canada B2G
   1C0

The Antioch Review, P.O. Box 148, Yellow Springs, OH 45387
The Apalachee Quarterly, P.O. Box 20106, Tallahassee, FL 32304
Applezaba Press, P.O. Box 4134, Long Beach, CA 90804
Arizona Quarterly, Univ. of Arizona, Tucson, AZ 85721
Artemis, P.O. Box 945, Roanoke, VA 24005
Ascent, 100 English Bldg., Univ. of Illinois, Urbana, IL 61801
Ashford Press, P.O. Box 246, Clinton, CT 06413
Asphodel, 613 Howard Ave., Pitman, NJ 08071
August House, Inc., 1010 West Third St., Little Rock, AR 72201

Bad Henry Review, P.O. Box 45, Van Brent Sta., Brooklyn,
    NY 11215
Balance Beam Press, Inc., 12711 Stoneridge Rd., Dayton,
    MN 55327
Barn Owl Books, 1101 Keeler Ave., Berkeley, CA 94708
The Barnwood Press, River House, RR2, Box 11C, Daleville,
    IN 47334
Bear Tribe Publishing, P.O. Box 9167, Spokane, WA 99209
Beginning, P.O. Box 2191, Iowa City, IA 52244
Bellingham Review, 412 N. State St., Bellingham, WA 98225
Beloit Poetry Journal, P.O. Box 2, Beloit, WI 53511
Berkeley Works Magazine, 2940 Seventh St., Berkeley, CA 94710
Beyond Baroque Foundation, P.O. Box 806, Venice, CA 90291
Biblio Press, P.O. Box 22, Fresh Meadows, NY 11365
Bieler Press, P.O. Box 3856, St. Paul, MN 55165
Bilingual Review Press, Graduate School, SUNY. Binghamton, NY
    13901
BITS Press, Dept. of Eng., Case Western Res. Univ., Cleveland,
    OH 44106
Bitteroot, P.O. Box 51, Blythebourne Sta., Brooklyn, NY 11219
Black Bart, P.O. Box 48, Canyon, CA 94516
Black Buzzard Press, 4705 South 8th Rd., Arlington, VA 22204
Black Market Press, 1516 Beverly Rd., Brooklyn, NY 11226
Black Oak Press, Box 4663, Univ. Pl. Sta., Lincoln, NE 68504
Bloodroot, P.O. Box 891, Grand Forks, ND 58206
The Bloomsbury Review, P.O. Box 8928, Denver, CO 80201
Blue Cloud Quarterly, Blue Cloud Abbey, Marvin, SD 57251
Bluefish, P.O. Box 1601, Southampton, NY 11968
Blueline, Blue Mountain Lake, NY 12812
Blue Unicorn, 22 Avon Rd., Kensington, CA 94707

BOA Editions, 92 Park Ave., Brockport, NY 14420

Books of a Feather, P.O. Box 3095, Terminal Annex, Los Angeles, CA 90051

Borgo Press, P.O. Box 2845, San Bernardino, CA 92406

Bottomfish Magazine, De Anza College, Cupertino, CA 95014

Bread & Butter Press, 2582 S. Clayton, Denver, CO 80210

Breitenbush Publications, Inc., P.O. Box 02137, Portland, OR 97202

Brick Books, P.O. Box 219, Ilderton, Ontario, Canada N0M 2A0

Bridges to the Sound Publishing Corp., P.O. Box 260607, Tampa, FL 33685

Burning Deck, 71 Elmgrove Ave., Providence, RI 02906

Cabbagehead Press, 1272 E. Loma Vista Dr., Tempe, AZ 85282

California Quarterly, University of California, Davis, CA 95616

California Street Books, 723 Dwight Way, Berkeley, CA 94710

Callaloo, English Dept., University of Kentucky, Lexington, KY 40506

Calliope, Creative Writing, Roger Williams College, Bristol, RI 02809·

Calyx, P.O. Box 8, Corvallis, OR 97330

Cambric Press, 312 Park, Huron, OH 44839

Capra Press, P.O. Box 2068, Santa Barbara, CA 93120

Cardamom Press, Box D, Richmond, ME 04357

Cardinal Press, 76 N. Yorktown, Tulsa, OK 74110

Carolina Quarterly, University of North Carolina, Chapel Hill, NC 27514

Carolina Wren Press, 300 Barclay Rd., Chapel Hill, NC 27514

Cat's Eye, 1005 Clearview Dr., Nashville, TN 37205

Ceilidh, 986 Marquette La., Foster City, CA 94404

The Centennial Review, 110 Morrill Hall, Mich. St. Univ., East Lansing, MI 48824

Center for Women's Studies & Services, 2829 Broadway, San Diego, CA 92102

Chase Avenue Press, 107 E. Spring St., Apt. 9, Oxford, OH 45056

Chattahoochee Review, DeKalb Community College, Dunwoody, GA 30338

Chestnut Hill Press, 5320 Groveland Rd., Genesee, NY 14454

Chiaroscuto, 108 N. Plain St., Ithaca, NY 14850

Cincinnati Poetry Review, Univ. of Cincinnati, Cincinnati, OH 45221

Circus Buffoon, P.O. Box 3684, Sarasota, FL 33578
City Lights Books, 261 Columbus Ave., San Francisco, CA 94133
The Clamshell Press, 160 California Ave., Santa Rosa, CA 95405
Clockwatch . . . see Driftwood Publications
Coevolution Quarterly, Box 428, Sausalito, CA 94961
Communica-Press, 1650 Piikoi St., Apt. 901, Honolulu, HI 96822
Confrontation, Long Island University, Brooklyn, NY 11201
Conjunctions, 33 West 9th St., New York, NY 10011
Contact, P.O. Box 500, Mendocino, CA 95460
Copper Beech Press, Box 1852, Brown University, Providence,
   RI 02912
Copper Canyon Press, P.O. Box 271, Port Townsend, WA 98368
Corona, Montana State Univ., Bozeman, MT 59717
Cotton Lane Press, 2 Cotton Lane, Augusta, GA 30902
Cottonwood Review, Box J, Kansas Union, Univ. of Kansas,
   Lawrence, KS 66044
Coyote Love Press, 27 Deering St., Portland, ME 04101
Crab Creek Review, 30 F St., NE, Ephrata, WA 98823
Crazyhorse, University of Arkansas, Little Rock, AR 72204
Creative with Words Publications, P.O. Box 223226, Carmel,
   CA 93922
Creativity Unlimited Press, 30819 Casilina, Rancho Palos Verdes,
   CA 90274
The Crescent Review, P.O. Box 15065, Winston-Salem, NC 27103
Crop Dust, Rte. 2, Box 389-1, Bealeton, VA 22712
Crosscurrents, 2200 Glastonbury Rd., Westlake Village, CA 91361
Crossing Press, Trumansburg, NY 14886
Croton Review, P.O. Box 277, Croton-on-Hudson, NY 10520
Cumberland Poetry Review, P.O. Box 120128, Acklen Sta.,
   Nashville, TN 37212
CutBank, University of Montana, Missoula, MT 59812
The Cypress Review, P.O. Box 673, Half Moon Bay, CA 94019

Darkhorse, Jones Hill Rd., Ashby, MA 01431
Dawn Valley Press, P.O. Box 58, New Wilmington, PA 16142
Dead Angel, 1206 Lyndale Dr., SE, Atlanta, GA 30316
Denver Quarterly, Univ. of Denver, Denver, CO 80208
Descant, Box 32872, TCU, Ft. Worth, TX 76129
Dooryard Press, P.O. Box 221, Story, Wyo 82842
Downtown Poets, GPO 1720, Brooklyn, NY 11202
Dragon Gate, Inc., 508 Lincoln St., Port Townsend, WA 98368

Dragonsbreath Press, Rt. 1, Sister Bay, WI 54234
Dragon's Teeth Press, Georgetown, CA 95634
Driftwood Publications, 737 Penbrook Way, Hartland, WI 53029
Dryad Press, 15 Sherman Ave., Takoma Park, MD 20912

Eagle Books, Rte. 1, Box 701, Bolivar, MO 65613
Ecology Digest, P.O. Box 60961, Sacramento, CA 95860
El Camino Publishers, 410 Calle Real, Suite 4, Santa Barbara,
    CA 93110
Electrum, 1435 Louise St., Santa Ana, CA 92706
Elizabeth Street Press, 240 Elizabeth St., New York, NY 10012
Epoch, Cornell University, Ithaca, NY 14853
Erespin Press, 920 East 50th, Austin, TX 78751
Erie Street Press, 642 S. Clarence Ave., Oak Park, IL 60304
Event, Kwantlen College, P.O. Box 9030, Surrey, B.C.,
    Canada V3T 5H8
Eye Prayers Press, P.O. Box 16616, San Diego, CA 92116

Farmer's Market, P.O. Box 1272, Galesburg, IL 61401
Felis-Hadiken Publications, 16C Division St., Glens Falls,
    NY 12801
Feminist Studies, c/o Women's Studies, Univ. of Md, College
    Park, MD 20742
Fiction Collective, Eng. Dept., Brooklyn College, Brooklyn,
    NY 11210
Fiction Monthly, 545 Haight St., Ste 67, San Francisco,
    CA 94117
Fiction Network, P.O. Box 5651, San Francisco, CA 94101
Field, Oberlin College, Oberlin, OH 44074
Fine Arts Press, P.O. Box 3491, Knoxville, TN 37927
Footwork, Passaic Co. Community College, Paterson, NJ 07509
Frontiers, Women Studies, Univ. of Colorado, Boulder, CO 80309

Galileo Press, P.O. Box 16129, Baltimore, MD 21218
Gambit, 608 Seventh St., Marietta, OH 45750
Gargoyle/Paycock Press, P.O. Box 3567, Washington, DC 20007
Garric Press, P.O. Box 517, Glen Ellen, CA 95442
General Hall, Inc., 23-45 Corporal Kennedy St., Bayside,
    NY 11360
The Georgia Review, University of Georgia, Athens, GA 30602

Ghost Pony Express, 2518 Gregory St., Madison, WI 53711

Grand Street, 50 Riverside Dr., New York, NY 10024

Gray Moose Press, 19 Elmwood Ave., Rye, NY 10580

Graywolf Press, P.O. Box 142, Port Townsend, WA 98368

Great River Review, 211 W. 7th St., Winona, MN 55987

Greenfield Review, RD 1, P.O. Box 80, Greenfield Center,
NY 12833

Greenhouse Review Press, 3965 Bonny Doon Rd., Santa Cruz,
CA 95060

Green's Magazine, P.O. Box 3236, Regina, Sask., Canada S4P 3H1

Griffin House Publications, Bagehot Council, P.O. Box 81,
Whitestone, NY 11357

Grimoire, 8181 Wayne Rd., Apt. H2084, Westland, MI 48185

Hanging Loose Press, 231 Wyckoff St., Brooklyn, NY 11217

The Harbor Review, Eng. Dept., Univ. of Mass., Boston, MA
02125

Heavy Evidence Press, c/o Caldwell, 1315 7th St., E, Menomonie,
WI 54751

Holmgangers Press, 95 Carson Ct., Shelter Cove, Whitethorn, CA
95489

Holy Cow! Press, P.O. Box 618, Minneapolis, MN 55440

Home Planet News, P.O. Box 415, Stuyvesant Sta., New York,
NY 10009

Horse and Bird Press, P.O. Box 67089, Los Angeles, CA 90067

Howe Street Press, 212 E. Howe, Seattle, WA 98102

Hubbub, 2754 S.E. 27th Ave., Portland, OR 97202

The Hudson Review, 684 Park Ave., New York, NY 10021

Humana Press, Inc., Crescent Manor, P.O. Box 2148, Clifton,
NJ 07015

Icare Press, Inc., P.O. Box 23340, Hollis, NY 11423

Images, Eng. Dept., Wright St. Univ., Dayton, OH 45435

Indiana Review, 316 N. Jordan Ave., Indiana Univ., Bloomington,
IN 47405

Individual Artists of Oklahoma, 2927 Paseo, Oklahoma City,
OK 73103

Intertext, P.O. Box 100014 DT, Anchorage, Alaska 99510

Invisible City/Red Hill Press, P.O. Box 2853, San Francisco, CA
94126

The Iowa Review, University of Iowa, Iowa City, IA 52242
Ironwood, P.O. Box 40907, Tucson, AZ 85717
Ithaca House, 108 N. Plain St., Ithaca, NY 14850

Jalmar Press, 45 Hitching Post Dr., Bldg. 2, Rolling Hills Estates,
   CA 90274
Jam Today, P.O. Box 249, Northfield, VT 05663
Journal of Canadian Studies, Trent Univ., Peterborough, Ont.,
   Canada K9J 7B8

Kalliope, 3939 Roosevelt Blvd., Jacksonville, FL 32205
Kansas Quarterly, Kansas State University, Manhattan, KS 66506
Kelsey St. Press, P.O. Box 9235, Berkeley, CA 94709
Kenyon Review, Kenyon College, Gambier, OH 43022
Michael Kesend Publishing, Ltd., 1025 Fifth Ave., New York,
   NY 10028
Kindred Joy Publications, 554 W. 4th St., Coquille, OR 97423
The Kindred Spirit, 808 Maple, Great Bend, KS 67530
Kitchen Table, Women of Color Press, Box 2753, Rockefeller Ctr.
   Sta., New York, NY 10185

Labyris Press, Box 16102, Lansing, MI 48933
Lake Street Review, Box 7188, Powderhorn Sta., Minneapolis,
   MN 55407
Landscape, P.O. Box 7107, Berkeley, CA 94707
Laughing Bear Press, P.O. Box 23478, San Jose, CA 95153
Laurel Review, W. Va. Wesleyan College, Buckhannon,
   W.VA 26201
Lips, P.O. Box 1345, Montclair, NJ 07042
The Literary Review, Fairleigh Dickinson University, Madison,
   NJ 07940
Little Free Press, Box 8201, Minneapolis, MN 55408
The Lockhart Press, Box 1207, Port Townsend, WA 98368
The Loft, 93 Grant Ave., Glens Falls, NY 12801
Long Pond Review, Eng. Dept., Suffolk Comm. College, Selden,
   NY 11784
The Long Story, 11 Kingston St., North Andover, MA 01845
Look Quick, P.O. Box 222, Pueblo, CO 81002
Lost & Found Times, (see Luna Bisonte Prods.)

Louisiana Writers Guild, P.O. Box 44370, Capitol Sta., Baton Rouge, LA 70804

Luna Bisonte Prods., 137 Leland Ave., Columbus, OH 43214

Lynx House Press, Box 800, Amherst, MA 01004

MFA in Writing Program, Vermont College, Montpelier, VT 05602

MSS, SUNY, Binghamton, NY 13901

Magical Blend, P.O. Box 11303, San Francisco, CA 94101

Maledicta, 331 S. Greenfield Ave., Waukesha, WI 53186

Manhattan Poetry Review, 36 Sutton Pl., So., (11D), New York, NY 10022

Manhattan Review, 304 Third Ave., Apt. 4A, New York, NY 10010

Man-Root, Box 982, So. San Francisco, CA 94083

Massachusetts Review, Univ. of Mass., Amherst, MA 01002

McFarland & Co., Inc., Publishers, Box 611, Jefferson, NC 28460

Meadow Press, 251 Parnassus Ave., #33, San Francisco, CA 94117

Mendocino Review, P.O. Box 888, Mendocino, CA 95460

Mey-House Books, P.O. Box 794, Stroudsburg, PA 18360

Micah Publications, 255 Humphrey St., Marblehead, MA 01945

Michigan Quarterly, University of Michigan, Ann Arbor, MI 48109

Mid-American Review, 2358 W. 63rd St., Chicago, IL 60636

Milkweed Chronicle, Box 24303, Minneapolis, MN 55424

Minnesota Review, Eng. Dept., Oregon St. Univ., Corvallis, OR 97331

Mirth & Merriment Publications, 821 N. Penna. St., #22, Indianapolis, IN 46204

Mississippi Review, Univ. of Southern Miss., Hattiesburg, MS 39406

Missouri Review, Eng. Dept., Univ. of Missouri, Columbia, MO 65211

Modern Poetry Studies, Widener Univ., Chester, PA 19013

Mogul Book & Filmworks, P.O. Box 2773, Pittsburgh, PA 15230

The Montana Review, (see Owl Creek Press)

Moonlighting: The Princeton Inn College Literary Magazine, Princeton Inn College, Princeton, NJ 08540

Moonsquilt Press, 16401 N.E. 4th Ave., N. Miami Beach, FL 33162

Moving Out, P.O. Box 21879, Detroit, MI 48221

Moving Parts Press, 419-A Maple St., Santa Cruz, CA 95060

Naked Man Press, c/o M. Smetzer, Eng. Dept., BGSU, Bowling Green, OH 43403

Negative Capability, 6116 Timberly Rd., N. Mobile, AL 36609

New Collage, 5700 N. Tamiami Trail, Sarasota, FL 33580

New England Review and Bread Loaf Quarterly, Box 170, Hanover, NH 03755

New Kauri, 2551 W. Mossman Rd., Tucson, AZ 85746

New Letters, 5100 Rockhill Rd., Kansas City, MO 62110

New Oregon Review, 537 N.E. Lincoln St., Hillsboro, OR 97123

New Renaissance, 9 Heath Rd., Arlington, MA 02174

New Rivers Press, 1602 Selby Ave., St. Paul, MN 55104

Night Horn Books, 495 Ellis St., San Francisco, CA 94102

Nikmal Publishing, 698 River St., Mattapan, MA 02126

Nimrod, 2210 S. Main, Tulsa, OK 74114

Nit & Wit Magazine, P.O. Box 14685, Chicago, IL 60614

The North American Review, Univ. of No. Iowa, Cedar Falls, IA 50614

Northern New England Review, Box 825, Franklin Pierce College, Rindge, NH 03461

Northwest Review, Eng. Dept., Univ. of Oregon, Eugene, OR 97403

Now it's Up to You Publications, 157 S. Logan, Denver, CO 80209

O.ARS, Box 179, Cambridge, MA 02238

Oberon Press, 401A Inn of the Provinces, Ottawa, Canada K1R 7S8

OBOE, (see Night Horn Books)

Ohan Press, 171 Maplewood St., Watertown, MA 02172

The Ohio Journal, OSU Dept. of Eng., 164 W. 17th Ave., Columbus, OH 43210

The Old Red Kimono, Floyd Jr. College, P.O. Box 1864, Rome, GA 30161

The Ontario Review, 9 Honey Brook Dr., Princeton, NJ 08540

Open Places, Box 2085, Stephens College, Columbia, MO 65215

Osiris, Box 297, Deerfield, MA 01342

Outreach, Eng. Dept., Morgan St. Univ., Baltimore, MD 21239

Owl Creek Press, P.O. Box 2248, Missoula, MT 59806

Ox Head Press, 414 N. 6th, Marshall, MN 56258

Oxymora Book Press, P.O. Box 429, Venice, CA 90294

OYEZ Review, 430 S. Michigan Ave., Chicago, IL 60603

The Pale Fire Review, 162 Academy Ave., Providence, RI 02908
Pancake Press, 163 Galewood Circle, San Francisco, CA 94131
Pangloss Papers, Box 18917, Los Angeles, CA 90018
The Paper, 1255 Nuuanu Ave., #1813, Honolulu, HI 96817
Parabola, 150 Fifth Ave., New York, NY 10011
Paris Review, 45-39 171 Place, Flushing, NY 11358
The Paseo Papers, c/o Renegade Artservices, 2927 The Paseo, Oklahoma City, OK 73103
Passages North, Bonifas Fine Arts Center, Escanaba, MI 49829
Passaic Review, Forstmann Library, 195 Gregory Ave., Passaic, NJ 07055
The Pawn Review, 2903 Windsor Rd., Austin, TX 78703
Pax, 217 Pershing Ave., San Antonio, TX 78209
Pentagram, Box 379, Markesan, WI 53946
Pequod, 536 Hill St., San Francisco, CA 94114
Performance Projects, P.O. Box 2495, Tucson, AZ 85702
Perivale Press, 13830 Erwin St., Van Nuys, CA 91401
Piedmont Literary Review, P.O. Box 3656, Danville, VA 24543
Pig Iron Press, P.O. Box 237, Youngstown, OH 44501
The Pikestaff Forum, P.O. Box 127, Normal, IL 61761
Pinchpenny, 4851 Q St., Sacramento, CA 95819
Pitcairn Press, 388 Franklin St., Cambridge, MA 02139
Pivot, 103 Burrowes, University Park, PA 16802
Plainview Press, 1509 Dexter, Austin, TX 78704
Ploughshares, Box 529, Cambridge, MA 02139
Plumbers Ink Books, P.O. Box 233, Cerrillos, NM 87010
Poet Lore, 4000 Albemarle St., NW, Washington, DC 20016
Poetic Justice, 8220 Rayford Dr., Los Angeles, CA 90045
Poetics Journal, 2639 Russell St., Berkeley, CA 94705
Poetry Center, Cleveland St. Univ., Cleveland, OH 44115
Poetry Northwest, Univ. of Washington, Seattle, WA 98105
Poultry, Box 727, Truro, MA 02666
Prairie Publ. Co., (see Winnipeg Free Press)
Prairie Schooner, 201 Andrews, Univ. of Neb., Lincoln, NE 68588
Press Me Close, P.O. Box 250, Farmingdale, NJ 07727
Primavera, Univ. of Chicago, 1212 E. 59th St., Chicago, IL 60637
Prism, c/o S. R. Jones, Rt. 2, Box 239, Corvallis, OR 97333
Prometheus, Box 14181, Austin, TX 78761
Pterodactyl Press, Main St., Cumberland, IA 50843
Ptolemy/Browns Mills Press, P.O. Box 908, Browns Mills, NJ 08015

Publication Fellowship, 3825 S. Seneca, #75B, Wichita, KS 67217
The Publishing Ward, Inc., 725 Breakwater Dr., Fort Collins,
  CO 80525
Pudding Magazine, 2384 Hardesty Dr., S, Columbus, OH 43204
Puerto Del Sol, New Mexico St. Univ., Box 3E, Las Cruces,
  NM 88003
The Pushkin Press, 1930 Columbia Rd., NW, Washington, DC
  20009

Quarterly West, University of Utah, Salt Lake City, UT 84112
Quorum Editions, Ten North Mill, Cranbury, NJ 08512

RFD, Rt. 1, Box 127-E, Bakersville, NC 28705
The Radical Reviewer, P.O. Box 24953, Sta. O, Vancouver, B.C.,
  Canada V5T 4G3
Raritan: A Quarterly Review, 165 College Ave., New Brunswick,
  NJ 08903
Raw Dog Press, 129 Worthington Ave., Doylestown, PA 18901
Realities Library, 2475 Monterey Rd., #76, San Jose, CA 95111
Red Cedar Review, Dept. of Eng., Michigan St. Univ.,
  E. Lansing, MI 48823
Reflect, 3306 Argonne Ave., Norfolk, VA 23509
Rhode Island Review, 85 Preston St., Providence, RI 02906
River City Review, P.O. Box 34275, Louisville, KY 40232
River Styx, 7420 Cornell, St. Louis, MO 63130

Sachem Press, P.O. Box 9, Old Chatham, NY 12136
St. Andrews Press, Laurinburg, NC 28352
Salthouse, P.O. Box 11537, Milwaukee, WI 53211
Samisdat, Box 129, Richford, VT 05476
Sands, 17302 Club Hill Dr., Dallas, TX 75248

Santa Susanna Press, Calif. St. Univ., Northridge, CA 91330
Sapiens, P.O. Box 209, Millburn, NJ 07041
Saturday Press, Inc., P.O. Box 884, Upper Montclair, NJ 07043
Scholia Satyrica, Eng. Dept., Univ. of So. Florida, Tampa,
  FL 33620
The Seal Press, 312 S. Washington, Seattle, WA 98104
Second Coming Press, P.O. Box 31249, San Francisco, CA 94131

Seneca Review, Hobart & William Smith Colleges, Geneva,
NY 14456

The Sewanee Review, University of the South, Sewanee,
TN 37375

Shadow Press, P.O. Box 8803, Minneapolis, MN 55408

Shankpainter, Box 565, Provincetown, MA 02657

Shearwater Press, Box 417, Wellfleet, MA 02667

Shenandoah, Box 722, Lexington, VA 24450

Shmate, Box 4228, Berkeley, CA 94704

Sign of the Times, P.O. Box 6464, Portland, OR 97228

Sing Heavenly Muse!, P.O. Box 14059, Minneapolis, MN 55414

Sisters, P.O. Box 14593, Minneapolis, MN 55414

The Small Pond Magazine, P.O. Box 664, Stratford, CT 06497

Small Press News, (see Stony Hills)

Smithereens Press, Box 1036, Bolinas, CA 94924

Smoke Signals, (see Black Market Press)

Snowy Egret, 205 S. Ninth St., Williamsburg, KY 40769

Sonora Review, Univ. of Arizona, Tucson, AZ 85721

South Carolina Review, Clemson Univ., Clemson, SC 29631

Southern Poetry Review, Eng. Dept., Univ. of N.C., Charlotte,
NC 28223

The Southern Review, Louisiana State Univ., Baton Rouge,
LA 70803

Southwest Review, Southern Methodist Univ., Dallas, TX 75275

Sou'wester Magazine, Southern Ill. Univ., Edwardsville, IL 62026

Spinsters Ink, 803 DeHaro St., San Francisco, CA 94102

Starchand Press, Box 468, Wainscott, NY 11975

State Street Press, 67 State St., Pittsford, NY 14534

Stone Country, P.O. Box 132, Menemsha, MA 02552

The Stone House Press, Box 196, Roslyn, NY 11576

Stony Hills, Weeks Mills, New Sharon, ME 04955

Stories, 14 Beacon St., Boston, MA 02108

Story Quarterly, P.O. Box 1416, Northbrook, IL 60062

Stronghold Press, Plains Poetry Journal, Box 2337, Bismarck,
ND 58502

The Sun, 412 W Rosemary St., Chapel Hill, NC 27514

Sun & Moon, 4330 Hartwick Rd., College Park, MD 20740

Sunstone Press, P.O. Box 2321, Santa Fe, NM 87501

Swallow Press, Scott Quadrangle, Athens, OH 45701

Swallow's Tale Magazine, P.O. Box 4328, Tallahassee, FL 32315

Syzygy, P.O. Box 183, Mill Valley, CA 94942

Talonbooks, 1019 East Cordova, Vancouver, B.C.,
   Canada V6A 1M8
Tamarisk, 319 Juniper St., Philadelphia, PA 19107
Tar River Poetry, East Carolina Univ., Greenville, NC 27834
Taylor Street Press, 60 Taylor, Fairfax, CA 94930
Tendril, Box 512, Green Harbor, MA 02041
Territory of Oklahoma, (see Individual Artists of Oklahoma)
Third Eye, 189 Kelvin Dr., Buffalo, NY 14223
13th Moon, 230 W. 105 St., New York, NY 10025
Three Continents Press, Inc., 1346 Connecticut Ave., NW,
   Washington, DC 20036
Threepenny Review, P.O. Box 9131, Berkeley, CA 94709
Thunder City Press, P.O. Box 600574, Houston, TX 77260
Thunder's Mouth Press, Box 780, New York, NY 10025
Top Stories, 700 Main St., Buffalo, NY 14202
Touchstone, P.O. Box 42331, Houston, TX 77042
Tri-Quarterly, 1735 Benson Ave., Northwestern Univ., Evanston,
   IL 60201
Truly Fine Press, P.O. Box 891, Bemidji, MN 56601
Turkey Press, 6746 Sueno Rd., Isla Vista, CA 93117
Tuumba Press, 2639 Russell St., Berkeley, CA 94705

United Artists, 172 E. 4th St., New York, NY 10009
University of Windsor Review, 401 Sunset Ave., Windsor, Ont.,
   Canada N9B 3P4
U.S.1 Worksheets (Poets Cooperative), 21 Lake Dr., Roosevelt,
   NJ 08555

Vagabond Press, 1610 North Water, Ellensburg, WA 98926
Vanity Press, 160 6th Ave., New York, NY 10013
Vol. No. Magazine, 24721 Newhall Ave., Newhall, CA 91321
Vortex Editions, P.O. Box 42698, San Francisco, CA 94101

Watchwords, 20 Becher St., London, Ont., Canada N6C 1A3
Water Mark Press, 175 East Shore Rd., Huntington Bay, NY 11743
Webster Review, Webster College, Webster Groves, MO 63119
West Branch, Bucknell Univ., Lewisburg, PA 17837
Western Humanities Review, Univ. of Utah, Salt Lake City,
   UT 84112
Wheat Forder's Press, P.O. Box 6317, Washington, DC 20015

White Cross Press, Rt. 1, Box 592, Granger, TX 76530
White Eagle Publisher, P.O. Box 1332, Dept. S-0111, Lowell,
  MA 01853
Wind Magazine, RFD #1, Box 809K, Pikeville, KY 41501
The Windless Orchard, Eng. Dept., Indiana Univ., Fort Wayne,
  IN 46805
Winnipeg Free Press, 300 Carlton St., Winnipeg, Canada R3C
  3C1
Wisconsin Academy Review, 1922 University Ave., Madison,
  WI 53705
The Word Works, P.O. Box 42164, Washington, DC 20015
Wormwood Review, P.O. Box 8840, Stockton, CA 95208
Writers Forum, Univ. of Colo., Colorado Springs, CO 80907

Yarrow, Eng. Dept., Kutztown Univ., Kutztown, PA 19530
Yellow Silk, P.O. Box 6374, Albany, CA 94706

Zyga Multimedia Research, 642 El Dorado, Oakland, CA 94611

ЬЬ ЬЬ ЬЬ

INDEX

The following is a listing in alphabetical order by author's last name of works reprinted in the first nine *Pushcart Prize* editions.

CONTRIBUTORS' NOTES

PHILIP APPLEMAN is the author most recently of the collection *Darwin's Ark* (Indiana University Press). He has also published two novels and five books of nonfiction.

DANIEL BERRIGAN S.J., peace activist and poet, won the Lamont Poetry Award in 1958. His most recent book is *Portraits of Those I Love*.

RICHARD BLESSING died last year. He was chairman of the graduate program in English at the University of Washington. His books include *Poems & Stories* (1983), two previous collections of poetry, critical studies of Theodore Roethke and Wallace Stevens and a novel, *A Passing Season*.

MICHAEL BLUMENTHAL's latest book is *Days We Would Rather Know* (Viking Penguin 1984). He lectures at Harvard University.

T. CORAGHESSAN BOYLE's most recent book is *Budding Prospects* (Viking Penguin, 1984).

PAMELA BRANDT studies at Stanford University. "L.A. Child" is her second published story.

CLARK BROWN is the author of the novel, *The Disciple*, 1968. He teaches at California State University, Chico.

HAYDEN CARRUTH's poetry has been featured in previous *Pushcart Prize* editions. This is his first nonfiction contribution.

RAYMOND CARVER is the author of several story collections published by Knopf. His stories have appeared in *Pushcart Prize* editions I, VI and VIII.

SIV CEDERING has published several collections of poetry and is also a novelist. Her poetry previously appeared in *Pushcart Prize* II.

STEPHEN COREY has published three collections of poetry from Water Mark Press, State Street Press and Night Owl Press. He is assistant editor of *The Georgia Review*.

CHRISTOPHER JANE CORKERY's first poetry collection, *Blessing*, will be published soon by Princeton University Press.

MALCOLM COWLEY's next book is *The Flower and The Leaf* (Viking Penguin), which will include his essay on John Cheever.

JOHN ENGELS' most recent book is *Weather-Fear: New and Selected Poems 1958-1982* (University of Georgia Press). He lives in Williston, Vermont.

TERRENCE DES PRES is the author of *The Survivor: An Anatomy of Life In The Death Camps* (Oxford University Press) and teaches at Colgate University.

SHARON DOUBIAGO is the author of the epic poem, *Hard Country* (West End Press, 1982). She lives in Port Townsend, Washington.

RICHARD EBERHART currently lives in Hanover, New Hampshire. For more biological information see Stephen Corey's Introduction to this selection.

MICHAEL FINLEY is the author of several collections of poetry and the novel, *Animal Fame*.

CELIA GILBERT's poem is from her book *Bonfire* (Alice James Books, 1983). She is the winner of a Discovery Award and an Emily Dickinson Award.

GAIL GODWIN is author of *A Mother and Two Daughters* and most recently *Mr. Bedford and The Muses*. She wrote the Introduction to *Pushcart Prize VIII*.

ALBERT GOLDBARTH's most recent collection of poetry, *Original Light: New & Selected Poems 1973-1983*, has just been published by Ontario Review Press. He lives in Austin, Texas and teaches at the University of Texas.

WILLIAM GOYEN's novel *Arcadio* was published in 1983 shortly after his death. He was the author of many novels and stories. His story "Arthur Bond" appeared in *Pushcart Prize VI*.

DONALD HALL is the author of *Weather for Poetry* and other books. He lives in Danbury, New Hampshire.

RODNEY JONES teaches at Virginia Intermont College and is the author of *The Story They Told Us of Light* (University of Alabama Press, 1980).

EDMUND KEELEY teaches at Princeton University. "Cambodian Diary" will appear as the first chapter of his novel, *A Wilderness Called Peace*, forthcoming from Simon & Schuster.

TADEUSZ KONWICKI lives in Poland. His novel, *A Minor Apocalypse*, was published last year by Farrar Straus and Giroux, translated by Richard Lourie.

TED KOOSER's most recent collection of poetry is *Sure Signs* (University of Pittsburgh Press).

LI-YOUNG LEE's second published poem appeared in last year's *Pushcart Prize*. He lives in Chicago.

CURZIO MALAPARTE died in 1957. "The Soroca Girls" is from his book *Kaputt*, published just after World War II. He was both a supporter and later a foe of Mussolini. During the war, he was a reporter for Milan's *Corriere della Sera* and he joined the Italian liberation forces after the death of Mussolini. *Kaputt* went through ten printings, was a bestseller of its time, and has been out of print until its reissue by Micah Publications in 1983.

THOMAS MCGRATH has held fellowships from The Guggenheim Foundation, The National Endowment for the Arts and others. He is the author of collections from Swallow Press, Holy Cow ! Press and Copper Canyon Press and was a founder of the magazine *Crazyhorse*.

BARBARA MILTON's *A Small Cartoon* was the 1983 winner of Word Beat Press' fiction contest. She lives in New York City and has published in *The Paris Review* and elsewhere.

SUSAN MINOT's first book will be published by E.P. Dutton. She lives in New York City.

SUSAN MITCHELL's first collection of poetry, *Water Inside The Water*, was published last year by Wesleyan University Press.

MARY MORRIS teaches at Princeton University and is the author of the novel, *Crossroads* (1983) and the short story collection, *Vanishing Animals* (1980). Her *Searching for Men In Seattle*, a collection of stories, is due from Houghton Mifflin soon.

JOAN MURRAY grew up near New York City's Harlem River. She now lives in Buffalo.

THOMAS RUSSELL served as fiction editor of *Cottonwood Review*. His stories have appeared in *Vanderbilt Review* and elsewhere.

NAOMI SHIHAB NYE's latest book, *Hugging The Jukebox*, was published by The National Poetry Series/E.P. Dutton. She lives in San Antonio, Texas.

JONATHAN PENNER received the Drue Heinz Literature Prize for his short story collection *Private Parties* (University of Pittsburgh Press, 1983). He has received fellowships from the Guggenheim Foundation and the National Endowment for the Arts.

JOE ASHBY PORTER is the author of the novel, *Eelgrass*, and a collection of short fiction, *The Kentucky Stories*. His work has appeared in many magazines and in *Best American Short Stories* and *Pushcart Prize IV*.

JOAN RETALLACK teaches at The University of Maryland. She has published poetry, fiction and critical articles in *London Magazine, Massachusetts Review, Sun & Moon* and elsewhere. She is the author of a book of poems, *Circumstantial Evidence*.

PATTIANN ROGERS' poems have appeared in *The Georgia Review, Virginia Quarterly Review, Poetry, Poetry Northwest* and elsewhere. Her book, *The Expectations of Light*, was published by Princeton University Press.

WILLIAM PITT ROOT's *Invisible Guests* has just been published by Confluence Press. He is the author of several poetry collections and teaches at the University of Montana.

TERI RUCH has published in various journals and lives in Texas. She is a graduate of the Johns Hopkins Writing Seminars.

THOMAS RUSSELL has served as fiction editor for *The Cottonwood Review*. His stories have appeared in *Vanderbilt Review* and elsewhere.

BETH TASHERY SHANNON's work previously appeared in *Pushcart Prize III*. She publishes in *The Chicago Review* and elsewhere.

LOUIS SIMPSON's awards include Columbia University's Medal for Excellence and the Pulitzer Prize for poetry. His latest collections of poetry were published by BOA Editions and Ticknor & Fields.

GILBERT SORRENTINO is the author of *Mulligan Stew* and *Aberration of Starlight,* plus other books. North Point Press will issue his collected essays, *Something Said*.

GARY SOTO is the author of poetry collections from Strawberry Hill Press and the University of Pittsburgh. He teaches at the University of California, Berkeley.

WILLIAM STAFFORD is the author of many poetry collections from Harper & Row, Confluence Press, West Coast Poetry Review Press, Perishable Press, Croissant Press, BOA Editions, Copper Canyon Press, David Godine, Sceptre Press and Graywolf Press. He is a hiker, biker, photographer, husband and father of four children.

BARBARA THOMPSON lived for sixteen years in Pakistan and has written several stories about her experiences there. Her "Tattoo" appeared in *Pushcart Prize VII,* also from *Shenandoah*.

DAVID WAGONER is a poet, novelist and professor. He is the editor of *Poetry Northwest*.

MICHAEL WATERS is the author of poetry collections from Ithaca House, BOA Editions and the current *The Stories In The Light* (Thunder City Press).

WILLIAM CARLOS WILLIAMS' poetry is available from New Directions and other publishers. He died in 1963. For more biographical information see the Introduction to this selection.

RICHARD YATES' collection of short stories, *Liars in Love,* was published in 1981 by Seymour Lawrence Inc. and included "Oh, Joseph, I'm So Tired." The story has appeared in *The Atlantic,* and won an O'Henry Award.

SAUL YURKIEVICH was born in Argentina in 1931 and now lives in Paris. He has published many books of poetry and criticism, widely translated into French. Cola Franzen has translated several of his works into English.